Concurrency Theory

Howard Bowman and Rodolfo Gomez

Concurrency Theory

Calculi and Automata for Modelling Untimed and Timed Concurrent Systems

With 126 Figures

 Springer

Howard Bowman
Rodolfo Gomez

Computing Laboratory
University of Kent at Canterbury
Canterbury
Kent
UK

British Library Cataloguing in Publication Data
A catalogue record for this book is available from the British Library

ISBN-13: 978-1-84996-951-2   e-ISBN-13: 978-1-84628-336-9

Printed on acid-free paper

Printed in the United States of America   (MVY)

9 8 7 6 5 4 3 2 1

Springer Science+Business Media
springer.com

To our friends and families.

Preface

In the world we live in concurrency is the norm. For example, the human body is a massively concurrent system, comprising a huge number of cells, all simultaneously evolving and independently engaging in their individual biological processing. In addition, in the biological world, truly sequential systems rarely arise. However, they are more common when manmade artefacts are considered. In particular, computer systems are often developed from a sequential perspective. Why is this? The simple reason is that it is easier for us to think about sequential, rather than concurrent, systems. Thus, we use sequentiality as a device to simplify the design process.

However, the need for increasingly powerful, flexible and usable computer systems mitigates against simplifying sequentiality assumptions. A good example of this is the all-powerful position held by the Internet, which is highly concurrent at many different levels of decomposition. Thus, the modern computer scientist (and indeed the modern scientist in general) is forced to think about concurrent systems and the subtle and intricate behaviour that emerges from the interaction of simultaneously evolving components.

Over a period of 25 years, or so, the field of concurrency theory has been involved in the development of a set of mathematical techniques that can help system developers to think about and build concurrent systems. These theories are the subject matter of this book.

Our motivation in writing this book was twofold. (1) We wished to synthesise into a single coherent story, a body of research that is scattered across a set of journal and conference publications. (2) We have also sought to highlight newer research (mainly undertaken by the authors) on concurrency theory models of real-time systems. The first of these aspects yields the text book style of the first three parts of the book, whereas the second has motivated the approach of the fourth part, which has more of the flavour of a research monograph.

There are other books on concurrency theory, but these have tended to have a different focus from this book. Most relevant in this respect are classic works by Milner on the Calculus of Communicating Systems (CCS) [148],

Hoare on first generation Communicating Sequential Processes (CSP) [96], Roscoe on the mature CSP theory [171] and Schneider on Timed CSP [176]. However, all of these have a tighter focus than this book, being directed at specific theories. Although one point of major focus in this book is the process calculus LOTOS (which, by the way, has not previously been presented in book format), our approach is broader in scope than these earlier texts. For example, we consider both untimed and timed approaches (in the same book), we highlight the process calculus approach along with communicating finite and infinite state automata and we present a spectrum of different semantic theories, including traces, transition systems, refusals and true concurrency models. The latter of these semantic models being particularly noteworthy, because the bundle event structure true concurrency theory we consider is not as well known as it should be.

Another difference with previous concurrency theory texts is that this book is less focused on proof systems. There are a number of reasons for this. First, proof systems are not as well behaved in LOTOS as they are in CCS and CSP; e.g. testing equivalence is not a congruence in LOTOS. Second, we would argue that the issue of finding complete proof systems has actually turned out to be less important than once seemed to be the case. This is because of the development of powerful state-space exploration methods, such as model-checking and equivalence-checking, which are not proof system dependent. As a reflection of this trend, we also consider finite and infinite state communicating automata approaches, which have recently taken a prominent place in concurrency theory, because of their amenability to formal verification. These techniques were not considered in the previous process calculus texts.

Due to the breadth of scope that we have sought in this book, by necessity, certain topics have had to be treated in less depth than would be optimum. As just discussed, one of these is the topic of proof systems. In addition, when, in a denotational style, we interpret recursive definitions semantically, we do not present the full details of the fixed point theories that we use. However, at all such points in the text, we give pointers to the required definitions and include references to complete presentations of the necessary theory.

In terms of target readership, this book is partially a textbook and partially a research monograph. It is particularly suitable for masters and doctoral level programmes with an emphasis on parallel processing, distributed systems, networks, formal methods and/or concurrency in general. We assume a basic knowledge of set theory, logic and discrete mathematics, as found in a textbook such as [86]. However, we do include a list of notation to help the reader.

The material presented here has partially grown out of a set of course notes used in an MSc-level course on formal methods taught in the Computing Laboratory at the University of Kent. Consequently, we would like to thank the students who have taken this course over a number of years. The feedback from these students has helped these notes to be refined, which has, in turn, benefited this book.

Preface   IX

We would also like to thank a number of our academic colleagues with whom we have discussed concurrency theory and who have contributed to the development of our understanding of this field. We would particularly like to mention Juan Carlos Augusto, Gordon Blair, Lynne Blair, Eerke Boiten, Tommaso Bolognesi, Jeremy Bryans, Amanda Chetwynd, John Derrick, Giorgio Faconti, Holger Hermanns, Joost-Pieter Katoen, Rom Langerak, Diego Latella, Su Li, Peter Linington, Mieke Massink, Tim Regan, Steve Schneider, Marteen Steen, Ben Strulo, Simon Thompson, Stavros Tripakis and Frits Vaandrager.

In addition, we would like to acknowledge the contribution of the following funding bodies who have provided financial support for our concurrency theory research over the last ten years: the UK Engineering and Physical Sciences Research Council, British Telecom, the European Union, under the Marie Curie and ERCIM programmes, Universities UK, through the Overseas Research Fund, and the Computing Laboratory at the University of Kent.

Finally, we would like to thank Catherine Drury and the Springer publishing team for their efficiency and patience with us.

Canterbury, Kent, UK,   *Howard Bowman*
June 2005   *Rodolfo Gomez*

Notation

The following is an account of some symbols commonly found in this book.

Numbers

$\mathbb{N}$: the natural numbers
$\mathbb{Z}$: the integer numbers
$\mathbb{R}$: the real numbers
$\mathbb{R}^+$: the positive real numbers
$\mathbb{R}^{+0}$: the positive real numbers, including zero

Sets and Functions

$|S|$: cardinality of (i.e. number of elements in) S
$\mathcal{P}(S)$: powerset of S (i.e. the set of all possible sets containing elements of S)
$\subseteq$ ($\subset$) : set inclusion (proper set inclusion)
$\cup$ ($\bigcup$) : set union (generalised union)
$\cap$ ($\bigcap$) : set intersection (generalised intersection)
$\backslash$: set difference
$\times$: Cartesian product: $S_1 \times S_2 \times \cdots \times S_n = \{(s_1, s_2, \ldots, s_n) \mid s_i \in S_i\}$
$^{-1}$: inverse relation: $b\,R^{-1}\,a$ iff $a\,R\,b$
$\lceil$: domain restriction: given $f : \mathcal{D} \to \mathcal{R}$, then $f\lceil S$ is s.t. $f\lceil S : \mathcal{D} \cap S \to \mathcal{R}$
        $f(x) = f\lceil S(x)$ for all $x \in \mathcal{D} \cap S$

where $S, S_1, S_2, \cdots, S_n$ are sets, R is a binary relation and f is a function.

Logic

$\wedge$ ($\bigwedge$) : conjunction (generalised conjunction)
$\vee$ ($\bigvee$) : disjunction (generalised disjunction)
$\neg$: negation
$\implies$: implication
$\iff$: double implication
$\forall$: universal quantification
$\exists$: existential quantification
$\models$: satisfiability relation

General Abbreviations and Acronyms

$\triangleq$: "defined as"
iff   : "if and only if"

s.t.	: "such that"
w.r.t.	: "with respect to"
LTS	: "Labelled Transition System"
BES	: "Bundle Event Structure"
TBES	: "Timed Bundle Event Structure"
TTS	: "Timed Transition System"
CA	: "(finite state) Communicating Automata"
ISCA	: "Infinite State Communicating Automata"
TA	: "Timed Automata"
DTA	: "Discrete Timed Automata"
RSL	: "Ready Simulation Logic"
HML	: "Hennessy-Milner Logic"
LOTOS	: "Language of Temporal Ordering Specification"
CCS	: "Calculus of Communicating Systems"
CSP	: "Communicating Sequential Processes"
pomset	: "partially ordered multiset"
lposet	: "labelled partially ordered set"

Process Calculi (Chapters 2,3,4,5,6,9 and 10)

Sets

In LOTOS

$Defs$	: the set of LOTOS definitions
$DefList$	: the set of lists of LOTOS definitions
$tDeflist$	: the set of tLOTOS definition lists
$PIdent$	: the set of process identifiers
Beh	: the set of LOTOS behaviours
$tBeh$	: the set of tLOTOS behaviours
$Der(B)$	: the set of behaviours that can be derived from B
Act	: the set of actions
$\mathcal{L}$	: the set of actions occurring in a given specification
$\mathcal{A}(B)$	: the set of actions which arise in B
$Gate$	: the set of gates
SN	: the set of semantic notations
SM	: the set of semantic mappings
DEV	: the set of development relations
$\mathcal{T}$	: the set of traces
A^*	: the set of traces from actions in A
$Tr(S)$	: the set of traces that can be derived from S
$\mathcal{LTS}$	: the set of labelled transition systems
$\mathcal{TTS}$	: the set of timed transition systems
$Ref_B(\sigma)$	: the set of refusals of B after σ

$S(B)$: the set of (RSL) observations that B can exhibit
Ξ : the set of time intervals

where B is a behaviour, σ is a trace and S is an LTS.

In Bundle Event Structures

BES : the set of bundle event structures
$TBES$: the set of timed bundle event structures
$\mathcal{U}_E$: the universe of events
$\$\rho$: the set of events underlying ρ
$\mathbf{cfl}(\rho)$: the set of events that are disabled by some event in ρ
$\mathbf{sat}(\rho)$: the set of events that have a causal predecessor in ρ
         for all incoming bundles
$\mathbf{en}(\rho)$: the set of events enabled after ρ
$\mathcal{PS}(\varepsilon)$: the set of proving sequences of ε
$\mathcal{CF}(\varepsilon)$: the set of configurations of ε
$\mathsf{L}(X)$: the multiset of labels of events in X
$Tr^{st}(\varepsilon)$: the set of step traces of ε
$\mathcal{LP}(\varepsilon)$: the set of lposets of ε
$PoS(\varepsilon)$: the set of pomsets of ε

where ρ is a proving sequence, ε is a BES and X is a set of events.

Relations (Functional and Nonfunctional)

In Traces and Labelled Transition Systems

$[\![\,]\!]$: a semantic map
$[\![\,]\!]_{tr}$: the trace semantic map
$[\![\,]\!]_{lts}$: the LTS semantic map
$[\![\,]\!]_{tts}$: the TTS semantic map
$\leq_{tr}$: trace preorder
$\asymp$: equivalence
$\asymp_{tr}$: trace equivalence
$\prec$: simulation
$\asymp_{\prec}$: simulation equivalence
$\prec_R$: ready simulation
$\sim_R$: ready simulation equivalence
$\sim$: strong bisimulation
$\sim_t$: timed strong bisimulation
$\approx$: weak bisimulation (or observational) equivalence
$\approx_c$: weak bisimulation congruence
$\approx_t$: timed weak bisimulation
$\approx_r^t$: timed rooted weak bisimulation

In Bundle Event Structures

$[\![\ ]\!]_{be}$: the BES semantic mapping
$[\![]\!]_{tbe}$: the TBES semantic mapping
ψ : a mapping from BES to $\mathcal{LTS}$
$\sim_{sq}$: sequential strong bisimulation
$\sim_{st}$: step strong bisimulation
$\preceq$: the causality partial order induced by bundles
$\preceq_C$: the causality partial order $\preceq$ restricted to C
$\otimes_C$: the independence relation between events w.r.t. C
$\asymp_{st}$: step trace equivalence
$\asymp_{PoS}$: pomset equivalence
$\asymp_{PS}$: proving sequence isomorphism
$\simeq$: the isomorphism between lposets

where C is a configuration.

In Testing Theory

$te\ (te^s)$: testing equivalence (stable testing equivalence)
$conf\ (conf^s)$: conformance (stable conformance)
$red\ (red^s)$: reduction (stable reduction)
$ext\ (ext^s)$: extension (stable extension)

Transitions

In Labelled Transition Systems

$B \xrightarrow{\ a\ } B'$: B evolves to B' after a
$B \xRightarrow{\ \sigma\ } B'$: B evolves to B' after σ $(\sigma \neq i)$
$B \xRightarrow{\ \sigma\ }\!\!\!\twoheadrightarrow B'$: B evolves to B' after σ $(\sigma = i$ is allowed)
$B \xRightarrow{\ \sigma\ }\!\!\!\twoheadrightarrow B'$: B evolves to B' after σ $(\sigma = i$ is allowed but $B \neq B')$
$B \overset{a}{\leftrightsquigarrow} B'$: B evolves to B' after a (considers undefinedness)

where B, B' are LOTOS behaviours, a is an action and σ is a trace.

In Bundle Event Structures

$\bullet\!\xrightarrow{\ a\ }$: denotes a sequential transition generated from a BES
$\blacktriangleright\!\xrightarrow{\ A\ }$: denotes a step transition generated from a BES

In Timed Transition Systems

$B \overset{t}{\leadsto} B'$: B evolves to B' after t

$B \overset{a}{\longrightarrow} B'$: B evolves to B' after a

$s \overset{a}{\longrightarrow} s'$ $(s \overset{t}{\leadsto} s')$: a TTS action (time) transition

$B \overset{v}{\longrightarrow\!\!\!\!\rightarrow} B'$: B evolves to B' after v

$B \overset{\sigma}{=\!\!\!=\!\!\!\ggg}_t B'$: B evolves to B' after σ

where B, B' are tLOTOS behaviours, s, s' are states, t is a delay, a is an action, v is either an action or a delay, and σ is either a trace, an internal action, or a delay.

Other symbols and acronyms

In LOTOS

pbLOTOS	: *primitive basic LOTOS*, a subset of bLOTOS
bLOTOS	: *basic LOTOS*, the complete language without data types
fLOTOS	: *full LOTOS*, the complete language with data types
i	: the internal action
δ	: the successful termination action
|||	: independent parallel composition
||	: fully synchronised parallel composition
$|[G]|$	: parallel composition with synchronisation set G
[]	: choice
;	: action prefix
>>	: enabling
[>	: disabling
ϵ	: the empty trace
Ω	: a LOTOS process with completely unpredictable behaviour
$\models_{RSL}$	: satisfiability under RSL
$\models_{HML}$	: satisfiability under HML
$[t, t']$	: time interval (also $[t, \infty)$, $[t]$ and (t))
$\oplus$	: time interval addition
$\ominus$	: time interval subtraction
$initI(a, B)$	: the set of intervals where B can initially perform a
$initI{\downarrow}(A, B)$	: the smallest instant where B can initially perform an action in A
$initI{\downarrow\uparrow}(A, B)$	: the smallest of the set of all maximum time points where B can initially perform an action in A

where B is a tLOTOS behaviour, a is an action and A is a set of actions.

In Bundle Event Structures

E	: the set of events of a given BES
$\#$	: the set of conflicts of a given BES
$\mapsto$	: the set of bundles of a given BES
l	: the labelling function of a given BES
$\varepsilon[C]$	: the remainder of ε after C
$\overline{C}$	: the lposet corresponding to C
$[\overline{C}]_{\simeq}$	: the pomset corresponding to the lposet $\overline{C}$
$\mathcal{A}$	: the event-timing function
$\mathcal{R}$	: the bundle-timing function
$init(\Psi)$	: the set of initial events of Ψ
$exit(\Psi)$	: the set of successful termination events of Ψ
$res(\Psi)$	: the events of Ψ whose timing is restricted
$rin(\Psi)$	: the set of initial and time restricted events of Ψ
$X \xmapsto{I} e$	: a timed bundle
$\mathcal{Z}(\sigma,e)$	: the set of instants where (enabled event) e could happen, after σ

where ε is a BES, C is a configuration, Ψ is a TBES, X is a set of events, I is a time interval, e is an event and σ is a timed proving sequence.

Automata (Chapters 8, 11, 12 and 13)

Sets

In Communicating Automata, Timed Automata and Timed Automata with Deadlines

Act	: the set of action labels
$CAct$	: the set of labels for completed actions
$HAct$	: the set of labels for half actions
$CommsAut$	: the set of product automata (CA)
TA	: the set of timed automata
L	: the set of locations in a given automaton
TL	: the set of transition labels of a given automaton
T	: the transition relation of a given automaton
$\mathbb{C}$	: the set of clocks
CC	: the set of clock constraints
C	: the set of clocks of a given automaton
CC_C	: the set of clock constraints restricted to clocks in C
$Clocks(\phi)$	: the set of clocks occurring in the constraint ϕ
$\mathbb{V}$	: the space of clock valuations
$\mathbb{V}_C$	: the space of valuations restricted to clocks in C
$Runs(A)$	: the set of runs of A
$ZRuns(A)$	: the set of zeno runs of A

$Loops(A)$: the set of loops in A
$Loc(lp)$: the set of locations of lp
$Clocks(lp)$: the set of clocks occurring in any invariant of lp
$Trans(lp)$: the set of transitions of lp
$Guards(lp)$: the set of guards of lp
$Resets(lp)$: the set of clocks reset in lp
$Act(lp)$: the set of transition labels in lp
$HL(|A)$: the set of pairs of matching half loops in $|A$
$CL(|A)$: the set of completed loops in $|A$
$Esc(lp)$: the set of escape transitions of lp

where A is an automaton, $|A$ is a network of automata and lp is a loop.

In Infinite State Communicating Automata, Discrete Timed Automata and Fair Transition Systems

$\mathcal{A}$: the set of actions of a given automaton
$COMP(\mathcal{A})$: the set of completed actions in $\mathcal{A}$
$IN(\mathcal{A})$: the set of input actions in $\mathcal{A}$
$OUT(\mathcal{A})$: the set of output actions in $\mathcal{A}$
V : the set of variables in a given automaton or fair transition system
$V'(e)$: the set of variables modified by effect e
V_L : the set of local variables of a given automaton
V_S : the set of shared variables of a given automata network
Θ : the initialisation formula
Θ_L : the initialisation formula for variables in V_L
Θ_S : the initialisation formula for variables in V_S

Transitions

In Communicating Automata, Timed Automata and Timed Automata with Deadlines

$l \xrightarrow{a} l'$: a CA transition
$s \xrightarrow{a} s'$: an LTS transition
$l \xrightarrow{a,g,r} l'$: a TA transition
$l \xrightarrow{a,g,d,r} l'$: a TAD transition
$s \xrightarrow{\gamma} s'$: a TTS transition from s to s'

where l, l' are automata locations, s, s' are states, γ is either an action or a delay, a is an action label, g is a guard, r is a reset set and d is a deadline.

Relations

Δ_1 : the mapping from product automata (CA) to pbLOTOS specifications
Δ_2 : a mapping from product automata (CA) to CCS^{CAct} specifications

Other Symbols and Acronyms

CCS^{CAct} : a CCS variant with completed actions
$|A$: a network of automata
$\langle u_1, \ldots, u_n \rangle$: a location vector
$u[l \rightarrow j]$: substitution of locations (the jth component in u, by location l)
$\backslash^{CAct}$: the CCS^{CAct} restriction operator
Π^{CAct} : the CCS^{CAct} parallel composition operator
E_V : an expression on variables in V
$[\![v]\!]_s$ ($[\![E_V]\!]_s$) : the value of variable v (expression E_V) in state s
l_0 : the initial location of a given automaton
$I(l)$: the invariant of l, where l is a location of a given TA
$[l, v]$: a state with location l and valuation v
(l, Z) : a symbolic state with location l and zone Z
$r(Z)$: reset of zone Z w.r.t. reset set r
$Z^\uparrow$: forward projection of zone Z
$norm(Z)$: normalisation of zone Z

Contents

Part III Concurrency Theory – Further Untimed Notations

Part IV   Concurrency Theory – Timed Models

Part I

Introduction

1

Background on Concurrency Theory

1.1 Concurrency Is Everywhere

There are two main axes to mathematical research,

1. Refining and building upon existing mathematical theories, e.g. trying to prove or disprove the remaining conjectures in well explored branches of mathematics (Andrew Wiles's proof of Fermat's Last Theorem is such an effort [179]), and
2. Developing mathematical theories for new areas of interest.

The mathematical theory of concurrency is an example of the latter. Although concurrent systems are ubiquitous in our world, no mathematical theory of concurrent systems existed until the pioneering work of Carl Petri in the 1960s [161,169] and the field did not really come to maturity until the 1980s. Thus, in terms of the history of mathematics, the area of concurrency can firmly be considered to be new.

With what then is the area concerned? For want of a better definition, we give the following.

> Concurrency theory concerns itself with the development of mathematical accounts of the behaviour of systems containing a number of components, each of which evolves simultaneously with the others, subject to (typically frequent) interaction amongst the components.

The ubiquity of concurrent systems should be clear. In fact, although concurrency theory was inspired by the needs of designers and developers of computer systems, where critical advances (such as the construction of reliable communication networks) were aided by its definition, concurrency is everywhere in our world: all entities, whether they be plants, animals, machines, or whatever, execute in parallel with one another.

To take a familiar example, a car engine is a concurrent machine: spark plugs spark in parallel, pistons fire in parallel, wheels turn in parallel and engine components run simultaneously. Also, driving a car is a concurrent process: we seamlessly adjust our steering, change gear and maintain a conversation in a coordinated stream of parallel activity.

Furthermore, the concurrent nature of the world we inhabit is reflected by the multimodal nature of our sensory and effector systems: tactile, visual, acoustic and olfactory (smell) sensations are simultaneously relayed to and processed by the brain. Indeed, in the brain, all levels of cognitive activity have a concurrent element. For example, at the lower levels of cognitive processing, neurons evolve concurrently, and so do the neural circuits that are built from them.

In fact, our world can be seen to be fundamentally concurrent and we would argue that it is best to view concurrency as the norm, rather than the exception. As a reflection of this, we would further argue that sequential systems are best viewed as a special case of concurrent systems and this is what we do in this book. It is just the history of the development of computer science, where it was initially easier to work with sequential paradigms, that led to the historical over-emphasis on sequential systems.

1.2 Characteristics of Concurrent Systems

Three particularly important characteristics of concurrent systems are:

1. **Interaction** – components interact with one another;
2. **Nontransformational** – the ongoing behaviour is critical; and
3. **Unbounded Execution** – placing an upper bound on the execution time of the system is typically inappropriate.

The conjunction of these characteristics yields a class of systems that is closely related to what Manna and Pnueli call *reactive systems* [136]. However, we do not explicity use this term here.

We consider each of the above three characteristics in turn.

1. **Interaction**

   It is possible that components evolve both in parallel and completely independently of one another; that is, they do not interact. However, this scenario is not very interesting as it implies that components are completely isolated from one another: in order to generate sophisticated behaviour, components must communicate. Indeed the richness of concurrent systems can be seen to arise from interaction.

   Many different interaction mechanisms have been considered, e.g. asynchronous communication [56], synchronous communication [148] and by shared memory [136]. In this book, we use a particular variety of synchronous (message passing) communication. One reason for choosing this model of interaction is that it can be shown to be primitive in the sense that other forms of interaction can be built out of it (see, for example, the spectrum of buffer implementations defined in CSP [171]).

Furthermore, we wish to allow the possibility that control is distributed. That is that, unless explicitly required, components are autonomous and there is no centralised controller or repository at which the global state of the system is recorded. Approaches that employ a shared memory, through which components interact, typically contradict this characteristic and concurrently evolving components do have access to a global view of the state of the entire system.

2. **Nontransformational**

   The early years of computer science research were focused on what we can broadly call *transformational systems*. These are systems that can be viewed as input to output transformers: input is presented to the system, the system executes according to this input and then the system terminates and outputs its results.

   However, concurrent systems are not transformational because components evolve in parallel with their environment (whereas in transformational systems, there is a sequential relationship between system and environment) [136]. Thus, the key concern with nontransformational systems is not defining functions, which characterise input to output behaviour, rather it is describing the "ongoing" behaviour of systems and what series of interactions they can perform.

   In fact, some prominent researchers, e.g. Peter Wegner [197], have suggested that the class of concurrent systems is in computability terms more expressive than the class of transformational systems. In other words there exist concurrent computations that cannot be expressed by Turing machines!

3. **Unbounded Execution**

   It is typically inappropriate to place an upper bound on the execution of concurrent systems. Consider, for example, the Internet. This is a highly concurrent system, however, predicting and enforcing a life span for it is not appropriate. This is particularly true of many noncomputing concurrent systems such as biological and physics systems, the world itself being one example.

As a reflection of these three points, an execution of a concurrent system can be viewed as a (possibly infinite[1]) sequence of events.[2]

For example, the ongoing behaviour of a person driving a car would contain fragments such as:

```
..brake, depress_clutch, change_gear,
```

---

[1]In fact, there are different ways to handle this potential for infinite execution, which sometimes do not imply an infinite sequence, but this becomes clearer in the body of this book.

[2]Here we use the term event in a nonspecific way. Later in the book it comes to have a particular meaning.

`release_clutch, accelerate..`

where each of the events in this sequence would yield an interaction between the driver and components of the car, e.g. the brake pedal.

However, you should notice that, when concurrent systems are considered, viewing the behaviour in terms of such sequences can be problematic because the execution of events may overlap. For example, when we drive, there may be an overlap between the first two events in this sequence, i.e. braking and depressing the clutch. However, if we view events as atomic markers then this problem does not arise. This is a central point that justifies interleaved interpretations of concurrency and we return to it in Section 2.3.6 of this book.

In addition, although for almost all this book issues of the physical distribution of components are not explicitly considered (although, we discuss the related topic of mobility very shortly, in Section 1.3.4), there is an implicit assumption that, with the approaches we consider, components are physically distributed. It is worth noting that distribution is closely related to the issue of nontransformational systems. Specifically, tightly coupled concurrent systems can often exhibit transformational behaviour, but the more loosely coupled the components of a system, the more unlikely it is that a transformational behaviour will emerge from the concurrent interaction of components.

1.3 Classes of Concurrent Systems

From within concurrency theory a number of different classes of system are considered. Typically, these focus on particular aspects of concurrency and abstract from other aspects. We can distinguish among these classes on a number of axes. For example, we can distinguish between the following three axes:

1. **Timing**
2. **Probabilistic choice**
3. **Mobility**

First we consider the primitive class of concurrent systems that these axes generalise. Then we discuss each of the three axes in turn.

1.3.1 Basic Event Ordering

One abstract view of concurrent systems is to model them purely in terms of the order in which events occur. This was, for example, the approach implicitly taken above when we wrote out the sequence of events involved in changing gear. However, this sequence of events says nothing about the relative timing of different events. For example, it does not indicate how soon after depressing the clutch we should start to change gear.

Thus, all this class of system allows us to state is that events must follow one another, but it makes no distinction between whether events follow immediately or a million years after one another. As a reflection of this characteristic, it is often said that basic event ordering allows the *qualititative*, rather than the *quantitative*, properties of systems to be described, where quantitative refers to timing.

We suggest that basic event ordering is the minimal level of expressiveness required in order to specify interesting aspects of concurrent systems. It is the focus of Parts II and III of this book.

Each of the axes that we consider in the following sections gives a path to increasing the level of expressiveness of basic event ordering. They each generalise the basic event ordering approach according to a particular characteristic of concurrent systems.

1.3.2 Timing Axis

In order that we can define quantitative aspects of concurrent systems we need to add ways of expressing relative timing between events. This is what the timing axis considers.

The standard way of doing this is to add constructs that enable *deterministic timing* to be expressed (the term deterministic is used to distinguish this approach from the *stochastic timing* approach, which we discuss shortly). There are a number of subtle issues surrounding this addition of timing properties and hence many different approaches exist. However, all broadly provide a means to associate timing intervals with the enabling of events; i.e. upper and lower time bounds are placed on the interval of time in which an event can occur.

Broadly speaking, approaches employing deterministic timing generalise those employing basic event ordering. Ignoring some subtle issues that arise with particular formalisms, if all events are given a timing interval of zero to infinity, then deterministically timed systems behave as if no distinction were made between the times at which events can occur.

Part IV of this book considers how deterministic timing can be added to techniques for describing basic event ordering.

A further class of timed system comes from allowing stochastic timing. According to this approach, the interval of time in which an event can occur is sampled from a probability distribution function. A number of such approaches exist, e.g. [18,93,94], most of which only allow sampling from exponential distributions. The reason for this restriction to exponential distributions is that it yields a much more tractable class of specifications. However, if generalised distributions (which, for example, allow timings to be sampled deterministically) are used, then stochastic models would be able to generalise deterministically timed approaches.

1.3.3 Probabilistic Choice Axis

Another axis is generalising the choice implicit in basic event ordering to allow probabilistic branching. When describing concurrent systems, choice points have to be specified. For example, in our gear changing example, after braking, we might have a choice between depressing the clutch (in order to change gear) and accelerating away in the same gear. Informally, this could be depicted by the branching shown in Figure 1.1.

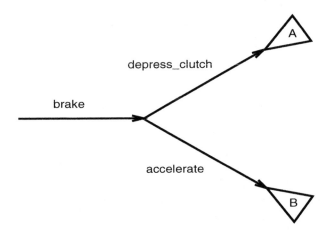

Fig. 1.1. A Choice Point

With basic event ordering, choices between different events are either offered to the environment for resolution or are resolved internally (and non-deterministically). For example, if we view the car as the system being described and the driver as the environment, the above choice between depressing the clutch and accelerating is an external choice, which the environment would make. However, we might wish to include the possibility that, due to a gear box failure, the gear cannot be changed and this would be modelled by an internal choice between the car offering the *change_gear* event and an event *lock_gear_box*.

Models can also be devised in which probabilities are associated with branches. Thus, in the above example, the probability of offering *change_gear* may be 0.999 and that of *lock_gear_box* 0.001.

In fact, probabilistic approaches and stochastic approaches (as considered in the last section) have a close relationship because sampling timings from probability distribution functions generates a race condition on branching. This race condition expresses the likelihood that one or other branch is likely to happen first, i.e. yields a form of probabilistic choice.

The main target of probabilistic branching is to give a more refined non-deterministic choice. Thus, rather than just stating that either branch could be taken internally, such approaches allow likelihoods to be associated with these internal choices. This is important when considering failure scenarios such as the gearbox locking example just highlighted. However, due to space limitations, we are not able to discuss this topic further in this book.

1.3.4 Mobility Axis

In their primitive form, approaches which just describe the basic event ordering of systems assume a static configuration of components. Thus, for example, it is not possible to change communication paths between components (if component A does not communicate with component B at the start of the execution of the system, it never will), and it is not possible for components to physically change locations.

Such mobility and dynamic reconfiguration, though, arises frequently in practice. For example, mobile phones and mobile computers or systems where autonomous agents move are typical examples of such systems.

There are now a number of ways to generalise basic event ordering models by adding mobility features, one of the most important being Milner's π-calculus [149]. In this book however, we do not consider such generalisations and restrict ourselves to considering timing generalisations.

1.4 Mathematical Theories

The previous sections of this introduction have clarified what we mean by concurrency theory. However, this leaves the question of what we mean by a *mathematical theory* of concurrency.

In a broad sense, our mathematical theory of concurrency has the same ingredients as the familiar mainstream mathematical theories, such as, for example, the theory of (counting) numbers (which is the heart of the mathematical discipline of number theory). We illustrate this by comparing the ingredients of the theory of numbers with those of concurrency theory.

1. **Values**

   These are the primitive elements in mathematical theories. They are the basic objects that the theory is about.

   The values in the theory of numbers are the integers,

   $$\ldots, -3, -2, -1, 0, 1, 2, 3, \ldots$$

   In contrast, values in concurrency theory denote the behaviour of concurrent systems. The event sequence that we illustrated earlier is related to such (concurrency theory) values. However, it is not wholly accurate to view a single trace as a value, because to characterise the behaviour of a system requires a number of traces. This is because systems will have choice points and thus, many traces could possibly result from a single system. In fact, a large part of this book is concerned with the issue of what constitute suitable values for concurrent systems and we show many different varieties of value: trace sets, trace-refusals sets, labelled transition systems, event structures etc.

By way of illustration, we present an example of a labelled transition system in Figure 1.2. Thus, nodes represent states that the system can be in, arcs represent that an event can occur and the labelling of arcs indicates which event occurs.

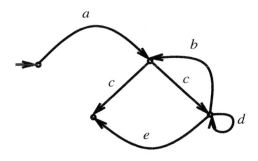

Fig. 1.2. A Labelled Transition System

One point to note is that the values in mathematical theories of computation (of which concurrency theory is a branch) are behaviours of systems: they code the possible executions of systems. This computational aspect of underlying mathematical objects is in contrast to standard mathematical theories, where values are static in nature. As a reflection of this, we use the term behavioural values to denote the values found in concurrency theory.

In one sense, standard mathematics typically provides a fixed static view of the world, whereas theories of computation are fundamentally dynamic, expressing how entities can evolve. Mathematical theories of computation must reflect this dynamic/behavioural aspect.

2. **Variables**

In the theory of numbers we use variables to symbolically denote values, e.g. X, Y or Z. In concurrency theory we do the same. Thus, we might denote the system that behaves as the labelled transition system in Figure 1.2 by P. In fact, we use variables to denote many different entities, e.g. action names (this becomes clear in the body of this book).

3. **Operators**

Arithmetic operators, e.g. $+$ and $\times$, are used in the theory of numbers to express how numbers can be transformed into other numbers. In concurrency theory we also have operators, e.g. $|||$ and $[]$. The former of these denotes a particular form of parallel composition and the second a choice between two alternatives.

4. **Expressions**

   Arithmetical expressions can be defined in the theory of numbers, e.g.

   $$(X + 73) \times 3$$

   These are built as "allowable" combinations of variables, values and operators. The same is true in concurrency theory. For example, we might write the following expression,

   $$(P \; [] \; Q) \; ||| \; R$$

   which states that two components, $P \; [] \; Q$ and R, are "run" independently in parallel with each other, where $P \; [] \; Q$ offers a choice between behaving as P and behaving as Q (the actual characteristics of this choice are clarified later).

   Notice that, due to the nature of our values, it is not possible to "quote" them inline in our expressions (although there are graphical notations which do something like this, e.g. Statecharts [87]). However, effectively, we can view the variables here, P, Q and R, as standing for particular labelled transition systems, i.e. behavioural values. In fact, once we have more operators, we will be able to code up labelled transition systems directly as expressions.

5. **Evaluating Expressions**

   If we give values to all free variables in an expression we can then evaluate it to get a (result) value. For example, if X is given the value 4, then $(X + 73) \times 3$ can be evaluated to yield 231 and the same applies to expressions in concurrency theory. So, for example, we will be able to take an expression such as,

   $$(P \; [] \; Q) \; ||| \; R$$

   and assign a labelled transition system value to it. This can be done because the definitions of the operators $[]$ and $|||$ state how a (result) labelled transition system can be built from two (argument) labelled transition systems. To be more precise, we define semantic mappings that define how (behavioural) values can be derived from (behaviour) expressions. This becomes clear during the next part of this book.

6. **Relations**

   In the same way that we can define relations between values in the theory of numbers, e.g. $<$ or $>$, and hence define relations between expressions, e.g. $X + 4 < X + 9$, we can do the same in concurrency theory. In particular, we define preorders and equivalences which characterise relationships between concurrency theory values. For example, we define a relation $\leq_{tr}$ (called trace preorder), which gives one interpretation of when a particular system (value) is "less than or equal to" a second system (value).

7. **Equality**

   Probably the most important relation is equality. For example, in the theory of numbers, $(X + 73) \times 3 = ((X + 72) \times 3) + 3$. The fact that these two expressions are equal is justified by the fact that whatever value you plug in for X, the two expressions evaluate to the same value.

In a similar way to equality in the theory of numbers, the theory of concurrency defines notions of equality, but this time it is between systems. In fact, there turn out to be many different possible notions of when two systems are indistinguishable and this is a significant element of the story of this book.

As we just stated, in the theory of numbers, evaluating to the same value is the sole justification for viewing two expressions as equal. However, in concurrency theory, equality between expressions is often more generous than the equality induced by evaluating to the same behavioural value. This means that there will be some expressions that we view as equal (in fact, equivalent) which are not semantically mapped to the same behavioural value.[3] One of the most important examples of such a relationship is *strong bisimulation* equivalence. This is denoted $\sim$ and if $P \sim Q$ then, broadly speaking, we can view P as strongly equivalent to Q. Once again, this is an issue that we return to later in this book.

8. **Proof Rules**

One of the most powerful techniques in mathematics is to identify proof systems. These are sets of rules about the particular mathematical theory under investigation, which allow equality (or other relations) to be demonstrated between expressions without recourse to evaluating the expressions. Thus, we can investigate the relationship between expressions at a more "abstract", syntactic, level. For example, in the theory of numbers we might have a rule such as the following,

$$X \times (1 + Y) = X + (X \times Y)$$

which states a general property about the relationship between multiplication and addition.

We can, once again, do the same in our theory of concurrency. For example, the following rule will turn out to hold,

$$a; P \,|||\, b; Q \ \sim \ a; (P \,|||\, b; Q) \,[]\, b; (a; P \,|||\, Q)$$

which the reader should not feel must be understood at this stage. It broadly shows how parallelism can be turned into sequence and choice and is justified by interleaving interpretations of concurrency. Such rules can be used to analyse systems; e.g. they can be used to determine that two descriptions of a system are behaviourally the same.

In fact, in this book, we are not strongly focused on proof rules. This is not because such rules cannot be devised in the domain of concurrency theory. Indeed a number of other texts give comprehensive presentations of proof rules for analysing concurrent systems, e.g. [148,171]. Rather, we focus on analysis methods that the power of modern computers have made feasible. That is, automatic verification techniques, such as equivalence-checking

---

[3]However, a particular relationship between their behavioural values must exist.

and model-checking. These are algorithms that undertake systematic exploration of the behaviour of a system description (i.e. its state-space). For example, equivalence checkers can determine when two descriptions of a system are equivalent by systematically traversing the labelled transitions arising from these descriptions, comparing what events the two descriptions can perform at each state.

The capacity to undertake such automatic verification arises naturally from the mathematical theory we develop[4] and is a major strength of modern concurrency theory. It is for this reason that automatic verification plays an important role in our presentation.

1.5 Overview of Book

The book comprises four parts. The first of these just contains this introduction. Then Part II presents a basic body of concurrency theory, focused on untimed models of concurrent systems. Specifically, Chapter 2 introduces a basic LOTOS calculus, denoted pbLOTOS. Then, in Chapters 3, 4 and 5, we consider a spectrum of different semantic models for this calculus. Following this, Part III considers a set of more advanced untimed modelling notations. Included are discussions of richer LOTOS calculi, which, in particular, have the capacity to define a spectrum of data types, in Chapter 6; a comparison with the calculi CCS and CSP in Chapter 7; and a consideration of communicating automata approaches in Chapter 8. Finally, Part IV of the book considers how the theory presented in previous parts of the book can be enhanced in order to model timed concurrent systems. Chapters 9 and 10 consider timed enhancements of the pbLOTOS theory developed in Part II, and the remaining three chapters (11, 12 and 13) consider timed versions of the communicating automata discussed in Chapter 8 and associated theoretical issues.

---

[4]Although, we consider infinite state frameworks (see the last section of Chapter 8 and the whole of Chapter 13) where automatic verification can only be applied to finite abstractions of full models.

Concurrency Theory – Untimed Models

This part contains core concurrency theory material. We present the process calculus pbLOTOS from first principles in Chapter 2, illustrating the approach with a number of running examples. Then, in Chapters 3, 4 and 5, we consider how this calculus can be interpreted semantically. In particular, we motivate the use of semantic models in concurrency theory in Chapter 3. Then, in the same chapter, we consider two simple semantic theories: (linear time) trace semantics and (branching time) labelled transition system semantics. Contrasting semantic theories are considered in Chapters 4, where we discuss true concurrency semantics, and 5, where we focus on testing theories.

2

Process Calculi: LOTOS

2.1 Introduction

A number of notations have been developed within concurrency theory for specification of concurrent systems, e.g. process calculi [96, 148],[1] temporal logics [136], Petri Nets [169] and extended finite state machines [105]. We will particularly focus on process calculi, as realised in the specification language LOTOS [101].

LOTOS (Language Of Temporal Ordering Specification) was defined during the 1980's by a standardisation committee chaired by Ed Brinksma of the University of Twente. The most significant influence on the design of the language was a number of previously defined process calculi, including CCS, CSP, CIRCAL [144] and ACP [15]. From amongst this list, the two most direct influences were CCS [148] and CSP [96]. In fact, the language is largely a composite of these two previous process calculi.

The language has two main parts: a behavioural part (sometimes also referred to as the process algebraic part) and a data part. The role of the behavioural part is to specify the order in which actions can occur; for example, you may specify that component B of a system receives messages from component A and then either passes the messages on to a further component, C, or loses the message. The data part on the other hand defines the data types that can be used in the behavioural part. For example, a queue data type might be defined. This queue type may then be used as an input queue by component B. Thus, when an action occurs at component B to indicate a message has arrived, the message will be added to the queue. The data part

---

[1]We prefer the term process calculus to process algebra, because in fact, the approach we present is not that advanced in algebraic terms. In particular, we do not consider algebraic proof systems. Although, the reader should be aware that the term, process algebra, is often used in the literature to describe very similar approaches to the one we highlight.

of LOTOS uses an abstract data typing language called ACT-ONE; see [24] for an introduction to this notation.

A process of restandardisation has been undertaken. One particular area of redefinition is the data part, which in its original form was seen to be very cumbersome and a hindrance to the uptake of the language. The ACT-ONE notation has been replaced with a functional notation. We discuss these revisions in Chapter 6.

It is quite easy though to view the behavioural and data parts as distinct. In fact, here we are almost exclusively interested in the behavioural part. We use the term *full LOTOS* (which we shorten to *fLOTOS*) to refer to the full language with data types and the term *basic LOTOS* (which we shorten to *bLOTOS*) to refer to the language without data types (i.e. just the behavioural part). We also subdivide basic LOTOS, because the full behavioural language contains a lot of syntax that is somewhat cumbersome to carry around when looking at the theoretical properties of the language. Thus, our main point of focus is a subset of bLOTOS that we call *primitive basic LOTOS* (which we shorten to *pbLOTOS*).

The next section (Section 2.2) introduces two specification examples that we use to illustrate formal description in LOTOS. Then Section 2.3 introduces pbLOTOS; and, finally, Section 2.4 presents example specifications written in pbLOTOS.

2.2 Example Specifications

A simple communication protocol and the Dining Philosophers problem are used as running examples. Both of these are standard examples of concurrent behaviour and readers who are familiar with them can safely skip this section.

2.2.1 A Communication Protocol

The communication protocol comprises three main components: a *sender process*, a *receiver process* and a *medium* (or channel). These components are depicted in Figure 2.1. The specification task here is to firstly model the behaviour of the medium (e.g. its ability to lose messages) and then to give sender and receiver process specifications that support reliable communication. The specification will use timeouts, sequence numbering and acknowledgement in order to do this.

The sender process obtains messages to send (also called packets or frames) from outside the protocol system (in terms of a layered protocol model, messages to send would be obtained from a previous layer in the protocol stack). The computation steps of the sender are: request a message from outside the system, successfully send the message (perhaps with some retransmission)

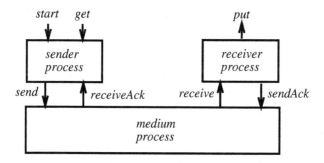

Fig. 2.1. Components in the Communication Protocol

and then request a new message. Thus, the protocol is a *stop and wait* protocol [187]; it waits for the current message to be successfully sent before it requests a new message to send.

Transmission using the protocol is initiated by a request to start from outside the protocol. The sender then obtains a message to send and sends it. Getting a message to send is identified by an event *get* being performed by the sender process with the environment and sending is identified by an event *send* occurring between the sending process and the medium. The medium then relays the message to the receiver. Successful transmissions cause an event *receive* to occur at the receiver process. However, the medium may lose the message, in which case no such event is able to occur. In addition, the receiver sends acknowledgements through the medium (so the medium is a duplex channel). Sending and receiving these acknowledgements are identified by the events *sendAck* and *receiveAck*, respectively. Successfully received messages are passed out of the system on the receiver side using the event *put*.

We consider two variants of this basic scenario. The first assumes a reliable acknowledgement medium. The second assumes that acknowledgements can be lost. We discuss these in turn.

- **Reliable Acknowledgement.** In this class of protocol, messages sent from the sender to the receiver may be lost, but acknowledgements will always be relayed successfully. This assumption simplifies the protocol considerably and avoids the necessity for sequence numbers. The sender process will still have to set a timer when it sends a message. If the timer expires, the message is assumed lost in transit and is resent.
- **Unreliable Acknowledgement.** The second variant assumes that acknowledgements may be lost. The troublesome scenario for such a protocol is that an acknowledgement is lost, the sender times out and retransmits the original message, which is successfully transmitted to the receiver. The receiver will have no way of knowing that this is a retransmission and will blindly pass it to higher layers, resulting in delivery of a duplicate message. Stop and wait protocols, which can lose acknowledgements, typically use

alternating bit sequence numbering in order to obtain reliable communication. A sequence number of zero or one is associated with every message. This means that retransmissions can be distinguished from transmission of new messages when an acknowledgement is lost, because the sequence number of a retransmission will have the same sequence number as the previously received message.

2.2.2 The Dining Philosophers

The Dining Philosophers scenario has been used for many years as an illustration of the problems associated with scheduling shared resources in concurrent systems. The version of the problem that we seek to specify is given by the following scenario.[2]

> Four philosophers (Aristotle, Buddha, Confucius and Descartes) are sitting around a table, which has a large plate of rice in the middle. Philosophers alternately think and eat. To be able to eat they must first pick up two chopsticks, one in their left hand and one in their right. They can pick up the chopsticks in any order, either right hand first or left hand first. Because there are only four chopsticks, not all of them can eat at the same time.

The table is depicted in Figure 2.2. A formal description of this problem will describe all the possible behaviours in which the four philosophers can engage.

2.3 Primitive Basic LOTOS

The Nature of LOTOS Specification. A major objective of formal description is not to over-specify and to allow implementation freedom by being non-prescriptive about aspects of realisation. Such avoidance of over-specification is at the heart of the process calculus approach. In particular, it is important that the correct interpretation is imposed on LOTOS descriptions. Specifically, they should be viewed as expressing the "externally visible possible behaviour" of a system. Specifications should be viewed as *black boxes*; they describe the order of possible external interaction, but do not prescribe how that interaction order is internally realised. Any physical system that realises the external behaviour is a satisfactory implementation.

The concept of the *environment* that a specification evolves in is central in obtaining this interpretation. The term environment refers to the behaviour that the *external observer* of a system wishes to perform. Note that this external observer could be either human or mechanical. Conceptually, a LOTOS

---

[2]This scenario is based upon a Dining Philosophers specification associated with the SEDOS tool set.

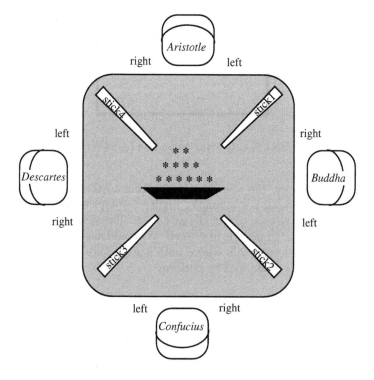

Fig. 2.2. The Dining Philosophers

specification only defines "possibilities" for evolution of a system and it is through interaction with a particular environment that these possibilities are resolved and realised. For example, if an environment cannot offer an action that a specification *must* perform, a deadlock will ensue.

As an illustration, we might view a LOTOS specification, called S, in the form depicted in Figure 2.3; i.e. as a black box with two interaction points between the specification and the environment, g and h. Such interaction points are called *gates* (the term *port* is also sometimes used). The set of all gates of a specification defines the *interface* to the specification. It is only through gates in this interface that an external observer can interact with the specified system.

Gates reference "locations" at which interactions can take place. At such gates, *actions* are performed. We say more shortly about this concept, but they can be thought of as interaction activities, e.g. passing a value, sending a message or pressing a button. In fact, the latter of these yields a nice pictorial representation of interaction between environment and specification. LOTOS descriptions define the order in which actions can be offered at gates; e.g. it might be that an action at gate g can only be offered once an action at gate h has been performed. Thus, typically, actions are only offered intermittently

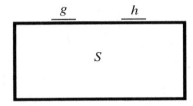

Fig. 2.3. Black Box Interpretation of a LOTOS Specification

at gates. We can view the offering of an action to the environment as the popping up of a button. For example, Figure 2.4 depicts the situation when an action is offered at gate g, but not at gate h. The environment can decide to push the button or to leave it unpushed. We could also have situations such as that depicted in Figure 2.5, where both buttons are up and the external observer has a choice of actions to perform.

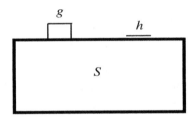

Fig. 2.4. Action Offering as Buttons Popping Up

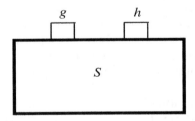

Fig. 2.5. Choice of Action Offers

We use this button-pushing analogy a number of times in our presentation of LOTOS.

Behaviour Expressions. As indicated already, we introduce pbLOTOS by working through the main constructs of the language. As also indicated already, we are interested in deriving *behavioural* specifications. As a reflection of this, the main unit of pbLOTOS specification is a *behaviour*. The operators that we introduce characterise the possible behaviour expressions that can be written in pbLOTOS. The set of all possible pbLOTOS behaviour expressions is denoted *Beh*; the variables B, B', B'', B_1, B_2, ... range over the set *Beh*; i.e. when we refer to such a variable it is implicitly assumed to be in *Beh*; e.g. $B \in Beh$.

There is one behaviour expression that we can highlight immediately; it is the null behaviour expression,

stop

which is a distinguished behaviour that performs no actions. In fact, it is synonymous with deadlock. *stop* is typically used to terminate a nonnull behaviour; i.e. it indicates that a point has been reached at which no more behaviour can be performed.

Behaviour Trees. We use a general notation, which we call behaviour trees, in order to depict the allowable evolutions of a behaviour expression. One of the semantics that we consider in the next chapter, *labelled transition systems*, has similarities to behaviour trees and can be seen as a formalisation of some aspects of behaviour trees.[3] Examples of behaviour trees are presented in Figure 2.6. The exact meaning of this graphical notation is made clear as we introduce the LOTOS constructs. Such a representation of behaviour is helpful for simple specifications, but becomes unmanageable when specifications become complex, e.g. if a large amount of recursive behaviour is included in a specification.

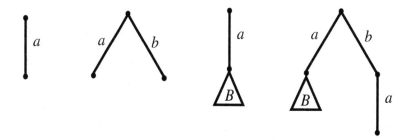

Fig. 2.6. Example Behaviour Trees

---

[3]In fact, labelled transition systems are more general than behaviour trees, because their underlying connectivity can be a graph; i.e. can contain cycles.

2.3.1 Abstract Actions

The first major principle is to assume the existence of a universe of *observable actions* (these are also called *external actions*). For example, in specifying a communication protocol we might assume the following observable actions exist.

- *send*, which references the instant that a message is transmitted from a sender process to a communication medium;
- *receive*, which references the instant that a message is passed from the communication medium to a receiver process;
- *timeout*, which references the instant that a sender process times out waiting for an acknowledgement;
- And similarly, *sendAck*, *receiveAck*, *get*, *put* etc;

and, in specifying the Dining Philosophers problem, we might assume the following observable actions:

- *pick*, which references the instant that a chopstick is picked up off the table; and
- *put*, which references the instant that a chopstick is put back onto the table.

The set of all such actions is denoted *Act*; i.e. this is the set of all possible actions that can be written; this set will clearly be infinite. *Act* is sometimes called the alphabet of actions. The variables u, v, x, y, z and their super- and subscripts, e.g. x', x'', x_1, x_2, ..., range over *Act*.[4] However, although *Act* is infinite, the set of actions used in a particular pbLOTOS specification is finite; i.e. a finite subset of *Act*. Assuming that a particular pbLOTOS specification is being considered, the set of all actions in the specification is denoted $\mathcal{L}$; i.e. the labels arising in the specification.

In pbLOTOS, actions and gates are synonymous. This is because no data is passed as part of an action, so, the name of the gate at which an action is performed completely defines the action performed at that gate. As a reflection of this, for pbLOTOS, the terms gate and action can be used interchangeably.

It is important to note that actions are *atomic*; they are atomic units of observation and cannot be divided in time. A consequence of this is that no two actions can occur at the same time and, thus, the occurrence of two actions cannot overlap. For example, a *send* and a *sendAck* or a *pick* and a *put* cannot happen at the same time. The atomicity of actions clearly has important consequences for the modelling of concurrency; we discuss these consequences in Section 2.3.6.

The restriction to atomic actions does not limit expressiveness, because nonatomic activities can be specified in terms of the actions that delimit the

---

[4]Not only is this convention employed in this chapter, it is followed throughout the book, unless otherwise stated.

activity; i.e. rather than defining an action that has duration, we can specify the atomic instant at which the activity starts and the atomic instant at which it stops. For example, rather than specifying that a philosopher eats, we specify that at some instant he starts eating (which could be marked with an action *pick*) and at some instant he stops eating (which could be marked with an action *put*).

Actions are a fundamental abstraction device. Systems are described in terms of such abstract entities rather than physical realisations; e.g. a communication protocol is described in terms of abstract actions rather than the physical mechanisms that realise the tasks of sending, receiving, timing-out etc.

A special distinguished action, i, is also used; it denotes an *internal action*; i.e. an action that is hidden from the external observer. The occurrence of an internal action is not externally visible. Thus conceptually, no button is raised when it is offered or pushed when it is performed. It is important to note though that although an i action is not externally visible, it may "indirectly" affect behaviour that is externally visible. Typically, an i action will represent an internal decision, resolution of which prescribes a particular visible behaviour.

The internal action has a number of roles. Firstly, it enables *information hiding*; actions that are observable at one level of specification can be transformed into hidden actions at another level. Thus, behaviour that should not be visible can be hidden. Such hiding supports a form of abstraction, because the complexity of a part of the system is abstracted away from, by hiding it, when specifying another part. In addition, internal actions play a central role in creating nondeterminism; see Section 2.3.4.

Internal actions also prove to be important when (behavioural) equivalences are defined. In particular, two specifications with different internal behaviour may achieve the same "observable" behaviour and could, thus, be considered equivalent.

Observable actions can be transformed into i using a hiding operator, which takes the form:

hide $x_1, \ldots, x_n$ *in* B

and states that wherever any of the actions $x_1, \ldots, x_n$ arise during the evaluation of the behaviour B they will be replaced by i. Thus, the gates $x_1, \ldots, x_n$ are removed from the interface of behaviour B. For example, if we assume B' models the behaviour of a sending process and contains an action *timeout*, we might wish to hide the *timeout* from all observers outside the sender; i.e.

hide timeout in B'

This hiding reflects the reality of networked communication, where, for example, the receiver process would be unable to observe a timer expiring in the sender. We use a, b, c, d, e and their super- and subscripts, e.g. a', a'', a_1, a_2, $\ldots$, to range over $Act \cup \{i\}$.

Actions are the basic unit of LOTOS specification and, typically, when performing a formal description using LOTOS, a set of actions in the problem domain would be located. Having identified the constituent actions of the specification we would like to order them in someway, i.e. to define the "temporal order" in which actions can occur (after all this is what basic event ordering models are about). The pbLOTOS operators allow us to do this. Thus, we postulate a universe of actions and then order them according to a set of primitive operators. Standard operators are: *sequence, choice, process instantiation* and *concurrency*.

2.3.2 Action Prefix

Basic sequencing of actions is defined in LOTOS using *action prefix*, which has the general form

   $a \,; B$

where a is an action from $Act \cup \{i\}$ and B is a behaviour. Thus, $a \,; B$ is a behaviour that will perform action a and then behave as B. We can depict the effect of this construct using the behaviour tree shown in Figure 2.7. Thus, action offers are attached to line segments in behaviour trees and unspecified behaviour, such as B, is depicted using a triangle.

In terms of pushing buttons, we can also view $a \,; B$ as a black box with a gate a (and gates for all the external actions in B). The button a is initially the only button raised; if the environment pushes a then the black box behaves as B (e.g. new buttons will be raised).

Fig. 2.7. A General Behaviour Tree Depicting Action Prefix

As an example, we may wish to specify that our medium process will perform a *send* action with the sender process and then perform a *receive* action with the receiver process (this behaviour is depicted in Figure 2.8):

   send ; *receive* ; *stop*

Notice the use of the distinguished behaviour *stop* to terminate the action offering of the sender. This behaviour states that the action *receive* cannot happen before the action *send* and, following the action *receive*, no more

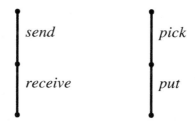

Fig. 2.8. Behaviour Trees of Action Prefix

actions will be offered. By way of clarification, this behaviour can be derived from the general form for action prefix by repeated application. In fact, as a reflection of this, the behaviour is actually a shorthand for the following fully bracketed behaviour

send ; (*receive* ; (*stop*))

where the repeated application is made explicit.

Alternatively, we might want to specify the following behaviour (depicted in Figure 2.8) for a dining philosopher

pick ; *put* ; *stop*

indicating that a philosopher cannot put his chopstick down until he has picked it up.

2.3.3 Choice

Choice is denoted

$B_1 \;[]\; B_2$

and states that either behaviour B_1 or behaviour B_2 will be performed. The choice of which behaviour to perform is determined by the initially offered action of the two behaviours. Typically, all such actions will be offered to the environment, which will choose which to perform; this decision will resolve the choice.

The necessity to offer such choices largely arises because of the move to systems that contain concurrency. A behaviour offering a choice of a number of observable actions to perform is really offering a menu of possible interactions from which concurrently executing objects can select. The behaviour is defining the set of actions to which it is willing to react. Such choices are not typically associated with sequential systems which are, in comparison to parallel systems, closed. The interaction choices between components are predetermined in sequential systems.

As an example of choice, we may wish to specify the sender behaviour depicted to the left in Figure 2.9:

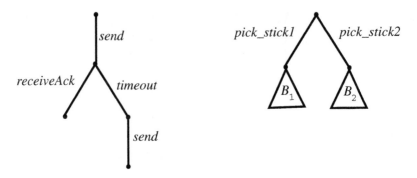

Fig. 2.9. Examples of Choice in Behaviour Trees

$send\,;\,(receiveAck\,;\,stop\,[]\,timeout\,;\,send\,;\,stop\,)$

This states that after a *send* the sender will either receive an acknowledgement or time out and retransmit, by performing another *send*. Each of the alternatives is completed by stopping.

We can also picture choice in terms of buttons popping up. For example, this behaviour yields a black box with gates *send*, *receiveAck* and *timeout* and it is initially in the state depicted in Figure 2.10(i). If the environment performs a *send* then the box progresses to the state depicted in Figure 2.10(ii). So, there is now a choice for the environment: does it press *receiveAck* or *timeout*? (In fact, in more advanced versions of this behaviour we hide *timeout* and do not make this choice externally visible, but for illustrative purposes we leave it visible here.) If the environment presses *receiveAck* no more actions will be offered; i.e. all buttons will be depressed. However, if *timeout* is pressed, the send button pops up and we progress to the (external) state depicted in Figure 2.10(i).

This is only a snapshot of the full behaviour of the sender and is far from complete. For example, after timing out we would actually like to specify that the behaviour recurses back to the start in order to resend. We have to wait until we have a few more constructs before we can express such behaviour.

In a similar way, we could specify the behaviour depicted on the right in Figure 2.9 as

$pick\_stick1\,;\,B_1\,[]\,pick\_stick2\,;\,B_2$

i.e. a philosopher can either pick up stick 1 or stick 2.

2.3.4 Nondeterminism

Nondeterminism goes hand in hand with concurrency. Because, in concurrent systems, components can evolve independently of one another, choices made

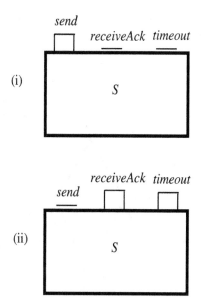

Fig. 2.10. Examples of Choice in Black Boxes

inside one component can create nondeterminism for the component's environment (i.e. all components that evolve in parallel with it). This is because components cannot "look inside" other components to see why they make a particular choice, thus, to the environment, hidden choices seem nondeterministic.

Another way of viewing this is that components are autonomous and thus, they make decisions for themselves, which are not "explained" to their environment. This does not mean that overall behaviour is nondeterministic; the emergent behaviour could be deterministic. Specifically, it will be deterministic if the environment can handle all the nondeterministic possibilities, i.e. if nothing is unexpected. Although many hidden choices are taking place in a car engine, (while faults do not occur) its emergent behaviour is predictable, once it has been explained to the driver by reading the car manual or passing a driving test.

Nondeterminism is defined in LOTOS as a special case of choice. Specific forms of choice yield a nondeterministic resolution of the alternatives. The main forms are:

(i) $i; B_1 [] i; B_2$

(ii) $i; B_1 [] x; B_2$

(iii) $x; B_1 [] i; B_2$

(iv) $x; B_1 [] x; B_2$

where x denotes an observable action and (ii) and (iii) are mirror images of each other; so, there are really three basic forms. Notice that these first three classes of nondeterminism could be created by hiding some actions in an otherwise deterministic behaviour. In addition, parallel composition can create nondeterminism, as we discuss in Section 2.3.6. The three basic forms are depicted in Figure 2.11.

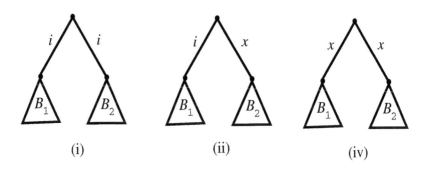

Fig. 2.11. General Forms of Nondeterminism in Behaviour Trees

The nondeterminism arises because selection between the two initial actions of the choice is beyond the control of the environment. For example, in (iv), when the external observer performs an x he or she has no control over whether the specification evolves to B_1 or to B_2. As a reflection of this, a nondeterministic choice is also referred to as an internal choice.

Each of these three forms yields a different variant of nondeterministic behaviour. Firstly, notice that forms (i) and (iv) are symmetric, while (ii) is nonsymmetric, in the sense that the left branch starts with an internal action, while the right branch starts with an observable action. We now consider each in turn.

- In (i), the initial evolution of the behaviour is completely hidden from the external observer; in terms of button-pushing, no buttons are raised. Thus, a wholly internal choice will be made to either evolve to behaviour B_1 or to evolve to behaviour B_2.
- In (ii), the initial evolution could also be completely hidden from the external observer; i.e. the left branch could be taken immediately and no buttons will be raised. However, if the external observer is quick enough to interact with the behaviour she could perform action x and evolve to B_2. However, if the external observer is either not quick enough or unable to perform an x, the behaviour will eventually evolve to B_1. Conceptually, the button x is raised, to see whether the environment can push it, and then, at some point, retracted (i.e. depressed). Critically though, because we are not yet in the business of quantitative time specification, the time

point at which x is retracted is not stated. Effectively, the specification says that, if the environment has not performed the x by some unspecified time point, it will be retracted.

- In (iv), the point of initial evolution of the behaviour is always externally visible; i.e. an x action will be offered and the corresponding button will be raised. However, the choice of evolving to B_1 or to B_2 after performing x is made internally and hence nondeterministically.

It is important to note the difference between a deterministic choice (sometimes referred to as an external choice) and a nondeterministic choice. For example, you should convince yourself that the following two behaviours, which are depicted in Figure 2.12, are different.

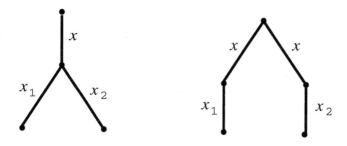

Fig. 2.12. A Deterministic and a Nondeterministic Choice

x ; (x_1 ; $stop$ [] x_2 ; $stop$) and x ; x_1 ; $stop$ [] x ; x_2 ; $stop$

Specifically, after performing an x action, the first behaviour will offer an external choice between performing an x_1 or an x_2, whereas, after performing an x action, the second behaviour will offer one of x_1 or x_2 to the environment, but, crucially, not the choice between both. In terms of button-pushing, we can depict the two behaviours as the two alternative sequences of black box states depicted in Figure 2.13, where the arrows indicate evolution of the system and, in particular, the two arrows in the nondeterministic black box indicate a choice of internal evolution.

Nondeterminism plays a number of roles in process calculi. In general it acts as an abstraction device. For example, nondeterminism is often introduced when, at a certain level of system development, we wish to abstract away from a particularly complex mechanism. A good example of this is in modelling loss in a communication medium. For example, the medium in our running example might be specified as follows,

$send$; (i ; B_1 [] $receive$; B_2)

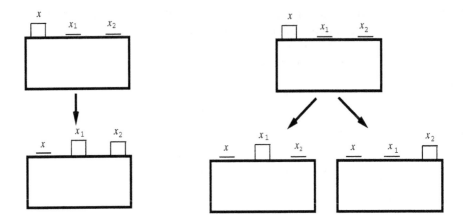

Fig. 2.13. Deterministic and Nondeterministic Choice in Black Boxes

which will perform a *send* action with the sender process (i.e. a message is sent to the medium) and then it will either nondeterministically decide to lose the message, represented by the i action, or pass the message on, represented by offering the *receive* action, with which the receiver process may interact.

What we are really doing here is abstracting away from the specific mechanism by which loss occurs in a communication medium. We are stating that some internal mechanism could occur and result in the message being lost, but, at the particular level of abstraction we are considering, we are not interested in how this happens. Notice that a complete specification of the mechanics of loss would probably require the physical laws of noise and attenuation on communication lines to be expressed.

There is also a sense in which nondeterminism is used in specification to allow implementation freedom. A nondeterministic choice between evolving to B_1 or to B_2 can be viewed as stating that implementations that behave as either B_1 or B_2 are satisfactory. Such a specification is stating that the specifier does not mind whether the system behaves as B_1 or as B_2. Such nondeterminism may then be refined out during development. This is the motivation behind refinement relations, such as reduction; see Section 5.1.6.2.

2.3.5 Process Definition

Basic Form. The basic unit of modularity is the process. The syntax for process definition is:

$$P[x_1, \ldots, x_n] := B$$

where $P \in PIdent$, the set of process identifiers. This states that the process identifier P is bound to the behaviour B. The list $x_1, \ldots, x_n$ indicates the

actions that are observable in B. $[x_1, \ldots, x_n]$ can be thought of as denoting
the interface of B, i.e. the actions that can be interacted with; it defines the
buttons that must be made available in a black box implementation of the
process P.

Instantiation of the behaviour B is performed through reference to P in
a behaviour expression (we also talk about invocation of processes; the terms
instantiation and invocation are interchangeable). In the process of instantiating P, we can alter the action names. For example, the definition

$$P[x, y, z] := B \quad \text{(a)}$$

could be invoked by referencing

$$P[u, x, w] \quad \text{(b)}$$

which has the effect of instantiating behaviour B in such a way that, whenever
it is specified to offer an x it offers a u, whenever it is specified to offer a y it
offers an x and whenever it is specified to offer a z it offers a w. The terms
formal and *actual* gates, are often used to refer to these action lists. Thus, in
the above example, x, y and z are formal gates of the process P, whereas u,
x and w are actual gates of the process instantiation.

In terms of black boxes, the definition of P, expression (a), can be depicted
as in Figure 2.14, whereas instantiation of P, expression (b), can be depicted
as in Figure 2.15.

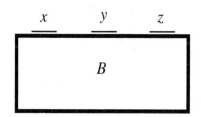

Fig. 2.14. Process Definition Black Box

Notice also that, in $P[x, y, z] := B$, the behaviour B can reference P and
thus create recursion. As an example, consider the behaviour

$$P[z, w] := z \,;\, w \,;\, P[w, z]$$

which, on invocation as

$$P[x, y]$$

yields the infinite behaviour depicted in Figure 2.16. Infinite behaviour is created by recursive process invocation. Notice also, recursive behaviour cannot

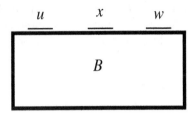

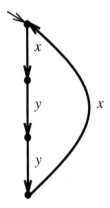

Fig. 2.15. Process Instantiation Black Box

be finitely represented in a tree. Thus, to denote such executions, we need to use what could be called behaviour graphs as a generalisation of the trees used to this point.

Fig. 2.16. An Infinite Behaviour

Sometimes when we use process definition and instantiation we drop the action list. So, we write

$P := B$

as a shorthand for

$P[x_1, \ldots, x_n] := B$

We only use this shorthand when the action list plays no role; i.e. action names are not renamed on process instantiation. Thus, a process definition such as

$P := x \, ; \, y \, ; \, stop$

cannot be invoked as

$P\,[z,w]$

Example. As an example of process definition and instantiation, the medium in the communication protocol example could be specified as a process called *Medium* and defined as follows.

$Medium[send, receive]$:=

    $send$; (i; $Medium\,[send, receive]$ [] $receive$; $Medium\,[send, receive]$)

This is actually a one-slot medium; i.e. it deals with one message at a time. A one-slot medium is suitable for a stop and wait protocol because only one message is in transit between the sender and receiver at any time. The process named *Medium* performs a *send* action with the sender. Then the medium will either nondeterministically lose the message or offer the action *receive* with which the receiver may interact. After either of these alternatives, the behaviour recurses by invoking *Medium* again, thus preparing the process for the next *send* action from the sender.

We can also specify a possible behaviour for the sender process as follows.

$Sender\,[get, send, receiveAck]$:=

    get; $send$; $Sending\,[get, send, receiveAck]$

$Sending\,[get, send, receiveAck]$:=

    $hide\ timeout\ in$ ($receiveAck$; $Sender\,[get, send, receiveAck]$

        []

        $timeout$; $send$; $Sending\,[get, send, receiveAck]$)

The top-level process here is *Sender*, which invokes the process *Sending*. We use the convention that process identifiers are written with a capital first letter, whereas action names are written with a small first letter. The process *Sender* obtains a message to deliver by performing the action *get* (remember this interaction takes place between the *Sender* and its environment); it transmits the message by performing *send* and then it invokes *Sending*.

The role of *Sending* is to ensure successful transmission of the message sent. In order to do this, *Sending* waits for an acknowledgement (the *receiveAck*) action; if it does not arrive in time a timeout occurs and the message is resent, modelled by offering the action *send* again. Notice that, if a *receiveAck* is successfully received then the recursive call takes us back to *Sender*, indicating that the message has been successfully transmitted, and we are ready to send another message. In contrast, after timing out and resending, we recurse back to the start of *Sending* and try for an acknowledgement to the resend.

Although they are the same actions, the two references to *send* are conceptually different: the *send* in *Sender* is an initial transmission, whereas the *send* in *Sending* is a retransmission of an old message. This distinction is justified because an initial transmission *send* is preceded by the action *get*.

You can think of the effect of the action *get* as being to fill the send buffer with a new message.

In this example, you should notice the approach of invoking a subprocess, which enables a repetition to be set up by recursing on the name of the subprocess. The definition and invocation of the process *Sending* is just such an example. In terms of state machines, *Sending* can be viewed as a state back to which the machine iterates. In fact, all constituent behaviours of a pbLOTOS specification can be viewed as states. For example, the behaviour expression:

$$get; \, send; \, Sending\,[\ldots]$$

can be viewed as a state from which a transition labelled *get* can be performed and the system evolves into state,

$$send; \, Sending\,[\ldots]$$

which is a state from which a transition labelled *send* can be performed and the system evolves into state,

$$Sending\,[\ldots]$$

To complete the set of processes in the communication protocol example, the receiver process and acknowledgement mediums can be specified as follows:

$$Receiver\,[put, receive, sendAck] :=$$
$$receive; \, put; \, sendAck; \, Receiver\,[put, receive, sendAck]$$

$$AckMedium\,[sendAck, receiveAck] :=$$
$$sendAck; \, receiveAck; \, AckMedium\,[sendAck, receiveAck]$$

As indicated earlier, we have assumed a reliable acknowledgement medium. Thus, the receiver simply receives messages and sends acknowledgements and the acknowledgement medium passes these messages on (and does not lose any of them).

Divergence. An important technical issue arising through recursion is the possibility of infinite internal behaviour, which is called *divergence*. The following behaviours give different examples of the phenomenon.

1. $P := i; \, P$
2. $P := x; \, stop \; [] \; i; \, P$
3. $P := x; \, stop \; [] \; y; \, hide \; y \; in \; P$
4. $hide \; x \; in \; (y; \, B \; [] \; z; \, P) \quad where \quad P := x; \, x; \, P$

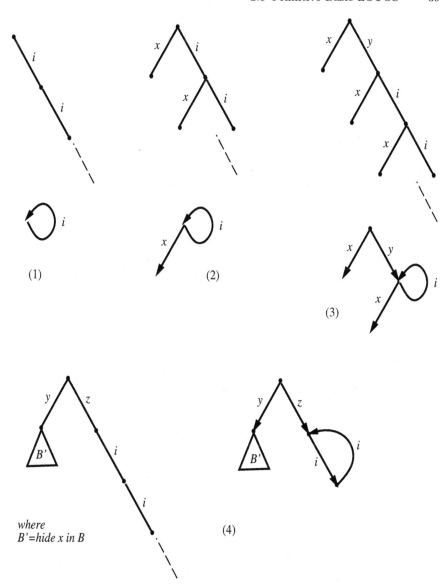

where
B'=hide x in B

Fig. 2.17. Divergent Behaviour

The behaviour of these expressions is depicted in Figure 2.17; both infinite expansions and cyclic depictions are presented.

Thus, (1) is a straightforward form of divergence; (2) offers the possibility, at every state, of not diverging by performing an x, but nonetheless it could diverge if the environment is never willing to perform an x; (3) shows how hiding can create divergence; and (4) shows how hiding can create divergence deep inside a subprocess.

The correct interpretation of divergence is a hotly debated issue, with one school of thought viewing divergence as degenerate in the extreme [96]. For example, extreme cases of divergence, where the recursive call is not even "guarded" by an internal action, are certainly problematic, viz:

$$P := P$$

We discuss these issues in some depth in Sections 5.1.4 and 7.2.6.

Relabelling. In order to correctly model the effect of process instantiation, another operator is required called *relabelling*. This has the form,

$$B\,[y_1/x_1,\ldots,y_n/x_n]$$

and has the effect of relabelling the x_is with the y_is in the behaviour B (i.e. buttons are renamed). Notice that $x_i \in Act$ for all $1 \leq i \leq n$, so internal actions cannot be relabelled; this also applies to the special (pseudo internal) action δ, which we introduce in Section 2.3.7. In the standard LOTOS language, the relabelling operator is not available to the specifier, rather it is used in defining the semantics of the language. This is because the basic form, i.e. renaming through binding actual gate names to formal gate names is viewed to be more usable from the specifier's point of view. However, the basic form is really just syntactic sugar for direct application of the relabelling operator. In particular, an invocation,

$$P\,[y_1,\ldots,y_n]$$

of a process definition,

$$P\,[x_1,\ldots,x_n] := B$$

can always be rewritten using our simplified form of process instantiation and relabelling, i.e.,

$$P\,[y_1/x_1,\ldots,y_n/x_n]$$

with a process definition,

$$P := B$$

This approach of completely dividing the mechanisms for process invocation and the mechanisms for relabelling leads to more elegant semantic definitions and is thus, generally used in our chapters on semantics. However, the basic form is kept for presentation of examples.

2.3.6 Concurrency

2.3.6.1 Independent Parallelism

We begin with a special case of concurrency; this is given by the operator $|||$, and has the general form,

$$B_1 \, ||| \, B_2,$$

which states that the two behaviours B_1 and B_2 evolve independently in parallel. Independent in this context means that there is no shared behaviour, which would arise if B_1 and B_2 performed some actions together.

We might, for example, use this construct to specify that the behaviour of two philosophers that do not share chopsticks are independent:

$$pick\_stick1 \, ; \, pick\_stick2 \, ; \, put\_stick1 \, ; \, put\_stick2 \, ; \, stop \, |||$$

$$pick\_stick3 \, ; \, pick\_stick4 \, ; \, put\_stick4 \, ; \, put\_stick3 \, ; \, stop$$

Of course, if they share a chopstick there would be some overlapping behaviour; we come to this situation shortly.

How though should we view such independent behaviour? In fact, the choice of interpretation to put on parallelism is one of the main issues in our discussion of semantics. However, here we focus on what is the standard interpretation: *interleaving*.

Interleaved interpretations of concurrency are justified by our assumption that all actions are atomic. Specifically, as discussed earlier, a direct consequence of actions being assumed to be atomic is that no two actions can occur simultaneously. Thus, in terms of action occurrences, there is no true simultaneity and any execution path through the specification will be a linear sequence of actions. As an illustration, consider the following simple example,

$$x \, ; \, stop \, ||| \, y \, ; \, stop$$

This behaviour specifies that the action x will be offered independently in parallel with the action y. Now, assuming atomicity of actions, we know that the occurrences of x and y cannot overlap, which implies that one must occur before the other. So, we obtain the following relationship,

$$x \, ; \, stop \, ||| \, y \, ; \, stop \, \equiv \, x \, ; \, y \, ; \, stop \, [] \, y \, ; \, x \, ; \, stop$$

where $\equiv$ means "are equivalent" (we make precise such notions of equivalence later in this book). This states that x occurring in parallel with y is the same as either the occurrence of x being followed by the occurrence of y or the occurrence of y being followed by the occurrence of x. Thus, interleaving allows parallelism to be expressed in terms of sequence and choice and although behaviours may be "truly in parallel", no two actions occur "truly" simultaneously. This interpretation allows us to depict independent concurrency very easily; a depiction of $x \, ; \, stop \, ||| \, y \, ; \, stop$ is given in Figure 2.18.

Figure 2.19 shows the following larger example of interleaved parallelism.

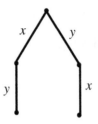

Fig. 2.18. Interleaved Parallelism

$(x ; y ; stop) ||| (y ; z ; stop)$

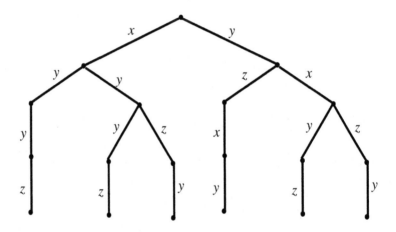

Fig. 2.19. Interleaved Parallelism 2

We have once again mapped concurrency to sequence and choice, but this time the possible alternatives are far greater. This is characteristic of interleaving: the number of states in the interleaved representation increases very rapidly as the complexity of the parallel behaviour increases. Also, notice that the y actions on both sides of the parallel behaviour occur independently. These two actions would have to be explicitly identified for synchronisation if they were to occur together. In addition, notice that some subbranches of the complete behaviour are repeated. Such repetitions could be pruned out.

Nondeterministic choices can also be created through parallel composition. For example, if the environment performs the action x, then the behaviour,

$(x ; stop) ||| (x ; y ; stop)$

will internally decide whether to offer just an x and then a y or an external choice between y and x, with the former evolving to offering an x and the latter evolving to offering a y. This behaviour is depicted in Figure 2.20. You should also notice that a similar instance of nondeterminism is embedded into the behaviour depicted in Figure 2.19; the nondeterminism is on the action y. Forms of nondeterminism based on internal actions can also be created through parallel composition.

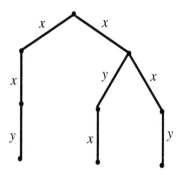

Fig. 2.20. Interleaving Creating Nondeterminism

2.3.6.2 General Form

As already stated, independent parallelism is one specific class of concurrent behaviour. Concurrency, in its most general form, is denoted

$$B_1 \; |[x_1, \ldots, x_n]| \; B_2$$

with the operator parameterised on the observable actions that must be synchronised, the $x_1, \ldots, x_n$. This behaviour states that B_1 and B_2 evolve independently in parallel subject to the synchronisation of actions $x_1, \ldots, x_n$; i.e. an action x_i ($1 \le i \le n$) appearing in either B_1 or B_2 can only be executed if it synchronises with an x_i in the other behaviour. Also notice that internal actions cannot synchronise; this is because they are not externally visible and, thus, cannot be interacted with.

As examples, consider the following behaviours.

(i) $(x; y; stop) \; |[y]| \; (y; z; stop)$

(ii) $(x; y; stop) \; |[x]| \; (x; z; stop)$

(iii) $(x; stop) \; |[y]| \; (z; stop)$

(iv) $(x; y; stop) \; |[y]| \; (z; stop)$

(v) $(x; y; w; stop) \; |[x,y]| \; (x; z; stop)$

(vi) $(x; y; stop) \; |[y]| \; (i; z; stop)$

Their behaviour trees are depicted in Figure 2.21. For each of the behaviours, independent parallelism is constrained by synchronisation of the actions in the gate set.

- (i) Synchronisation on y results in a totally sequential behaviour. In particular, notice that the y on the right-hand side of the behaviour cannot occur without the left-hand side offering a y with which to synchronise. Thus, the x must be performed first.
- (ii) Synchronisation on x still allows y and z to be arbitrarily interleaved once x has occurred.
- (iii) The interleaving of the two behaviours is unconstrained because y does not appear in either behaviour.
- (iv) The interleaving of x and z is unconstrained, but because the y action is identified for synchronisation and does not appear on both sides of the parallel operator, it does not occur. The behaviour on the left-hand side is, in fact, unable to proceed once the x action has been performed; i.e. it is locally deadlocked.
- (v) Firstly, the x action is synchronised on, then the z action can occur, but, once again, the y action is deadlocked. The inability to perform a y blocks the w action from being offered as well.
- (vi) The interleaving of x and i is unconstrained by the synchronisation on y and the z action can follow the occurrence of i. However, the y action is blocked from being offered.

Generalised parallelism, $|[\ldots]|$, has two special cases, one of them we have seen already:

$$B_1 \;|||\; B_2,$$

which is equivalent to writing, $B_1 \;|[\;]|\; B_2$, i.e. general parallel composition with an empty synchronisation set; and,

$$B_1 \;||\; B_2$$

which is equivalent to generalised parallelism with a synchronisation set containing all the actions of B_1 and B_2 or alternatively containing all the actions in $\mathcal{L}$. Thus, $|||$ gives the composition of independent concurrent threads and $||$ gives fully synchronised parallelism.

As illustrations of fully synchronised parallelism, consider the following behaviours (behaviour trees for which are presented in Figure 2.22).

- (i) $(\,x\,;\,y\,;\,stop\,)\;||\;(\,x\,;\,y\,;\,z\,;\,stop\,)$
- (ii) $(\,x\,;\,y\,;\,z\,;\,stop\,)\;||\;(\,z\,;\,y\,;\,z\,;\,stop\,)$
- (iii) $(\,x\,;\,stop\,[]\,y\,;\,stop\,[]\,z\,;\,w\,;\,stop)\;||\;(\,x\,;\,stop\,[]\,i\,;\,y\,;\,stop\,)$

Thus, (i) can successfully synchronise on x and then y, but then is unable to progress, as the z action is only offered on one side of the parallel composition.

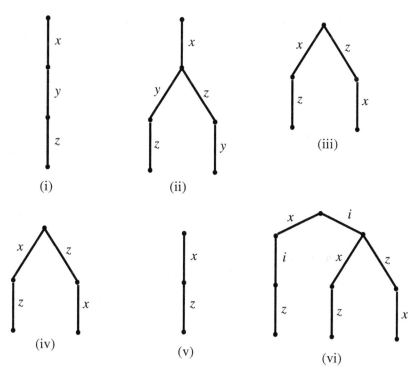

Fig. 2.21. Generalised Parallelism

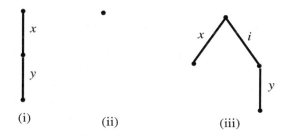

Fig. 2.22. Fully Synchronised Parallelism

In contrast, (ii) can perform no actions and thus induces the indicated trivial behaviour tree, because it cannot even synchronise on an initial action. (iii) illustrates how choice and internal actions behave through fully synchronised parallelism. In particular, notice how one of the branches of the left-hand choice is blocked because z is not offered as an initial action of the right-hand choice. In addition, the internal action is not subject to synchronisation, so appears in the resultant behaviour.

As a reflection of the relationship between generalised parallelism and the two operators $|||$ and $||$, only $|[\ldots]|$ is included in pbLOTOS; $|||$ and $||$ are viewed as derived operators; i.e. $||| = |[\ ]|$ and $|| = |[x_1,\ldots,x_n]|$ where $\{x_1,\ldots,x_n\} = \mathcal{L}$.

2.3.6.3 Example

As a more concrete illustration of parallel composition, in the communication protocol example we might compose the two mediums together to form a duplex medium as follows,

$$DupMedium\,[send, receive, sendAck, receiveAck] :=$$

$$Medium\,[send, receive]\,|||\,AckMedium\,[sendAck, receiveAck]$$

This states that the behaviour of the two mediums is independent, which is as expected, because the two directions of communication do not affect each other. We can now define the top-level behaviour of the protocol as follows:

$$(\,(\,Sender\,[get, send, receiveAck]\,|||\,Receiver\,[put, receive, sendAck]\,)$$

$$|[send, receive, sendAck, receiveAck]|$$

$$DupMedium\,[send, receive, sendAck, receiveAck]\,)$$

So, the *Sender* and *Receiver* processes evolve independently, but communicate by synchronising on the commmon gates *send, receive, sendAck* and *receiveAck* through the duplex medium.

2.3.6.4 Why Synchronous Communication?

As indicated already, in LOTOS concurrent threads of control interact by *synchronous communication*. Synchronous message passing is chosen because it can be viewed as the primitive mechanism from which other communication paradigms, e.g. asynchronous communication or remote procedure call, can be defined.

The particular class of synchronous communication employed in LOTOS is *multiway* synchronisation. Thus, any number of behaviour expressions can be involved in a synchronous communication. For example, in the following behaviour,

$$P\,[x,y]\,|[x]|\,Q\,[x]\,|[x]|\,R\,[x,z]$$

all three of the processes, P, Q and R, have to synchronise in order to perform the action x.

The LOTOS multiway synchronisation plays an important role in the *constraint-oriented* style of specification [171, 195]. The term constraint-oriented is used to refer to an incremental system development style in which system specifications are refined by imposing behavioural constraints on the system. This is done by composing the system in parallel with a piece of behaviour, which reflects this constraint. It is suggested that such an approach offers a powerful incremental development methodology [195].

You should also be aware of the important role that hiding plays in relation to multiway synchronisation. Specifically, hiding is used to "close off" an interaction and prevent further synchronisation on a particular action. This implies a very specific order to the application of operators in constraint-oriented styles of specification. In particular, an interaction cannot be hidden until the behaviour has been fully constrained through parallel composition.

2.3.7 Sequential Composition and Exit

Action prefix defines sequencing for actions, however, we would also like to define sequential composition of complete behaviours. This is supported by the *sequential composition* operator (also called *enabling*),

$$B_1 >> B_2$$

which will evolve as B_1 then; if B_1 terminates successfully, it will behave as B_2. The concept of successful termination is pivotal here. We do not wish $B_1 >> B_2$ to evolve to B_2 unless B_1 completes its evolution. In particular, if B_1 is in a deadlock state we would wish $B_1 >> B_2$ to evolve to the same deadlock state. Thus, we introduce a special distinguished behaviour,

exit

to denote successful termination. For example, consider the following behaviour expressions.

(i) $(x; y; exit) >> (z; stop)$

(ii) $(x; y; stop) >> (z; stop)$

(iii) $(x; stop \, [] \, y; exit) >> (x; stop)$

(iv) $(x; exit \, ||| \, y; exit) >> (z; stop)$

(v) $(x; stop \, ||| \, y; exit) >> (z; stop)$

(vi) $(x; exit \, |[x]| \, y; exit) >> (z; stop)$

(vii) $x; y; exit$

Behaviour trees for expressions (i) to (vi) are depicted in Figure 2.23 and expression (vii) is shown in Figure 2.24. We consider each of the examples in turn.

- (i) The left-hand behaviour is performed first (x followed by y), then an internal action is performed (reflecting the successful termination at *exit*) and this is followed by the right-hand behaviour (performing the z action).

- (ii) Only the left-hand behaviour is performed here. This is because the left-hand behaviour does not successfully terminate, i.e. there is no *exit*, so, the right-hand behaviour is not enabled.
- (iii) Only one branch of the choice successfully terminates and thus, only this branch is postfixed with the right-hand behaviour.
- (iv) It is important to note that, in the behaviour on the left side of $>>$ both sides of the parallel composition successfully terminate. Thus, in whatever state the left-hand behaviour terminates, it will be followed by the right-hand behaviour.
- (v) In contrast to (iv), because only one side of the parallel composition concludes with an exit, the behaviour on the left of $>>$ cannot successfully terminate and, thus, the right-hand behaviour cannot follow. This is an important aspect of sequential composition. Both branches of a parallel composition must successfully terminate in order for the whole of a parallel composition to successfully terminate. With some thought you will be able to convince yourself that this correctly reflects the behaviour of concurrent threads of execution.
- (vi) Because it is in deadlock after performing action y, the left-hand side of this behaviour is not able to successfully terminate.
- (vii) The behaviour successfully terminates by performing a δ action (see Figure 2.24). However, there is no behaviour to enable, thus, the δ action is left dangling. δ is a special action used to signal successful termination and, thus, enable a sequential composition. It is really a semantic device, which enables sequential composition to work. We postpone a full discussion of its behaviour until we consider actual semantic approaches. However, you should note that δ cannot be explicitly used by a specifier, thus, $\delta \notin Act$; it is a distinguished event, which has some similarities to i.

As a more concrete example of the use of successful termination, consider the Dining Philosophers example. We might want to specify that a philosopher can only perform the behaviour of putting his chopsticks down once he has performed the behaviour of picking his chopsticks up:

$$(pick\_stick1\,;\, exit \,|||\, pick\_stick2\,;\, exit)$$
$$>> (put\_stick1\,;\, stop \,|||\, put\_stick2\,;\, stop)$$

Notice that this expresses that the chopsticks can be picked up and put down in any order, modelled by actions on stick 1 and stick 2 being placed independently in parallel. But, it is only after both chopsticks have been picked up that a successful termination can occur and we can evolve to putting down the chopsticks. This behaviour is depicted in Figure 2.25.

As suggested by this example, the main role of the sequential composition operator is in enabling specifiers to subdivide their specifications into phases. Here we have decomposed into a picking-up phase and a putting-down phase and there will be a synchronisation (the successful termination) before moving between phases. We could specify this example using just action prefix and

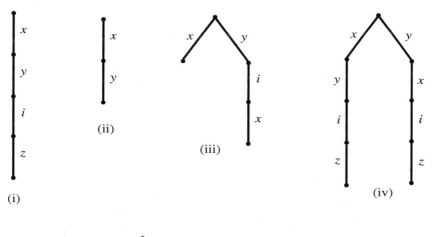

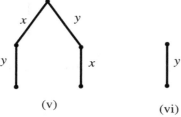

Fig. 2.23. Sequential Composition and Exit

(vii)

Fig. 2.24. Further Sequential Composition and Exit Illustration

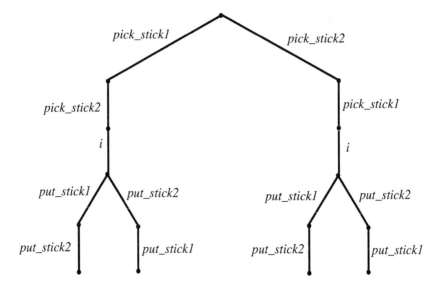

Fig. 2.25. Sequential Composition in the Dining Philosophers

choice (and possibly concurrency), but the specification would be far more complex and difficult to understand without the high-level description provided by >>. For example, the following is a specification of this behaviour that avoids the use of >>,

$$(\textit{pick\_stick}1 \,;\, \textit{pick\_stick}2 \,;\, i \,;\, (\textit{put\_stick}1 \,;\, \textit{stop} \,|||\, \textit{put\_stick}2 \,;\, \textit{stop}))$$
$$[] \,(\textit{pick\_stick}2 \,;\, \textit{pick\_stick}1 \,;\, i \,;\, (\textit{put\_stick}1 \,;\, \textit{stop} \,|||\, \textit{put\_stick}2 \,;\, \textit{stop}))$$

and more complex specifications can be given.

2.3.8 Syntax of pbLOTOS

This section brings together the constructs that we have introduced to give an abstract syntax for pbLOTOS. The syntax defines an arbitrary pbLOTOS specification $S \in pbLOTOS$ as follows.

$$S \ ::= \ B \ | \ B \ where \ D$$
$$D \ ::= \ (P[x_1, \ldots, x_n] := B) \ | \ (P[x_1, \ldots, x_n] := B) \, D$$
$$B \ ::= \ stop \ | \ exit \ | \ a \,;\, B \ | \ B_1 \, [] \, B_2 \ | \ B_1 \, |[x_1, \ldots, x_n]| \, B_2 \ |$$
$$\qquad \quad B_1 \, >> \, B_2 \ | \ hide \ x_1, \ldots, x_n \ in \ B \ | \ B \, [y_1/x_1, \ldots, y_n/x_n] \ |$$
$$\qquad \quad P[x_1, \ldots, x_n]$$

$a \in Act \cup \{i\}$, $x_i, y_i \in Act$, $D \in DefList$ (the set of pbLOTOS definition lists), $P \in PIdent$ (the set of process identifiers) and $B \in Beh$. The set of pbLOTOS definitions is denoted *Defs*. Also note that the body of a definition (denoted *B* above) could contain a reference to the process identifier (*P*), thus setting up a recursive behaviour.

So, the top-level structure of a *pbLOTOS* specification (the first clause) is either a behaviour or a behaviour and an associated list of process definitions. Definitions have the expected form. There can be many such definitions. Behaviours are the main syntactic construct; they can be constructed using any of the operators and constructs that we have introduced.

In many circumstances we simplify the expression of action sets and mappings in parallel composition, hiding and relabelling operators, as follows,

$$B_1 \ |[G]| \ B_2 \ \triangleq \ B_1 \ |[x_1, \ldots, x_n]| \ B_2$$

$$\text{where, } G = \{ x_1, \ldots, x_n \}$$

$$hide \ G \ in \ B \ \triangleq \ hide \ x_1, \ldots, x_n \ in \ B$$

$$\text{where, } G = \{ x_1, \ldots, x_n \}$$

$$B\,[H] \ \triangleq \ B\,[y_1/x_1, \ldots, y_n/x_n]$$

$$\text{where, } \ H \ : \ Act \cup \{i, \delta\} \ \longrightarrow \ Act \cup \{i, \delta\}$$

$$\text{and} \quad H(a) \ \triangleq \ if \ a = x_i \ (1 \le i \le n) \ then \ y_i \ else \ a$$

We typically simplify presentation, by assuming the following operator precedences,

action prefix > choice > parallel composition > enabling > hiding > relabelling

where *A > B* states that *A* binds more tightly than *B*. So, for example, the expression:

$$hide \ y \ in \ y \,; \ x \,; \ stop \ [] \ z \,; \ exit \ ||| \ x \,; \ exit \ >> \ z \,; \ stop$$

would be fully parenthesised as:

$$hide \ y \ in \ (\,(\,(\,(y \,; \ (x \,; \ stop)) \ [] \ (z \,; \ exit)\,) \ ||| \ (x \,; \ exit)\,) \ >> \ (z \,; \ stop)\,)$$

It should also be pointed out that the different operators of pbLOTOS can be subdivided according to their character. For example, we can view the operators, *stop*, action prefix, choice and process instantiation as "low-level" (more primitive) operators, whereas the operators, such as parallel composition, enabling, hiding and relabelling, can be viewed as more "high-level" operators. This is in the sense that the high-level operators facilitate high-level specification structuring. Such high-level structuring may, for example, reflect real-world identifiable components. Identification of such components in specifications using just low-level operators is often less straightforward.

In fact, a behaviour expressed using high-level operators can typically be mapped to an equivalent behaviour expressed purely in terms of the low-level operators. A very important example of such a mapping is the *expansion* law for a calculus [101, 148], which relates parallel composition to action prefix and choice. In effect, the expansion law realises the interleaved interpretation of parallelism. As a reflection of this, parallel composition cannot so naturally be viewed as a high-level operator when true concurrency semantics are being considered, which they are in Chapter 4.

The term *monolithic* specification is often associated with a specification expressed purely in terms of the low-level operators. Thus, there is a clear distinction between specifications expressed in a constraint-oriented style, as highlighted in Section 2.3.6.4, and those expressed in a monolithic style.

2.4 Example

The following is a specification in pbLOTOS of the behaviour of the communication protocol with reliable acknowledgement. The top-level behaviour of the protocol is specified as a process called *Protocol*.

$Protocol\,[start, get, put] :=$

  $start$;

   $hide\ send,\ receive,\ sendAck,\ receiveAck\ in$

    $(\,(\,Sender\,[get, send, receiveAck]\ |||\ Receiver\,[put, receive, sendAck]\,)$

     $|[send, receive, sendAck, receiveAck]|$

    $DupMedium\,[send, receive, sendAck, receiveAck]\,)$

So, the action *start* initiates the behaviour of the protocol. This causes the processes *Sender*, *Receiver* and *DupMedium* to be invoked according to the required parallel composition. Notice, all the actions *send*, *receive*, *sendAck* and *receiveAck* are hidden from outside the protocol. Such hiding reflects the fact that the actions involved in implementing the protocol are hidden from users of the protocol. The behaviour of the sender could be specified as follows (this is the behaviour we discussed earlier).

$Sender\,[get, send, receiveAck] :=$

  get ; $send$; $Sending\,[get, send, receiveAck]$

$Sending\,[get, send, receiveAck] :=$

  $hide\ timeout\ in\ (\,receiveAck$; $Sender\,[get, send, receiveAck]$

    $[]\ timeout$; $send$; $Sending\,[get, send, receiveAck]\,)$

The behaviour of the receiver could be specified as follows.

$Receiver\,[put, receive, sendAck] :=$

  $receive$; put ; $sendAck$; $Receiver\,[put, receive, sendAck]$

The top-level behaviour of the medium could be specified as

$DupMedium\,[send, receive, sendAck, receiveAck] :=$
    $Medium\,[send, receive] \;|||\; AckMedium\,[sendAck, receiveAck]$

which in turn uses the following sending medium,

$Medium[send, receive] :=$
    $send\,;$
        $(\,i\,;\,Medium\,[send, receive]$
        $[]\; receive\,;\,Medium\,[send, receive]\,)$

and the following acknowledgement medium,

$AckMedium\,[sendAck, receiveAck] :=$
    $sendAck\,;\, receiveAck\,;\, AckMedium\,[sendAck, receiveAck]$

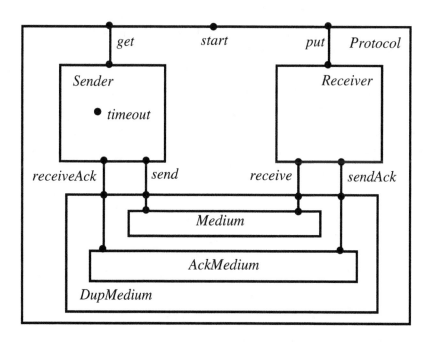

Fig. 2.26. Box Diagram of the Communication Protocol

We can explicitly depict the structure of the protocol specification using a box diagram, such as in Figure 2.26. This diagram shows the process structure of the specification; you should notice that the structure closely resembles our original depiction of the protocol in Figure 2.1. The process *Sending* is not included in this diagram as it sets up a mutual recursion with *Sender*, which is difficult to depict. Such diagrams as these are only really useful for representing static process structure, the dynamics of process instantiation quickly become unrepresentable.

The interface of each process is directly represented. For example, the process protocol has three external gates, *start*, *get* and *put*, which are distinguished from internal gates by being linked to the exterior of the *Protocol* box. In addition, the fact that subprocesses interact on external gates is indicated by a line segment, e.g. the attachment of *get* to *Sender*. In contrast, *start* is not interacted with by any subprocess. All actions in the specification are depicted (apart from the *i* action in *Medium*). Notice also that the diagram shows that *timeout* is completely internal to the process *Sender* and that the gates *receiveAck*, *send*, *receive* and *sendAck* are hidden from the interface of the process *Protocol*.

Finally, the top-level behaviour of the protocol specification will invoke the process *Protocol* and thus initiate its evolution, e.g.

Protocol [*sstart*, *ssend*, *rreceive*]

where the external gates of the protocol have been renamed, *start* to *sstart*, *get* to *ssend* and *put* to *rreceive*.

3

Basic Interleaved Semantic Models

This chapter considers two of the main semantic models that can be associated with LOTOS. We begin by discussing the motivation for giving semantics to specification notations and then we discuss the relevant semantics: *trace semantics* (in Section 3.2) and *labelled transition systems* (in Section 3.3). Note also that two further semantics are introduced, *event structures*, in Chapter 4, and trace-refusals, in Chapter 5.

In addition, as an illustration of the value of semantic models, Section 3.4 considers how tools to analyse the behaviour of specifications (i.e. verification tools) can be developed from these semantic models.

3.1 A General Perspective on Semantics

3.1.1 Why Semantics?

The constructs of specification and programming languages are chosen to ease the task of system specification. They are "natural" at the level of the system developer's view of computer systems. This is reflected in the "high-level" specification constructs offered by LOTOS, e.g. parallel composition, sequential composition etc. In contrast, semantic models are not intended to be natural vehicles for specification; rather they express the "meaning" of specifications. This is similar to the way in which execution of a program expresses the meaning of a program; it is what the program does; e.g. the meaning of a hello world program is to output the words "hello world" and then terminate. In this sense, semantics are the machine code of formal specification; they express what a specification does. This interpretation is reflected in the terminology that is often associated with semantics; a semantics is sometimes referred to as a *model* or even an *implementation* of a specification.

It is mportant to note though that, semantics define *mathematical models* of the meaning of specifications and, thus, the meaning of specifications can be analysed. As an initial example, we might define the meaning of the LOTOS behaviour,

x ; y ; $stop$ [] z ; w ; $stop$

as the following set,

{ ϵ , x , z , xy , zw }

which defines the possible "linear" sequences of actions, or executions, that the behaviour can perform. The symbol ϵ denotes an empty sequence / trace. Notice, the set reflects all possible positions in the evaluation of the behaviour, even before any evaluation has occurred, i.e. after ϵ. Thus, it represents all possible complete or partial executions of a system. This reflects the characteristics of nontransformational (reactive) systems, as discussed in Section 1.2.

Perhaps the most significant value of semantics is that they enable the meaning of different specifications to be compared and allow us to answer questions such as: are two specifications the same or alternatively are they developments / refinements of each other? For example, we might want to view the following pairs of LOTOS behaviours as equal, because "intuitively" we can see that they have the same meaning.

$(x$; y ; $stop)$ [] $(z$; w ; $stop)$ and $(z$; w ; $stop)$ [] $(x$; y ; $stop)$

$(x$; x ; $stop)$ and $(x$; x ; $stop)$ [] $(x$; x ; $stop)$

$(x$; y ; $stop)$ || $(y$; x ; $stop)$ and $stop$

$(x$; $stop$ [] y ; $stop)$ || x ; $stop$ and x ; $stop$

Such relating of specifications is not possible without semantics, because purely syntactic comparison will distinguish the pairs. In contrast, if we were to compare the trace sets of the pairs, they would be equal. Thus, a trace semantics would equate the two specifications in each pair, as we require.

It is also worth pointing out that the flip side of knowing what syntactic structures are equivalent is locating what structures are to be differentiated. For example, an obvious approach to obtaining equality in a syntactic setting is to directly identify syntactic laws that characterise how behaviours relate, in the spirit of the proof rules we discussed in Section 1.4. An obvious such law is distributivity of ; through []. However, this does not in general hold. That is,

x ; $(B$ [] $B')$ and x ; B [] x ; B'

should be distinguished because they have different observable behaviour. Other behaviours that we may or may not want to equate are:

$$x;\,stop \mathbin{|||} y;\,stop \quad \text{and} \quad (\,x;\,y;\,stop\,) \mathbin{[]} (\,y;\,x;\,stop\,)$$

$$(\,x;\,y;\,stop\,) \mathbin{[]} (\,x;\,z;\,stop\,) \quad \text{and} \quad (\,i;\,x;\,y;\,stop\,) \mathbin{[]} (\,i;\,x;\,z;\,stop\,)$$

A principle, which all our semantics adhere to, and which is illustrated in the above trace semantics examples, is to abstract away from syntactic comparison and rather express the meaning of syntactic expressions in terms of how they "can behave." We model expressions in terms of what actions they can or cannot perform and in what order these actions can be performed. Thus, in analogy with state machines, where behaviour expressions are seen as states and actions offers as transitions from states to states, we are interested in relating the "labelled transitions", rather than the states (which are the syntactic structures). It is in fact possible to regain syntactic relationships between expressions by axiomatizing particular semantic relationships, i.e. identifying proof rules. But, this would only be done alongside identification of a "behavioural" semantic relationship, which would be used as a yardstick for assessing the correctness of the syntactic rules.

We should also point out that equality is not the only relationship that we are interested in verifying. For example, we might want to show that a particular specification is a refinement of a second specification. As a reflection of this, a semantic model for a specification language will typically have a number of *correctness relations* associated with the semantics. These characterise certain intuitive relationships between specifications. For example, notions of equivalence based on the observable behaviour are defined. These characterise when two processes cannot be distinguished by some external observer. There are also equivalences based on the testing of processes; see [89] and Chapter 5.

3.1.2 Formal Definition

More formally, we can think of a semantic notation as just a set of descriptions, each description being a particular model in the semantics. We denote the set of all semantic notations as SN and for a particular semantic notation $sn \in SN$, a semantic map, typically denoted $[\![\ ]\!]$, maps specifications in a formal technique, say ft, into the semantic notation. Thus, the semantic map is typed as follows,

$$[\![\ ]\!] : ft \longrightarrow sn$$

So, a semantic map is just a function from elements of ft to elements of sn; it defines how formal specifications can be mapped to semantic descriptions. For example, in Section 3.2 we define a semantics,

$$[\![\ ]\!]_{tr}$$

which, if applied to the behaviour

$$P := (\, x \, ; \, y \, ; \, stop \,) \; [] \; (\, z \, ; \, w \, ; \, stop \,)$$

will map it to the trace set that we highlighted earlier; i.e.

$$[\![\, P \,]\!]_{tr} \; = \; \{ \, \epsilon \, , \, x \, , \, z \, , \, xy \, , \, zw \, \}$$

As stated already, a semantics will typically incorporate an associated set of development relations. Thus, we can think of a semantics for a formal technique *ft*, which we denote $\mathcal{S}$, as having the following general form,

$$\mathcal{S} \in SN \times SM \times \mathcal{P}(DEV)$$

where *SN* is the set of all semantic notations, *SM* is the set of all semantic maps and *DEV* is the set of all development relations (we use the term development relation to embrace all possible correctness relations, e.g. equivalences and refinement relations, and to emphasise their role in the process of system development). Thus,

$$\mathcal{S}_{tr} \; = \; (\, \mathcal{P}(\mathcal{T}) \, , \, [\![\,]\!]_{tr} \, , \, \{\leq_{tr}, \asymp_{tr}\} \,)$$

is a typical semantics. $\mathcal{T}$ is the trace-setting notation that we have been referring to and $\leq_{tr}$ and $\asymp_{tr}$ are development relations, which we discuss in Section 3.2.3.

As yet, we have not put any constraints on the properties that the chosen development relations should have. However, different classes of development will typically have different properties. In particular, *DEV* contains *refinement* relations, *equivalences* and relations that can broadly be classed as *implementation* relations [122], such as the LOTOS conformance relation *conf*; see Section 5.1.6.1. These different classes of development are best distinguished by their basic properties. Refinement is reflexive and transitive (i.e. a preorder); equivalences are reflexive, symmetric and transitive; and implementation relations only need to be reflexive. The distinction between refinement and implementation relations is particularly significant; transitivity is a crucial property in enabling incremental development of specifications towards realisations and implementation relations are typically lacking in this respect.

We must also consider what interpretation of equivalence (which we denote $\asymp$) we should adopt. The interpretation that we choose is

$$X \asymp_{dv} X' \text{ iff } \forall Y, \, Y \; dv \; X \iff Y \; dv \; X'$$

where *dv* is a development relation; i.e. $dv \in DEV$ and $\asymp_{dv} \in DEV$. Thus, two equivalent descriptions have identical development sets; i.e. every description that is a development of one will be a development of the other. This demonstrates that during system development we really can choose any one of a set of equivalent specifications without affecting the possibilities of future development.

$\asymp_{dv}$ can easily be shown to be an equivalence and, in addition, no properties are required of *dv* for $\asymp_{dv}$ to be an equivalence. In particular, even if *dv* is not reflexive or transitive, $\asymp_{dv}$ will be an equivalence.

Another standard interpretation of equivalence between specifications is that they are developments of each other. With transitivity of dv, this interpretation gives us that two specifications in any cycle by the relation dv are equivalent.

However, if dv is in fact a preorder, we can obtain that $\asymp_{dv} = dv \cap dv^{-1}$. Thus, we use these two interpretations interchangeably if development is a preorder. We summarise these results in the following proposition.

Proposition 1

(i) $\asymp_{dv}$ *is an equivalence.*

(ii) If dv is a preorder then $\asymp_{dv} = dv \cap dv^{-1}$.

(iii) If dv is a preorder and $\asymp_{dv}$ is taken as identity then dv is a partial order.

Proof
The only part of this proposition that is not completely trivial is (ii), so we include this proof. Firstly, assume $X \asymp_{dv} X'$, but because, by reflexivity, $X\ dv\ X$, this gives us $X\ dv\ X'$ and similarly, $X'\ dv\ X$. Secondly, assume $X\ dv \cap dv^{-1}\ X'$ and take Y, such that $Y\ dv\ X$, but using our assumption and transitivity of dv we get $Y\ dv\ X'$ and similarly, we can show that $Y\ dv\ X'$ implies $Y\ dv\ X$.
○

Congruence. A property that would be particularly nice for development relations to satisfy is congruence. This has a very basic relationship to incremental development. We apply the term *congruence* to equivalence relations and *precongruence* to preorders. Let us consider congruence first. This is best explained in terms of behaviours with holes. For example, the following behaviour,

$(x\,;\,y\,;\,stop\,)\ []\ [\cdot]$

contains a hole, indicated by $[\cdot]$. An arbitrary behaviour can be inserted into this hole; for example,

$z\,;\,stop$ (*)

could be inserted to obtain,

$(x\,;\,y\,;\,stop\,)\ []\ (z\,;\,stop\,)$ (+)

Behaviours with holes are called *contexts* and denoted $C[\cdot]$. For example, if,

$C[\cdot] = (x\,;\,y\,;\,stop\,)\ []\ [\cdot]$

then $C[\cdot]$ is the context into which the behaviour (*) can be placed, i.e. $C[z\,;\,stop]$, to obtain behaviour (+).

Definition 1
Congruence states that given B and B' such that $B \asymp B'$ (where $\asymp$ is an equivalence), then, for any context C,

$$C[B] \asymp C[B']$$

Thus, equivalence is preserved when placed in any context. This property is actually a constraint on the operators of a language. To preserve it, we need to know that for any operator, $+$ say (here we consider only binary operators, but this can be generalised to any arity), and any behaviour B, if $B' \asymp B''$ then

$$B + B' \asymp B + B''$$

Thus, $B + [\cdot]$ plays the role of the context. If this property holds, we say that $\asymp$ is a congruence over the operators of the particular language being considered.

Although in some places in this book we use the term more liberally, mathematically speaking, an equivalence does not have the right to be viewed as an identity relation unless it can be shown to be a congruence. The defining property of equality is that like can be substituted for like without changing the meaning of an expression. Congruence is the property that ensures this is indeed the case.

We can similarly define a precongruence, by replacing the relation $\asymp$ with a preorder, say $\sqsubseteq$.

Definition 2
A preorder $\sqsubseteq$ is a precongruence if, for any context $C[\cdot]$, if $B \sqsubseteq B'$ then $C[B] \sqsubseteq C[B']$.

One reason why congruence is such an important property is that it enables incremental system development. For example, if we wish to develop a component of a complete system, then congruence implies that, if we can derive a relationship between the component and its replacement, then we will obtain the same relationship between the entire system and the system with the component replaced.

Two particular ways in which congruence is important are in (i) reusing known relationships and (ii) enabling strategies of stepwise refinement to implementation. Specifically, (i), if a property, such as equivalence or refinement, can be determined between two specifications B and B', by perhaps some complex proof, we can infer a property between larger specifications, if the two specifications are placed in a particular context. This suggests that, if known results are stored, significant reuse can be obtained.

Congruence enables us to, (ii), employ a stepwise refinement strategy in which we assume some initial specification is identified, S say. Then we can construct implementations as follows. First, decide on a construction C to use and write a subspecification, S', such that $C[S']$ is equivalent to S. Now, if we can identify an implementation of S', I say, we know how $C[I]$ is related to S. In addition, if at any stage it is not feasible to implement the identified component, the refinement process can be applied recursively.

Axiomatisation. One consequence of defining behavioural semantics, such as those being considered here, is that syntactic rules (i.e. proof rules, as discussed in Section 1.4) between behaviours can be derived that reflect these semantics. The identification of such a set of rules is called an axiomatisation of a language. For example, a rule that we might want to hold of a particular behavioural equivalence $\asymp$ is

$$a \,;\, i \,;\, B \asymp a \,;\, B$$

i.e. a hidden action, which is guarded by another action, can be removed. This rule could be justified because the observable behaviour of the two syntactic expressions would be the same. Two properties associated with axiomatisation are *soundness* and *completeness*.

The former of these is an absolute requirement, whereas the latter is desirable, but sometimes not achievable. Intuitively, soundness requires that all the laws in an axiomatisation are valid and completeness ensures that every true statement, in a particular domain, can be verified using the laws. Axiomatisation is extremely important and amongst other things plays a central role in proof-based verification.

The following three books [96], [171] and [148] have made extensive investigations of axiomatisation of behavioural semantics in process calculi settings. In particular, the rule we quoted above is an example of one of Milner's tau laws (i is written τ in CCS). We do not cover the topic of proof rules as extensively. One reason for this is because so much attention has been given to such approaches in the CCS and CSP settings. However, in addition, axiomatisation of LOTOS is in fact difficult (as indicated by the difficulty in finding congruence relations for LOTOS; see, for example, Section 5.1.7). Furthermore, as discussed in Section 1.4, our emphasis in this book is on automatic verification rather than proof.

3.1.3 Modelling Recursion

One of the most difficult aspects of defining semantics is modelling recursive behaviour. One reason for this is that some pbLOTOS specifications are inherently infinite state and, thus, all semantic models must be capable of handling infinite structures. This implies that infinite trees, infinite graphs and infinite sets of traces must be considered.

In our handling of recursion we only consider directly recursive definitions, such as $P := x \,;\, y \,;\, P$, rather than mutually recursive definitions, such as $P := x \,;\, y \,;\, Q$ and $Q := z \,;\, P$. However, the approaches that we present could easily be extrapolated to sets of mutually recursive definitions.

Modelling recursion typically implies that fixed point theory must be used. This concerns finding solutions of equations of the form:

$$E = F(E)$$

i.e. given some function F, find an object E such that application of the function to the object leaves the object unchanged. In our setting, the solution E here is a semantic model. The point is that we can think of a recursive definition as having the form,

$$P := F(P)$$

where F is the body of the behaviour of the definition. For example, F would correspond to the context x ; y ; $[\cdot]$ in the process definition $P := x$; y ; P. A solution for P will be a semantic structure that is a fixed point of F.

In certain circumstances we have to impose constraints on the recursive definitions that we can interpret in this way. For example, consider a definition such as,

$$P := P$$

In terms of our abstract syntax, this is syntactically well formed, but as a recursive definition there is something odd going on: this definition has more than one solution. In fact, any arbitrary model can be seen as a solution of the equation. The problem is that the equation is under-defined and does not identify a solution precisely enough. There are a number of approaches to handling this problem; one is to ban such definitions and only characterise the meaning of more well-behaved recursive definitions; alternatively, a unique solution to the definition can be selected from the set of possible solutions in some uniform way. For example, in [96] both approaches are considered. First in defining a trace semantic meaning for CSP, Hoare imposes a guardedness condition on processes, whereas, in defining a full failures semantics, the most nondeterministic process is selected as the solution.

The concept of guardedness is quite straightforward.

Definition 3 (Guarded)
A process invocation P is guarded in B if each reference to P is within some behaviour expression a ; B', where $a \in Act \cup \{i\}$.

Notice that the guard here can be either an internal or external action. This will not always be sufficient. In circumstances where we only want to model external behaviour, e.g. we might have a syntactic rule such as,

$$B \equiv i\,;\,B$$

our guardedness constraint will have to be stronger than Definition 3. In such circumstances definitions such as

$$P := i\,;\,P \quad \text{and} \quad P := i\,;\,P \,[\!]\, B$$

would have to be ruled out. Stronger notions of guardedness can be defined to do this, although hiding can make this problematic. Such definitions are beyond the scope of this book.

3.1.4 What Makes a Good Semantics?

We look at a number of different semantic models for LOTOS. Before we do this, it is worth considering what constitutes a "good" semantics, and what criteria we can apply to the choice of semantics. The following issues can be highlighted.

- A semantics should enable properties of a specification to be verified, e.g. that the specification cannot do a particular "bad thing," such as deadlock.
- The semantics should be unambiguous; i.e. it should not be possible to relate a specification to two different meanings.
- The semantics must be intuitively meaningful. Perhaps the most important criterion for the choice of semantics is that it correctly reflects the "meaning" that is trying to be extracted from a specification. Thus, the semantics should relate specifications that are "intuitively" the same.
- A semantics must distinguish specifications that are different. This is just as important as the previous point. If a semantic map relates two "intuitively" different specifications to the same semantic model we would not be able to differentiate between the specifications in our semantic world. This would, for example, mean that any property that held about one of the specifications would hold for the other. Thus, we must be careful to ensure that our semantics are fully expressive, in the sense that they distinguish between enough specifications.

An obvious question that arises from these points is: what is an appropriate intuitive meaning? There are actually a number of different such intuitions. Most of our semantics though seek to describe only the observable behaviour of systems (this applies less to the true concurrency model). Thus, we seek to locate semantics that model the observable behaviour of systems and that abstract from the internals of how this behaviour is obtained.

3.2 Trace Semantics

3.2.1 The Basic Approach

This is the first semantic model that was considered for process calculi [95] and it remains the simplest approach that is in use. The idea is to model the semantics of specifications as the set of all possible linear sequences (or traces) of actions that the specification can perform. The "all possible" here is important. In particular, you should notice that we are not solely interested in complete traces, i.e. sequences of actions that cannot be extended. Rather, we are interested in all possible intermediate and complete traces.

As a reflection of the fact that trace semantics consider *linear traces*, such approaches are frequently referred to as *linear time* models. As suggested earlier, we denote the trace semantic map as

$$[\![\ ]\!]_{tr} \ : \ pbLOTOS \ \longrightarrow \ \mathcal{P}(\mathcal{T})$$

i.e. it maps primitive basic LOTOS specifications to trace sets. The following pbLOTOS behaviours,

$P_0 := x \, ; \, y \, ; \, stop$

$P_1 := (\, x \, ; \, y \, ; \, stop \,) \, [] \, (\, z \, ; \, w \, ; \, stop \,)$

$P_2 := (\, z \, ; \, w \, ; \, stop \,) \, [] \, (\, x \, ; \, y \, ; \, stop \,)$

$P_3 := x \, ; \, x \, ; \, stop$

$P_4 := (\, x \, ; \, x \, ; \, stop \,) \, [] \, (\, x \, ; \, x \, ; \, stop \,)$

$P_5 := stop$

are mapped to the following trace sets,

$[\![P_0]\!]_{tr} \ = \ \{ \ \epsilon \, , \ x \, , \ xy \ \}$

$[\![P_1]\!]_{tr} \ = \ \{ \ \epsilon \, , \ x \, , \ z \, , \ xy \, , \ zw \ \}$

$[\![P_2]\!]_{tr} \ = \ \{ \ \epsilon \, , \ x \, , \ z \, , \ xy \, , \ zw \ \}$

$[\![P_3]\!]_{tr} \ = \ \{ \ \epsilon \, , \ x \, , \ xx \ \}$

$[\![P_4]\!]_{tr} \ = \ \{ \ \epsilon \, , \ x \, , \ xx \ \}$

$[\![P_5]\!]_{tr} \ = \ \{ \ \epsilon \ \}$

Notice that we have now equated two of the pairs of specifications that we highlighted as intuitively equal; i.e. $[\![P_1]\!]_{tr} = [\![P_2]\!]_{tr}$ and $[\![P_3]\!]_{tr} = [\![P_4]\!]_{tr}$. The properties of sets play an important role in making these semantic descriptions equal; i.e. sets are unordered and duplicates are removed.

Also notice that the behaviour *stop* is mapped to the trace set which includes just one trace: ϵ, the empty trace. It is a rule of trace semantics that the trace set of any behaviour will contain the empty trace, because all behaviours can perform an empty trace.

Process invocation and action relabelling can also be easily modelled using trace semantics. Consider the following recursive process definition,

$$P \, [z, w] := z \, ; \, w \, ; \, P \, [w, z]$$

Notice how the action names are flipped on recursive invocation. So, invocation of this behaviour with the action z relabelled to x and the action w relabelled to y will have the following infinite trace model,

$$[\![P \, [x, y]]\!]_{tr} \ = \ \{ \ \epsilon \, , \ x \, , \ xy \, , \ xyy \, , \ xyyx \, , \ xyyxx \, , \ xyyxxy \, , \ xyyxxyy \, , \ \ldots \}$$

Infinite models typically arise when recursive behaviour is considered. We consider how to handle such behaviour shortly.

As already indicated, we are interested in modelling just the observable behaviour of pbLOTOS specifications. As a reflection of this, internal actions do not find their way into trace sets. For example, the behaviours

$P_0 := i\,;\, y\,;\, stop$

$P_1 := (\,x\,;\, i\,;\, stop\,)\,[]\,(\,z\,;\, w\,;\, stop\,)$

$P_2 := i\,;\, i\,;\, stop$

$P_3 := hide\ z\ in\ (\,x\,;\, z\,;\, y\,;\, stop\,)$

are mapped to the trace sets:

$[\![\,P_0\,]\!]_{tr} \;=\; \{\ \epsilon\ ,\ y\ \}$

$[\![\,P_1\,]\!]_{tr} \;=\; \{\ \epsilon\ ,\ x\ ,\ z\ ,\ zw\ \}$

$[\![\,P_2\,]\!]_{tr} \;=\; \{\ \epsilon\ \}$

$[\![\,P_3\,]\!]_{tr} \;=\; \{\ \epsilon\ ,\ x\ ,\ xy\ \}$

Notice that this gives us equality between behaviours such as

$i\,;\, i\,;\, stop\ ,\quad i\,;\, stop$ and $stop$

and also, between behaviour such as

$x\,;\, y\,;\, stop$ and $hide\ z\ in\ (\,x\,;\, z\,;\, y\,;\, stop\,)$.

Because of the suppression of internal actions, the point of sequential composition is not directly reflected in trace semantics. Remember that successful termination in pbLOTOS has the form:

$B_1 >> B_2$

where the behaviour B_1 enables the behaviour B_2 when all concurrent threads in B_1 have performed an *exit* and an internal action is generated when control is handed from B_1 to B_2. For example, the behaviour,

$P := (\,x\,;\, y\,;\, exit\,[]\,z\,;\, exit\,) >> (\,w\,;\, stop\,)$

will map to the following trace set,

$[\![\,P\,]\!]_{tr} \;=\; \{\ \epsilon\ ,\ x\ ,\ z\ ,\ xy\ ,\ zw\ ,\ xyw\ \}$

However, successful termination actions, denoted δ, can arise in trace sets. Such actions will only appear when an exit is left "dangling" in a behaviour, i.e. is not matched by a sequential composition. Thus, the behaviour

$Q := (\,x\,;\, y\,;\, exit\,)\,[]\,(\,z\,;\, exit\,)$

will map to the following trace set,

$[\![\,Q\,]\!]_{tr} = \{\ \epsilon\ ,\ x\ ,\ z\ ,\ xy\ ,\ z\delta\ ,\ xy\delta\ \}$

Trace semantics typically model concurrency using interleaving (an exception is found in [139]). This view of concurrency fits naturally with the linear trace approach. For example, the behaviours

$$P_0 := x\,;\,stop\,|||\,y\,;\,stop$$
$$P_1 := (\,x\,;\,stop\,)\,|||\,(\,y\,;\,z\,;\,stop\,)$$
$$P_2 := (\,x\,;\,z\,;\,stop\,)\,|[z]|\,(\,y\,;\,z\,;\,stop\,)$$
$$P_3 := (\,x\,;\,y\,;\,z\,;\,stop\,)\,||\,(\,x\,;\,y\,;\,stop\,)$$

are mapped to the following trace sets,

$$[\![\,P_0\,]\!]_{tr} = \{\ \epsilon\,,\ x\,,\ y\,,\ xy\,,\ yx\ \}$$
$$[\![\,P_1\,]\!]_{tr} = \{\ \epsilon\,,\ x\,,\ y\,,\ xy\,,\ yx\,,\ yz\,,\ xyz\,,\ yxz\,,\ yzx\ \}$$
$$[\![\,P_2\,]\!]_{tr} = \{\ \epsilon\,,\ x\,,\ y\,,\ xy\,,\ yx\,,\ xyz\,,\ yxz\ \}$$
$$[\![\,P_3\,]\!]_{tr} = \{\ \epsilon\,,\ x\,,\ xy\ \}$$

3.2.2 Formal Semantics

This section gives a formal interpretation of trace semantics, which reflects the intuition that we have presented in the examples of the previous section.

3.2.2.1 Preliminaries: Traces

First we need to formalise what we mean by a trace and a set of traces. The set of all traces is denoted $\mathcal{T}$; it contains the special distinguished trace ϵ (which denotes an empty trace) and all sequences,

$$x_0 x_1 x_2 x_3 \ldots x_n, \ \text{where} \ x_i \in Act \cup \{\delta\}$$

of observable actions or successful terminations.[1] Notice that these traces are finite; i.e. each trace represents a finite sequence of behaviour. However, the set of all traces of a computation is likely to be infinite. Thus, we model behaviour as a (potentially) infinite set of finite computations. We use $\sigma, \sigma', \sigma'', \sigma_1, \sigma_2, \ldots$ to range over $\mathcal{T}$ and we define a number of basic operations on traces.

- *Concatenation.* Two traces σ and σ' can be concatenated by performing the operation, $\sigma.\sigma'$. Formally, we can define concatenation as:

$$(\sigma_1 = \epsilon \implies \sigma_1.\sigma_2 = \sigma_2) \ \wedge$$
$$(\sigma_2 = \epsilon \implies \sigma_1.\sigma_2 = \sigma_1) \ \wedge$$
$$(\sigma_1 = x_1 x_2 \ldots x_n \ \wedge \ \sigma_2 = y_1 y_2 \ldots y_n)$$
$$\implies \sigma_1.\sigma_2 = x_1 x_2 \ldots x_n y_1 y_2 \ldots y_n$$

As a slight abuse of notation, we write x to mean both a single action and the singleton trace; the correct interpretation is clear from the context.

---

[1]In fact, our semantics will ensure that successful termination actions only arise as the last element of a trace, however, for ease of presentation, we use a more liberal definition here.

- *Star.* Given a set $A \subseteq Act$, we denote the set of all traces that can be formed using actions from the set A as A^*. Formally,

$$A^* \triangleq \{\epsilon\} \cup \{\, x_0 x_1 \ldots x_n \mid x_i \in A \,\}$$

Using this notation we can note that $\mathcal{T} = (Act \cup \{\delta\})^*$.

A wealth of additional operators on traces is defined in [96].

3.2.2.2 A Denotational Trace Semantics for pbLOTOS

The following rules define a, so called, denotational semantics for pbLOTOS. This will realise the semantic map $[\![\ ]\!]_{tr}$ and, thus, define a function from pbLOTOS specifications to trace sets. The function is expressed by defining the meaning of all the syntactic elements of the language. This is done by traversing the abstract syntax of pbLOTOS. The mathematically correct phrase is that the mapping is defined by induction over the syntax of the language. So, the rules work construct by construct through the language. The rules we give are based on those presented in [120] with some influence from similar rules presented for CSP in [96].

What we are interested in is the meaning of an arbitrary pbLOTOS specification, i.e. to evaluate $[\![\, S\,]\!]_{tr}$, where $S \in$ pbLOTOS and $[\![\ ]\!]_{tr}$ has the form:

$$[\![\ ]\!]_{tr} \; : \; pbLOTOS \; \longrightarrow \; \mathcal{P}(\mathcal{T})$$

The function $[\![\ ]\!]_{tr}$ is defined according to the syntactic alternatives a top-level pbLOTOS specification can be constructed from, i.e. according to the first clause in the pbLOTOS abstract syntax. Thus, we have the following rules, which handle the two alternative forms that a top-level specification can take.

$$[\![\, B\,]\!]_{tr} \triangleq \mathcal{B}[\![\, B\,]\!]_{(\emptyset)}$$

$$[\![\, B \; where \; D\,]\!]_{tr} \triangleq \mathcal{B}[\![\, B\,]\!]_{(\mathcal{D}[\![\, D\,]\!])}$$

$\mathcal{B}[\![\ ]\!]$ is the semantic function that maps behaviour expressions to trace sets. The function $\mathcal{B}[\![\ ]\!]$ has two parameters: the behaviour expression to evaluate (here B) and a set of process definitions (the second parameter is written as a subscript of the application, e.g. $[\![\ ]\!]_{(d)}$). This set of definitions is used in the evaluation of the behaviour B, thus enabling processes defined in D to be instantiated in B. In analogy with programming language semantics d is an environment.

The rules state that if the specification just contains a behaviour expression, with no process definitions, then the trace model of the specification is given by applying $\mathcal{B}[\![\, B\,]\!]_{(\emptyset)}$ (with the definition parameter empty). Alternatively, if the specification is a behaviour followed by a *where* clause, then the trace model of the specification is given by applying $\mathcal{B}[\![\, B\,]\!]_{(\mathcal{D}[\![\, D\,]\!])}$, i.e. evaluating behaviour B according to the declarations in D.

Now we step down one level in the pbLOTOS abstract syntax to define the meaning of lists of definitions. All we do here is to place the list of definitions into a set, which can be accessed at a deeper level in the semantics. Thus, we define the function

$$\mathcal{D}[\![\ ]\!]\ :\ \mathit{DefList} \longrightarrow \mathcal{P}(\mathit{Defs})$$

which is defined as

$$\mathcal{D}[\![\,(P := B)\,]\!] \triangleq \{\,P := B\,\}$$
$$\mathcal{D}[\![\,(P := B)\ D\,]\!] \triangleq \{\,P := B\,\} \cup \mathcal{D}[\![\,D\,]\!]$$

We can now step down another level in the syntax to define the trace meaning of behaviour expressions. This is the major part of the semantics and it involves defining the meaning of the function,

$$\mathcal{B}[\![\ ]\!]_{(d)}\ :\ \mathit{Beh}\ \times\ \mathcal{P}(\mathit{Defs}) \longrightarrow \mathcal{P}(\mathcal{T})$$

which evaluates behaviour expressions. Notice that the two parameters to the function are made explicit in the typing.

In a similar way to earlier, $\mathcal{B}[\![\ ]\!]$ is defined by working through the possible syntactic forms that a behaviour expression can take. Thus, we define the meaning of all possible formats that a behaviour expression can take.

Stop. The semantics of this behaviour are trivial; it simply yields the set containing the empty trace. This indicates that the behaviour *stop* cannot perform any nontrivial traces.

$$\mathcal{B}[\![\,stop\,]\!]_{(d)} \triangleq \{\epsilon\}$$

Exit. The semantics of *exit* are only marginally more complex:

$$\mathcal{B}[\![\,exit\,]\!]_{(d)} \triangleq \{\epsilon, \delta\}$$

exit is a behaviour which can perform one of two traces: the empty trace or a singleton trace just containing an action δ. The δ action is the special distinguished action which denotes successful termination. The action is used as a signal to indicate successful termination. This becomes clear when we consider the semantics of enabling, $>>$, which use the δ action to initiate the transfer of control to the enabled behaviour.

Action Prefix. There are two clauses for action prefix; the first deals with observable actions and the second deals with internal actions. The first is as follows,

$$\mathcal{B}[\![\,x\,;\,B\,]\!]_{(d)} \triangleq \{\epsilon\} \cup \{\,x.\sigma \mid \sigma \in \mathcal{B}[\![\,B\,]\!]_{(d)}\,\}$$

The trace set for action prefix is defined by taking the traces that can be derived from B (thus, $\mathcal{B}[\![\ ]\!]$ is a recursive definition) and prepending the action x on the front of all of them. The empty trace must also be added, because, although $\mathcal{B}[\![\ B\ ]\!]_{(d)}$ will contain an empty trace, it will be lost when x is prepended.

The second clause is as follows.

$$\mathcal{B}[\![\ i\ ;\ B\ ]\!]_{(d)} \triangleq \mathcal{B}[\![\ B\ ]\!]_{(d)}$$

Because i is not observable in trace semantics, the occurrence of such an action is simply ignored.

Choice. Choice yields a straightforward trace semantics; it simply corresponds to taking the union of the trace sets derived from the two alternative behaviours.

$$\mathcal{B}[\![\ B_1\ [\!]\ B_2\ ]\!]_{(d)} \triangleq \mathcal{B}[\![\ B_1\ ]\!]_{(d)} \cup \mathcal{B}[\![\ B_2\ ]\!]_{(d)}$$

Notice that any traces that can be performed by both B_1 and B_2 will be represented by a single trace in $\mathcal{B}[\![\ B_1\ [\!]\ B_2\ ]\!]_{(d)}$ and that choice points are not explicitly reflected in the semantics.

Enabling. The semantic rule for sequential composition centres on the handling of the δ action.

$$\mathcal{B}[\![\ B_1\ >>\ B_2\ ]\!]_{(d)} \triangleq$$
$$\{\ \epsilon\ \}\ \cup\ \{\ \sigma.x\ |\ \sigma.x \in \mathcal{B}[\![\ B_1\ ]\!]_{(d)}\ \wedge\ x \neq \delta\ \}\ \cup$$
$$\{\ \sigma.\sigma'\ |\ \sigma.\delta \in \mathcal{B}[\![\ B_1\ ]\!]_{(d)}\ \wedge\ \sigma' \in \mathcal{B}[\![\ B_2\ ]\!]_{(d)}\ \}$$

Firstly, any trace from B_1 that does not successfully terminate, i.e. does not have δ as the last element, is included directly in the semantics of $B_1 >> B_2$. These traces reflect the noncomplete evaluations of B_1, in other words, all the traces that B_1 performs before it terminates. Secondly, all traces from B_1 that finish with δ are concatenated with all traces from B_2. It is important to note that the δ action does not appear in the concatenated trace (unless it appears in B_2). In terms of the informal definition of pbLOTOS, the δ should be transformed into an internal action. However, because internal actions are not depicted in trace semantics, this replacement is not visible.

Parallel Composition. The semantics of parallel composition are somewhat more complex. We need to compose the traces of B_1 and B_2 in such a way that the resultant traces reflect the parallel composition of the two behaviours. The basic rule is

$$\mathcal{B}[\![\ B_1\ |[x_1, \ldots, x_n]|\ B_2\ ]\!]_{(d)} \triangleq$$
$$\{\ \sigma\ |\ \exists\sigma_1 \in \mathcal{B}[\![\ B_1\ ]\!]_{(d)},\ \exists\sigma_2 \in \mathcal{B}[\![\ B_2\ ]\!]_{(d)}\ s.t.\ \sigma \in \sigma_1|\{x_1, \ldots, x_n, \delta\}|\sigma_2\ \}$$

which returns the set of all traces that are in $\sigma_1|\{x_1, \ldots, x_n, \delta\}|\sigma_2$ for all possible traces σ_1 in $\mathcal{B}[\![\, B_1 \,]\!]_{(d)}$ and σ_2 in $\mathcal{B}[\![\, B_2 \,]\!]_{(d)}$. Thus, we determine the traces of B_1 and the traces of B_2; then we apply $|\{x_1, \ldots, x_n, \delta\}|$ to each possible pair of traces from the two. For each of these pairs, $|\{x_1, \ldots, x_n, \delta\}|$ derives the set of possible interleavings of the two traces subject to synchronisation on actions from $\{x_1, \ldots, x_n, \delta\}$. Notice, in particular, that δ is included in this synchronisation set. This is because a parallel composition only successfully terminates when both its constituent threads have terminated (see the discussion in Section 2.3.7).

So, the central aspect of this definition is the mapping $|\{x_1, \ldots, x_n, \delta\}|$; it is a function with the following type,

$$|A| \; : \; \mathcal{T} \times \mathcal{T} \; \longrightarrow \; \mathcal{P}(\mathcal{T})$$
$$\text{where } A \subseteq Act \cup \{\delta\}$$

The operator is written infix, as $\sigma_1|A|\sigma_2$, and, broadly, it denotes the set of possible interleavings of σ_1 and σ_2 that identify actions in A. The operator is defined as follows, where $x, x' \in A$, $x \neq x'$ and $y, y' \notin A$,

$$\sigma_1|A|\sigma_2 \; \triangleq$$
$$\quad if \; (\sigma_1 = x.\sigma_1' \wedge \sigma_2 = \epsilon) \vee (\sigma_1 = \epsilon \wedge \sigma_2 = x'.\sigma_2') \vee$$
$$\quad\quad (\sigma_1 = \sigma_2 = \epsilon) \vee (\sigma_1 = x.\sigma_1' \wedge \sigma_2 = x'.\sigma_2')$$
$$\quad then \; \{\epsilon\}$$
$$\quad otherwise \; \{\; y.\sigma \mid \sigma \in \sigma_1'|A|\sigma_2 \wedge \sigma_1 = y.\sigma_1' \;\} \; \cup$$
$$\quad\quad\quad\quad\quad \{\; y'.\sigma \mid \sigma \in \sigma_1|A|\sigma_2' \wedge \sigma_2 = y'.\sigma_2' \;\} \; \cup$$
$$\quad\quad\quad\quad\quad \{\; x.\sigma \mid \sigma \in \sigma_1'|A|\sigma_2' \wedge \sigma_1 = x.\sigma_1' \wedge \sigma_2 = x.\sigma_2' \;\}$$

This definition mirrors, in some respects, the operational semantics definition of parallel composition that we present in Section 3.3.2.2. The operator is best illustrated through an example. Consider the behaviour

$$(\, y \,;\, x \,;\, z \,;\, stop \,) \; |[x]| \; (\, x \,;\, w \,;\, stop \,)$$

Evaluation of the two component behaviours yields the following two trace sets,

$$\{\, \epsilon \,,\, y \,,\, yx \,,\, yxz \,\} \quad and \quad \{\, \epsilon \,,\, x \,,\, xw \,\}$$

where the first is the trace set for the left-hand behaviour and the second is the trace set for the right-hand behaviour. Our definition of

$$\mathcal{B}[\![\, B_1 \; |[x_1, \ldots, x_n]| \; B_2 \,]\!]_{(d)}$$

would apply $|\{x\}|$ to all possible pairings of traces from the two sets (in fact, it would apply $|\{x, \delta\}|$, but because there is no $exit$ in the original behaviour, δ can be safely ignored). The results of these applications are:

$$\epsilon|\{x\}|\epsilon = \{\epsilon\} \qquad y|\{x\}|\epsilon = \{y\} \qquad yx|\{x\}|\epsilon = \{y\} \qquad yxz|\{x\}|\epsilon = \{y\}$$

$$\epsilon|\{x\}|x = \{\epsilon\} \qquad y|\{x\}|x = \{y\} \qquad yx|\{x\}|x = \{yx\} \qquad yxz|\{x\}|x = \{yxz\}$$

$$\epsilon|\{x\}|xw = \{\epsilon\} \qquad y|\{x\}|xw = \{y\} \qquad yx|\{x\}|xw = \{yxw\} \qquad yxz|\{x\}|xw = \{yxzw, yxwz\}$$

The definition of $\mathcal{B}[\![\, B_1 \,||[x_1,\dots,x_n]|\, B_2 \,]\!]_{(d)}$ accumulates traces from the sets, to yield

$$\mathcal{B}[\![\, y\,;\, x\,;\, z\,;\, stop \,||[x]|\, x\,;\, w\,;\, stop \,]\!]_{(d)} =$$
$$\{\,\epsilon\,,\, y\,,\, yx\,,\, yxz\,,\, yxw\,,\, yxzw\,,\, yxwz\,\}$$

as required.

Hiding. We need an auxiliary operator in defining the semantics of hiding. The operator is denoted / and it has the type:

$$/\ :\ \mathcal{T}\ \times\ (Act \cup \{\delta\} \longrightarrow \mathcal{T})\ \longrightarrow\ \mathcal{T}$$

The operator is written infix and has two arguments: a trace and a function from actions to traces, which is total on $Act \cup \{\delta\}$. The operator returns a new trace. Given that $\lambda \in Act \cup \{\delta\} \longrightarrow \mathcal{T}$, then σ/λ is defined as

$$\epsilon/\lambda \triangleq \epsilon \ \wedge$$
$$(x.\sigma')/\lambda \triangleq \lambda(x).(\sigma'/\lambda)$$

Thus, the application,

$$\sigma/\lambda' \quad where \quad \lambda'(x) \triangleq if\ x = x_i\,(1 \le i \le n)\ then\ \sigma_i\ else\ x$$

has the effect of searching along the trace σ and replacing every occurrence of an action x_i with the trace σ_i.

The trace semantics for hiding derives all the traces from B and then removes all occurrences of the (to be hidden) actions $x_1,\dots,x_n$ from the generated traces, by replacing x_i with ϵ.

$$\mathcal{B}[\![\, hide\ x_1,\dots,x_n\ in\ B \,]\!]_{(d)} \triangleq \{\ \sigma/\lambda^{hide} \mid \sigma \in \mathcal{B}[\![\, B \,]\!]_{(d)}\ \} \quad where,$$
$$\lambda^{hide}(x) \triangleq if\ x = x_i\,(1 \le i \le n)\ then\ \epsilon\ else\ x$$

Relabelling. The semantics of relabelling follow very much the same lines as the semantics for hiding. However, rather than replacing actions with a null trace, we replace them with the required relabelling.

$$\mathcal{B}[\![\, B[y_1/x_1,\dots,y_n/x_n] \,]\!]_{(d)} \triangleq \{\ \sigma/\lambda^{rel} \mid \sigma \in \mathcal{B}[\![\, B \,]\!]_{(d)}\ \} \quad where,$$
$$\lambda^{rel}(x) \triangleq if\ x = x_i\,(1 \le i \le n)\ then\ y_i\ else\ x$$

Process Instantiation. The semantics of process instantiation are complicated by the need to interpret recursion. In fact, we only give a partial definition of such behaviour, as the full semantics are relatively complex. In particular, we do not consider mutual recursion, i.e. indirect recursion resulting from a series of process instantiations (although, generalisation to such definitions can easily be given) and our presentation is informal. A full formal treatment is beyond the scope of this book.

Nonrecursive process definitions can be handled very easily; i.e.

$$\mathcal{B}[\![\, P \,]\!]_{(d)} \triangleq \mathcal{B}[\![\, B \,]\!]_{(d)}$$

where $P := B$ is a definition in d and P is not referenced in B

Notice that it is here, in defining the meaning of process instantiation, that we use the definitions contained in d. This rule states that the meaning of a process instantiation is the meaning of the corresponding process body.

In contrast, the semantics of recursion (in fact, only direct recursion) is defined by

$$\mathcal{B}[\![\, P \,]\!]_{(d)} \triangleq \bigcup_{n \in \mathbb{N}} \mathcal{B}[\![\, f_B^n(stop) \,]\!]_{(d)}$$

where $P := f_B(P)$ is a definition in d

Firstly, we have written the process definition in an unusual manner; viz,

$$P := f_B(P)$$

f_B denotes a function, which takes a process instantiation and evaluates it in place in the body of B. In fact, f_B can be thought of as a context corresponding to the behaviour B, with holes where P is referenced. Filling these holes corresponds to instantiating a behaviour in place for P.

We can think of a recursion as generating a series of models, which are increasingly large; each successive model corresponds to a further unfolding of the recursive call. This series of models is infinite; i.e. we will keep on making recursive calls and increasing the size of the resulting model. We refer to such a series of models as a chain.

The semantic model for this behaviour will have to be an infinite set; it will be an infinite set which contains all the models from all the recursive calls, i.e. every model in the chain. The expression:

$$\bigcup_{n \in \mathbb{N}} \mathcal{B}[\![\, f_B^n(stop) \,]\!]_{(d)} \qquad (*)$$

turns out to yield the least upper bound of this chain, i.e. a model which is larger than all elements in the chain, but does not contain more than is found in elements of the chain. It is the union of all models in the chain.

The notation f_B^n is defined as follows.

$$f_B^0(B') \triangleq B'$$
$$f_B^1(B') \triangleq f_B(B')$$
$$f_B^2(B') \triangleq f_B(f_B(B'))$$

$$\cdots$$
$$\cdots$$

$$f_B^n(B') \triangleq f_B(f_B \ldots (f_B(B')) \ldots)$$

where there are n f_Bs on the right-hand side

This construction generates the infinite chain to which we have been referring. The chain requires a "bottom" behaviour to start from; it can be shown that *stop* is the required bottom or null behaviour. Thus, in our above definition, the chain is given by:

$$f_B^0(stop) , \ f_B^1(stop) , \ f_B^2(stop) , \ldots$$

In order to prove that our definition yields the least upper bound of such a chain we would have to consider fixed point theory. This is beyond the scope of this book; the interested reader is referred to [199].

In addition, it can be shown that, as long as the behaviour f_B is guarded, this definition of recursion is the only solution [96,120]. In fact, we would need a strong guardedness property, because internal behaviour is not reflected in trace semantics. For example, the definition:

$$P := (\, x\,;\, stop\,) \ [] \ (\, i\,;\, P\,)$$

will have an infinite number of solutions. In fact, for any B',

$$x\,;\, stop \ [] \ B'$$

is a solution as

$$(\, x\,;\, stop\,) \ [] \ (\, i\,;\, (\, x\,;\, stop \ [] \ B'\,)\,) = x\,;\, stop \ [] \ B'$$

in trace semantics.

3.2.3 Development Relations

As previously indicated, a semantics typically has three constituents: a notation in which to express semantic models, a semantic map and a set of development relations. We have presented the first two of these, the trace notation $\mathcal{T}$ and the semantic map $[\![\ ]\!]_{tr}$. In this section we consider the third: development relations for trace semantics. We consider the two classic relations: *trace preorder* and *trace equivalence*. These relations define how pbLOTOS specifications can be related using trace semantics.

3.2.3.1 Trace Preorder

Trace preorder is the basic refinement relation of trace semantics; it is denoted $\leq_{tr}$, and defined as follows.

$S \ \leq_{tr} \ S'$ *if and only if* $[\![\, S \,]\!]_{tr} \subseteq [\![\, S' \,]\!]_{tr}$

So, S is a trace refinement of S' if and only if the traces of S are a subset of or equal to the traces of S'. Firstly, it is easy to show that this relation is a preorder.

Proposition 2
$\leq_{tr}$ is (i) reflexive and (ii) transitive.

Proof
(i) This is trivial, because the traces of a specification are equal to the traces of the same specification. (ii) This follows from transitivity of subset inclusion; i.e. if $[\![\, S\,]\!]_{tr} \subseteq [\![\, S'\,]\!]_{tr}$ and $[\![\, S'\,]\!]_{tr} \subseteq [\![\, S''\,]\!]_{tr}$ then $[\![\, S\,]\!]_{tr} \subseteq [\![\, S''\,]\!]_{tr}$.
$\bigcirc$

The fact that the trace preorder is not symmetric is also easy to verify. Consider for example the two behaviours:

$$Q := stop \quad \text{and} \quad P := x\,;\, stop$$

we have,

$$[\![\, Q\,]\!]_{tr} = \{\, \epsilon\, \} \quad \text{and} \quad [\![\, P\,]\!]_{tr} = \{\, \epsilon\,,\, x\, \}$$

which implies that $[\![\, Q\,]\!]_{tr} \subseteq [\![\, P\,]\!]_{tr}$ but $[\![\, P\,]\!]_{tr} \not\subseteq [\![\, Q\,]\!]_{tr}$. So, $Q \leq_{tr} P$, but, $P \not\leq_{tr} Q$. As illustration of the trace preorder, consider the LOTOS behaviours:

$$P_1 := y\,;\, stop$$
$$P_2 := x\,;\, stop$$
$$P_3 := (\,x\,;\, stop\,) [] (\,y\,;\, stop\,)$$
$$P_4 := hide\ y, z\ in\ (\,(\,y\,;\, x\,;\, z\,;\, stop\,) [] (\,z\,;\, x\,;\, stop\,)\,)$$
$$P_5 := (\,x\,;\, y\,;\, stop\,) |[y]| (\,z\,;\, stop\,)$$
$$P_6 := (\,x\,;\, y\,;\, stop\,) ||| (\,z\,;\, stop\,)$$

The following is a subset of the trace refinement relations amongst these behaviours.

$$P_1 \not\leq_{tr} P_2 \quad \text{and} \quad P_2 \not\leq_{tr} P_1$$
$$P_1 \leq_{tr} P_3 \quad \text{and} \quad P_2 \leq_{tr} P_3$$
$$P_4 \leq_{tr} P_3 \quad \text{and} \quad P_5 \not\leq_{tr} P_3 \quad \text{and} \quad P_3 \not\leq_{tr} P_5$$
$$P_2 \leq_{tr} P_6 \quad \text{and} \quad P_4 \leq_{tr} P_6 \quad \text{and} \quad P_5 \leq_{tr} P_6$$

You should also notice that the behaviour *stop* is more refined (by trace preorder) than any other pbLOTOS specification. This is because its trace set only contains the empty trace, which is included in the trace set of all specifications. Thus, we can refine any pbLOTOS specification to *stop*. This is clearly not very satisfactory, as it means that during development, we can just throw all the content of a specification away.

The theoretical justification for the trace preorder is that it preserves so-called *safety properties*. These are properties which state that "something bad does not happen." For example, we might want to ensure that a particular unwanted action, perhaps one called **crash**, never happens. Refinement by trace preorder cannot introduce actions. Thus, if our abstract specification satisfies a particular safety property, we know that all refinements of the specification will satisfy the property. But, this does not prevent us from refining out all the *wanted* behaviour.

3.2.3.2 Trace Equivalence

As stated by Proposition 1 earlier, a preorder development relation will naturally induce an equivalence between specifications. In trace semantics, the trace equivalence, denoted $\asymp_{\leq_{tr}}$ (or $\asymp_{tr}$ for presentational simplicity), is induced; it is defined as follows.

$$S \asymp_{\leq_{tr}} S' \text{ if and only if } S \leq_{tr} S' \text{ and } S' \leq_{tr} S$$

$\asymp_{\leq_{tr}}$ is reflexive, symmetric and transitive, so, it is an equivalence; it plays the role of identity in the trace theory of pbLOTOS. From the definition of the trace preorder, it can easily be seen that

$$S \asymp_{\leq_{tr}} S' \iff [\![S]\!]_{tr} = [\![S']\!]_{tr}$$

Thus, any two specifications with equal traces are trace equivalent. This is actually the identity that we have been using informally already; see, for example, the discussion in Section 3.2.1.

3.2.4 Discussion

So, we have defined a simple linear time semantics for pbLOTOS, $\mathcal{S}_{tr}$. In its entirety, the semantics comprises:

$$\mathcal{S}_{tr} \triangleq (\ \mathcal{P}(\mathcal{T})\ ,\ [\![\ ]\!]_{tr}\ ,\ \{\leq_{tr}, \asymp_{tr}\}\ )$$

Thus, it contains $\mathcal{P}(\mathcal{T})$ (a notation of semantic models), a semantic map $[\![\ ]\!]_{tr}$ and two development relations, $\leq_{tr}$ and $\asymp_{tr}$. The semantics is relatively crude; in particular, we can make two observations.

Firstly, although preserving safety is a useful property of development, there are many different classes of property that we would like to preserve during refinement and safety is only one of these. For example, we would like to preserve liveness properties, i.e. statements that "something good must eventually happen." The trace preorder cannot guarantee such properties, as the required "good thing" may simply be refined out during application of $\leq_{tr}$.

Secondly, the trace semantics equate too many specifications. They do not enable branching points to be distinguished; in particular, they do not enable deterministic and nondeterministic choice to be distinguished. This is highly unsatisfactory as, from our discussions already, we have noted that deterministic and nondeterministic choices yield a very different observable behaviour. We discuss this issue in more depth in Section 3.3.1.

However, in a completely deterministic setting, trace semantics are quite satisfactory and fully characterise the behaviour of pbLOTOS. This is witnessed by the fact that in [96] a reduced process calculus, which is deterministic, is completely characterised by a trace semantics.

As presented in [96], the trace equality relation can be axiomatised for this deterministic language. We conjecture that similar trace-based axiomatisations could be developed for pbLOTOS.

We do not consider congruence issues with either trace preorder or trace equivalence. This is for two reasons. Firstly, for the reasons just discussed, neither are particularly useful development relations and secondly, in order to prove congruence in recursive contexts we would have to work from a complete fixed point theory. In the absence of such a theory, we wait for the, more useful, bisimulation relations before considering congruence issues.

3.3 Labelled Transition Systems

A more distinguishing semantics than trace semantics can be given using labelled transition systems. This is in fact the standard semantics for LOTOS and the one presented in the LOTOS standard [101]. It is also the most commonly used semantics throughout the process calculi domain.

3.3.1 The Basic Approach

We have already seen a notation that is similar to labelled transition systems (LTS), viz the behaviour trees presented in Chapter 2 (although in the general case we deal with graphs, rather than trees). For example, the two trees depicted in Figure 3.1 could be viewed as labelled transition systems. In such systems, the arcs of the tree are called *transitions* and the actions associated with arcs give the *labelling*. LTS model systems solely in terms of sequence and choice. In particular, a branching point indicates a choice and sequence is denoted by transitions following one another.

What though resides at the nodes of a labelled transition system? Nodes represent states; these are locations in the computation that are nonatomic and can consume time (remember actions and, thus, transitions are atomic). Such states are equated with the behaviour expression reached at that point in evaluation. Thus, the two labelled transition systems depicted in Figure 3.1 can more fully be depicted as in Figure 3.2.

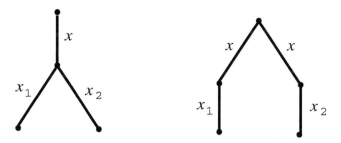

Fig. 3.1. Labelled Transition Systems (Deterministic and Nondeterministic)

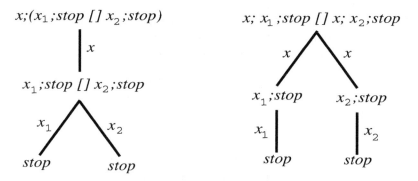

Fig. 3.2. Labelled Transition System with States Explicitly Represented

The term *branching time* model is often associated with approaches such as labelled transition systems, where choice is explicitly represented; this is in contrast to *linear time* models. As a reflection of this, labelled transition systems can be seen to be more discriminating than trace semantics. For example, the two behaviours,

$$x\,;\,(x_1\,;\,stop\,[]\,x_2\,;\,stop) \quad \text{and} \quad (x\,;\,x_1\,;\,stop)\,[]\,(x\,;\,x_2\,;\,stop)$$

cannot be distinguished in trace semantics; the two behaviours will both have the trace semantic model,

$$\{\,\epsilon\,,\,x\,,\,xx_1\,,\,xx_2\,\}$$

However, they can be distinguished with labelled transition systems, as made apparent in Figure 3.2. This example is a particularly good one, because from our earlier discussion, it should be clear that we would like to differentiate these two behaviours. This is because the first expresses a deterministic choice, whereas the second expresses a nondeterministic choice. If you are not happy that these two should be distinguished, look again at Section 2.3.4 and, in particular, consider the illustration of these two behaviours in terms of black boxes offering interactions at buttons. Thus, branching time models, such as LTS, can distinguish different forms of choice, whereas trace semantics cannot.

3.3.2 Formal Semantics

3.3.2.1 Preliminaries: Labelled Transition Systems

We begin by giving a formal definition of a labelled transition system. The set of all labelled transition systems is denoted $\mathcal{LTS}$ and $\forall Sys \in \mathcal{LTS}$, Sys is a four tuple (S, A, T, s_0), where

- S is a nonempty set of states; these are the behaviour expressions derived from evaluation of the specification;
- A is a set of actions; A contains all the actions that the specification can perform, including i and δ, thus, $A \subseteq Act \cup \{i, \delta\}$;
- T is a set of transition relations; one relation, T_a, is included for each $a \in A$; and
- $s_0 \in S$ is the starting state for Sys.

A *transition relation* T_a is a set of triples of the form (s, a, s'); i.e.

$$T_a \subseteq S \times \{a\} \times S$$

where (s, a, s') states that a transition from state s to state s' exists, which is labelled with action a. Transitions are usually denoted

$$s \xrightarrow{a} s'$$

The labelled transition system contains sufficient information to construct transition system diagrams such as those that we have seen already:

- S defines the nodes of the diagrams;
- A defines the allowable labels for arcs in the diagrams;
- T defines the arcs in the diagrams; and
- s_0 defines the start point of the diagram.

A final point to notice is that internal actions do get represented in labelled transition systems. This is in contrast to the situation with trace semantics, where all internal actions are ignored. This may seem surprising, as it seems to indicate that labelled transition systems depict more than just the externally visible behaviour of the system. This view is to some extent true. However, in general, the occurrence of internal actions is needed in order that different varieties of choice (in particular, forms of nondeterminism) can be distinguished. Section 3.3.3 shows how development relations can be used to equate the labelled transition systems that cannot realistically be distinguished by the external observer. Thus, the approach in labelled transition systems is to give a distinguishing and expressive underlying semantic notation and then to equate, using equivalence relations, models in the notation that should be viewed as the same.

3.3.2.2 An Operational Semantics for LOTOS

The following rules define a, so-called, operational semantics for pbLOTOS. This will realise the semantic map $[\![\ ]\!]_{lts}$,

$$[\![\ ]\!]_{lts} \ : \ pbLOTOS \ \longrightarrow \ \mathcal{LTS}$$

i.e. define a function from pbLOTOS specifications to labelled transition systems. As was the case with the denotational approach, these semantics will traverse the abstract syntax of pbLOTOS. However, the rules for the semantics are expressed very differently from those in the denotational setting (for a comprehensive discussion of different forms of semantics see [199]). Specifically, they are expressed as a series of inference rules. A set of inference rules defines a derivation system, which characterises how behaviours can be mapped to transition systems.

Inference rules have the form:

$$R : \ \frac{P_1 \dots P_n}{Q} \ C$$

where $P_1, \dots, P_n, Q$ are assertions. The R here is merely a label for the rule, the assertions $P_1, \dots, P_n$ are called the *premises* of R and the assertion Q is called the *conclusion* or *consequence* of R. C is optional; it is used to express conditions on the variables used in the inference rule (e.g. a variable v might be stated to be in a set V). The informal meaning of the rule is that if $P_1, \dots, P_n$ hold then the assertion Q will hold. If the list of premises is empty, i.e.

$$R : \ \frac{}{Q}$$

then the inference rule defines an axiom of the derivation system; the consequence Q will always hold, as it does not depend upon any premises.

Now we come to the operational semantics for pbLOTOS. The derivation system that we define characterises how to derive transition relations from a pbLOTOS behaviour. The top-level structure of a pbLOTOS specification is either B or B *where* D, with D a list of process definitions. In the former case, we can interpret the behaviour directly; in the latter case, we have to interpret the behaviour B subject to the bindings set up in D. In our semantics, the process definitions of D are assumed to be available throughout the derivation system, enabling us to reference them in our inference rules. We could add a mechanism to transmit these definitions through the inference rules. However, in order not to complicate our mathematical constructions, we have not included this. The basic derivation system follows.

Stop. The behaviour *stop* has no inference rule. This is because, as it cannot perform any actions, it cannot be derived further.

Exit. The behaviour *exit* has the following inference rule,

$$(EX): \quad \frac{}{exit \xrightarrow{\delta} stop}$$

This rule defines an axiom stating that a behaviour $exit$ can always perform a δ (remember δ is a hidden action used to signal successful termination, as discussed in Section 3.2.2.2) and evolve to $stop$. So, the sole purpose of $exit$ is to signal successful termination and then evolve no further.

Action Prefix. Sequencing by action prefix also yields an axiom of the derivation system,

$$(AP): \quad \frac{}{a \, ; \, B \xrightarrow{a} B} \quad (a \in Act \cup \{i\})$$

i.e. a behaviour $a \, ; \, B$ can always perform action a and evolve to behaviour B. Notice, a may be an external or internal action, reflecting that i actions are represented in LTS.

Choice. The behaviour of choice is expressed using two rules, which are symmetric. They are not axioms, because they are both dependent upon a single premise.

$$(CH.i): \quad \frac{B_1 \xrightarrow{a} B_1'}{B_1 \, [] \, B_2 \xrightarrow{a} B_1'} \quad (a \in Act \cup \{i, \delta\})$$

$$(CH.ii): \quad \frac{B_2 \xrightarrow{a} B_2'}{B_1 \, [] \, B_2 \xrightarrow{a} B_2'} \quad (a \in Act \cup \{i, \delta\})$$

The rules state that, if either of the alternatives can perform a transition a and evolve into a state B', then the whole behaviour can perform a and evolve into B'. This correctly models the effect of choice, which is to select between the two possible alternatives. Notice also that δ actions are included; thus, successful termination of one alternative can resolve the choice.

As these are our first nonaxiomatic inference rules it is worth at this point clarifying the manner in which transitions are derived using such rules. So, consider for example, the behaviour,

$$P := (\, x \, ; \, y \, ; \, stop \,) \, [] \, (\, x \, ; \, stop \,)$$

We are seeking to apply one of the two rules (CH.i) or (CH.ii) in order to determine what transitions this behaviour is able to perform. However, both rules require properties to hold of one of the two constituent behaviours. Thus, determining the behaviour of P induces evaluation of the behaviour of,

$$x \, ; \, y \, ; \, stop \quad \text{and} \quad x \, ; \, stop$$

We can apply our action prefix rule (AP) to determine what transitions can be derived from these behaviours; i.e.,

$$x \, ; \, y \, ; \, stop \xrightarrow{x} y \, ; \, stop \quad \text{and} \quad x \, ; \, stop \xrightarrow{x} stop$$

The former of these enables us to apply (CH.i) and determine that

$$P \xrightarrow{x} y \, ; \, stop$$

whereas the latter enables us to apply (CH.ii) and determine that

$$P \xrightarrow{x} stop$$

Thus, P offers a choice of transitions (as we would expect). From this discussion it should be straightforward to see that the complete transition system for this behaviour is as depicted in Figure 3.3. Thus, the approach is, at each stage, to apply exhaustively as many rules as possible. We can in fact put a derivation of behaviour together into an inference tree in a similar way to that found in logical deduction; see, for example [148].

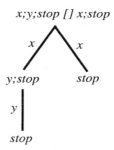

Fig. 3.3. Derivation of Labelled Transition Systems from Inference Rules

Parallel Composition. The parallel composition operator has three rules. The first two are symmetric.

$$(PA.i): \quad \frac{B_1 \xrightarrow{a} B_1'}{B_1|[x_1, \ldots, x_n]|B_2 \xrightarrow{a} B_1'|[x_1, \ldots, x_n]|B_2} \quad (a \notin \{x_1, \ldots, x_n, \delta\})$$

$$(PA.ii): \quad \frac{B_2 \xrightarrow{a} B_2'}{B_1|[x_1, \ldots, x_n]|B_2 \xrightarrow{a} B_1|[x_1, \ldots, x_n]|B_2'} \quad (a \notin \{x_1, \ldots, x_n, \delta\})$$

These state how parallel composition can evolve for actions not in the synchronisation set $x_1, \ldots, x_n$ or equal to δ. The rules state that, if one of the constituent behaviours, say B_1, can perform an action that is not in the synchronisation set and evolve into B_1', then the whole behaviour can perform the action and evolve into $B_1'|[x_1, \ldots, x_n]|B_2$. It is important to note that, in contrast to the situation with choice, an evolution of the whole behaviour does not exclude one of the constituent behaviours. This reflects the nature of parallel behaviour: B_1 and B_2 continue evolving in parallel.

Also notice that a δ action cannot be performed from these two rules. This reflects the fact that successful termination must be synchronised on by all parallel threads.

The final rule for parallel composition defines synchronisation behaviour,

$$(PA.iii): \quad \frac{B_1 \xrightarrow{a} B_1' \quad B_2 \xrightarrow{a} B_2'}{B_1|[x_1,\ldots,x_n]|B_2 \xrightarrow{a} B_1'|[x_1,\ldots,x_n]|B_2'} \quad (a \in \{x_1,\ldots,x_n,\delta\})$$

It states that an action in the synchronisation set can only be performed if both constituent behaviours can perform the action and, as a consequence, both sides of the parallel composition will evolve. The rule implies that, if one of the behaviours is ready to perform an action in the synchronisation set (or δ), if there are no alternative actions, it must wait for its "partner" behaviour to offer the same action. Notice also that δ actions can only be performed if both threads can perform the action.

We have only presented inference rules for the general form of parallel composition. The two derived operators, $|||$ and $||$, can be given very simple direct operational semantics. These are left as an exercise (note: you should be careful of how you handle δ).

Enabling. There are two rules for enabling.

$$(EN.i): \quad \frac{B_1 \xrightarrow{a} B_1'}{B_1 >> B_2 \xrightarrow{a} B_1' >> B_2} \quad (a \neq \delta)$$

$$(EN.ii): \quad \frac{B_1 \xrightarrow{\delta} B_1'}{B_1 >> B_2 \xrightarrow{i} B_2}$$

(EN.i) states that B_1 can evolve by performing an action a as long as the action is not a successful termination. (EN.ii) states that B_1 performing a successful termination will cause $B_1 >> B_2$ to perform an internal action and then evolve to B_2. Thus, as stated in Section 2.3.7, successful termination is represented by the occurrence of an i action. So, the δ action is used to signal the point of successful termination, but, that point is represented by an i action.

Hiding. There are two rules for hiding,

$$(HD.i): \quad \frac{B \xrightarrow{x} B'}{hide\ x_1,\ldots,x_n\ in\ B \xrightarrow{i} hide\ x_1,\ldots,x_n\ in\ B'} \quad (x \in \{x_1,\ldots,x_n\})$$

$$(HD.ii): \quad \frac{B \xrightarrow{a} B'}{hide\ x_1,\ldots,x_n\ in\ B \xrightarrow{a} hide\ x_1,\ldots,x_n\ in\ B'} \quad (a \notin \{x_1,\ldots,x_n\})$$

(HD.i) states that, if an action in the hiding set can be performed, it will be replaced by an internal action. (HD.ii) states that any action not in the hiding set can be performed as normal.

Relabelling. This again has two forms.

$$(RL.i): \quad \frac{B \xrightarrow{x_j} B'}{B[y_1/x_1,\ldots,y_n/x_n] \xrightarrow{y_j} B'[y_1/x_1,\ldots,y_n/x_n]} \quad (1 \leq j \leq n)$$

$$(RL.ii): \quad \frac{B \xrightarrow{a} B'}{B[y_1/x_1, \ldots, y_n/x_n] \xrightarrow{a} B'[y_1/x_1, \ldots, y_n/x_n]} \quad (a \notin \{x_1, \ldots, x_n\})$$

These rules are similar to the hiding rules.

Process Instantiation. There is just one rule for process instantiation; it assumes that the relevant process definition can be accessed.

$$(PI): \quad \frac{B \xrightarrow{a} B'}{P \xrightarrow{a} B'} \quad (P := B \text{ is in definition list } D \ \wedge \ a \in Act \cup \{\delta, i\})$$

Thus, the transitions of a process instantiation are those of the body of the process B.

One important issue to note is that recursive behaviour is treated in a very direct manner. In particular, a fixed point characterisation is not given, as is typically presented for a denotational semantics; rather recursion falls out of the inference rules of process instantiation. Thus, infinite behaviour of a pbLOTOS specification is mimicked directly in the derivation rules it induces.

Deriving a Labelled Transition System. From the inference rules defined above we can quite easily derive a labelled transition system. Firstly, we determine the set of states of the transition system; we denote this as $Der(S)$. Assuming S has the form

$B \ where \ D$

(if S is just a behaviour expression, B, this can be viewed as an expression of the above form, but with an empty definition list) we define

- $B \in Der(S)$
- $B' \in Der(S) \wedge \exists a \in Act \cup \{i, \delta\} \ s.t. \ B' \xrightarrow{a} B'' \implies B'' \in Der(S)$

where $\xrightarrow{a}$ is the smallest relation closed under the inference rules just presented. Thus, all possible derivations from B, according to transitions induced by the above inference rules, are included. We also need to define a function that maps behaviour expressions to their constituent actions. This is denoted $\mathcal{A}$ and is defined by induction over the structure of pbLOTOS behaviours, as shown in Figure 3.4.

Notice that this will actually give an upper bound on the actions that a behaviour can perform, as some actions may be prevented from happening by parallel composition. Now we are in a position to derive a labelled transition system for an arbitrary pbLOTOS specification S. Once again assuming, without lose of generality, that S has the form $B \ where \ D$ then $[\![S]\!]_{lts}$ is defined as

$$[\![S]\!]_{lts} \triangleq (Der(B), \mathcal{A}(B), T, B)$$

where

$$\mathcal{A}(stop) \triangleq \emptyset$$

$$\mathcal{A}(exit) \triangleq \{\delta\}$$

$$\mathcal{A}(a\,;\,B) \triangleq \mathcal{A}(B) \cup \{a\}$$

$$\mathcal{A}(B_1 \,[]\, B_2) \triangleq \mathcal{A}(B_1) \cup \mathcal{A}(B_2)$$

$$\mathcal{A}(B_1 \,|[x_1,\dots,x_n]|\, B_2) \triangleq \mathcal{A}(B_1) \cup \mathcal{A}(B_2)$$

$$\mathcal{A}(B_1 >> B_2) \triangleq \mathcal{A}(B_1) \cup \mathcal{A}(B_2)$$

$$\mathcal{A}(hide\ x_1,\dots,x_n\ in\ B) \triangleq \mathcal{A}(B) \setminus \{x_1,\dots,x_n\}$$

$$\mathcal{A}(B[y_1/x_1,\dots,y_n/x_n]) \triangleq \{\,H(a) \mid a \in \mathcal{A}(B)\,\}\ \ \text{where,}$$

$$H(a) \triangleq if\ a = x_i\ (1 \leq i \leq n)\ then\ y_i\ else\ a$$

$$\mathcal{A}(P) \triangleq \mathcal{A}(B)\ \ \text{assuming } P := B \text{ is in } D$$

Fig. 3.4. Function for Extracting Labels from a Behaviour

$$T \triangleq \{\ \xrightarrow{a}\ \subseteq\ Der(B) \times Der(B) \mid a \in \mathcal{A}(B)\ \}$$
$$\text{where}\ \xrightarrow{a}\ \triangleq\ \{\ (B_1, B_2) \mid B_1 \xrightarrow{a} B_2\ \wedge\ B_1, B_2 \in Der(B)\ \}$$

This completes our derivation of labelled transition systems from pbLOTOS specifications.

3.3.2.3 Deriving Trace Semantics from Labelled Transition Systems

We have already suggested that labelled transition systems are a more distinguishing semantics than trace semantics; i.e. they identify fewer pbLOTOS specifications. This relationship is reflected by the fact that we can derive trace semantics from labelled transition systems. We define a mapping from labelled transition systems to trace sets. The mapping is standard and, in fact, many researchers prefer to derive trace semantics for LOTOS indirectly via labelled transition systems, rather than defining a direct denotational semantics, such as the one we presented in Section 3.2.2.2.

We denote the mapping,

$$Tr : \mathcal{LTS} \longrightarrow \mathcal{P}(\mathcal{T})$$

which is defined, for a particular LTS, say (S, A, T, s_0), using a relation,

$$\Longrightarrow\ \subseteq S \times A^* \times S$$

which is usually written $\xRightarrow{\sigma}$, where σ is a trace in A^*. Typical applications of the relation might be:

$s \stackrel{\sigma}{\Longrightarrow} s'$ where $s, s' \in S$ or,

$B \stackrel{\sigma}{\Longrightarrow} B'$ where $B, B' \in Beh$

Remember, states and behaviour expressions are identified in labelled transition systems. So, the relation can be defined interchangeably over either. The relation $s \stackrel{\sigma}{\Longrightarrow} s'$ should be read: from state s, the trace σ can be performed to reach state s'. Performing a trace σ means performing the sequence of observable actions included in the trace. The relation $\Longrightarrow$ is derived from the relation $\longrightarrow$; it corresponds to zero or more occurrences of the relation $\longrightarrow$, with internal actions possibly interleaved. To be more formal, we first define the meaning of applying $\stackrel{\sigma}{\Longrightarrow}$ with the empty trace.

$$s \stackrel{\epsilon}{\Longrightarrow} s' \;\textit{iff}\; s = s' \;\vee$$

$$(\exists s_0, \ldots, s_n \in S \,.\, s \stackrel{i}{\longrightarrow} s_0 \;\wedge\; s_0 \stackrel{i}{\longrightarrow} s_1 \;\wedge\; \ldots \;\wedge\; s_n \stackrel{i}{\longrightarrow} s')$$

So, $s \stackrel{\epsilon}{\Longrightarrow} s$ and $s \stackrel{\epsilon}{\Longrightarrow} s'$ if s' can be reached from s by a sequence of internal actions. The former of these reflects the fact that an empty trace can always be performed and leave the LTS in the same state, whereas the latter reflects the fact that internal behaviour is not represented in trace semantics. In mathematical terms, the relation $\stackrel{\epsilon}{\Longrightarrow}$ is the reflexive and transitive closure of $\stackrel{i}{\longrightarrow}$.

We are now able to define $\stackrel{\sigma}{\Longrightarrow}$ for any nonempty trace σ.

$$s \stackrel{x.\sigma}{\Longrightarrow} s' \;\textit{iff}\; \exists s_1, s_2 \,.\, s \stackrel{\epsilon}{\Longrightarrow} s_1 \;\wedge\; s_1 \stackrel{x}{\longrightarrow} s_2 \;\wedge\; s_2 \stackrel{\sigma}{\Longrightarrow} s'$$

This definition is (tail) recursive; it defines the relation by stating how the head of the trace, the x, should be handled and then considers recursively the tail of the trace, the σ. The relation states that $s \stackrel{\sigma}{\Longrightarrow} s'$ if and only if s' can be reached from s by performing the zero or more actions of the trace σ, with internal actions possibly interleaved.

We can now define the function Tr; it is very simply expressed as

$$Tr((S, A, T, s_0)) \triangleq \{ \, \sigma \mid \exists s \in S \text{ s.t. } s_0 \stackrel{\sigma}{\Longrightarrow} s \, \}$$

So, this defines the set of all possible traces that can be derived from the labelled transition system, (S, A, T, s_0).

3.3.3 Development Relations

3.3.3.1 Basic Equivalence Relations

In some circumstances, labelled transition systems can be seen to be too discriminating. For example, consider the following two pbLOTOS behaviours (these were highlighted in [148]),

$$P_1 := x \,;\, y \,;\, stop \quad \text{and} \quad P_2 := (\,x \,;\, (\,y \,;\, stop \,[]\, y \,;\, stop\,)\,)\,[]\,(\,x \,;\, y \,;\, stop\,)$$

which have the labelled transition systems depicted in Figure 3.5. Although these transition systems are different, in fact, they should not be distinguished, as their observable behaviour will be the same. This is because, although there are a number of different alternative paths that can be taken through P_2, whereas there is only one possible path through P_1, all these alternative paths generate the same external behaviour.

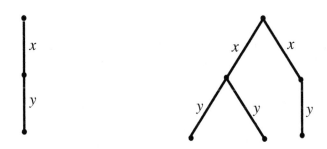

Fig. 3.5. Two Labelled Transition System: P_1 on the Left and P_2 on the Right

What is required then is to define an identity relation that equates behaviours that we want to consider as identical, such as P_1 and P_2. So, the approach with LTS is to define a semantics that differentiates many pbLOTOS specifications and then to identify processes again by equating LTS models.

There are two relations that are typically used to identify LTS. These are *strong* and *weak bisimulation*;[2] they are the main development relations defined over labelled transition systems. The latter of these is also often called *observational equivalence*. The distinction between the two equivalences reflects two different views of the observability of systems. We discuss the two in turn. We follow relatively closely the treatment to be found in [148], which is the classic text on the topic.

Strong Bisimulation. As reflected in its name, this relation characterises a strong interpretation of observation and, thus, induces a strong equivalence. The following defines a strong bisimulation relation.

Definition 4   (Strong Bisimulation Relations)
A binary relation $\mathcal{R} \subseteq Beh \times Beh$ is a strong bisimulation if $(B_1, B_2) \in \mathcal{R}$ implies $\forall a \in Act \cup \{i, \delta\}$,

1. $\forall B_1' \in Beh, \ B_1 \xrightarrow{a} B_1' \implies \exists B_2' \in Beh \ . \ B_2 \xrightarrow{a} B_2' \wedge (B_1', B_2') \in \mathcal{R} \ \wedge$
2. $\forall B_2' \in Beh, \ B_2 \xrightarrow{a} B_2' \implies \exists B_1' \in Beh \ . \ B_1 \xrightarrow{a} B_1' \wedge (B_1', B_2') \in \mathcal{R}.$

---

[2]Although, we will also consider a derivation of this latter relation, called weak bisimulation congruence, which is technically more well behaved.

Informally, the definition states that $B_1 \mathcal{R} B_2$ (which we have written above as $(B_1, B_2) \in \mathcal{R}$) implies that any transition that B_1 can perform, B_2 can perform as well and they will evolve into bisimilar states and the converse; i.e. any transition that B_2 can perform, B_1 can perform and they will evolve into bisimilar states. Bisimulation requires the states in the two specifications to be related in such a way that the transition property holds at all states. However, it is important to note that this relation is not driven in any way by the syntactic relationship between states. For example, the two behaviour expressions:

$$(x ; y ; stop) \| (x ; z ; stop) \quad \text{and} \quad x ; stop$$

could quite reasonably be identified by a strong bisimulation relation $\mathcal{R}$, even though they are syntactically very different. This aspect illustrates how bisimulation relations abstract away from syntactic equality. Notice that the definition matches internal actions and successful terminations. Thus, in order to characterise externally observable behaviour, the strong bisimulation relation delves into the internals of specifications. We have more to say about this shortly.

The concept is best illustrated by example. Consider the following behaviours.

$$P_1 := (x ; y ; stop) [] (z ; stop)$$
$$P_2 := (z ; stop) [] (x ; y ; stop)$$
$$P_3 := (x ; y ; stop)$$
$$P_4 := (x ; (y ; stop [] y ; stop)) [] (x ; y ; stop)$$
$$P_5 := (x ; y ; stop) [] (x ; (y ; stop [] y ; stop [] y ; stop))$$

We can identify strong bisimulation relations between a number of these behaviours. For example, if we denote behaviours in the evaluation of these expressions as

$$P_1^2, P_1^3, P_2^1, P_2^3, P_3^2, P_3^3, P_4^2, P_3^5, P_5^4 = stop$$
$$P_1^1, P_2^2, P_3^1, P_4^2, P_5^1 = y ; stop$$
$$P_4^1 = y ; stop [] y ; stop$$
$$P_5^2 = y ; stop [] y ; stop [] y ; stop$$

then we can demonstrate the following strong bisimulation, denoted $\mathcal{R}'$, between P_1 and P_2.

$$\mathcal{R}' = \{ (P_1, P_2), (P_1^1, P_2^2), (P_1^3, P_2^1), (P_1^2, P_2^3) \}$$

This relation is depicted in Figure 3.6(i); P_1 is on the left and P_2 is on the right and the arcs between the two derivation trees highlight the states that are identified by $\mathcal{R}'$. You should convince yourself that the relationship between states highlighted does yield a strong bisimulation relation. In fact, the bisimulation between these two behaviours is very straightforward and all the states that are related are syntactically equal (i.e. denote the same behaviour expression) apart from the root states. This, however, is not always the case, as we show shortly.

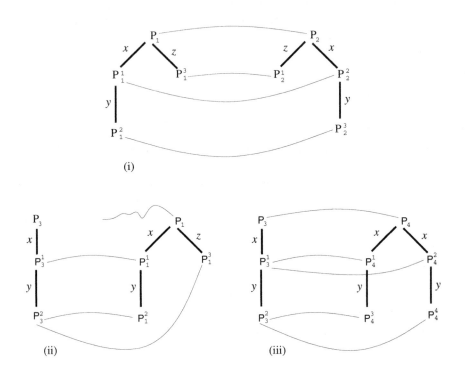

Fig. 3.6. Examples of Strong Bisimulation Relations

It is also easy to locate two behaviours that cannot be related by a strong bisimulation. For example, Figure 3.6(ii) depicts an attempt to relate the states in the two behaviours P_3 and P_1. All states can be related apart from the root states. We can show this by considering Condition (2) of Definition 4. Specifically, $P_1 \xrightarrow{z} P_1^3$, but P_3 can perform no transition with this labelling; i.e. $P_3 \xrightarrow{z}\!\!\!\!/\ $. In this example, strong bisimilarity is prevented by an initial action offer, but differences in action offers farther down the derivation tree will similarly prevent strong bisimulation. Because of the recursive nature of the definition, states that cannot be related inside derivation trees will prevent the root states from being related by bisimulation.

We can also show that the two behaviours that we identified earlier as candidates for being equated are related by strong bisimulation. Figure 3.6(iii) highlights a strong bisimulation between P_3 and P_4. Notice that we have compressed the two branches of P_4 following state P_4^1 into a single branch. This is because the two branches are actually identical. Further notice that, apart from initial states, the relation equates single states in P_3 to multiple states in P_4. This reflects the increased branching of P_4.

Definition 4 does not yet give us an equivalence though. In particular, many relations, including the null relation, will satisfy Definition 4. For example, we can show that there is more than one strong bisimulation relation between the behaviours P_4 and P_5; Figure 3.7 highlights two strong bisimulations for P_4 and P_5.

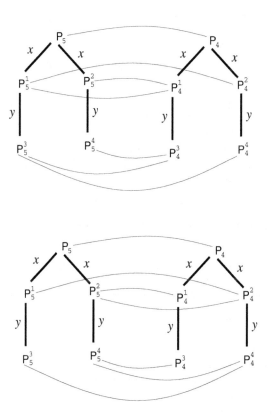

Fig. 3.7. Two Strong Bisimulation Relations

In general, there can be many strong bisimulation relations between pairs of specifications. These arise when there is a choice of states to which to relate. However, what we are actually interested in, is that a strong bisimulation exists. If it does exist, we should equate the two specifications. Thus, we take as our equivalence relation, the largest relation that satisfies Definition 4. This amounts to taking the union of all possible strong bisimulation relations and states that two specifications are equivalent if at least one strong bisimulation relation can be found between the two specifications.

Definition 5   (Strongly Bisimilar)
Two behaviours B and B′ are strongly bisimilar (also called strongly equivalent), denoted B ∼ B′, if there exists a strong bisimulation relation $\mathcal{R}$ such that B $\mathcal{R}$ B′, or equivalently,

$$\sim \triangleq \bigcup \{ \, \mathcal{R} \mid \mathcal{R} \text{ is a strong bisimulation relation } \}$$

The following relationships between our example behaviours can be identified.

$$P_1 \sim P_2 \, , \quad P_3 \sim P_4 \, , \quad P_4 \sim P_5 \, , \quad P_3 \sim P_5$$
$$P_1 \nsim P_3, \; P_2 \nsim P_3 \, , \; P_1 \nsim P_4, \; P_2 \nsim P_4 \, , \; P_1 \nsim P_5 \text{ and}$$
$$P_2 \nsim P_5$$

Definition 5 induces a relation with a number of useful properties; see, for example, [148]. In particular, the relation can easily be shown to be an equivalence and, in addition, the relation is a congruence for the pbLOTOS operators. A proof of this fact is presented in Theorem 14.1 of Section 14.2 in the appendix.

Theorem 3.1.
∼ *is a congruence over the pbLOTOS operators.*

Weak Bisimulation. As indicated already, ∼ induces a strong notion of identity. In particular, it matches internal behaviour in the two specifications. For example, none of the following three behaviours,

$$x \, ; y \, ; stop \quad , \quad i \, ; x \, ; y \, ; stop \quad \text{and} \quad x \, ; i \, ; y \, ; stop$$

are strongly bisimilar. However, in reality, there is no way that these three behaviours can be distinguished by an external observer. In particular, the only way in which internal behaviour could alter a linear sequence of actions in respect of an observer is that an action might be slowed. However, such slowing is not observable in the untimed world. Implicitly, the length of time the environment may have to wait before performing an action is not distinguishable in the semantic models of this part.

In response to this observation, we introduce the notion of a *weak bisimulation* between behaviours. This uses a slight enhancement of the relation $\overset{\sigma}{\Longrightarrow}$, which was introduced in Section 3.3.2.3. This is denoted $\overset{\sigma}{\Longrightarrow\!\!\!\!\twoheadrightarrow}$ and formally,

$$B_1 \overset{\sigma}{\Longrightarrow\!\!\!\!\twoheadrightarrow} B_2 \quad \textit{iff} \quad (\, B_1 \overset{\sigma}{\Longrightarrow} B_2 \,) \; \vee \; (\, B_1 \overset{\epsilon}{\Longrightarrow} B_2 \; \wedge \; \sigma = i \,)$$

Thus, $\sigma \in (Act \cup \{\delta\})^*$ or $\sigma = i$.[3] Definition of this equivalence follows the same lines as that of strong bisimulation. Thus, we begin by defining what it means for a relation to be a weak bisimulation relation.

Definition 6   (Weak Bisimulation Relations)
A binary relation $\mathcal{S} \subseteq Beh \times Beh$ is a weak bisimulation if $(B_1, B_2) \in \mathcal{S}$ implies, $\forall a \in Act \cup \{i, \delta\}$,

1. $\forall B_1' \in Beh,\ B_1 \xrightarrow{a} B_1' \implies \exists B_2' \in Beh . B_2 \overset{a}{\Longrightarrow\!\!\!\!\!\Rightarrow} B_2' \wedge (B_1', B_2') \in \mathcal{S} \wedge$
2. $\forall B_2' \in Beh,\ B_2 \xrightarrow{a} B_2' \implies \exists B_1' \in Beh . B_1 \overset{a}{\Longrightarrow\!\!\!\!\!\Rightarrow} B_1' \wedge (B_1', B_2') \in \mathcal{S}.$

Informally, the definition states that $B_1\ \mathcal{S}\ B_2$ implies that any transition that B_1 can perform B_2 can perform as well, with internal actions "skipped over" and they evolve into weakly bisimilar states and the converse. So, the definition is identical to that given for a strong bisimulation relation apart from the fact that the double arrow, $\overset{a}{\Longrightarrow\!\!\!\!\!\Rightarrow}$, is used in the target behaviour. Remember the definition of $\overset{\sigma}{\Longrightarrow}$ that we gave in Section 3.3.2.3; i.e. it denotes the occurrence of the sequence of actions in σ with internal actions possibly interleaved. Here we are only considering singleton traces, i.e. traces of one element. So, the definition states that, if we are trying to find a transition which matches $\xrightarrow{x}$ say, we can use a transition that has internal actions before and after x, i.e. one that satisfies $\overset{x}{\Longrightarrow\!\!\!\!\!\Rightarrow}$ and hence $\overset{x}{\Longrightarrow}$.

This concept is also best illustrated by example. Consider the following behaviours,

$P_1 := x\,;\,y\,;\,stop$

$P_2 := i\,;\,x\,;\,y\,;\,stop$

$P_3 := x\,;\,i\,;\,y\,;\,stop$

There are weak bisimulation relations between all these three behaviours. Consider, for example, P_1 and P_2. The weak bisimulation relation between these two behaviours is:

$$\mathcal{S}' = \{\ (P_1, P_2), (P_1, P_2^1), (P_1^1, P_2^2), (P_1^2, P_2^3)\ \}$$

which is depicted in Figure 3.8(i). You should be able to convince yourself that,

$$(P_1^2, P_2^3), (P_1^1, P_2^2), (P_1, P_2^1)$$

are weakly bisimilar. So, the interesting issue is relating P_1 and P_2, assuming the pairs of behaviour just highlighted are related by weak bisimulation. First, we consider how to relate P_1 to P_2 from left to right. We have,

$P_1 \xrightarrow{x} P_1^1$ is matched by $P_2 \overset{x}{\Longrightarrow\!\!\!\!\!\Rightarrow} P_2^2$ and $(P_1^1, P_2^2) \in \mathcal{S}'$

---

[3]The abuse of notation here, whereby σ is used to denote both a trace and an internal action, does not cause any difficulties.

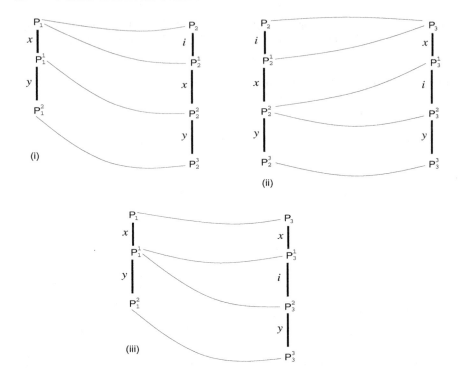

Fig. 3.8. Weak Bisimulation Relations

and second, we consider how to relate P_1 to P_2 from right to left. We have,

$$P_2 \xrightarrow{i} P_2^1 \text{ is matched by } P_1 \xRightarrow{\ \ \ } P_1 \text{ and } (P_1, P_2^1) \in \mathcal{S}'$$

(This is why we need to move from $\Longrightarrow$ to $\xRightarrow{\ \ \ }$, because $\xRightarrow{i}$ is not defined, as i is not an observable trace.)

which gives us that $(P_1, P_2) \in \mathcal{S}'$ as required. Figures 3.8(ii) and 3.8(iii) highlight the, slightly more complex, weak bisimulation relations between P_2 and P_3 and P_1 and P_3.

It would though be wrong to suggest that internal behaviour cannot prevent two behaviours from having a weak bisimulation relation between them; the definition is more subtle than that. For example, consider whether a weak bisimulation can be found which relates P_1 and P_4, where

$$P_4 := (x\,;\,y\,;\,stop)\, [] \,(i\,;\,stop)$$

An attempt to identify states to locate a weak bisimulation relation, $\mathcal{S}''$ say, between P_1 and P_4 is shown in Figure 3.9. You should be able to convince yourself that the following pairs of states are weak bisimilar,

$(P_1^1, P_4^1), (P_1^2, P_4^3), (P_1^2, P_4^2),$

but what about P_1 and P_4? Where this fails is in trying to relate P_1 and P_4 from right to left. In particular, from P_4 we have

$P_4 \xrightarrow{i} P_4^2$

So, we require a state in P_1 that will be related to P_4^2 after $\overset{i}{\Longrightarrow}$ is performed. The only candidate for such a state is P_1 itself as $P_1 \overset{i}{\Longrightarrow} P_1$, but, P_1 and P_4^2 are not weak bisimilar, because P_4^2 cannot offer an x. So, P_1 and P_4 cannot be related by weak bisimulation.

We can give similar arguments to show that none of the following behaviours can be related by a weak bisimulation.

$x \,; stop \,[] \, y \,; stop,$

$(\,x \,; stop\,) \, [] \, (\,i \,; y \,; stop\,)$ and

$(\,i \,; x \,; stop\,) \, [] \, (\,i \,; y \,; stop\,)$

So, weak bisimulation relations do distinguish nondeterminism due to internal behaviour from deterministic behaviour and also different varieties of nondeterminism due to internal behaviour. This relatively closely reflects the capabilities of the external environment to observe a pbLOTOS behaviour, as we have discussed previously. However, it should be pointed out, that some researchers believe that even weak bisimulation induces an unrealistically strong equivalence; they advocate a relation called *testing equivalence*, which we consider in Chapter 5.

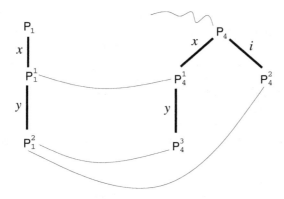

Fig. 3.9. A Failed Weak Bisimulation Relation

As was the case for strong bisimulation, there can be many bisimulation relations between pairs of specifications. So, once again, we take as our equivalence relation, the largest relation that satisfies Definition 6.

Definition 7   (Weakly Bisimilar)
Two behaviours B and B' are weakly bisimilar (also called observationally equivalent), denoted $B \approx B'$ if there exists a weak bisimulation relation S such that $B \, S \, B'$, or equivalently,

$$\approx \triangleq \bigcup \{ \, S \mid S \text{ is a weak bisimulation relation} \, \}$$

Definition 7 induces a relation with a number of useful properties; see [148]. In particular, the relation can easily be shown to be an equivalence. In addition, it can be shown that strong bisimulation implies weak bisimulation, but not the converse; i.e.

$$\sim \, \subset \, \approx$$

Weak Bisimulation Congruence. However, $\approx$ is only substitutive for a subset of the pbLOTOS operators. The context that prevents $\approx$ from being a congruence is choice. As an illustration, consider the two behaviours:

$x \, ; \, stop$ and $i \, ; \, x \, ; \, stop$

These are weakly bisimilar, because the internal action at the start of the second expression does not affect the observable behaviour. However, the two behaviours,

$x \, ; \, stop \, [] \, y \, ; \, stop$ and $(\, i \, ; \, x \, ; \, stop \,) \, [] \, (\, y \, ; \, stop \,)$

are not weakly bisimilar. The internal action in the second expression now affects the external behaviour, because an asymmetric nondeterministic choice is created. This is an unfortunate result; however, a number of alternative relations have been devised in order to obtain a congruent equivalence with the flavour of weak bisimulation.

Typically, these constrain the initial moves of the relation. For instance, they may require that, if the initial states of one of the behaviours can perform an internal action, then the other must be able to do at least one internal action and change state, thus, preventing behaviours of the form

$i \, ; \, x \, ; \, B$ and $x \, ; \, B$

from being related. Typical examples of such relations include Milner's observational congruence [148] and rooted bisimulations [120].

We follow Milner [148] and define a relation, which we call weak bisimulation congruence. It uses a new double arrow transition relation, which is defined as follows.

$$B_1 \stackrel{\sigma}{\Longrightarrow} B_2 \;\; \textit{iff} \;\; (\, B_1 \stackrel{\sigma}{\Longrightarrow} B_2 \,) \, \vee \, (\, \sigma = i \, \wedge \, B_1 \stackrel{\epsilon}{\Longrightarrow} B_1' \, \wedge \, B_1' \stackrel{i}{\longrightarrow} B_2 \,)$$

where $\sigma \in (Act \cup \{\delta\})^*$ or $\sigma = i$. Thus, $\Longrightarrow\!\!\!\!\Longrightarrow$ strengthens $\Longrightarrow\!\!\!\!\rightarrow$ in one crucial case; that is,

$$\forall B, \; B \stackrel{i}{\Longrightarrow\!\!\!\!\rightarrow} B, \;\; but, \;\; B \stackrel{i}{\Longrightarrow\!\!\!\!\not\!\rightarrow} B$$

Thus, $\Longrightarrow\!\!\!\!\rightarrow$ allows i moves that stay in the same state, whereas $\Longrightarrow\!\!\!\!\Longrightarrow$ rules out this possibility; it can only perform an i move if there is a concrete i transition (by $\longrightarrow$). It is straightforward to show that

$$\Longrightarrow \; \subset \; \Longrightarrow\!\!\!\!\Longrightarrow \; \subset \; \Longrightarrow\!\!\!\!\rightarrow$$

Thus, $\Longrightarrow$ does not allow i moves (i.e. moves of the form $B_1 \stackrel{i}{\Longrightarrow} B_2$), however, $\Longrightarrow\!\!\!\!\Longrightarrow$ does allow such moves, but only when an i transition (i.e. $\stackrel{i}{\longrightarrow}$) can be made and, finally, $\Longrightarrow\!\!\!\!\rightarrow$ also allows "null" i moves between the same state.

Now, we can define weak bisimulation congruence as follows.

Definition 8   (Weak Bisimulation Congruence)
Two pbLOTOS behaviours, B_1 and B_2, are weak bisimulation congruent, written $B_1 \approx_c B_2$, if $\forall a \in Act \cup \{i, \delta\}$,

1. $\forall B_1' \in Beh, \; B_1 \stackrel{a}{\longrightarrow} B_1' \; \Longrightarrow \; \exists B_2' \in Beh \, . \, B_2 \stackrel{a}{\Longrightarrow\!\!\!\!\Longrightarrow} B_2' \; \wedge \; B_1' \approx B_2' \; \wedge$

2. $\forall B_2' \in Beh, \; B_2 \stackrel{a}{\longrightarrow} B_2' \; \Longrightarrow \; \exists B_1' \in Beh \, . \, B_1 \stackrel{a}{\Longrightarrow\!\!\!\!\Longrightarrow} B_1' \; \wedge \; B_1' \approx B_2'.$

It is important to note that when compared with weak bisimulation, this definition only imposes the stronger ($\Longrightarrow\!\!\!\!\Longrightarrow$) constraint on initial moves. In particular, once initial transitions have been successfully matched, the definition reverts to checking weak bisimulation (hence the use of $\approx$ rather than $\approx_c$). Through this stronger constraint on initial moves, weak bisimulation congruence prevents a behaviour with an initial i transition from being matched with a behaviour that offers no such transition. For example, the following two behaviours,

$$x\,;\, stop \quad \text{and} \quad i\,;\, x\,;\, stop$$

are not related by $\approx_c$. However, the following,

$$y\,;\, x\,;\, stop \quad \text{and} \quad y\,;\, i\,;\, x\,;\, stop$$

are weak bisimulation congruent.

Our choice of the name weak bisimulation *congruence* is justified by Theorem 14.2 of Section 14.3 in the Appendix.

Discussion. The area of bisimulation semantics is extremely rich and the presentation in this book has only been able to reflect a small part of this area of study. We offer the following pointers to other important topics.

- In [148], Milner investigates axiomatic laws for bisimulation equivalences and gives sound and complete axiomatisations for finite processes.

- In [148], Milner defines notions of strong and weak bisimulation up to $\sim$ (respectively, $\approx$). These relations simplify the process of locating bisimulation relations.
- Weak bisimulation can be presented in terms of just the double arrow relation; remember we have presented it in terms of $\longrightarrow$ and $\Longrightarrow\!\!\!\!\gg$. In fact, presentation using only the double arrow predominates in the LOTOS community. However, the presentations induce the same relation, although, the definition we have favoured can be easier to handle, because it does not require as many states to be matched.

It is also worth pointing out that bisimulation relations do not distinguish divergent behaviour. This is in contrast to CSP failure semantics. We discuss this issue in some depth in Chapter 7.

In summary, it should be apparent that identifying specifications based on bisimulation equivalences is far more discriminating than using trace equality. In particular, as noted earlier, trace-based semantics can only ensure safety properties are preserved. However, bisimulation semantics ensure both safety and liveness properties are preserved. For example, the following two behaviours would be identified by trace equality,

$$(i \,;\, x \,;\, stop) \,[\!]\, (i \,;\, stop) \quad \text{and} \quad x \,;\, stop$$

but, they clearly would not be identified by any of the bisimulation equivalences, because the second behaviour cannot evolve into a deadlock state after performing the i action by any of the transition relations, $\longrightarrow$, $\Longrightarrow$, $\Longrightarrow\!\!\!\!\gg$ or $\Longrightarrow\!\!\!\!\gg$.

3.3.3.2 Refinement Relations and Induced Equivalences

The relations that we have considered in the previous section have all been equivalences. However, in some circumstances, we would like to use refinement relations. Such relations can also be defined for labelled transition systems. Although, there has been less work on defining nonequivalence relations in the bisimulation setting (this is in contrast to the situation with trace semantics and trace-refusals semantics), thus, our presentation is not as in depth as was the case in the previous section. References for the relations that we consider in this section include [73, 118, 148].

The first relation we consider is called simulation and it was actually one of the first correctness relations that was explored with regard to process calculi. The relation is something like half of bisimulation; i.e. bisimulation in just one direction. It could be formulated in a *weak* manner, analogously to how weak bisimulation is defined, however, here we restrict ourselves to a *strong* formulation. It is defined as follows.

Definition 9   (Simulation Relations)
A binary relation $S \subseteq Beh \times Beh$ is a simulation relation if $B_1 \, S \, B_2$ implies

$\forall a \in Act \cup \{i, \delta\}$,

$\forall B_1' \in Beh,\ B_1 \overset{a}{\longrightarrow} B_1' \implies \exists B_2' \in Beh\ s.t.\ B_2 \overset{a}{\longrightarrow} B_2' \wedge B_1'\ \mathcal{S}\ B_2'.$

Definition 10 (Similar)
Behaviour B' simulates behaviour B, denoted $B' \prec B$ if there exists a simulation relation $\mathcal{S}$ such that $B\ \mathcal{S}\ B'$, or equivalently,

$$\prec \triangleq \bigcup\{\ \mathcal{S}^{-1} \mid \mathcal{S}\ \text{is a simulation relation}\ \}$$

Notice that, in defining $\prec$, we have flipped the order of relations $\mathcal{S}$. This is to bring the relation into line with the direction LOTOS refinement relations are typically written. Thus, in Definition 9, B_2 is the more concrete specification (i.e. closer to an implementation) and B_1 is the abstract specification.

It can be verified that $\prec$ does indeed satisfy the requirements of a refinement relation; i.e. it is a preorder. In fact, the relation is a precongruence.

Proposition 3

(i) $\prec$ is a preorder.

(ii) $\prec$ is a precongruence.

Proof
The proof of (i) is straightforward. (ii) could be verified using an adaptation of the line of reasoning given in Section 14.2 to justify that strong bisimulation is a congruence. In fact, the required proof is a simplification of the line of reasoning given there in which only one direction of deduction is used.
$\bigcirc$

To illustrate the relation, consider the following behaviours.

$P_1 := x\,;\, y\,;\, stop$

$P_2 := (\,x\,;\, y\,;\, stop\,) \ []\ (\,z\,;\, stop\,)$

$P_3 := (\,x\,;\, y\,;\, z\,;\, stop\,)$

$P_4 := (\,x\,;\, y\,;\, stop\,) \ []\ (\,x\,;\, stop\,)$

$P_5 := x\,;\, stop$

The following relationships hold:

- $(P_2 \prec P_1)$. This example shows that a new branch in a choice can be added. In this respect, simulation is related to the extension relation, which we consider in Section 5.1. The reason that new branches can be added is that the relation is only checked in one direction; i.e. from P_1 to P_2, so, any extra behaviour of P_2 is not considered.
- $(P_3 \prec P_1)$. This example demonstrates that extra behaviour can be added to the end of a complete trace. This is because, after performing x and y, P_1 evolves to $stop$ and $stop \overset{a}{\not\longrightarrow}$ for any a. Thus, state $z\,;\, stop$ vacuously simulates state $stop$. This is another illustration of the fact that simulation allows traces to be extended.

- $(P_4 \prec P_1)$. This shows that deadlocks can be added by simulation. That is, an environment can always perform a y after an x when interacting with P_1, but it may deadlock after performing x with P_4. Simulation behaves in this way because there only has to be one match for the transitions of P_1 in P_4. Thus, the x; *stop* branch of P_4 is not involved in the derived simulation relation.
- $(P_5 \not\prec P_1)$. These are not related because, after performing x, P_5 cannot perform a y.

It should be clear from these examples that simulation is not a well-behaved refinement relation. It does not preserve safety properties (i.e. traces can be extended) and it does not preserve liveness properties (i.e. deadlocks can be added).[4] The relation is largely included here for completeness and as a historical artefact.

An obvious notion of equivalence that can be obtained from simulation is the following.

Definition 11   (Simulation Equivalent)
B and B′ are simulation equivalent iff $B \prec B′$ and $B′ \prec B$; i.e. simulation equivalence is the relation: $\prec \cap \prec^{-1}$, which, in terms of the notation introduced earlier, would be written as $\asymp_\prec$.

This turns out to be an inappropriate definition of equivalence in the same way that $\prec$ was an inappropriate notion of refinement. For example, $P_4 \asymp_\prec P_1$ because we have already justified that $P_4 \prec P_1$ and a simulation in the other direction would relate the rightmost P_4 behaviour *stop* to y; *stop* in P_1. Notice that the simulation relations used to justify $P_4 \prec P_1$ and to justify $P_1 \prec P_4$ are different. This example demonstrates that simulation equivalence does not always preserve liveness properties.

It can be shown that, if the same relation is used in both directions, strong bisimulation is obtained.

Proposition 4
$\mathcal{R} \subseteq Beh \times Beh$ is a strong bisimulation if and only if $\mathcal{R}$ and $\mathcal{R}^{-1}$ are simulations.

Proof
See [160].
○

An alternative refinement relation to simulation is *ready simulation* [192], which coincides with, what has been called, 2/3-bisimulation [118].

Definition 12   (Ready simulation)
$\mathcal{R} \subseteq Beh \times Beh$ is a ready simulation if $B_1 \, \mathcal{R} \, B_2$ implies $\forall a \in Act \cup \{i, \delta\}$,

---

[4]Chapter 5 elaborates on the relationship between liveness and deadlocks.

1. $\forall B_1' \in Beh, \ B_1 \xrightarrow{a} B_1' \implies \exists B_2' \in Beh \ . \ B_2 \xrightarrow{a} B_2' \ \wedge \ B_1' \ \mathcal{R} \ B_2'$,

2. $B_2 \xrightarrow{a} \ \implies B_1 \xrightarrow{a}$.

Definition 13   (Ready similar)
$\preceq_R \triangleq \bigcup\{\ \mathcal{R}^{-1} \mid \mathcal{R} \ is \ a \ ready \ simulation \ \}$

In terms of the examples presented earlier,

$$P_2 \not\prec_R P_1, \quad P_3 \not\prec_R P_1$$

These indicate that, as a result of adding Condition 2 in Definition 12, traces cannot be extended with ready simulation. However we can still add deadlocks; e.g. $P_4 \prec_R P_1$.

Ready simulation induces an equivalence.

Definition 14   (Ready Simulation Equivalence)
B and B' are ready simulation equivalence iff there exist ready simulations $\mathcal{R}$ and $\mathcal{R}'$ such that $B \ \mathcal{R} \ B'$ and $B' \ \mathcal{R}' \ B$. This equivalence is denoted $\sim_R$.

To illustrate the difference between $\sim_R$ and the other two "strong" equivalences that we have discussed (strong bisimulation and simulation), consider the following processes (where the first two were also considered as P_4 and P_1 earlier in this section).

$$R_1 := (x\,;\,y\,;\,stop)\ [\!]\ (x\,;\,stop)$$
$$R_2 := x\,;\,y\,;\,stop$$
$$R_3 := (x\,;\,y\,;\,stop)\ [\!]\ (x\,;\,z\,;\,stop)$$
$$R_4 := x\,;\,(y\,;\,stop\ [\!]\ z\,;\,stop)$$
$$R_5 := x\,;\,(y\,;\,z\,;\,stop\ [\!]\ y\,;\,w\,;\,stop)$$
$$R_6 := x\,;\,(y\,;\,z\,;\,stop\ [\!]\ y\,;\,w\,;\,stop)\ [\!]\ x\,;\,y\,;\,z\,;\,stop$$

Corresponding transition systems are depicted in Figure 3.10. It can be shown that the following relationships hold between these processes.

$$R_1 \asymp_\prec R_2, \quad R_1 \not\prec_R R_2 \quad and \quad R_1 \not\sim R_2$$
$$R_3 \not\asymp_\prec R_4, \quad R_3 \not\prec_R R_4 \quad and \quad R_3 \not\sim R_4$$
$$R_5 \asymp_\prec R_6, \quad R_5 \sim_R R_6 \quad and \quad R_5 \not\sim R_6$$

Most of these relationships are straightforward. Thus, we only discuss a subset of the relationships in more depth.

$R_1 \not\prec_R R_2$ is because $R_2 \not\prec_R R_1$ (whereas $R_1 \prec_R R_2$; in fact, this is the same as $P_4 \prec_R P_1$ discussed earlier in this section). The reason that $R_2 \not\prec_R R_1$ is that $R_2^1 \not\prec_R R_1^2$ (see Figure 3.10), because the second condition of Definition 12 requires $R_1^2 \xrightarrow{y}$.

Now, in order to justify $R_3 \not\asymp_\prec R_4$, we can see that $R_3 \not\prec R_4$. This is because for $R_3 \prec R_4$ to hold, we would need to relate R_3^1 to one of R_4^2 or

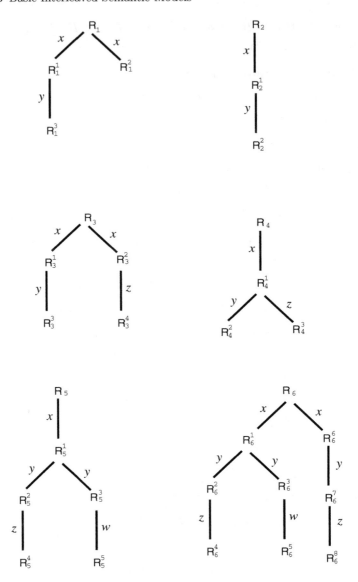

Fig. 3.10. Ready Simulation Illustrations

R_3^1. That is, either $R_3^2 \prec R_4^1$ or $R_3^1 \prec R_4^1$, but neither of these hold, because $R_4^1 \xrightarrow{y}$ and $R_4^1 \xrightarrow{z}$.

Finally, the fact that $R_5 \not\sim R_6$ follows, because to show bisimulation from right to left requires that R_6^6 be related to R_5^1. However, this is not the case, because, after performing a y, R_5^1 reaches a state (R_5^3) where it can perform a w; this sequence of actions is not available to R_6^6. In fact, this is an example of a situation in which strong bisimulation could be argued to be too distinguishing with respect to the branching structure of the transition system, in that it is not clear that an external observer could distinguish between R_5 and R_6. Indeed, it is examples of this variety that motivate our exploration of testing theories and trace-refusals semantics in Chapter 5.

The following proposition summarises the relationship between $\asymp_\prec$, $\sim_R$ and $\sim$.

Proposition 5
Strong bisimulation is strictly stronger than ready simulation equivalence, which is strictly stronger than simulation equivalence. That is, more formally, $\sim \subset \sim_R \subset \asymp_\prec$.

Proof
See [118].

○

3.4 Verification Tools

A number of mature and powerful verification tools have been developed for process calculi. Typically, the centre point of these tools is decision procedures that check development relations of the kind introduced in this chapter. Accordingly, these tools are often based upon semantic theories such as those just presented. The most prominent approach is to use branching time theories, such as the labelled transition systems we introduced in Section 3.3, and, thus, to compare pairs of process calculus specifications by checking their underlying transition systems according to one of the spectrum of bisimulation equivalences. This approach is typically employed, because trace semantic models are considered not to be discriminating enough (for the reasons introduced in this chapter), whereas true concurrency and refusals-based models (which we discuss in the next two chapters) are often argued to be more complex to check.

As a representative example of such a verification tool, we briefly consider the salient features of the CADP tool suite [81]. The acronym now stands for Construction and Analysis of Distributed Processes, although it was formerly known as the CAESAR / ALDEBARAN Development Package.

We begin, in Section 3.4.1, by giving a brief overview of the tool suite and then, in Section 3.4.2, we focus more directly on bisimulation checking in this environment, which is one of the key strengths of CADP.

3.4.1 Overview of CADP

The CADP tools have been developed as a verification suite for analysing LOTOS specifications. However, for some time, the tools have additionally supported other input notations, including finite state machines and communicating automata. In particular, the latter of these is realised by the EXP notation, in which labelled transition systems are combined using LOTOS-style parallel composition and hiding operators. This yields a notation for describing networks of communicating automata, similar to the formalism we introduce in Chapter 8, although the synchronisation primitives are slightly different.

Furthermore, the recent development of the OPEN / CAESAR environment provides an open and extensible means to interface with the CADP tools. For example, this has been applied to interface languages such as μCRL, SDL and UML / RT.

The CADP suite is a state of the art formal development framework; it includes compilers that translate LOTOS to C code (the CAESAR tools), which can be used for simulation, verification and generation of test purposes. For example, the simulators provide a number of facilities to step through specifications. In addition, a spectrum of verification algorithms is supported, such as deadlock detection, reachability analysis, model-checking and assessment of bisimulation equivalences. These facilities are supported by representations for compact encoding of the behaviour of specifications. In particular, BCG (Binary Coded Graphs) provide a compact labelled transition system description format together with efficient and useful tools and libraries.

One of the strengths of CADP is its use of on-the-fly analysis of statespaces. On-the-fly techniques have been developed to limit the state-space explosion problem. The key idea is to avoid building the transition system of the entire system, unless absolutely necessary. The transition system of the top-level behaviour of the system is often called the product transition system and, with interleaving semantics, it is likely to be prohibitively large. This is because the size of the top-level transition system can grow as a product of the size of its parallel components. Thus, rather than building the product at the start of verification, on-the-fly techniques derive transitions as and when they are required during exploration (i.e. on-the-fly) and this derivation is driven by the verification question at hand.

In addition to bisimulation-checking, which we discuss in the next section, model-checking is a key verification mechanism that CADP supports. In particular, the EVALUATOR 3.0 tool provides a state of the art on-the-fly model-checker for regular alternation free μ-calculus formulae [138]. This logic provides a "machine code" for temporal logic model-checking; i.e. a low-level notation, to which higher-level, more user-friendly notations can be mapped. For example, CADP provides a mapping by which computation tree logic (see Section 8.2.5) can be mapped to the μ-calculus. The tool also generates a diagnostic portion of the LTS under evaluation, which serves as a counter-example when a model-check fails. For the interested reader, more detailed explanations of model-checking can be found elsewhere in this book, particularly in Section 8.2.5.

The tool suite also benefits from the EUCALYPTUS graphical user interface, which integrates with the CADP tools, providing user-friendly interaction with the system. For more details on all the aspects of CADP discussed in this section, the interested reader is referred to the following CADP overview [81].

3.4.2 Bisimulation Checking in CADP

Perhaps the most valuable verification technique available in CADP is the checking of bisimulation and simulation-based equivalences over labelled transition systems. The key transformation provided is the minimisation of a labelled transition system modulo such an equivalence. Critically, for bisimulation and simulation equivalences, a canonical (smallest) transition system always exists. That is, there is a unique minimal transition system modulo such an equivalence. The CADP minimisation techniques generate such canonical transition systems for a spectrum of equivalences, which includes strong and weak bisimulation, branching bisimulation and safety equivalence [81].

CADP offers three different algorithms to minimise transition systems: an approach based on the Paige–Tarjan algorithm for computing the relational coarsest partition [159], an on-the-fly technique developed by Fernandez and Mournier [75, 76] and a recently developed approach that works on symbolic representations of labelled transition systems using Binary Decision Diagrams (BDDs) [54]. These algorithms also provide counterexample-based diagnostic support when an equivalence check fails. We discuss the Paige–Tarjan-based relational coarsest partition approach further now, and the interested reader is referred to the literature for explanation of the other two algorithms.

The states of a labelled transition system can be partitioned according to an equivalence relation, such that all elements of each partition are equivalent. The Paige–Tarjan-based algorithm extracts the coarsest such partition; i.e. in which the partitions are maximal. It does this by applying an iterative algorithm that repeatedly refines a given partition to a coarser one. The algorithm is initiated with a single partition containing all states in the labelled transition system and, due to the existence of a canonical transition system for the equivalences under investigation, is known to terminate with the coarsest partition. Because all states in a given partition are equivalent, they can be treated as a single state in the minimal transition system.

This algorithm can also be used to check that two transition systems are equivalent by including all states of the two transition systems in the starting partition. If the transition systems are equivalent, their start states will appear together in the same partition when the algorithm terminates.

A simple, but elegant, illustration of CADP bisimulation checking is the alternating bit protocol verification, which is undertaken in demo 2 of the standard release of the tool suite. A LOTOS specification of the alternating bit protocol is provided, which is similar to the communication protocol running example that we have used to illustrate pbLOTOS.[5] The correctness of this specification is verified in a number of steps. Firstly, a (BCG-format) labelled transition system is generated, which is surprisingly large and unwieldy for such a relatively small specification. Secondly, reduction by strong bisimulation is applied, which dramatically reduces the LTS, despite which, the LTS is still too large for meaningful evaluation.

The resulting labelled transition system is then further reduced by applying minimisation according to weak bisimulation (called observational equivalence in CADP). This generates a further dramatic reduction of the size of the transition system. In fact, this reduction could be argued to be the main step in the verification scenario. In particular, in the specification, all communications that are not visible to the environment are hidden. Thus, the only observable actions are *get* and *put* (or CADP analogues thereof). Critically, minimisation due to weak bisimulation removes all internal actions that do not affect externally visible behaviour. Because the protocol is correctly specified and thus, ensures reliable communication (i.e. all messages eventually get delivered), all internal behaviour can be removed without changing what is externally observed. Thus, external behaviour of the original LOTOS specification, the strong bisimulation reduced transition system and the weak bisimulation reduced transition system are all the same; they implement a one-place buffer; i.e. each *get* is eventually followed by a *put*.

As a reflection of this observable behaviour, the final step in the verification scenario is to compare the weak bisimulation reduced transition system with a one-place buffer specification. The fact that the reduced communication protocol and requirements specification transition systems are bisimilar formally justifies the correctness of the protocol specification.

Due to the similarity of the CADP alternating bit protocol and the communication protocol running example that we have used to illustrate pbLOTOS, this CADP verification serves as an illustration of how our communication protocol could be formally verified.

---

[5]The reader comparing the CADP communication protocol with ours should though beware of a number of differences between the two. Firstly, actions *PUT* and *GET* in the CADP specification actually play the opposite role to *put* and *get* in our protocol specification. Thus, in the CADP example, *PUT* plays the role of putting into the protocol (at the sender end), whereas in our specification, *put* plays the role of putting into the layer above the protocol (at the receiver end). Secondly, the CADP specification also includes the possibility that the mediums can knowingly lose a message; i.e. with an indication that the message has been lost, and, in this situation, the mediums notify the sender and receiver of this loss, which resend accordingly. Finally, there are two further differences, which, actually, make the CADP example more similar to the full LOTOS communication protocol version we consider in 6.3.1. First, the CADP version assumes that messages can be lost in both directions and, second, it also includes explicit data passing.

4

True Concurrency Models: Event Structures

4.1 Introduction

So far we have considered two semantic notations for pbLOTOS, trace semantics and LTS semantics. We have argued that these give increasingly discriminating models for pbLOTOS descriptions. Specifically, trace semantics cannot distinguish certain (behaviourally distinct) varieties of choice, whereas LTS semantics can. However, we can go one step further and notice that, although LTS do distinguish different forms of choice, they are unable to distinguish concurrency from certain forms of choice and sequence. For example, the following two behaviours would be equated under both trace semantics and LTS semantics,

$$ x\,;\, stop \parallel\!\parallel\!\parallel y\,;\, stop \quad (1) \quad \text{and} \quad (\,x\,;\,y\,;\, stop\,) \, [] \, (\,y\,;\,x\,;\, stop\,) \quad (2) $$

There is no way of differentiating between these two behaviours using these semantics. This identification of concurrency and choice / sequence is typical of models that employ an interleaved interpretation of parallelism.

A body of researchers has argued that this is not a realistic assumption and has considered, so-called, *true concurrency* notations, where concurrency is fully distinguished from behaviour that uses just choice and sequence. There are a number of reasons for advocating a true concurrency approach.

- Interleaving semantics abstract away from the decomposition of systems into components and, thus, they abstract from aspects of "physical" distribution. However, such abstraction may or may not reflect the intention of the specification being semantically modelled. Interleaving semantics model a global view of "observable behaviour." This is reflected in the fact that independence of components is not distinguished from forms of choice and sequence (as highlighted above). For example, in the behaviours above, x and y in (1) could be quite independent actions (e.g. x could happen in Japan and y could happen in the U.K.), whereas in (2) the two actions are causally related; e.g. one causes the other in each branch of the choice, and they could, conceptually, be viewed as being offered in the same logical component (probably in the same interface).

This discussion reflects the classic distinction between the *extensionalist* and *intensionalist* view of formal specification. The former argues that systems can be modelled purely in terms of the externally visible behaviour, whereas the latter argues that the internal decomposition of systems must be reflected in modelling, see [147].

- The previous point suggests that full independence and autonomy of components can only be expressed with true concurrency semantics. Furthermore, this enables parts of systems to be isolated and studied; i.e. a local view can be taken, as opposed to the typically global view enforced by interleaving.

- A strong argument is that the different approaches are applicable at different levels of abstraction. Thus, interleaving is most applicable at early stages of system development, where global systemwide requirements are being identified, whereas true concurrency is more applicable when components need to be identified and made visible, in preparation for implementation. It could be said that interleaving implies a *black box* approach, whereas true concurrency implies a *white box* approach.

- True concurrency models are less susceptible to "state-space explosion" than interleaved models. This is because the number of states in a truly concurrent (independent) parallel composition is a sum of the number of states in its components, rather than a product, as is the case with interleaving. State explosion is currently the major hindrance to the development of verification tools.

- An area of refinement that we do not have a chance to cover in these notes is *action refinement*; i.e. refining by replacing a single action by some composite behaviour, however, we simply note that there are strong arguments in favour of true concurrency models when action refinement is being considered [191].

In response to these observations, we consider a true concurrency approach called *event structures*. The next section (Section 4.2) introduces event structures and the particular form of this model that we use: *bundle event structures*. In Section 4.3 we illustrate, by example, how the behaviour of pbLOTOS specifications can be modelled using bundle event structures. Section 4.4 presents a denotational semantics for mapping pbLOTOS specifications to bundle event structures. Section 4.5 shows how labelled transition systems can be generated from event structures. Then Section 4.6 describes some of the development relations that can be associated with event structure semantics and Section 4.7 gives a brief review of the different event structures models. Finally, Section 4.8 presents a concluding discussion.

4.2 The Basic Approach – Event Structures

The event structures model dates back to work by Winskel and co-workers [155], which sought to reconcile Scott domain theory and Petri Nets. In fact, event structures have a very close link with Petri Nets and have been successfully used to give domain-theoretic interpretations of a number of classes of Petri Net. However, our presentation does not focus on this aspect of event structures; rather we consider how they can be used to give a semantics to process calculi.

Three basic concepts are at the heart of event structures:

Events,   Conflict and **Causality**

We consider each of these in turn.

1. *Events.* It is important to note that the notion of event is not the same as that of action. The latter of these models a particular *kind* of interaction, e.g. picking up a fork. Thus, there can be many instances of an action in a specification. For example, the behaviour

   pick ; *put* ; *pick* ; *stop*

   enables the action *pick* to be performed twice. In contrast, an event denotes a *unique* instance of an interaction. In the above example, the two instances of action *pick* would be differentiated and modelled as distinct events. This reflects the fact that they are different occurrences and may, for example, be differentiated in time; e.g. in the above behaviour the first occurrence of *pick* represents one instance at which the fork is picked up, which perhaps occurs at 5 PM, and the second represents a different instance, which perhaps occurs at 6 PM. The capacity to distinguish different instances of an action reflects the intensionalist's view alluded to above. Intensionalist approaches imply that the internal decomposition of a system is reflected in semantic models. Events reflect this by distinguishing the different internal occurrences of the same external action.

2. *Conflict.* This identifies events that cannot occur together in the same evaluation of the event structure. Such events are said to be in conflict. So, for example, two events which identify actions that are on either side of a choice would be in conflict with each other.

3. *Causality.* This is a relationship between events, which characterises how events enable (or cause) other events. For example, we might specify that event e causes event e', which states that e' cannot happen until e has. In addition, more than one event can cause a particular event. For example, event e might only be able to occur once both events e' and e'' have occurred. Causality is defined on events rather than on actions, because different action occurrences may have different causes.

The literature contains a spectrum of event structure models, e.g. *Prime Event Structures* [155], *Stable Event Structures* [198] and *Flow Event Structures* [31].

The particular event structure model that we consider was developed by Rom Langerak [114] and is called *Bundle Event Structures* (BES). The work of Joost-Pieter Katoen has also served as valuable source material [107]. Bundle event structures extend classic event structures in order to model the LOTOS multiway synchronisation. We define the model as follows.

The set of all bundle event structures is denoted *BES* and $\varepsilon \in BES$ has the form $\varepsilon = (E, \#, \mapsto, l)$, where

1. E is a set of unique *events*;
2. $\# \subseteq E \times E$ is the *conflict relation*;
3. $\mapsto \subseteq \mathcal{P}(E) \times E$ is the *bundle relation*; and
4. $l : E \rightarrow Act \cup \{i, \delta\}$ is the *labelling function*;

subject to the constraint that:

(1) $\#$ is irreflexive and symmetric, and,
(2) $\forall X \subseteq E, \ \forall e \in E, \ (\ X \mapsto e \implies (\forall e', e'' \in X, \ e' \neq e'' \implies e' \# e''))$.

The first two of these, events and conflict, are much as described above and are relatively standard. Notice that conflict is expressed as a binary relation between events. In addition, we assume a universe of events, denoted $\mathcal{U}_E$, which is such that $\forall e, e' \in \mathcal{U}_E, \ (e, *), (*, e), (e, e') \in \mathcal{U}_E$. This structure of events is used in the representation of parallel composition, as clarified later in this section.

The other two constituents of this structure require some explanation.

1. *Bundle Relation.* This set expresses the causality relation. However, this is not a binary causality relation, as it often is in event structure models; rather a *many-to-one* relation is used. This relation is called the *bundle relation*, denoted $\mapsto$. A typical member of $\mapsto$ is a pair, which has the form

   (X, e)

   where X is a set of events and e is an event; i.e. $X \subseteq E$ and $e \in E$. The meaning of this pair is that the event e cannot happen until one of the events in X has occurred. In addition, only one of the events in X can take place and this is realised in bundle event structures by imposing the constraint that all the events in X must be in conflict, which is the second constraint (see above) associated with bundle event structures.

   Notice that, if the set X here is a singleton, we obtain the standard binary causality relation. In fact, in most cases, X will be a singleton. However, there are circumstances, arising from modelling multiway synchronisation, where X will contain more than one element. In addition, it is also possible for X to be empty; this has a special meaning which we discuss shortly. As a shorthand, we often write

   $X \mapsto e$

   in place of

$(X, e) \in \mapsto$

The set $\mapsto$ is called either the *bundle set* or *bundle relation*; in $X \mapsto e$, X is called the *bundle enabling set* or simply the *enabling set* and e is called the *enabled event*.

2. *Labelling.* As bundle event structures are used to model pbLOTOS specifications, a labelling function is also included. This associates an action name with every event in the bundle event structure; it states that a particular event indicates the occurrence of a particular action. However, the same action can be associated with more than one event and in addition, there will be circumstances in which actions are not mapped to by any event; thus, the function is neither one-to-one nor onto.

For a BES $\varepsilon = (E, \#, \mapsto, l)$, we use the notation, $E_\varepsilon = E$, $\#_\varepsilon = \#$, $\mapsto_\varepsilon = \mapsto$ and $l_\varepsilon = l$. Bundle Event Structures (BES) have a very natural pictorial representation; Figure 4.1 shows a number of simple BES. We discuss each of the structures in turn.

1. This structure models the fragment of Dining Philosophers behaviour highlighted earlier. Events are depicted as black dots and bundles are represented as arrows between events. Labelling is shown separately.

2. This is a BES with one event labelled x. Note that event labelling for all BES in this figure, apart from the Dining Philosophers BES, is shown at the bottom right of the diagram.

3. In this structure, the event e'' is caused by e, but, neither is related in any way to the event e'. This BES depicts independent parallelism. In particular, e must occur before e'', however, e' can occur at any point relative to e and e''; i.e. before e, at the same time as e, between e and e'', at the same time as e'' or after e''. Thus, concurrency is reflected by events that are not related by either of the relations $\#$ or $\mapsto$.

4. Conflict is represented by a dotted line between events. This event structure can either perform the event e or the event e'. If the former of these is selected then the event e'' will be enabled. In addition, the event not selected will be permanently prevented from occurring; i.e. will be disabled. Thus, no evaluation / run of this event structure will contain both the events e' and e. In addition, if e' is in an evaluation, then e'' cannot occur either, as its occurrence is guarded by e. This is called *the conflict inheritance property* and some event structure models include the resultant inherited conflicts explicitly, e.g. between e' and e''. Prime event structures, which we discuss in Section 4.7, is such an approach.

5. This depicts our first example of a bundle with a nonsingleton enabling set. This BES contains a single bundle, which has the form $\{e, f\} \mapsto e''$. The line segment just above the two arrow heads indicates that a single bundle is being depicted. Notice that the events of the bundle enabling set are in conflict, as required by constraint (2) on BES. The behaviour of this structure is to enable e'' only after one of e or f has been selected.

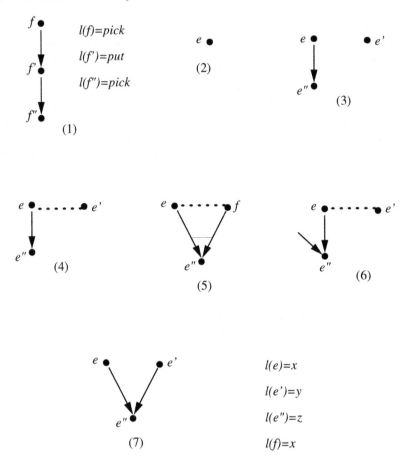

Fig. 4.1. Simple Bundle Event Structures

6. The behaviour of this BES is the same as (4) except the event e'' is prevented from happening, because a bundle with a null enabling set, $\emptyset \mapsto e''$, causes e''. Thus, a bundle with an empty enabling set blocks the event to which it points.

7. It is important to note that this structure defines quite a different behaviour to that depicted in (5). It states that e'' can only occur once both e and e' have occurred and the two occur independently in parallel with each other. This structure and the structure in (6) are examples of BES in which an event is enabled by multiple bundles.

In future, where it does not lead to confusion, we depict BES with action labels as event names or by associating action labels as subscripts of events.

An obvious concept that we consider is that of an evaluation or run of a BES. This yields the concept of a proving sequence for a BES, which is a linear run of the events of a BES. This turns out to be a very expressive model, because event names are referenced in proving sequence semantics as opposed to actions (which is the case with interleaving trace models). We need some preliminaries before we define this concept.

Let $\mathcal{ET}$ denote the set of all finite *event traces* (sequences); i.e.

$$\mathcal{ET} \triangleq \{\, e_0 e_1 \ldots e_n \mid n \in \mathbb{N} \ \wedge\ e_i \in \mathcal{U}_E \,\} \cup \{\, \epsilon \,\}$$

where ϵ is the empty event trace. σ ranges over $\mathcal{ET}$ and we denote the prefix of σ up to the $i - 1$st element by σ_i; i.e. if $\sigma = e_0 e_1 \ldots e_n$ then $\sigma_i = e_0 e_1 \ldots e_{i-1}$ for $0 \leq i \leq n$ and for $i = 0$, $\sigma_i = \epsilon$. Notice, the symbols σ and ϵ have already been used in action traces. However, no confusion will result from this overloading.

We also define the set of events underlying an event trace by:

$$\$e_0 e_1 \ldots e_n \triangleq \{\, e_0, e_1, \ldots, e_n \,\} \quad \text{and} \quad \$\epsilon \triangleq \emptyset$$

Now we can define a proving sequence as follows.

Definition 15
Given a BES $\varepsilon = (E, \#, \mapsto, l)$, then $\sigma \in \mathcal{ET}$ is a proving sequence for ε iff $\sigma = \epsilon$ or $\sigma = e_0 e_1 \ldots e_n$ and $\forall i\ (0 \leq i \leq n)$,

$$e_i \in E \ \wedge\ e_i \in \mathbf{sat}(\sigma_i) \setminus (\mathbf{cfl}(\sigma_i) \cup \$\sigma_i)$$

where

$$\mathbf{cfl}(\sigma) \triangleq \{\, e \in E \mid \exists e_j \in \$\sigma \ \text{s.t.}\ e_j \# e \,\} \quad and$$
$$\mathbf{sat}(\sigma) \triangleq \{\, e \in E \mid \forall X \subseteq E,\ X \mapsto e \implies X \cap \$\sigma \neq \emptyset \,\}$$

This definition is due to Katoen [107] and is defined in terms of $\mathbf{cfl}(\sigma)$, which generates the set of all events that are in conflict with an event in σ and $\mathbf{sat}(\sigma)$, which generates the set of all events that are completely enabled by events in σ. $\mathbf{sat}(\sigma)$ ensures that an event in each of the enabling sets of each bundle has already occurred.

Definition 16
The set of all proving sequences of a BES $\varepsilon = (E, \#, \mapsto, l)$ is defined as

$$\mathcal{PS}(\varepsilon) \triangleq \{\, \sigma \mid \sigma \text{ is a proving sequence for } \varepsilon \,\}$$

By way of illustration of this concept, the sets of proving sequences associated with each of the BES depicted in Figure 4.1 are as follows.

- BES (1) - $\{\, \epsilon,\ f,\ ff',\ ff'f'' \,\}$
- BES (2) - $\{\, \epsilon,\ e \,\}$

- BES (3) - { ϵ , e , e' , ee' , $e'e$, ee'' , $ee'e''$, $e'ee''$, $ee''e'$ }
- BES (4) - { ϵ , e , e' , ee'' }
- BES (5) - { ϵ , e , f , ee'' , fe'' }
- BES (6) - { ϵ , e , e' }
- BES (7) - { ϵ , e , e' , ee' , $e'e$, $ee'e''$, $e'ee''$ }

We can also define the notion of a configuration, which is the set of events that have occurred at a particular point in the evaluation of a BES.

Definition 17
$C \subseteq E$ is a configuration of a BES $\varepsilon = (E, \#, \mapsto, l)$ iff $\exists \sigma \in \mathcal{PS}(\varepsilon)$. $C = \$\sigma$.
The set of all configurations of a BES is denoted $\mathcal{CF}(\varepsilon)$.

For example, BES (7) in Figure 4.1 has the following configurations,

$$\{ \emptyset , \{e\} , \{e'\} , \{e, e'\} , \{e, e', e''\} \}$$

Both the concepts of a proving sequence and a configuration are used when we define event structure-based development relations for pbLOTOS.

4.3 Event Structures and pbLOTOS

This section illustrates informally how event structures relate to pbLOTOS specifications. It considers a number of typical pbLOTOS behaviours and shows how they would be modelled in a BES. We begin by considering the examples that motivated our investigation of true concurrency models:

(1) $x ; (y ; stop \parallel\!\parallel\!\parallel z ; stop)$ and   (2) $x ; (y ; z ; stop [\,] z ; y ; stop)$

These behaviours would be bisimulation equivalent under LTS and trace equivalent under trace semantics. The corresponding bundle event structures are depicted in Figure 4.2. The left-hand BES models behaviour (1) and the right-hand BES models behaviour (2). The labelling in these two bundle event structures is as follows.

$l(e) = x$, $l(e') = y$, $l(e'') = z$ and

$l(e_1) = x$, $l(e_2) = y$, $l(e_3) = z$, $l(e_4) = z$, $l(e_5) = y$

Thus, in general, action prefix in pbLOTOS gets modelled using causality, choice is modelled using conflict and concurrency is modelled by independence of events; e.g. the events e' and e'' can evolve concurrently because they are not related by conflict or causality. So, bundle event structures clearly give us a more discriminating semantics in terms of distinguishing concurrency.

In fact, most of the interesting BES models arise through parallel composition and synchronisation between parallel components. As an illustration, the BES for the following behaviour,

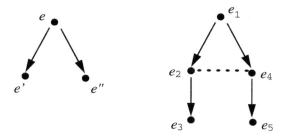

Fig. 4.2. Two Bundle Event Structures

$(\, y\, ;\, x\, ;\, z\, ;\, stop\,)\ |[x]|\ (\, x\, ;\, w\, ;\, stop\,)$

is depicted in Figure 4.3(1) (labelling is indicated by subscripting). Thus, a single event labelled x is created from the synchronisation over $|[x]|$.

In order to show why the causality relation is not a binary relation, first consider the following behaviour,

$(\, x\, ;\, y\, ;\, stop\ |||\ x\, ;\, stop\,)\ |||\ (\, x\, ;\, z\, ;\, stop\,)$

which has the BES model shown in Figure 4.3(2). Notice how the three occurrences of the (nonsynchronised) action x are modelled as separate events, in contrast to the previous example where x is synchronised. Two instances of the same actions occurring in parallel is called *autoconcurrency*. Now, if we replace the second parallel composition by a synchronised parallel context, as follows,

$(\, x\, ;\, y\, ;\, stop\ |||\ x\, ;\, stop\,)\ |[x]|\ (\, x\, ;\, z\, ;\, stop\,)$

then the BES shown in Figure 4.3(3) results. The event g_x results from synchronisation on x between events e_x and e_x'' and g_x' results from synchronisation on x between events e_x' and e_x''. It is important to note though that, the conflict between g_x and g_x' arises because only one of the independent events e_x and e_x' can synchronise with e_x'' at a time. Thus, a bundle of the form $\{\, g_x, g_x'\, \} \mapsto f_z'$ results. As a point of comparison, consider the labelled transition system that would be generated from this behaviour; this is depicted in Figure 4.4.

As a further example of the use of bundle enabling sets, Figure 4.3(4) depicts the BES model of the behaviour:

$(\, y\, ;\, x\, ;\, stop\ []\ z\, ;\, x\, ;\, stop\,)\ |[x]|\ (\, x\, ;\, w\, ;\, stop\,)$

Our next example illustrates how null enabling sets can be created in order to model deadlock situations. The BES depicted in Figure 4.3(5) models the behaviour:

$(\, y\, ;\, stop\,)\ |[x]|\ (\, x\, ;\, z\, ;\, w\, ;\, stop\,)$

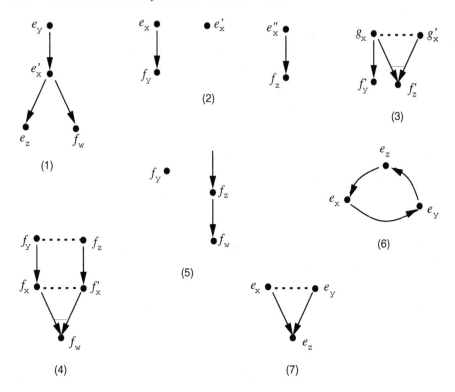

Fig. 4.3. Bundle Event Structures

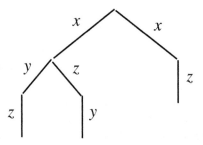

Fig. 4.4. Labelled Transition System Example

Notice that no event labelled x appears because the action is deadlocked. In addition, all events that would be caused by such an event are either directly or indirectly caused by a bundle with a null enabling set. Thus, they are also deadlocked.

Another example of a deadlock behaviour is

$$(x \,;\, y \,;\, stop) \;|[x,y]|\; (y \,;\, z \,;\, x \,;\, stop)$$

the model for which is depicted in Figure 4.3(6). This cycle of causality prevents any of the three generated events from occurring.

Our final example shows another way in which an event can be prevented from occurring. The model for the following behaviour is depicted in Figure 4.3(7),

$$(x \,;\, stop \;[]\; y \,;\, z \,;\, stop) \;|[x,z]|\; (x \,;\, z \,;\, stop)$$

Event e_z can never occur, as its two enabling bundles cannot both be satisfied; it is caused by two conflicting events.

4.4 An Event Structures Semantics for pbLOTOS

This section presents a denotational semantics for pbLOTOS in bundle event structures. We define a mapping,

$$[\![\ ]\!]_{be} \;:\; pbLOTOS \longrightarrow BES$$

This mapping is based upon the semantics given by Langerak in [114]. The top-level machinery of the semantics is much the same as that presented for our other denotational semantics, the trace semantics. We define:

$$[\![\, B \,]\!]_{be} \triangleq \mathcal{B}'[\![\, B \,]\!]_{(\emptyset)}$$

$$[\![\, B \; where \; D \,]\!]_{be} \triangleq \mathcal{B}'[\![\, B \,]\!]_{(\mathcal{D}[\![D]\!])}$$

where $\mathcal{D}$ is as defined in Section 3.2.2.2; i.e.

$$\mathcal{D}[\![\, (P := B) \,]\!] \triangleq \{\, P := B \,\}$$

$$\mathcal{D}[\![\, (P := B) \; D \,]\!] \triangleq \{\, P := B \,\} \cup \mathcal{D}[\![\, D \,]\!]$$

Once again, the main part of the semantics is the interpretation of behaviour expressions. But, before we consider this, we need some preliminary definitions.

• We use two auxiliary functions which, assuming $\varepsilon = (E, \#, \mapsto, l)$, are defined as follows.

$$init(\varepsilon) \triangleq \{\, e \in E \mid \not\exists X \subseteq E \text{ s.t. } X \mapsto e \,\}$$
$$exit(\varepsilon) \triangleq \{\, e \in E \mid l(e) = \delta \,\}$$

So, *init* yields the set of initial (or immediately enabled) events of a BES, whereas *exit* yields the set of successful termination events; i.e. those labelled with δ.

Given that

$$\mathcal{B}'[\![\, B_1 \,]\!]_{(d)} = \varepsilon_1 = (E_1, \#_1, \mapsto_1, l_1) \text{ and}$$
$$\mathcal{B}'[\![\, B_2 \,]\!]_{(d)} = \varepsilon_2 = (E_2, \#_2, \mapsto_2, l_2)$$

and assuming that $E_1 \cap E_2 = \emptyset$ (which, if necessary, can be obtained through systematic renaming of events), then the mapping of pbLOTOS to *BES* is as follows.

Stop. The behaviour *stop* induces the null BES:

$$\mathcal{B}'[\![\, stop \,]\!]_{(d)} \triangleq (\emptyset, \emptyset, \emptyset, \emptyset)$$

Exit. The semantics of successful termination are also relatively straightforward:

$$\mathcal{B}'[\![\, exit \,]\!]_{(d)} \triangleq (\{e\}, \emptyset, \emptyset, \{(e, \delta)\}) \quad \text{for an arbitrary } e \in \mathcal{U}_E$$

Thus, a single event is generated, which is labelled by δ.

Action Prefix. This construct cannot introduce conflicts, but events, bundles and labelling are all changed.

$$\mathcal{B}'[\![\, a \,; B_1 \,]\!]_{(d)} \triangleq (E, \#_1, \mapsto, l) \quad \text{where,}$$
$$E = E_1 \cup \{e\} \quad \text{for some } e \in \mathcal{U}_E \setminus E_1$$
$$\mapsto \; = \; \mapsto_1 \cup \left(\{\{e\}\} \times init(\varepsilon_1) \right)$$
$$l = l_1 \cup \{(e, a)\}$$

A new event is added and labelled a. In addition, bundles from the new event to all initial events in B_1 are included. Thus, the new event is grafted onto the front of the BES generated from B_1. We can illustrate this with a simple example. Consider the behaviour:

$$x \,; (\, y \,; z \,; stop \,[\!] \, z \,; stop \,)$$

Two of the stages in the generation of the BES for this behaviour are depicted in Figure 4.5. Notice in particular that the events labelled e_y and e_z are the initial events of the behaviour:

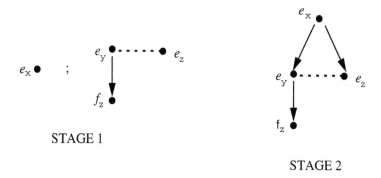

STAGE 1

STAGE 2

Fig. 4.5. Depiction of Action Prefix Semantics

$(y; z; stop) [] (z; stop)$

You should also notice that there is only one action prefix rule, so, internal and external actions are treated identically. Thus, internal actions can appear in BES in the same way that they appear in LTS.

Another point about this definition is that, not only is the selection of e from $\mathcal{U}_E$ unique in terms of the behaviour $a; B_1$, it is also assumed to be unique in terms of the entire pbLOTOS specification. Each instance of a pbLOTOS action will have a unique event denotation. To actually define this precisely over the binary pbLOTOS operators would require a more sophisticated mechanism than we have presented here. However, such mechanisms are relatively standard, would only complicate the presentation and have thus not been included.

Choice. This construct affects all elements of the bundle event structure.

$$\mathcal{B}'[\![\, B_1 [] B_2 \,]\!]_{(d)} \triangleq (E, \#, \mapsto, l) \quad \text{where}$$

$$E = E_1 \cup E_2$$

$$\# = \#_1 \cup \#_2 \cup (\, init(\varepsilon_1) \times init(\varepsilon_2)\,)$$

$$\mapsto = \mapsto_1 \cup \mapsto_2$$

$$l = l_1 \cup l_2$$

The events, bundles and labels of $\mathcal{B}'[\![\, B_1 [] B_2 \,]\!]_{(d)}$ are obtained by unioning the events, bundles and labels arising from the two constituent behaviours. This reflects the natural relationship between choice, logical or and set-theoretic union.

As might be expected, the definition for conflict is slightly more involved. Specifically, conflicts from either $\mathcal{B}'[\![\, B_1 \,]\!]_{(d)}$ or $\mathcal{B}'[\![\, B_2 \,]\!]_{(d)}$ are preserved and conflicts are added between initial events of $\mathcal{B}'[\![\, B_1 \,]\!]_{(d)}$ and $\mathcal{B}'[\![\, B_2 \,]\!]_{(d)}$. Thus, events at the choice point are put into conflict with one another.

Parallel Composition. The definition of parallel composition is somewhat more involved than the definitions we have seen so far. We use the following notation.

- Given $\mathcal{B}'[\![B_1]\!]_{(d)} = (E_1, \#_1, \mapsto_1, l_1)$ and $\mathcal{B}'[\![B_2]\!]_{(d)} = (E_2, \#_2, \mapsto_2, l_2)$ then, for a parallel composition $B_1 \, |[G]| \, B_2$,

$$E_i^s \triangleq \{ e \in E_i \mid l_i(e) \in G \cup \{\delta\} \} \quad \text{for } i = 1, 2 \quad \text{and}$$

$$E_i^f \triangleq E_i \setminus E_i^s \quad \text{for } i = 1, 2$$

which distinguishes between events that synchronise on parallel execution and those that are free (i.e. do not synchronise). Notice that successful termination events synchronise over parallel composition, as required by the standard LOTOS semantics.

Parallel composition can now be defined as

$$\mathcal{B}'[\![B_1 \, |[G]| \, B_2]\!]_{(d)} \triangleq (E, \#, \mapsto, l) \quad \text{where}$$

$$
\begin{aligned}
E = \; & (E_1^f \times \{*\}) \cup (\{*\} \times E_2^f) \cup \\
& \{ (e_1, e_2) \in E_1^s \times E_2^s \mid l_1(e_1) = l_2(e_2) \}
\end{aligned}
$$

$$
\begin{aligned}
(e_1, e_2) \, \# \, (e_1', e_2') \; \textit{iff} \; & (e_1 \#_1 e_1') \vee (e_2 \#_2 e_2') \vee \\
& (e_1 = e_1' \neq * \; \wedge \; e_2 \neq e_2') \vee \\
& (e_2 = e_2' \neq * \; \wedge \; e_1 \neq e_1')
\end{aligned}
$$

$$
\begin{aligned}
X \mapsto (e_1, e_2) \; \textit{iff} \; & \exists X_1 \subseteq E_1 . (X_1 \mapsto_1 e_1 \; \wedge \; X = \{ (e_i, e_j) \in E \mid e_i \in X_1 \}) \vee \\
& \exists X_2 \subseteq E_2 . (X_2 \mapsto_2 e_2 \; \wedge \; X = \{ (e_i, e_j) \in E \mid e_j \in X_2 \})
\end{aligned}
$$

$$l(e_1, e_2) = \textit{if } e_1 = * \textit{ then } l_2(e_2) \textit{ else } l_1(e_1)$$

We explain the definitions for events, conflict, bundles and labelling in turn.

- **Events.** All free events are paired with $*$, whereas all synchronising events; i.e. those labelled by an action in the gate set G or labelled δ, are paired with events with which they synchronise. This construction ensures that events generated from a parallel composition are unique and justifies the earlier definition concerning the structure of events in $\mathcal{U}_E$.
- **Conflict.** Component conflict creates conflict between paired events. In addition, different events with a component unequal to $*$ in common are made conflicting. This situation arises, for example, if an action offered independently in parallel on two sides of a parallel composition is synchronised with the same action in a third thread of parallel execution. See the examples in Section 4.3 for an illustration of this situation.
- **Bundles.** This states that a bundle is introduced between paired events if, when we project on the *ith* component ($i = 1,2$) of events in the bundle, we obtain a bundle in $\mathcal{B}[\![B_i]\!]_{(d)}$.

- **Labelling.** Event pairs constructed from free events are labelled with the label of their only proper component; for example, an event pair $(e, *)$ would inherit the label of e. Event pairs constructed from synchronising events must, by the definition of event pairing, have the same labelling and will thus, inherit it.

We present five illustrations of the semantics, through presentation in Figure 4.6 of the stages in evaluation of the following behaviours (uniqueness of events is obtained by superscripting action names; this informality does not cause ambiguity here).

1. $(x; y; stop) \,|||\, (y; z; stop)$
2. $(x; y; w; stop) \,|[y]|\, (y; z; stop)$
3. $(x; y; stop \,[]\, x; z; stop) \,|[x]|\, (x; w; stop)$
4. $(x; y; stop \,|||\, x; stop) \,|[x]|\, (x; w; stop)$
5. $(x; y; stop \,|||\, x; stop) \,|[x]|\, (x; x; stop)$

The bundle event structures for the first two behaviours are relatively straightforward. So, we only provide explanation of the last three. Behaviour (3) illustrates how component conflict is inherited by the parallel composition, as stated in the first two disjuncts of the clause defining $\#$ above. Thus, $(x, x'')\#(x', x'')$, because $x\#x'$. In addition, notice that the component bundle from x'' to w yields a bundle from $\{(x, x''), (x', x'')\}$ to $(*, w)$ in the parallel composition; i.e. one (and only one) of the events $(x, x''), (x', x'')$ can cause $(*, w)$; the clause defining $\mapsto$ above ensures that the bundle enabling set has this form.

Now consider behaviour (4) above, parallel composition of which is depicted in Figure 4.6(4). The generation of conflict between events (x, x'') and (x', x'') in the parallel composition arises from the last two disjuncts of the clause defining $\#$ above. That is, x'' can only synchronise with one of x and x' and, in so doing, prevents the other from becoming possible. Thus, this is a situation in which the requirement to synchronise on an action and the availability of only one instance of the action in one parallel component, turns independent parallelism in the other component into choice / conflict in the parallel composition. This phenomenon can also be seen in the labelled transition that would be generated from this behaviour (see Figure 4.4), which arises when interleaving semantics are applied.

Finally, consider behaviour (5) above, parallel composition of which is depicted in Figure 4.6(5). This example is similar to behaviour (4), except here, the inclusion of a further instance of action x, which yields the event denoted $x^\wedge$ in Figure 4.6(5), generates an extra level of conflict and causality. In addition, for comparison purposes, Figure 4.7 shows the labelled transition system that would arise from behaviour (5), if the interleaving semantics of Section 3.3 were applied.

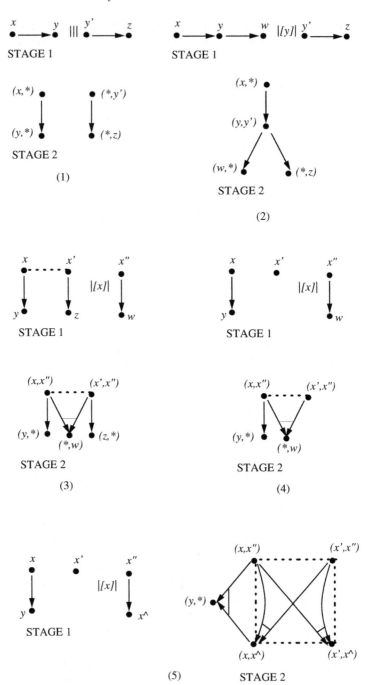

Fig. 4.6. Parallel Composition Semantics

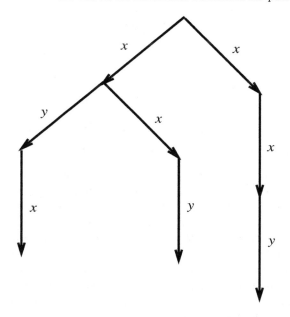

Fig. 4.7. Labelled Transition System of Behaviour (5)

The approach presented here will generate some impossible events; i.e. that cannot happen, e.g. events enabled by null bundles. It is shown in [114] that a mapping can be applied to remove all such events from a generated BES. An alternative approach would be to generate only events that are not impossible. This, for example, is the approach taken in [131] when modelling parallel composition in CSP. However, this approach leads to a more involved definition of the semantics of parallel composition.

Hiding and Relabelling. These definitions are straightforward.

$$\mathcal{B}'[\![\, hide \; G \; in \; B_1 \,]\!]_{(d)} \triangleq (E_1, \#_1, \mapsto_1, l) \quad \text{where}$$

$$l(e) = if \; l_1(e) \in G \; then \; i \; else \; l_1(e)$$

$$\mathcal{B}'[\![\, B_1[y_1/x_1, \ldots, y_n/x_n] \,]\!]_{(d)} \triangleq (E_1, \#_1, \mapsto_1, l) \quad \text{where}$$

$$l(e) = if \; \exists i \, (1 \leq i \leq n) \, . \, l_1(e) = x_i \; then \; y_i \; else \; l_1(e)$$

Sequential Composition/Enabling. The semantics for this construct are defined as follows.

$$\mathcal{B}'[\![\,B_1 >> B_2\,]\!]_{(d)} \triangleq (E, \#, \mapsto, l) \quad \text{where}$$

$$E = E_1 \cup E_2$$

$$\# = \#_1 \cup \#_2 \cup \{\, (e, e') \mid e, e' \in exit(\varepsilon_1) \wedge e \neq e' \,\}$$

$$\mapsto \; = \; \mapsto_1 \cup \mapsto_2 \cup (\,\{exit(\varepsilon_1)\} \times init(\varepsilon_2)\,)$$

$$l = (\,l_1 \cup l_2 \setminus (\,exit(\varepsilon_1) \times \{\delta\}\,)\,) \cup (\,exit(\varepsilon_1) \times \{i\}\,)$$

This definition can be explained in the following points.

- **Events** in either of the constituent BES are events of the combined BES.
- **Conflicts** in either of the constituent BES are preserved in the combined BES, but in addition, distinct exit events are placed mutually in conflict. This reflects the fact that in B_1, only one successful termination event needs to be performed for the whole behaviour to successfully terminate.
- **Bundles** in either of the constituent BES are preserved and in addition, initial events in B_2 become caused by a bundle from all the exit events of B_1. Notice that the definition of $\#$ above ensures that all events in $exit(\varepsilon_1)$ are in conflict and thus, $exit(\varepsilon_1)$ is a valid bundle enabling set. So, we attach the BES generated from B_2 to the BES generated from B_1 by connecting "final" events of B_1 (i.e. exit events) to "starting" events of B_2 (i.e. initial events).
- **Labelling** in either of the constituent BES is preserved in the combined BES, but in addition, the labelling of exit events with δ is replaced by i. Thus, successful termination is referenced by an internal action occurring at the point of sequential composition, as is normal.

We give one illustration of these semantics. The behaviour that we consider is

$$(\,x\,;\,(\,y\,;\,exit\,|||\,z\,;\,exit\,)\,) \; >> \; (\,w\,;\,stop\,)$$

the semantics of which are depicted in Figure 4.8.

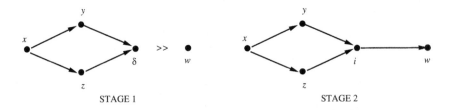

STAGE 1   STAGE 2

Fig. 4.8. Depiction of Sequential Composition Semantics

Process Instantiation and Recursion. The bundle event structure semantics for process instantiation and recursion are relatively complex. This complexity centres on the definition of a bundle event structure fixed point for recursive processes. As a consequence, we are not able to present this theory here, but the interested reader is referred to [114]. However, general points that should be noted are firstly, strong guardedness is not an issue in defining this fixed point, because internal actions are included in BES. Secondly, the semantic rules for all the pbLOTOS constructs are compositional; this property is crucial if a fixed point theory is to be presented.

We simply quote the definition of process instantiation:

$$\mathcal{B}[\![\, P \,]\!]_{(d)} \triangleq \bigsqcup\nolimits_i F_B^i(\bot)$$

where $(P := B) \in d$, $\bigsqcup_i$ is the least upper bound operator for chains of BES, F_B is a function, which re-expresses pbLOTOS behaviours as BES behaviours and $\bot$ is a "bottom" BES in a complete partial ordering between BES.[1]

4.5 Relating Event Structures to Labelled Transition Systems

In a similar way to which LTS were related to trace models, we can relate bundle event structures to labelled transition systems. This is realised by defining a transition relation over bundle event structures.

Firstly, let us remember the constituents of a labelled transition system. A LTS is a four-tuple (S, A, T, s_0), where S is a set of states, A is a set of actions, T is a set of transition relations and s_0 is a start state. So, we must derive all of these four constituents from a bundle event structure. This immediately prompts the question: what is our notion of state for BES? Basically, each state in our transition system will be a BES, with the starting state being the BES that we are modelling and other states being the BES that result from evolving the initial BES.

Central to this approach is the *remainder* function, which takes a BES and a configuration and derives the remainder of the BES after performing all the events in the configuration. This remainder will itself be a BES.

Definition 18
Let $\varepsilon = (E, \#, \mapsto, l)$; then the remainder of ε after the configuration C, denoted $\varepsilon[C]$, is as follows, where $\varepsilon[C] \triangleq (E', \#', \mapsto', l')$,

$$E' = E \setminus C$$

$$\#' = \# \cap (E' \times E')$$

$$\mapsto' = (\mapsto \setminus \{ (X, e) \in \mapsto \mid X \cap C \neq \emptyset \}) \cup \{ (\emptyset, e) \mid \exists e' \in C . e \# e' \}$$

$$l' = l \lceil E'$$

---

[1]We elaborate on the BES and timed BES fixed point constructions in section 10.2.3.6.

We explain the changes made to events, conflict, bundles and labelling in turn.

- **Events.** Only events that are not in the configuration are included in the remainder.
- **Conflict.** Only conflicts that are between events in the remainder are preserved.
- **Bundles.** All bundles are preserved apart from those that are enabled by an event in the configuration, which are removed. In addition, an empty bundle is included to all events that are in conflict with an event in the configuration; such events will be disabled by the execution of the configuration.
- **Labelling.** The labelling function is restricted to a domain, which is the events of the remainder.

It can be checked that $\varepsilon[C]$ is indeed a BES [114].

As an illustration of the function, Figure 4.9 presents the possible remainders of the bundle event structure derived from the behaviour:

$$P := (\, x \,;\, y \,;\, stop \,\|\|\, x \,;\, stop\,) \,\|[x]\|\, (\, x \,;\, x \,;\, stop\,)$$

The depicted event structures are identified as follows:

(1) is $\mathcal{B}'[\![\, P \,]\!]_{(d)} = \varepsilon = \varepsilon[\emptyset]$

(2) is $\varepsilon[\{e\}]$

(3) is $\varepsilon[\{e, e''\}]$

(4) is $\varepsilon[\{e, f'\}]$

(5) is $\varepsilon[\{e, e'', f'\}]$

(6) is $\varepsilon[\{e'\}]$

(7) is $\varepsilon[\{e', f\}]$

(8) is $\varepsilon[\{e', f, f'\}]$

So, in deriving transition systems, BES model states; BES can perform some configuration C and evolve to a new state $\varepsilon[C]$. In the transition systems that we give, the configurations considered are singleton sets. We define the basic transition relation as follows.

Definition 19

Given that $\varepsilon = (E, \#, \mapsto, l)$, for all $a \in Act \cup \{i, \delta\}$ we define

$$\varepsilon \xrightarrow{\;\;a\;\;} \varepsilon[\{e\}] \quad iff \quad \{e\} \in \mathcal{CF}(\varepsilon) \,\wedge\, l_\varepsilon(e) = a.$$

Using this transition relation, we can introduce a mapping from BES to LTS, which we denote $\psi : BES \longrightarrow \mathcal{LTS}$, and define as follows.

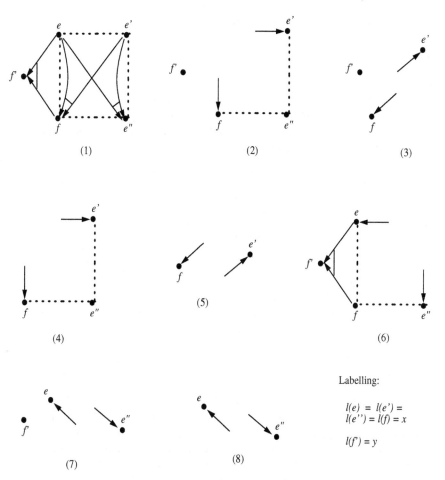

Fig. 4.9. Illustration of Remainder Function

$\psi(\varepsilon) = (S, A, T, s_0)$ where

$S = \{ \varepsilon[C] \mid C \in \mathcal{CF}(\varepsilon) \}$

$A = image(l)$ where $image(f) = \{ r_2 \mid (r_1, r_2) \in f \}$

$T = \{ \bullet\!\stackrel{a}{\longrightarrow} \, \subseteq BES \times BES \mid a \in A \}$ where,

$\qquad\qquad \bullet\!\stackrel{a}{\longrightarrow} \, = \{ (\varepsilon_1, \varepsilon_2) \mid \exists \varepsilon_1, \varepsilon_2 \in S \, . \, \varepsilon_1 \star\!\stackrel{a}{\longrightarrow} \varepsilon_2 \}$

$s_0 = \varepsilon$

Transition systems can also be derived from BES by making states configurations of events that have occurred up to a certain point, e.g. [191, 193].

4.6 Development Relations

In the same way that we defined development relations for trace semantics and labelled transition systems we can define such relations for bundle event structures. Unfortunately, we do not have sufficient space to consider refinement relations for BES, so, we concentrate on equivalences.

The spectrum of equivalences for BES is very large; this reflects the expressiveness of the model. We give a selection of relations, which spans this spectrum. See [191] for a more complete presentation.

Isomorphism of BES. A very strong identity between bundle event structures is given by *isomorphism*.

Definition 20
Let ε and ε' be BES; then an event structure isomorphism between ε and ε' is a bijection,

$$\phi : E_\varepsilon \longrightarrow E_{\varepsilon'}$$

such that

1. $\forall e, e' \in E_\varepsilon$, $e \#_\varepsilon e' \iff \phi(e) \#_{\varepsilon'} \phi(e')$;
2. $\forall X \subseteq E_\varepsilon, \forall e \in E_\varepsilon$, $X \mapsto_\varepsilon e \iff \{ \phi(e') \mid e' \in X \} \mapsto_{\varepsilon'} \phi(e)$ *and*
3. $\forall e \in E_\varepsilon$, $l_\varepsilon(e) = l_{\varepsilon'}(\phi(e))$

According to this definition, BES are identified if an event renaming function can be identified, which preserves the structure of BES. This is in the sense that the mapping is a bijection, so the set of events is preserved; and it preserves conflict, bundles and labelling. Thus, BES are identified if they have the same *structure*; in particular, there is no consideration of the behaviour of the BES. Consequently, two event structures with the same behaviour may be distinguished.

For example, consider the four BES depicted in Figure 4.10. BES (1) and (2) are clearly not isomorphic, because it is not even possible to define a bijective mapping between the events of the two BES. However, the behaviour of the two BES is the same: neither can evolve. Thus, they have identical proving sequences and configurations, viz $\{\varepsilon\}$ and $\{\emptyset\}$, respectively. In addition, (3) and (4) in Figure 4.10 would not be identified by isomorphism, as, although there is an obvious bijective mapping between events, which satisfies the labelling and conflict conditions, the bijection will not satisfy the bundles condition, as $\{f_x\} \mapsto f_z$, but $\{e_x\} \not\mapsto e_z$. However, their behaviour is clearly equivalent.

So, we seek weaker equivalences than isomorphism that identify bundle event structures according to their behaviour. We begin with a weak interpretation and then work in the direction of, generally, stronger equivalences; none of which though will be stronger than isomorphism.

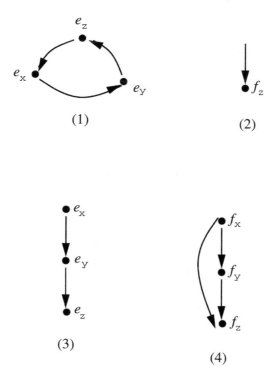

Fig. 4.10. Nonisomorphic Event Structures

Sequential Bisimulations. Using the mapping between BES and LTS defined in Section 4.5, we can define BES equivalences, which correspond to the bisimulations considered earlier for labelled transition systems.

We could define equivalences, which are weak in the sense of weak bisimulation; i.e. only identify according to the observable behaviour, however, in accordance with the intensionalist true concurrency view, we do not do this and internal actions are treated as any other action. See [131] for the definition of an equivalence that abstracts from internal actions. Thus, the relation that we consider corresponds to strong bisimulation.

Definition 21   (Sequential Strong Bisimulation Relation)
A binary relation $\mathcal{R} \subseteq BES \times BES$ is a sequential strong bisimulation if $(\varepsilon_1, \varepsilon_2) \in \mathcal{R}$ implies $\forall a \in Act \cup \{i, \delta\}$,

1. $\forall \varepsilon_1' \in BES, \varepsilon_1 \bullet\!\!\xrightarrow{a} \varepsilon_1' \implies \exists \varepsilon_2' \in BES . \varepsilon_2 \bullet\!\!\xrightarrow{a} \varepsilon_2' \wedge (\varepsilon_1', \varepsilon_2') \in \mathcal{R} \wedge$
2. $\forall \varepsilon_2' \in BES, \varepsilon_2 \bullet\!\!\xrightarrow{a} \varepsilon_2' \implies \exists \varepsilon_1' \in BES . \varepsilon_1 \bullet\!\!\xrightarrow{a} \varepsilon_1' \wedge (\varepsilon_1', \varepsilon_2') \in \mathcal{R}$

Definition 22   (Sequential Strong Bisimilar)
$\sim_{sq} \triangleq \bigcup \{ \mathcal{R} \mid \mathcal{R}$ *is a sequential strong bisimulation* $\}$

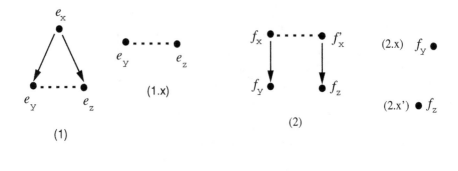

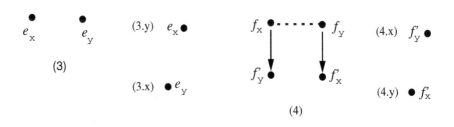

(5) The empty BES

Fig. 4.11. Event Structures Illustrating Equivalence Relations

As illustrations of this definition, consider the bundle event structures depicted in Figure 4.11, where impossible events, i.e. with a null incoming bundle, are simply not depicted. The BES are identified as follows.

(1) depicts ε_1;   (1.x) depicts $\varepsilon_{1.x}$;

(2) depicts ε_2;   (2.x) depicts $\varepsilon_{2.x}$;   (2.x') depicts $\varepsilon_{2.x'}$;

(3) depicts ε_3;   (3.y) depicts $\varepsilon_{3.y}$;   (3.x) depicts $\varepsilon_{3.x}$;

(4) depicts ε_4;   (4.x) depicts $\varepsilon_{4.x}$;   (4.y) depicts $\varepsilon_{4.y}$;   and

(5) depicts $\varepsilon_{3.0} = \varepsilon_{4.0}$.

As would be expected, sequential bisimulation over BES distinguishes branching points; thus, $\varepsilon_1 \not\sim_{sq} \varepsilon_2$. This is because, for example, $\varepsilon_2 \bullet\!\!\xrightarrow{x} \varepsilon_{2.x}$, for which the only matching transition in ε_1 is $\varepsilon_1 \bullet\!\!\xrightarrow{x} \varepsilon_{1.x}$. However, $\varepsilon_{1.x} \not\sim_{sq} \varepsilon_{2.x}$ as $\varepsilon_{1.x} \bullet\!\!\xrightarrow{z}$, but $\varepsilon_{2.x} \bullet\!\!\not\!\xrightarrow{z}$.

The transition relation $\bullet\!\!\longrightarrow$ offers an interleaved interpretation of BES; thus, as its name suggests, sequential bisimulations do not distinguish independent parallelism from choice and sequence. For example, $\varepsilon_3 \sim_{sq} \varepsilon_4$, because the relation,

$$\mathcal{R} = \{\, (\varepsilon_3, \varepsilon_4), (\varepsilon_{3.y}, \varepsilon_{4.y}), (\varepsilon_{3.x}, \varepsilon_{4.x}), (\varepsilon_{3.0}, \varepsilon_{4.0}) \,\}$$

is a sequential strong bisimulation.

In a true concurrency setting, where we are seeking to distinguish concurrency from interleaving, sequential bisimulation is an unsuitable equivalence. The remaining relations all distinguish concurrency from interleaving.

Step Equivalences. Step semantics offer a simple means to distinguish concurrency from interleaving. Before we define the induced equivalence relations, we need some preliminary concepts.

First, we define a partial order causality relation over bundle event structures, which has a similar character to the classic causality relation of prime event structures (see the discussion in Section 4.7).

Definition 23   (Causality)
Given a BES ε, we define a causality partial order, denoted $\preceq$, as follows,

$$e \prec e' \ \text{iff} \ \exists X \subseteq E_\varepsilon \ s.t. \ e \in X \ \wedge \ X \mapsto_\varepsilon e' \ and$$

$\preceq$ *is the reflexive and transitive closure of* $\prec$

The restriction of $\preceq$ to a particular configuration C of ε is denoted $\preceq_C$.

So, $\preceq$ is the causality partial order induced by the bundle relation.

A standard relation in event structures theory is that of *independence*. This states when events are not related by causality or conflict, are thus, independent of one another, and can evolve independently in parallel.

Definition 24   (Independence in a Configuration)
Given a configuration $C \in \mathcal{CF}(\varepsilon)$, then events e and e' in C are independent, denoted $e \otimes_C e'$ if and only if $\neg(e \preceq_C \cup \succeq_C e')$.

Notice that the fact that e and e' are in the same configuration implies that they are not related by $\#$.

In order to define a step semantics-based equality, we use the notion of a step transition relation, $\blacktriangleright\!\!\xrightarrow{A} \ \subseteq \ BES \times BES$, where A is a multiset over $Act \cup \{i, \delta\}$. A multiset is a function $A : Act \cup \{i, \delta\} \to \mathbb{N}$ where $A(a)$ denotes the number of occurrences of the action a in the multiset. Remember, multiple instances of an action may occur in parallel with one another; this is called *autoconcurrency*. The required transition relation is defined as follows.

Definition 25
We use the auxiliary function $\mathsf{L}(X) : Act \cup \{i, \delta\} \to \mathbb{N}$, which for $\varepsilon \in BES$ and $X \subseteq E_\varepsilon$, denotes the multiset of labels of events from X, and is defined as $\mathsf{L}(X)(a) \triangleq |\{e \in X \mid l_\varepsilon(e) = a\}|$.

Now, for a given BES ε, we can define the transition relation:

$\forall A$ s.t. $A : Act \cup \{i, \delta\} \to \mathbb{N}$,

$$\varepsilon \blacktriangleright^{A} \varepsilon[C] \quad iff \quad C \in \mathcal{CF}(\varepsilon) \wedge \forall e, e' \in C, \ e \otimes_C e' \wedge \mathsf{L}(C) = A$$

$\varepsilon \blacktriangleright^{A} \varepsilon'$ states that the BES ε can concurrently perform the multiset of actions A and evolve to ε'.

This construction enables us to define, first, the notion of a step trace and then, a step bisimulation; a multiset is called a step.

Definition 26
A multiset sequence, $A_1 \dots A_n$, is a step trace of $\varepsilon \in BES$ iff $\exists \varepsilon_0, \dots, \varepsilon_n \in BES$ such that $\varepsilon = \varepsilon_0 \wedge \varepsilon_{i-1} \blacktriangleright^{A_i} \varepsilon_i$ for $1 \leq i \leq n$. If we let

$$Tr^{st}(\varepsilon) = \{ \rho \mid \rho \ is \ a \ step \ trace \ of \ \varepsilon \}$$

then, this induces an equivalence:

$$S \asymp_{st} S' \quad iff \quad Tr^{st}(\llbracket S \rrbracket_{be}) = Tr^{st}(\llbracket S' \rrbracket_{be})$$

Definition 27   (Step Strong Bisimulation Relation)
$\forall \varepsilon_1, \varepsilon_2 \in BES$, $\mathcal{R} \subseteq BES \times BES$ is a step strong bisimulation if $(\varepsilon_1, \varepsilon_2) \in \mathcal{R}$ implies $\forall A$ s.t. $A : Act \cup \{i, \delta\} \to \mathbb{N}$,

1. $\forall \varepsilon_1' \in BES, \ \varepsilon_1 \blacktriangleright^{A} \varepsilon_1' \implies \exists \varepsilon_2' \in BES . \ \varepsilon_2 \blacktriangleright^{A} \varepsilon_2' \wedge (\varepsilon_1', \varepsilon_2') \in \mathcal{R} \wedge$
2. $\forall \varepsilon_2' \in BES, \ \varepsilon_2 \blacktriangleright^{A} \varepsilon_2' \implies \exists \varepsilon_1' \in BES . \ \varepsilon_1 \blacktriangleright^{A} \varepsilon_1' \wedge (\varepsilon_1', \varepsilon_2') \in \mathcal{R}$

Definition 28   (Step Strong Bisimilar)
$\sim_{st} \triangleq \bigcup \{ \mathcal{R} \mid \mathcal{R} \ is \ a \ step \ strong \ bisimulation \}.$

In a general sense, step trace equivalence is related to step bisimulation in a similar way to which strong trace equivalence (in which, internal actions are not collapsed) would be related to strong bisimulation in LTS. Thus, we do not discuss step trace equivalence further; it is largely included for completeness.

Step bisimulation is more discriminating than sequential bisimulation. With regard to the examples presented in Figure 4.11, $\varepsilon_1 \not\sim_{st} \varepsilon_2$ and $\varepsilon_3 \not\sim_{st} \varepsilon_4$. The first of these arises because $\sim_{st} \subseteq \sim_{sq}$, which can be verified quite easily, whereas the second arises because

$$\varepsilon_3 \blacktriangleright^{\{(x,1),(y,1)\}} \quad but, \quad \varepsilon_4 \blacktriangleright^{\{(x,1),(y,1)\}} \not\rightarrow$$

where we have denoted the multiset by its underlying set of pairs. Thus, step bisimulation semantics are more discriminating than sequential bisimulation semantics; i.e. $\sim_{st} \subset \sim_{sq}$.

Pomset Equivalence. Partially ordered multisets, or pomsets, are a well-known truly concurrent semantic model. In deriving pomsets and their induced equivalence, we take the approach employed in [114], which is to define an even more expressive semantics, labelled partially ordered sets, or lposets, and then derive pomsets from this model. This is also similar to the approach taken in [131].

Lposet semantics for BES were presented in [114] and are based on ideas investigated in [170]. The approach is to model events as well as actions (all previous approaches have only modelled actions) and, in addition, to include causality relations. Thus, an lposet is a configuration of a BES with labelling and causalities between events included. We have the following definition.

Definition 29   (Lposets)
Take $\varepsilon \in BES$; then if $C \in \mathcal{CF}(\varepsilon)$, there is a labelled partially ordered set (or lposet) corresponding to C, denoted $\overline{C}$, defined as $\overline{C} = (C, \preceq_C, l_\varepsilon \lceil C)$.
$\mathcal{LP}(\varepsilon)$ denotes the set of all lposets of a BES ε.

Lposets are denoted lp and the elements of lp can be accessed using E_{lp}, $\preceq_{lp}$ and l_{lp}.

So, an lposet is a triple containing a set of events, a partially ordered causality relation and a labelling. In fact, an lposet can be viewed as a (labelled) conflict-free prime event structure (see discussion of event structure models in Section 4.7). Each lposet corresponds to a single system run and includes the causalities that have contributed to the run. Because $\preceq$ is a partial ordering, independence of events will be reflected in the lposet.

From lposets we define pomsets using the notion of an lposet isomorphism.

Definition 30
lp is isomorphic to lp', denoted $\simeq$, iff there exists a bijection $\phi : E_{lp} \to E_{lp'}$ such that

1. $e \preceq e' \iff \phi(e) \preceq \phi(e')$
2. $l(e) = l(\phi(e))$

The isomorphism class of an lposet is a pomset over *Act*. The pomset corresponding to an lposet $\overline{C}$ is denoted by $[\overline{C}]_\simeq$. $PoS(\varepsilon)$ denotes the set of all pomsets of ε; i.e.

$$PoS(\varepsilon) \triangleq \{ [\overline{C}]_\simeq \mid C \in \mathcal{CF}(E_\varepsilon) \}$$

Now we can define pomset equivalence.

Definition 31   (Pomset Equivalent)
Two event structures, ε and ε', are pomset equivalent, denoted $\varepsilon \asymp_{PoS} \varepsilon'$, if and only if $PoS(\varepsilon) = PoS(\varepsilon')$.

Pomsets are trace-based semantics, so they do not distinguish forms of choice. For example, $\varepsilon_1 \asymp_{PoS} \varepsilon_2$ (see Figure 4.11), because they both have the maximal pomsets $\{[x \to y], [x \to z]\}$ (each pomset is denoted inside square brackets; for example, $[x \to y]$ denotes the isomorphism class of pomsets with two events labelled x and y, respectively, and a causality between the events). Notice, the maximal lposets of ε_1 are $\{[e_x \to e_y], [e_x \to e_z]\}$ and the maximal lposets of ε_2 are $\{[f_x \to f_y], [f'_x \to f_z]\}$; so, they are not lposet equivalent. This is reflected in our consideration of equality of proving sequences. However, $[e_x \to e_y]$ and $[f_x \to f_y]$ are in the same isomorphism class and similarly, $[e_x \to e_z]$ and $[f'_x \to f_z]$ are isomorphic.[2] Thus, we have a pair of BES, $(\varepsilon_1, \varepsilon_2)$, such that $\varepsilon_1 \asymp_{PoS} \varepsilon_2$, but $\varepsilon_1 \not\sim_{st} \varepsilon_2$. Thus, $\asymp_{PoS} \not\subseteq \sim_{st}$.

Furthermore, we can show that $\sim_{st}$ does not imply $\asymp_{PoS}$, by considering the two behaviours:

$$P := (x;\ stop) \,|||\, (y;\ stop)$$

$$Q := (x;\ stop \,|||\, y;\ stop) \,[]\, (x;\ y;\ stop) \,[]\, (y;\ x;\ stop)$$

The underlying bundle event structures for these two behaviours are step equivalent, however, they are not pomset equivalent. The resulting bundle event structures are depicted as (1), respectively, (2) in Figure 4.12. Note, this example reveals a limitation of step equivalence. This difficulty arises because, in addition to maximal steps (i.e. multisets that reflect as many independent events as possible at a particular state), it is also possible to take submaximal steps. For example, if we let ε_P denote the BES arising from P and assume $\varepsilon_{x;\,stop}$ and $\varepsilon_{y;\,stop}$ similarly, then, although $\varepsilon_P \blacktriangleright\!\!\xrightarrow{\{(x,1),(y,1)\}}$, it is also the case, for example, that $\varepsilon_P \blacktriangleright\!\!\xrightarrow{\{(y,1)\}} \varepsilon_{x;\,stop}$ and $\varepsilon_{x;\,stop} \blacktriangleright\!\!\xrightarrow{\{(x,1)\}}$. Critically, in P, this possibility to perform such submaximal steps, effectively, covers the interleaving of x and y, found as an alternative to the independent parallel behaviour, in Q. It is for this reason that P and Q are indistinguishable according to step semantics.

In Figure 4.12, (3) and (4) give another such example; they are step bisimulation equivalent, but not pomset equivalent (this example is due to Van Glabbeek [191]).[3] So, $\sim_{st}$ and $\asymp_{PoS}$ are incomparable; that is, neither implies the other.

Proving Sequence Equivalence. Now we come to what is our most discriminating event structure development relation: equality of proving sequences, denoted $\asymp_{PS}$. Firstly, we have the following important result.

Proposition 6
$\mathcal{PS}(\varepsilon) = \mathcal{PS}(\varepsilon') \iff \mathcal{LP}(\varepsilon) = \mathcal{LP}(\varepsilon') \iff \mathcal{CF}(\varepsilon) = \mathcal{CF}(\varepsilon')$.

Proof
See [114].
○

So, equality of proving sequences is equivalent to equality of lposets and to equality of configurations. Thus, without loss of generality we can use

---

[2]The key point is that a different bijection, ϕ in definition 30, is used in each pomset, which is quite legitimate.

[3]Although, it is not clear what process calculus specification would generate the event structure in Figure 4.12(4).

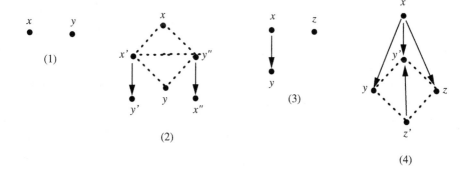

Fig. 4.12. More Event Structures Illustrating Equivalence Relations

these three equalities interchangeably. Here we focus on equality of proving sequences.

$\asymp_{PS}$ is a discriminating equality, not only does it discriminate concurrency and interleaving, it also distinguishes choice points. The discriminating power over choice is obtained because events are referenced rather than actions. Such event references imply an inherently more intensionalist equality than those we have considered so far.

Implicitly $\asymp_{PS}$ is defined modulo an isomorphism, but it is a different isomorphism to that used to generate pomsets.

Definition 32   (Proving Sequence Isomorphic)
Given $E = \{e \mid \exists \sigma \in \mathcal{PS}(\varepsilon) \ . \ e \in \$\sigma\}$ and $E' = \{e \mid \exists \sigma \in \mathcal{PS}(\varepsilon') \ . \ e \in \$\sigma\}$, where $\$\sigma$ returns the set of elements in a sequence, then ε and ε' are proving sequence isomorphic, denoted $\asymp_{PS}$, if and only if there exists a bijection,

$$\phi : E \to E',$$

such that,

$$l_\varepsilon(e) = l_{\varepsilon'}(\phi(e)) \quad and$$

$$e_1 \ldots e_n \in \mathcal{PS}(\varepsilon) \iff \phi(e_1) \ldots \phi(e_n) \in \mathcal{PS}(\varepsilon').$$

Notice how this isomorphism behaves differently to that used to derive pomsets. In pomsets, the isomorphism is between the events in a single lposet. However, here our isomorphism is between the events of the entire set of proving sequences. For example, if we consider ε_1 and ε_2 again, which are pomset equivalent, as indicated earlier, the maximum lposets of ε_1 are $[e_x \to e_y]$ and $[e_x \to e_z]$ and the maximum lposets for ε_2 are $[f_x \to f_y]$ and $[f'_x \to f_z]$. Now, individually, $[e_x \to e_y]$ and $[f_x \to f_y]$ are isomorphic; i.e. $\phi = \{(e_x, f_x), (e_y, f_y)\}$ will work, and in addition, $[e_x \to e_z]$ and $[f'_x \to f_z]$ are isomorphic, but only by a different isomorphism, viz $\phi' = \{(e_x, f'_x), (e_z, f_z)\}$. However, there does not exist a single bijection between the two sets of lposets

$\{[e_x \to e_y], [e_x \to e_z]\}$ and $\{[f_x \to f_y], [f'_x \to f_z]\}$ as the latter contains two events labelled x, whereas the former contains only one such event. Similarly, the induced sets of maximal proving sequences, $\{e_x e_y, e_x e_z\}$ from ε_1, and $\{f_x f_y, f'_x f_z\}$ from ε_2, are not isomorphic.

So, in terms of the examples presented in Figure 4.11, $\varepsilon_1 \not\asymp_{PS} \varepsilon_2$ and $\varepsilon_3 \not\asymp_{PS} \varepsilon_4$. In addition, the two pairs of BES highlighted in Figure 4.12 are distinguished by $\asymp_{PS}$. But, the more significant observation is that proving sequence equality often differentiates BES with identical external behaviour. For example, the two BES depicted in Figure 4.13 are distinguished by proving sequence equality. A justification for such a strong notion of equality is that, although behaviourally the two BES are the same, in terms of implementation they are not the same, in the sense that (2) is a more resilient solution, because it has some built-in redundancy.

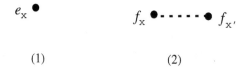

(1)   (2)

Fig. 4.13. BES with the Same Behaviour

4.7 Alternative Event Structure Models

We discuss three event structure models, which are to be found in the literature: *prime event structures*, *stable event structures* and *flow event structures*. We relate each of these to the BES model we have just presented.

Prime Event Structures. These were the original event structures model, as defined in [155]. They are called "prime" event structures because, when the model is related to domain theory, it yields a *Prime Algebraic Coherent Partial Order* [155]. Ignoring labelling, which could easily be added, prime event structures have the following basic form.

A *prime event structure* is a triple: $\varepsilon = (E, \#, \leq)$, where
- E is a set of events;
- $\# \subseteq E \times E$ is a conflict relation (irreflexive and symmetric); and
- $\leq \subseteq E \times E$ is a causality relation (a partial order).

The structure is subject to the following two conditions.

1. *Finite Causes* – $\{ e' \mid e' \leq e \}$ is finite

2. *Conflict Inheritance* – $e \# e' \wedge e' \leq e'' \Rightarrow e \# e''$

There are two basic aspects of prime event structures that differ from BES: the definition of causality and the conflict inheritance property.

- *Causality.* This is a binary partial order relation between events. It is denoted $e \leq e'$, which, if equality of events is factored out, induces a relation $<$, which states that "e *must* happen before e' can happen" or, alternatively, "e' depends upon the previous occurrence of the event e." This is a naturally transitive interpretation and, thus, $\leq$ is a partial order.
- *Conflict Inheritance.* The conflict relation has the same form as in BES; i.e. it is a binary relation between events. However, an additional constraint is imposed. This is the conflict inheritance property, which states that, if an event is in conflict with a second event, all causal successors of the event must be in conflict with the second event.

Prime event structures are a very simple true concurrency model with nice mathematical properties, but they are not well suited to modelling a process calculus like pbLOTOS. As acknowledged by [198], they offer a limited interpretation of parallel composition. This is because the model does not allow events to have multiple possible enablings. Consider the behaviour:

$(x; y; stop \, [] \, x; stop) \, |[x]| \, (x; z; stop) \quad (*)$

which generates the BES depicted in Figure 4.14(1), where the event g_z could be enabled by either g_x or g'_x. The obvious representation in an event structure with binary causality is depicted in Figure 4.14(2). However, this structure contradicts the conflict inheritance property, which would require that g_z be in conflict with both g_x and g'_x.

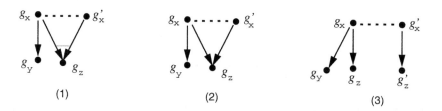

(1)   (2)   (3)

Fig. 4.14. Event Structures with Multiple Enablings

Prime event structures have the nice property that each event is enabled by a unique set of events, which immediately prevents choices of enabling from being modelled. However, it should be pointed out that copying of events can be used to model the behaviour we are seeking in prime event structures. For example, we could duplicate the event g_z to obtain the structure depicted in Figure 4.14(3). This is the solution employed in [131] for modelling CSP parallel composition. This solution has been argued against even by Winskel [198], because a conceptually "single" piece of computation, the event g_z, has been subdivided.

Stable Event Structures. These are an enhancement of prime event structures, which overcomes the problem highlighted in the previous section. The main difference to prime event structures is that the binary causality relation is replaced by a, nonbinary, *enabling* relation:

$$\vdash \subseteq Con \times E$$

where Con is the set of all finite conflict-free subsets of E; i.e.

$$Con \triangleq \{\, X \subseteq E \mid \forall e, e' \in X,\ \neg(e \# e')\,\}$$

So, for example, for $X \in Con$ and $e \in E$ we could have $X \vdash e$, which states that, if all the events in X have occurred, then e can occur. In accordance with this interpretation, we impose the following constraint,

$$X \vdash e \ \wedge\ X \subseteq Y \ \wedge\ Y \in Con \ \implies\ Y \vdash e$$

i.e. e is enabled by any conflict-free set, which contains more than the minimum number of events required to enable e. An enabling relation is depicted in a similar way to a bundle; e.g. $\{e, e'\} \vdash e''$ would be depicted as in Figure 4.15. However, it should be apparent that the enabling relation has quite a different meaning to the bundle relation in BES.

Fig. 4.15. An Enabling Relation

A stable event structure has the following structure.

> A *stable event structure* is a triple: $\varepsilon = (E, \#, \vdash)$ where
> - E is a set of events;
> - $\# \subseteq E \times E$ is a conflict relation (irreflexive and symmetric); and
> - $\vdash \subseteq \mathcal{P}(E) \times E$ is the enabling relation.

Stable event structures can model behaviours such as (*), which was highlighted in the subsection on prime event structures. This is because they do

Fig. 4.16. Concurrent Enablings

not include the conflict inheritance property. In fact, the stable event structure for (*) would be the structure depicted in Figure 4.14(2).

However, without more constraints, structures of the form depicted in Figure 4.16 can be defined. This structure has two enabling relations $\{e\} \vdash e''$ and $\{e'\} \vdash e''$. Conceptually, this is a slightly odd structure as both the sets $\{e\}$ and $\{e'\}$ enable e'', but their union, $\{e, e'\}$, does not, even though $\{e, e'\}$ is conflict-free. Another way of looking at this structure is that the enabling of e'' is not unique; i.e. in a configuration $\{e, e', e''\}$ we do not know whether e'' is immediately caused by $\{e\}$ or $\{e'\}$. In response to this observation, [198] imposes the, so-called, stability condition on the basic event structure construction, hence the name stable event structures. This condition states the following,

$$X \vdash e \wedge Y \vdash e \wedge X \cup Y \cup \{e\} \in Con \implies X \cap Y \vdash e$$

which would not be satisfied by the structure depicted in Figure 4.16, because $\{e\} \cap \{e'\} = \emptyset \nvdash e''$. A unique minimal enabling set can always be found, which is obtained by taking the intersection of enabling sets, as suggested by the above property.

Winskel [198] defines a stable event structure semantics for parallel composition and a semantics for pbLOTOS based on stable event structures could be defined. However, we have chosen to use bundle event structures, as their link with LOTOS has been more extensively explored than is the case with stable event structures. In addition, [114] argues against stable event structures on a number of technical grounds.

Flow Event Structures. These offer an alternative approach to resolving the problems prime event structures have in modelling parallel composition. The main workers are Boudol and Castellani, and a good reference to the work is [31].

The basic idea of flow event structures is to drop the conflict inheritance property of prime event structures, but maintain a binary causality relation, although this will have a different character.

A *flow event structure* is a triple: $\varepsilon = (E, \#, \prec)$ where

- E is a set of events;

- $\# \subseteq E \times E$ is a conflict relation (symmetric, but not necessarily irreflexive); and
- $\prec \subseteq E \times E$ is an irreflexive binary flow relation.

It is important to note that the flow relation has a different interpretation to the causality relation of prime event structures. Specifically, $e \prec e'$ means "if e occurs e' cannot have already occurred." This does not induce a transitive relation; for example, consider the flow event structure depicted in Figure 4.17, which could have been generated from the pbLOTOS behaviour:

$$(y \,;\, x \,;\, stop \;|||\; x \,;\, stop) \;|[x]|\; (x \,;\, z \,;\, stop)$$

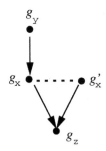

Fig. 4.17. A Flow Event Structure

Although, $g_y \prec g_x$ and $g_x \prec g_z$ it is clear that $g_y \not\prec g_z$. In particular, a legitimate evaluation of this event structure could perform g_x' first, then g_z and finally g_y. Thus, g_z has occurred before g_y. $\prec$ is a local, nontransitive relation, which expresses immediate enabling.

Another important aspect of flow event structures is the concept of self-conflicting events; i.e. events e such that $e \# e$. These are used to model events that cannot occur and, thus, to create deadlock situations (in a related way to the use of empty bundles in BES). Flow event structure semantics could also be given for LOTOS. However, [114] argues against this on a number of grounds, most significantly, because self-conflicting events cannot be removed from flow event structures; i.e. a transformation cannot be found which removes such events, but yields an equivalent event structure in terms of possible configurations. This is in contrast to the situation with BES, where empty bundles can be transformed out.

4.8 Summary and Discussion

Bundle event structures are a more discriminating semantics than the interleaving semantics that we have considered in Chapter 3. In particular, they allow us to distinguish between concurrent behaviour and forms of choice and sequence which model interleaving. Conceptual justifications for event structure approaches emphasise the importance of the intensionalist view of modelling concurrent systems. The added expressiveness of bundle event structures is reflected in the increased complexity of the semantic mapping from pbLOTOS.

A spectrum of development relations can be identified for bundle event structures. Each of these, to a different degree, abstracts away from the expressiveness of the basic bundle event structures. In particular, interleaving equivalences and relations can be regained. In addition, more discriminating relations, which distinguish concurrency from interleaving can be highlighted. Even relations which differentiate according to the internal construction of specifications can be defined.

Testing Theory and the Linear Time – Branching Time Spectrum

There is a whole spectrum of alternative approaches to the three semantic models we considered in Chapters 3 and 4. This chapter discusses a number of these alternatives, within the context of a powerful conceptual framework for investigating the meaning of concurrent systems: *testing theory*. Central to this approach is the principle that has dominated our treatment of concurrency theory; that is, that two systems / processes are considered to be equivalent if they cannot be distinguished by an external observer or, in other words, by an agent testing the system. This statement leaves open a number of issues; perhaps most significantly, what capacity does the observer have to test / interrogate the system? Note that, in Chapter 2, we informally (and implicitly) took a position on this question, when we explained the behaviour of pbLOTOS operators and specifications in terms of performing button-pressing actions on a black box representation of systems.

We only have room to describe one of these models in depth; this is the *trace-refusals* model, which we discuss in Section 5.1. This approach arises out of a very natural interpretation of the capacity of an observer to test a process, which we discuss in Section 5.2. Then, in Section 5.3, we review the spectrum of testing theoretic interpretations of different equivalences and preorders. Finally, in Section 5.4, we show how the testing theory discussed in this chapter can be applied in the context of object-oriented distributed systems.

It is also important to note that this chapter focuses exclusively on interleaving semantics. This is because testing theories have been far more extensively explored in this context than in the true concurrency domain.

5.1 Trace-refusals Semantics

5.1.1 Introduction

LOTOS trace-refusals semantics were derived from the failure semantics defined for CSP [96]. However, in LOTOS, the model is formulated in a subtly different way to the CSP definition. We discuss this formulation here and give a comparison with the CSP approach in Section 7.2.6.

Trace-refusals semantics are a hybrid approach, which extends trace semantics. Remember, trace semantics cannot distinguish certain forms of branching; in particular, they identify some behaviours that have quite different deadlock properties (i.e. one could deadlock where the other could not). Thus, a second concept is added, which characterises the possible deadlocks of a behaviour at a certain point in its evaluation. This is the notion of a refusal; it records what a behaviour can refuse to do; i.e. a set of actions, which, if offered by the environment, would result in a deadlock.

The equality induced by trace-refusals is weaker than the bisimulation equalities; it responds to the observation that weak bisimulation unrealistically distinguishes certain behaviours. For example, the behaviours:

$$P := (x \,;\, x \,;\, y \,;\, stop) \; [] \; (x \,;\, x \,;\, z \,;\, stop) \quad \text{and}$$
$$Q := x \,;\, (x \,;\, y \,;\, stop \; [] \; x \,;\, z \,;\, stop),$$

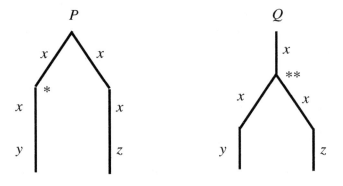

Fig. 5.1. Labelled Transition Systems with Two Levels of Nondeterminism

LTS for which are depicted in Figure 5.1, are not weak bisimilar. This is because P can perform an x and evolve into the state marked *. In addition, after x, Q must evolve into the state marked **, but these two states are not weak bisimilar, as * cannot perform an x and get into a state where it can perform a z. A similar example was discussed in Section 3.3.3.2: processes R_5 and R_6 in the discussion of ready simulation.

The problem is that bisimulation is too discriminating with regard to branching. Both P and Q contain a nondeterministic choice; in P it is immediate, whereas in Q it is after one x. However, the point at which this internal choice is made will not be observable, because both can perform two xs and then reach a state where they can either only perform a y or only perform a z. Thus, there is strong intuitive justification for equating these two behaviours.

Trace-refusals semantics will not distinguish these two behaviours. In fact, we show a number of behaviours that trace-refusals identifies, but $\approx$ does not.

5.1.2 The Basic Approach

The central concept in trace-refusals semantics is that of a refusal. A set of actions X is a refusal at a particular state if none of the actions can be performed at that state; i.e. they are all refused. Thus, if you consider the behaviour:

$$P_1 := x\,;\,y\,;\,stop,$$

which has alphabet of actions $\{x, y\}$, at its initial state, it can refuse the sets $\emptyset$ and $\{y\}$ (each of these sets is called a refusal), but it cannot refuse x. After performing an x, the behaviour can refuse $\emptyset$ and $\{x\}$. Finally, after performing xy, the behaviour will have four possible refusals: $\emptyset$, $\{x\}$, $\{y\}$ and $\{x, y\}$.

We typically talk about a refusal after a certain trace. Thus, P_1 will refuse $\{x, y\}$ after the trace xy. Notice that the empty set is a refusal of all states, because any state can refuse to perform all actions in the empty set.

An intuitive justification for the trace-refusals formulation is in terms of testing. Assume that we are a tester who is observing how a particular specification behaves. We have the capacity to record the actions that are performed; this is the trace part of trace-refusals. In addition, we can observe when a deadlock has occurred. A finite observation of a specification either yields a trace or a trace followed by deadlock. In the latter case, a trace may be recorded along with a set of actions, which indicates the set of actions offered by the environment at the point where deadlock ensued; it is a refusal of the specification after the recorded trace. We elaborate on this intuition in Section 5.2.

A complete trace-refusals characterisation of a specification B is a pair, which records the set of traces B can perform and the set of all possible refusals of B after any trace. We denote the set of all refusals of a behaviour B after a trace σ by

$$Ref_B(\sigma)$$

and this will be a subset of $\mathcal{P}(Act \cup \{\delta\})$. Notice that, because it cannot be synchronised on, the internal action cannot be included in a refusal set. So, the observer cannot test a system with regard to i. This also reflects the fact that we are once again only interested in observable behaviour.

Thus, a refusals model for a specification S is a pair:

$$(\llbracket S \rrbracket_{tr}, Ref_S) \in \mathcal{P}(\mathcal{T}) \times (\mathcal{T} \to \mathcal{P}(\mathcal{P}(Act \cup \{\delta\})))$$

with first element a set of traces and second element a function from traces to sets of refusals. In CSP, this is written differently; each refusals set is associated with a specific trace, to generate a failure. Thus, the basic model is a set of pairs, where the elements of each pair are a trace and a refusal. However, the two are isomorphic formulations and one can trivially be regained from the other. For example, the following function will map a LOTOS-style trace-refusals characterisation to a CSP-style set of failures, where T is a set of traces and Ref is a function from traces to sets of refusal sets.

$$toF((T, Ref)) \triangleq \bigcup_{\sigma \in T} \{(\sigma, X) \mid X \in Ref(\sigma)\}$$

We present a series of examples to illustrate the LOTOS trace-refusals concept.

5.1.2.1 Example 1

$P_1 := stop$

$[\![P_1]\!]_{tr} = \{\epsilon\}, \quad Ref_{P_1}(\epsilon) = \mathcal{P}(\mathcal{L})$

The deadlock behaviour will perform nothing and refuse everything.

5.1.2.2 Example 2

$P_2 := x\,;\, y\,;\, stop \quad$ assuming $\mathcal{L} = \{x, y\}$

$[\![P_2]\!]_{tr} = \{\epsilon, x, xy\},$

$Ref_{P_2}(\epsilon) = \{\emptyset, \{y\}\}$

$Ref_{P_2}(x) = \{\emptyset, \{x\}\}$

$Ref_{P_2}(xy) = \{\emptyset, \{x\}, \{y\}, \{x, y\}\} = \mathcal{P}(\mathcal{L})$

As suggested by this example, refusal sets are subset closed, because, if a set of actions is refused, clearly, all subsets of the set of actions will also be refused.

5.1.2.3 Example 3

$P_3 := x\,;\, (y\,;\, stop \,[\!]\, z\,;\, stop) \quad$ assuming $\mathcal{L} = \{x, y, z\}$

$[\![P_3]\!]_{tr} = \{\epsilon, x, xy, xz\},$

$Ref_{P_3}(\epsilon) = \mathcal{P}(\mathcal{L} \setminus \{x\})$

$Ref_{P_3}(x) = \{\emptyset, \{x\}\}$

$Ref_{P_3}(xy) = Ref_{P_3}(xz) = \mathcal{P}(\mathcal{L})$

At a choice point, e.g. after the trace x, every action, apart from the actions offered in the choice, are refused.

5.1.2.4 Example 4

$P_4 := (x\,;\,y\,;\,stop\,)\;[]\;(x\,;\,z\,;\,stop\,)$ assuming $\mathcal{L} = \{x, y, z\}$

$[\![\,P_4\,]\!]_{tr} = \{\epsilon, x, xy, xz\}$,

$Ref_{P_4}(\epsilon) = \mathcal{P}(\mathcal{L} \setminus \{x\})$

$Ref_{P_4}(x) = \{\emptyset, \{x\}, \{y\}, \{z\}, \{x, y\}, \{x, z\}\}$

$Ref_{P_4}(xy) = Ref_{P_4}(xz) = \mathcal{P}(\mathcal{L})$

This illustrates that choice points are distinguished, because the refusals of P_3 and P_4 are different (notice their trace sets are the same). The two behaviours are differentiated by the refusals after the trace x. P_3 only refuses x, whereas P_4 refuses all subsets of $\{x, y\}$ and $\{x, z\}$. This is because the refusals of P_4 after the trace x are a composite of the refusals at the two states that can be reached after the trace x. So, after a particular trace, a behaviour might be able to get into a number of different states and a refusal at each of these states is a refusal of the behaviour after the trace. This is an important point, which generates much of the subtlety of refusals. Such situations are characteristic of nondeterministic behaviour. However, the set $\{y, z\}$ is not a refusal of P_4 after x, because if the environment offers both y and z, one of them will be able to be performed and thus, a deadlock will not result. In addition, note that actions can be both performed and refused after a particular trace; e.g. y can be offered after x, but it can also be refused. We postpone considering examples of how internal behaviour is represented until we have presented the trace-refusals concept formally.

5.1.3 Deriving Trace-refusal Pairs

There are basically two approaches to deriving trace-refusals pairs from pbLO-TOS specifications. The first is via labelled transition systems and the second is through a direct semantics. We consider these in turn.

5.1.3.1 Deriving Trace-refusals from Labelled Transition Systems

The standard semantics for LOTOS are labelled transition systems; this is the semantic model presented in the defining standard [104]. Thus, a natural approach is to derive trace-refusals semantics indirectly via labelled transition systems. Thus, LOTOS specifications are first mapped to labelled transition systems and then a trace-refusals characterisation is derived from the labelled transition system. In fact, this is the standard approach for deriving trace-refusals for LOTOS.

The heart of the labelled transition system to trace-refusals mapping is the double arrow transition relation defined in Section 3.3.2.3, which was used there to generate trace sets from labelled transition systems. Our approach here is a natural extension of the mapping of Section 3.3.2.3.

An important mapping used in constructing trace-refusals is *after*, which is defined as,

$$B \ after \ \sigma \triangleq \{ \ B' \mid B \stackrel{\sigma}{\Longrightarrow} B' \ \}$$

which denotes the set of all states reachable from B, after performing the trace σ. Using this mapping, we can define the refusals of a behaviour after a particular trace:

$$Ref_B(\sigma) \triangleq \{ \ X \mid \exists B' \in B \ after \ \sigma \ s.t. \ \forall x \in X, \ B' \stackrel{x}{\nRightarrow} \ \}$$

This denotes the set of all sets, X say, such that a state can be reached after σ, at which all actions in X are refused. It is important to notice that this is a set of sets; i.e. all possible refusals after performing the trace σ. Also notice that, as indicated earlier, the refusals after a particular trace are a composite of the refusals at each state reachable after that trace.

5.1.3.2 Direct Denotational Semantics

The failures semantics for CSP are defined using a direct denotational semantics [171]. Thus, the effect of each operator on the traces and refusals is defined directly. Leduc [120] attempts to give a similar direct semantics for LOTOS, however, it is important to note that the modelling of divergence in his semantics is very different from that employed in the CSP semantics (as discussed in the next section). In particular, he seeks to give a noncatastrophic interpretation of divergence, which is in accordance with the standard LOTOS interpretation of the concept. However, this turns out to be problematic and Leduc shows that the LOTOS hiding operator cannot be fully modelled in this setting. The problem is that it is very hard to see how to give hiding a compositional semantics. Due to this complexity we do not present a direct denotational semantics here; the interested reader is referred to Leduc's thesis [120].

5.1.4 Internal Behaviour

The handling of internal behaviour in trace-refusals semantics leads to much of the subtlety and power of the approach. This section presents examples of how pbLOTOS behaviours with internal actions map to trace-refusals models. These follow on from the examples presented in Section 5.1.2.

The pbLOTOS behaviours:

$P_1 := i \, ; \, i \, ; \, x \, ; \, y \, ; \, stop$

$P_2 := x \, ; \, i \, ; \, y \, ; \, stop$

$P_3 := x \, ; \, stop \ [] \ y \, ; \, stop$

$P_4 := (\, i \, ; \, x \, ; \, stop \,) \ [] \ (\, i \, ; \, y \, ; \, stop \,)$

$P_5 := (\, i \, ; \, x \, ; \, stop \,) \ [] \ (\, y \, ; \, stop \,)$

with $\mathcal{L} = \{x, y\}$, have the following trace-refusals characterisations.

$[\![\, P_1 \,]\!]_{tr} = \{\ \epsilon\ ,\ x\ ,\ xy\ \}$

$Ref_{P_1}(\epsilon) = \{\ \emptyset\ ,\ \{y\}\ \}$

$Ref_{P_1}(x) = \{\ \emptyset\ ,\ \{x\}\ \}$

$Ref_{P_1}(xy) = \mathcal{P}(\mathcal{L})$

$[\![\, P_2 \,]\!]_{tr} = \{\ \epsilon\ ,\ x\ ,\ xy\ \}$

$Ref_{P_2}(\epsilon) = \{\ \emptyset\ ,\ \{y\}\ \}$

$Ref_{P_2}(x) = \{\ \emptyset\ ,\ \{x\}\ \}$

$Ref_{P_2}(xy) = \mathcal{P}(\mathcal{L})$

$[\![\, P_3 \,]\!]_{tr} = \{\ \epsilon\ ,\ x\ ,\ y\ \}$

$Ref_{P_3}(\epsilon) = \{\ \emptyset\ \}$

$Ref_{P_3}(x) = Ref_{P_3}(y) = \mathcal{P}(\mathcal{L})$

$[\![\, P_4 \,]\!]_{tr} = \{\ \epsilon\ ,\ x\ ,\ y\ \}$

$Ref_{P_4}(\epsilon) = \{\ \emptyset\ ,\ \{x\}\ ,\ \{y\}\ \}$

$Ref_{P_4}(x) = Ref_{P_4}(y) = \mathcal{P}(\mathcal{L})$

$[\![\, P_5 \,]\!]_{tr} = \{\ \epsilon\ ,\ x\ ,\ y\ \}$

$Ref_{P_5}(\epsilon) = \{\ \emptyset\ ,\ \{y\}\ \}$

$Ref_{P_5}(x) = Ref_{P_5}(y) = \mathcal{P}(\mathcal{L})$

We discuss each of these in turn.

1. The trace-refusals characterisation of P_1 is the same as the trace-refusals characterisation for x; y; $stop$; this is because the internal actions do not create any nondeterminism. Also, because refusals are defined in terms of the $\Longrightarrow$ transition relation, the internal actions guarding x will be skipped over and all states reachable after the empty trace; i.e. i; i; x; y; $stop$, i; x; y; $stop$ and x; y; $stop$, will have the same refusals; i.e. $\emptyset$ and $\{y\}$.

2. The point to note here is that the trace-refusals of P_2 are identical to those of P_1, because once again, the internal action does not affect the observable behaviour.

3. P_3 is included as a point of comparison with the refusals of P_4 and P_5. Notice in particular that, after the empty trace, P_3 does not refuse any actions. This is because both actions in the alphabet of the behaviour are offered.

4. In contrast, P_4 offers a symmetric nondeterministic choice created through internal behaviour. Thus, we would expect that P_4 would have a different refusal characterisation after the empty trace to P_3. In explaining the refusal sets derived, you should first notice that P_4 *after* ϵ contains three

states: the initial state, which we reference as P_4, x; *stop* and y; *stop*. This is because $P_4 \overset{\epsilon}{\Longrightarrow}$ can map to any of these states. Thus, a refusal at any one of these states will be a refusal of P_4 after ϵ. In the initial state, only the empty set can be refused, because $P_4 \overset{x}{\Longrightarrow}$ and $P_4 \overset{y}{\Longrightarrow}$. So, the initial state does not contribute any "proper" refusals. However, in state x; *stop*, both the empty set and $\{y\}$ are refusals and, similarly, in state y; *stop* both the empty set and $\{x\}$ are refusals. Thus, these are all members of $Ref_{P_4}(\epsilon)$. What this refusal characterisation is modelling is the fact that, after the empty trace, P_4 could be in a state where it refuses $\{x\}$ and it could be in a state where it refuses $\{y\}$. However, it cannot be in a state where it refuses $\{x, y\}$.

5. Our final example is that of an asymmetric nondeterministic choice. Once again the interesting refusals are those after the empty trace. Notice that P_5 *after* ϵ will contain two states: P_5 and x; *stop*. As was the case for P_4, P_5 has no proper refusals, but y can be refused at state x; *stop*.

In understanding refusal characterisations of nondeterministic behaviour you should remember that we are working in an untimed setting. Thus, it is assumed, that, if an environment / tester is offering a particular action, this offer will wait for any finite period necessary for the behaviour being observed to complete any internal evolution. Thus, in P_5, the action x cannot be refused after the empty trace, because any tester will wait an arbitrarily long period for P_5 to evolve to state x; *stop*.

In a similar vein, consider the following processes with cyclic behaviour, transition systems for which are shown in Figure 5.2.

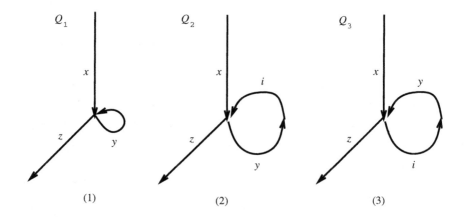

Fig. 5.2. Processes with Cyclic Behaviour

1. $Q_1 := x\,;\,Q$ and $Q := y\,;\,Q\,[]\,z\,;\,stop$

2. $Q_2 := x\,;\, Q'$ and $Q' := y\,;\, i\,;\, Q' \,[\!]\, z\,;\, stop$

3. $Q_3 := x\,;\, Q''$ and $Q'' := i\,;\, y\,;\, Q'' \,[\!]\, z\,;\, stop$

Assuming $\mathcal{L} = \{x, y, z\}$ and that Y is the set of all (nonempty) sequences containing a finite repetition of y; i.e. y, yy, yyy, ..., we have the following trace-refusals characterisations.

$$[\![Q_1]\!]_{tr} = [\![Q_2]\!]_{tr} = [\![Q_3]\!]_{tr} =$$
$$\{ \epsilon,\, x \} \cup \{ x\sigma \mid \sigma \in Y \} \cup \{ x\sigma z \mid \sigma \in Y \}$$

$$Ref_{Q_1}(\epsilon) = Ref_{Q_2}(\epsilon) = Ref_{Q_3}(\epsilon) = \{ \emptyset,\, \{y\},\, \{z\},\, \{y, z\} \}$$

$$Ref_{Q_1}(x) = Ref_{Q_2}(x) = \{ \emptyset,\, \{x\} \}$$

$$Ref_{Q_3}(x) = \{ \emptyset,\, \{x\},\, \{z\},\, \{x, z\} \}$$

$$\forall \sigma \in Y,\, Ref_{Q_1}(x\sigma) = Ref_{Q_2}(x\sigma) = \{ \emptyset,\, \{x\} \}$$

$$\forall \sigma \in Y,\, Ref_{Q_3}(x\sigma) = \{ \emptyset,\, \{x\},\, \{z\},\, \{x, z\} \}$$

$$\forall \sigma \in Y,\, Ref_{Q_1}(x\sigma z) = Ref_{Q_2}(x\sigma z) = Ref_{Q_3}(x\sigma z) = \mathcal{P}(\mathcal{L})$$

Thus, Q_1 and Q_2 are indistinguishable in trace-refusals semantics. This is because the internal action in Q_2 does not create nondeterminism, thus, it is important to note that after performing $x\sigma$ (for $\sigma \in Y$), Q_2 is either in state Q' or $i\,;\, Q'$ and neither of these states can refuse z. However, the state $y\,;\, Q''$, reachable by Q_3 after performing $x\sigma$ (for $\sigma \in Y$), and actually also after performing x, refuses z. Consequently, an observer that, for example, wishes to perform the trace $xyyyz\delta$, will always manage to reach δ (here used as a signal of successful completion of an observation) with Q_1 or Q_2, whereas, with Q_3, it may deadlock attempting to perform the z and thus, not reach the δ.

Much of the difference between alternative refusal-based semantic models is associated with the interpretation of infinite internal behaviour. This, for example, is a major difference between the CSP failures model and LOTOS trace-refusals, which we discuss in some depth in Section 7.2.6. However, as a precursor to that discussion, here we consider the nature of the LOTOS trace-refusals interpretation of cyclic internal behaviour.

The first point to note is that, unlike many other approaches (see [192] and especially CSP [171]), there is no extra semantic item, such as a set of divergences, added to the basic trace-refusals pair. Thus, divergence; i.e. infinite internal behaviour, is semantically handled by the trace-refusals structure.

This is best understood by example. Consider the following behaviours, transition systems for which are shown in Figure 5.3.

1. $R_1 := x\,;\, stop$

2. $R_2 := x\,;\, R$ and $R := i\,;\, R$

3. $R_3 := x\,;\, R'$ and $R' := i\,;\, i\,;\, R'$

4. $R_4 := x\,;\, i\,;\, R$ and $R := i\,;\, R$

5. $R_5 := x \,; y \,; stop$
6. $R_6 := x \,; R''$ and $R'' := (\, y \,; stop \,) \,[] \, (\, i \,; R'' \,)$
7. $R_7 := x \,; R'''$ and $R''' := (\, i \,; y \,; stop \,) \,[] \, (\, i \,; R''' \,)$

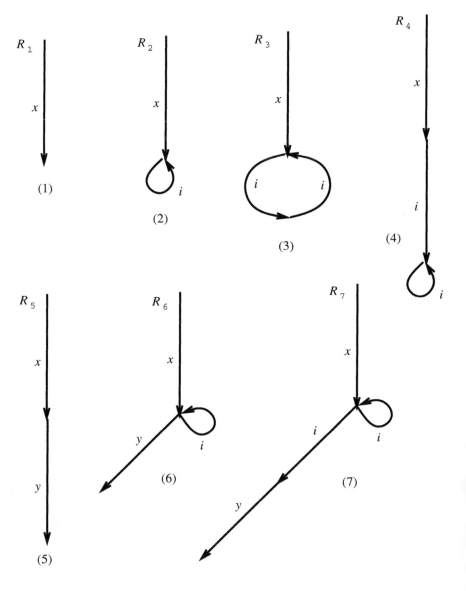

Fig. 5.3. Processes with Infinite Internal Behaviour

Now, assuming that $\mathcal{L} = \{x\}$, we have the following trace-refusals characterisations for the first four processes.

$$[\![R_1]\!]_{tr} = [\![R_2]\!]_{tr} = [\![R_3]\!]_{tr} = [\![R_4]\!]_{tr} = \{ \epsilon , x \}$$
$$Ref_{R_1}(\epsilon) = Ref_{R_2}(\epsilon) = Ref_{R_3}(\epsilon) = Ref_{R_4}(\epsilon) = \{ \emptyset \}$$
$$Ref_{R_1}(x) = Ref_{R_2}(x) = Ref_{R_3}(x) = Ref_{R_4}(x) = \mathcal{P}(\mathcal{L})$$

So, these four behaviours are indistinguishable by LOTOS trace-refusals. Thus, with regard to the notion of observability inherent in these semantics, the internal behaviour included fails to render R_2, R_3 or R_4 distinguishable from R_1. The intuition for this is that, although a process may be infinitely evolving internally, this is not externally visible and is, thus, indistinguishable from a process that has deadlocked.

Now, assuming that $\mathcal{L} = \{x, y\}$, we have the following trace-refusals characterisations for the final three processes above.

$$[\![R_5]\!]_{tr} = [\![R_6]\!]_{tr} = [\![R_7]\!]_{tr} = \{ \epsilon , x , xy \}$$
$$Ref_{R_5}(\epsilon) = Ref_{R_6}(\epsilon) = Ref_{R_7}(\epsilon) = \{ \emptyset , \{y\} \}$$
$$Ref_{R_5}(x) = Ref_{R_6}(x) = Ref_{R_7}(x) = \{ \emptyset , \{x\} \}$$
$$Ref_{R_5}(xy) = Ref_{R_6}(xy) = Ref_{R_7}(xy) = \mathcal{P}(\mathcal{L})$$

So, again, including divergent loops is not detectable in these processes according to LOTOS trace-refusals. For example, the reason that R_5 and R_7 are indistinguishable is that, although, after performing trace x, R_7 may be in a state where y is not immediately offered, it will eventually (i.e. in a finite period of time) evolve into a state where y is offered. This intuition of eventually evolving into a state in which an action is offered, is encapsulated in the $\implies$ transition relation, as used in the definition of Ref; see Section 5.1.3.1. Thus, according to the intuition of untimed semantics, whereby, effectively, the observer is always willing to wait as long as necessary, an observer wishing to perform a y after an x will be as satisfied with R_7 as with R_5. In other words, they are indistinguishable and consequently, they both yield the same trace-refusals characterisation.

A theoretical key to the handling of divergence in LOTOS trace-refusals is a fairness assumption, which states that, if there is a path out of a tau cycle,[1] as is the case in R_6 and R_7, then that path cannot be infinitely often ignored. In other words, if an action is repeatedly enabled, a process cannot infinitely often refuse to take that path. This is commonly called Kooman's Fair Abstraction property [8] and it is an issue we return to when we compare the LOTOS and the CSP handling of divergence, the latter of which is typically described as a catastrophic interpretation of divergence.

---

[1]Internal actions are denoted τ in CCS; consequently, the term tau cycle has been inherited from this earlier process calculus and is used in preference to the term i cycle.

5.1.5 Development Relations: Equivalences

We can identify a number of development relations, which are defined in terms of trace-refusals semantics. We begin by considering equivalence.

The basic equivalence induced by trace-refusals semantics is *testing equivalence*.

Definition 33   (Testing Equivalence)
Behaviours B and B' are testing equivalent, denoted B te B', if and only if,

- $[\![B]\!]_{tr} = [\![B']\!]_{tr}$ *and*

- $\forall \sigma \in [\![B]\!]_{tr}$, $Ref_B(\sigma) = Ref_{B'}(\sigma)$

Proposition 7
te is an equivalence relation.

Proof
The result is clear from the properties of set equality.
○

So, specifications are testing equivalent if they have the same trace-refusals characterisation; in other words, if they have the same trace and deadlock properties.

A particularly interesting aspect of testing equivalence is how it relates to weak bisimulation equivalence. First, let us consider the example that we identified at the start of this section.

$P := x\,;\,x\,;\,y\,;\,stop \; [\!]\; x\,;\,x\,;\,z\,;\,stop$ and

$Q := x\,;\,(\,x\,;\,y\,;\,stop\; [\!]\; x\,;\,z\,;\,stop\,)$

It is clear that P and Q are trace equivalent, but, in addition, after any trace, they have the same refusals. The crucial point is the refusals after the trace x: in both cases, everything apart from x is refused. Trace-refusals identify these behaviours because these semantics are not as distinguishing with regard to branching as bisimulations. In this respect, trace-refusals seem a more realistic semantic interpretation.

The following are all examples of specifications that are testing equivalent, but not weak bisimilar; (1) is taken from [104] and (2) is taken from [120].

(1) $P_1 := x\,;\,(\,x\,;\,x\,;\,stop\; [\!]\; x\,;\,stop\,)$ and
   $Q_1 := (\,x\,;\,x\,;\,x\,;\,stop\,)\; [\!]\; (\,x\,;\,x\,;\,stop\,)$

(2) $P_2 := x\,;\,y\,;\,stop\; [\!]\; x\,;\,z\,;\,stop$,
   $Q_2 := i\,;\,x\,;\,y\,;\,stop\; [\!]\; i\,;\,x\,;\,z\,;\,stop$ and
   $R_2 := x\,;\,(\,i\,;\,y\,;\,stop\; [\!]\; i\,;\,z\,;\,stop\,)$

(3) $P_3 := i\,;\,x\,;\,stop\; [\!]\; y\,;\,stop$ and
   $Q_3 := i\,;\,x\,;\,stop\; [\!]\; i\,;\,(\,x\,;\,stop\; [\!]\; y\,;\,stop\,)$

These examples demonstrate that $te \not\subseteq \approx$. However, it is a well-known result that $\approx \subseteq te$ [52]. Thus, we have the following important relationship between bisimulation equivalences and testing equivalences.

Theorem 5.1.
$\approx \subset te$

However, unfortunately, testing equivalence is not a congruence. As was the case with weak bisimulation, choice is an offending context. For example,

$x; stop$ and $i; x; stop$

are testing equivalent, but it is not the case that the following are testing equivalent.

$x; stop \,[]\, y; stop$ and $i; x; stop \,[]\, y; stop$

In addition, Leduc has shown [120] that hiding contexts that create divergence are not always substitutive. For example, consider P and Q, depicted in figure 5.4 and defined as follows,

$P := x; P_1 \,[]\, x; P_2$ where
$P_1 := w; P_1 \,[]\, y; stop$ and $P_2 := w; P_2 \,[]\, z; stop$

$Q := x; Q_1 \,[]\, x; Q_2$ where
$Q_1 := w; Q_2 \,[]\, y; stop$ and $Q_2 := w; Q_1 \,[]\, z; stop$

P and Q are testing equivalent. In particular, after either the trace x or $x\sigma$ (where σ is a finite repetition of w), the refusals of both P and Q are $\{ \emptyset, \{x\}, \{y\}, \{z\}, \{x,y\}, \{x,z\} \}$, noticing especially that although y and z can be refused individually, they cannot be refused together, because both of the states in P after x and P after $x\sigma$ (and Q after x and Q after $x\sigma$) can perform one or the other of these actions.

However, P' and Q', defined as follows, and depicted in Figure 5.4, are not testing equivalent.

$P' := hide\ w\ in\ P$ and $Q' := hide\ w\ in\ Q$

It is important to note that after the trace x, P' can refuse y and it can refuse z (although, it cannot refuse the two together), but Q' can refuse neither action.

As we discuss in Section 7.2.6, it turns out that a catastrophic interpretation of divergence (as found in CSP) does not suffer substitutivity difficulties in hiding contexts such as these. Thus, in this sense, enforcement of Kooman's fair abstraction property [8] leads to a theoretically less clean handling of divergent behaviour. Although, there may, nonetheless, be good conceptual reasons for sticking with the property and indeed we believe there are such reasons.

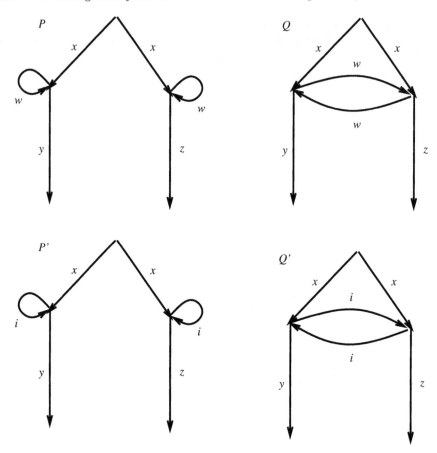

Fig. 5.4. Testing Equivalence Is Not a Congruence in the Hiding Context

5.1.6 Nonequivalence Development Relations

A number of development relations based on trace-refusals semantics that are not equivalences have been defined. We consider three of these, here: *conf*, *red* and *ext*. These were defined by Brinksma and co-workers [50], [52] and [53]. We consider each of these relations in turn.

5.1.6.1 Conformance

This relation was devised as a formal instantiation of the conformance testing process. It is defined as follows.

Definition 34   (Conformance)
$\forall B, B' \in pbLOTOS,\ B\ conf\ B'\ \textit{iff}\ \forall \sigma \in [\![B']\!]_{tr}\ ,\ Ref_B(\sigma) \subseteq Ref_{B'}(\sigma).$

Thus, B conforms to B' if and only if, for the traces of B', B cannot refuse more than B'; i.e. it cannot deadlock in an environment that B' cannot. Thus, deadlock properties are not worsened for any trace in B'.

Brinksma argues that *conf* corresponds to a restricted notion of testing, which is practically feasible to realise. In accordance with this view, *conf* has been used as the basis of much work on test case generation from LOTOS specifications [50].

Unfortunately, the properties of the relation are not very pleasing. In particular, *conf* is not transitive. As an illustration, consider the specifications:

$$P_1 := x\,;\, stop \,[\!]\, i\,;\, y\,;\, stop \quad,\quad P_2 := i\,;\, y\,;\, stop \quad \text{and}$$
$$P_3 := x\,;\, z\,;\, stop \,[\!]\, i\,;\, y\,;\, stop$$

We claim that P_1 *conf* P_2 and P_2 *conf* P_3, but $\neg(P_1$ *conf* $P_3)$. We can justify these as follows.

- P_1 *conf* P_2 follows because the traces of P_2 are $\{\ \epsilon\ ,\ y\ \}$ and the refusals after both are equal: after ϵ they both refuse all actions apart from y and after y they both refuse all actions.
- To show that P_2 *conf* P_3 holds, consider the traces of P_3: $\{\ \epsilon\ ,\ y\ ,\ x\ ,\ xz\ \}$. The interesting traces are those that are not in $Tr(P_2)$; i.e. x and xz. However, refusals are defined in such a way that after a trace that a behaviour cannot perform, the empty set is refused; i.e. $\mathit{Ref}_{P_2}(x) = \mathit{Ref}_{P_2}(xz) = \emptyset$. Thus, the refusals of P_2 after x and xz are trivially a subset of the refusals of P_3 after the same traces.
- However, $\neg(P_1$ *conf* $P_3)$ because P_1 can refuse z after the trace x, but P_3 cannot refuse z after the same trace.

Another aspect of the *conf* relation is that it does not induce an equivalence in the manner that preorder refinement relations do. In particular, the relation *confSy* (standing for *conf* symmetric) defined as

$$confSy = conf \cap conf^{-1}$$

is not an equivalence. In particular, P_1, P_2 and P_3 above serve as a counterexample to *confSy* being transitive. This is because P_1 *confSy* P_2 and P_2 *confSy* P_3, but $\neg(P_1$ *confSy* $P_3)$.

However, an equivalence relation can be defined, if we use our original, more general, formulation of $\preceq_{dv}$; i.e.

$$B_1 \preceq_{conf} B_2 \quad \textit{iff} \quad \{\, B_1' \mid B_1'\ conf\ B_1\,\} = \{\, B_2' \mid B_2'\ conf\ B_2\,\}$$

This was justified in the general case in Section 3.1.2.

It should be clear from this discussion that *conf* is a poorly behaved relation. However, it should also be pointed out that its role is somewhat different from that of the other development relations. In fact, it has been argued that conformance testing is not an inherently transitive process, because it concerns the one-step mapping from a specification to a real physical implementation. Thus, incremental development is not an issue. The term implementation relation is often associated with development relations such as *conf*, which are concerned with relating specifications directly to real implementations [120].

5.1.6.2 Reduction

Probably the most important of the LOTOS trace-refusals development relations is reduction, *red*. This is an almost direct import from CSP, where the corresponding relation is simply called refinement; we discuss how this relates to reduction in Section 7.2.6.

Reduction is defined as follows.

Definition 35   (Reduction)
$\forall B, B' \in pbLOTOS$, B *red* B' iff,

- $[\![B]\!]_{tr} \subseteq [\![B']\!]_{tr} \ \wedge \ \forall \sigma \in [\![B']\!]_{tr} , \ Ref_B(\sigma) \subseteq Ref_{B'}(\sigma)$,

- or, alternatively, $B \leq_{tr} B' \ \wedge \ B$ *conf* B'.

Reduction requires that, in addition to deadlocks not being added, traces are not added. Thus, a concrete behaviour is a reduction of an abstract behaviour as long as the concrete behaviour does not perform traces that the abstract behaviour cannot and after any trace of the abstract behaviour, the concrete behaviour cannot deadlock in an environment where the abstract behaviour cannot deadlock.

Reduction can also be thought of in terms of reducing nondeterminism; a reduction cannot add nondeterminism to that defined in the abstract specification. This is in accordance with the view that nondeterminism is a device applicable to abstract stages in specification and the observation that it is generally viewed as bad if implementations contain nondeterminism (although, see [185]).

We can give the following examples of reduction. Consider the behaviours:

- $P_1 := x\,;\, stop$
- $P_2 := x\,;\, stop\ [\!]\ x\,;\, y\,;\, stop$
- $P_3 := i\,;\, x\,;\, stop\ [\!]\ y\,;\, stop$
- $P_4 := x\,;\, stop\ [\!]\ y\,;\, stop$
- $P_5 := i\,;\, x\,;\, stop\ [\!]\ i\,;\, y\,;\, stop$
- $P_6 := y\,;\, stop$

The following relationships can be determined,

$$P_1 \ red \ P_2 \quad P_1 \ red \ P_3 \quad P_4 \ red \ P_3 \quad P_4 \ red \ P_5 \quad P_3 \ red \ P_5$$
$$\neg(P_1 \ red \ P_4) \quad \neg(P_6 \ red \ P_3) \quad \neg(P_3 \ red \ P_4) \quad \neg(P_5 \ red \ P_3) \quad \neg(P_5 \ red \ P_4)$$

In addition, the following result is clear.

Proposition 8
red is a preorder (in fact, it is a partial order with identity te).

Proof
Reflexivity: clear from properties of subsetting. Antisymmetry: P_1 *red* P_2 and
P_2 *red* P_1 if and only if P_1 *te* P_2. Transitivity: assuming P_1 *red* P_2 and
P_2 *red* P_3, then, clearly, $[\![\, P_1\,]\!]_{tr} \subseteq [\![\, P_3\,]\!]_{tr}$ by transitivity of subsetting. But,
in addition, $\forall \sigma \in [\![\, P_3\,]\!]_{tr}$ if $\sigma \in [\![\, P_1\,]\!]_{tr}$ then $\sigma \in [\![\, P_2\,]\!]_{tr}$ (because, P_1 *red* P_2)
and so, $Ref_{P_1}(\sigma) \subseteq Ref_{P_2}(\sigma) \subseteq Ref_{P_3}(\sigma)$, as required; otherwise, $\sigma \notin [\![\, P_1\,]\!]_{tr}$
and then, $Ref_{P_1}(\sigma) = \emptyset$ and, thus, trivially, $Ref_{P_1}(\sigma) \subseteq Ref_{P_3}(\sigma)$, as required.
The result follows.
$\bigcirc$

However, unfortunately, reduction is not a precongruence. Choice and hiding
are the offending contexts once again. This said, reduction is the most important, well behaved and widely accepted of the nonequivalence development
relations introduced in this section.

Subject to the handling of divergence, reduction can be shown to correspond, not only to the CSP refinement relation, but also *Must Testing* [89].

5.1.6.3 Extension

Implicit in the definition of reduction is the condition that traces cannot be
added during refinement. Adding traces can be viewed as adding behaviour;
i.e. extending the possible computations that a specification can perform.
There are development situations in which such addition of functionality is
required. For example, a subclass in an OO-type system may add operations
to the interface of a superclass. Operations can be interpreted as actions in
process calculi and, thus, the relationship of the subclass to the superclass is
one of adding traces [33]. We return to these issues in Section 5.4.

The extension relation is a direct realisation of this idea of extending behaviour.

Definition 36   (Extension)
$\forall B, B' \in pbLOTOS$, B *ext* B' *iff,*

- $[\![\, B\,]\!]_{tr} \supseteq [\![\, B'\,]\!]_{tr} \; \wedge \; \forall \sigma \in [\![\, B'\,]\!]_{tr}$, $Ref_B(\sigma) \subseteq Ref_{B'}(\sigma)$,

- *or alternatively,* $B \geq_{tr} B' \; \wedge \; B$ *conf* B'.

Thus, a concrete behaviour is an extension of an abstract one if and only if the
concrete behaviour does not contain fewer traces than the abstract behaviour,
and, for the traces of the abstract behaviour, the concrete behaviour does not
add deadlocks. Thus, behaviour can be extended, but subject to the normal
refusals property being preserved, as reflected in the *conf* relation.

As an illustration of the relation, consider the following behaviours.

- $P_1 := x\,;\,y\,;\,stop$
- $P_2 := x\,;\,y\,;\,stop\ []\ z\,;\,stop$
- $P_3 := x\,;\,y\,;\,stop\ []\ x\,;\,stop$
- $P_4 := x\,;\,y\,;\,stop\ []\ i\,;\,z\,;\,stop$

The following properties hold,

$$P_2\ ext\ P_1\quad,\quad \neg(P_3\ ext\ P_1)\quad,\quad \neg(P_4\ ext\ P_1)\quad,\quad P_2\ ext\ P_4$$

The first of these relationships shows that extension typically allows the addition of branches. An alternative behaviour, $z\,;\,stop$, has been added in P_2 and placed at a choice point. Thus, P_2 could behave as P_1 or it could behave as the added behaviour. It is important to note though that this extension does not add nondeterminism; in particular, x cannot be refused after the empty trace. This is in contrast to P_3 and P_4, which although they do not reduce the traces of P_1, they do add nondeterminism. Specifically, after performing x, y can be refused by P_3, but it could not be refused after x by P_1 and P_4 can refuse x after the empty trace.

So, extension allows behaviour to be added, as long as nondeterminism is not added, as this would invalidate the refusals constraint. Unfortunately, extension is also not a precongruence. The offending contexts are choice and hiding once again. Although, ext is a preorder.

Proposition 9
ext is a preorder (in fact, it is a partial order with identity te).

Proof
Reflexivity: clear from properties of subsetting. Antisymmetry: $P_1\ ext\ P_2$ and $P_2\ ext\ P_1$ if and only if $P_1\ te\ P_2$. Transitivity: assuming $P_1\ ext\ P_2$ and $P_2\ ext\ P_3$, then, clearly, $[\![\,P_1\,]\!]_{tr} \supseteq [\![\,P_3\,]\!]_{tr}$ by transitivity of subsetting. But, in addition, $\forall \sigma \in [\![\,P_3\,]\!]_{tr},\ \sigma \in [\![\,P_1\,]\!]_{tr}$ (because $[\![\,P_1\,]\!]_{tr} \supseteq [\![\,P_3\,]\!]_{tr}$, as just verified) and so, $Ref_{P_1}(\sigma) \subseteq Ref_{P_2}(\sigma) \subseteq Ref_{P_3}(\sigma)$, as required. The result follows.
○

5.1.7 Explorations of Congruence

An approach similar to that used to obtain observational congruence from weak bisimulation can be applied to the trace-refusals relations. This is done by restricting the initial behaviour of related specifications. As an example, we consider stable testing equivalence.

Definition 37
$B\ te^s\ B'$ iff $B\ te\ B' \wedge stable(B) \Longleftrightarrow stable(B')$, where $stable(B)$ iff $B \xrightarrow{\ i\ }\!\!\!\!/\ $.

So, te^s is a stronger equivalence than testing equivalence; it adds the condition that, either both specifications must be stable, or both specifications must be unstable. Behaviours are stable if and only if they do not offer any initial i transitions.

A consequence of this is that the following two behaviours are not viewed as equivalent under te^s,

x ; $stop$ and i ; x ; $stop$

Definitions similar to te^s can be given for red and ext. The induced relations are called red^s and ext^s.

However, as Leduc demonstrated [120], and we discussed in Section 5.1.5, hiding contexts that create divergence can also fail to be substitutive. Thus, te^s is also not a congruence. The interested reader is referred to [120] for further discussion of this point.

5.1.8 Summary and Discussion

Trace-refusals semantics offer a model of semantic behaviour that intuitively sits between trace semantics and bisimulation semantics. In particular, the induced equivalence, testing equivalence, is weaker than weak bisimulation and has been argued to be a more realistic instantiation of observational identity.

The trace-refusals development relations are more discriminating than their trace counterparts. This is because they preserve liveness properties as well as safety properties. Remember trace semantics only preserve safety properties.

However, the LOTOS development relations induced from trace-refusals, although similar in spirit to the CSP failures relations, are in fact different. A major reason for this is that trace-refusals employ a (CCS-like) noncatastrophic interpretation of divergent behaviour. We elaborate on this issue in Chapter 7.

Tool support for LOTOS-style trace-refusals semantics is not, to the authors' knowledge, currently available. One reason for this is that bisimulation equivalences have dominated verification strategies for LOTOS specifications, as indicated by the power and maturity of the CADP tool set; see Section 3.4. However, CSP does boast a powerful refusals-based tool environment: the FDR (Failures Divergences Refinement) suite [171]. Although, as should now be clear, differences between CSP and LOTOS, in particular, in respect of handling divergence, mean that LOTOS specifications cannot be mapped to this framework without a good deal of care.

5.2 Testing Justification for Trace-refusals Semantics

Testing theory is extremely rich. In fact, it is possible to place the spectrum of process calculi correctness relations into a hierachy of strength;[2] i.e. in terms of their level of discrimination, and this is what we consider in the next section (5.3). The relative strengths of particular correctness relations are tied to the intrusive capabilities of the tester to observe the specification.

In this section, we consider a notion of testing in which the tester has the power of a standard process calculus process, here a pbLOTOS process. In this respect we follow the work of Brinksma and Scollo [52], who were, in turn, inspired by the pioneering work of De Nicola and Hennessy [153].

The following results justify this intuitive interpretation of this form of testing.

Theorem 5.2.
For all pbLOTOS processes P_1 and P_2, the following are equivalent.

1. $P_1 \; red \; P_2$,   *and,*

2. $\forall P \in pbLOTOS, \; G \subseteq Act, \; \sigma \in \mathcal{T}$,
$$(P_1 \; |[G]| \; P \stackrel{\sigma}{\Longrightarrow} \approx stop \; \; implies \; \; P_2 \; |[G]| \; P \stackrel{\sigma}{\Longrightarrow} \approx stop).$$

Proof
Brinksma and Scollo [52] provide a proof of this result with the assumption that $[\![P_1]\!]_{tr} \subseteq [\![P_2]\!]_{tr}$. Thus, all we need to consider is the situation in which $[\![P_1]\!]_{tr} \not\subseteq [\![P_2]\!]_{tr}$. So, take $\sigma \in [\![P_1]\!]_{tr} \setminus [\![P_2]\!]_{tr}$. Now, $P_1 \; red \; P_2$ must be false, by definition. However, in addition, condition (2) fails, because, if we take G to be all the labels of P_1 and P to be the process that performs the sequence of actions encapsulated by σ and then stops, then $P_1 \; |[G]| \; P \stackrel{\sigma}{\Longrightarrow} \approx stop$, but $P_2 \; |[G]| \; P \stackrel{\sigma}{\Longrightarrow} \approx stop$ fails to hold, because $P_2 \; |[G]| \; P \stackrel{\sigma}{\nRightarrow}$. Thus, conditions (1) and (2) will always both be false when $[\![P_1]\!]_{tr} \not\subseteq [\![P_2]\!]_{tr}$ and therefore, the two conditions are also equivalent in this situation. The result follows.
◯

Corollary 5.3.
For all pbLOTOS processes P_1 and P_2, the following are equivalent.

1. $P_1 \; te \; P_2$,   *and,*

2. $\forall P \in pbLOTOS, \; G \subseteq Act, \; \sigma \in \mathcal{T}$,
$$(P_1 \; |[G]| \; P \stackrel{\sigma}{\Longrightarrow} \approx stop \iff P_2 \; |[G]| \; P \stackrel{\sigma}{\Longrightarrow} \approx stop).$$

Proof
Follows from Theorem 5.2 and the fact that $te = red \cap red^{-1}$.
◯

---

[2]Although, to date, the emphasis has been placed on interleaving theories.

In these results, we use the following concepts that have been previously introduced, $||[G]||$ is the LOTOS parallel composition operator, $\approx$ is weak bisimulation equivalence, *stop* is the deadlock process and σ is a trace of observable actions. In addition, relation composition is denoted by juxtaposition.[3] Theorem 5.2 states that P_1 reduces P_2 if and only if, for all possible tester processes (denoted P), if P_1 can perform a trace σ and then deadlock, then, under the control of the same tester, P_2 could also have performed σ and then deadlocked. Thus, even more informally, when observed / interacted with, P_1 does not add any new deadlocks to those that could already arise from P_2.

Furthermore, in a similar vein, Corollary 5.3 states that P_1 and P_2 are testing equivalent if and only if, for any tester process and trace, one will perform the trace and deadlock if and only if the other will do the same. Thus, when observed / interacted with, P_1 and P_2 have the same deadlocks.

The importance of these results is that they link semantic models to the capacity of pbLOTOS processes to observe other pbLOTOS processes. For example, Corollary 5.3 ensures that, if two processes are testing equivalent, then no process (when run as an observer) can tell them apart. Thus, *red* and *te* characterise the testing power of the behavioural specification notation itself! Because of this natural intuitive characterisation, testing equivalence has a claim to being the most appealing of the LOTOS equivalence relations, as does reduction in respect of nonequivalence development relations.

The following (more restrictive) result characterises extension in a similar manner.

Proposition 10
For all processes P_1 and P_2 such that $[\![P_1]\!]_{tr} \supseteq [\![P_2]\!]_{tr}$ and assuming that $\mathcal{L}(Q)$ denotes the labels of process Q, the following are equivalent.

1. P_1 ext P_2,   and,

2. $\forall P \in pbLOTOS, G \supseteq \mathcal{L}(P_2), \sigma \in [\![P_2]\!]_{tr}$,
$$P_1 \,||[G]|\, P \overset{\sigma}{\Longrightarrow} \approx stop \text{ implies } P_2 \,||[G]|\, P \overset{\sigma}{\Longrightarrow} \approx stop.$$

Proof
See [52].
○

Thus, extension only ensures that deadlocks are not added when restricting to traces of the abstract specification.

5.3 Testing Theory in General and the Linear Time – Branching Time Spectrum

As should be becoming clear, testing theory is a rich and extensively investigated branch of concurrency theory [2,153,192]. Testing theory systematically

---

[3]That is, $S \,||[G]|\, P \overset{\sigma}{\Longrightarrow} \approx stop$ means $\exists Q \,.\, S \,||[G]|\, P \overset{\sigma}{\Longrightarrow} Q \wedge Q \approx stop$.

considers how the behaviour of processes can be observed by their environment / observer. Such observations naturally yield preorders and equivalences between processes. Two processes P and Q might be related by such a preorder if all the observations that can be made of P can also be made of Q; similarly, the processes might be related by equivalence if they generate the same observations.

5.3.1 Sequence-based Testing

Testing relations can be characterised by comparing the set of *observations* that can be made of a process. The observations that characterise reduction and testing equivalence are trace-refusals. This is easiest to see if the trace-refusals of a process are expressed (isomorphically) as a set of failure pairs, the mapping, *toF*, introduced in Section 5.1.2, performs this transformation. Thus, a failure (σ, X) of a process indicates an observation in which a sequence of actions (corresponding to the trace) was observed, followed by the process deadlocking in response to an environment that attempts to perform the set of actions X. Using *toF*, it is not hard to show the following.

$P_1 \, red \, P_2$ if and only if every failure of P_1 is also a failure of P_2

$P_1 \, te \, P_2$ if and only if the failures of P_1 are equal to those of P_2

In fact, trace-refusals are just one class of observation and we can explore testing in a more general context by viewing processes as closed systems with some form of interface to the outside world. Then, the process is observed through this interface. By varying the nature of the interface, one can conceptually vary the "blackness" of the box. Thus, some classes of interface offer a very limited capacity to interact with the process, whereas others allow highly invasive interaction.

In this way, different notions of testing can be obtained, each supporting a different level of invasiveness and more important, each can be characterised by a different style of observation, yielding different preorders and equivalences. For example, in *trace preorder* and *trace equivalence* the observations are traces, the observations in *failure traces* are traces with failures information throughout, and the observations in *readiness preorder* and *equivalence* consider the actions that may be accepted rather than those that may be refused. Furthermore, this spectrum of testing preorders and equivalences can be placed in a hierarchy of strength; see [192].

We use the term *sequence-based testing* to embrace all forms of testing that yield linear sequences of observations, which, in all but the pure traces case, are entwined or terminated with some refusal or ready information. Thus, this form of testing corresponds to the linear time portion of the linear time – branching time spectrum.

5.3.2 Tree-based Testing

An alternative way to relate processes is to match transitions in the inductive style of (bi)simulation relations; see Section 3.3.3. This yields a further spectrum of preorders and equivalences, e.g. simulation, ready simulation, weak and strong bisimulation, and the strength of these relations can be compared to the sequence based testing relations, yielding an enlarged hierarchy of relations; see [192] again.

Here, in fact, we concentrate on equivalences. This is because preorders have not been extensively studied in the (bi)simulation setting, which is partially because the natural preorders that arise are not always that well behaved, especially in respect of preservation of deadlock properties. In fact, this aspect of (bi)simulation relations was alluded to in Section 3.3.3.2.

Testing categorizations of these simulation relations can also be given. However, because these relations are more discriminating with regard to the branching structure of labelled transition systems, sequence-based testing is not sufficient; rather observations have to be constructed as trees. This can be viewed as giving the environment the capability that, at any time during the run of a process, an arbitrary (but finite) number of copies of the process, in its current state, can be taken and all observed independently. This copying yields the branches in the observation tree. We call such testing *tree-based testing*, which comprises the branching time portion of the linear time – branching time spectrum.

Ready Simulation Testing. As an example of tree-based testing, we consider ready simulation testing. The resulting observations of the behaviour of processes are constructed using a simple modal logic, which codes up observation trees.

Definition 38 *The logic, denoted RSL, is called Ready Simulation Logic and an arbitrary formula ϕ is characterised by the following syntax,*

$$\phi := True \mid \phi \wedge \phi \mid a\phi \mid X$$

where $a \in Act \cup \{i, \delta\}$ and $X \subseteq Act \cup \{i, \delta\}$.

Note that the ready simulation framework we consider here is *strong* and thus, internal actions are treated identically to observable actions. However, this framework could easily be adapted to yield a *weak* interpretation (in the same manner that weak bisimulation adapts strong bisimulation in respect of the handling of internal evolutions).

The elements of the logic are straightforward. In particular, we can assert the statement *True*, which any process satisfies and conjunction is also inherited from propositional logic. However, we can also make statements that are specific to transition systems. That is, $a\phi$ holds over a process that can perform an a and reach a state where ϕ holds and a process satisfies X if all the actions in X are immediately offered. The element X is often termed a *ready set* (or an acceptance set), because it characterises the set of actions that a process is ready to perform / accept.

As an example of ready simulation, the following are some of the observations that can be performed by both the behaviours P and Q,

$$P := x\,;\,x\,;\,y\,;\,stop \;[]\; x\,;\,x\,;\,z\,;\,stop \quad \text{and}$$
$$Q := x\,;\,(\,x\,;\,y\,;\,stop \;[]\; x\,;\,z\,;\,stop\,)$$

which were first highlighted in Section 5.1.1 (see also Figure 5.1) as archetypal processes that are distinguished by bisimulation relations and not distinguished by trace-refusals semantics,

$$xxyTrue \quad xx\{y\} \quad x\{x\} \quad xxTrue \wedge xTrue \quad xx\{y\} \wedge xTrue$$

The generalisation of sequence-based testing arises because, not only can we express traces, the action sequences, and ready / acceptance properties,[4] the set of actions X, we can also express branching, using $\wedge$.

The capability of a process to yield an observation is expressed using logical satisfaction, $\models_{RSL} \subseteq pbLOTOS \times RSL$. Thus, $R \models_{RSL} \phi$ means intuitively that, when tested, the transition system $[\![R]\!]_{lts}$ (see Section 3.3.2.2) can exhibit the observable behaviour expressed by ϕ. Satisfaction is defined inductively over the structure of formulae, as follows,

$$R \models_{RSL} True$$
$$R \models_{RSL} \phi \wedge \psi \quad \text{iff} \quad R \models_{RSL} \phi \text{ and } R \models_{RSL} \psi$$
$$R \models_{RSL} a\phi \quad \text{iff} \quad \exists R' \text{ s.t. } (R \xrightarrow{a} R' \text{ and } R' \models_{RSL} \phi)$$
$$R \models_{RSL} X \quad \text{iff} \quad out(R) = X$$

where $out(R) = \{\, a \mid \exists R' .\, R \xrightarrow{a} R' \,\}$. Using $\models_{RSL}$, we define the mapping $S : pbLOTOS \rightarrow \mathcal{P}(RSL)$, which yields the set of formulae that a particular process satisfies; i.e. $S(R) = \{\, \phi \mid R \models_{RSL} \phi \,\}$. In other words, $S(R)$ is the set of all observations that R can exhibit.

Now, because ready simulation employs tree-based testing, it should be able to distinguish P and Q (highlighted above and in Section 5.1.1) and indeed it does. For example,

$$Q \models_{RSL} \phi, \quad \text{but} \quad P \not\models_{RSL} \phi, \quad \text{where} \quad \phi = x(xyTrue \wedge xzTrue)$$

In fact, it can be shown (see [192]) that this testing characterisation yields the same equivalence as that highlighted inductively in Definition 14 of Chapter 3; i.e.,

$$P_1 \sim_R P_2 \quad \text{iff} \quad S(P_1) = S(P_2)$$

That is, $P_1 \sim_R P_2$ (i.e. P_1 and P_2 are ready simulation equivalent) if and only if, the observations of P_1 and P_2 are the same.

---

[4]Note, tree-based testing formulations that use refusals, rather than ready sets can also be given; see [192].

Bisimulation. The move from sequence-based testing to tree-based testing corresponded to an increased capacity of the tester to observe the system. That is, additionally, the observer could, at any time during the investigation of the system, take a finite, but arbitrarily large, number of copies of the process under test (in its current state) and observe them all separately. This capacity is afforded by the inclusion of conjunction in the modal observation language *RSL*.

However, bisimulations are even more discriminating than ready simulations; see Proposition 5 of Section 3.3.3.2. What then is the further testing capacity that comes with a move to this setting?

Well, it turns out that what is required is the additional capacity to perform what has been called *global testing*. The key aspect that global testing gives is the capability to selectively explore all branches of a nondeterministic choice. This amounts to a significant increase in the invasiveness of the testing process, because, in this setting, the observer really can look inside the black box and view the taking of internal decisions. The unrealistic nature of such testing is illustrated by the fact that, when describing this form of testing, Milner drew an analogy with the famously unpredictable issue of forecasting the weather, according to which he argued that global testing assumes the capability to control the weather [145]!

In terms of modal (observation) logics, global testing adds to *RSL* the capacity to take negations, which yields Hennessy-Milner logic (*HML*) [90]. For example, the following two processes,

$$T := x \, ; \, x \, ; \, y \, ; \, stop \, [] \, x \, ; \, (\, x \, ; \, y \, ; \, stop \, [] \, x \, ; \, z \, ; \, stop\,) \quad \text{and}$$
$$U := x \, ; \, (\, x \, ; \, y \, ; \, stop \, [] \, x \, ; \, z \, ; \, stop\,),$$

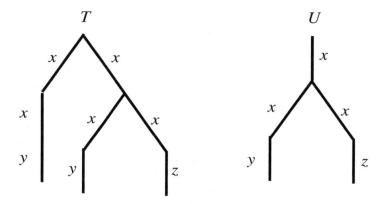

Fig. 5.5. Ready Simulation Equivalent, but Not Bisimulation Equivalent Processes

which are depicted in Figure 5.5, are distinguished by *HML*, but not by *RSL*.[5]
A formula / observation that distinguishes the two is as follows.

$$T \models_{HML} \psi, \quad \text{but} \quad U \not\models_{HML} \psi, \quad \text{where} \quad \psi = x(xyTrue \wedge \neg(xzTrue))$$

The fact that *HML* distinguishes more processes than *RSL* is, of course, consistent with Proposition 5 of Section 3.3.3.2.

5.4 Applications of Trace-refusals Relations in Distributed Systems

Testing theory in general and the trace-refusals development relations in particular have been used to investigate the theoretical properties of modern distributed systems. Providing formal frameworks for such domains has been a major objective of recent formal methods research. This section gives a brief pointer to some of the work in this area. Bowman and Derrick [41] and Bowman [33] give reviews of this field that are broader in scope than we present here.

We consider three topics in the general area of LOTOS testing theory applied to modern Object-Oriented (OO) distributed systems: (1) a basic relating of OO concepts to LOTOS; (2) the behavioural subtyping problem; and (3) viewpoint models of distributed systems and consistency-checking. These are discussed in the next three sections. One reason for including this material is to illustrate application of the theory highlighted in this chapter.

5.4.1 Relating OO Concepts to LOTOS

It is worth clarifying how LOTOS specifications relate to OO concepts. This section highlights some basic relationships.

Class. A class describes the common behaviour of a set of objects. As noted by a number of authors (e.g. [70, 173, 180]), in LOTOS, the natural counterpart to a class is a process definition. This describes the common behaviour of instantiations of the process definition.

Object. In OO programming, objects are instantiations of a class. Thus, a simple interpretation of class instantiation in LOTOS is as process instantiation.

However, more sophisticated interpretations of object instantiation can also be given. For example, [61, 173] interpret instantiation as the LOTOS implementation relation *conf*. Thus, any process that conforms to the specification of a class is seen as an instantiation of the class. Although, as discussed

---

[5]Note, the pattern of nondeterminism in T and U that leads to this result is effectively the same as that to be found in R_5 and R_6, which we considered in Section 3.3.3.2 to distinguish $\sim$ and $\sim_R$.

in Section 5.1.6.1, *conf* has a number of undesirable properties as a development relation, in principle, such an interpretation of instantiation is richer and more flexible than simple process instantiation. In particular, when working in a behavioural setting, it seems sensible to interpret instantiation in behavioural terms, rather than as a purely syntactic operation. Although we do not consider this issue of instantiation further here, implicitly, instantiations in our setting are related to their class definition much more strongly than by *conf*, perhaps by testing equivalence.

Operations. The basic units of interaction between objects are operations, also called method invocations, member function calls or feature calls. In process calculi, the basic units of interaction between processes are actions. The affinity between these two concepts is witnessed by the number of workers in this area who have related the two, e.g. [61, 70, 156, 173, 180]

However, it should be pointed out that this similarity may not be exact, because process calculi actions are atomic, whereas, in many OO models, operations have duration. The assumption of atomicity is highly significant in the process calculi setting, because it justifies the modelling of concurrency as interleaving, as discussed in Section 2.3.6.1. Nonatomic interpretations of actions lead to more complex semantic theories. A simplifying assumption that Nierstrasz makes [156] is only to model method requests. Such an assumption effectively justifies an atomic interpretation of actions when modelling operations. In accordance with this majority of workers, we also enforce a simplifying atomic interpretation of actions / operations.

Finally, the parameters of operations may be modelled using LOTOS's data passing attributes, "!" and "?", which are introduced in Section 6.2.4.

Interface. An object-oriented class definition will usually contain a statement of the interface to objects of that class: usually a list of calls that may be made on the objects. The LOTOS equivalent is the set of all nonhidden actions in the process definition.

The above are only the most basic correspondences; there are many more that can be made. For example, Rudkin [173] describes how inheritance and *self* might be introduced into LOTOS and Najm et al [151] consider how object mobility may be obtained. The interested reader is also referred to part IV of [106], which relates OO modelling concepts to LOTOS constructs in the open distributed processing setting [41].

5.4.2 Behavioural Subtyping

The concept of subtyping is familiar from object-oriented programming languages [80]; it is defined as substitutability: type A is a subtype of type B if and only if objects of type A may be used in any situation where an object of type B was expected, without the object's environment being able to tell the difference. Thus, an object of any particular type can *masquerade* as, or stand in for, an object of any of its supertypes. Subtyping is naturally a reflexive and transitive relation; i.e. a preorder.

However, in client–server distributed systems, the state of the art in service matching is signature-based subtyping; see Chapter 11 of [41]. Unfortunately, such matching is not rich enough to ensure the safety of object interactions in a heterogeneous distributed processing environment. For example, two object types may have methods with the same name but quite different meaning. To take a rather frivolous example, consider the analogy of an artist and a cowboy. Both are able to perform an operation "draw", but the results in each case will be rather different! Thus, it is possible that, although signatures match, compatibility, in terms of the behaviour of services, is not obtained. What is actually required is a more powerful interpretation of service matching based on (stronger) *behavioural* notions of subtyping. Here we investigate possible definitions of such *behavioural subtyping* in LOTOS.

Relating OO terms to process calculus terms, the following is a semiformal definition of behavioural subtyping.

> S_1 *is a behavioural subtype of* S_2 *if and only if, any client (tester), using* S_1 *according to any interface (synchronisation set), can only perform a sequence of interactions (a trace) and then refuse to perform further interactions (deadlock), if, when using* S_2 *(with the same interface), the client could observe the same sequence of interactions followed by a deadlock.* [6]

Assuming more explicitly that S_1 and S_2 are LOTOS processes, we can make this definition more precise as follows.

> S_1 *is a behavioural subtype of* S_2 *iff, for all, processes* P, *finite sets of observable actions* G, *and traces* σ, $S_1 \,|[G]|\, P \stackrel{\sigma}{\Longrightarrow}\approx$ stop *implies* $S_2 \,|[G]|\, P \stackrel{\sigma}{\Longrightarrow}\approx$ stop.

In terms of OO, P reflects possible client specifications / program and G reflects the possible interfaces between S_1 and the client; i.e. the actions by which they can communicate.

Thus, it is clear that behavioural subtyping is just a reformulation, in a new context, of the classic testing theory interpretation of when a more concrete process (the subtype) is observationally indistinguishable from a more abstract process (the supertype). Consequently, the results we justified in Section 5.2, can be used to inform our discussion of behavioural subtyping. The choice of this interpretation of testing from within the linear time – branching time spectrum arises because, in the setting being considered here, clients are LOTOS processes. Thus, the capacity of a client to observe a server object is that of a LOTOS tester process.

---

[6]Because we test against all possible clients (and not just those that have a subset of the operations of S_2) we get a strong notion of subtyping. This strength is necessary, e.g. when there is concurrent interaction between objects.

This leaves the question of which exactly of the LOTOS development relations does indeed correspond to behavioural subtyping. From amongst the LOTOS development relations, a direct application of reduction does not in fact yield a sufficient definition of behavioural subtyping. This is because, behavioural subtyping in the OO context allows *extension of functionality*; e.g. a subtype can offer more operations than its supertype.

In the process calculi setting, extending functionality implies addition of traces. However, reduction enforces a trace subsetting property and thus, does not allow functionality to be extended. In response to this observation, a number of previous workers [61, 156, 173] have based their interpretation of subtyping upon extension. However, we argue against using this relation; rather we show how to reinterpret LOTOS specifications in order that reduction is the appropriate relation.

5.4.2.1 Relating LOTOS Relations and Subtyping

In this section, we attempt to locate an interpretation of behavioural subtyping from amongst the existing LOTOS development relations. Firstly, because subtyping is reflexive and transitive, but not symmetric (a symmetric relation would suggest substitutability in both directions, which is too strong), we only consider the preorder relations. This choice rules out the equivalences: weak bisimulation ($\approx$), strong bisimulation ($\sim$), simulation equivalence ($\asymp_{\prec}$), ready simulation equivalence ($\sim_R$) and testing equivalence (te) and the implementation relation, *conf*, which is not transitive.

Trace Subsetting and Supersetting. We first consider trace preorder. This is inappropriate, because it does not allow the subtype to have any more traces than the supertype, which contradicts the extension of functionality involved in subtyping.

An alternative to $\leq_{tr}$ is trace extension: $P_1 \leq_{tre} P_2$ iff $Tr(P_1) \supseteq Tr(P_2)$. This *does* allow new operations to be added and, in fact, is the interpretation of subtyping used in [163]. In Puntigam's work, trace extension serves as a valid check for type safety, where, in this context, type safety ensures that the subtype can understand all operations that the supertype can. However, the relation is not a suitable instantiation of the stronger notion of behavioural subtyping, because it allows deadlocks to be added. For example, if X and Y are defined as

$$X := x\,;\, stop \,[]\, y\,;\, stop$$

$$Y := x\,;\, stop \,[]\, y\,;\, stop \,[]\, i\,;\, stop$$

then $Y \leq_{tre} X$. However, Y is not a behavioural subtype of X. When placed in synchronisation with the process / client $x\,;\, stop$, X will perform action x, but Y may perform x, or may perform an internal action and then deadlock. If Y deadlocks in a situation where X would not, Y is distinguishable from X and is therefore not a behavioural subtype of X. Indeed, of course, the same criticism can be levelled at all solely trace-based correctness relations, including trace preorder.

Reduction. As discussed earlier in this chapter, reduction adds consideration of liveness properties to trace preorder; see Section 5.1.6.2. Indeed, Theorem 5.2 in Section 5.2 ensures the deadlock property we are seeking. However, as discussed earlier, reduction fails to allow extension of functionality. So, as it stands, it is not a suitable instantiation of subtyping.

Extension. Because extension is sensitive to deadlock properties and supports extension of functionality (see Section 5.1.6.3) it appears, at first sight, to be an ideal candidate for the subtyping relation. This is witnessed by the large number of workers who have used it as the basis for definitions of subtyping [61, 156, 173].
Consider two LOTOS processes, X and Y:

$$X := x\,;\, stop \,[]\, y\,;\, stop$$

$$Y := x\,;\, stop \,[]\, y\,;\, stop \,[]\, z\,;\, stop$$

We see that Y *ext* X. Y can perform every trace that X does (and more), and, after any trace that X can perform, X refuses at least everything that Y refuses. Conceptually, Y defines a class that adds an operation to class X, viz. the action z. Thus, extension enables interface enlargement.

Unfortunately, extension does not satisfy our requirements for behavioural subtyping, because it does not guarantee the deadlock property we require. For example, the tester $z\,;\, stop$, with synchronisation set $\{z\}$, serves as a counterexample, because,

$$Y \,|[z]|\, z\,;\, stop \xRightarrow{z}\approx stop \quad \text{but} \quad X \,|[z]|\, z\,;\, stop \overset{z}{\xRightarrow{\hspace{0.6em}}\!\!\!\!\!/}$$

By Proposition 10 in Section 5.2, extension only ensures the deadlock property we require when restricting to traces of the supertype. However, we require that it hold for all traces.

Another way of looking at this problem is that our definition of behavioural subtyping is based on the principle that a subtype must be usable in any situation where the supertype could be used, and not be seen to behave differently. If we have a process that may be an X or a Y, we can detect which it is by trying to perform the action z on the process. If the z is accepted, we have Y, but if z is refused, we must have X. Because it is possible to tell that we have a Y, Y is not a subtype of X.

Interestingly, this problem with extension is one that Nierstrasz has observed [156]. His illustrative example is that of a one-place buffer supertype and a deleting buffer subtype. We can express his example in pbLOTOS as follows,

$$Buf1 := put\,;\, get\,;\, Buf1 \ \text{and} \ DelBuf := put\,;\, (\,get\,;\, DelBuf \,[]\, del\,;\, stop\,)$$

Thus, *DelBuf* behaves as *Buf1* does, but it adds the possibility to delete the element in the buffer and then evolve to deadlock.[7] The tester / client that distinguishes the two is analogous to the LOTOS process:

$T := Prod \,|||\, Cons \,|||\, del\, ;\, stop$ where,

$Prod := put\, ;\, Prod$

$Cons := get\, ;\, Cons$

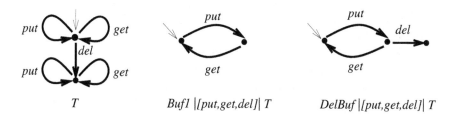

$$T \qquad Buf1 \,|[put,get,del]|\, T \qquad DelBuf \,|[put,get,del]|\, T$$

Fig. 5.6. LOTOS Buffers, with Grey Arrows Denoting Start States

which yields the composite behaviour shown in Figure 5.6. Now, *DelBuf* is clearly an extension of *Buf1*, however, Nierstrasz observes that, with the interface $\{put, get, del\}$ and the tester T, *Buf1* cannot reach a deadlock state, whereas *DelBuf* can. Specifically,

$$DelBuf|[put, get, del]|\, T \xrightarrow{\;put\ del\;}\approx stop \quad \text{but}$$

$$Buf1\,|[put, get, del]|\, T \xrightarrow{\;put\ del\;}\!\!\!\!\!\!\!\!\not\rightarrow$$

In fact, the problem here is exactly the same as that which we highlighted with behaviours X and Y above. Nierstrasz develops a number of concepts such as *request substitutability* and a notion of *restriction* in order to contain this problem. In contrast, our approach is to reject extension as an interpretation of behavioural subtyping.

5.4.2.2 Functionality Extension and Undefined

Undefined Operations in Object–oriented Methods. In order to inform this problem let us consider how functionality extension and particularly adding operations works in OO specification and programming methods.

---

[7]Note that, because we have not yet introduced data passing behaviours, no actual data is associated with these data structures. However, these could be added in a full LOTOS version of these behaviours.

- *OO Specification Techniques.* A number of OO specification notions exist, for example, OO versions of Z, such as Object-Z [41, 172] and ZEST [60], OO versions of VDM, such as VDM++ [115] and Liskov and Wing's notation [41, 130]. Subtyping is not handled in a uniform way throughout these techniques, so, let us focus on the Liskov and Wing approach, which has considered the topic in some depth. In [130] and Chapter 12 of [41], a number of conditions are highlighted, which must all hold in order to ensure subtyping between a pair of specifications. However, the part of the definition that concerns us here is the pre- and postcondition relationship between operations. The definition requires that, for every operation in the supertype, there must exist a corresponding operation in the subtype (although, the subtype may contain extra operations) such that, for corresponding operations, the following holds.

  1. The precondition of the supertype operation implies the precondition of the subtype operation, and
  2. The postcondition of the subtype operation implies the postcondition of the supertype operation.

  Thus, through subtyping, preconditions can be weakened and postconditions can be strengthened. In informal terms, weakening of preconditions enables operations to be applied (i.e. terminate) in more states, whereas strengthening of postconditions reduces nondeterminism. This really does give us what we seek: addition of traces and reduction of refusals when we take subtypes. In spirit, subtyping behaves as does refinement in state-based specification notations such as Z [69].

  It is important to note though that this interpretation of subtyping only works because applying an operation outside its precondition has a very different meaning from the analogous occurrence in process calculi. In process calculi, the analogue of applying an operation outside its precondition is the environment trying to perform an action when it is not currently offered, which has the result *deadlock*. In contrast, in state-based specification notations, such as Z or Liskov and Wing's notation, applying an operation outside its precondition is *undefined*; i.e. is completely unpredictable. In an "operational sense," anything could occur and the choice between these alternatives is nondeterministic.

- *OO Programming Methods.* In strongly typed object-oriented systems, it is not possible to call an operation that is not offered by an object. However, other OO systems produce error messages when a program calls an undefined operation, or result in undefined behaviour (such as the program crashing or giving incorrect results), e.g. Smalltalk [83].

So, both these OO settings give justification for the argument that attempting to apply an operation that is not currently offered should result in undefined behaviour and not deadlock.

Undefinedness and LOTOS. What, then, would be the consequence of adapting LOTOS specifications to behave in an undefined fashion if an action that is not currently offered is performed? Unpredictable behaviour can be modelled in LOTOS using nondeterminism. In fact, we can highlight the following process,

$$\Omega := (\, choice \; x \; in \; Act \cup \{\delta\} \; [] \; i \,; x \,; \Omega \,) \; [] \; (\, i \,; stop \,)$$

where $choice \; x \; in \; \{\, x_1 \,, \ldots, x_n \,\} \; [] \; B = B[x_1/x] \; [] \; \ldots \; [] \; B[x_n/x]$ and $B[y/z]$ denotes B with all occurrences of z replaced by y.[8] Ω offers a completely nondeterministic behaviour; at every point in its evolution it could offer any action and refuse any set of actions. Because (1) $Tr(\Omega) = (Act \cup \{\delta\})^*$ and (2) $\forall \sigma \in (Act \cup \{\delta\})^*$, $Ref_\Omega(\sigma) = \mathcal{P}(Act \cup \{\delta\})$, we know that Ω is at the top of the reduction preorder: every behaviour is a reduction of it.[9]

It turns out that we are able to use reduction as the subtyping relation if the LOTOS definitions of our objects' behaviours are modified using Ω. We show how the modification is done with two examples.

Example 1. A one-place buffer, *Buf1*, was defined earlier. A two-place buffer may be defined as follows.

$$Buf2 := \; put \,; Buf2a \qquad Buf2a := \; get \,; Buf2 \; [] \; put \,; get \,; Buf2a$$

The labelled transition systems corresponding to *Buf1* and *Buf2* are given on the left side in Figure 5.7. For these definitions, $\mathcal{L} = \{put, get\}$.

We would like the two-place buffer to be a subtype of the one-place buffer. Notice that, for the same reasons that we highlighted in our earlier example, as they stand, the two-place buffer is not a subtype of the one-place buffer. To achieve this, we modify the two processes as shown in the right-hand labelled transition systems of Figure 5.7.

We have added transitions such that every node has at least one transition leading away from it for every possible action in $\mathcal{L}$. Following any of the transitions we have added, the process evolves to Ω (this is in fact a relatively standard technique in process calculi, which is used to enable parts of specifications to be extended when refining; see, for example, [119]).

Using the fact that any behaviour reduces Ω, these two processes are now related in the way we wish. With the addition of undefined behaviour, *Buf2* is both a reduction and a subtype of *Buf1*. To justify this, firstly observe that the traces of T(*Buf2*) and T(*Buf1*) (we define the mapping T, that adds undefined behaviour shortly) are the same; i.e. $\mathcal{L}^*$. This is because our transformation has ensured that, at any state, each process "may" perform any action in $\mathcal{L}$. Secondly, observe that, for any trace in $\mathcal{L}^*$, the refusals of T(*Buf2*) are a subset of those of T(*Buf1*). Informally, T(*Buf1*) and T(*Buf2*) have identical refusals apart from those for traces of the form $\rho \, put \, put \, \sigma$, where, $\sigma \in \mathcal{L}^*$

---

[8] Actually, Ω enables δ to arise directly in action prefix (i.e. $i \,; \delta \,; \Omega$), which is not strictly allowed in LOTOS, but this abuse of notation does not cause problems. Also, this choice notation is discussed in some depth in Section 6.1.

[9] Although, Ω does not uniquely characterise the top of the reduction preorder. See [38] for a fuller discussion of this issue.

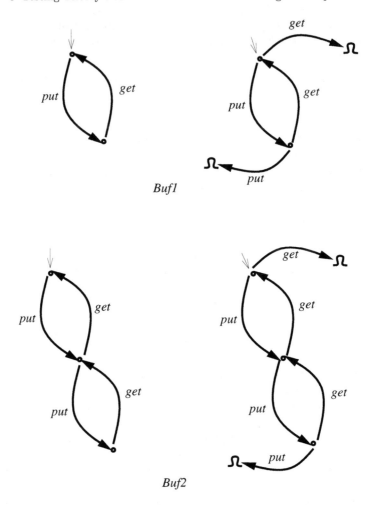

Fig. 5.7. *Buf1* and *Buf2* Without and with Undefined Added and Start States Marked with Gray Arrows

and $\rho \in \{\epsilon\} \cup \{\rho_0 \ldots \rho_n \mid n \in \mathbb{N} \wedge \forall i (0 \le i \le n) . \rho_i = put\,get\,\}$. For such traces, $\mathrm{T}(Buf1)$ will have evolved to undefined, and will thus refuse everything, whereas $\mathrm{T}(Buf2)$ may still be performing defined behaviour, in which case it will refuse nothing. In addition, $\mathrm{T}(Buf1)$ is not a reduction / subtype of $\mathrm{T}(Buf2)$ because, for example, $\mathrm{T}(Buf1)$ can perform the trace *put put* and then refuse anything, whereas, after the same trace, $\mathrm{T}(Buf2)$ cannot refuse anything.

Example 2. Interestingly, using the label set $\{put, get, del\}$, when transformed, *DelBuf* will be a subtype of *Buf1*. This is because, in either of its defined states, the transformed *Buf1* can perform a *del* and evolve to Ω. This contrasts with the approach taken in [156], where Nierstrasz attempts to develop conditions that show that, in their untransformed form, *DelBuf* is not a subtype of *Buf1*.

5.4.2.3 Adding Undefinedness to LOTOS Specifications

Transforming Specifications. Having introduced the concept of undefined behaviour we have to consider how to add this behaviour to LOTOS specifications in an automated way. Our approach is to take the labelled transition system of a LOTOS process and derive a new transition relation, which we denote,

$$\overset{a}{\nrightarrow}.$$

This new relation will add states and transitions that reflect the required undefined behaviour. Where $\mathcal{L}$ is the label set of the specification, we generate the relation that satisfies the inference rules:

$$R1 : \frac{P \xrightarrow{a} P', \quad a \in \mathcal{L} \cup \{\delta, i\}}{P \overset{a}{\nrightarrow} P'} \qquad R2 : \frac{x \in (\mathcal{L} \cup \{\delta\}) \setminus initials(P)}{P \overset{x}{\nrightarrow} \Omega}$$

$$R3 : \frac{x \in \mathcal{L} \cup \{\delta\}}{\Omega \overset{i}{\nrightarrow} x ; \Omega} \qquad R4 : \frac{-}{x ; \Omega \overset{x}{\nrightarrow} \Omega} \qquad R5 : \frac{-}{\Omega \overset{i}{\nrightarrow} stop}$$

where $initials(P) = \{ x \in \mathcal{L} \cup \{\delta\} \mid \exists P' . P \xrightarrow{x} P' \}$. $R1$ ensures that the new relation contains the relation $\longrightarrow$. $R2$ adds the possibility to evolve to Ω when applying an action that is not currently offered. Rules $R3$, $R4$ and $R5$ code up the behaviour of the undefined process Ω.

Nondeterminism. These inference rules define a simple means to add undefinedness to a labelled transition system. For deterministic processes, the consequences of applying these rules are very straightforward. For example, the rules will map the two labelled transition systems to the left in Figure 5.7 to the two labelled transition systems to the right. However, application of the rules is more subtle in the presence of nondeterminism. Consider the following examples of the three archetypal forms of LOTOS nondeterminism, with $\mathcal{L} = \{x, y, z\}$,

$$X := x ; y ; stop [] x ; z ; stop$$
$$Y := i ; x ; stop [] i ; y ; stop$$
$$Z := i ; x ; stop [] y ; z ; stop$$

Labelled transition systems resulting from adding undefinedness for each of these processes are shown as (1), (2) and (3) of Figure 5.8. This transformation has the virtue of being extremely simple, however, it does not generate the

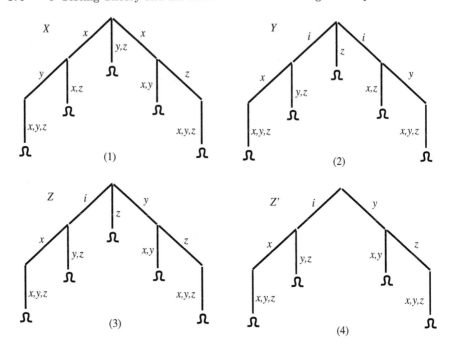

Fig. 5.8. Transformed Behaviours

minimum (in terms of least number of transitions) labelled transition system. For example, in (3), the transition labelled z, emanating from the start state, is in fact redundant and (3) and (4) of Figure 5.8 are testing equivalent.

A consequence of applying this transformation is that (modulo the addition of undefined behaviour) more processes are reductions than they would normally be. For example, once transformed, all of the following behaviours would be reductions of Z.

x; $stop$ [] y; z; $stop$ [] z; $stop$

x; $stop$ [] z; $stop$

x; $stop$ [] y; x; $stop$

The last of these is perhaps the most surprising as the defined behaviour of the resulting specification requires an x action to be performed after the trace y, whereas Z requires a z action to be performed after the same trace. However, according to our intuition of subtyping in OO, this is correct, as the transformed Z can refuse the y action at the root that leads to z, but cannot refuse the y action reached via i, which leads to Ω. Thus, this situation is only odd if the processes are interpreted without undefinedness.

Further Examples. It is important to note though that, although transforming LOTOS specifications in this way yields a more generous relationship between processes, which was after all our original intention, the resulting notion of subtying still remains sensitive to incompatible behaviour.

Consider two examples from [156]: a variable and a nondeterministic stack, although both these definitions are rather abstract and underspecified, because we do not have data types in pbLOTOS.

$$Var := \; put \, ; Var2 \qquad Var2 := \; put \, ; Var2 \, [] \; get \, ; Var2$$

$$NDstack := \; put \, ; NDstack2$$

$$NDstack2 := \; put \, ; NDstack2 \, [] \; get \, ; NDstack2 \, [] \; get \, ; NDstack$$

Now, it can be checked that $\mathtt{T}(Var)$ *red* $\mathtt{T}(NDstack)$ and $\mathtt{T}(NDstack)$ *red* $\mathtt{T}(Buf1)$, but $\neg(\mathtt{T}(NDstack) \; red \; \mathtt{T}(Var))$ and $\neg(\mathtt{T}(Buf1) \; red \; \mathtt{T}(NDstack))$. The latter two of these are because

$$Ref_{\mathtt{T}(NDstack)}(put \, get \, get) = \mathcal{P}(\mathcal{L}) \not\subseteq \{\emptyset\} = Ref_{\mathtt{T}(Var)}(put \, get \, get)$$

$$Ref_{\mathtt{T}(Buf1)}(put \, put) = \mathcal{P}(\mathcal{L}) \not\subseteq \{\emptyset\} = Ref_{\mathtt{T}(NDstack)}(put \, put)$$

Bowman et al [38] who consider the issue discussed here in more depth, also explore how this transformation works in the presence of data.

As these examples demonstrate, transformed behaviours have a very precise trace / refusal character. Transformed specifications can perform any trace in $(\mathcal{L} \cup \{\delta\})^*$ and after all traces either refuse nothing or refuse everything. One consequence of this is that, for transformed specifications, $red \; = \; ext \; = \; conf$.

Finally, it is worth noting that the issue of how to handle undefinedness is also one of the main hurdles that has to be tackled when behavioural specifications, such as those arising from LOTOS, and state-based specifications, such as those arising from Z, are related. For a detailed discussion of this issue, see [40].

5.4.3 Viewpoints and Consistency

Viewpoints are becoming a dominant structuring concept in a number of areas of computer science, e.g. requirements engineering [79], OO design methodologies [27], formal system development [203], in the Unified Modelling Language (see Chapter 7 of [41]) and in software engineering in general [182]. The idea is that, rather than having a single thread of system development, in the style of the classic waterfall approach, multiple partial specifications (i.e. viewpoints) of a system are considered during system development. Each particular specification represents a different perspective on the system under development and, in fact, may well be written by a different specifier and be in a different notation.

A distributed systems context in which viewpoints are particularly significant is *Open Distributed Processing (ODP)*, which is a joint ITU / ISO standardisation framework for constructing distributed systems in a multi-vendor environment. The interested reader is referred to published introductions, e.g. [129] and Chapters 1 and 2 of [41], and the standards documents themselves [106]. It is beyond the scope of this chapter to give a complete introduction to ODP, however, we summarise the basic ODP viewpoints model to frame our presentation.

ODP uses five predefined viewpoints – *the enterprise viewpoint, the information viewpoint, the computational viewpoint, the engineering viewpoint* and *the technology viewpoint*. They have the following respective roles.

- The *Enterprise Viewpoint* supports capture of global "business" requirements;
- The *Information Viewpoint* enables the generic information structures and flows of the system to be defined;
- The *Computational Viewpoint* is an object-oriented design model targeted at the applications programmer;
- The *Engineering Viewpoint* enables the engineering structures supporting the computational and information viewpoints to be defined;
- The *Technology Viewpoint* identifies how and where existing technologies can be used in the target system.

ODP is not prescriptive about which language each viewpoint should be specified with; rather the standard defines the basic structures and concepts that would be used in each viewpoint. It is assumed that, through a process of instantiation, the basic concepts of each viewpoint will be related to the constructs of particular specification languages.

One of the consequences of adopting a multiple viewpoints approach to development is that descriptions of the same, or related, entities can appear in different viewpoints and must co-exist. *Consistency* of specifications across viewpoints thus becomes a central issue. The problem is complicated by the fact that we can expect viewpoint specifications to be written in different languages, viz. languages particularly suited for the viewpoint at hand, e.g. Z for the information viewpoint and LOTOS for the computational viewpoint.

Thus, providing techniques to check viewpoint consistency is a major research topic surrounding ODP viewpoints modelling. A number of workers have responded to this challenge [17, 42, 74].

5.4.3.1 Consistency Definition

An initial challenge of work on viewpoints was to locate a definition of consistency that was general enough to be used in the ODP context. Bowman et al [37] proposed such a definition.

The intuition is that we can view n specifications $X_1, X_2, \ldots, X_n$ as consistent if there exists a physical implementation which is a realisation of all the specifications; i.e. X_1, X_2 through to X_n can be implemented in a single

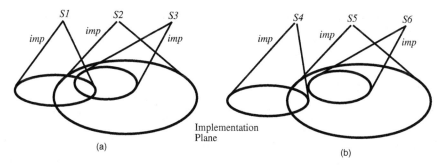

Fig. 5.9. Common Implementation Models

system. This interpretation has similarities to satisfaction in a logical setting. A conjunction of propositions $\phi_1 \wedge \phi_2 \wedge \ldots \wedge \phi_n$ is satisfiable if there exists a single model that individually satisfies all the propositions.

Figures 5.9(a) and 5.9(b) illustrate this; in both depictions specifications are related to their set of possible realisations by a relation implements (denoted *imp*). Thus, the Venn diagrams in the implementation plane depict the set of possible realisations of each specification. It should be clear that the three specifications in Figure 5.9(a) are consistent, because their set of possible implementations intersect. In contrast, the three specifications in Figure 5.9(b) are not consistent, although the pairs S4 and S5 and S5 and S6 are mutually consistent.

However, rather than talk explicitly about implementation, as this interpretation does, it is necessary to work purely in the formal setting and define consistency solely in terms of specifications and relations between specifications. Thus, we define consistency in terms of a common (formal) specification, X, and a list of development relations, $dv_1, dv_2, \ldots, dv_n$. n specifications are consistent, denoted $\mathcal{C}(dv_1, X_n) \ldots (dv_n, X_n)$ if there exists a specification that is a development of X_1 according to dv_1, X_2 according to dv_2, through to X_n according to dv_n; i.e.

$$\mathcal{C}(dv_1, X_n) \ldots (dv_n, X_n) \quad \textit{iff} \quad \exists X \text{ s.t. } X \ dv_1 \ X_1 \wedge \ldots \wedge X \ dv_n \ X_n.$$

Notice that we allow the descriptions to be related to their common development in different ways; i.e. if $dv_i \neq dv_j$. This is inherent in the nature of ODP viewpoints modelling, where, for example, one viewpoint could be related to the common implementation by conformance, another by direct implementation and a third by functionality extension. In addition, there is nothing preventing the specifications from being in different languages.

One central issue that we do not have space to discuss here is that of obtaining global consistency from a series of binary consistency checks. It turns out that the choice of common implementation between viewpoint specifications is crucial to obtaining such incremental consistency checking [48].

This definition of consistency is very general, being parameterised, firstly, on the choice of specification language and secondly, on the notion of development used. In the following we consider consistency in the LOTOS setting.

5.4.3.2 Consistency in LOTOS

What makes consistency checking between viewpoint specifications in LOTOS a particularly challenging task is the existence and use of multiple development relations. Consistency checking using combinations of these development relations has been investigated [48, 184], which characterises consistency checks that result when different LOTOS development relations are used.

As a *very* simple illustration, consider the consistency check,

$$\mathcal{C}(ext, P)(red, Q)$$

where *ext* is the extension relation, introduced in Section 5.1.6.3, and *red* is the reduction relation, introduced in Section 5.1.6.2. We can give the following examples of consistent and inconsistent pairs of "buffer" specifications.

$$\neg \mathcal{C}(ext, Inbuf)(red, blockbuf) \quad \text{and} \quad \mathcal{C}(ext, 1buf)(red, blockbuf)$$

where

$$Inbuf := put\,;\, Inbuf$$

$$1buf := put\,;\, get\,;\, 1buf$$

$$blockbuf := put\,;\, get\,;\, blockbuf \; [] \; put\,;\, stop$$

We can justify the former of these, because any extension, call it R, of *Inbuf* must be able to perform the trace *put put* (for example), but R cannot be a reduction of *blockbuf*, because *put put* $\notin [\![\, blockbuf \,]\!]_{tr}$. In addition, the latter holds because *1buf* extends itself (*ext* is reflexive) and it reduces *blockbuf*. This is, of course, a rather trivial illustration of consistency checking; a larger example is considered in [22, 48]. Furthermore, [48] gives a complete characterisation of consistency checking using LOTOS development relations.

5.4.3.3 Discussion

Our discussion here of consistency checking has been presented as a taster of the topic. In particular, it is beyond the scope of this book to go into what is a very complex topic in full depth. However, the interested reader is referred to the literature for more details. In particular, [23] considers how consistency can be checked between pairs of Z specifications; [48] presents a theoretical framework for viewpoints and consistency checking; the same paper instantiates this framework in the LOTOS context; and, finally, [70] shows how LOTOS specifications can be translated into Z specifications and then consistency checking can be performed in Z.

Part III

Concurrency Theory – Further Untimed
Notations

This part builds from Part II by considering a set of more advanced untimed modelling notations, which enhance the capabilities of the methods developed in Part II. Specifically, Chapter 6 discusses enhanced LOTOS calculi, which are syntactically richer and interface with data typing notations. Then in Chapter 7, a comparison with the calculi CCS and CSP is made. Finally, a consideration of communicating automata approaches is presented in Chapter 8.

Beyond pbLOTOS

Chapter 2 defined a relatively restricted subset of LOTOS. The main reason for isolating this subset is that it is a suitable size to consider formally and the chapters of the previous part that discuss semantics restrict themselves to this subset. However, the complete language contains a number of other constructs and a somewhat more verbose syntax. This chapter presents bLOTOS (i.e. LOTOS without data types), which is discussed in Section 6.1, and fLOTOS (i.e. the full language, with data types), which is discussed in Section 6.2. Included are the full syntactic forms for a number of the constructs that we have already discussed and some completely new constructs. We give operational semantics rules for each new construct, which map to labelled transition systems. However, these semantics are presented as a taster, rather than as an exhaustive semantic definition, which would require us to be more detailed in respect of our treatment of data than we are able to be within this book. We also illustrate the fLOTOS constructs with examples in Section 6.3.

fLOTOS is effectively the language (minus the data typing notation) that was standardised in 1987 in [104]. However, there has been a further standardisation activity focused on enhancing LOTOS by adding features and responding to perceived problems in the original language. Unfortunately, it is beyond the scope of this book to give a full presentation of the resulting E-LOTOS notation, however, we give a short review of the main extensions and highlight pointers to literature on the topic in Section 6.4.

6.1 Basic LOTOS

We begin by looking at bLOTOS. We work construct by construct through the new operators and then we define an abstract syntax for bLOTOS.

6.1.1 Disabling

Disabling has the general form:

$$B_1 \mathrel{[>} B_2$$

which states that behaviour B_2 can disable behaviour B_1. We call B_1 the *normal behaviour* and B_2 the *exception behaviour*. At any point during the evolution of B_1, the first action of B_2 can be performed, causing B_1 to be stopped and $B_1 \mathrel{[>} B_2$ to behave as B_2. In fact, even before B_1 has performed an action, B_2 can disable it. Once B_1 has successfully terminated, it can no longer be disabled.

For example, consider the following behaviours.

(i) $x\,;\,y\,;\,exit \mathrel{[>} w\,;\,z\,;\,stop$

(ii) $P \mathrel{[>} w\,;\,z\,;\,stop$ where, $P := x\,;\,y\,;\,P$

(iii) $x\,;\,y\,;\,stop \mathrel{[>} w\,;\,z\,;\,stop$

(iv) $x\,;\,y\,;\,exit \mathrel{[>} i\,;\,z\,;\,stop$

(v) $(\,x\,;\,y\,;\,exit \mathrel{[>} w\,;\,z\,;\,stop\,) \mathrel{>>} v\,;\,stop$

Behaviour trees for these expressions are depicted in Figure 6.1. The following points can be made on each example behaviour.

(i) The exception behaviour, $w\,;\,z\,;\,stop$, is offered as an alternative to performing any action in the normal behaviour. Thus, at any point, the normal behaviour can be disabled, that is, until a successful termination action is performed.

(ii) Because the normal behaviour has an infinite character, there is no successful termination to disable the exception behaviour.

(ii) This behaviour cannot successfully terminate, thus, the exception behaviour cannot be disabled and *must* happen after the normal behaviour has completed.

(iv) An asymmetric nondeterministic choice is generated between performing the normal behaviour observably or internally evolving to the exception behaviour.

(v) This behaviour illustrates the interplay of disabling and successful termination. Specifically, successful termination of the normal behaviour enables the new behaviour $v\,;\,stop$.

The disable operator is not a standard process calculus operator (although, its origins date back to [96]); rather it is targeted at the specific application domain of LOTOS: description of communication protocols. In this context, it is used to express the disrupting effect of error and exception behaviour, e.g. a connection being unexpectedly disconnected. We have not included disabling in pbLOTOS because it has some unpleasant semantic consequences. For example, disabling cannot be expressed easily using the bundle event structure true concurrency semantics that were considered in Chapter 4.

Three simple operational semantics rules can be given for the behaviour of the disabling operator.

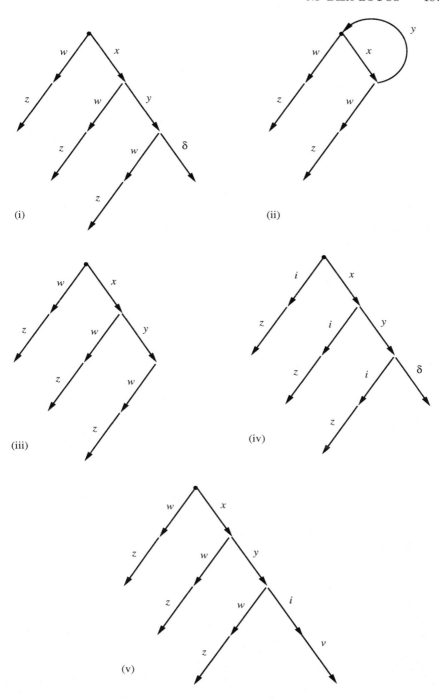

Fig. 6.1. Disabling Examples

$$(DIS.i): \quad \frac{B_1 \xrightarrow{a} B_1'}{B_1 [> B_2 \xrightarrow{a} B_1' [> B_2} \quad (a \neq \delta)$$

$$(DIS.ii): \quad \frac{B_1 \xrightarrow{\delta} B_1'}{B_1 [> B_2 \xrightarrow{\delta} B_1'}$$

$$(DIS.iii): \quad \frac{B_2 \xrightarrow{a} B_2'}{B_1 [> B_2 \xrightarrow{a} B_2'} \quad (a \in Act \cup \{i, \delta\})$$

Thus, rule *(DIS.i)* ensures that any nonterminating action that B_1 can perform, can be performed by $B_1 [> B_2$ and the capacity to disable remains. Rule *(DIS.ii)* states that a successful termination on the part of B_1, will successfully terminate the disabling. Finally, rule *(DIS.iii)* indicates how a transition of B_2 can disable the evolution of B_1.

6.1.2 Generalised Choice

Generalised choice has the form,

> *choice* $ge_1, \ldots, ge_n$ [] B

where ge_i is a gate expression of the form:

> x *in* $[x_1, \ldots, x_m]$

which states that the variable x ranges over the set $[x_1, \ldots, x_m]$; i.e. can be instantiated with any of the actions $x_1, \ldots, x_m$. Generalised choice allows us to express behaviour such as

> *choice* x *in* $[v, z, w]$, y *in* $[u, w]$ [] B'

which is equivalent to the following

> $B'[v/x, u/y]$ [] $B'[z/x, u/y]$ [] $B'[w/x, u/y]$ []
> $B'[v/x, w/y]$ [] $B'[z/x, w/y]$ [] $B'[w/x, w/y]$

So, the choice of a series of instances of B' is generated, where each instance reflects a particular instantiation of x and y.

As suggested by this example, generalised choice enables us to express a large class of behaviours significantly more succinctly than they would be expressed with basic (binary) choice. In addition, we can express infinite choices using generalised choice (such behaviour cannot be expressed using basic choice). This particularly becomes clear when we discuss the integration of data with generalised choice in the next section. However, a specific case of infinite choice is given by the following behaviour,

> *choice* x *in* Act [] B where B usually refers to x

which defines an infinite choice of behaviour B instantiated with actions from the (infinite) set of all possible LOTOS actions.

A simple operational semantics rule can be given for the behaviour of generalised choice.

$$\frac{B[x_i/x] \xrightarrow{a} B'}{choice\ x\ in\ [x_1,\ldots,x_n]\ [] \ B \xrightarrow{a} B'} \ (1 \le i \le n)$$

This rule assumes just a single action binder, $x\ in\ [x_1,\ldots,x_n]$, however, it can easily be generalised to multiple action binders.

6.1.3 Generalised Parallelism

Generalised parallelism has the form,

$$par\ ge_1,\ldots,ge_n\ |[x_1,\ldots,x_m]|\ B$$

For example, the behaviour:

$$par\ x\ in\ [v,z,w],\ y\ in\ [u,w]\ |[w]|\ B'$$

is equivalent to:

$$B'[v/x,u/y]\ |[w]|\ B'[z/x,u/y]\ |[w]|\ B'[w/x,u/y]\ |[w]|$$
$$B'[v/x,w/y]\ |[w]|\ B'[z/x,w/y]\ |[w]|\ B'[w/x,w/y]$$

It should be noted that the parallel composition operator, $|[w]|$ above, cannot be affected by the instantiation of action names. This construct plays a similar role to generalised choice, but in the context of parallel behaviour.

Rather than giving inference rules specific to this operator, as we did for generalised choice, we simply provide a mapping from generalised parallelism to a sequence of normal binary parallel compositions. This is possible because the number of parallel threads that can be generated with this operator is always finite (in contrast, generalised choice can yield infinite choices).

$$par\ x\ in\ [y_1,\ldots,y_n]\ |[x_1,\ldots,x_m]|\ B \triangleq$$
$$B[y_1/x]\ |[x_1,\ldots,x_m]|\ \ldots\ |[x_1,\ldots,x_m]|\ B[y_n/x]$$

Again our rule is specific to a single action binder, but it could also easily be generalised to multiple action binders. Another reason why this mapping is well-formed is because in pbLOTOS, parallel composition is associative when synchronisation sets are repeated. That is, an expression of the form, $B_1\ |[x_1,\ldots,x_m]|\ \ldots\ |[x_1,\ldots,x_m]|\ B_n$ defines a unique behaviour, because any bracketing that decomposes the expression into a sequence of binary compositions would be equivalent up to strong bisimulation.

6.1.4 Verbose Specification Syntax

The top-level syntax for a bLOTOS specification has the following form,

> *specification I* $[x_1, \ldots, x_n]$: *F*
> *behaviour*
> ...
> ...
> *endspec*

where I is an identifier that names the specification, $x_1, \ldots, x_n$ are the observable actions of the entire specification and F denotes the functionality of the specification. These extensions to the top-level specification syntax of pbLOTOS are largely syntactic sugar. The body of the specification appears between the keywords *behaviour* and *endspec*. This behaviour will have the form:

> *B*
> *where*
> D_1
> ...
> ...
> D_n

where B is an arbitrary behaviour and D_i is a process definition. Although the list of declarations could be empty.

The functionality parameter, F, states that the specification either has the functionality *exit* or *noexit*. A specification that can successfully terminate has the functionality *exit*, whereas a specification that is unable to successfully terminate has the functionality *noexit*. Rules for determining the functionality of specifications are given in [24].

6.1.5 Verbose Process Syntax

In a similar way, a verbose process syntax is used in bLOTOS,

> *process P* $[x_1, \ldots, x_n]$: *F* :=
> ...
> ...
> *endproc*

where P is the process identifier; $x_1, \ldots, x_n$ are the observable actions of the process; F denotes the functionality of the process; i.e. *exit* or *noexit* in the same way as for complete specifications; and the body of the process is between the symbol := and *endproc*. This behaviour will typically have the form:

B
where
D_1
$\ldots$
$\ldots$
D_n

where B is an arbitrary behaviour and D_i is a process definition. In fact, the
similarity between the syntax of process definitions and the top-level structure
of specifications is not surprising, because a specification, as a whole, can be
seen to be a process. A specification is a special kind of process, but only by
virtue of its name.

6.1.6 Syntax of bLOTOS

This section brings together the constructs that we have introduced to give
an abstract syntax for bLOTOS. The syntax defines an arbitrary specification
$S \in bLOTOS$ as follows.

S ::= *specification* I $[x^\times]$: F *behaviour* U *endspec*

U ::= B | B *where* D^+

D ::= *process* P $[x^\times]$: F := U *endproc*

B ::= *stop* | *exit* | a ; B | B_1 [] B_2 | B_1 |[$x^\times$]| B_2 |

　　　$B_1 >> B_2$ | B_1 [> B_2 | *choice* ge^+ [] B | *par* ge^+ |[$x^\times$]| B |

　　　hide x^+ *in* B | $B[(x/y)^+]$ | $P[x^\times]$

F ::= *exit* | *noexit*

ge ::= y *in* $[x^+]$

where

- We have used BNF notation in which X^+ denotes a finite number, bigger
  than zero, of repetitions of X and $Y^\times$ denotes a finite number, including
  zero, of repetitions of Y, which are separated by commas, if there is more
  than one;
- S is the domain of specifications, U is the domain of top-level behaviours,
  D is the domain of definitions, B is the domain of behaviour expressions,
  F is the domain of functionality parameters and ge are action binders;
- The domain D has changed from pbLOTOS; here we are using it to range
  over single definitions; and
- $a \in Act \cup \{i\}$, $x, y \in Act$, $I, P \in PIdent$.[1]

---

[1]Note, we do not distinguish the domain of specification names from that of
process names.

6.2 Full LOTOS

As indicated earlier, full LOTOS integrates the constructs introduced above with a data typing notation, ACT-ONE. A complete presentation of this notation is inappropriate for a number of reasons.

- Our main interest in this book is the behavioural part of LOTOS.
- The ACT-ONE data language has proved a troublesome part of full LO-TOS. There are a number of reasons for this, which we do not have room to consider here; see, for example, [150] for a discussion of this issue. However, a central issue is that ACT-ONE is not in practice easy to use. In particular, even trivial specifications, such as that of the natural numbers, prove complex to express in ACT-ONE.
- LOTOS restandardisation has designed a new data language to replace ACT-ONE; see Section 6.4. Thus, in the LOTOS context, ACT-ONE is largely obsolete.

However, we now give a flavour of the interface between data and behaviour provided by full LOTOS. In order to do this, we assume a basic set of data types that are not tied to any particular data language; i.e. natural numbers, Booleans and enumerated types. We show how these can be interfaced with LOTOS. So, we assume the following primitive set of data domains.

- A set *nat* of natural numbers, with $0, 1, 2, 3, \ldots \in nat$ and operations $+$ and relations $=$, $>$, $<$, etc. defined on *nat*; we also have an operator *comp*, which takes the complement of 0 and 1; i.e. $comp(0) = 1$ and $comp(1) = 0$;
- A set *int* of integers, with $\ldots, -3, -2, -1, 0, 1, 2, 3, \ldots \in int$ and operations $+, -$ and relations $=$, $>$, $<$, etc. defined on *int*;
- A set *bool* of Booleans, with two elements, *true* and *false*, and operations *not*, *and*, *or* etc. defined on *bool*; and
- Four enumerated types that are used in the Dining Philosophers example:

$$name \quad ::= \quad Aristotle \mid Buddha \mid Confucius \mid Descartes$$

$$side \quad ::= \quad left \mid right$$

$$action \quad ::= \quad eat \mid think$$

$$chopstick \quad ::= \quad stick1 \mid stick2 \mid stick3 \mid stick4$$

These are presented in a standard way using BNF. These definitions state that the type *name* can have four constant values, *Aristotle*, *Buddha*, *Confucius* and *Descartes*, and similarly for *side*, *action* and *chopstick*.

As was the case with bLOTOS, for each of the new constructs we introduce, we provide operational semantics rules to illustrate how these constructs are interpreted in a labelled transition systems semantics. However, as stated earlier, these semantics are presented as a taster, rather than as an exhaustive semantic definition.

We present the fLOTOS extensions to bLOTOS construct by construct.

6.2.1 Guarded Choice

Conditional selection based on the value of variables can be defined. There are three basic ways to define data conditionals in fLOTOS: *guarded commands*, *selection predicates* and *generalised choice*. We consider the first of these here. The other two are considered when we have described value passing actions.

Guarded choice is derived from Dijkstra's guarded commands notation; it has the following general form,

$$[be] \rightarrow B$$
$$[]$$
$$[be'] \rightarrow B'$$

where be and be' are Boolean expressions. The meaning of this construct is: if the guard be holds, behave as B, otherwise, if the guard be' holds, behave as B'. Notice that if the guards overlap, nondeterminism can be created.

In fact, any arbitrary piece of behaviour can be prefixed with a guard. Thus, the choice here is not even required and the basic syntactic enhancement that arises with guards is the capacity to "prefix" any arbitrary behaviour with a guard. Thus,

$$[be] \rightarrow B$$

Semantically, this construct is interpreted via the following inference rule,

$$\frac{B \xrightarrow{a} B' \quad beval(be)}{([be] \rightarrow B) \xrightarrow{a} B'}$$

where $a \in Act \cup \{i, \delta\}^2$ and $beval$ evaluates the Boolean expression be in the obvious way. Notice that the LOTOS semantics ensure that be only contains ground terms. Thus, $beval$ does not require a state or environment in order to evaluate a Boolean expression.

6.2.2 Specification Notation

The top-level syntax for an fLOTOS specification has the following form,

$$specification\ I\ [x_1, \ldots, x_n](n_1 : T_1, \ldots, n_m : T_m) :\ F$$
$$\qquad\qquad TD$$
$$behaviour$$
$$\qquad\qquad B$$
$$where$$
$$\qquad\qquad TD$$
$$\qquad\qquad D^\times$$
$$endspec$$

---

[2]Although, with fLOTOS actions are more complex, because they carry data attributes. This is an issue we elaborate on shortly.

where TD is a list of type definitions and D^+ is a list of process definitions. The TDs in the above specification indicate places where ACT-ONE definitions can legally be placed in LOTOS specifications. The type definitions that follow the specification header would be global, over the entire specification, whereas the type definitions following the *where* keyword only range over the list of process definitions.

In addition, the list $(n_1 : T_1, \ldots, n_m : T_m)$ parameterises the specification on a group of data variables with associated types, which can be instantiated on execution of the specification. So, these are data values that are input to the specification.

6.2.3 Process Definition and Invocation

The fLOTOS syntax for process definition is:

$$process\ P\ [x_1, \ldots, x_n](n_1 : T_1, \ldots, n_m : T_m)\ :\ F\ :=$$
$$B$$
$$where$$
$$TD$$
$$D^\times$$
$$endproc$$

Thus, process definition takes a very similar form to the top-level specification syntax. In particular, processes are parameterised on certain variables and local data type and process definitions can be included following the keyword *where*; although, these are all optional.

This parameterisation means that process invocation takes on a somewhat more complicated form than it did for pbLOTOS and bLOTOS. Given the above process definition, process invocation takes the following general form,

$$P[y_1, \ldots, y_n](E_1, \ldots, E_m)$$

where E_i is a value expression of type T_i. The effect of this invocation is to textually substitute the expressions E_i in place into the process body for their corresponding formal parameter; i.e. n_i. This class of parameter passing is similar to call by name as used in standard programming languages.

6.2.4 Value Passing Actions

In fLOTOS, actions can exchange data. As a reflection of this, we distinguish between gates and actions and we assume variables $g, g', g'', g_1, g_2, \ldots$ ranging over the set *Gate*. Actions now have the general form:

$$g\, d_1 \ldots d_n$$

i.e. action instances comprise a gate and a list of *value* and *variable decla-rations*, denoted d_i (these are sometimes called *experiment offers* and what we call value and variable declarations are called *value experiments* and *vari-able experiments*). For example, in the communication protocol example, we might want to specify that, when a *send* is performed, a natural number is passed with the *send*. This number could, for example, be used to associate a sequence number with messages. The following are typical data valued action instances occuring in this setting,

$$send!5 \;,\; send!(10+2) \;,\; send!n \;,\; send!(10+n) \;,\; send?m : nat$$

In these action instances, *send* is the gate name and !5, !(10+2), !n, !(10+n) and ?m : nat are data passing declarations. In particular, !5, !(10+2), !n and !(10+n) are value declarations, whereas ?m : nat is a variable declaration. The effect of a value declaration is to pass a data value (here a natural number). So, the effect of *send*!20 is to offer an interaction at the gate named *send* and associate the value 20 with that interaction, whereas *send*!n offers interaction on the same gate, but, this time, the value of the variable n is associated with the interaction. In contrast, the effect of a variable declaration is to offer a variable to which a binding can be made. So, the effect of *send*?m : nat is to offer an interaction at the gate named *send* and associate a binding to variable m with that interaction. In effect, the declaration ?m : nat states that m can take any value from the natural numbers.

Notice that one implication of value passing is that specifications will now typically have an infinite set of possible actions. Thus, the set $\mathcal{L}$ can now be infinite. For example, for the behaviour,

$$P := send?m : nat\,;\, stop$$

$\mathcal{L} = \{\, send\_0, send\_1, send\_2, \ldots \,\}$, where $send\_v$ denotes interaction at gate *send* with an associated data value v.

In fact, this style of action denotation plays a central role in the fLOTOS semantics. Specifically, labels in transition systems will now have the form,

$$g\_v_1\_v_2 \ldots \_v_n$$

where the v_is are data values. Thus, effectively, data is "flattened out" when the semantics are applied. For example, the transition system arising from process P above is shown in Figure 6.2.

One beneficial consequence of this flattening of data is that the standard development relations introduced in Part II can be applied in this context, subject to the problems that may arise with infinite branching.[3] Effectively, these relations just treat the complex flattened labels that arise from fLOTOS in the same way as the pure action names that arise from pbLOTOS. Thus,

---

[3]Of course, we are here talking from a theoretical perspective, because it is clear that such infinite branching is a major difficulty for the development of verification tools for data passing calculi.

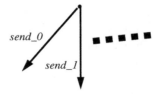

$send\_0$

$send\_1$

Fig. 6.2. Flattening of Data

reassuringly, all theory developed in the pbLOTOS setting is still applicable in the fLOTOS setting.

In our general form of action, the d_is can have one of the following forms,

$!E$ or $?n : T$

where E is a value expression and T is a type name. The n here is described as a *binding* occurrence of the variable, whereas instances of variables in E would, in this context, be described as *free*.

As a consequence, action prefix has the general form:

$g\,d_1 \ldots d_m\,;\ B$

The variables declared in d_i can be used in B. In fact, the scope for these declarations is exactly the extent of B. We assume that, for any $i\,(1 \leq i \leq m)$, if d_i is a binding occurrence of n, then n does not appear in any $d_j\ (j \neq i)$ or occur as a binder in B. Note, systematic renaming can always be used to resolve any such name clashes.

In the behaviour of the medium, we might want to express that, once a *send* has been performed, with a certain sequence number, a *receive* is performed with the same sequence number. This models the successful transmission by the medium of a message from sender to receiver. We can express this as

$send\,?m : nat\,;\ receive\,!m\,;\ B$

which states that the variable m will be bound to a value in *nat* when an interaction at *send* occurs and then the value of m will be associated with interaction on the *receive* gate. We could also specify that, after a *receiveAck* action is performed in the sender process, a *send* action is performed with an incremented sequence number. This could be specified as follows,

$receiveAck\,?m : nat\,;\ send\,!(comp(m))\,;\ B$

where *comp* is the complement operator introduced earlier, as appropriate for alternating bit sequence numbering.

In addition, a single gate can have a number of value or variable declarations associated with it. For example, the action, *receive*!*seqno*?*d* : *data*?*c* : *checksum*

offers interaction on gate *receive* with a specified sequence number, an arbitrary data unit and error checksum.

The semantic interpretation of this construct is as follows.

$$g \, d_1 \ldots d_n \, ; B \xrightarrow{\overline{g \, \text{-}v_1 \, \cdots \, \text{-}v_n}} B(\text{rewrite}(J))$$

where $m \leq n \ \wedge \ \forall i (1 \leq i \leq n), \ j(1 \leq j \leq m)$,

- $v_i \triangleq eval(E) \ \ if \ d_i = !E;$
- $v_i \in T \ \ if \ d_i = ?r' : T;$
- $J \triangleq \{ (u_j, r_j) \mid d_i = ?r_j : T \ \wedge \ u_j = v_i \};$
- $\text{rewrite}(\{ (s_1, t_1), \ldots, (s_k, t_k) \}) \triangleq [s_1/t_1, \ldots, s_k/t_k];$

where v_i and u_j are data values, types are treated as sets, which is appropriate in this setting, there are m variable declarations in the list $d_1 \ldots d_n$, i ranges over all data passing declarations, j ranges over variable declarations, $[u_1/r_1, \ldots, u_m/r_m] \triangleq [u_1/r_1] \ldots [u_m/r_m]$ [4] and *eval* evaluates data expressions in the obvious manner. Note, that, as was the case with Boolean expressions, by the time *eval* is applied in the semantics, all data expressions will only contain ground terms.

6.2.4.1 Value Passing and Synchronisation

As indicated earlier, communication between parallel threads of control is performed through actions synchronising on parallel composition. What happens then when data passing actions synchronise? Well, in general, some form of value binding occurs. However, there are a number of possibilities for such synchronisation. The following are the basic forms of data passing synchronisation.[5]

    (i) $g!E \, ; B \ |[g]| \ g!F \, ; B'$

    (ii) $g!E \, ; B \ |[g]| \ g?n : T \, ; B'$

    (iii) $g?m : T \, ; B \ |[g]| \ g?n : T' \, ; B'$

We explain these in turn, when the pbLOTOS parallel composition rules (defined in Section 2.3.6) are applied with the (flattened) actions that arise from our value passing calculus.

---

[4]Notice that, because we assume there is no possibility of a name clash, these renamings could actually be performed in any order.

[5]We assume that static checks, such as those considered in [104], have already been applied in order to ensure type correctness.

1. If $eval(E) = eval(F)$ then the action $g\_eval(E)$ will be performed. However, if $eval(E) \neq eval(F)$ then interaction on gate g cannot take place and deadlock will result. This form of synchronisation is called *value synchronisation*.

2. Assuming the type of E is T, the action $g\_eval(E)$ will be performed and, as a by-product, on the right-hand side of the behaviour, the variable n will be bound to $eval(E)$. This form of synchronisation is called *value passing*.

3. Assuming $T = T'$, this behaviour will offer an interaction on gate g with all values from T associated. This form of synchronisation is called *value generation*. It is important to note that synchronisation on gate g in this way will not prescribe a particular value from T. In effect, a (potentially infinite) choice is made available to the environment between performing g with each of the data values of T. In particular, because multiway synchronisation is allowed on gate g, a further behaviour that constrains the value to be associated with the interaction (e.g. a gate $g!E$) could be composed in parallel and, thus, resolve the choice. As an illustration of this form of value synchronisation, Figure 6.3 depicts the choice of possible immediate evolutions of a typical behaviour of this form.

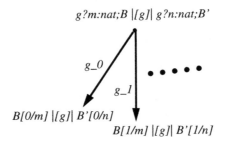

Fig. 6.3. Value Generation Example

6.2.4.2 Value Passing and Internal Behaviour

Hidden behaviour is also affected by value passing. Firstly, it is syntactically illegal to associate a data attribute with an internal action, e.g. the behaviour:

  $i!5; stop$

is not syntactically well formed. This is because an internal action is not able to interact with the environment and thus, passing values to and from the environment is not meaningful. However, data passing can be associated with internal actions through hiding. This reflects that an observable interaction with data can be hidden. Thus, the interaction and its data experiments still occur, but are made internal and hidden from the environment. For example, all the following behaviours are syntactically well formed,

(i) *hide g in g!5 ; stop*

(ii) *hide g in (g!5 ; B |[g]| g?n : nat ; B')*

(iii) *hide g in (g?m : nat ; B |[g]| g?n : nat ; B')*

and we depict them in Figure 6.4. Although, (i) is rather a silly specification, because no other party can view the value 5.

However, in all these behaviours, the data value associated with each internal action is not visible to the external observer; they can be thought of as being transmitted inside some internal communication channel. You should also notice that behaviour (iii) amounts to an infinite nondeterministic choice; the nondeterminism arises because the choice is over a hidden gate. Thus, an internal action will be performed and the same arbitrary value will be bound to both m in B and n in B'.

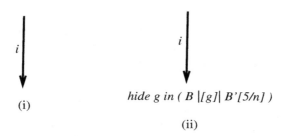

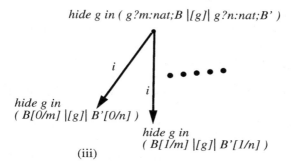

Fig. 6.4. Value Generation Examples and Internal Behaviour

6.2.4.3 Illustration of Value Passing

Examples of the use of value passing synchronisation can be found in the communication protocol example. As an illustration, consider first the receiver process:

$$process\ Receiver\ [put, receive, sendAck](m : nat)\ :\ noexit\ :=$$
$$\quad hide\ timeout\ in$$
$$\quad\quad (\ timeout\,;\ sendAck!comp(m)\,;$$
$$\quad\quad\quad\quad\quad Receiver[put, receive, sendAck](m)$$
$$\quad\quad []$$
$$\quad\quad receive?n : nat\,;$$
$$\quad\quad\quad (\ [m = n]\ ->\ put\,;\ sendAck!n\,;$$
$$\quad\quad\quad\quad\quad\quad\quad Receiver[put, receive, sendAck](comp(m))$$
$$\quad\quad\quad []$$
$$\quad\quad\quad [m \neq n]\ ->\ sendAck!n\,;$$
$$\quad\quad\quad\quad\quad\quad\quad Receiver[put, receive, sendAck](m)\ )\ )$$

$$\quad endproc$$

Note that the protocol example we discuss in this chapter is slightly more complex than the version considered in Chapter 2. In particular, here we add the difficulty that the acknowledgement medium may lose messages. As a result, the receiver is never sure that its acknowledgements get through to the sender.

Notice that sequence numbers are transmitted in the specification; thus, for example, when the receiver performs the action *receive*, the variable n is bound to the sequence number of the received message. Then, depending upon the value of n, either the message is relayed to higher layers, by performing a *put*, or it is dropped. In both cases, an acknowledgement is sent and then the process recurses.

The reason for the conditional is that the message may be a retransmission of a previously received message, which has had its acknowledgement lost. In this case, the expected sequence number, m, and the received sequence number, n, will not be equal, the message will not be relayed to higher layers and acknowledgement of the previously received message will be resent on the *sendAck* gate.

In addition, in this specification, the *Receiver* is initially waiting to receive a message from the medium. However, if the message does not arrive "in time", it can timeout, in which case it sends an acknowledgement for the previous message. This is because it assumes that its previous acknowledgement must have been lost in transit.

In the more complex protocol example considered here, on receipt of an acknowledgement (on gate *sendAck*), the acknowledgement medium can either relay the acknowledgement (ensuring that the same sequence number is used) or it can lose the acknowledgement in transit. This behaviour is realised in the following specification.

process AckMedium [*sendAck, receiveAck*] : *noexit* :=
    sendAck?n : nat ;
      (*receiveAck!n* ; *AckMedium*[*sendAck, receiveAck*]
      []
      i ; *AckMedium*[*sendAck, receiveAck*])
endproc

As a fragment of the communication protocol, we can consider the following parallel composition.

    Receiver[*put, receive, sendAck*](0)
      |[*sendAck*]|
    AckMedium[*sendAck, receiveAck*]

It is important to note that synchronisation on the gate *sendAck* now has the effect of binding the value of *n* or *comp(m)* (depending upon the instance of *sendAck*) in the process *Receiver* to the variable *n* in *AckMedium*. Thus, the sequence number of the message being acknowledged is passed through the medium.

It is also worth noting that there is a good deal of redundancy in LOTOS concerning how conditional data passing behaviours can be expressed. For example, the following fragment of behaviour from the *Receiver* process,

    receive?n : nat ;
      ([*m = n*] −> *put* ; *sendAck!n* ;
                      Receiver[*put, receive, sendAck*](*comp(m)*)
      []
      [*m ≠ n*] −> *sendAck!n* ;
                      Receiver[*put, receive, sendAck*](*m*))

could also be expressed as follows,

    receive!m ; *put* ; *sendAck!m* ;
                Receiver[*put, receive, sendAck*](*comp(m)*)
    []
    receive!(comp(m)) ; *sendAck!(comp(m))* ;
                Receiver[*put, receive, sendAck*](*m*)

where branching according to the sequence number received is pushed into the action instances. In fact, although these two fragments are equivalent in the context of the communication protocol example, which only uses two numbers, 0 and 1, they are not equivalent in every context. This is because, the second fragment will deadlock with an environment that attempts to perform a *receive* with a value greater than 1, however, the original version will not deadlock on that receive, although it is likely to deadlock immediately afterwards.

6.2.5 Local Definitions

We can associate value expressions with free variables using the let construct, which has the following general form,

$$let\ m_1 : T_1 = E_1, \ldots, m_n : T_n = E_n\ in\ B$$
$$where,\ for\ i \neq j,\ m_i \neq m_j\ and,\ in\ general,\ B\ references\ m_1, \ldots, m_n$$

This states that the behaviour B is performed with the variables m_i of type T_i replaced by the value expressions E_i.

Now, assuming that the construct is well typed and that there are no binding occurrences of the m_is in B (note, if necessary, systematic renaming of bound variables could be applied to ensure this holds), then the following inference rule can be applied for this construct.

$$\frac{B[E_1/m_1, \ldots, E_n/m_n] \xrightarrow{a} B'}{(let\ m_1 : T_1 = E_1, \ldots, m_n : T_n = E_n\ in\ B) \xrightarrow{a} B'}$$

where $B[E_1/m_1, \ldots, E_n/m_n] \triangleq B[E_1/m_1] \ldots [E_n/m_n]$ and $a \in Act \cup \{i, \delta\}$.

6.2.6 Selection Predicates

We introduce two more forms of conditional in this and the next sections. The first of these is the selection predicate. This gives the final enhancement to action prefix, which in fLOTOS has the general form:

$$g\, d_1 \ldots d_n [be]\, ;\ B$$

This allows the values of variables in the declaration list, $d_1 \ldots d_n$, to be constrained by the Boolean expression be. For example, the Boolean expression may specify that a variable declared in d_i to be of type nat, can only take values between 4 and 10.

The semantic interpretation of this construct generalises that of action prefix. As previously, we assume that, for any $i\,(1 \leq i \leq n)$, if d_i is a binding occurrence of n, then n does not appear in any $d_j\,(j \neq i)$ or occur as a binder in B.

$$\frac{beval(be[u_1/r_1, \ldots, u_m/r_m])}{g\, d_1 \ldots d_n\, [be]\, ;\, B \xrightarrow{g\, \_v_1 \ldots \_v_n} B(\mathsf{rewrite}(J))}$$

where $m \leq n\ \wedge\ \forall i(1 \leq i \leq n),\ j(1 \leq j \leq m)$,

- $v_i \triangleq eval(E)\ \ if\ d_i = !E$;
- $v_i \in T\ \ if\ d_i = ?r' : T$;
- $J \triangleq \{\, (u_j, r_j) \mid d_i = ?r_j : T\ \wedge\ u_j = v_i \,\}$;
- $\mathsf{rewrite}(\{\, (s_1, t_1), \ldots, (s_k, t_k) \,\}) \triangleq [s_1/t_1, \ldots, s_k/t_k]$;

where v_i and u_j are data values, there are m variable declarations in the list $d_1 \ldots d_n$, i ranges over all data passing declarations and j ranges over variable declarations.

As an illustration of this construct, in the communication protocol example, we may wish to enforce an exception behaviour on receipt of an out of range sequence number. For example, we may re-express our receiving fragment of behaviour as follows.

$$receive?n : nat\,[n \leq 1]\,;$$
$$(\,[m = n]\,->\,put\,;\,sendAck!n\,;$$
$$Receiver[put, receive, sendAck](comp(m))$$
$$[]$$
$$[m \neq n]\,->\,sendAck!n\,;$$
$$Receiver[put, receive, sendAck](m)\,)$$
$$[>$$
$$receive?n : nat\,[n > 1]\,;\,B_{except}$$

6.2.7 Generalised Choice

We can further generalise choice, enabling it to be defined over a number of variable declarations. Thus, it can take the following form,

$$choice\ m_1 : T_1, \ldots, m_n : T_n\ []\ B$$

where for $i \neq j$, $m_i \neq m_j$, B will typically refer to $m_1, \ldots, m_n$ and there are no binding occurrences of m_i in B. Thus, $m_i : T_i$ is a declaration, which specifies that the variable m_i ranges over the type T_i. This allows us to express infinite choices, such as the following,

$$choice\ n : nat\ []\ B \qquad \text{where typically } B \text{ references } n$$

which states that B will be performed with n instantiated by one of $0, 1, \ldots$.

The following inference rule interprets this operator.

$$\frac{B[v_1/m_1, \ldots, v_n/m_n] \xrightarrow{a} B'}{(choice\ m_1 : T_1, \ldots, m_n : T_n\ []\ B) \xrightarrow{a} B'}\ (v_1 \in T_1, \ldots, v_n \in T_n)$$

It should also be noted that the generalised choice,

$$choice\ n : T\ []\ a!n\,;\,B$$

is equivalent to the action prefix $a?n : T\,;\,B$.

As an example of the relationship between ! and ?, we could re-express the fragment of receiver behaviour highlighted at the end of the previous Section (6.2.6) as follows.

$choice\ n : nat$ []
   ($[n = m] ->$ $receive!n$; put ; $sendAck!n$;
                    $Receiver[put, receive, sendAck](comp(m))$

   []
   $[n \neq m \land n \leq 1] ->$ $receive!n$; $sendAck!n$;
                        $Receiver[put, receive, sendAck](m)$

   []
   $[n > 1] ->$ $receive!n$; B_{except})

Notice that, because we do not use disabling here, the exception behaviour can only occur at the initial choice point, where the behaviour is waiting to perform an action on gate *receive*. In contrast, the use of disabling in the fragment highlighted at the end of the previous section (6.2.6), allows the exception behaviour to be initiated at any point during the execution of the normal behaviour.

In conclusion then, generalised choice can either be parameterised on sets of actions (see Section 6.1.2) or data types.

6.2.8 Parameterised Enabling

Sequential composition, also called enabling,

$$B_1 >> B_2$$

may also be parameterised. This has the effect of binding data values from B_1 to variables contained in B_2 on successful termination. However, in order for this to happen we need some extra syntax to enable us to match up the values generated from B_1 with the variables contained in B_2. There are three aspects to this syntax; firstly, a parameterised *exit* notation,

$$exit(e_1, \ldots, e_n)$$

which defines the list of values that are generated from a behaviour on successful termination; secondly, the functionality parameter referenced in process and specification headers (the F in the abstract syntax of Section 6.2.9) is enhanced in order to define the typing associated with successful termination of that process; i.e.

$$exit(T_1, \ldots, T_n)$$

Thirdly, a special construct, *accept*, is introduced in order that the enabled behaviour can accept the values passed through sequential composition. This gives us the following general form for sequential composition,

$$B_1 >> accept\ m_1 : T_1, \ldots, m_n : T_n\ in\ B_2$$

which states that, on successful termination of B_1, the variables $m_1, \ldots, m_n$, of the specified types, will be bound in B_2 to the exit values of behaviour B_1. We again assume that there are no binding occurrences of the m_is in B_2 and that for $i \neq j$, $m_i \neq m_j$.

Determining the functionality of a behaviour is not completely straightforward. In particular, in order for the functionality of a process to be identified, all *exits* in the process must have compatible functionality. For example, *exit(true)* and *exit(5)*, as used in, say,

        $a\,;\, exit(true) \;|||\; b\,;\, exit(5)$

are clearly not compatible. However, in order to give some flexibility in defining exit parameters, the construct *any* is introduced. This can be used to state that any value from a type is an acceptable exit parameter. For example, *exit(5, any bool)* and *exit(any nat, true)* would match with functionality *(nat,bool)* and would terminate with the values *(5, true)*. In contrast, *exit(5, any bool)* and *exit(4, true)* would not match.

There is a set of rules that enable the functionality of a behaviour to be defined. These rules express how the functionality of the constituent operators of a process are determined. For more details, the interested reader is referred to [24, 101].

The following inference rules interpret these operators. Firstly, we interpret parameterised successful termination.

$$\frac{-}{exit(e_1, \ldots, e_n) \xrightarrow{\;\delta\_v_1\ldots\_v_n\;} stop}$$

where $\forall i (1 \leq i \leq n)$,

$$v_i = eval(E) \quad if \quad e_i = E$$

$$v_i \in T \quad if \quad e_i = any\ T$$

Using the function *name*, which returns the underlying gate name of a data passing action, we have two rules for the accept operator. We begin with a rule that allows behaviour B_1 to evolve.

$$\frac{B_1 \xrightarrow{\;a\;} B_1'}{B_1 >> accept\ m_1 : T_1, \ldots, m_n : T_n\ in\ B_2 \atop \xrightarrow{\;a\;}} \quad (name(a) \neq \delta)$$

$$B_1' >> accept\ m_1 : T_1, \ldots, m_n : T_n\ in\ B_2$$

Thus, B_1 can perform any action, as long as it is not a successful termination. The final rule characterises the point of successful termination.

$$\frac{B_1 \xrightarrow{\;\delta\_v_1\ldots\_v_n\;} B_1'}{B_1 >> accept\ m_1 : T_1, \ldots, m_n : T_n\ in\ B_2 \atop \xrightarrow{\;i\;}}$$

$$B_2[v_1/m_1, \ldots, v_n/m_n]$$

So, a successful termination action passes control to B_2, subject to the bindings arising from the accept construction.

Parameterised enabling is illustrated in the Dining Philosophers example shortly.

6.2.9 Syntax of fLOTOS

This section brings together the constructs that we have introduced to give an abstract syntax for fLOTOS. The syntax defines an arbitrary specification $S \in fLOTOS$ as follows.

$$S ::= specification \ I \ [g^\times]((n:T)^\times) \ : \ F \ \ TD \ behaviour \ U \ endspec$$

$$U ::= B \ | \ B \ where \ \ TD \ D^+$$

$$D ::= process \ P \ [g^\times]((n:T)^\times) \ : \ F \ := \ U \ endproc$$

$$B ::= stop \ | \ exit(e^\times) \ | \ i \ ; \ B \ | \ g \ d^\#[be] \ ; \ B \ | \ B_1 \ [] \ B_2 \ | \ [be] \rightarrow B \ |$$
$$B_1 \ ||[g^\times]|| \ B_2 \ | \ B_1 >> accept \ (n:T)^\times \ in \ B_2 \ | \ hide \ g^+ \ in \ B \ |$$
$$B[(g/h)^+] \ | \ P[g^\times](E^\times) \ | \ B_1 \ [> B_2 \ | \ choice \ df \ [] \ B \ |$$
$$par \ (g \ in \ [h^+])^+ \ ||[g^\times]|| \ B \ | \ let \ (n:T=E)^+ \ in \ B$$

$$F ::= noexit \ | \ exit(T^\times)$$

$$df ::= (g \ in \ [h^+])^+ \ | \ (n:T)^+$$

$$d ::= !E \ | \ ?n:T$$

$$e ::= any \ T \ | \ E$$

where $Z^\#$ is the same as $Z^\times$, except the repetitions are not separated by commas, $g, h \in Gate$, $I, P \in PIdent$,[6] n is a data variable, T is a data type, E is a data expression, be is a Boolean expression, TD is a data type declaration (the syntax of which is left unspecified), F are functionality parameters, e are exit parameters and d are data passing declarations.

We also assume the following defined special cases of operators.

$$exit \ \triangleq \ exit(\ )$$

$$g \ d_1 \ ... \ d_n \ ; \ B \ \triangleq \ g \ d_1 \ ... \ d_n \ [true] \ ; \ B$$

$$B_1 >> B_2 \ \triangleq \ B_1 >> accept \ in \ B_2$$

6.2.10 Comments

Comments can appear anywhere in fLOTOS specifications and are enclosed in starred brackets as follows,

$$(* \ ... \ *)$$

---

[6] Again, we do not distinguish the domain of specification names from that of process names.

6.3 Examples

As an illustration of fLOTOS, we present complete specifications of the two running examples that we have been using: the communication protocol and the Dining Philosophers.[7] Together, these specifications illustrate the major features of fLOTOS.

6.3.1 Communication Protocol

The top-level behaviour of the communication protocol is as follows:

> *specification protocol* [*start, get, put*] : *noexit*
>
> > *(* Type Definitions *)*
>
> *behaviour*
>
> > *start*;
> >
> > > *(hide send, receive, sendAck, receiveAck in*
> > >
> > > > *((Sender*[*get, send, receiveAck*](0)
> > > >
> > > > ||| *Receiver*[*put, receive, sendAck*](0))
> > > >
> > > > |[*send, receive, sendAck, receiveAck*]|
> > > >
> > > > *DupMedium*[*send, receive, sendAck, receiveAck*]))
>
> *where*
>
> > *(* Definition of Sender *)*
> >
> > *(* Definition of Receiver *)*
> >
> > *(* Definition of DupMedium *)*
>
> *endspec*

The protocol has three external actions, *start*, *get* and *put*. The first of these starts the communication system. The *get* action is used to request transmission of a message from outside the protocol, e.g. from the previous layer in a protocol stack. Notice that the sender and receiver processes are instantiated with the value of the starting sequence number as their actual parameters.

The behaviour of the sender could be specified as follows.

> *process Sender* [*get, send, receiveAck*](*n* : *nat*) : *noexit* :=
>
> > *get*; *send*!*n*; *Sending*[*get, send, receiveAck*](*n*)
>
> *endproc*

---

[7]The Dining Philosophers specification is taken from the SEDOS tool set, which is, in turn, based upon a similar specification to be found in [96].

process Sending [*get, send, receiveAck*](*m : nat*) : *noexit* :=

 hide timeout in

  (*timeout*; *send*!*m*; *Sending*[*get, send, receiveAck*](*m*)

  []

  receiveAck?*n : nat*;

   ([*m = n*] −> *Sender*[*get, send, receiveAck*](*comp*(*m*))

   []

   [*m* ≠ *n*] −> *send*!*m*;

      Sending[*get, send, receiveAck*](*m*)))

 endproc

One point to observe is that, although we model sequence numbers directly, using natural numbers, we still do not model the data elements of a message. These could easily be added, yielding action instances of the form *send*!*d*!*n* and *receive*?*d : data*?*n : nat*, where *data* is a new data type. However, because this communication layer is blind to the contents of these data items and just relays them through as encapsulated packets, message data has no effect on the behaviour of the protocol and is thus abstracted away at this level.

 The sender behaviour here has a similar structure to that encoded in the nondata passing version of the protocol considered in Section 2.4. However, now *receiveAck*s are not always assumed to be acknowledgements of the expected message, as they were in the pbLOTOS example. Rather, now, an incorrect acknowledgement is assumed to indicate that the receiver has resent an acknowledgement to the previous message. This could arise if the receiver times out waiting for a message. In response to this situation, the sender will resend the current message (assuming its previous transmission of the same message was lost in the medium).

 As discussed in Section 6.2.4.1, the behaviour of the receiver could be specified as follows.

process Receiver [*put, receive, sendAck*](*m : nat*) : *noexit* :=

 hide timeout in

  (*timeout*; *sendAck*!*comp*(*m*);

     Receiver[*put, receive, sendAck*](*m*)

  []

  receive?*n : nat*;

   ([*m = n*] −> *put*; *sendAck*!*n*;

      Receiver[*put, receive, sendAck*](*comp*(*m*))

   []

   [*m* ≠ *n*] −> *sendAck*!*n*;

      Receiver[*put, receive, sendAck*](*m*)))

 endproc

The top-level behaviour of the medium (which is now a duplex communication channel) could be specified as

> *process DupMedium* [*send, receive, sendAck, receiveAck*] : *noexit* :=
>   *Medium*[*send, receive*] ||| *Medium*[*sendAck, receiveAck*]
> *endproc*

which in turn uses the following medium.

> *process Medium* [*in, out*] : *noexit* :=
>   *in?n* : *nat*;
>   (*i*; *Medium*[*in, out*]
>   []
>   *out!n*; *Medium*[*in, out*])
> *endproc*

Notice that both directions of transmission can be modelled using the same behaviour, with some simple renaming. This is because both mediums pass on and lose messages in the same way.

This represents a typical LOTOS specification of a communication protocol, however, the specification is not wholly satisfactory, because timeouts in communication protocols make such specifications time dependent. Hence, to give a completely representative specification of this protocol, we would like to associate a time value with the action *timeout* and, hence, make the offering of this action dependent upon the time at which other actions can occur. This is not possible in LOTOS, because the language only considers "qualitative timing"; see Section 1.3. We discuss extensions to LOTOS that support quantitative timing in Part IV.

As was the case for our nondata passing protocol example, the specification presented here is very similar to that investigated in demo 2 of the standard release of the CADP tools [81]; see our earlier discussion in Section 3.4.2. Once again, the verification presented in the CADP demo can be viewed as an illustration of how a protocol specification such as ours could be formally verified against a requirements description.[8]

---

[8]The reader comparing the CADP communication protocol with ours should though beware of a number of differences between the two. Firstly, the CADP version does include a data component to message transmissions, however, we have abstracted from this detail; see the discussion earlier in this section. Secondly, rather than using guarded commands, the CADP specification uses data passing conditionals in the style of the fragment at the end of Section 6.2.4.3. Thirdly, actions *PUT* and *GET* in the CADP specification actually play the opposite role to *put* and *get* in our protocol specification. Thus, in the CADP example, *PUT* plays the role of putting into the protocol (at the sender end), whereas in our specification, *put* plays the role of putting into the layer above the protocol (at the receiver end). Finally, the CADP specification also includes the possibility that the mediums can

6.3.2 Dining Philosophers

Assuming the definition of the constant data types, *name*, *side*, *action* and *chopstick*, introduced at the beginning of Section 6.2, the top-level behaviour of the Dining Philosophers can be specified as follows.

> *specification philo [pick, put] : noexit*
>
> > *(* Type Definitions *)*
>
> *behaviour*
>
> > *ThinkTank [pick, put] || ChopSticks [pick, put]*
>
> *where*
>
> > *(* Definition of ThinkTank *)*
> >
> > *(* Definition of ChopSticks *)*
>
> *endspec*

Thus, the specification is composed of the collection of philosophers, which reside in process *ThinkTank*, and the collection of chopsticks, which reside in process *ChopSticks*. These two components are run together fully synchronised in parallel. As a result, the actions of the specification, which are all either on gates *pick* or *put*, can only be performed jointly by the *ThinkTank* and the *ChopSticks* components. In other words, an eating implement can only be moved (to a mouth or back to the table) by a philosopher.

ThinkTank is defined as follows.

> *process ThinkTank [pick, put] : noexit :=*
>
> > *phil [pick, put] (Aristotle, stick1, stick4)*
> > |||
> > *phil [pick, put] (Buddha, stick2, stick1)*
> > |||
> > *phil [pick, put] (Confucius, stick3, stick2)*
> > |||
> > *phil [pick, put] (Descartes, stick4, stick3)*
>
> *endproc*

This process simply runs the four philosophers independently in parallel, with the appropriate instantiation of data values. The use of independent parallelism here reflects the fact that the philosophers do not communicate amongst themselves; our philosophers have simple needs: they are only motivated to

---

knowingly lose a message; i.e. with an indication that the message has been lost, and, in this situation, the mediums notify the sender and receiver of this loss, which resend accordingly.

sustain themselves by eating and by (self-) reflecting on their theories. How-ever, they have no desire to subject their ideas to the competing views of their co-thinkers.

All philosophers have the same basic behaviour, which is coded in process *phil*.

> *process phil [pick, put] (n:name, l,r:chopstick): noexit :=*
>
>> *(pick !n !l !left; exit(n, eat)*
>> |||
>> *pick !n !r !right; exit(n, eat))*
>>> *>> accept n1:name, ac: action in*
>>> *(put !n !l !left; exit(n, think)*
>>> |||
>>> *put !n !r !right; exit(n, think))*
>>>> *>> accept n1:name, ac:action in*
>>>> *phil [pick, put] (n,l,r)*
>
> *endproc*

Thus, philosophers repeatedly perform a sequence of phases. The first of these involves picking up (in either order) the two pieces of cutlery required to eat. Once these have been acquired, the philosopher enters an eating state.[9] Then, once the philosopher is satiated, he decides to put his two sticks down (again in either order) so that he can liberate his mind from the demands of controlling his eating implements and can satisfy his other needs: to think. This sequence of phases repeats ad infinitum.

The chopsticks also exist independently in parallel with each other.

> *process ChopSticks [pick, put] : noexit :=*
>
>> *stick [pick, put] (stick1)*
>> |||
>> *stick [pick, put] (stick2)*
>> |||
>> *stick [pick, put] (stick3)*
>> |||
>> *stick [pick, put] (stick4)*
>
> *endproc*
>
> *process stick [pick, put] (chs:chopstick): noexit :=*
>
>> *pick ?n:name !chs ?s:side;*

---

[9]Note, the data values passed through the sequential composition, here bound to *n1* and *ac*, are actually superfluous, because they are not used in the enabled behaviour. Thus, they are included here as a, somewhat artificial, demonstration of the successful termination syntax.

$$put\ ?n:name\ !chs\ ?s:side;\ stick\,[pick,\ put]\,(chs)$$

endproc

endspec

So, each chopstick simply makes itself available to be picked up and then put down.

This specification correctly models the behaviour of the Dining Philosophers scenario, however, it contains a deadlock. For example, because there are only four chopsticks shared amongst four philosophers and each philosopher requires two sticks to eat, the following trace will yield a deadlock,

$$pick\_Confucius\_stick3\_left\quad pick\_Aristotle\_stick1\_left$$
$$pick\_Descartes\_stick4\_left\quad pick\_Buddha\_stick2\_left$$

The result of this sequence (and there are a number of others) is that all philosophers hold a single stick (actually, all in the same hand) and there are no more sticks left on the table. However, two sticks are required in order to eat and, thus, every philosopher is blocked in his effort to satisfy his appetite and the system is deadlocked. The upshot of which is that all the philosophers will eventually starve to death!

There are many known solutions to the Dining Philosophers problem. However, we only have room to focus on one of these approaches. This adds a constraining process that limits the capacity of philosophers to pick up sticks.[10]

behaviour
    ThinkTank [pick, put]
    ||
    ChopSticks [pick, put]
    ||
    StickConstraint [pick, put] (0, 0)

This added constraint keeps track of the total number of chopsticks that are in left, respectively, right-hands, which it does by maintaining a global count of the number of left (nl), respectively, right (nr), stick allocations.

process StickConstraint [pick, put] (nl, nr: int) : noexit :=

    pick ?n:name ?chs:chopstick !left [nl < 3];
        StickConstraint [pick, put] (nl + 1, nr)
    []
    pick ?n:name ?chs:chopstick !right [nr < 3];
        StickConstraint [pick, put] (nl, nr + 1)

---

[10] Note, this is a nice example of the value of multiway synchronisation, which enables constraining behaviours to be run in parallel, synchronising on existing interactions in the constrained system. Thus, it enables the *constraint-oriented* specification style [196].

[]
put ?n:name ?chs:chopstick !left;
            StickConstraint [pick, put] (nl − 1, nr)
[]
put ?n:name ?chs:chopstick !right;
            StickConstraint [pick, put] (nl, nr − 1)

    endproc

This constraint prevents the occurrence of deadlock: a chopstick may only be picked up as right or left chopstick, if there are less than three chopsticks picked up as left, respectively, right chopstick. Thus, the transition system arising from this constrained Dining Philosophers will be the same as that for the original (nonconstrained) Dining Philosophers, except that, branches that lead to four chopsticks being placed in four left (respectively, right) hands will not arise. Thus, traces of the form of the deadlock causing trace we highlighted earlier will not arise.

6.4 Extended LOTOS

The E-LOTOS restandardisation activity was completed in 2001 [103]. It is beyond the scope of this format to present an exhaustive discussion of the notation, the interested reader is referred to an overview of the language presented as Chapter 5 of [41]. Thus, we merely give a very brief summary of the extensions.

    The list of features added is extensive; it includes the following,

- A modules facility,
- A new (ML-based) data language,
- Real-time features (which are discussed in more depth in Part IV),
- A re-evaluation of sequential composition,
- Entwining of the process and data parts,
- Imperative features (such as assignment and loops),
- A more general parallel composition operator,
- A suspend / resume operator (a generalisation of the disabling operator),
- Exception handling, and
- Subtyping and typed gates.

Thus, although backward compatibility with LOTOS has been maintained, in many respects, E-LOTOS is a completely new language. Each of the new features is individually elegant and well justified. However, because the resulting complete language is now rather large, it is not clear how the features will sit together. In particular, the basic semantic definitions are now rather complex.

This can be argued to be unavoidable for an "industrially usable" language. However, it certainly contrasts with standard LOTOS, which has a simple semantic interpretation. Consequently, theoretical investigations of standard LOTOS are feasible, e.g. axiomatisation [28]. Such investigations will be harder with E-LOTOS.

In fact, in some respects, E-LOTOS is running against the tide of concurrency theory research, which has been moving in the direction of pared down tractable notations; i.e. that are amenable to formal verification. In contrast, E-LOTOS adds functionality at the expense of ease of verification and tractability.

This said, the added features certainly enhance the specification power of the language. For example, it is clear that ACT-ONE (the "original" LOTOS data language) was a major hindrance to the industrial uptake of LOTOS [150] and the new data language resolves many of the concerns raised by users. Furthermore, the real-time features are very powerful and enable application of the language to a whole new class of systems.

7

Comparison of LOTOS with CCS and CSP

There are now many process calculi, all in some way inspired by the pioneering work of Milner, Hoare and, a little later, Roscoe. Prominent within this family of basic calculi are, CCS, CSP, CIRCAL [144], ACP [15], LOTOS and SCCS [146].[1] A small portion of the history of the development of these calculi is depicted in Figure 7.1. As this diagram indicates, LOTOS can largely be seen as a syntactic and semantic composite of CSP and CCS. In fact, one of the most interesting aspects of LOTOS is how it seeks to reconcile the two different approaches. This chapter makes a broad comparison between LOTOS and each of these other two techniques. Although, we make no claims to be exhaustive in this comparison. Rather, our focus is on a small set of key differences between the approaches.

This material has been prepared with reference to the CCS notation defined in [148] and the CSP notation defined in [96] and in [171]. Although, in the latter case, there are actually a number of differences between Hoare's 1985 presentation of CSP and Roscoe's updating of the approach in 1997. As a result, our comparison between LOTOS and CSP is somewhat longer and more caveat laden than our CCS comparison. In addition, the unpublished notes associated with the tutorial [77] have proved valuable source material.

In terms of motivation, the three techniques have some differences.

- In CCS, Milner sought to identify a minimal calculus from which all useful behaviour and operators can be defined. Thus, the base language is deliberately small.
- CSP is, in some respects, an investigation into the spectrum of possible "useful" operators for expressing concurrent behaviour. Thus, [96] and [171] contain a large number of operators, which they characterise mathematically.

---

[1]Note again that we are not considering here an important branch of process calculi focused on mobility of processes and communication channels, e.g. [149].

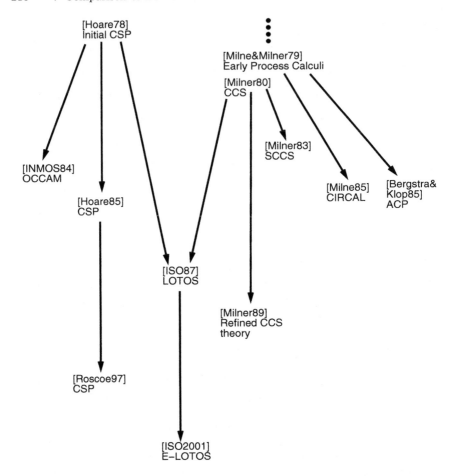

Fig. 7.1. Portion of the History of Process Calculi

- LOTOS has sought to standardise a "canonical" set of operators, where they are canonical both in terms of usability and in terms of primitiveness. In this respect, LOTOS could be argued to sit between CCS and CSP.

Before we compare the approaches, it is important not to overlook that, despite the impression that our comparisons may give, the three calculi are, in a broader sense, very similar. This is because all the notations are built upon the basic idea of atomic actions, their combining operators and interleaving (branching-time) semantics. This is the starting point for all the calculi.

We relate CCS and CSP to LOTOS separately.

7.1 CCS and LOTOS

We begin with Table 7.1, which summarises how LOTOS and CCS relate construct by construct. Bold in the table indicates syntactic constructs that are very closely related, whereas constructs not in bold are only approximately related. However, the comparison here is not exhaustive in respect of LOTOS operators, which are, as a reflection of the different intents of the notations, a lot more numerous than in CCS. We particularly concentrate on differences between the notations as they are most revealing with regard to the character of the LOTOS approach.

As indicated in this table, a number of the CCS and LOTOS constructs are analogous, e.g. ports and gates, agents and behaviours and action prefix. However, some of the operators have subtly different and some significantly different behaviour. We consider these differences in the following sections.

7.1.1 Parallel Composition and Complementation of Actions

It is here that the greatest differences exist between LOTOS and CCS. With regard to parallel composition, LOTOS is much more akin to CSP. CCS employs a *biparty* synchronous communication paradigm, whereas LOTOS uses *multiway* synchronisation.

In CCS, each observable action, x say, has a complement, $\overline{x}$, with which it can synchronise. Such annotation of actions defines the communication patterns within a specification. The concept is best illustrated by example. Consider the CCS behaviour:

$$X \stackrel{def}{=} (x.A \mid \overline{x}.A' \mid \overline{x}.A'')$$

which yields the derivation tree depicted in Figure 7.2. Thus, any of the actions that are initially offered by the three constituent behaviours, $x.A$, $\overline{x}.A'$ and $\overline{x}.A''$, are offered individually by the composite behaviour (and suitable evolution of the complete behaviour takes place). In addition, the action x could synchronise with either of the two complement actions and evolve accordingly. Thus, the derivation allows x to interact with either of the $\overline{x}$ actions, but, it is important to note that the two $\overline{x}$ actions cannot interact together.

In addition, notice the use of internal (or perfect) actions to identify a synchronisation / communication in CCS, the τ actions in Figure 7.2. The implication of this is that an interaction between two parties is closed to any third party. This also motivates the preference for restriction rather than hiding, which we discuss shortly.

Thus, in CCS, we obtain a biparty form of synchronisation, which contrasts with the multiway synchronisation offered by LOTOS. For example, in LOTOS, we could give an example which, at least superficially, looks related to the above, viz,

$$Q := x; B \mid [x] \mid x; B' \mid [x] \mid x; B''$$

Construct	CCS	LOTOS
Computation Units	Agents $(A_1, A_2,\dots)$	Behaviours $(B_1, B_2,\dots)$
Interaction Points	Ports $(p_1, p_2,\dots)$	Gates $(g_1, g_2,\dots)$
Units of Observation	Observable Actions $(x_1, x_2,\dots)\ (\overline{x}_1, \overline{x}_2,\dots)$	Observable Actions $(x_1, x_2,\dots)$
Internal Actions	τ	i
Action Prefix	$a.A$	$a; B$
Inaction	0	$stop$
Binary Choice	$A + A'$	$B\ []\ B'$
Parallel Composition	$A \mid A'$ (+ action complementation)	$B\ |[G]|\ B'$
Hiding	$A \backslash G$ (restriction)	$hide\ G\ in\ B$ (hiding)
Process Definition	$X \stackrel{def}{=} A$	$P := B$
Recursion	$fix\ (X = A)$	$P := B$ (P referenced in B)
Relabelling	$A[f]$ or $A[x'_1/x_1,\dots,x'_n/x_n]$	$B[x'_1/x_1,\dots,x'_n/x_n]$
Generalised Choice	$\sum_{j \in I} A_j$	$choice\ x\ in\ G\ []\ B$
Successful Termination	Not in basic calculus	$exit$
Enabling	Not in basic calculus	$B_1 >> B_2$
Generalised Parallelism	$\Pi_{j \in I}\ A_j$	$par\ x\ in\ G\ |[H]|\ B$
Value Passing Actions	$x(r),\quad \overline{x}(E)$	$x\,?r : T,\quad x\,!E$

Table 7.1. Relating CCS and LOTOS Constructs

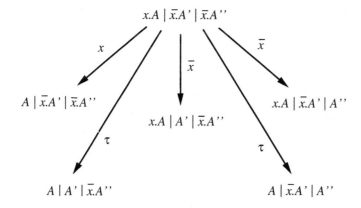

Fig. 7.2. Derivation of CCS Parallel Composition

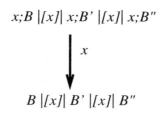

Fig. 7.3. Derivation of LOTOS Parallel Composition

which can only perform a single transition, as depicted in Figure 7.3. This aspect of LOTOS is often vaunted as a motivation for preferring the language; in particular, it enables the constraint-oriented style of specification, discussions of which can be found in [171, 196].

Returning to the CCS communication mechanism, you can also view actions such as x as input actions, and complemented actions, $\bar{x}$, as output actions. This becomes evident when the data passing calculus is considered and the values of expressions are associated with $\bar{x}$, e.g. $\bar{x}(r+5)$, and variable bindings are associated with x, e.g. $x(n)$. Thus, complementation has a relation to ! and ? in LOTOS. Although, through their interplay with multiway synchronisation, LOTOS ! and ? are more general, e.g. value generation can be created; see Section 6.2.4.1.

Another aspect of relating LOTOS concurrency to CCS concurrency is to find equivalents of the extreme forms of LOTOS parallel composition, ||| and ||. The first of these is, in effect, duplicated by CCS parallel composition; i.e.

$$A_1 \mid A_2$$

when $\mathcal{L}(A_1) \cap \overline{\mathcal{L}}(A_2) = \emptyset$; i.e. when the two sides of the parallel composition do not have any complementary actions. However, the generation of τ actions by CCS synchronisation prevents an equivalent of $\parallel$ from existing.

7.1.2 Restriction and Hiding

The CCS equivalent of hiding is called restriction, however, this operator does not generate internal actions; rather it removes actions (and the labelled transition system subgraph rooted at that transition) altogether. For example, the transitions that can be performed by $X\backslash\{x\}$, where X was defined in the previous section, are depicted in Figure 7.4. Thus, all actions, or complements of actions, in the restriction set are literally blocked from occurring. The related hiding of x in the LOTOS behaviour Q would yield the transition depicted in Figure 7.5.

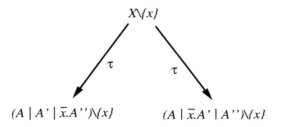

Fig. 7.4. Derivation of CCS Parallel Composition with Restriction

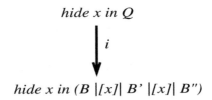

Fig. 7.5. Derivation of LOTOS Parallel Composition with Hiding

This difference in interpretation arises because restriction is typically used in CCS to limit evolution of a behaviour to just synchronisation transitions; i.e. the τ transitions. Thus, a typical specification strategy is to define synchronisation between an action and its complement and then restrict the specification in terms of that action.

7.1.3 Internal Behaviour

Modulo the differences discussed in the last two sections; i.e. the direct generation of internal actions as markers of synchronisation and the use of restriction rather than hiding, CCS and LOTOS treat internal actions in similar ways. In particular, the LOTOS handling of internal behaviour in choice contexts is directly inherited from CCS; i.e. in respect of the creation of symmetric and asymmetric internal choices.

In addition, LOTOS's "fair" (rather than catastrophic) treatment of divergence (see Section 5.1.4) is also largely inherited from CCS. This issue really comes down to how divergence is handled in bisimulation relations, which are the key means of semantic interpretation in CCS. By not adding an explicit divergence term or condition and simply relying on the capacity of the double arrow ($\Longrightarrow$) relation to pass through tau cycles, weak bisimulation (in particular) satisfies Kooman's Fair Abstraction property [8]; see our discussion in Section 5.1.4.

In addition, CCS obtains a "weak" congruence relation. This is typically called observational congruence [145]. It is a little stronger than weak bisimulation, because it constrains the initial internal moves of the two behaviours in order to prevent the classic nonsubstitutive choice context, viz, that, using CCS syntax,

$\tau.x.0$ and $x.0$ are weak bisimilar

but

$\tau.x.0 + y.0$ and $x.0 + y.0$ are not.

Thus, CCS observational congruence uses the same trick we used in our bisimulation congruence introduced in Section 3.3.3.1.

Finally, it is also interesting that use of the restriction operator in CCS, rather than hiding, may make the quest for congruences more straightforward. For example, nonsubstitutive cases, such as were highlighted in Figure 5.4 with regard to LOTOS testing equivalence, do not carry over to the restriction operator.

7.1.4 Minor Differences

There are a number of further minor (and mainly syntactic) differences between CCS and LOTOS, some of which we document here.

- *Relabelling.* The only point to make here is that CCS relabelling can be arbitrarily placed between other operators in a behaviour expression, whereas, in LOTOS, relabelling syntactically arises through action parameter binding on process invocation. In addition, the LOTOS equivalent of CCS relabelling (i.e. $B[x_1/y_1, \ldots, x_n/y_n]$) is syntactically hidden from the specifier.

- *Generalised Choice.* This takes a somewhat different form in the two notations. The CCS *summation* operator is indexed over some indexing set. So, for example,

  $\sum_{j\in\{1,2,3\}} A_j = A_1 + A_2 + A_3$

  If the indexing set is infinite, an infinite choice is generated. In contrast, the LOTOS generalised choice operator is parameterised on gates or variable names. Two typical examples are:

  choice x in [y, z, w] [] x ; P
  choice n : [1 ... 10] [] z !n ; Q

- *Exit and Enabling.* Neither successful termination nor sequential composition is included as primitive in CCS. However, Milner shows how similar forms can be derived from the basic CCS calculus (see [148] Chapter 9) by running the enabling and enabled behaviours together in parallel, subject to synchronisation on a distinguished action that signals termination of the enabling behaviour and plays the role of the LOTOS action δ. We reuse this approach in Section 14.1. In a value passing calculus, data values could be passed with this distinguished action, thus yielding a derived analogue of fLOTOS's parameterised *exit* and *accept* constructs.

- *Recursion.* CCS defines recursion using a fixed point notation and explicit self-reference interchangeably. This is because the fixed point notation:

  fix $(X = A)$

  is more easy to deal with in certain formal situations.

7.2 CSP and LOTOS

In general, in terms of parallel composition, LOTOS and CSP are similar, and CCS is different, whereas in terms of choice, LOTOS and CCS are similar, and CSP is different. In addition, it should be noted that, in a number of respects, time has brought CSP and LOTOS closer together. In particular, the presentation of CSP in [171] is more similar to LOTOS than the version of the language discussed in [96]. For example, the parallel composition stories are a good deal closer in [171].

We present a list of LOTOS and CSP comparisons in Tables 7.2 and 7.3. In the following sections, we consider in more depth key constructs that are different.

7.2.1 Alphabets

An initial point that is worth making is the important role that alphabets play in CSP. All processes have an explicitly associated alphabet of actions and the operators of the language are each defined to have specific effects on alphabets. The notation αP denotes the alphabet of process P. As an example, the following rule is associated with the parallel composition operator $\|$.

Construct	CSP	LOTOS
Computation Units	Processes $(P_1, P_2,\ldots)$	Behaviours $(B_1, B_2,\ldots)$
Interaction Points	Channels $(c_1, c_2,\ldots)$	Gates $(g_1, g_2,\ldots)$
Units of Observation	Events $(x_1, x_2,\ldots)$	Observable Actions $(x_1, x_2,\ldots)$
Internal Actions	Not directly referencible	i
Action Prefix	$x \to P$	$a\,;\,B$
Inaction	*stop*	*stop*
Deterministic Choice	$x_1 \to P_1 \mid x_2 \to P_2$ $x_1 \neq x_2$	$x_1\,;\,B_1\ []\ x_2\,;\,B_2$ $x_1 \neq x_2 \neq i$
Generalised Deterministic Choice	$?x : A \to P(x)$ (A a set of actions)	*choice* x *in* $G\ []\ x\,;\,B$
External Choice	$P_1\ []\ P_2$	$B_1\ []\ B_2$
Nondeterministic Choice	$P_1 \sqcap P_2$	$i\,;\,B_1\ []\ i\,;\,B_2$
Generalised Non-deterministic Choice	$\sqcap S$ (S a set of processes)	*choice* x *in* $G\ []\ i\,;\,B$ *choice* $r : T\ []\ i\,;\,B$
Independent Parallel	$P_1 \mid\mid\mid P_2$	$B_1 \mid\mid\mid B_2$
Alphabetised Parallel	$P_1\ _{\alpha P_1}\|_{\alpha P_2}\ P_2$ (although, see caption)	$B_1\ \|[G]\|\ B_2$ $(G = \mathcal{L}(B_1) \cap \mathcal{L}(B_2))$
Fully Synchronised	$P_1\ _\Sigma\|_\Sigma\ P_2$ (Σ the set of all actions)	$B_1 \mid\mid B_2$

Table 7.2. Relating CSP and LOTOS Constructs (continued in Table 7.3). Note though that, in fact, the alphabetised parallel considered here is the one used in [96], Roscoe generalises the operator by allowing it to be parameterised on sets of actions other than the intrinsic alphabet of the constituent processes [171].

Construct	CSP	LOTOS
Generalised Parallel	$P_1 \parallel_A P_2$	$B_1 \,|[G]|\, B_2$
Hiding	$P\backslash A$ (concealment)	$hide\ G\ in\ B$ (hiding)
Process Definition	$X = P$	$P := B$
Recursion	$\mu X.F(X)$ or $X = P$ (X referenced in P)	$P := B$ (P referenced in B)
Relabelling	$f(P)$ f a one-to-one function (although, see caption)	$B[x_1'/x_1, \ldots, x_n'/x_n]$
Successful Termination	$skip$ and $\sqrt{}$	$exit$ and δ
Enabling	$P_1 \,;\, P_2$	$B_1 >> B_2$
Disabling	$P_1 \wedge P_2$	$B_1\ [> B_2$
Value Passing Actions	$x\,!E$, $x\,?r:T$	$x\,!E$, $x\,?r:T$

Table 7.3. Relating CSP and LOTOS Constructs continued. Note, the restriction here that relabelling is a one-to-one function is actually dropped in [171]

$$\alpha(P||Q) = \alpha P \cup \alpha Q$$

In fact, the reason for explicitly recording alphabets is to enable the alphabetised parallel composition operator to be defined[2], because it is expressed explicitly in terms of the alphabets of its constituent processes. We return to this point shortly.

7.2.2 Internal Actions

Internal actions are used for many roles, for example, in CCS τ is used to denote a synchronisation; in LOTOS and CCS it is used to create nondeterminism and it is also used to denote some internal behaviour, perhaps resulting, in LOTOS, from hiding. In CSP, an internal action cannot be directly referenced by the specifier. Although, it can be created through hiding

---

[2]In fact, this was more of an issue for Hoare's 1985 presentation of the language [96], which was particularly strongly focused on the alphabetised parallel operator. In contrast, Roscoe's 1997 presentation [171] reflects the expressive power of generalised parallel, which corresponds to LOTOS's generalised parallel; see Section 7.2.4.

(called concealment in CSP). A consequence of this is that nondeterminism and concealment must be handled differently in CSP compared to LOTOS and we discuss both of these in future sections.

7.2.3 Choice

As already suggested, some major differences between CSP and LOTOS reside in the definition of choice. CSP contains a spectrum of choice operators, each of which captures a different class of choice. One motivation for this is to locate the particular characteristics and laws applicable to each of these classes. In contrast, LOTOS (and CCS as well) uses a single general notion of choice, specialisations of which reflect different forms of CSP choice. We consider each of the CSP choice operators in turn.

7.2.3.1 Deterministic Choice (also Called Guarded Alternative)

This is the most basic form of choice offered in CSP and its binary form is denoted

$$x_1 \to P_1 \mid x_2 \to P_2$$

which is only defined if $x_1 \neq x_2$. Thus, this operator can only express deterministic choices. Remember, internal actions cannot be explicitly referenced, so asymmetric nondeterminism cannot be directly defined with this operator (although, it can be created in combination with concealment).

Using deterministic choice in [96], Hoare is able to define a completely deterministic subcalculus of CSP which he fully characterises using trace semantics. Clearly, a LOTOS equivalent of this operator is given by

$$x_1; B_1 \; [] \; x_2; B_2$$

where nondeterminism is not allowed; i.e. $x_1 \neq x_2$ and neither x_1 or x_2 are internal actions.

CSP allows a generalisation of the binary deterministic choice, denoted

$$?x : A \to P(x)$$

where A is a set of action names; e.g.,

$$?x : \{y, z, w\} \to P(x) \; = \; y \to P(y) \mid z \to P(z) \mid w \to P(w)$$

Notice that, because A is a set, once again, a nondeterministic choice cannot be defined. An obvious equivalent of this behaviour is given by:

$$choice \; x \; in \; A \; [] \; x \, ; \; B$$

7.2.3.2 External Choice

The CSP operator [] strictly generalises deterministic choice. In particular, it adds the possibility that certain forms of nondeterminism can arise, because in

$$P_1 \; [] \; P_2$$

the processes P_1 and P_2 can have any arbitrary form. Thus, a behaviour such as

$$(a \rightarrow Q_1) \; [] \; (a \rightarrow Q_2)$$

is legal. However, because internal actions cannot be explicitly referenced, we cannot directly create internal action induced nondeterminism with this operator. Although, using CSP concealment / hiding, some varieties of such nondeterminism can be created, which we discuss in Section 7.2.5. In summary then, although [] in CSP is certainly the closest to the LOTOS [] operator, due to differences in the languages, it is not quite an analogue of LOTOS choice.

7.2.3.3 Nondeterministic Choice

CSP also includes a pure form of symmetric nondeterministic choice, denoted ⊓, where

$$P_1 \sqcap P_2$$

will internally decide to either behave as P_1 or as P_2. It is not hard to see that the LOTOS equivalent of this behaviour is:

$$i; B_1 \; [] \; i; B_2$$

In addition, a generalised nondeterministic choice is offered in CSP, which is denoted

$$\sqcap S$$

where S is a set of processes. In fact, LOTOS generalised choice cannot be parameterised over sets of processes, so, neither of the following is quite an analogue of this operator.

$$choice \; x \; in \; G \; [] \; i; B \quad or \quad choice \; r : T \; [] \; i; B$$

However, of course, if S is finite, $\sqcap S$ can be expressed as a number of binary nondeterministic choices.

So, we have considered how CSP models the symmetric forms of nondeterminism that were introduced for LOTOS. This only leaves asymmetric nondeterminism:

$$i; B_1 \; [] \; x; B_2$$

The CSP analogue is modelled using a combination of $[]$ and $\sqcap$; i.e,

$$P_1 \; [] \; (x \to P_2 \; \sqcap \; stop)$$

which will initially offer an external choice between P_1 and $x \to P_2$, but, at some point, may nondeterministically decide to evolve to P_1 (actually, $P_1 \; [] \; stop$, which is equivalent).

7.2.4 Parallelism

The basic principles of CSP and LOTOS parallel composition are very similar. Although, the earlier presentations of CSP parallel composition, particularly [96], used alphabetised parallelism. However, by the time of [171], an operator equivalent to LOTOS generalised parallel composition was employed as the primitive form.

Indeed, it is clear that alphabetised parallel can be generated from generalised parallel. Specifically, the alphabetised parallel introduced in [171],

$$P_{1 \; A_1}||_{A_2} \; P_2$$

states that P_1 and P_2 evolve independently in parallel, subject to synchronisation on any events in $A_1 \cap A_2$. The equivalent of this operator is a LOTOS composition:

$$B_1 \; |[G]| \; B_2$$

where G is exactly the set of actions in both A_1 and A_2. In the special case where $A_1 = A_2 = \Sigma$ (Σ is the CSP analogue of Act), the CSP parallel composition is equivalent to the LOTOS fully synchronised parallel composition:

$$B_1 \; || \; B_2$$

In addition, CSP contains an explicit independent parallelism operator $|||$, which is clearly equivalent to the LOTOS parallel composition:

$$B_1 \; ||| \; B_2$$

7.2.5 Hiding

CSP concealment, denoted

$$P \backslash G$$

conceptually has a similar effect to

$$hide \; G \; in \; B$$

In particular, nondeterminism can be created through concealment. For example,

$$(a \rightarrow P_1 \mid b \rightarrow P_2)\backslash\{a,b\}$$

is equivalent to

$$P_1 \sqcap P_2$$

and is, thus, analogous to the LOTOS behaviour,

$$i; B_1 \; [] \; i; B_2$$

This also means that asymmetric nondeterminism can be created using concealment. In particular,

$$(a \rightarrow P_1 \mid b \rightarrow P_2)\backslash\{a\}$$

is analogous to the LOTOS behaviour

$$i; B_1 \; [] \; b; B_2 \qquad (*)$$

However, a subtle, but important distinction is that a concealed action cannot resolve a choice. So,

$$(a \rightarrow P_1)\backslash\{a\} \mid (b \rightarrow P_2)$$

is not equivalent to (*) above. This behaviour is, in fact, analogous to the LOTOS behaviour:

$$B_1 \; [] \; b; B_2$$

This different interpretation of how internal behaviour affects choice turns out to be crucial as it is one reason why CSP is a congruence for refusal-based refinement and equivalence, but LOTOS is not; see [120] and our discussion in Section 7.2.6.2.

7.2.6 Comparison of LOTOS Trace-refusals with CSP Failures-divergences

Of the refusal-based semantics, the CSP failures model [96, 171] is the most well known and has the longest history. As indicated earlier, LOTOS refusal semantics are based upon CSP failures. However, the approaches are different in important respects.

7.2.6.1 Divergence

A fundamental difference between LOTOS trace-refusals and CSP failures is the handling of divergence. In fact, it is in this area that many of the semantic models associated with process calculi can be differentiated [192].

CSP is extreme in its handling of divergence; it employs a, so called, *catastrophic* interpretation, reflecting a strong view of the undesirability of divergence; to quote [96]:

"... divergence is never the intended result of the attempted definition
of a process."

This interpretation of divergence is a reflection of Hoare's concern for imple-
mentability and, clearly, implementation of divergent behaviour is an issue.
However, this view of infinite internal behaviour is not universally accepted,
as exemplified by Kooman's Fair Abstraction property [8] (see Section 5.1.4)
which the LOTOS handling of divergence reflects.

The CSP view of divergence is reflected in the important role the process
CHAOS plays. *CHAOS* is a process that can perform any trace, can refuse
anything after any trace and can diverge after any trace. It is the top element
of the failures–divergences preorder; i.e. every other process is a refinement of
CHAOS, in the sense that, every other process is more deterministic than it. In
fact, *CHAOS* can be viewed as the most nondeterministic and unpredictable
process and, in CSP terms, the "worst" process.

Another important aspect of the catastrophic handling of divergence is
that, if a divergence could occur during a computation, the complete computation is viewed to be divergent. That is, even if a computation can pass
through a divergent state; i.e. one that offers the chance of diverging, but
could also reach a nondivergent state, the computation is viewed to be divergent (and, hence, chaotic); some of the examples we considered in Section
5.1.4, e.g. (6) and (7) in Figure 5.3, have this character. Put another way, any
suffix of a divergent trace is itself divergent. This again reflects the view that
any computation containing the possibility of divergence is unintended.

Divergence is handled quite differently in CCS, and LOTOS inherits this
interpretation: a noncatastrophic approach is employed. For example, in terms
of weak bisimulation, a definition such as

$$R := i; R \; [] \; x; stop$$

is equivalent to the behaviour:

$$T := x; stop$$

even though the R could possibly diverge. Also, see the examples previously
highlighted in Section 5.1.4. As previously suggested, this is often called a
"fair" interpretation of divergence, in the sense that R cannot refuse the observable action x infinitely many times in favour of i. Thus, there must exist
a finite time in the future at which x is offered, hence, Kooman's Fair Abstraction property [8].

The LOTOS trace-refusals semantics reflect this fair (noncatastrophic)
interpretation. Divergence is not distinguished in trace-refusals semantics. For
example, in the above behaviours,

$$[\![\, R \,]\!]_{tr} = [\![\, T \,]\!]_{tr} = \{\, \epsilon \,,\, x \,\} \quad \text{and} \quad Ref_R(\epsilon) = Ref_T(\epsilon) = \mathcal{P}(\mathcal{L} - \{x\})$$

In particular, notice that R does not refuse x after ϵ; this is a direct consequence of employing the Fair Abstraction property. Furthermore, $R \approx T$, because,

$$\{ (R, T), (stop, stop) \}$$

is a suitable weak bisimulation relation.

A consequence of this handling of divergence is that weak bisimularity does not imply CSP failures–divergences equivalence. However, weak bisimularity does imply testing equivalence in the LOTOS setting.

As an illustration of the difference between LOTOS and CSP in respect of handling divergence, consider the weak bisimulation reduction of the CADP LOTOS alternating bit protocol discussed in Section 3.4.2. The resulting transition system generated is very small and also does not contain any "tau" loops; i.e. cycles in the transition system that only involve internal actions. However, the nonreduced transition system of the example did contain tau loops, which could arise, for example, because the system could enter the following pattern of infinite behaviour, the sender sends a message, it is lost in the medium, the sender times out and resends, the resend is again lost etc. Because only *put* and *get* actions are observable, all such cyclic behaviour is divergent.

The reason that such tau loops can be removed under weak bisimulation is due to the noncatastrophic interpretation of divergence. That is, the fairness assumption implies that a process cannot infinitely often select a transition of the loop at the expense of a transition that escapes the divergence; i.e. in our example, a transition that escapes the continuous sequence of retransmission and loss.

This difference between the LOTOS and CSP approaches is reflected in the way that the alternating bit protocol has to be specified in CSP; see Section 5.3 of [171]. Specifically, Roscoe has to go to great lengths to prevent the sort of sequences of loss, timeout and retransmission, highlighted above, from generating divergence. This adds to the complexity of the specification. In contrast, the Fair Abstraction approach is to allow such tau loops to arise unconstrained at the specification level, but to impose a fairness assumption at the level of the transition system that ensures they will be exited in finite time.

7.2.6.2 Development Relations and Congruence

The complete CSP semantic model identifies the failures of a process (i.e. traces and refusals) and its divergences (i.e. the traces from which it could diverge). Then the CSP refinement relation is subsetting of each of the constituents of this semantic model. Thus, a refinement must not have any failures or divergences that the abstract specification does not. This leads to a relation that, modulo the handling of divergence, is very close in spirit to the LOTOS reduction relation and refinement corresponds to reduction of nondeterminism.

However, an important aspect of CSP refinement is that it is a precongruence over the CSP operators and the induced equivalence (failures equivalence) is a congruence. Two issues contribute to this; the first is related to the handling of divergence and how such divergence can be created through concealment and the second is due to the capacity of internal actions to resolve choice in CSP. As an illustration of the former of these; i.e. that a catastrophic interpretation of divergence helps the quest for congruence, consider the example processes at the end of Section 5.1.5 depicted in Figure 5.4; i.e.

$$P := x \,;\, P_1 \,[]\, x \,;\, P_2 \quad \text{where}$$
$$P_1 := w \,;\, P_1 \,[]\, y \,;\, stop \quad \text{and} \quad P_2 := w \,;\, P_2 \,[]\, z \,;\, stop$$

$$Q := x \,;\, Q_1 \,[]\, x \,;\, Q_2 \quad \text{where}$$
$$Q_1 := w \,;\, Q_2 \,[]\, y \,;\, stop \quad \text{and} \quad Q_2 := w \,;\, Q_1 \,[]\, z \,;\, stop$$

which demonstrate that te is not a congruence in hiding contexts. Specifically, P and Q are testing equivalent. However, P' and Q', defined as follows, and also depicted in Figure 5.4, are not testing equivalent.

$$P' := hide \ w \ in \ P \quad \text{and} \quad Q' := hide \ w \ in \ Q$$

However, not only are the CSP analogues of P and Q failures equivalent (in a similar way to which P and Q are testing equivalent), but, the CSP analogues of P' and Q' are also failures equivalent. This is because, according to a CSP interpretation, they both perform an x and then become equivalent to $CHAOS$, because, even only the possibility to diverge, collapses to catastrophe; i.e. the capacity to perform any trace and refuse anything at any point. For a further discussion of this issue see [120].

Finally, with regard to the capacity of internal actions to resolve choice in CSP, we can see that the fact that internal actions generated from process arguments do not resolve $[]$ helps the quest for congruence. Specifically, let us return to our classic illustration of why choice is not a congruence for "weak" LOTOS equivalences; i.e.,

$$R_1 := x \,;\, stop \quad \text{and} \quad R_2 := i \,;\, x \,;\, stop$$

are testing and weak bisimulation equivalent, but

$$R_1 \,[]\, y \,;\, stop \quad \text{and} \quad R_2 \,[]\, y \,;\, stop$$

are not. However, the CSP analogues would be

$$R_1 = x \to stop \quad \text{and} \quad R_2 = (z \to x \to stop)\backslash\{z\} \quad \text{and}$$
$$Q_1 = R_1 \,[]\, (y \to stop) \quad \text{and} \quad Q_2 = R_2 \,[]\, (y \to stop)$$

both pairs of which are failures–divergences equivalent, because the initial τ generated by R_2 cannot resolve the choice in Q_2 and, thus, does not generate asymmetric nondeterminism. This is, for example, apparent in the operational semantics of CSP choice on page 162 of [171].

8

Communicating Automata

8.1 Introduction

This chapter focuses on a class of concurrency theory notations that can be seen as an alternative to process calculi. These notations are a rather natural adaptation of classic automata theory (see e.g. [5]), which are broadly classified as Communicating Automata (CAs). The basic idea is to model the components in a concurrent system using automata and interaction between components is modelled using message passing communication. Although not universally the case, interaction in these techniques is typically modelled using synchronous message passing, similar to that employed in process calculi. Indeed, we introduce a communicating automata notation based upon CCS-style binary synchronisation.

Communicating automata are the most prominent modelling technique when exhaustive verification of concurrent systems is applied, which is witnessed by model-checking, one of the most successful applications of formal methods in practice. Given a system represented as a network of communicating automata, and a correctness requirement expressed in some temporal logic (e.g. Linear time Temporal Logic (LTL) [162] or Computation Tree Logic (CTL) [57]), the model-checking algorithm will explore the network's state-space in order to determine whether the property is satisfied (in other words, whether the state-space represents a model for the formula). Depending on the formula, the model-checking algorithm might also return a justification for the answer, typically in the form of a system execution (a sequence of states). Usually, temporal logic formulae will denote safety or liveness properties (important among these are *reachability* formulae); informally speaking, these properties denote the reachability (or unreachability) of certain states of interest (or executions characterised by certain ordering of relevant states).

Despite being ubiquitous in the modelling of concurrent systems, communicating automata can only describe systems for which a finite state-space abstraction can be found (a limitation inherited by model-checking). Nevertheless, many systems of interest naturally present infinite state behaviour (e.g.

those systems where the modelling of data in infinite domains is important). This motivates the presentation of infinite state communicating automata (IS-CAs), a basic framework in which infinite state systems can be modelled. In this respect, we also comment on a typical deductive verification approach for this kind of systems, which is representative of those commonly found in the literature and practice.

Finally, a further reason for introducing communicating automata is that they play a particularly important role in the timed concurrency theory setting, where timed automata, and their associated model-checking algorithms, are one of the most commonly used methods for specifying and verifying time critical systems. Chapters 11, 12 and 13 focus on such timed extensions of communicating automata.

The rest of the chapter is organised around finite and infinite state communicating automata. Section 8.2 describes networks of (finite state) communicating automata; this includes formal definitions of components in Section 8.2.1, parallel composition in Section 8.2.2, and a comparison with process calculi in Section 8.2.6. Semantics and development relations are discussed in Section 8.2.4, and verification of networks of CAs is addressed in Section 8.2.5 (in particular, temporal logic and model-checking are discussed). The presentation of infinite state communicating automata in Section 8.3 follows a similar layout.

8.2 Networks of Communicating Automata

We begin by describing a basic automata model in which components are finite-state automata and there is one level of such components. This approach is called networks of communicating automata.

8.2.1 Component Automata

The finite-state automata components have much in common with the labelled transition systems discussed as a semantic model of process calculi in Section 3.3. Specifically, automata components have the following general form,

$$(L, TL, T, l_0)$$

where

- L is a finite set of locations; the automaton can only be in one location at a time;
- TL is a finite set of transition labels;
- $T \subseteq L \times TL \times L$ is the transition relation, where $(l, a, l') \in T$ states that a transition from location l to location l' exists, which is labelled with a. Note

that more than one transition may contain the same label.[1] Transitions are typically denoted

$$l \xrightarrow{a} l'$$

• And $l_0 \in L$ is the initial location of the automaton.

As an illustration of component automata, Figure 8.1 depicts a *Medium* and a *Sender* automaton for the communication protocol introduced in Section 2.2.1. In this depiction, initial locations are denoted with a double circle and transition labels are action names. In particular, there is a distinction between communication actions (here called half actions) and internal actions (here called completed actions). The former are indicated by the annotations ! and ?. We discuss this distinction further shortly.

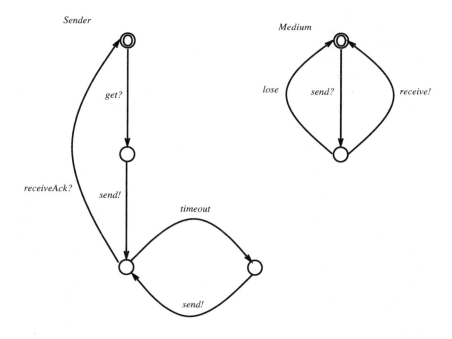

Fig. 8.1. Example Communicating Automata

These automata follow the same pattern as the pbLOTOS specification of the same components introduced in Section 2.4. Thus, the *Medium* waits for a *send* action (from the *Sender*), then it either loses the transmission or it

---

[1]Alternatively, T could have been defined as a set of sets T_a, where every set T_a contains all transitions labelled with $a \in TL$, which is the approach we took in Section 3.3.2.1.

passes it on by performing a *receive* action (with the *Receiver*). In both cases, the automaton evolves back to the initial location.

The *Sender* automaton *gets* a message to send from its environment; it then passes the message to the *Medium* by performing the *send* action. The automaton then waits for an acknowledgement, which it either receives (through the action *receiveAck*) or it times out and resends the message.

8.2.2 Parallel Composition

8.2.2.1 Basic Notation

Notice in Figure 8.1 that we are using binary synchronisation in our networks of CAs. Thus, we are taking inspiration from CCS and assuming that each interaction involves only two automata. Consequently, we distinguish between instances of half actions, indicated by the symbols ! and ?, and completed actions, denoted without input/output annotations.

In this notation, ! marks an output synchronisation and ? an input synchronisation.[2] Although, it is important to realise that we are using these symbols here in a different way from their use in full LOTOS (and indeed CSP). Thus, in our network of CAs notation, ! and ? are not denoting data passing communication attributes, as they do in full LOTOS and CSP. Indeed, the variety of networks that we consider in this book do not support data passing communication.

Many of the different parallel composition strategies considered in the process calculus setting could be applied between component automata. One reason for focusing on binary synchronisation is that it is used in the timed automata notation, which we are working up to introducing (and which we present in Chapter 11).

Perhaps the most significant difference between parallel composition in the networks of CAs and process calculus setting is that the former is typically defined over a vector of component automata, rather than as a binary operator. Thus, the main semantic mapping applied to networks of CAs is the generation of a single automaton from a vector of interacting component automata. This single automaton characterises the global behaviour that results from running the component automata in parallel. The automaton that arises from this parallel composition is called the product automaton, because its locations are generated from the Cartesian product of the component locations.

In fact, the focus on a vector of components is another reason why binary synchronisation is often employed in communicating automata. For example, LOTOS-style multiway synchronisation is more naturally applied as a compositional binary operator, rather than over a vector of components.

---

[2]These are distinguished with overlining in CCS.

8.2.2.2 Formal Definition

In order to define parallel composition over the vector of automata, we need some notation. *CAct* is a set of *completed* (or internal) actions. $HAct = \{x?, x! \mid x \in CAct\}$ is a set of *half* (or *uncompleted*) actions. These give a simple CCS-style [148] point-to-point communication similar, for example, to the synchronisation primitives found in Uppaal [16]. Thus, two actions, $x?$ and $x!$ can synchronise and generate a completed action x. $Act = HAct \cup CAct$ is the set of *all* actions.

Network of Communicating Automata. Networks are intended to model *closed* systems, that is, systems where synchronisation is defined solely in terms of their components. Thus, the term *closed* here refers to the fact that the interaction between the system and the environment is not modelled, or equivalently, where the environment is modelled as another component (i.e. every possible interaction is known at design-time). This is an important distinction between automata and process calculi; processes may specify interactions with the environment, without necessarily modelling the environment itself (in this sense, process calculi model *open* systems).

Formally, a network of CAs is modelled by a vector of automata denoted $|A = |\langle A_1, \ldots, A_n \rangle$, where, for $1 \leq i \leq n$, $A_i = (L_i, TL_i, T_i, l_{i,0})$ is a communicating automaton and $TL_i \subseteq Act$.

Note, we write $s \leq k \neq r \leq t$ in place of $s \leq k \leq t \ \wedge \ s \leq r \leq t \wedge \ k \neq r$; and denote $(l, a, l') \in T_i$ as $l \xrightarrow{a}_i l'$. In addition, we let u, u' etc. range over the set of location vectors $L_1 \times \cdots \times L_n$, which are written, $\langle u_1, \ldots, u_n \rangle$. We use a substitution notation as follows,

$$\langle u_1, \ldots, u_j, \ldots, u_n \rangle[l \to j] \ = \ \langle u_1, \ldots, u_{j-1}, l, u_{j+1}, \ldots, u_n \rangle$$

and we write

$$u[l_1 \to i_1] \ldots [l_m \to i_m] \quad \text{as} \quad u[l_1 \to i_1, \ldots, l_m \to i_m]$$

Product Automaton. The product automaton, which characterises the behaviour of $|A$, is given by

$$\Pi = (L, TL, T, l_0)$$

where

- $L = \{l_0\} \ \cup \ \{u' \mid \exists\, u \in L, a\,.\, u \xrightarrow{a} u'\}$;

- $l_0 = \langle l_{1,0}, \ldots, l_{n,0} \rangle$;

- $TL = \bigcup_{i=1}^{n} TL_i$; and

- T is as defined by the following two inference rules ($1 \leq i \neq j \leq n$),

$$(\text{R1}) \quad \frac{u_i \xrightarrow{x?}_i l \quad u_j \xrightarrow{x!}_j l'}{u \xrightarrow{x} u[l \rightarrow i, l' \rightarrow j]} \qquad (\text{R2}) \quad \frac{u_i \xrightarrow{x}_i l \quad x \in CAct}{u \xrightarrow{x} u[l \rightarrow i]}$$

Thus, the locations of the product automaton are vectors of component locations, which are reachable from the initial location of the product. The recursive nature of the definition of L and its use of the product transition relation ($\xrightarrow{a}$) ensures that only reachable locations are included.

In addition, the two inference rules determine the transitions between product locations. The first rule (R1) governs when the product can perform a synchronised transition, which two of the component automata interact in performing. Thus, if the product reaches a location in which two components offer matching half actions ($x?$ and $x!$ in the inference rule), then the product can perform the corresponding completed action (x above).[3] As a result, the product moves to a new vector of locations in which the locations of the synchronising components have both moved accordingly.

The second rule (R2) defines independent parallel execution in the product. Thus, completed actions in components are performed independently of any other transition and the corresponding component automaton moves on accordingly in the product.

It should be apparent that these rules follow a similar pattern to the LOTOS parallel composition operational semantics discussed in Section 3.3.2.2. Specifically, the synchronisation rule (R1) plays the role of (PA.iii) in the LOTOS semantics and the independent parallel execution rule (R2) plays the role of rules (PA.i) and (PA.ii) in the LOTOS semantics.

As an illustration of this product construction, consider the example in Figure 8.2. Fragments of each of the two components of the communication protocol shown in Figure 8.1 are highlighted to the left of the Figure. These fragments have been extracted from the Figure 8.1 components by removing all half actions that synchronise with components other than the sender and medium.

The resulting product automaton (denoted $|\langle Sender', Medium' \rangle$) is shown to the right of Figure 8.2. Because it characterises the global behaviour of the network, the product only contains completed actions. Furthermore, the product reflects the expected emergent behaviour of the network. Thus, the rather degenerate behaviour of the product is for a message to be sent, followed by an interleaving of the message being lost at the medium and the sender timing out. This sequence is repeated ad infinitum.

---

[3]Note that, as is in fact also the case with CCS demarcation of half actions using overlining, because nothing is actually transmitted over the communication channel, the directionality of communication here is rather artificial. Despite this, we describe half actions annotated ! as output and ? as input.

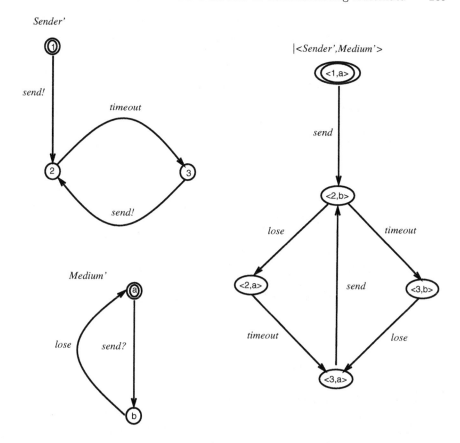

Fig. 8.2. Product Automaton Example

8.2.3 Example Specifications

As an illustration of networks of CAs, we present the full (nondata passing version of the) communication protocol example, as presented for LOTOS in Section 2.4. This full specification is shown in Figure 8.3. We must observe that the network is not complete: an *Environment* automaton (not shown in the Figure), which provides the *get!* and *put?* actions, is also assumed to be a component of the network.

The components, over and above those presented in Figure 8.1, are a reliable acknowledgement medium (*AckMedium*), which relays acknowledgements from the receiver back to the sender, and a receiver, which receives messages (action *receive?*), passes them to the environment (action *put!*) and then sends an acknowledgement (action *sendAck!*).

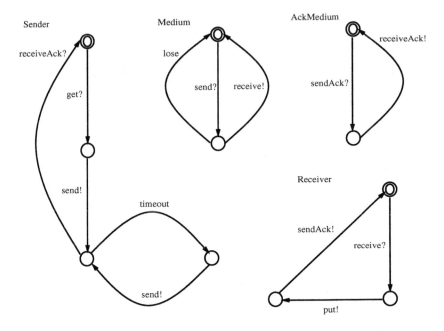

Fig. 8.3. Communication Protocol Example as a Network of CAs

8.2.4 Semantics and Development Relations

Labelled transition systems are the standard semantics for networks of CAs. This is consistent with the dominant role that transition systems semantics also play in process calculi. Indeed, due to the close relationship between automata and transition systems, the product automata generation rules, which we highlighted in Section 8.2.2.2, effectively play the role of a semantic map for networks of CAs. Furthermore, the labelled transition systems generated in this way play a central role in verification methods. For example, bisimulation equivalences can be applied directly over product automata.

However, it should also be noted that, although not typically explored, it is easy to map to semantic models other than labelled transition systems. For example, trace semantics and trace-refusals semantics can both be straightforwardly generated from networks of CAs, via the product automata; the mappings considered in Sections 3.3.2.3 and 5.1.2 could be used for this purpose. In addition, true concurrency semantics could be generated in two steps. Firstly, the network of CAs to process calculi mapping, considered in Section 8.2.6, could be applied and then, secondly, a process calculus to event structures mapping could be applied.

Finally, and to complete the overview of CA semantics, we must mention that a general liveness hypothesis is implicitly assumed in CA models: at any given state, some enabled action will always eventually be taken. More formally, a path in the labelled transition system represents a valid (complete) system execution only if either (a) it is infinite or (b) it is finite and there is no enabled transition in its last state (i.e. a deadlock state).

This liveness hypothesis represents a typical communicating automata interpretation for system executions (also called computations; see e.g. [136]). Although we do not discuss this topic any further, in principle, CA models could also be augmented with fairness conditions. For example, a common way [136] to add fairness conditions to labelled transition systems, is to mark certain transitions as "just" or "compassionate". Infinite paths in the labelled transition system will not be considered valid executions if just transitions are continuously enabled without being eventually taken, or if compassionate transitions are enabled infinitely often, but taken only a finite number of times (an overview of fair transition systems [136] is given in Section 13.2.1). The model-checker SMV[4] is a good example of how fairness is dealt with in practice; in SMV, the user may specify fairness assumptions as part of the model.

8.2.5 Verification of Networks of Communicating Automata

Efficient verification of networks of CAs (in their practical incarnations) can be achieved through model-checking: correctness requirements are expressed as formulae in some temporal logic, and, typically, an algorithm is run on the product automaton, which checks whether the property is satisfied. Depending on the formula, model-checkers might also return a justification for their answers, typically in the form of a sequence of states validating (or invalidating) the verified property.

This informal description of model-checking corresponds to the most widespread verification technique for finite-state systems. In practice, most model-checkers choose either CTL (Computation Tree Logic) [57,58] or LTL (Linear Time Temporal Logic) [128, 136, 162] as property specification languages (or some variants of these temporal logics).

This section discusses, briefly, the main features of CTL and the basics of CTL-based model-checking. We refer the reader interested in LTL and LTL-based model-checking to [128] and [97].[5] Vardi [194] compares CTL and LTL on a number of technical grounds, including the expressiveness of the logics as property specification languages, and the efficiency of the related model-checking algorithms.

8.2.5.1 Computation Tree Logic (CTL)

Informally, CTL formulae can be seen as statements about system executions.

---

[4]http://www-2.cs.cmu.edu/~modelcheck/smv.html

[5]See also the SPIN site at http://spinroot.com/spin/whatispin.html

- States of interest can be characterised by atomic propositions and logical connectives. For example, and with respect to the network of CAs shown in Figure 8.2, the formula $SL1 \lor SL3 \Rightarrow MLa$ denotes a set of states in which *Medium'* is in location a (prop. MLa) whenever *Sender'* is either in location 1 or 3 (props. $SL1$ and $SL3$). Clearly, more interesting characterisations can be obtained in richer automata models, e.g. those which include shared variables.
- The sequencing of states in a particular execution can be seen as a temporal ordering of events, and thus can be characterised by temporal operators. For example, the CTL formula $G\phi$ denotes an execution in which every state satisfies the formula ϕ.
- Properties of interest might range over all or just some of the system executions; hence, CTL includes operators which quantify over the set of possible executions. For example, the CTL formula $A\phi$ denotes a system in which ϕ is satisfied on all possible executions.

In consequence, many interesting properties can be naturally expressed in CTL. For example, a possible correctness requirement for the system of Figure 8.2 may state that *Sender'* is always allowed to send packets. This is the same as saying that whenever a *send!* action is enabled in *Sender'*, a *send?* action is also enabled in *Medium'*. This can be expressed in CTL as

$$\mathsf{AG}(SL1 \lor SL3 \Rightarrow MLa)$$

Notice that $SL1 \lor SL3 \Rightarrow MLa$ characterises exactly the set of states where action *send?* in *Medium'* is enabled, provided any of the two *send!* actions in *Sender'* is also enabled.

Syntax. A CTL formula ϕ_{state} is typically given in the following syntax (where p is an atomic proposition),

$$\phi_{state} ::= p \mid \neg\phi_{state} \mid \phi_{state} \land \phi_{state} \mid \{\mathsf{A}, \mathsf{E}\}\phi_{path}$$
$$\phi_{path} ::= \phi_{state} \mid \{\mathsf{F}, \mathsf{G}\}\phi_{state}$$

We also assume the usual logical connectives ($\lor$, $\Rightarrow$, etc.) and tautologies. Other important operators, not considered here, include X (next) and U until (see e.g. [58] for a complete presentation). Notice that "temporal operators", F and G, can only occur under the immediate scope of a "path quantifier", A or E. Simple examples of CTL formulae include $\mathsf{EF}p$ and $\mathsf{AG}(p \Rightarrow \mathsf{EF}q)$, where p and q are atomic propositions.

Semantics. CTL is a logic interpreted on Kripke structures, essentially, finite-state automata of the form $(S, T, P, \mathcal{M}, s_0)$, where

- S is a finite set of states (and $s_0 \in S$ the initial state);
- $T \subseteq S \times S$ is a transition relation, which is total on S; i.e. for every $s \in S$ there exists $s' \in S$ s.t. $(s, s') \in T$;

- P is a finite set of atomic propositions; and
- $\mathcal{M} : S \to \mathcal{P}(P)$ is a mapping which relates every state in the automaton with a valuation for propositions in P. Equivalently, $\mathcal{M}$ can be seen as relating every state with a subset of P, which includes only those atomic propositions which are considered *true* in that state.

A Kripke structure can be unfolded into an infinite tree (called a *computation tree*) where every state in the structure corresponds to at least one node in the tree (with the initial state being the root), and every path in the tree corresponds to the infinite traversal of consecutive transitions. Because the transition relation is total, every state in the Kripke structure has at least one outgoing transition, which guarantees the existence of infinite paths in the computation tree. This unfolding is illustrated in Figure 8.4, where the initial state is distinguished with a double circle.

It is not difficult to see that a mapping between networks of CAs and Kripke structures (and correspondingly, computation trees) can be readily obtained. Effectively, a product automaton, $\Pi = (L, TL, T_\Pi, l_0)$, can be interpreted as a Kripke structure $K = (S, T_K, P, \mathcal{M}, s_0)$, where

- $S = L$ (and $s_0 = l_0$);

- $T_K = \{ (l, l') \mid l \xrightarrow{a}_\Pi l' \} \cup \{ (l, l) \mid \nexists a \in TL, l' \in L . l \xrightarrow{a}_\Pi l' \}$

  This states that labels in the product transitions are disregarded; and that locations in the product with no outgoing transitions result in reflexive states in the Kripke structure (this ensures that T_K is total on S).

- P and $\mathcal{M}$ can be arbitrarily defined; they usually depend on the application domain (i.e. the interpretation of states and transitions of the network of CAs) and the properties to be verified.

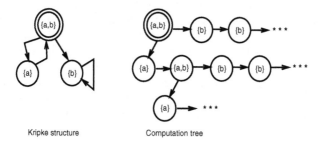

Kripke structure   Computation tree

Fig. 8.4. A Kripke Structure and Its Related Computation Tree (Fragment)

The satisfiability of a CTL formula is defined with respect to a given state s in a computation tree. Path quantifiers A and E refer to all paths, or some path starting at s, respectively. Temporal operators G and F refer to all states, or some state in a given path, respectively. Finally, propositional formulae are interpreted over the valuation which defines a particular state. For example, the formula EFp will be satisfied in a state s where there exists at least one path starting from s (E), which contains at least one state (F) where p holds. Similarly, the more interesting AG$(p \Rightarrow$ EF$q)$ is satisfiable at s if in every state s', which satisfies p, of every possible path starting at s, there exists at least one path starting at s' along which some state satisfies q.

By way of example, Figure 8.5 illustrates the satisfiability of EFϕ, AGϕ, EGϕ and AFϕ, over computation trees. In these, we assume that the uppermost node is the root, that black nodes denote states satisfying the CTL formula ϕ and that dashed lines denote repetition in the tree structure.

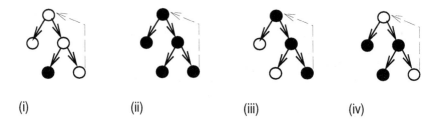

(i)   (ii)   (iii)   (iv)

Fig. 8.5. Fragments of Computation Trees, (i) EFϕ, (ii) AGϕ, (iii) EGϕ, (iv) AFϕ

Notice that a temporal interpretation can be given to CTL formulae, if we consider that a sequence of states represents the evolution of a system in time. According to this view, then, the formula EFp can be said to be satisfiable in s if there exists a possible execution of the system in which, *eventually*, a state where p holds can be reached.

Table 8.1 gives formal semantics for CTL operators. We assume a Kripke structure $K = (S, T, P, \mathcal{M}, s_0)$, and $\mathcal{C}$ the computation tree arising from K; $s \in S$ denotes a node in $\mathcal{C}$; $\sigma \triangleq \sigma_0 \sigma_1 \sigma_2 \dots$, an infinite path in $\mathcal{C}$ (not necessarily starting at the root) where $\sigma_i \in S$, $i \geq 0$ and $\sigma_0 \in S$ is the initial state of the path. We use $p \in s$, where $p \in P$, to denote that p is *true* in s with respect to $\mathcal{M}$. CTL formulae are state formulae, ϕ_{state}, and are interpreted over a pair (K, s). Correspondingly, path formulae ϕ_{path} are interpreted over a pair (K, σ). We use $\models$ to denote both the satisfiability relations for state and path formulae.

Correctness Properties as CTL Formulae. CTL formulae can be classified according to the kind of correctness properties they can express. Typically (see e.g. [14]), the literature distinguishes among the following.

$$
\begin{array}{lll}
(K,s) & \models p & \text{iff } p \in s \\
(K,s) & \models \neg\phi_{state} & \text{iff } (K,s) \not\models \phi_{state} \\
(K,s) & \models \phi_{state} \wedge \phi'_{state} & \text{iff } (K,s) \models \phi_{state} \text{ and } (K,s) \models \phi'_{state} \\
(K,s) & \models \mathbf{E}\phi_{path} & \text{iff } \text{exists } \sigma \text{ s.t. } \sigma_0 = s \text{ and } (K,\sigma) \models \phi_{path} \\
(K,s) & \models \mathbf{A}\phi_{path} & \text{iff } \text{for all } \sigma \text{ s.t. } \sigma_0 = s,\ (K,\sigma) \models \phi_{path} \\
(K,\sigma) & \models \phi_{state} & \text{iff } (K,\sigma_0) \models \phi_{state} \\
(K,\sigma) & \models \mathbf{F}\phi_{state} & \text{iff } \text{exists } \sigma_i,\ i \geq 0,\ \text{s.t. } (K,\sigma_i) \models \phi_{state} \\
(K,\sigma) & \models \mathbf{G}\phi_{state} & \text{iff } \text{for all } \sigma_i,\ i \geq 0,\ (K,\sigma_i) \models \phi_{state}
\end{array}
$$

Table 8.1. Semantics of CTL Formulae

- *Reachability* properties are usually expressed as a CTL formula of the form $\mathbf{EF}\phi$. This formula states that a certain event of interest (characterised by ϕ) may eventually occur, i.e. is reachable.
- *Safety* properties are typically of the form $\mathbf{AG}\neg\phi$. This formula states that an error-state (characterised by ϕ) is never reached.
- *Liveness* properties (other than reachability) express, in general, that some event will always eventually occur. It is common to find liveness expressed by CTL formulae such as $\mathbf{AGEF}\phi$ or $\mathbf{AG}(\phi \Rightarrow \mathbf{EF}\psi)$, where ϕ and ψ usually denote propositional formulae.

A reachability property of interest in the system shown in Figure 8.2, may state that a *timeout* is possible. This can be expressed as $\mathbf{EF}SL3$; we recall that *SL3* is a proposition denoting that *Sender'* is currently in location 3. We have already seen an example of a safety property, $\mathbf{AG}\ (SL1 \vee SL3 \Rightarrow MLa)$, which states that *Sender'* is always allowed to send messages to *Medium'*. Equivalently, the property states that *Sender'* is never prevented from sending the messages; i.e.,

$$\mathbf{AG}\neg((SL1 \vee SL3) \wedge \neg MLa)$$

Safety properties can be expressed as reachability properties, because CTL operators $\mathbf{A}$ and $\mathbf{E}$, and $\mathbf{F}$ and $\mathbf{G}$, are duals.[6] Following the previous example, the safety property in question can be expressed in terms of reachability,

$$\neg\mathbf{EF}((SL1 \vee SL3) \wedge \neg MLa)$$

which denotes that a state where a *send!* action is enabled, and a *send?* action is not, cannot be reached. As for examples of liveness properties, consider the following.

- The property which states that *Sender'* will always eventually attempt to send messages, can be expressed as $\mathbf{AGEF}(SL1 \vee SL3)$; i.e. a state is always eventually reached in which some *send!* action in *Sender'* is enabled.

---

[6] $\mathbf{A}\phi$ and $\neg\mathbf{E}\neg\phi$ are logically equivalent, and so are $\mathbf{G}\phi$ and $\neg\mathbf{F}\neg\phi$.

- The property which states that every time after a *timeout* occurs a packet is eventually sent (at least to *Medium'*, can be expressed as AG($SL3 \Rightarrow$ AF$SL2$).

8.2.5.2 Model-checking CTL

Although, in practice, much more efficient algorithms have been implemented (e.g. [140]), CTL model-checking can be conceptually described in terms of a labelling procedure which works on Kripke structures [58].

Given a system represented as a Kripke structure $K = (S, T, P, \mathcal{M}, s_0)$, and a correctness property expressed as a CTL formula ϕ, we can state the model-checking problem as a search for those states in S which satisfy ϕ. If $s_0 \in S$ represents the system's initial state, then the system satisfies ϕ if ϕ is satisfied at s_0. This search can be performed in many ways. Consider, for example, a procedure which labels each state $s \in S$ with the set of subformulae of ϕ (which are themselves state formulae) that are satisfied in s. Let $label(s)$ be such a set. Then, the set of states which satisfy ϕ is given by

$$\{\, s \in S \mid \phi \in label(s) \,\}$$

The labelling procedure can be thought of as working in stages. Initially, and for every $s \in S$, $label(s)$ is just the set of propositions which are *true* in s; then states are labelled according to subformulae in ϕ until eventually ϕ is processed. As the satisfiability of a CTL formula ϕ can be defined in terms of the satisfiability of its subformulae (see table 8.1), the labelling of states with respect to ϕ can be defined in terms of a labelling with respect to subformulae of ϕ.

To illustrate this procedure, Figure 8.6 sketches a possible implementation for the labelling of EFϕ on the states of K, where ϕ is a CTL formula. The function $labelEF(\phi, s, Visited)$ will label all states in S with respect to EFϕ, assuming that,

- K is strongly connected;
- $Successors(s) = \{\, s' \mid (s, s') \in T \,\}$;
- ϕ has been "marked" already; i.e. for every state $s \in S$, $\phi \in label(s)$ if and only if ϕ has been found to be satisfiable in s; and
- initially, $Visited = \emptyset$ and $s = s_0$.

8.2.6 Relationship to Process Calculi

8.2.6.1 Encoding Networks of CAs into Process Calculi

Networks of CAs can be viewed as a specialisation of process calculi and they can be encoded into the sort of notation we discussed in Chapters 2 and 7.

Function *labelEF*(ϕ, s, *Visited*)
begin
       Visited $\leftarrow$ *Visited* $\cup$ { s };
       if $\phi \in$ *label*(s) **then**
         label(s) $\leftarrow$ *label*(s) $\cup$ { **EF**ϕ };
       else
           for all $s' \in$ *Successors*(s), $s' \notin$ *Visited* **do**
              labelEF(ϕ, s', *Visited*);
           end for
           if $\exists$ $s' \in$ *Successors*(s) . **EF**$\phi \in$ *label*(s') **then**
            label(s) $\leftarrow$ *label*(s) $\cup$ { **EF**ϕ };
           end if
       end if
       return;
end.

Fig. 8.6. Model-checking CTL: The Labelling of **EF**ϕ Formulae.

However, in general, process calculi are too expressive to be encoded into networks of CAs.

As an initial illustration, we consider a mapping,

$$\Delta_1 : CommsAut \longrightarrow pbLOTOS,$$

from product automata to pbLOTOS specifications, which is defined as follows.

1. Given an automaton $A = (L, TL, T, l_0)$, we assume n is the cardinality of L and we introduce n process identifiers indexed by locations in L, each denoted P_l for $l \in L$.
2. For all $l, l' \in L$, define,
   $$P_l := []\{ x; P_{l'} \,|\, l \xrightarrow{x} l' \}$$
   where
   $$[]\{ E_1, \ldots, E_r \} = E_1 [] \ldots [] E_r$$
3. Now, P_{l_0} is the top-level pbLOTOS behaviour corresponding to the initial location of the product automaton.

However, the Δ_1 mapping requires transitions to be labelled with completed actions. In particular, the disparity in communication mechanisms (binary communication vs. multiway synchronisation), prevents us from being able to give a compositional transformation of networks of CAs into LOTOS. However, we can give such a compositional mapping if the target of the translation is a CCS-style calculus; remember, CCS employs a binary synchronisation mechanism very similar to that employed in our networks of CAs. In fact, the CCS dialect we map to is slightly nonstandard, in the sense that completed actions (as characterised by the set *CAct*) play the role of internal,

τ, actions (as classically used in CCS). We denote the completed actions x^τ (where $x \in CAct$) in this CCS variant, which we call CCS^{CAct}.

Thus, we consider a compositional mapping,

$$\Delta_2 : CommsAut \longrightarrow CCS^{CAct},$$

which is defined as follows.

1. Given a vector $|\langle A_1, \ldots, A_m \rangle$ of component automata, where $A_i = (L_i, TL_i, T_i, l_{0,i})$ for $1 \leq i \leq m$ and n_i is the cardinality of L_i. For each $i \, (1 \leq i \leq m)$ we assume n_i process identifiers indexed by locations in L_i, each denoted $X_{i,l}$ for $l \in L_i$.
2. For all $i \, (1 \leq i \leq m)$, $l, l' \in L_i$, let,

$$X_{i,l} \overset{def}{=} \Sigma \{ \alpha(a). X_{i,l'} \mid l \overset{a}{\longrightarrow}_i l' \}$$

where

$$\Sigma \{ E_1, \ldots, E_r \} = \underset{j \, (1 \leq j \leq r)}{\Sigma} E_j$$

and, for $x \in CAct$,

$$\alpha(x?) = x$$
$$\alpha(x!) = \overline{x}$$
$$\alpha(x) = x^\tau$$

3. $X_{i,l_{0,i}}$ gives the top-level behaviour of the CCS^{CAct} agent corresponding to the ith component automaton.
4. Finally, the following defines a process variable, X, which is the top-level CCS^{CAct} agent corresponding to running the network of CAs in parallel.

$$X \overset{def}{=} (\Pi_{i \, (1 \leq i \leq m)}^{CAct} X_{i,l_{0,i}}) \backslash^{CAct} (\bigcup_{i=1}^{m} TL_i)$$

where Π^{CAct} enforces the usual CCS generalised parallel composition, with the one alteration being that synchronisation generates the corresponding completed action, rather than τ, and $A \backslash^{CAct} G$ enforces the usual CCS restriction, with one alteration being that only half actions are restricted (and, it is important to note, completed actions are not).

Thus, X runs the agents generated from each component automaton in parallel. In addition, CCS^{CAct} parallel composition ensures that matching half actions synchronise and restriction removes branches from leftover instances of half actions.

Although we do not provide a formal proof to justify the statement, it should be clear that, through Δ_2, networks of CAs can be compositionally encoded into process calculi.

8.2.6.2 Comparing Communicating Automata Networks and Process Calculi

Although communicating automata networks are an elegant (and simple) model of concurrent systems, they are expressively limited when compared with process calculi. In particular, they only offer one level of parallel components. Consequently, it is typically more difficult to describe large systems in networks of CAs than in process calculi. In particular, with process calculi, a decompositional strategy of system specification can be employed, in which complex systems can be incrementally described. That is, the system developer can focus on specifying a part of the entire system, then she can hide all internal behaviour and wrap that part of the system up as a process, which can be composed with other parts of the system at the next level of decompositional structure. In addition, processes (and thus, arbitrarily complex behaviour) can be nested to any arbitrary depth.

This is a serious limitation of networks of CAs. However, these expressiveness limitations are often accepted, because verification of such restricted notations is more straightforward than for arbitrary process calculi. For example, this is one of the reasons for the widespread use of networks of CAs in the timed model-checking domain; see Section 11.3.

In addition, it is worth noting that, although not considered here, data typing primitives could be added to networks of CAs, to yield a more powerful specification notation. In particular, data passing could be associated with networks of CAs in a similar manner to that employed in fLOTOS. In fact, Section 11.2 discusses timed automata, which have an expressive data notation in their most mature practical incarnation: the Uppaal specification language [16]. Although, because Uppaal employs shared data variables, it does not include data passing in the basic communication primitives.

State-based and Action-based Formalisms. We can also compare communicating automata and process calculi from the perspective of state-based and action-based formalisms. Process calculi are usually considered to be action-based formalisms in the sense that actions play the most important role in the representation of both the system behaviour and the correctness requirements of interest. For example, we have seen that LOTOS specifications are interpreted over sequences of actions (i.e. semantics are usually given in terms of LTSs, traces, etc.), but states are regarded as subordinated to actions, in the sense that they simply denote a stage in the behaviour of the system, which lies between the execution of two consecutive actions. From another point of view, states can also be considered as black boxes which carry no visible structure or relevant information about the system behaviour, and so one can argue that states are "indistinguishable", where one can only observe (and given the whole execution context) the sequences of actions which led to them, and those which may possibly follow from them.

Action-based formalisms have also encouraged a verification method where correctness is stated operationally, and one is usually interested in determining whether the behaviour of two systems is equivalent according to some development relation (where the second system describes the "correct" behaviours the first system can perform). For example, the CADP tool is able to check, given two LOTOS specifications, whether a bisimulation exists between them.

This is in contrast to state-based formalisms, such as communicating automata. Here (and even more so in CA models augmented with shared variables), the behaviour of a system is interpreted in terms of sequences of states which carry the relevant information, e.g. the current location in the automaton and a valuation for its variables. Thus, states have a certain structure and are distinguishable, defining precisely those points in system execution where the system can be observed. Actions, on the other hand, are viewed mostly as the means by which different states in execution can be reached. Consequently, verification is concerned with states and sequencing of interesting states in a given execution; these elements are the building blocks in the specification of correctness properties as temporal logic formulae (e.g. in CTL and LTL).

To conclude, let us mention that choosing either an action-based or a state-based model depends on the system at hand, and the type of properties we are interested in verifying. Also, and in particular for complex systems, it is usually the case that both viewpoints are necessary, and so they complement each other. For example, it may be the case that the system in question is more naturally modelled in terms of networks of CAs, but some correctness requirements are better expressed in terms of actions rather than states. In addition, we must point out that verification methods are not, per se, exclusive to one type of formalism or another. For example, determining the existence of a bisimulation between two CAs is a common practice to verify correctness; on the other hand, LOTOS specifications can be model-checked in CADP with respect to properties written in the μ-Calculus logic [112].

8.3 Infinite State Communicating Automata

Communicating automata (in their many incarnations) stand, probably, as the most widely used formal methods for the specification of concurrent systems. Despite their limitations in expressiveness (and to a great extent, thanks to these limitations), communicating automata allow for efficient, exhaustive verification of systems. As we have seen, an automatic verification technique, such as model-checking, is made possible because the state-space is finite.

Nevertheless, many systems of interest cannot be model-checked, because no finite state-space abstraction can be obtained for them. This infinite state behaviour is common in systems where data play a central role (and so the specification language must deal with infinite domains of some sort). For example, this is commonly found in the verification of software or parameterised communication protocols, to name just two.

Many frameworks have been proposed to deal with infinite state systems, and the literature on the topic is very rich (e.g. see the prominent work of Manna and Pnueli on transition systems and LTL [136, 137], and Lynch et al. on I/O automata [132, 133]). The main disadvantage of infinite state frameworks has been, traditionally, the expertise required in the verification process.

The expressiveness of these notations is such that verification must be performed in the form of deductive proofs, where theorem provers provide the (semi automatic) tool support.

This section presents an abstract notation, named Infinite State Communicating Automata (ISCAs), which embodies many of the principles found in this area. In addition, the reason for introducing this notation here is similar to that which we offered for communicating automata: ISCAs are a good starting point to understand discrete timed automata (Chapter 13), a notation for (infinite state) timed systems.

We hope this gives the reader a good idea about how infinite state systems can be specified, without burdening them too much with technical details (which are, in most cases, particular to each notation). Having said that, by all means the reader is encouraged to consult the bibliography and compare between different frameworks (e.g. Manna and Pnueli's fair transition systems [136], and Lynch and Tuttle's I/O automata [132]), and their related verification techniques.

8.3.1 Networks of Infinite State Communicating Automata

In this model, systems are described by a network where the components are infinite state communicating automata. As for communicating automata, there is only one level of such components, and networks of ISCAs represent closed systems (synchronisation is specified only among the network's components).

8.3.1.1 Component Automata

Let the sets *CAct*, *HAct* and *Act* be defined as in Section 8.2.2.2. An infinite state communicating automaton is a tuple $A = (V, \Theta, TL, \mathcal{A})$, where

- V is a finite set of variables;
- Θ is a formula in first-order language (FOL), which denotes the initial valuation for variables in V;
- $TL \subseteq Act$ is a set of action labels; and
- $\mathcal{A}$ is a finite set of actions with labels in TL .

Actions in $\mathcal{A}$ are triples[7], (a, p, e), where $a \in TL$ is the action's label, p (the action's *precondition*) is a FOL-formula on variables in V, and e (the action's *effect*) is a FOL-formula on variables in V and their primed versions. The precondition denotes a set of possible valuations which enable the action; in other words it represents a set of states where the action may be performed.

---

[7]Notice, in contrast with the meaning assigned in process calculi, that here actions have a structure (a label, a precondition and an effect). This is a direct consequence of the notation being state-based: actions explicitly denote how the state of a system evolves during execution.

The effect denotes the valuation which results after the action has been taken (denoted by valuations of primed variables). Although more general forms can be given, we adopt a simple deterministic behaviour for actions; i.e. actions, when performed, will always result in single next state (e.g. as in [136]). Let e be an effect formula, and $V'(e) \subseteq V$ be the set of variables modified by e (i.e. those whose valuations change as the result of performing the corresponding action). Then, e has the form,

$$e \triangleq \bigwedge_{v \in V'(e)} v' = E_V$$

where E_V is an expression on variables in V. Notice that any variable not in $V'(e)$ is assumed unchanged when the corresponding action is performed. In other words, the above expression for e is a shorthand for

$$e \triangleq \bigwedge_{v \in V'(e)} v' = E_V \wedge \bigwedge_{y \in V \setminus V'(e)} y' = y$$

Binary synchronisation between automata (as in finite state communicating automata) will be achieved by partitioning $\mathcal{A}$ into sets of completed (or internal), input and output actions; that is,

$$\mathcal{A} = COMP(\mathcal{A}) \cup IN(\mathcal{A}) \cup OUT(\mathcal{A})$$

Completed, input and output actions will be labelled with $a \in CAct$, $x?, x! \in HAct$, respectively. Collectively, input and output actions can be thought of as the half actions of the model (with a similar role as that in Communicating Automata). Note, also, that more than one action in the same partition (completed, input or output actions) may share labels. This allows the representation of actions which have different effects depending on the state where they are enabled. In the following definitions, we may refer to actions simply by their labels. For example, we use $x? \in \mathcal{A}$ to denote any input action $(x?, p, e) \in IN(\mathcal{A})$.

Figure 8.7 illustrates a network of component automata (ISCAs) corresponding to (a fragment of) the communication protocol example of Figure 8.2.

8.3.1.2 Parallel Composition

Here we follow the synchronisation model of communicating automata (Section 8.2.2.2). For any given network, parallel composition results in a product automaton that represents the semantics of the network. By construction (and well-formedness of the network), this product automaton contains just completed actions. These concepts (both networks of ISCAs and product automaton) are formalised by the following definitions.

Network: $|\langle Sender', Medium' \rangle$

ISCA: *Sender'*
$V :\ SenderState \in \{1, 2, 3\}$
$\Theta :\ SenderState = 1$
$TL = \{send!,\ timeout\}$
$\mathcal{A} :\ send!$
   prec: $SenderState = 1$
   eff: $SenderState' = 2$
  timeout
   prec: $SenderState = 2$
   eff: $SenderState' = 3$
  send!
   prec: $SenderState = 3$
   eff: $SenderState' = 2$

ISCA: *Medium'*
$V :\ MediumState \in \{a, b\}$
$\Theta :\ MediumState = a$
$TL = \{send?,\ lose\}$
$\mathcal{A} :\ send?$
   prec: $MediumState = a$
   eff: $MediumState' = b$
  lose
   prec: $MediumState = b$
   eff: $MediumState' = a$

Fig. 8.7. Example Infinite State Communicating Automata

Network of Infinite State Communicating Automata. A network of
ISCAs is a vector of components $|A = \langle A_1, \ldots, A_n \rangle$, where, for $1 \leq i \leq n$,
$A_i = (V_i, \Theta_i, TL_i, \mathcal{A}_i)$ is an ISCA. A network is well-formed if both variables
and completed actions are local to components; that is,

$$\forall i, j\, (1 \leq i \neq j \leq n)\,, V_i \cap V_j = \emptyset$$

$$\forall i, j\, (1 \leq i \neq j \leq n)\,, COMP(\mathcal{A}_i) \cap \mathcal{A}_j = \emptyset$$

Product Automaton. Let $|A = \langle A_1, \ldots, A_n \rangle$ be a network of ISCAs, where
$A_i = (V_i, \Theta_i, TL_i, \mathcal{A}_i)$, for $1 \leq i \leq n$. The product automaton, which results
from the parallel composition of the network's components, is given by

$$\Pi = (V, \Theta, TL, \mathcal{A})$$

where

- $V = \bigcup\limits_{i=1}^{n} V_i;$

- $\Theta = \bigwedge\limits_{i=1}^{n} \Theta_i$;

- $TL = (CAct \cap \bigcup\limits_{i=1}^{n} TL_i) \cup \{ x \mid \exists x? \in TL_i\,,\, x! \in TL_j\,.\, 1 \le i\ \ne j \le n \}$; and

- $COMP(\mathcal{A}) = \bigcup\limits_{i=1}^{n} COMP(\mathcal{A}_i) \cup$
$\{\, (x, p, e) \mid \exists\, i, j\, (1 \le i \ne j \le n)\,.$
$\qquad (x?, p_i, e_i) \in IN(\mathcal{A}_i) \wedge (x!, p_j, e_j) \in OUT(\mathcal{A}_j) \wedge$
$\qquad (p \triangleq p_i \wedge p_j) \wedge$
$\qquad (e \triangleq e_i \wedge e_j) \,\}$

- $IN(\mathcal{A}) = OUT(\mathcal{A}) = \emptyset$

Notice that all actions in the product automaton are completed, where synchronisation has been resolved by producing one completed action from every two matching input/output actions in the components. By way of example, Figure 8.8 shows the product automaton corresponding to the network of Figure 8.7. In particular, observe that the automaton includes two completed actions *send*, each one representing a possible synchronisation between one of the *send!*s in *Sender* and the *send?* action in *Medium* (see Figure 8.7 again), but just one *timeout* and one *lose*.

This is worth comparing with the product automaton in the CA setting (Figure 8.2), where the interleaving between these two completed actions is explicit. Unlike in communicating automata, the interleaving of completed actions in the ISCA setting does not cause an explosion in the size of the resulting product automaton. This is so because preconditions implicitly model a set of states; for example, the precondition of the *timeout* action denotes that this action is only enabled in those states where $SenderState = 2$, but it does not specify what the value of $MediumState$ is. Consequently, *timeout* is enabled both in states,

$$s_1 = (SenderState = 2, MediumState = a) \text{ and}$$
$$s_2 = (SenderState = 2, MediumState = b)$$

On the other hand, and in order to represent the same information with finite state communicating automata, the product automaton in Figure 8.2 must produce two *timeout* transitions, one for every possible location vector denoting that $Sender'$ is in location 2 (that is, vectors $\langle 2, a \rangle$ and $\langle 2, b \rangle$).

8.3.2 Semantics of ISCAs as Labelled Transition Systems

The semantics of a network of ISCAs is evident from the product automaton; nevertheless the distinction between syntax and semantics will acquire more importance in timed automata notations (both for finite- and infinite-state systems). It is interesting, then, to present a formalisation for the semantics of networks of ISCAs, in terms of labelled transitions systems.

ISCA: Π
V : $SenderState \in \{1, 2, 3\}$, $MediumState \in \{a, b\}$
Θ : $SenderState = 1 \wedge MediumState = a$
$TL = \{send, \ timeout, \ lose\}$
$\mathcal{A}$: $send$
        prec: $SenderState = 1 \wedge MediumState = a$
        eff: $\ SenderState' = 2 \wedge MediumState' = b$
    $send$
        prec: $SenderState = 3 \wedge MediumState = a$
        eff: $\ SenderState' = 2 \wedge MediumState' = b$
    $timeout$
        prec: $SenderState = 2$
        eff: $\ SenderState' = 3$
    $lose$
        prec: $MediumState = b$
        eff: $\ MediumState' = a$

Fig. 8.8. Communication Protocol - Product Automaton (ISCA).

Let $A = (V, \Theta, TL, \mathcal{A})$ be an ISCA where all actions are completed (i.e. $\mathcal{A} = COMP(\mathcal{A})$). The semantics of A are given by the LTS (S, TL, T, s_0), where

- S is the state-space defined by all possible valuations for variables in V. We use $[\![v]\!]_s$ (resp. $[\![E_V]\!]_s$) to denote the value of the variable $v \in V$ in $s \in S$ (resp. the result of evaluating the expression E_V in s).
- $s_0 \in S$ s.t. $s_0 \models \Theta$, is the starting state (for convenience, we assume there is a unique starting state).
- $T \subseteq S \times TL \times S$ is the transition relation, where transitions $(s, a, s') \in T$ are denoted $s \xrightarrow{a} s'$. The transition relation is defined by the following rule,

$$\frac{(a, p, e) \in \mathcal{A} \quad s \models p \quad (s, s') \models e}{s \xrightarrow{a} s'}$$

where $s \models \phi$ denotes that $s \in S$ satisfies the formula ϕ (under FOL semantics). Similarly, $(s, s') \models e$ denotes that s' is the state which results from s by applying the effect formula e, and where every variable not modified by e remains unchanged. Formally, $(s, s') \models e$ if, for every $v \in V$, s' satisfies the following.

$$[\![v]\!]_{s'} = \begin{cases} [\![E_V]\!]_s & \text{if } v \in V'(e) \\ [\![v]\!]_s & \text{otherwise} \end{cases}$$

The set of reachable states in any possible execution of A is, then,

$$S_{reach} = \{s_0\} \cup \{s' \mid \exists a \in TL, s \in S_{reach} \cdot s \xrightarrow{a} s'\}$$

Part IV

Concurrency Theory – Timed Models

This part considers the important issue of real-time extensions to concurrency theory.[8] The need for such models was discussed in Section 1.3.

If you consider the historical development of the field of timed concurrency theory, it is clear that, broadly speaking, there were two phases. Initially, from the mid-1980s to the early 1990s, there was considerable investigation of how time could be added to the first generation of (untimed) process calculi. As a result, timed extensions of all the major process calculi were explored, e.g. timed extensions of CCS [167, 201], CSP [64, 177] and LOTOS [26, 59, 125, 164] and important new timed calculi were proposed [154]. Due to the algebraic focus of process calculi there were accompanying explorations of proof systems for such languages, e.g. [176].

This initial thrust of timed concurrency theory research had great theoretical value. However, as is also, to some extent, the case in the untimed setting, the expressive power of the resulting calculi made the search for tractable verification algorithms very difficult. Thus, in the second phase of timed concurrency theory research, focus was placed on more restricted (communicating automata-based) notations, for which tractable (region-based) verification methods could be developed [7, 13, 16, 91, 189, 202]. Thus, for example, the resulting timed automata notations typically do not support hierarchical decomposition of process structure; they offer a flat model of parallel components.

The format of this part reflects this historical progression of the field. Thus, we begin, in Chapters 9 and 10, by discussing timed extensions of the process calculus LOTOS. The first of these chapters considers mainly syntactic issues of how time should be added to such a calculus, whereas the second explores formal semantic interpretations of the resulting timed LOTOS. Both branching time and true concurrency interpretations are presented. We then move to considering real-time communicating automata notations in Chapters 11, 12 and 13. Chapter 11 considers a basic timed communicating automata model and associated region-based model-checking. Chapter 12 considers the thorny issue of how timelocks should be handled in timed communicating automata. Then, finally, Chapter 13 considers a new notation for infinite-state models of timed communicating automata.

---

[8]Notice, the term *temporal* is often used confusingly in this domain. For example, the use of the term in the context Language of Temporal Order Specification (LOTOS) does not imply real-time, but rather, what we called basic event ordering in Section 1.3.

9
Timed Process Calculi, a LOTOS Perspective

9.1 Introduction

The need to incorporate quantitative time into formal specification languages has been widely recognised. This is essential in order that applications that are time dependent can be correctly modelled at early stages in system development. Typical classes of such applications are communication protocols, real-time control systems and real-time distributed systems (e.g. multimedia applications). A spectrum of classic examples are used to test the expressiveness of specification techniques; typical examples are, the Alternating Bit Protocol [167], Train Gate examples [175], the Tick Tock Protocol [127], Dying Dining Philosophers [183] and Lip Synchronisation [21]. A number of time dependent computation structures arise repeatedly in these examples, e.g. standard timeouts [167], symmetric timeouts [26], watchdog timers [154], continuous media (streams) [21] and quality of service constraints [21]. Timed formal description notations must support specification of all these computation structures. Parts II and III have justified that process calculi [148] provide an appropriate means to specify the functional aspects of concurrent and distributed systems (i.e. what we called basic event ordering in Section 1.3) and convincing arguments for the approach have been given elsewhere [147].

The first generation of process calculi did not support specification of real-time constraints. Consequently, there has been much interest in extending process calculi in this direction, e.g. [64, 154, 167, 177, 201]. In particular, a plethora of timed extensions to LOTOS have been proposed, e.g. [25, 26, 59, 123, 125, 143, 164, 166, 168] and the experience of these proposals has been fed into the standardisation of the enhanced LOTOS language E-LOTOS; see Section 6.4. The revised language, amongst a number of other extensions, adds support for the expression of quantitative time; see Section 9.5.

This chapter presents a timed extension to LOTOS that uses a number of the proposed enhancements, with particular emphasis being placed on the following approaches, [26, 99, 102, 125, 143]. Thus, the chapter surveys the main design decisions involved in extending LOTOS with real-time and then presents a particular approach.

The main requirements for time-extended LOTOS are reviewed and alternative design choices are contrasted with reference to a number of the main proposals. One important point to note is that adding quantitative time has an impact on the nature of formal description in process calculi. Specifically, standard process calculus specification gives an abstract expression of "possible" behaviour, whereas real-time specification, by its nature, is more prescriptive; it grounds action possibilities in real-time and defines when actions will happen, rather than the possibility that they may occur [36]. This is exacerbated by the enforcement of urgency properties in timed process calculi (an observation also made by [78, 165] and further discussed in Section 9.2.2). Thus, we view timed calculi as a more low-level formalism than classic process calculi, less an abstract specification notation and more a design notation.

Section 9.2 contains the review of requirements and issues surrounding timed extension to LOTOS. Section 9.3 presents the timed LOTOS notation that we are proposing. Then Section 9.4 discusses some anomalous behaviours that can arise in timed LOTOS. Finally, Section 9.5 briefly reviews the timed extensions in E-LOTOS.

9.2 Timed LOTOS – The Issues

The now extensive field of timed process calculi has revealed a number of design choices involved in extending LOTOS with real-time. These choices are discussed in the following sections, each of which is devoted to a particular feature of extending LOTOS with real-time. The following features are discussed.

- Timed action enabling;
- Urgency;
- Persistency;
- Nondeterminism;
- Synchronisation;
- Timing domains;
- Time measurement;
- Timing of nonadjacent actions;
- Timed interaction policies; and
- Forms of internal urgency.

9.2.1 Timed Action Enabling

In a most basic sense, the enabling of LOTOS actions (i.e. when they are offered to the environment for interaction) needs to be tied to the passage of time. This section considers the different classes of timed action enabling that can be employed and highlights notational extensions to standard LOTOS that can be used to support these classes. First we consider two basic choices.

- **Instantaneous (Atomic) Actions vs. Durational Actions**
  As previously indicated, the atomic actions principle is central to standard process calculus theory; see Section 2.3.6.1. However, the move to real-time has prompted a minority of workers to consider noninstantaneous actions, e.g. [4]. By their very nature, approaches with action duration are truly concurrent; it would be unrealistic to prevent the interval of execution of any action from overlapping with any other action. However, largely in order to remain in line with the majority of timed process calculi workers, and, to our knowledge, all timed LOTOS workers, we remain faithful to the concept of atomic (and temporally instantaneous) actions.

- **Relative vs. Global (Absolute) Time**
  The distinction here is between approaches in which timing constraints are expressed relative to the execution of a causally preceding action (relative timing) and approaches in which all actions are timed relative to an absolute global clock (global timing). The former of these two approaches has dominated the time extended LOTOS work and can be seen to be most appropriate, because specification of ordering is expressed relatively; thus it is natural to interpret timing constraints in the same manner.

In accordance with these choices, the remainder of this chapter considers timed specification based on relative timings of atomic instantaneous actions. Expression of such real-time behaviour is generally facilitated by notational extensions to action prefix. Thus, some variety of timed action prefix is introduced, which has the general form,

$$a\, T\,;\, B$$

i.e. an action followed by a time constraint, denoted T, and a behaviour B. T expresses a time constraint that defines when a is offered relative to the execution of a predecessor action or the start of execution (when there is no predecessor). Once a has been executed, $a\, T$; B behaves as B. The different notational conventions for T and the different interpretations of these conventions reflect the class of timed action enabling being employed. The different classes of enabling are as follows.

- **Simple Enabling**
  This is the simplest approach. It allows the instant an action becomes enabled to be constrained by real-time, but, note, it does not allow any constraint to be placed on how long this enabling lasts. Thus, no upper bound can be imposed on enabling and the timing constraint associated with action prefix simply states the time that an action starts being offered relative to a predecessor action. So, a behaviour such as

  $$a\,[0]\,;\, b\,[5]\,;\, stop$$

states that the action a is enabled immediately, whereas action b is enabled 5 time units after action a is taken (note: the T discussed previously has been instantiated with the syntax $[t]^1$). This approach only very loosely prescribes when actions are taken. For example, from 5 time units after the execution of a, b can be taken at any time, e.g. 6 time units after a, 12 time units after a or 10000007 time units after a. Thus, this approach offers a minimal timing capability and it is easy to think of real-time examples that require a richer timing model. The advantage of this class is that it imposes minimal alterations to the classic process calculus model. In particular, once enabled, an action behaves as a standard process calculus action. An important consequence of this is that parallel composition rules (both interleaved and synchronised) are only minimally changed. Simple enabling is adopted as the main class of timing in [51].

- **Initiation and Termination of Enabling**
  In this class, both lower and upper time bounds can be imposed on enabling. Thus, the region of time in which an action is offered is bounded by an initiating and a terminating time constraint. The class is typically modelled using timing intervals. For example, a behaviour such as

  $a\,[0,2]\,;\,b\,[5,12]\,;\,stop$

  states that a is enabled immediately and will be offered for 2 time units; b will be enabled 5 time units after a is taken and will be offered for 7 time units. Clearly, an issue is what happens if the environment does not allow the action to be taken in the region in which it is enabled. This issue is discussed when we consider the possibilities for parallel composition and synchronisation in Section 9.2.5.

- **Punctual Enabling**
  The final class is punctual enabling, i.e. instantaneous initiation and then retraction of enabling. The action prefix of [143] uses this class of timing. So, a behaviour such as

  $a\,[0]\,;\,b\,[5]\,;\,stop$

  states that a is instantaneously offered and that 5 time units after a is taken, b is offered instantaneously. Punctual enablings are used as abstractions of real-world systems. An important class of applications that use punctual enabling is those employing periodic behaviour, e.g, isochronous transmissions, which are central to multimedia applications based on continuous media, and clocks. For example, the following behaviour,

  $Clock := tick\,[100]\,;\,Clock$

  will offer a *tick* every 100 time units. Once again, an issue to consider is what happens if the environment is not willing to engage in the action when it is instantaneously offered. This issue is discussed in Section 9.2.5.

---

[1]This syntax should not be confused with a selection predicate, as discussed in Section 6.2.6.

It should be clear that a fully expressive timed LOTOS should support all these classes of enabling. Thus, the central issue to consider is which class should be adopted as primitive. Clearly, only a class for which all the other classes can be derived would be suitable. The different classes can be related as follows.

- **Simple Enabling as Primitive**
  This choice is not appropriate as neither intervals of enabling nor punctual enabling can be derived.
- **Initiation and Termination of Enabling as Primitive**
  If we allow intervals to have upper bounds of infinity then simple enabling can be directly defined using this class; e.g. the simple enabling behaviour $a\,[0]$; $b\,[5]$; *stop* is equivalent to $a\,[0, \infty)$; $b\,[5, \infty)$; *stop* using intervals. In addition, punctual enabling can be defined by giving the interval the same lower and upper bound; e.g. the behaviour $a\,[0]$; $b\,[5]$; *stop* with punctual enabling is equivalent to $a\,[0, 0]$; $b\,[5, 5]$; *stop* using intervals.
- **Punctual Enabling as Primitive**
  It is more difficult to see how the other classes of enabling can be defined from punctual enabling, but they can. The timed LOTOSs built using punctual enabling typically use generalised choice in order to derive richer real-time scenarios, e.g. [143]. See Section 6.2.7 for an introduction to generalised choice. A typical example of the use of generalised choice to define timing intervals from punctual timing behaviour is

  $$choice\ t : nat\ []\ (\ [5 \le t \le 12]\ -> b\,[t]\,;\,B\ )$$

  which states that b is enabled after 5 time units and is then offered for the next 7 time units, when the offer is retracted. Thus, the behaviour is equivalent to the interval behaviour $b\,[5, 12]$; B. In addition, placing an infinite upper bound on generalised choice facilitates definition of simple enabling; e.g. the punctual timing behaviour,

  $$choice\ t : nat\ []\ (\ [5 \le t]\ -> b\,[t]\,;\,B\ )$$

  is equivalent to the simple enabling $b\,[5]$; B.

There are actually more notational alternatives than we have revealed in the discussion so far; some of these are considered in more depth later, e.g. in Sections 9.2.8 and 9.2.9, but we consider two alternatives now.

- **Delays**
  An alternative to adding time through action prefix is to include a delay operator, such as $\Delta\,t$ or $Wait\ t$; see [99, 123]. The behaviour $\Delta\,t\,B$ will idle for t time units and then behave as B. On its own, a delay operator does not yield a rich enough timing notation. However, in addition to other timed extensions, a fully expressive timed calculus can be devised. A good example of such an approach is the proposal [125], which supports two primary timing constructs, the "dream team" as Leduc refers to them, a delay operator $\Delta\,t$ and the, so-called, "life reducer". The latter of these is

an action prefix notation that bounds the length of enabling of an action; i.e. $a[t]$; B will offer a for a time period t, i.e. until the life reducer expires. With these two operators, lower bounds on enabling can be defined using the delay operator and upper bounds can be imposed using the life reducer, e.g. $\Delta\, 5\, b\,[10]$; B corresponds to $b\,[5,15]$; B in interval notation.

Leduc's motivation for including an explicit delay operator is to enable delays to be imposed that do not resolve choice on expiry of the delay. For example, the following behaviour $\Delta\, 5\, B\, [] \,\Delta\, 7\, B'$ imposes 5 time unit (respectively 7 time unit) delays on B (resp. B'), but, it is important to note that the choice between B and B' cannot be resolved solely by the expiry of either of the delays. This is in contrast to the solution that would have to be employed in a model without delays: $i\,[5,5]$; $B\, [] \,i\,[7,7]$; B', where the delay is overloaded on a hidden action. (Assuming maximal progress, which we discuss shortly) this solution will perform an i and behave as B after 5 time units have been reached. Thus, the choice is resolved by the i action with the smallest timing.

In actual fact, we would like to have a delay interval available, e.g. $\Delta\,[t1,t2]\,B$, which will wait for a time period nondeterministically chosen from the interval $t1$ to $t2$. This can be obtained using a single valued delay and offering an internal action during an interval, but this again has the problem of resolving choice. Typically, models do not support such a delay interval.

The reason for this is that it is difficult to define semantically. Specifically, a semantics would have to distinguish between the following two behaviours,

$$\Delta\,[0,2]\,x\,[0,2]\,;\,B \quad \text{and} \quad x\,[0,4]\,;\,B$$

because the first selects a delay (nondeterministically) from the interval $[0,2]$, waits that period of time and then (and only then) starts to offer x, which it offers for 2 time units. In contrast, the second behaviour offers x for 4 time units.

These are behaviourally very different processes; in particular, a tester process that wishes to perform x after 1 time unit, i.e. $x\,[1]$; $exit$, can never deadlock with the second process, but it can with the first. However, because we will have no semantic way of distinguishing deterministic and nondeterministic timing we will not be able to distinguish the two semantically. As a reflection of this, we do not include interval delays in our model. Thus, in this respect, we have the same limitation as E-LOTOS.

- **"High-level" Operators**

  Another approach is to incorporate "high-level" timing operators, such as timeouts and watchdog timers, directly in the language. One of Leduc's proposals emphasizes such operators. For example, [123] introduces an operator of the form $\lfloor P\rfloor^{t,x}(Q)$, which enables a timeout of value t to be imposed on all instances of action x in P; if a timeout expires, Q is activated (the operator is a generalisation of the timeout operator of TCSP [175], which is usually also introduced as primitive). Leduc's operators are related to the timed interaction operators of Bolognesi, which is discussed in Section 9.2.9.

In particular, one of Leduc's motivations in introducing these operators was to support specification of time constraints over interactions and thereby to support structured specification styles, such as the constraint-oriented style [24]. However, the introduction of operators such as timeouts and watchdogs as primitive leads to semantic complexity and is somehow not in keeping with the standard LOTOS operators, which provide a lower level of behavioural specification. Thus, our approach does not consider such high-level operators as primitive, but rather derives realisations of timeouts and watchdog timers in terms of more low-level primitive constructs. This is the approach taken in the majority of timed LOTOSs; in particular, later Leduc proposals have largely rejected the high-level operators.

In summary then, we have highlighted a number of different classes of timed enabling and a number of different notational conventions that can realise these classes. The debate between these notations concerns which is the most expressive and which will support all other classes of timed enabling. It is clear from our discussion that punctual timing and intervals could both be employed as primitive. However, the derivation from intervals is more straightforward and does not rely on an additional LOTOS construct, the generalised choice operator. Thus, we employ time intervals as our primitive timing notation. In addition, as justified above, we incorporate a delay operator similar to that in E-LOTOS.

9.2.2 Urgency

The previous section has highlighted a number of classes of timed action enabling. However, even a model that supports all these classes is only expressive enough to model a subset of real-time systems. The classic process calculus model expresses possibilities; it enables specification of what a system may do. The interpretation of choice in process calculi directly reflects this characteristic. Specifically, there is no point at which one of the two branches of a choice, such as a ; $stop$ [] b ; $stop$, is forced to happen; it really is the case that the behaviour may do a or it may do b and at no point (until the environment dictates) must it perform one in preference to the other. In addition, although internal actions are not waiting for environmental influence, in untimed calculi, they also express a may (rather than a must) execution policy. Thus, there is no point at which an internal action can be forced to happen. All we know is that it will eventually (at some finite point in time) happen.

The domain of real-time specification requires a revision of this interpretation. For many important classes of time-dependent systems, it is necessary to express that a particular behaviour *must* happen. As discussed at the end of Section 6.3.1, the classic example of this is a protocol containing a timeout; e.g. in our running communication protocol example, the sender behaviour,

$Sender\,[get, send, receiveAck] :=$

   $get\,;\; send\,;\; Sending\,[get, send, receiveAck]$

$Sending\,[get, send, receiveAck] :=$

   $receiveAck\,;\; Sender\,[get, send, receiveAck]$

   $[]\;\; i\,[t, t]\,;\; send\,;\; Sending\,[get, send, receiveAck]$

will perform an action *send* and then wait for an acknowledgement (the action *receiveAck*). If the acknowledgement arrives before a timer has expired, modelled here as the internal action i, which occurs punctually t time units after the *send*, then the behaviour recurses and makes its next transmission. If the behaviour times out waiting for *receiveAck* it will resend the message. Superficially, this seems a suitable solution, however, unless we can force the action i to occur urgently we cannot guarantee that the specification behaves correctly. Thus, we must actively rule out evolutions of the behaviour in which a *receiveAck* is offered at times greater than or equal to t time units after the *send* and force the i action to occur at time t. This requires some form of *urgency* to be imposed on timed actions, i.e. to define that an action must occur by some point in time.

Urgency is now a well-accepted and extensively documented requirement [123, 154, 167] and many different solutions exist. Three main approaches have been identified. These are differentiated by where urgency is placed in the model.

- **Urgent Actions**
  In this approach, all actions (both those that are observable and those that are unobservable) are interpreted as urgent. This approach can lead to some counterintuitive scenarios. Specifically, a main premise of process calculi is that the environment should dictate when observable actions are selected. With urgent actions, it is possible that observable actions will become urgent, but will be prevented from executing by an environment that is not offering the action. A consequence of this interpretation is that timelocks, i.e. situations in which time is not able to pass, may occur, because the specification may not allow time to pass because it wants to perform an action urgently, but the environment is not able to perform the action. Timed calculi have been considered that assume urgent actions, but allow nonurgency to be enforced explicitly, e.g. ATP [154], and this approach was reflected in an early timed LOTOS proposal by Leduc [121], which has not been taken further. In addition, some of the early Spanish proposals adopted urgent actions (e.g. [164]). However, urgent actions are now largely rejected in timed process calculi.
- **Explicit Urgency Operator**
  In this approach, a specific operator is incorporated into the language that enables actions to be made into urgent actions. So, for example, an operator *urge* may be introduced, which, in the following behaviour,

urge y in (x [2, 10] ; y [4, 6] ; stop)

will make the *y* urgent, i.e. force it to be offered urgently 4 time units after the execution of *x*. This approach clearly constrains the environment more selectively than the urgent actions approach, however, timelocks can still occur. Bolognesi [25, 26], the main advocate of explicit urgency operators, argues that timelocks reflect a specification error and should be accepted in timed calculi. Brinksma et al [51] provide another notable approach that employs an explicit urgency construct, although, urgency in this model is defined over action instances rather than over interactions as advocated in Bolognesi's proposals.

- **Urgent Internal Actions**
  All of the following terms have been used in the literature in order to describe variants of this class of urgency: *Maximal Progress*, *asap (as soon as possible)* and *Minimal Delay*. The approach restricts urgency to internal actions. Thus, unless an extra paradigm is incorporated into the language, all observable actions are interpreted as nonurgent, whereas internal actions are interpreted urgently. The intuition behind this is that all external actions are subject to the control of the environment, which should not be constrained by the imposition of urgency on offered behaviour, whereas internal actions are not so constrained. Thus, an internal action can always execute and it can always execute urgently (and without the possibility of timelocks arising). This is now the most common approach; see, for example, [99, 102, 125, 127, 143, 168]. However, it is worth pointing out that there are limitations to this approach. In particular, a specifier may want to constrain an action to be urgent, but still leave it available for synchronisation. With maximal progress, when an action is selected as urgent, the specifier is forced to hide the action and thus constraints can no longer be added to the action. This imposes a strict order of steps on the development process; all parallel constraints must be added first before urgency of interactions, and hence hiding, is considered.

It should be clear from the discussion above that incorporating urgency in LOTOS enables more "prescriptive" specifications than one classically offered by standard LOTOS. Urgency constraints prescribe that particular actions must happen in preference to other offered actions. In fact, some authors have viewed all forms of urgency as encouraging overspecification. Although we acknowledge this argument, we feel that the pragmatic case for forms of urgency (i.e. that certain classes of timed specification are only possible with it) is powerful. In accordance with what is now the majority of researchers, we prefer urgent internal actions over the other approaches.

However, there is still a choice to be made over the type of internal urgency that we recommend and we return to this issue in Sections 9.2.4 and 9.2.10.

9.2.3 Persistency

Action persistency is the property that the passage of time cannot cause an offered action to be retracted. In transition notation, action persistency can be defined as

$$\forall B, B', t, a \in Act \cup \{i, \delta\}, (B \overset{t}{\rightsquigarrow} B' \wedge B \overset{a}{\longrightarrow} \implies B' \overset{a}{\longrightarrow})$$

where B and B' are behaviour expressions, t is a time delay and $\overset{t}{\rightsquigarrow}$ is a time passing transition. The property states that, if a behaviour B can perform an action a, after idling, it will still be able to perform the action a.

Persistency enforces the standard untimed process calculus retraction of an enabled action, i.e. by action occurrence. The timed LOTOS community is split over the value of this property. Proposals which support persistency include [25, 26, 123], and proposals which do not support the property include [99, 102, 143]; in addition, [125] contains two proposals; the first does not support the property and the second does.

The strongest advocate of the principle is certainly Bolognesi [26], who argues for what he calls a strong timing policy (although, he does also recognise the need for a weak timing policy). He obtains this strong timing policy by enforcing a hard or strict upper bound on intervals of action enabling. Thus, time cannot pass beyond this upper bound without the action being executed or being disabled by the execution of an alternative action; e.g. if the action a is strongly timed, in the absence of an alternative action offer, the time constraint $a\,[2, 10]$ means that a becomes enabled two time units after the previous action and must have been taken within eight time units of this enabling. Thus, a *must* timing constraint is enforced, in a similar way as for urgency.

As was the case with imposing urgency on external actions, Bolognesi's strong timing policy has some counterintuitive consequences, such as the possibility of timelocks. In addition, specification of a choice between two actions with nonoverlapping intervals, e.g.

$$(x\,[5, 10]\,;\,B)\ [] \ (y\,[15, 20]\,;\,B')\qquad(*)$$

will only offer the environment the possibility of interacting with the first enabled action, i.e. the action x. This is because the upper bound on enabling of x is strict and, thus, either the x is taken within its time constraint or a timelock ensues; the y can never be offered. This seems a surprising interpretation of the interplay of choice and intervals of action enabling and suggests that the consequences of enforcing action persistency can be severe. A solution which would work in Bolognesi's model is

$$(x\,[5, 10]\,;\,B)\ [] \ (i\,[10, 10]\,;\,y\,[5, 10]\,;\,B')$$

where an internal action is introduced, execution of which will give an action persistent alternative to the execution of x at its upper bound. However, this solution becomes cumbersome if a choice contains many alternatives with nonoverlapping timing intervals.

So, in accordance with a number of the other timed LOTOS workers, we believe this is a situation in which timed LOTOS should diverge from the standard untimed language and, in situations such as the above example, we would like time to pre-empt action offers. Thus, the interpretation of the behaviour (*) that we would advocate is that after 10 time units have passed the offer of action x is retracted; 5 time units pass and then action y is offered. We advocate, in Bolognesi's terminology, a weak timing policy. A consequence of this is that we must decide what happens when an upper bound on an action expires without the environment having been able to interact with the offered action. We adopt what is now a relatively standard approach: to interpret a behaviour $x\,I;\,B$ as *stop* if the upper bound of the interval I expires; i.e. the offer of action x is retracted and no further action offers can be made. Importantly, this evolution to *stop* avoids timelocks as *stop* allows time to pass.

9.2.4 Nondeterminism

This section considers the implications of real-time on nondeterminism. In general, we seek to preserve the standard untimed behaviour of nondeterminism. This is reflected in the requirement of the following property, which is called time determinism,

$$\forall B, B', B'', t,\, (\, B \overset{t}{\leadsto} B' \,\wedge\, B \overset{t}{\leadsto} B'' \implies B' = B'' \,)$$

where equality here is syntactic equality. This states that the progression of time cannot create nondeterminism, i.e. cannot force B to evolve to two distinct behaviours. This is a reasonable property to require of a timed LOTOS and one that our extension will uphold.

In addition, the argument is often made that urgency of internal actions must be carefully defined. For some real-time behaviours, we would like to impose an interval of enabling on internal actions, i.e. to interpret a behaviour,

$$i\,[t,t'];\,B$$

as i is performed in the interval t to t'. The choice of instant that the internal action occurs is made nondeterministically. This is in keeping with the fact that internal actions are beyond the control of the environment. The implication of supporting this nondeterministic internal action is that i actions become urgent when they reach their upper time bounds. With strict maximal progress, they become urgent as soon as they are enabled.

The strict upper bound could though be circumvented through reference to an infinite upper bound,

$$i\,[t,\infty);\,B$$

Furthermore, maximal progress can be regained through a behaviour such as:

$i\,[t,t]\,;\,B$

ET-LOTOS [102] has adopted this approach of only enforcing urgency on the upper bound of time intervals for explicitly referenced internal actions (it employs maximal progress on hidden actions, as we discuss in Section 9.2.10). However, it should also be noted that the effect of a nondeterministic timed i action could be obtained through the combination of a delay operator and strict maximal progress on internal actions. For example, $\Delta\,[t,t']\,i\,;\,B$, where i occurs as soon as possible, in the classic sense of maximal progress. However, as discussed in Section 9.2.1 we do not include such an interval delay in our calculus. So this is not a solution we can employ.

9.2.5 Synchronisation

The basic difficulty surrounding synchronisation is that the timing intervals of synchronising actions may conflict (i.e. not overlap). We discuss this issue for each category.

- **Simple Enabling**
  For this class of enabling, synchronisation causes no problem. Conflicting timings cannot be specified as actions are enabled permanently from a particular point. For example, in the behaviour:

  $(\,x\,[5]\,;\,stop\,)\,|[x]|\,(\,x\,[3000]\,;\,stop\,)$

  the interaction on x would be offered after 3000 time units (the maximum of 5 and 3000).
- **Punctual Enabling**
  Timing conflicts arise if the instants of enabling of two synchronised actions are not identical. Thus,

  $(\,x\,[5]\,;\,stop\,)\,|[x]|\,(\,x\,[6]\,;\,stop\,)$

  will be in conflict on the interaction x.
- **Initiation and Termination of Enabling**
  As for punctual enabling, conflicting synchronisations can be easily illustrated; e.g.

  $(\,x\,[5,10]\,;\,stop\,)\,|[x]|\,(\,x\,[11,15]\,;\,stop\,)$

  However, the timing constraints do not have to be identical to enable synchronisation, as was the case for punctual enabling. Consider,

  $(\,x\,[5,10]\,;\,stop\,)\,|[x]|\,(\,x\,[8,15]\,;\,stop\,)$

  here the intersection of the two intervals, i.e. [8, 10], defines a constraint on the interaction x, which can satisfy the original intervals of enabling of the left- and right-hand instances of action x.

Similar alternatives are available for handling synchronisation conflicts with both punctual enabling and initiation and termination of enabling. The two standard alternatives are to enforce a timelock when synchronisations conflict or to enforce a deadlock (which would allow time to pass). The choice surrounding these two alternatives is clearly tied to the choices surrounding urgency and persistency already discussed. In keeping with our conclusions on these issues, we advocate that conflicting synchronisations deadlock rather than timelock.

9.2.6 Timing Domains

There are three realistic options for the choice of time domain: discrete, dense (but countable) and continuous, i.e. isomorphic to the natural numbers, the nonnegative rationals or the nonnegative reals. Many early approaches used discrete time domains [167] because they were simple and on the grounds that computers are discrete digital artefacts and so computer specifications should reflect this. However, the limitation of the discrete approach is that a minimal time unit must be assumed and no subdivision of this grain size can be made. This brings problems, because it may be difficult to determine what a suitable indivisible grain is for a specification. Employing refinement during system development accentuates the problem, because evolving a specification may reveal that the grain size chosen is too coarse.

This said, in certain contexts, the simplicity of discrete time models, especially in respect of how easily they can be analysed, outweighs these limitations. As a reflection of this, we consider a discrete time model in Chapter 13.

However, it is important to note that dense and continuous time domains do not suffer these problems concerning the granularity of timing. So, the problem could be resolved with either. However, continuous time domains have been argued for in order to support specification of systems combining analogue and digital elements. Thus, because it will not generate any technical problems for our approach, we employ the nonnegative reals as our time domain. Notice that discrete time (and time isomorphic to the rationals) can be recovered as a special case.

9.2.7 Time Measurement

The ability to reference the time instant at which an action occurs is important in certain classes of real-time specification. This facility enables constraints on action offers to be made subject to the time instant at which a previous action is taken. More generally, it enables time measurements to be undertaken.

A number of the timed LOTOS proposals incorporate facilities to reference the instant at which an action is executed. Miguel et al [143], for example, were the first to define timing domains as standard ACT-ONE data types and then timing variables were defined as any normal data variable. This enables the generalised choice operator to be used to reference the instant an action is taken; e.g.

$$send; (\ choice\ t : nat\ []\ receive\ [t]\ ;\ B\ )$$

will record the time between send and receive (the propagation delay of a protocol) in the variable t. Time measurement facilities are also available in [152], but perhaps the most important proposal in this area is that by [125]; a variant of which has been adopted in the E-LOTOS standard [99, 102]. The notation is based upon that used by Wang Yi [201] in his time-extended CCS; it enables an @t attribute to be associated with timed action prefix. The construction $a@t; B$ states that the value of variable t is the relative time instant at which a occurred; i.e. t records the duration that the action a is offered before it is taken. The lifetime of the binding to t is the whole of B. A typical example that uses the @ attribute is the specification of a global time clock:

$$Clock(time : nat) :=$$
$$current\_time\ ?cur : nat\ @t\ [cur = time + t]\ ;\ Clock(cur)$$

This discrete time (because it uses the naturals as a time domain) behaviour offers the current time of a global clock as a data attribute of the action $current\_time$ and then recurses with the new global time as argument.

9.2.8 Timing of Nonadjacent Actions

The majority of timed extensions to process calculi incorporate a notion of timed action prefix, similar to those discussed in Section 9.2.1. These paradigms express time constraints relative to the occurrence of a causally preceding action. However, some real-time problems require time constraints to be defined between actions, which are not direct predecessor and successor of one another. For example, we might want to specify that action z will occur between 10 and 15 time units after action x in the following behaviour $x; y; z; stop$. This constraint, of course, assumes that y happens between 0 and 15 time units after x. We can specify such a behaviour using parallel composition; e.g.

$$(\ x; y; z; stop)\ |[x, z]|\ (\ x; z\ [10, 15]\ ;\ stop)$$

This solution fits nicely into a constraint-oriented style of specification, where constraints on system behaviour are added through parallel composition. However, this approach does not work so well when the nonadjacent timing spans a choice or parallel composition. For example, specifying that z is time-constrained by x in the behaviour,

$$x; (y; z; stop\ []\ w; z; stop)$$

in such a way that the reference to z on the left of the choice has a different time constraint to the reference to z on the right of the choice, is difficult to envisage.

In addition, there is no way to *directly* express nonadjacent timing in calculi that only support a restricted notion of timed action prefix. For some workers this is a significant limitation of the standard approach [152]. Time measurement attributes such as the @t discussed in the last section aid direct expression of this class of property. For example, the above behaviour could be expressed as

$$x \, ; \, y@t \, ; \, z \, [10 - t, 15 - t] \, ; \, stop$$

but, if many intermediate actions exist between the nonadjacent actions, this can be cumbersome. For example, the behaviour,

$$x \, ; \, y@t1 \, ; \, z@t2 \, ; \, w@t3 \, ; \, u@t4 \, ;$$
$$v \, [10 - (t1 + t2 + t3 + t4), 15 - (t1 + t2 + t3 + t4)] \, ; \, stop$$

expresses that v will be enabled between 10 and 15 time units after x, with intermediate actions, y, z, w and u.

Nakata et al [152] directly address the issue of timing on nonadjacent actions with a proposal that rejects relative timing and where timing constraints in first-order predicate logic are associated with action offers. For example, the previous example would be expressed as

$$x \, [c = t] \, ; \, y \, ; \, z \, ; \, w \, ; \, u \, ; \, v \, [10 + c \le t \le 15 + c] \, ; \, stop$$

where t is a distinguished variable that denotes the current global time. t is used twice in this example, first to express the time at which x occurs and second to express the time at which v occurs. The use of t is akin to the use of clock variables in explicit clock temporal logics such as RTTL [157]. This approach certainly enables a rich set of nonadjacent timing constraints to be defined, but it also brings not insignificant added complexity, mainly centred on checking satisfiability of first-order predicate logic. Although, it should be noted, [152] argues that the logic is amenable to formal verification.

9.2.9 Timed Interaction Policies

Bolognesi and co-workers have consistently argued for a timed interaction policy, rather than the more common timed action policy. This preference has been reflected in a series of timed LOTOS proposals leading up to the extension presented in [26]. The choice is between the local application of timing constraints, as exemplified by approaches based on timed action prefix, and the more global application of timing constraints to interactions. The timed interaction policy enables a timer to be started at the precise moment that two parties begin interaction over a parallel composition. Bolognesi argues that specification of such behaviour is important and not possible with timed action policies. He draws analogies with the mature timing model offered by Merlin and Farber Petri nets [141].

As an illustration of the timed interaction approach, the following behaviour,

$$time\ y\,(5,8)\ in\ (\,x\,;\,y\,;\,stop\ |[y]|\ y\,;\,z\,;\,stop\,)$$

will offer y between 5 and 8 time units after the synchronisation of y across $|[y]|$ becomes possible. Thus, the timing constraint is imposed on the interaction y, rather than on the instances of action y, as would be the case with a timed action policy. Quantitative time in such a timed interaction policy is introduced into the language in a similar way to hiding in standard LOTOS. In fact, Bolognesi imposes both timing constraints and urgency constraints on interactions in preference to on actions; see the *urge* operator of Section 9.2.2

The, so-called, high-level timing operators of one of Leduc's early timed LOTOS proposals [123], which were discussed in Section 9.2.1, have many similarities to Bolognesi's timed interaction notation. However, in later proposals, Leduc has largely rejected these operators, stating that experience they have gained from extensive case studies suggests timed interaction operators are not in fact necessary.

9.2.10 Forms of Internal Urgency

As previously suggested, there are a number of different ways in which internal actions can be made urgent. We highlight the two main approaches.

1. **Maximal Progress**
   With pure maximal progress, as soon as an internal action becomes possible it must be taken. Thus, for example, (assuming that x does not appear in B), the following behaviours,

   $$i\,[2,10]\,;\,B\quad,\quad i\,[2,4]\,;\,B\quad and\quad hide\,x\,in\,(\,x\,[2,\infty)\,;\,B\,)$$

   are "behaviourally equivalent"[2] to each other and to the behaviour,

   $$i\,[2]\,;\,B$$

   Internal actions occurs *as soon as possible*.

2. **Urgent on Upper Bounds**
   With this approach, internal actions only become urgent when they reach the upper bound of their enabling. Thus, (again assuming that x does not appear in B) the behaviours,

   $$i\,[2,10]\,;\,B\quad,\quad i\,[2,4]\,;\,B\quad and\quad hide\,x\,in\,(\,x\,[2,\infty)\,;\,B\,)$$

   are no longer "behaviourally equivalent", because the first becomes urgent after 10 time units, the second after 4 and the third will never become urgent.

---

[2]For the moment we use this term informally. However, we formalise it in Chapter 10.

There are arguments in favour of both approaches, for example, as previously suggested, the latter allows nondeterministic timing of internal actions, e.g. the i action in,

$i\,[2,10]\,;\,B$

will happen at any time from 2 to 10, with the choice being made nondeterministically and this cannot be expressed with pure maximal progress. Furthermore, since we do not include an interval delay we cannot mimic this effect using it.

In contrast, maximal progress allows an important form of urgency on interactions to be defined. This can be seen from a scenario devised by Bolognesi, called the symmetric timeout. The timeout is built from two similar processes, each of which independently performs an unpredictably long activity (completion of which is signalled by w below). Then it wishes to synchronise on a given action (the x below) with its partner process as soon as possible (i.e. as soon as both are ready). However, the process sets a timer on how long it waits to synchronise and if synchronisation does not happen quickly enough it times out and retracts its offer of the synchronisation.

The general process is defined as follows:

$P\,[w, timeout, x]\ :=$

    $w\,;$

        $(\ x\,;\ P\,[w, timeout, x]$

        $[]\ timeout\,[t]\,;\ stop\ )$

and two copies of this process are run in parallel, subject to synchronisation on x (note: we could give each process a different timeout value, but we avoid this for simplicity of presentation).

$Q\ :=$

    $hide\ timeout1, timeout2\ in$

        $(\ P\,[w1, timeout1, x]\ |[x]|\ P\,[w2, timeout2, x]\ )$

Now importantly, the effect we seek is that, as soon as the two processes can synchronise on x, they do so. Thus, urgency is enforced at the point of the synchronisation being fulfilled and to do this we need to impose urgency on the interaction x, rather than each of the instances of x. We can do this with maximal progress using hiding, i.e.

    $hide\ x\ in\ Q$

However, it is not clear how to obtain the same effect when urgency is enforced on the upper bounds of internal actions. This observation has lead some workers to include both scenarios [102]. Thus, explicitly referenced internal actions, e.g. $i\,[0,5]\,;\,B$ are made urgent on their upper time bound (here 5), while hiding yields maximal progress. Thus, using $\equiv$ to denote our informal notion of behavioural equivalence (and assuming no references to x in B),

$$hide \; x \; in \; (\, x\,[0,5]\,;\, B\,) \;\; \equiv \;\; hide \; x \; in \; (\, x\,[0]\,;\, B\,) \;\; \not\equiv \;\; i\,[0,5]\,;\, B$$

which is an unpleasant compromise that advocates of this approach would accept.

Our approach is to handle internal actions consistently (whether explicit or hidden) and employ urgency on the upper time bound of all internal actions. We acknowledge that this reduces the expressiveness of our approach in terms of examples such as the symmetric timeout above.

9.2.11 Discussion

Combinations of the highlighted options have been incorporated into different proposals. However, no approach has incorporated all the options. In fact, such an all-embracing language is almost certain to be unsatisfactorily complex. With the desire not to over-complicate in mind we have made the following choices for our timed LOTOS.

- *Timed Action Enabling* – initiation and termination of enabling using intervals and a punctual delay operator;
- *Urgency* – urgency is imposed on internal actions;
- *Persistency* – nonpersistent;
- *Nondeterminism* – timing intervals associated with internal actions;
- *Synchronisation* – behaviours evolve to deadlock if the intervals of synchronising actions do not overlap;
- *Timing Domains* – isomorphic to the nonnegative reals;
- *Time Measurement* – not included;
- *Timing of Nonadjacent Actions* – no new operator included;
- *Timed Interaction Policies* – not included; and
- *Forms of Internal Urgency* – on upper bounds.

The absence of time measurement is a limitation, however, we do not see any technical reason why it could not be included in our model, with a certain amount of added complexity. In addition, we have not included a specific notation to obtain timing of nonadjacent actions, however, incorporation of time measurement would resolve this deficiency (although the @t construct and intervals are not a wholly natural combination). One reason for not including these facilities is that our semantic model will not support data.

9.3 Timed LOTOS Notation

9.3.1 The Language

The timed LOTOS that we introduce is denoted tLOTOS; it reflects a "core" subset of LOTOS operators, which excludes data and some high-level constructs, e.g. disabling, generalised choice and generalised parallelism.[3] Handling disabling would require richer semantic models than we consider (e.g. extended bundle event structures; see [114]) and we avoid the added complexity of considering these here. However, what we present can easily be extended to these models. tLOTOS is ostensibly a timed version of pbLOTOS; see Chapter 2. In accordance with what we have argued so far, we add intervals as our basic timing syntax. More formally, Ξ is the set of all possible timing intervals and $I \in \Xi$ has the form:

$$[t, t'] \quad \text{or} \quad [t, \infty)$$

where $t, t' \in \mathbb{R}^{+0}$ and $\mathbb{R}^{+0}$ is the positive reals with zero (and $\mathbb{R}^{+}$ will denote the positive reals without zero). So, these are (continuous) intervals on the nonnegative real numbers, either closed or half-open with an upper bound of infinity[4]. If $t > t'$ in $[t, t']$ then an empty interval results, denoted $\emptyset$. We use the notation $\uparrow I$ to yield the upper bound of I and $\downarrow I$ to yield the lower bound. For half open intervals, $\uparrow [t, \infty) = \infty$. In addition, by convention, we assume that $\uparrow \emptyset = 0$ and $\downarrow \emptyset = \infty$.

We define addition on intervals as follows,

$$I \oplus J = \{ t_1 + t_2 \mid t_1 \in I \land t_2 \in J \}$$

where, because $t + \infty = \infty$, infinite bounds are preserved.

We define subtraction on intervals in a similar way,

$$I \ominus J = \{ (t_1 - t_2) \in \mathbb{R}^{+0} \mid t_1 \in I \land t_2 \in J \}$$

which avoids negative values being generated by enforcing that $(t_1 - t_2) \in \mathbb{R}^{+0}$. Clearly, we can obtain constant addition and subtraction as a specialisation of these operators. Thus, we write,

$$I \ominus d \text{ for } I \ominus [d, d] \text{ and } I \oplus d \text{ for } I \oplus [d, d]$$

Observe also that $I \ominus d$ does not necessarily have the same cardinality as I. In particular, $I \ominus d = \emptyset$ if $d > \uparrow I$.

The set of all tLOTOS descriptions is defined as follows. Thus, all $S \in tLOTOS$ satisfy the following rules.

$$S ::= B \mid B \text{ where } D$$

$$D ::= (P := B) \mid (P := B) \, D$$

$$B ::= stop \mid exit \, I \mid wait \, [t] \, B \mid a \, I \, ; \, B \mid B_1 \, [] \, B_2 \mid B_1 \, |[G]| \, B_2 \mid$$
$$\quad B_1 >> B_2 \mid hide \, G \, in \, B \mid B \, [y_1/x_1, \ldots, y_n/x_n] \mid P$$

---

[3]Strictly speaking, we should call this language tpbLOTOS, but we use the more concise tLOTOS for presentational convenience.

[4]Note, we do not allow half-open intervals in any other circumstances, since they can generate timelocks. For example, enforcing urgency at the upper bound of an interval, which has no proper upper bound, would prevent time passing.

where $a \in Act \cup \{i\}$, $x_i, y_i \in Act$, $t \in \mathbb{R}^{+0}$, $I \in \Xi$, $D \in tDeflist$ (the set of tLOTOS definition lists), $G \subseteq Act$, $P \in PIdent$ and $B \in tBeh$ (the set of all tLOTOS behaviour expressions).

Thus, we have a deadlock behaviour, *stop*; timed successful termination, *exit I*; a delay operator, *wait* $[t]B$; timed action prefix, $a\,I\,;\,B$; binary choice, $B_1 \,[]\, B_2$; parallel composition, $B_1 \,||G||\, B_2$; sequential composition, $B_1 >> B_2$; hiding, *hide* $x_1, \ldots, x_n$ *in* B; relabelling, $B[y_1/x_1, \ldots, y_n/x_n]$; and process instantiation, P.

In order to simplify presentation, we often write relabelling as $B[H]$ where H is a relabelling function. It is assumed to be total on $Act \cup \{i, \delta\}$ and can be obtained from a relabelling vector, $y_1/x_1, \ldots, y_n/x_n$, by defining $H(x_i) = y_i$ for all $1 \leq i \leq n$ and $H(a) = a$ for all $a \in (Act \setminus \{x_1, \ldots, x_n\}) \cup \{i, \delta\}$. Also, for ease of presentation, in some examples we associate gate lists with process definitions and instantiations even though this is not in the base language.

The construct *wait* $[t]\ B$ is our delay; it will idle for t time units and then behave as B. Timed action prefix, $a\,I\,;\,B$, will offer a (which ranges over internal and observable actions) in the interval of enabling defined by I and, if a is taken, it will behave as B. Thus,

- $x\,[t, t']\,;\,B$ will offer x between t and t' inclusive;
- $x\,[t, \infty)\,;\,B$ defines simple enabling of x; and
- $x\,[t, t]\,;\,B$ defines punctual enabling of x.

We can create nondeterministic intervals of internal behaviour such as

$$i\,[10, 20]\,;\,B$$

More usable operators can be derived from the basic tLOTOS constructs. We assume the following derivations.

- $a\,(t)\,;\,B \triangleq a\,[t, \infty)\,;\,B$;
- $x\,;\,B \triangleq x\,(0)\,;\,B$ for $x \in Act$;
- $a\,[t]\,;\,B \triangleq a\,[t, t]\,;\,B$;
- $i\,;\,B \triangleq i\,[0]\,;\,B$;
- $exit\,(t) \triangleq exit\,[t, \infty)$;
- $exit \triangleq exit\,[0, \infty)$;
- $exit\,[t] \triangleq exit\,[t, t]$; and
- $B \rhd_t B' \triangleq B\,[]\,(\,wait\,[t]\,i\,;\,B'\,)$.

Notice that nontime-constrained action prefix is interpreted differently dependent upon whether the action is internal or external; i.e. $x\,;\,B \triangleq x\,[0, \infty)\,;\,B$ while $i\,;\,B \triangleq i\,[0, 0]\,;\,B$. This reflects the standard interpretational distinction between external and internal behaviour arising from urgency. Notice also that the last of these derived operators is a timeout, which will behave as B

if the first action of B is performed before t time units expire; if t time units do pass before this action is performed, the behaviour evolves to B'. Central to the definition of this operator is the interpretation of internal actions as urgent, which ensures that the timeout really does expire after t time units and the exception behaviour is performed.

9.3.2 Example Specifications

This section discusses specification of two typical real-time constructs, a time-out and a multimedia stream.

Simple Timeout. From the communication protocol example, the following behaviour,

$Sender\,[get, send, receiveAck] :=$
  $get\,;\, send\,[0]\,;\, Sending\,[get, send, receiveAck]$

$Sending\,[get, send, receiveAck] :=$
  $receiveAck\,;\, Sender\,[get, send, receiveAck]$
  $\rhd_t\, send\,[0]\,;\, Sending\,[get, send, receiveAck]$

defines a simple *Sender* process, which sends a message immediately and then goes into state *Sending*. In this state it will either receive an acknowledgement and restart the transmission process or it will timeout after t time units, resend and try again for an acknowledgement.

Multimedia Stream. Distributed multimedia computing is an important area of real-time systems and the application of timed formal techniques to this area is being widely considered [21]. Distributed multimedia systems contain continuous flows of data with strict associated timing constraints, e.g. flows of audio or video. A multimedia stream is an abstraction of such flows of data. We consider a very simple example of such a stream, comprising a data source and a data sink communicating asynchronously over a channel; see Figure 9.1. The channel is assumed to be infinite and may lose messages. Time units are milliseconds.

The top-level behaviour of the stream could be specified as

  $start;$
    $hide\ sourceOut, sinkIn\ in$
      $(\ (\ (\ sourceOut\,[0]\,;\, Source\ )\ |||\ Sink\ )$
        $|[sourceOut, sinkIn]|$
      $Channel\ )$

This composes the *Source*, *Sink* and *Channel* processes into a form equivalent to that depicted in Figure 9.1. The gates *sourceOut* and *sinkIn* are hidden from the external observer. The *start* action is offered until it is taken and

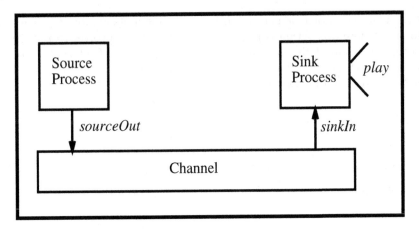

Fig. 9.1. A Multimedia Stream

the *sourceOut* action is offered immediately following *start* (as long as the *Channel* is willing).

The *Source* process has a very simple behaviour,

$$Source := sourceOut\,[50]\,;\,Source$$

sourceOut actions are repeatedly offered at 50 ms intervals. Notice that no error recovery is incorporated, i.e. acknowledgement or timeout schemes. This is typical of multimedia data, where temporal integrity is most important and retransmission is of limited value, since it would typically invalidate temporal integrity. The behaviour of the *Channel* can be specified as follows,

$$
\begin{aligned}
&Channel := \\
&\quad sourceOut\,; \\
&\qquad (\ (\ i\,[80, 90]\,;\,sinkIn\,[0]\,;\,stop \\
&\qquad\quad []\ i\,[0, 90]\,;\,stop\ ) \\
&\qquad |||\ Channel\ )
\end{aligned}
$$

So, the *Channel* will always offer a *sourceOut* and then either a *sinkIn* will be offered or the *Channel* will internally decide to lose the message, indicated by an internal action. In addition, the channel imposes a latency delay of between 80 and 90 ms on each transmission. The action *sinkIn* will be offered at a time instant nondeterministically chosen from the interval [80, 90]. The independent parallel recursive call ensures that the channel is nonblocking.

The data sink could be specified as

$$
\begin{aligned}
&Sink := \\
&\quad (\ sinkIn\,;\,(\ play\,[5]\,;\,stop\ |||\ Waiting\ )\ )
\end{aligned}
$$

$\rhd_{90}$ (i ; $error$; $stop$)

$Waiting$:=

($sinkIn$; ($play$ [5] ; $stop$ ||| $Waiting$))

$\rhd_{50}$ (i ; $error$; $stop$)

which either receives a $sinkIn$ and $play$s the frame or returns an error. The process takes 5 ms to process frames, i.e. the time between frames arriving and being played. If either the first frame does not arrive within 90 ms of the action $start$ occurring or a future frame does not arrive within 50 ms of a previous frame, the $Sink$ will go into error.

9.4 Timing Anomalies in tLOTOS

The fact that observable actions cannot be forced to be urgent, prevents a major source of timelocks, i.e. those that arise through mismatched synchronisations, where one partner in a synchronisation wishes to force the action to occur at a particular point, but the other partner does not offer the action at that instant. However, other forms of timelocks can occur. These are analogues of what we call zeno-timelocks in Chapter 12, where we discuss these issues in some depth in the timed automata setting. They all occur through the interplay of recursion and the passage of time and they correspond to situations in which an infinite number of transitions can be performed in a finite (even zero) amount of time.

Firstly, instantaneous tau loops can stop time. For example,

$P := i$; P (remember, i ; $B \triangleq i [0,0]$; B)

will perform an infinite number of i transitions without passing time. Note, the urgency of internal transitions is critical in generating this behaviour. In particular, although

$R := x (0)$; R

has a trace whereby an infinite number of xs are performed at time zero (i.e. a zeno run), at all points during that trace, there is a future point at which it can allow time to pass arbitrarily. Indeed, this arbitrary idling will, at some point, become the only possibility for the process unless the environment is also willing to undertake an infinite number of x actions at time zero. Thus, through its choice of action offers, the environment can "force" R out of its zeno run. Consequently, R never actually locks time; it is not an example of a timelock.

Secondly, unguarded recursion can generate timelocks. For example,

$Q := Q$

will block time. This is because the labelled transition system semantics for tLOTOS take the *smallest* relation satisfying the operational semantics inference rules (which are given in Section 10.1.2). Consequently, Q yields the null transition system, which can neither pass time nor perform any actions; i.e. it is timelocked (actually, time-action locked in the terminology of Chapter 12).

Indeed, any tLOTOS process containing an unguarded recursion will block time. For example,

$$unguarded := (\, x \, [2, 6] \, ; \, stop \,) \, ||| \, unguarded$$

cannot pass time.

Finally, if we imagine our language has data typing capabilities, we can define pure zeno processes. First, the following is a process with zeno runs.

$$zeno := zzeno(1)$$
$$zzeno(k : nat) := x \, ; \, wait \, [2^{-k}] \, zzeno(k+1)$$

This process can perform an x, delay for 0.5 time units, then perform another x, wait 0.25 time units, and so on, ad infinitum. Thus, if x is repeatedly selected instantaneously, the process gets infinitely close to an absolute time of 1, but it never actually gets there. However, because it uses observable actions, it will not generate a timelock; that is, repeatedly, during a zeno run it will reach points from which it could pass time, i.e. when x is enabled.

Notice, the following process also does not create a zeno timelock, even though it does have zeno runs.

$$zeno' := zzeno'(1)$$
$$zzeno'(k : nat) := x \, [0] \, ; \, wait \, [2^{-k}] \, zzeno'(k+1)$$

In this case, idling will make x unavailable, but, nonetheless, any point in a zeno run is followed by a point at which the process can idle arbitrarily.

However, the following behaviour does timelock.

$$zeno\_urgent := zzeno\_urgent(1)$$
$$zzeno\_urgent(k : nat) := i \, ; \, wait \, [2^{-k}] \, zzeno\_urgent(k+1)$$

It never reaches a state where it can idle to an absolute time not less than 1. Once again, the urgency of internal actions is critical in obtaining this effect.

A key characteristic of timelocks is that they prevent a completely independent process from evolving [34,35]. Accordingly, *zeno* and *zeno'* have paths in which time passes arbitrarily and thus, they will not block a completely independent process. However, *zeno_urgent* will. For example,

$$zeno\_urgent \, ||| \, (\, i \, [2] \, ; \, success \, ; \, stop \,)$$

can never perform the action *success*. However,

zeno ||| (*i* [2] ; *success* ; *stop*)   and

zeno' ||| (*i* [2] ; *success* ; *stop*)

can both reach *success*. We do not view behaviours with zeno runs as, automatically, degenerate, however, behaviours with *only* zeno runs, i.e. zeno timelocks, are clearly very dangerous.

Whereas timing anomalies, such as those highlighted here, are not a pleasing part of tLOTOS, our position is that such zeno timelocks should not be prevented by construction (this is in contrast with our position with respect to nonzeno timelocks, which, as discussed throughout this chapter, we believe should be ruled out by construction). Indeed, it has been observed in [65] that such behaviour can have an important role in a constraint-oriented specification style [195]. We thus prefer the application of analytical methods, which can detect such degenerate behaviour. We highlight such an analysis technique, which detects zeno timelocks in timed automata specifications in Chapter 12. It should be possible to devise similar techniques that can be applied in the tLOTOS setting.

9.5 E-LOTOS, the Timing Extensions

E-LOTOS was briefly discussed in Section 6.4. In addition to the extensions discussed there, the language also has a number of extensions that allow the specification of real-time behaviour; these include the following.

- E-LOTOS has the capacity to define timing domains in the data language. This yields a type *time*, with appropriate operations defined on it. Typically, the data domain chosen will be a renaming of either the non negative naturals or the nonnegative rationals.
- A wait operator, similar to tLOTOS' wait operator, is included. Thus, behaviours such as

    x ; $wait(5)$; y

and, more interestingly,

    x ; ($?t := any\ time\ [t <= 10]$) ; $wait(t)$; y

can be specified. The former just enforces a 5 time unit delay between x and y (note, in E-LOTOS ; denotes sequential composition, rather than action prefix and action instances implicitly generate successful terminations). The latter enforces a delay between x and y that is a randomly chosen value less than 10 (note, in E-LOTOS $?t$ denotes a binding occurrence of variable t).
- A powerful time capture enhancement of action prefix (as discussed earlier in this chapter) is included. Thus, in

    $x\ @?t$; $wait(20 - t)$; y

t captures the time elapsed between when x started being offered and when it is taken. Assuming that x occurs within 20 time units of being enabled, the above behaviour ensures that y becomes enabled 20 time units after x initially became enabled.

When combined with the selection predicate, the time capture operator can also be used to recover punctual and interval enabling; e.g.

$$x \, @?t \, [t = 5] \, ; \, y \quad \text{and} \quad x \, @?t \, [2 <= t <= 5] \, ; \, y$$

The left-hand behaviour requires x to happen at time 5, or not at all and the right-hand behaviour offers x between times 2 and 5.

- The maximal progress principle is employed. Thus, internal actions generated through hiding must occur as soon as possible and observable actions cannot be urgent.

E-LOTOS certainly offers a powerful set of timing operators. In particular, the time measurement capacities of the $@t$ attribute give E-LOTOS advantages over tLOTOS. However, we have selected the pure intervals approach of tLOTOS because of its simplicity and because semantic treatments of it in both the interleaved and true concurrency setting have been given, which is not the case for time capture.

Semantic Models for tLOTOS

We need to consider semantic models for timed process calculi for just the same reason that we had to consider semantics for untimed process calculi. In particular, in order to know definitively when we can view two specifications of timed systems as behaviourally equivalent, we need to relate their semantic models. Syntactic equivalence is again much too fine a means of comparison.

As was the case in the untimed setting, many different semantic interpretations have been devised, each of which induces a particular notion of equivalence. In fact, timed versions of all the semantic models we considered in Part II can be presented. However, due to the limits of this presentational format, we restrict ourselves to timed versions of labelled transition systems and of bundle event structures. The interested reader can, for example, consider the timed CSP theory [176] for details of timed extensions of trace-based and trace-refusals based theories.

The material presented in this chapter follows closely work performed by Joost-Pieter Katoen and co-workers [51, 108, 109]; Bowman [32, 39] and, particularly closely, Bowman and Katoen [47]. The chapter is divided into two sections. The first (Section 10.1) considers labelled transition system semantics for tLOTOS and the second (Section 10.2) considers bundle event structure semantics for the calculus.

10.1 Branching Time Semantics

10.1.1 Timed Transition Systems

In order to give a branching time semantics for tLOTOS we need an enhancement of labelled transition systems that not only allows us to describe the order in which actions occur, but also allows us to express relative timing between actions. The semantic structure that we use is what has been called a *time action transition* system [26], although, when there is no chance of confusion, we use the simpler term "timed transition system". Bolognesi [26] gives a justification for why this approach is preferable to the other common approach, which he calls timed-action transition systems.

The set of all time action transition systems is denoted $\mathcal{TTS}$ and we require that $\forall Sys \in \mathcal{TTS}$, Sys is a four tuple (S, TL, T, s_0) where

- S is a nonempty set of states.
- $TL \subseteq A \cup \mathbb{R}^+$ is a set of transition labels. Notice that real numbers as well as actions (from the set A) can label transitions (for tLOTOS A will be set to $Act \cup \{i, \delta\}$).
- T is a set of transition relations. One relation, T_v, is included for each $v \in TL$.
- $s_0 \in S$ is the starting state of Sys.

In the normal way, a *transition relation* T_v is a set of triples of the form (s, v, s'),[1] i.e.

$$T_v \subseteq S \times \{v\} \times S$$

where (s, v, s') states that a transition from state s to state s' exists, which is labelled by v. Thus, transitions in time action transition systems not only denote when actions occur, but, by placing values (in the reals) on transitions, they also denote time passing. For example, Figure 10.1 shows a very simple time action transition system. The system will idle for 1.5 time units, then it will perform a nondeterministic choice on x, as a result of which it will either idle 0.9 time units and offer a y or it will idle 2.8 time units and then offer a z. Thus, time and action transitions are scattered throughout the resulting graph, indicating that the offering of atomic actions can be interleaved with the passage of time.

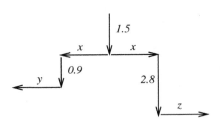

Fig. 10.1. A Time Action Transition System

As a notational convention, we distinguish between transitions labelled with actions, which we denote

---

[1]Although, rather than explicitly subdividing T into subrelations by label, we could analogously have given a flat definition of the transition relation, as we did in Section 8.2.1. Indeed, our use of a nested transition relation in the process calculus setting, and a flat relation with automata, is largely historical.

$$s \xrightarrow{a} s'$$

and those labelled with time steps, which we denote

$$s \xrightarrow{d} s'$$

where $d \in \mathbb{R}^+$.

In contrast to the illustration we gave in Figure 10.1, the time action transition systems derived from a nontrivial specification will almost certainly contain infinite branching. In particular, for a specification such as

$$P := x[0,1]; B$$

the following will hold

$$\forall d \in \mathbb{R}^+ . P \xrightarrow{d}$$

and because our time domain is the reals, the number of possibilities for d will not only be infinite, but it will also be uncountable!

10.1.2 Operational Semantics

We present an operational semantics that maps tLOTOS specifications to time action transition systems. The inference rules presented in this section realise the semantic map $[\![\ ]\!]_{tts}$,

$$[\![\ ]\!]_{tts} : tLOTOS \longrightarrow \mathcal{TTS}$$

The inference rules we give are based upon the (event-based) operational semantics given in [47], which were, in turn, based on those given in Katoen's PhD thesis [107]. Although, our rules are adapted to the calculus tLOTOS, they work on action labels, rather than event labels and they resolve some subtle difficulties with the earlier semantics, which we discuss in the next few paragraphs.

We need some preliminary definitions before we give our inference rules. Let $initI(a, B)$ be the set of time intervals at which B is allowed to initially perform a (this function is based upon the mapping denoted al in [47], which was originally defined in [107][2]). The interpretation of $initI(a, B)$ being equal to $\emptyset$ or $\{\emptyset, \ldots, \emptyset\}$ is that B cannot initially perform a.

For tLOTOS expression B and $a \in Act \cup \{i, \delta\}$, function $initI(a, B)$ is defined as the smallest set satisfying the rules in Figure 10.2. The rules define a relatively straightforward induction on the structure of tLOTOS specifications. Note in particular, that the wait operator merely delays the initial times

---

[2]Although it is important to note that we take the set of initial intervals, rather than collapsing these intervals together to obtain the set of initial time points. It turns out that a correct interpretation of urgency generated by hiding and enabling requires this richer representation, as discussed further in the next few paragraphs.

$$initI\,(a, stop) \triangleq \emptyset$$

$$initI\,(a, exit\,I) \triangleq \begin{cases} \emptyset & \text{if } a \neq \delta \\ \{I\} & \text{if } a = \delta \end{cases}$$

$$initI\,(a, b\,I\,;\,B) \triangleq \begin{cases} \emptyset & \text{if } a \neq b \\ \{I\} & \text{if } a = b \end{cases}$$

$$initI\,(a, B \;[\!]\; B') \triangleq initI\,(a, B) \cup initI\,(a, B')$$

$$initI\,(a, wait\,[t]\,B) \triangleq \{\, t \oplus I \mid I \in initI\,(a, B)\,\}$$

$$initI\,(a, B \gg B') \triangleq \begin{cases} \emptyset & \text{if } a = \delta \\ initI\,(a, B) & \text{if } a \notin \{i, \delta\} \\ initI\,(a, B) \cup initI\,(\delta, B) & \text{if } a = i \end{cases}$$

$$initI\,(a, B \;|[G]|\; B') \triangleq \begin{cases} initI\,(a, B) \cup initI\,(a, B') & \text{if } a \notin G \cup \{\delta\} \\ \{\,I \cap I' \mid I \in initI\,(a, B) \,\wedge\, I' \in initI\,(a, B')\,\} & \text{if } a \in G \cup \{\delta\} \end{cases}$$

$$initI\,(a, B[H]) \triangleq \{\, I \in initI\,(b, B) \mid a = H(b)\,\}$$

$$initI\,(a, hide\,G\,in\,B) \triangleq \begin{cases} \emptyset & \text{if } a \in G \\ initI\,(a, B) & \text{if } a \notin G \,\wedge\, a \neq i \\ \{\, I \in initI\,(b, B) \mid b \in G \cup \{i\}\,\} & \text{if } a = i \end{cases}$$

$$initI\,(a, P) \triangleq initI\,(a, B) \;\text{ for }\; P := B$$

Fig. 10.2. Definition of *initI*

to perform an action of the behaviour it prefixes. In addition, the lower clause for $|[G]|$ defines the initial intervals for synchronised actions. Thus, such an action can only be performed at a time point that is initial for both component behaviours. Finally, consider the third clause of the rule for hiding. It states that any initial instant of an action, which will be or, indeed, has been, hidden, becomes an initial instant of the internal action.

One important point to note about this definition is that $initI\,(a, B)$ returns a set, each element of which is an interval. In particular, $initI\,(a, B)$ cannot yield an item that is a discontinuous subset of the real number line. Thus, for each $I \in initI\,(a, B)$, the upper bound of enabling is straightforwardly characterised, which is important with respect to enforcing urgency on i actions generated by hiding and sequential composition, see the discussion of hiding later in this section.

As an example of the application of $initI\,(a, B)$, the following two processes,

$$R_1 := x\,[5]\,;\,stop \;[\!]\; x\,[2, 4]\,;\,stop$$

$$R_2 := x\,;\,stop \;[\!]\; x\,[2, 4]\,;\,stop$$

would be interpreted as follows.

$$initI\,(x, R_1) = \{\,[5, 5]\,,\,[2, 4]\,\}$$

$$initI\,(x, R_2) = \{\,[0, \infty)\,,\,[2, 4]\,\}.$$

We have introduced *initI* in order to derive two other functions, which play an important role in defining the operational semantics of hiding (and, indeed, sequential composition). The first identifies the smallest initial instant at which a particular action can be performed. That is, for $A \subseteq Act \cup \{i, \delta\}$ let

$$initI\!\downarrow(A, B) \triangleq Min(\bigcup\bigcup_{a \in A} initI(a, B))$$

We write $initI\!\downarrow(a, B)$ for $initI\!\downarrow(\{a\}, B)$ and we assume $Min(\emptyset) = \infty$. We also use the smallest of the set of all maximum time points at which an action in a set of actions can initially be performed. Thus, for $A \subseteq Act \cup \{i, \delta\}$,

$$initI\!\downarrow\!\uparrow(A, B) \triangleq Min(\{\uparrow I \mid I \in \bigcup_{a \in A} initI(a, B) \wedge I \neq \emptyset\})$$

As illustration of these definitions, the two processes R_1 and R_2 introduced earlier would be interpreted as follows.

$$initI\!\downarrow(x, R_1) = 2$$

$$initI\!\downarrow(x, R_2) = 0$$

$$initI\!\downarrow\!\uparrow(x, R_1) = initI\!\downarrow\!\uparrow(x, R_2) = 4$$

The relations $\longrightarrow$ and $\rightsquigarrow$ are the smallest relations that satisfy the inference rules defined below.

Stop / Inaction. This behaviour cannot perform any action, but permits any amount of time to pass.

$$(tST) \quad \frac{}{stop \overset{d}{\rightsquigarrow} stop}$$

This is consistent with the intuition that we have of what, in the untimed setting, would have been called a deadlock. Such locks fail to offer further actions, but, it is important to note that they still allow time to pass. Thus, they cannot *stop* time; i.e. generate timelocks; see Sections 9.4 and 10.2.4.

Successful Termination / Exit. The I in *exit I* governs the time points at which the successful termination, marked δ, can occur. Thus, *exit I* can perform a δ action if sufficient time has elapsed, i.e. if $0 \in I$. If time advances by d time units, it evolves into $exit(I \ominus d)$.

$$(tEX.i) \quad \frac{}{exit\, I \overset{\delta}{\longrightarrow} stop} \; (0 \in I) \qquad (tEX.ii) \quad \frac{}{exit\, I \overset{d}{\rightsquigarrow} exit\, (I \ominus d)}$$

Rule (tEX.ii) implies that δ actions are not interpreted urgently. This is because nothing prevents the rule from being applied in a situation in which $d > \uparrow I$. In which circumstance, *exit I* will become strongly equivalent to *stop*. For example, $exit\, [2, 10] \overset{12}{\rightsquigarrow} exit\, \emptyset$.

Observable Action Prefix. Because it is only internal actions that are treated urgently, we consider external and internal action prefix separately. As was the case for successful termination, $x\,I\,;\,B$ can perform x if $0 \in I$; i.e. it is enabled at the current time point (see rule (tAP.i)). It allows any amount of time to pass, with the possibility that x is no longer offered. This will arise if $d >\uparrow I$, which ensures that $0 \notin (I \ominus d) = \emptyset$, i.e. if time has passed beyond the enabling of x.

$$\text{(tAP.i)} \quad \frac{}{x\,I\,;\,B \xrightarrow{x} B} \ (0 \in I) \qquad \text{(tAP.ii)} \quad \frac{}{x\,I\,;\,B \xrightarrow{d}\rightsquigarrow x\,(I \ominus d)\,;\,B}$$

Internal Action Prefix. The difference between internal and external action prefix is that internal actions are urgent. This is reflected in rule (tIAP.ii), which allows delays up to $\uparrow I$, but not beyond. The only possibility to evolve after a maximal delay is to perform i (whereas for the observable case the possibility of further delay also exists; see rule (tAP.ii)). Thus, rule (tIAP.ii) ensures that internal actions become urgent on the upper bound of their time interval, which was the approach that we motivated in Section 9.2.10.

$$\text{(tIAP.i)} \quad \frac{}{i\,I\,;\,B \xrightarrow{i} B} \ (0 \in I)$$

$$\text{(tIAP.ii)} \quad \frac{}{i\,I\,;\,B \xrightarrow{d}\rightsquigarrow i\,(I \ominus d)\,;\,B} \ (d \le \uparrow I)$$

Delay. Behaviour $wait\,[t]\,B$ waits for t time units and then evolves into B. It either waits for more than t time units in one step (rule (tD.iii)) or by delaying precisely t time units, thus reaching $wait\,[0]\,B$ (using rule (tD.ii)). When the delay has been satisfied, the wait construct can perform action transitions (rule (tD.i)).

$$\text{(tD.i)} \quad \frac{B \xrightarrow{a} B'}{wait\,[0]\,B \xrightarrow{a} B'}$$

$$\text{(tD.ii)} \quad \frac{}{wait\,[t]\,B \xrightarrow{d}\rightsquigarrow wait\,[t-d]\,B} \ (d \le t)$$

$$\text{(tD.iii)} \quad \frac{B \xrightarrow{d}\rightsquigarrow B'}{wait\,[t]\,B \xrightarrow{d+t}\rightsquigarrow B'}$$

Choice. The action rules for [] are as per the untimed case; see Section 3.3.2.2. With regard to passing time, if B_1 and B_2 permit time to pass, then so will their choice $B_1 \;[]\; B_2$. Note that, the passage of time cannot resolve choice. However, time passing can cause action offers to be retracted. Thus, in combination with the action prefix rules, we obtain a nonpersistent semantics. For example, if

$$R := (x\,[2]\,;\, B_1) \;[]\; (y\,[4]\,;\, B_2)$$

then

$$R \overset{3}{\rightsquigarrow} B$$

where B is "strongly equivalent" to $y\,[1]\,;\, B_2$; i.e., because x has missed its interval (/point) of enabling, the option to perform this branch disappears.

$$\text{(tCH.i)} \quad \frac{B_1 \overset{a}{\rightarrow} B_1'}{\begin{array}{c} B_1 \;[]\; B_2 \overset{a}{\rightarrow} B_1' \\ B_2 \;[]\; B_1 \overset{a}{\rightarrow} B_1' \end{array}} \qquad \text{(tCH.ii)} \quad \frac{B_1 \overset{d}{\rightsquigarrow} B_1' \quad B_2 \overset{d}{\rightsquigarrow} B_2'}{B_1 \;[]\; B_2 \overset{d}{\rightsquigarrow} B_1' \;[]\; B_2'}$$

Notice, for presentational simplicity we combine the two symmetric action rules into a single rule (tCH.i). We use the same format in rule (tPA.i) for parallel composition.

Parallel Composition. As was the case for choice, $B_1 \;|[G]|\; B_2$ allows time to pass by some amount, if both components permit that evolution of time. Thus, parallel components synchronise on the passage of time (rule (tPA.iii)). In addition, parallel components may perform actions not in the synchronisation set $G \cup \{\delta\}$ independently (rule (tPA.i)), whereas, if both B_1 and B_2 can participate in a synchronisation action, $x \in G \cup \{\delta\}$, then so can their parallel composition (rule (tPA.ii)).

$$\text{(tPA.i)} \quad \frac{B_1 \overset{a}{\rightarrow} B_1'}{\begin{array}{c} B_1 \;|[G]|\; B_2 \overset{a}{\rightarrow} B_1' \;|[G]|\; B_2 \\ B_2 \;|[G]|\; B_1 \overset{a}{\rightarrow} B_2 \;|[G]|\; B_1' \end{array}} \;(a \notin G \cup \{\delta\})$$

$$\text{(tPA.ii)} \quad \frac{B_1 \overset{x}{\rightarrow} B_1' \quad B_2 \overset{x}{\rightarrow} B_2'}{B_1 \;|[G]|\; B_2 \overset{x}{\rightarrow} B_1' \;|[G]|\; B_2'} \;(x \in G \cup \{\delta\})$$

$$\text{(tPA.iii)} \quad \frac{B_1 \overset{d}{\rightsquigarrow} B_1' \quad B_2 \overset{d}{\rightsquigarrow} B_2'}{B_1 \;|[G]|\; B_2 \overset{d}{\rightsquigarrow} B_1' \;|[G]|\; B_2'}$$

Relabelling. If B can perform action a and evolve into B', then $B[H]$ can perform $H(a)$ and evolve into $B'[H]$ (tRL.i), whereas the passage of time is unaffected by relabelling (tPA.ii).

$$\text{(tRL.i)} \quad \frac{B \overset{a}{\rightarrow} B'}{B[H] \overset{H(a)}{\longrightarrow} B'[H]} \qquad \text{(tRL.ii)} \quad \frac{B \overset{d}{\rightsquigarrow} B'}{B[H] \overset{d}{\rightsquigarrow} B'[H]}$$

Hiding. This operator is strongly affected by the choices made concerning urgency, because, effectively, it turns nonurgent (observable) actions into urgent (hidden) ones. However, the action rules are inherited unchanged from the untimed case. That is, any actions that B can perform, can also be performed by *hide G in B*, subject to actions in the hiding set being turned into internal actions (rules (tHD.i) and (tHD.ii)). Because hidden actions become urgent on their upper bound (see Section 9.2.10) time cannot pass beyond this bound. This is reflected in rule (tHD.iii), which allows *hide G in B* to pass time by d time units only if there is no hidden action that must be performed earlier.

$$\text{(tHD.i)} \quad \frac{B \xrightarrow{x} B'}{hide\ G\ in\ B \xrightarrow{i} hide\ G\ in\ B'} \quad (x \in G)$$

$$\text{(tHD.ii)} \quad \frac{B \xrightarrow{a} B'}{hide\ G\ in\ B \xrightarrow{a} hide\ G\ in\ B'} \quad (a \notin G)$$

$$\text{(tHD.iii)} \quad \frac{B \stackrel{d}{\rightsquigarrow} B'}{hide\ G\ in\ B \stackrel{d}{\rightsquigarrow} hide\ G\ in\ B'} \quad (d \leq initI \Downarrow \Uparrow (G, B))$$

As an example of how (tHD.iii) "prunes" the passage of time in order to enforce urgency, consider the following behaviour,

$$P := (\,x\,[5, 10]\,;\,D\,)\,[]\,(\,y\,[12, 15]\,;\,D'\,)$$

Now, not only can P (initially) pass time by 10 time units, it can also pass time by 15 and, indeed, it will have a transition $P \stackrel{d}{\rightsquigarrow}$ for any $d \in \mathbb{R}^+$. This is the nonpersistent interpretation we have alluded to a number of times. However,

   hide x in P

can only pass time up to 10 time units, at which point, it must perform the internal action that has arisen from hiding x. As a result, *hide x in P* can never perform a y.

Notice that internal actions inherited from B do not have to be explicitly treated in (tHD.iii), because their urgency will be taken into account in the delay that B allows, i.e. the premise of rule (tHD.iii). For example, if,

$$Q := (\,i\,[5, 10]\,;\,B\,)\,[]\,(\,y\,[12, 15]\,;\,B'\,)$$

then

   hide y in Q

will only be able to initially pass time by 10 time units, which was also the case for Q.

It is also important to note that the appropriate smallest interval upper bound, which governs (tHD.iii) and, thus, the enforcement of urgency has to be carefully considered. For example, consider R_1 and R_2, which we introduced earlier in this section. That is

$$R_1 := x\,[5]\,;\, stop\,[]\;x\,[2,4]\,;\, stop$$

$$R_2 := x\,;\, stop\,[]\;x\,[2,4]\,;\, stop$$

In addition, consider

$$S_1 := hide\; x\; in\; R_1$$

$$S_2 := hide\; x\; in\; R_2$$

Now, (tHD.iii) ensures that,

$$\forall d > 4,\; S_1 \not\xrightarrow{d} \wedge S_2 \not\xrightarrow{d},$$

because,

$$initI{\downarrow\uparrow}(x, R_1) = initI{\downarrow\uparrow}(x, R_2) = 4$$

This interpretation is justified because we wish urgency created through explicit reference to i actions and through hiding to behave consistently. For example, for,

$$T_1 := i\,[5]\,;\, stop\,[]\;i\,[2,4]\,;\, stop$$

$$T_2 := i\,;\, stop\,[]\;i\,[2,4]\,;\, stop$$

we would expect T_1 and S_1 to be behaviourally indistinguishable and similarly T_2 and S_2. However, this is only the case if S_1 and S_2 cannot pass time beyond 4 time units, which our use of $initI{\downarrow\uparrow}$ in (tHD.iii) ensures. Note, in fact,

$$S_1 \sim_t S_2 \sim_t T_1 \sim_t T_2 \sim_t (\,i\,[2,4]\,;\, stop\,),$$

where $\sim_t$ denotes timed strong bisimulation equivalence, which we will introduce shortly (see Section 10.1.3). It is also important to note that this interpretation of urgency in hiding contexts is consistent with the interpretation arising from timed bundle event structures, see Section 10.2.

You should also notice that, as discussed in Section 9.2.10, this handling of hidden actions is different to the approach taken in ET-LOTOS [126] and in E-LOTOS [102]. In both of these, strict maximal progress is enforced on hidden actions. Thus, time can only pass up to the *lower* bound of the first enabled hidden action.

However, our semantics could be adjusted to bring them into line with these other approaches, yielding a pure maximal progress handling of hiding. We could do this by replacing (tHD.iii) with the following rule,

$$\frac{B \stackrel{d}{\rightsquigarrow} B'}{hide\ G\ in\ B \stackrel{d}{\rightsquigarrow} hide\ G\ in\ B'} \quad (d \leq initI{\downarrow}(G, B))$$

Enabling. Action transitions of $B_1 \gg B_2$ are the same as those of the untimed case: if B_1 can evolve to B_1', by performing a ($a \neq \delta$), then $B_1 \gg B_2$ can do the same, and evolve into $B_1' \gg B_2$. In addition, if B_1 successfully terminates, control passes to B_2. If B_1 can pass time by d time units then, as long as d does not pass beyond the upper bound of enabling of δ, $B_1 \gg B_2$ can also pass d time units. Thus, we allow the passage of time as long as the internal action resulting from the implicit hiding of the successful termination of B_1 (when control is passed to B_2) must not occur earlier. Notice that we maintain our policy that internal actions should become urgent on the upper bound of their enabling. Again this contrasts with the approach of ET-LOTOS and E-LOTOS.

$$(\text{tEN.i}) \quad \frac{B_1 \stackrel{a}{\rightarrow} B_1'}{B_1 \gg B_2 \stackrel{a}{\rightarrow} B_1' \gg B_2} \quad (a \neq \delta)$$

$$(\text{tEN.ii}) \quad \frac{B_1 \stackrel{\delta}{\rightarrow} B_1'}{B_1 \gg B_2 \stackrel{i}{\rightarrow} B_2}$$

$$(\text{tEN.iii}) \quad \frac{B_1 \stackrel{d}{\rightsquigarrow} B_1'}{B_1 \gg B_2 \stackrel{d}{\rightsquigarrow} B_1' \gg B_2} \quad (d \leq initI{\downarrow}{\Uparrow}(\delta, B_1))$$

Process Instantiation. The rules for process instantiation are a straightforward extrapolation from the untimed rules.

$$(\text{PI.i}) \quad \frac{B \stackrel{a}{\rightarrow} B'}{P \stackrel{a}{\rightarrow} B'} \quad (P := B) \qquad (\text{PI.ii}) \quad \frac{B \stackrel{d}{\rightsquigarrow} B'}{P \stackrel{d}{\rightsquigarrow} B'} \quad (P := B)$$

It is straightforward to derive a timed transition system from a tLOTOS behaviour using these inference rules. In particular, exactly the same steps as were used at the end of Section 3.3.2.2 to derive a labelled transition system from a pbLOTOS behaviour, could be applied in this context.

Properties of Operational Semantics. There are a number of properties satisfied by the timed transition systems that these inference rules generate. These are relatively standard "well behavedness" properties.

The first of these is time continuity (also often called time additivity, e.g. [126]); it states that a behaviour can pass time by a certain amount if and only if it can pass time by any intermediate amount and reach a state from which it can pass time the remaining amount.

Proposition 11   **(Time Continuity)**

$\forall B_1, B_2, \forall d_1, d_2 \in \mathbb{R}^+ , ((\exists B . B_1 \overset{d_1}{\leadsto} B \wedge B \overset{d_2}{\leadsto} B_2) \Leftrightarrow B_1 \overset{d_1+d_2}{\leadsto} B_2)$

Proof

We proceed by induction on the structure of B_1.

Base Case. The axioms of the inference system (i.e. the rules without hypotheses) give the base cases, that is, the rules for *Inaction*, *Successful Termination*, *Observable Action Prefix* and *Internal Action Prefix*. These all hold straightforwardly. However, by way of illustration, we give the proof for internal action prefix.

So, take $B_1, B_2, D \in tBeh$, $d_1, d_2 \in \mathbb{R}^+$ and assume that $B_1 = i\,I\,;\,D$; we can argue as follows.

$\qquad (B_1 \overset{d_1}{\leadsto} B \wedge B \overset{d_2}{\leadsto} B_2)$

$\Leftrightarrow \quad \{ \text{ by rule (tIAP.ii) } \}$

$\qquad (B = i\,(I \ominus d_1)\,;\,D) \wedge (B_2 = i\,((I \ominus d_1) \ominus d_2)\,;\,D) \wedge$

$\qquad (d_1 \leq \uparrow I) \wedge (d_2 \leq \uparrow (I \ominus d_1))$

$\Leftrightarrow \quad \{ \text{ mathematics } \}$

$\qquad (B_2 = i\,(I \ominus (d_1+d_2))\,;\,D) \wedge ((d_1+d_2) \leq \uparrow I)$

$\Leftrightarrow \quad \{ \text{ by rule (tIAP.ii) } \}$

$\qquad B_1 \overset{d_1+d_2}{\leadsto} B_2$

Inductive Case. Now we consider the nonaxiomatic rules of the inference system, i.e. *Delay*, *Choice*, *Parallel Composition*, *Relabelling*, *Hiding*, *Enabling* and *Process Instantiation*. Very similar inductive arguments can be applied in all these cases. By way of illustration, we consider the argument for parallel composition.

So, take $B_1, B_2, D_1, D_2, D_1', D_2', D_1'', D_2'' \in tBeh$, $d_1, d_2 \in \mathbb{R}^+$ and assume that $B_1 = D_1 \,||[G]||\, D_2$; we can argue as follows.

$\qquad (B_1 \overset{d_1}{\leadsto} B \wedge B \overset{d_2}{\leadsto} B_2)$

$\Leftrightarrow \quad \{ \text{ by rule (tPA.iii) } \}$

$\qquad (B = D_1' \,||[G]||\, D_2') \wedge (B_2 = D_1'' \,||[G]||\, D_2'') \wedge$

$\qquad (D_1 \overset{d_1}{\leadsto} D_1') \wedge (D_2 \overset{d_1}{\leadsto} D_2') \wedge (D_1' \overset{d_2}{\leadsto} D_1'') \wedge (D_2' \overset{d_2}{\leadsto} D_2'')$

$\Leftrightarrow \quad \{ \text{ inductive hypothesis } \}$

$\qquad (B_2 = D_1'' \,||[G]||\, D_2'') \wedge (D_1 \overset{d_1+d_2}{\leadsto} D_1'') \wedge (D_2 \overset{d_1+d_2}{\leadsto} D_2'')$

$\Leftrightarrow \quad \{ \text{ by rule (tPA.iii) } \}$

$\qquad B_1 \overset{d_1+d_2}{\leadsto} B_2$

The result follows.

$\bigcirc$

In addition, as discussed in Section 9.2.4, the following property demonstrates that the time-passing transitions generated from our semantics cannot create nondeterminism; i.e. it is not possible to evolve to two different states with identically timed transitions.

Proposition 12   (Time Determinism)

$$\forall B_1, B_2, B, \ \forall d \in \mathbb{R}^+ , \ (B \overset{d}{\leadsto} B_1 \ \wedge \ B \overset{d}{\leadsto} B_2 \ \Rightarrow \ B_1 = B_2).$$

Proof

We proceed by induction on the structure of B.

Base Case. The axioms of the inference system give the base cases, that is, the rules for *Inaction*, *Successful Termination*, *Observable Action Prefix* and *Internal Action Prefix*. These all hold straightforwardly. However, by way of illustration, we give the proof for internal action prefix.

So, take $B_1, B_2, B \in tBeh$ and $d \in \mathbb{R}^+$; we can argue as follows.

$$i\,I\,;\, B \overset{d}{\leadsto} B_1 \ \wedge \ i\,I\,;\, B \overset{d}{\leadsto} B_2$$
$$\Rightarrow \quad \{ \text{ by rule (tIAP.ii) } \}$$
$$B_1 = i\,(I \ominus d)\,;\, B \ \wedge \ B_2 = i\,(I \ominus d)\,;\, B \ \wedge \ d \leq \uparrow I$$
$$\Rightarrow \quad \{ \text{ syntactic equality } \}$$
$$B_1 = B_2$$

Inductive Case. Now, we consider the nonaxiomatic rules of the inference system, i.e. *Delay*, *Choice*, *Parallel Composition*, *Relabelling*, *Hiding*, *Enabling* and *Process Instantiation*. Very similar inductive arguments can be applied in all these cases. By way of illustration, we consider the argument for parallel composition.

So, take $B_1, B_2, B_1', B_2', B_1'', B_2'', D_1, D_2 \in tBeh$ and $d \in \mathbb{R}^+$; we can argue as follows.

$$B_1 \ |[G]| \ B_2 \overset{d}{\leadsto} D_1 \ \wedge \ B_1 \ |[G]| \ B_2 \overset{d}{\leadsto} D_2$$
$$\Rightarrow \quad \{ \text{ by rule (tPA.iii), we know the form of } D_1 \text{ and } D_2 \ \}$$
$$(\, B_1 \ |[G]| \ B_2 \overset{d}{\leadsto} D_1 \,) \ \wedge \ (\, B_1 \ |[G]| \ B_2 \overset{d}{\leadsto} D_2 \,) \ \wedge$$
$$(\, D_1 = B_1' \ |[G]| \ B_2' \,) \ \wedge \ (\, D_2 = B_1'' \ |[G]| \ B_2'' \,)$$
$$\Rightarrow \quad \{ \text{ by rule (tPA.iii) } \}$$
$$(\, B_1 \overset{d}{\leadsto} B_1' \,) \wedge (\, B_2 \overset{d}{\leadsto} B_2' \,) \wedge (\, B_1 \overset{d}{\leadsto} B_1'' \,) \wedge (\, B_2 \overset{d}{\leadsto} B_2'' \,) \wedge$$
$$(\, D_1 = B_1' \ |[G]| \ B_2' \,) \ \wedge \ (\, D_2 = B_1'' \ |[G]| \ B_2'' \,)$$
$$\Rightarrow \quad \{ \text{ by inductive hypothesis } \}$$
$$(\, B_1' = B_1'' \,) \ \wedge \ (\, B_2' = B_2'' \,) \wedge$$
$$(\, D_1 = B_1' \ |[G]| \ B_2' \,) \ \wedge \ (\, D_2 = B_1'' \ |[G]| \ B_2'' \,)$$
$$\Rightarrow \quad \{ \text{ syntactic equality } \}$$
$$D_1 = D_2$$

The result follows.

○

Finally, as discussed in Section 9.2.3, tLOTOS is not action persistent.

Proposition 13   (Not Action Persistent)
The following does not hold.

$$\forall B, B', d \in \mathbb{R}^+, \forall a \in Act \cup \{i\}, (B \stackrel{d}{\leadsto} B' \wedge B \stackrel{a}{\longrightarrow} \implies B' \stackrel{a}{\longrightarrow})$$

Proof
By example, for $B = x\,[0,5]$; *stop*, it is clear that $B \stackrel{6}{\leadsto} B'$, where our inference rules ensure that $B' = x\,\emptyset$; *stop* and $\neg(B' \stackrel{x}{\longrightarrow})$, whereas $B \stackrel{x}{\longrightarrow}$.

○

10.1.3 Branching Time Development Relations

The need to define equivalence and, more generally, preorder relations between specifications, still applies in the timed setting. In particular, syntactic correspondence of specifications is again much too strong. In fact, the problem is accentuated by the addition of timing constraints and there are many specifications that are behaviourally equivalent (informally denoted $\equiv$ here) even though the syntax of their timing differs. For example, for

$$P_1 := wait\,[0]\;stop \quad \text{and} \quad P_2 := wait\,[2]\;stop \quad \text{and} \quad P_3 := stop$$

we have

$$P_1 \equiv P_2 \equiv P_3$$

Thus, it is necessary to define timed counterparts to the equivalences that we introduced in Section 3.3.3. We do not though consider (nonequivalence) preorders in this timed setting. This is because little work on such refinement relations has been undertaken in the timed LOTOS domain. Although, failure-based refinement for timed CSP has been explored; see [176].

   Returning to the issue of equivalences, many such relations have in fact been explored in the timed process calculus domain, e.g. timed traces [176], timed failures [176], etc. However, here we restrict ourselves to consideration of bisimulation equivalences.

   In fact, it turns out that the strong and weak bisimulation definitions that we already have can be almost directly reused in the timed setting. This is because, in timed transition systems, both time passing and action offering are expressed in terms of transitions. Consequently, if we wish to ensure that the timing behaviour from two states is equivalent, we can match up time passing transitions in a similar way to how we matched up action transitions in the untimed setting, Section 3.3.3.1.

Definition 39   (Timed Strong Bisimulation Relations)

A binary relation $\mathcal{R} \subseteq tBeh \times tBeh$ is a timed strong bisimulation if whenever $(B_1, B_2) \in \mathcal{R}$ the following holds $\forall v \in Act \cup \{i, \delta\} \cup \mathbb{R}^+$,

1. $\forall B_1' \in tBeh$, $B_1 \xrightarrow{v}\!\!\!\twoheadrightarrow B_1' \implies \exists B_2' \in tBeh . B_2 \xrightarrow{v}\!\!\!\twoheadrightarrow B_2' \wedge (B_1', B_2') \in \mathcal{R} \wedge$

2. $\forall B_2' \in tBeh$, $B_2 \xrightarrow{v}\!\!\!\twoheadrightarrow B_2' \implies \exists B_1' \in tBeh . B_1 \xrightarrow{v}\!\!\!\twoheadrightarrow B_1' \wedge (B_1', B_2') \in \mathcal{R}.$

The only difference to the (untimed) definition of strong bisimulation (Definition 4 in Section 3.3.3.1) is that we need to ensure that both time and action transitions are matched; we do this by using a relation $\longrightarrow\!\!\!\twoheadrightarrow$, which is defined as follows,

$$\longrightarrow\!\!\!\twoheadrightarrow \;\triangleq\; \rightsquigarrow \cup \rightarrow$$

and by quantifying v over time values as well as actions.

Furthermore, in the standard way, we take as our equivalence, the largest relation that satisfies Definition 39.

Definition 40   (Timed Strongly Bisimilar)

Two behaviours B and B' are timed strongly bisimilar, denoted $B \sim_t B'$, if there exists a timed strong bisimulation relation $\mathcal{R}$, such that $B \,\mathcal{R}\, B'$, or, equivalently,

$$\sim_t \;\triangleq\; \bigcup \{\, \mathcal{R} \mid \mathcal{R} \text{ is a timed strong bisimulation relation } \}$$

It is clear that $\sim_t$ is indeed an equivalence relation.

As an illustration of this relation, with regard to the examples at the beginning of this section, $P_1 \sim_t P_2 \sim_t P_3$. In particular, to justify $P_1 \sim_t P_3$, observe that $\{\, (wait\,[0]\; stop\,,\; stop\,),\; (\,stop\,,\; stop\,)\,\}$ is a timed strong bisimulation, because $wait\,[0]\; stop$ can pass any length of time and evolve to $stop$. In addition, to see that $P_2 \sim_t P_3$, you should note that the following is a timed strong bisimulation $\{\, (wait\,[d]\; stop\,,\; stop\,)\mid 0 \leq d \leq 2\,\} \cup \{\, (\,stop\,,\; stop\,)\,\}$ and $P_1 \sim_t P_2$ can be shown in a similar way or using transitivity and symmetry of $\sim_t$.

In the same way as was discussed in depth in Section 3.3.3, $\sim_t$ induces a strong notion of identity, which equivalently matches internal as well as external behaviour in the two specifications. The same issues concerning the need for a weak matching of i actions apply in the timed setting and thus, we consider timed weak bisimulation.

However, before we can give our definition, we need to adapt the relation, $\xLongrightarrow{\sigma}\!\!\!\twoheadrightarrow$, which we introduced in Section 3.3.3, to accommodate the passage of time (related definitions can be found in Leonard [124]). Thus, assuming that $d, d_1, \ldots, d_n \in \mathbb{R}^+$ and $\sigma \in \mathcal{T}$ we define $\Longrightarrow\!\!\!\twoheadrightarrow_t$ as follows.

$$B_1 \xLongrightarrow{d}\!\!\!\twoheadrightarrow_t B_2 \;\; iff \;\; B_1(\xLongrightarrow{\epsilon}) \overset{d_1}{\rightsquigarrow} (\xLongrightarrow{\epsilon}) \overset{d_2}{\rightsquigarrow} \ldots \overset{d_n}{\rightsquigarrow} (\xLongrightarrow{\epsilon}) B_2 \wedge d = \sum_{1 \leq j \leq n} d_j$$

$$B_1 \xLongrightarrow{\sigma}\!\!\!\twoheadrightarrow_t B_2 \;\; iff \;\; B_1 \xLongrightarrow{\sigma}\!\!\!\twoheadrightarrow B_2$$

Thus, not only can $\overset{\sigma}{\Longrightarrow\!\!\!\gg}_t$ run over internal actions, so can $\overset{d}{\Longrightarrow\!\!\!\gg}_t$. However, in the latter case, we also have to ensure that the accumulated delays sum appropriately.

We define timed weak bisimulation in the obvious way.

Definition 41   (Timed Weak Bisimulation Relations)
A binary relation $\mathcal{S} \subseteq tBeh \times tBeh$ is a timed weak bisimulation if whenever $(B_1, B_2) \in \mathcal{S}$ it follows that $\forall v \in Act \cup \{i, \delta\} \cup \mathbb{R}^+$,

1. *$\forall B_1' \in tBeh, \ B_1 \overset{v}{\longrightarrow\!\!\!\!\rightarrow} B_1' \implies \exists B_2' \in tBeh \ . \ B_2 \overset{v}{\Longrightarrow\!\!\!\gg}_t B_2' \land (B_1', B_2') \in \mathcal{S} \ \land$*

2. *$\forall B_2' \in tBeh, \ B_2 \overset{v}{\longrightarrow\!\!\!\!\rightarrow} B_2' \implies \exists B_1' \in tBeh \ . \ B_1 \overset{v}{\Longrightarrow\!\!\!\gg}_t B_1' \land (B_1', B_2') \in \mathcal{S}.$*

As was the case for timed strong bisimulation, there can be many timed weak bisimulation relations between pairs of specifications. So, once again, we take as our equivalence relation, the largest relation which satisfies Definition 41.

Definition 42   (Timed Weakly Bisimilar)
Two behaviours B and B' are timed weakly bisimilar, denoted $B \approx_t B'$ if there exists a timed weak bisimulation relation $\mathcal{S}$ such that $B \ \mathcal{S} \ B'$, or, equivalently,

$$\approx_t \triangleq \bigcup \{ \ \mathcal{S} \mid \mathcal{S} \text{ is a timed weak bisimulation relation } \}$$

As an example of this relation at work, consider the following two processes.

$$Q_1 := i\,[2]\,;\,i\,[0,2]\,;\,x\,;\,stop \quad \text{and} \quad Q_2 := i\,[2,4]\,;\,x\,;\,stop$$

Depictions of timed transition systems of these processes are shown in Figure 10.3.[3] In particular, the reader should note that the two states marked * in the left-hand transition system are both timed weakly bisimilar to the state marked + in the right-hand transition system.

As a justification of the use of the term strong and weak, it is clear that

$$\sim_t \ \subset \ \approx_t$$

In particular, any timed strong bisimulation relation also satisfies the definition of timed weak bisimulation and, for example,

$$i\,;\,stop \ \approx_t \ stop, \quad \text{but} \quad i\,;\,stop \ \not\sim_t \ stop$$

We also consider a generalisation of weak bisimulation congruence, which we discussed in Definition 8 of Section 3.3.3.1. This new equivalence is called timed rooted weak bisimulation. The reason that we do not use the term congruence here is discussed in Section 14.7 in the appendix.

---

[3]Although, due to the continuous nature of the time domain, it is often difficult to represent timed behaviours perfectly accurately. Thus, figures such as these should be taken as approximate (schematic) depictions.

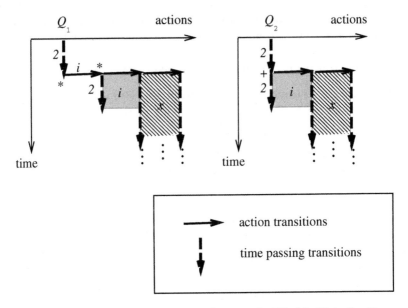

Fig. 10.3. Depiction of Timed Transition Systems for Weakly Bisimilar Processes

Definition 43   (Timed Rooted Weak Bisimulation)
A binary relation $S \subseteq tBeh \times tBeh$ is a timed rooted weak bisimulation if $(B_1, B_2) \in S$ implies $\forall a \in Act \cup \{i, \delta\}, \ d \in \mathbb{R}^+$,

1. $\forall B_1' \in tBeh$,
    a) $B_1 \xrightarrow{d} B_1' \implies \exists B_2' \in tBeh \,.\, B_2 \stackrel{d}{\leadsto} B_2' \wedge (B_1', B_2') \in S \ \wedge$
    b) $B_1 \xrightarrow{a} B_1' \implies \exists B_2' \in tBeh \,.\, B_2 \stackrel{a}{\Longrightarrow} B_2' \wedge B_1' \approx_t B_2'$ *and*

2. $\forall B_2' \in tBeh$,
    a) $B_2 \xrightarrow{d} B_2' \implies \exists B_1' \in tBeh \,.\, B_1 \stackrel{d}{\leadsto} B_1' \wedge (B_1', B_2') \in S \ \wedge$
    b) $B_2 \xrightarrow{a} B_2' \implies \exists B_1' \in tBeh \,.\, B_1 \stackrel{a}{\Longrightarrow} B_1' \wedge B_1' \approx_t B_2'$.

In addition, in standard fashion, we define timed rooted weak bisimulation as follows.

Definition 44   (Timed Rooted Weak Bisimilar)
Two behaviours B and B' are timed rooted weak bisimilar, denoted $B \approx_r^t B'$, if there exists a timed rooted weak bisimulation relation S such that $B \,S\, B'$, or equivalently,

$$\approx_r^t \triangleq \bigcup \{\, S \mid S \text{ is a timed rooted weak bisimulation relation} \,\}$$

As an explanation of this definition we have the following points.

1. By analogy with the untimed case, we match $B_1 \xrightarrow{a} B_1'$ with $B_2 \xRightarrow{a} B_2'$ and then require $B_1' \approx_t B_2'$. This ensures that initial i transitions are not mapped to $\xRightarrow{\epsilon}$, as justified late in Section 3.3.3.1 (the discussion of weak bisimulation congruence).

2. We match $B_1 \xrightarrow{d} B_1'$ with $B_2 \xrightsquigarrow{d} B_2'$ and require $(B_1', B_2') \in \mathcal{S}$, rather than matching to $B_2 \xRightarrow{d}_t B_2'$ and requiring $B_1' \approx_t B_2'$, since skipping over initial i transitions, when passing time, would prevent substitutivity in choice contexts. As an illustration of this, if it were the case that $B_1 \xrightarrow{d} B_1'$ was matched with $B_2 \xRightarrow{d}_t B_2'$ and $B_1' \approx_t B_2'$ then, for example, with the following definitions,

$$Q_1 := wait\,[2]\,x\,;\,stop$$

$$Q_2 := wait\,[2]\,i\,;\,x\,;\,stop$$

$$C[.] \triangleq [.]\,[]\,y\,;\,stop$$

Q_1 and Q_2 would be equivalent, but $C[Q_1]$ and $C[Q_2]$ would not be equivalent. To illustrate this, we can see that

$$C[Q_1] \xrightsquigarrow{3} Q \sim_t (\,(\,x\,;\,stop\,)\,[]\,(\,y\,;\,stop\,)\,)$$

but,

$$\forall R \in tBeh,\,(\,C[Q_2] \xRightarrow{3}_t R \implies (\,R \sim_t x\,;\,stop \wedge Q \not\sim_t R\,)\,)$$

In response to this issue, we strongly match all initial time transitions and also require $(B_1', B_2') \in \mathcal{S}$ (i.e., timed rooted weak bisimilar), rather than $B_1' \approx_t B_2'$, because we want to ensure that an initial i action, even when preceded by a delay, is matched by "proper" i (rather than $\xRightarrow{\epsilon}$) derivations. That is, we strongly match time passing transitions, until the first discrete / action transition is reached, after which we enforce the more liberal $\approx_t$ relationship.

We have the following simple relationship between the weak bisimulation relations we are considering

Proposition 14

$$\approx_r^t \subset \approx_t$$

Proof

This follows because,

$$\forall d \in \mathbb{R}^+,\,\xrightsquigarrow{d}\,\subset\,\xRightarrow{d}_t$$

and,

$$\forall a \in Act \cup \{i, \delta\},\,\xRightarrow{a}\,\subset\,\xRightarrow{a}_t,$$

which is as required.

○

10.2 True Concurrency Semantics

10.2.1 Introduction

The work presented here is based upon previous work on true concurrency semantics for timed LOTOS, e.g. [32, 39, 51, 108, 109]. The thread of research represented by these publications took much of its impetus from Katoen's PhD thesis [107], although similar ideas were independently developed by Bowman et al [32, 39]. We begin by reiterating the motivation for giving true concurrency semantics to process calculi; see Chapter 4 for a more detailed justification.

Interleaved semantics reflect the *extensionalist* [147] view that formal specification should just describe the "observable behaviour" of systems. This inherently means that some aspects of causality are abstracted away from. For example, the following two behaviours would be identified,

$$x\,;\,y\,;\,stop\,[]\,y\,;\,x\,;\,stop \quad \text{and} \quad x\,;\,stop\,|||\,y\,;\,stop$$

even though the first contains two causalities, an instance of action x causing an instance of action y and an instance of action y causing an instance of action x, and the second contains no causalities. Abstracting, in this way, from the internal relationships between components fits well into early phases of system development, such as the specification stage. Such phases typically involve the description of the global observable behaviour of systems and this is exactly what interleaved approaches model.

However, at later stages of system development, explicit links to implementations have to be made. At these stages, semantic models must be capable of modelling the decomposition of systems into components, which each have their own *local* state. In other words, they must accurately reflect the *distribution aspects* of the system under development. True concurrency models reflect such nonglobal interpretation; they are often categorised as *intensionalist*, because they model the *internal* decomposition of systems. A further benefit of true concurrency models is that, when exhaustive state exploration is being undertaken, such models limit the state-space explosion problem: parallel composition generates the sum of the component's states as opposed to the product, which is the case with interleaving semantics.

The motivation for true concurrency models carries over to the real-time setting. In fact, it has been argued that the incorporation of real-time properties fits naturally with both the move to true concurrency models and with the focus on lower levels of system development [36, 78, 107]. In order to realise the benefits of the true concurrency approach in the timed LOTOS setting, we present a true concurrency semantics for tLOTOS.

We build our timed true concurrency model from the bundle event structures semantics that we introduced in Section 4. The approach is inspired by the (several) real-time enhancements to bundle event structures to be found in the literature [32, 39, 51, 108, 109], Katoen's thesis being a particular source of inspiration [107].

10.2.2 Timed Bundle Event Structures

There are two aspects to adding time to bundle event structures. Firstly, to define delays between causally related events, time is associated with bundles, and, secondly, in order to enable timing of events that have no incoming bundles (i.e., the initial events of a timed bundle event structure), time is also associated with events.[4]

Definition 45   (Timed Bundle Event Structure)
A timed bundle event structure has the form $\langle \varepsilon, \mathcal{A}, \mathcal{R} \rangle$*, where*

- ε *is a bundle event structure* $(E, \#, \mapsto, l)$
- $\mathcal{A} : E \longrightarrow \Xi$*, is an* event-timing *function*
- $\mathcal{R} : \mapsto \longrightarrow \Xi$*, is a* bundle-timing *function, and*

for ease of presentation, we sometimes write, $\langle E, \#, \mapsto, l, \mathcal{A}, \mathcal{R} \rangle$*, as a shorthand for* $\langle \varepsilon, \mathcal{A}, \mathcal{R} \rangle$ *and* $\varepsilon = (E, \#, \mapsto, l)$*.*

We denote the set of Timed Bundle Event Structures as *TBES*. Note, event timing specifies a time relative to the start of the TBES, which is assumed to be time zero. In contrast, bundle-timings specify time relative to a causal predecessor.

A bundle $X \mapsto e$ where $\mathcal{R}((X, e)) = I$ is denoted $X \overset{I}{\mapsto} e$. When diagrammatically represented, bundle and event timings are depicted near to the corresponding bundle and event, respectively. In addition, intervals of the form $[0, \infty)$ are usually omitted and intervals $[t, \infty)$ are abbreviated to t.

An example timed bundle event structure is shown in figure 10.4(2). This is a timed extension of the bundle event structure in Figure 10.4(1). More precisely, we have the following event timings, $\mathcal{A}(e_i) = [2, 8]$, $\mathcal{A}(e_y) = [5, 10]$ and $\mathcal{A}(e_w) = [4, \infty)$ and the following bundle timings, $\mathcal{R}((\{e_i, e_y\}, e_z)) = [10, \infty)$ and $\mathcal{R}((\{e_w\}, e_v)) = [2, \infty)$ [5].

What though do these timings intuitively mean? Well, an event can only happen when all its bundle and event timing constraints are satisfied; e.g. $\mathcal{A}(e_z) = I$ constrains e_z to happen at a time $t_z \in I$ from the beginning of the execution of the system, which is assumed to be time 0. Suppose, in addition, that there is a single bundle entering e_z, which is such that

$$\{e_x\} \overset{I'}{\mapsto} e_z$$

Assuming that e_x happens at time t_x, this bundle further constrains the occurrence of e_z to any t_z such that $t_z \in t_x \oplus I'$. Thus, I' specifies the relative delay between e_x and e_z. Now, putting these two timing constraints together, we get that $t_z \in (t_x \oplus I') \cap I$, which characterises the timing of e_z. Further

---

[4]An alternative to event delays is to explicitly model the start of the system by a "fictitious" event; see [32].

[5]For presentational ease, where it does not cause confusion, we represent events by their labelling, while noting that this is, of course, informal.

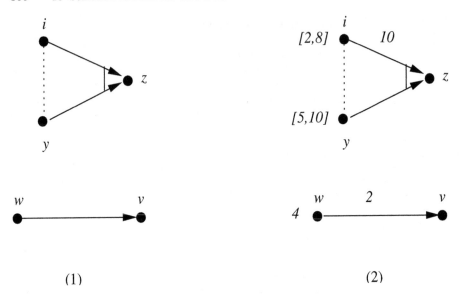

(1)   (2)

Fig. 10.4. Example Timed Bundle Event Structure

note that, if the intersection of a number of interval timing constraints is empty, then that event can never happen.

The notion of *timed proving sequence* (called a timed event sequence in [47]) formalises this intuition; it is a (timed) generalisation of the notion of a proving sequence; see Definition 15 in Section 4.2. However, before defining this concept we introduce some notation.

Firstly, let (e, t) denote that e happened at (absolute) time t. For sequences of timed events $\sigma = (e_1, t_1) \ldots (e_n, t_n)$, let $[\sigma]$ denote the (untimed) proving sequence of σ; i.e. $[\sigma] \triangleq e_1 \ldots e_n$.

Now, the following concepts were defined in Definition 15 in Section 4.2. For an (untimed) proving sequence ρ, $\mathbf{cfl}(\rho)$ is the set of events that are disabled by some event in ρ and $\mathbf{sat}(\rho)$ is the set of events that have a causal predecessor in ρ for all incoming bundles. That is, for events in $\mathbf{sat}(\rho)$, all bundles (i.e. causal constraints) are "satisfied".

We use $\mathbf{en}(\rho)$, which is defined in terms of $\mathbf{cfl}$ and $\mathbf{sat}$. It characterises the set of events enabled after ρ and is defined as follows $\mathbf{en}(\rho) \triangleq \mathbf{sat}(\rho) \setminus (\mathbf{cfl}(\rho) \cup \$\rho)$.

Now, assuming that σ is a timed proving sequence, $\mathcal{Z}(\sigma, e)$ (which has its roots in Katoen's PhD thesis [107]) is used to denote the set of time instants at which $e \in \mathbf{en}([\sigma])$ could happen, given that each event e_j in σ occurred at time t_j. Thus, event e can occur if,

1. the event delay, $\mathcal{A}(e)$, is satisfied, and

2. the bundle delays from all immediate causal predecessors are satisfied.

Formally, with regard to a timed bundle event structure, $\langle \varepsilon, \mathcal{A}, \mathcal{R} \rangle$, $\mathcal{Z}$ is defined as follows.

$$\mathcal{Z}(\sigma, e) \triangleq \bigcap (\{ \mathcal{A}(e) \} \cup H) \quad \text{where,}$$

$$H \triangleq \{ t_j \oplus I \mid \exists X \subseteq E . (X \overset{I}{\mapsto} e \wedge X \cap \$[\sigma] = \{ e_j \}) \}$$

where $\mathcal{A}(e)$ represents the first constraint above and H represents the second. Notice that H is a set of intervals, one per incoming bundle. Consistent with our intuition, $\mathcal{Z}(\sigma, e)$ is obtained by intersecting the interval constraint $\mathcal{A}(e)$ with the interval constraints arising from H.

A timed proving sequence is now defined as follows, where we have the convention that $Max(\emptyset) = \infty$ and, also, recall that the prefix of σ up to the $j - 1$st element is denoted σ_j.

Definition 46   (Timed Proving Sequence)
$\sigma = (e_1, t_1) \ldots (e_n, t_n)$ is a timed proving sequence of $\Psi = \langle \varepsilon, \mathcal{A}, \mathcal{R} \rangle$ if and only if, for all $k \ (0 < k \leq n)$, $e_k \in E$, $t_k \in \mathbb{R}^{+0}$, and,

1. $e_1 \ldots e_n$ is a proving sequence of ε, by Definition 15 in Section 4.2,
2. $\forall j . (k < j \implies t_k \leq t_j)$,
3. $t_k \in \mathcal{Z}(\sigma_k, e_k)$, and
4. $\forall e \in \mathbf{en}([\sigma_k]) , (l(e) = i \implies t_k \leq Max(\mathcal{Z}(\sigma_k, e)))$.

The first condition ensures consistency with the untimed model; i.e. if all timings are deleted from σ, a proving sequence of ε is obtained. The second condition requires time consistency, i.e. that time does not decrease through the sequence,[6] and the third requires that events happen at one of their possible timings. The first three conditions do not recognise the possibility that urgent events may prevent other events from occurring at certain times. The last condition enforces such urgency. It states that trace σ_k may be extended by (e_k, t_k) if and only if there is no urgent (i.e., internal) event enabled after σ_k that must occur earlier than e_k.

By way of illustration, the (nonempty) timed proving sequences of the timed bundle event structure in Figure 10.5 are (e_i, t), where $2 \leq t \leq 6$, (e_x, t), where $5 \leq t \leq 6$ and $(e_x, t) (e_y, t')$, where $5 \leq t \leq 6$ and $t \leq t'$. Notice that, for example, $(e_x, 7)$ is not a timed proving sequence, because the event labelled i will be forced at time 6, thus disabling e_x.

---

[6] Although, consistently with all our timed models, time can stay the same between adjacent points in the sequence, reflecting that multiple events / actions can occur at the same time instant.

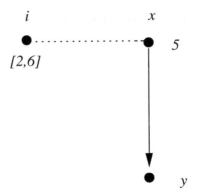

Fig. 10.5. Example Timed Bundle Event Structure for Consideration of Urgency in Timed Proving Sequences

10.2.3 Causal Semantics for tLOTOS

In this section we present a noninterleaving semantics for tLOTOS using timed bundle event structures. We define a mapping,

$$[\![\ ]\!]_{tbe} : tLOTOS \longrightarrow TBES$$

This mapping is based upon the semantics given in [47] and [46]. Many of these definitions first appeared in Katoen's thesis [107]. The top-level machinery of the semantics is the same as that presented for (untimed) bundle event structures. Thus, we define:

$$[\![\, B \,]\!]_{tbe} \triangleq \mathcal{B}''[\![\, B \,]\!]_{(\emptyset)}$$
$$[\![\, B \ where \ D \,]\!]_{tbe} \triangleq \mathcal{B}''[\![\, B \,]\!]_{(\mathcal{D}[\![\, D \,]\!])}$$

where $\mathcal{D}$ is as defined in Section 3.2.2.2; i.e.

$$\mathcal{D}[\![\, (P := B) \,]\!] \triangleq \{P := B\}$$
$$\mathcal{D}[\![\, (P := B) \ D \,]\!] \triangleq \{P := B\} \cup \mathcal{D}[\![\, D \,]\!]$$

Throughout these semantics, for an arbitrary TBES, $\Psi = \langle E, \#, \mapsto, l, \mathcal{A}, \mathcal{R} \rangle$, we use $init(\Psi)$, which denotes the set of initial events of Ψ; $exit(\Psi)$, which denotes the set of successful termination events; and $res(\Psi)$, which denotes the events whose timing is restricted. The definitions of $init$ and $exit$ in Section 4.4 are lifted to timed bundle event structures in the obvious way, whereas $res(\Psi) \triangleq \{e \in E \mid \mathcal{A}(e) \neq \mathbb{R}^{+0}\}$, i.e. the set of events that do not have a completely unrestricted timing. Furthermore, we abbreviate $init(\Psi) \cup res(\Psi)$ by $rin(\Psi)$. As previously, $\mathcal{U}_E$ denote the universe of events.

The main part of the semantics is the interpretation of behaviour expressions. Thus, in the rest of this section we assume that $\mathcal{B}''[\![\, B_1 \,]\!]_{(d)} = \Psi_1 = \langle \varepsilon_1, \mathcal{A}_1, \mathcal{R}_1 \rangle$ with $\varepsilon_1 = (E_1, \#_1, \mapsto_1, l_1)$ and $\mathcal{B}''[\![\, B_2 \,]\!]_{(d)}$ has a corresponding format. Furthermore, for B_1 and B_2 we assume that $E_1 \cap E_2 = \emptyset$; in case of name clashes, renaming can be used to obtain this property.

10.2.3.1 Inaction, Successful Termination and Action Prefix

These are defined as follows.

$$\mathcal{B}''[\![\, stop \,]\!]_{(d)} \triangleq \langle \emptyset, \emptyset, \emptyset, \emptyset, \emptyset, \emptyset \rangle$$

$$\mathcal{B}''[\![\, exit\, I \,]\!]_{(d)} \triangleq \langle \{\, e \,\}, \emptyset, \emptyset, \{\, (e, \delta) \,\}, \{\, (e, I) \,\}, \emptyset \rangle$$
$$\text{where } e \in \mathcal{U}_E$$

$$\mathcal{B}''[\![\, a\, I \,;\, B_1 \,]\!]_{(d)} \triangleq \langle E, \#_1, \mapsto, l, \mathcal{A}, \mathcal{R} \rangle \quad \text{where}$$
$$E = E_1 \cup \{\, e \,\} \quad \text{for, } e \in \mathcal{U}_E \setminus E_1$$
$$\mapsto \;=\; \mapsto_1 \cup \; (\{\, \{\, e \,\} \,\} \times rin(\Psi_1))$$
$$l = l_1 \cup \{\, (e, a) \,\}$$
$$\mathcal{A} = \{\, (e, I) \,\} \cup (E_1 \times \{\, \mathbb{R}^{+0} \,\})$$
$$\mathcal{R} = \mathcal{R}_1 \cup \{\, ((\{\, e \,\}, e'), \mathcal{A}_1(e')) \mid e' \in rin(\Psi_1) \,\}$$

Thus, $stop$ yields the empty timed bundled event structure and $exit\, I$ is mapped to a single event, labelled δ with timing I.

With regard to $a\, I \,;\, B_1$, a bundle is added from a new event e (labelled a) to events in Ψ_1 that are, either, initial (e will now causally precede these events) or time-restricted. For all such initial and time-restricted events, e' say, the delay is now relative to e, so a time delay $\mathcal{A}_1(e')$ is associated with each bundle $\{\, e \,\} \mapsto e'$ and $\mathcal{A}(e')$ becomes $\mathbb{R}^{+0}$; i.e. e' becomes time-unrestricted. In addition, I becomes the timing of e.

It is sufficient in the untimed case to introduce only bundles from e to the initial events of Ψ_1; c.f. Section 4.2. However, in the timed case, new bundles to time-restricted events of Ψ_1 are used to make delays relative to e. Notice that the above construction applies to both observable and internal events.

As an example, Figure 10.6(b) provides the semantics of $x\,[5, 6]\,;\, P$, where the semantics of P is given as Figure 10.6(a). The following behaviour would yield an event structure consistent with figure 10.6(a).

$$P := (\,(\, y\,(2)\,;\, z\,(8)\,;\, (\, w\,(2)\,;\, stop \,|\!|\!|\, exit\,(18)\,)\,)$$
$$|[w]|\; w\,[8, 25]\,;\, stop\,)$$
$$|\!|\!|\; i\,[12, 14]\,;\, v\,;\, stop$$

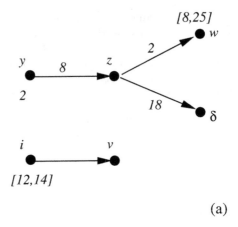

(a)

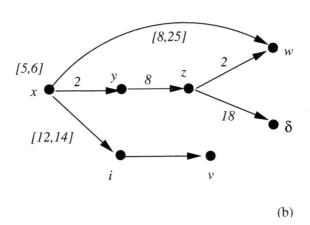

(b)

Fig. 10.6. Semantics of Action Prefix

10.2.3.2 Delay, Hiding and Relabelling

The semantics for these constructs are as follows.

$$\mathcal{B}''[\![\, wait\ [d]\ B_1\,]\!]_{(d)} \triangleq \langle E_1, \#_1, \mapsto_1, l_1, ((+d) \circ \mathcal{A}_1), \mathcal{R}_1 \rangle$$

$$\mathcal{B}''[\![\, hide\ G\ in\ B_1\,]\!]_{(d)} \triangleq \langle E_1, \#_1, \mapsto_1, l, \mathcal{A}_1, \mathcal{R}_1 \rangle \quad \text{where ,}$$
$$(\, l_1(e) \in G \implies l(e) = i\,) \ \wedge$$
$$(\, l_1(e) \notin G \implies l(e) = l_1(e)\,))$$

$$\mathcal{B}''[\![\, B_1[H]\,]\!]_{(d)} \triangleq \langle E_1, \#_1, \mapsto_1, (H \circ l_1), \mathcal{A}_1, \mathcal{R}_1 \rangle$$

Semantically, *wait* $[d]$ B_1 is identical to $\mathcal{B}''[\![\,B_1\,]\!]_{(d)}$, but with event delays incremented by d (∘ denotes function composition; i.e. $f \circ g\,(x) = f(g(x))$). Bundle delays express relative delays between events, and, thus, are unaffected. $\mathcal{B}''[\![\,hide\ G\ in\ B_1\,]\!]_{(d)}$ simply takes $\mathcal{B}''[\![\,B_1\,]\!]_{(d)}$ and turns events with labels in G into internal events. $\mathcal{B}''[\![\,B_1[H]\,]\!]_{(d)}$ is identical to $\mathcal{B}''[\![\,B_1\,]\!]_{(d)}$, but with events relabelled according to H.

As an example of these denotational semantics, consider the timed bundle event structure depicted in figure 10.7(a). After the hiding of actions y and v the event structure of Figure 10.7(b) results.

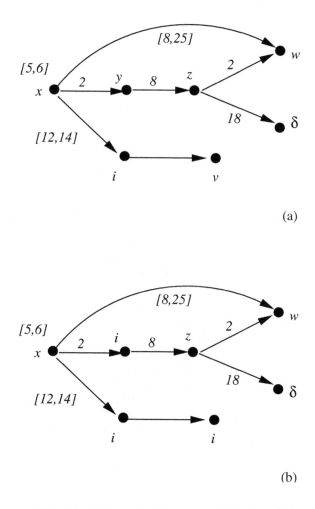

(a)

(b)

Fig. 10.7. Example of Semantics for Hiding

10.2.3.3 Choice

The semantics of choice are straightforward.

$$\mathcal{B}''[\![\, B_1 \,[\!]\, B_2 \,]\!]_{(d)} \triangleq \langle E_1 \cup E_2, \#, \mapsto_1 \cup \mapsto_2, l_1 \cup l_2, \mathcal{A}_1 \cup \mathcal{A}_2, \mathcal{R}_1 \cup \mathcal{R}_2 \rangle$$
$$\# = \#_1 \cup \#_2 \cup (init(\Psi_1) \times init(\Psi_2))$$

$\mathcal{B}''[\![\, B_1 \,[\!]\, B_2 \,]\!]_{(d)}$ takes the componentwise union of $\mathcal{B}''[\![\, B_1 \,]\!]_{(d)}$ and $\mathcal{B}''[\![\, B_2 \,]\!]_{(d)}$ subject to the addition of conflicts between initial events of $\mathcal{B}''[\![\, B_1 \,]\!]_{(d)}$ and $\mathcal{B}''[\![\, B_2 \,]\!]_{(d)}$. This ensures that, in the resulting structure, only one of B_1 or B_2 can happen. Timing is unaffected by this construct.

10.2.3.4 Enabling

The semantics of enabling are as follows.

$$\mathcal{B}''[\![\, B_1 \gg B_2 \,]\!]_{(d)} \triangleq \langle E_1 \cup E_2, \#, \mapsto, l, \mathcal{A}, \mathcal{R} \rangle$$
$$\# = \#_1 \cup \#_2 \cup (exit(\Psi_1) \times exit(\Psi_1)) \setminus \mathrm{Id}$$
$$\mapsto = \mapsto_1 \cup \mapsto_2 \cup (\{\, exit(\Psi_1)\,\} \times rin(\Psi_2))$$
$$l = ((l_1 \cup l_2) \setminus (exit(\Psi_1) \times \{\, \delta \,\})) \cup (exit(\Psi_1) \times \{\, i \,\})$$
$$\mathcal{A} = \mathcal{A}_1 \cup (E_2 \times \{\, \mathbb{R}^{+0} \,\})$$
$$\mathcal{R} = \mathcal{R}_1 \cup \mathcal{R}_2 \cup \{\, ((exit(\Psi_1), e), \mathcal{A}_2(e)) \mid e \in rin(\Psi_2) \,\}$$

Thus, the event set of $\mathcal{B}''[\![\, B_1 \gg B_2 \,]\!]_{(d)}$ is the union of those for $\mathcal{B}''[\![\, B_1 \,]\!]_{(d)}$ and for $\mathcal{B}''[\![\, B_2 \,]\!]_{(d)}$. Component conflicts are inherited, with the addition of conflicts between nonidentical successful termination events of $\mathcal{B}''[\![\, B_1 \,]\!]_{(d)}$ (the identity relation (Id) is subtracted in order to avoid generating self-conflicts). These mutual conflicts between successful termination events ensure that newly introduced bundles really are bundles, i.e. have mutually in conflict enabling sets. These new bundles are introduced from the successful termination events of $\mathcal{B}''[\![\, B_1 \,]\!]_{(d)}$ to the initial and time-restricted events of $\mathcal{B}''[\![\, B_2 \,]\!]_{(d)}$. Bundles to the initial events of $\mathcal{B}''[\![\, B_2 \,]\!]_{(d)}$ reflect that B_2 can only start if $\mathcal{B}''[\![\, B_1 \,]\!]_{(d)}$ has successfully terminated. In a similar way as with action prefix, new bundles to time-restricted events of $\mathcal{B}''[\![\, B_2 \,]\!]_{(d)}$ are required to enforce that event delays become relative to the termination of $\mathcal{B}''[\![\, B_1 \,]\!]_{(d)}$. Finally, in standard fashion, successful termination events of $\mathcal{B}''[\![\, B_1 \,]\!]_{(d)}$ are relabelled as internal events.

Figure 10.8 illustrates these semantics. The diagram depicts stages in semantic interpretation of the behaviour,

$P \gg Q$ where

$P := (\, y\,;\, exit\,(5)\,) \,[\!]\, (\, x\,;\, exit\,(2)\,),$ and

$Q := (\, z\,;\, w\,(10)\,;\, stop\,) \,|[w]|\, (\, w\,[5,7]\,;\, stop\,)$

The exact reason why $\mathcal{B}''[\![\, Q \,]\!]_{(d)}$ generates the enabled structure, shown to the left of the equals in Figure 10.8 becomes clear when we discuss the semantics of parallel composition. However, for the moment, the main point to note is how the enabling event structure is appended on the front of the enabled event structure. Notice also that e_z is an initial event of $\mathcal{B}''[\![\, Q \,]\!]_{(d)}$, whereas e_w is a time-restricted event of $\mathcal{B}''[\![\, Q \,]\!]_{(d)}$.

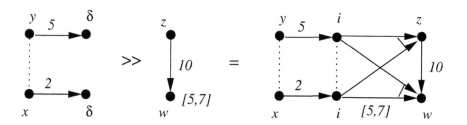

Fig. 10.8. Example of Semantics for Enabling

10.2.3.5 Parallel Composition

The first four clauses of the definition of parallel composition (shown in Figure 10.9) are inherited unchanged from the untimed setting; see Section 4.4. However, we briefly re-iterate their explanation for completeness.

Firstly, the events of $\mathcal{B}''[\![\, B_1 \,|[G]|\, B_2 \,]\!]_{(d)}$ comprise events arising through the pairing of (i) the symbol $*$ with events of $\mathcal{B}''[\![\, B_1 \,]\!]_{(d)}$ or $\mathcal{B}''[\![\, B_2 \,]\!]_{(d)}$ that do not need to synchronise (E_1^f and E_2^f, respectively), and (ii) events labelled with actions in $G \cup \{\delta\}$ with identically labelled events in the other process (as determined by E_1^s and E_2^s). Thus, parallel composition events are non-synchronising component events paired with $*$ and synchronising events of $\mathcal{B}''[\![\, B_1 \,]\!]_{(d)}$ and $\mathcal{B}''[\![\, B_2 \,]\!]_{(d)}$ paired with each other. E_k^s and E_k^f (for $k \in \{1,2\}$) were defined in Section 4.4.

Events are put in conflict if (i) any of their components are in conflict or (ii) distinct events have a common proper component (i.e. other than $*$). The latter case arises if a number of events in one process synchronise with the same event in the other process.

With regard to causality, bundles in the parallel composition are such that, if a projection on B_1 (or B_2) of all events in the bundle is taken, a bundle in $\mathcal{B}''[\![\, B_1 \,]\!]_{(d)}$ (or $\mathcal{B}''[\![\, B_2 \,]\!]_{(d)}$), respectively, results. Labelling is straightforward.

The new clauses are the last two, which were originally highlighted by Katoen [107]. Firstly, the event timing function is the intersection of component event timings, with $*$ events yielding null timing constraints. Secondly, bundle timings are defined to be the intersection of the time sets associated with the bundles obtained by projecting on the events of B_1 (or B_2), subject to the requirement that this projection yields a bundle in $\mathcal{B}''[\![\,B_1\,]\!]_{(d)}$ (or $\mathcal{B}''[\![\,B_2\,]\!]_{(d)}$), respectively.

$$\mathcal{B}''[\![\,B_1\,|[G]|\,B_2\,]\!]_{(d)} \triangleq \langle E, \#, \mapsto, l, \mathcal{A}, \mathcal{R} \rangle \quad \text{where,}$$

$$E = (E_1^f \times \{\,*\,\}) \cup (\{\,*\,\} \times E_2^f) \cup$$
$$\{\,(e_1, e_2) \in E_1^s \times E_2^s \mid l_1(e_1) = l_2(e_2)\,\}$$

$$(e_1, e_2) \# (e_1', e_2') \Leftrightarrow (e_1 \#_1 e_1') \vee (e_2 \#_2 e_2') \vee$$
$$(e_1 = e_1' \neq * \wedge e_2 \neq e_2') \vee$$
$$(e_2 = e_2' \neq * \wedge e_1 \neq e_1')$$

$$X \mapsto (e_1, e_2) \Leftrightarrow (\exists X_1 . (X_1 \mapsto_1 e_1 \wedge X = \{\,(e, e') \in E \mid e \in X_1\,\})) \vee$$
$$(\exists X_2 . (X_2 \mapsto_2 e_2 \wedge X = \{\,(e, e') \in E \mid e' \in X_2\,\}))$$

$$l((e_1, e_2)) = \textit{if } e_1 = * \textit{ then } l_2(e_2) \textit{ else } l_1(e_1)$$

$$\mathcal{A}((e_1, e_2)) = \mathcal{A}_1(e_1) \cap \mathcal{A}_2(e_2) \quad \text{where,} \quad \mathcal{A}_1(*) = \mathcal{A}_2(*) = \mathbb{R}^{+0}.$$

$$\mathcal{R}((X, (e_1, e_2))) = \text{if } X = \emptyset \text{ then } \mathbb{R}^{+0}$$

$$\text{otherwise,} \quad \bigcap_{X_1 \in S_1} \mathcal{R}_1(X_1, e_1) \cap \bigcap_{X_2 \in S_2} \mathcal{R}_2(X_2, e_2)$$

$$\text{where,}$$

$$S_1 = \{\,X_1 \subseteq E_1 \mid X_1 \mapsto_1 e_1 \wedge$$
$$X = \{\,(e, e') \in E \mid e \in X_1\,\}\,\}$$

$$S_2 = \{\,X_2 \subseteq E_2 \mid X_2 \mapsto_2 e_2 \wedge$$
$$X = \{\,(e, e') \in E \mid e' \in X_2\,\}\,\}$$

Fig. 10.9. TBES Semantics for Parallel Composition

Our first illustration of parallel composition (see Figure 10.10) highlights how events are constructed when there is no synchronisation. Note, in contrast to earlier event structure depictions in this chapter, event labels are explicitly represented. This is required to avoid ambiguity, because here, multiple events have the same label. Events are denoted e, f, g etc. and their primed versions. The following tLOTOS behaviour could yield the event structures shown in Figure 10.10.

$$P \mid\mid\mid Q \quad \text{where}$$
$$P := x\,;\, z\,[2, 10]\,;\, \textit{stop} \quad \text{and}$$
$$Q := (\,y\,;\, z\,(5)\,;\, \textit{stop}\,) \mathbin{[\!]} (\,w\,;\, \textit{stop}\,)$$

Because no causal or conflict relationships cross component event structures, the parallel composition yields two disconnected and, thus, independently evolving, event structures.

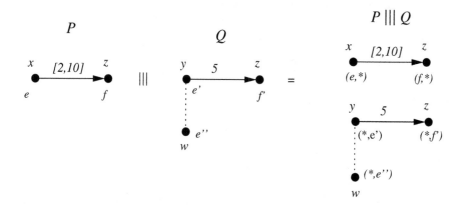

Fig. 10.10. Example Without Synchronisation, Illustrating Semantics for Parallel Composition

Next, we consider an example containing synchronisation. This yields pairing of component events and intersection of component event timings; see Figure 10.11. This structure could arise from the following behaviour,

$P \, |[z]| \, (Q \, |[z]| \, R)$ where

P and Q are as defined above and

$R := z \, [2, 5] \, ; \, stop$

The final example (see Figure 10.12) could arise from the following tLOTOS behaviour,

$S \, |[x]| \, T$ where

$S := (x \, [2, 8] \, ; \, i \, (10) \, ; \, stop) \, [] \, (x \, [3, 10] \, ; \, stop)$ and

$T := (x \, [2, 7] \, ; \, z \, (9) \, ; \, stop) \, [] \, (w \, [2, 12] \, ; \, stop)$

The example shows how bundles can result from synchronisation. In particular, because two in conflict events (e and f) both labelled x in the left component event structure are synchronised with a single event (e') labelled x in the right-hand component, a single bundle is generated of the form,

$\{ (e, e'), (f, e') \} \mapsto (*, g')$.

In addition, this example demonstrates how event timings are intersected during parallel composition. For example, $\mathcal{A}_{(S \, |[x]| \, T)}((f, e')) = \mathcal{A}_S(f) \cap \mathcal{A}_T(e')$.

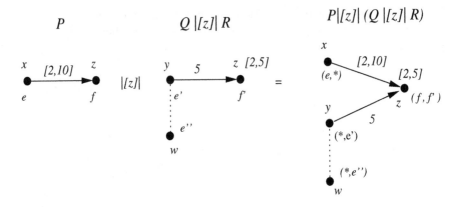

Fig. 10.11. Example with Synchronisation, Illustrating Semantics for Parallel Composition

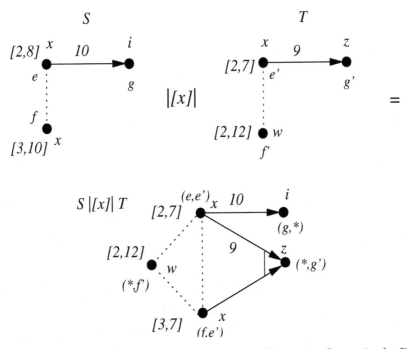

Fig. 10.12. Further Example with Synchronisation, Illustrating Semantics for Parallel Composition

10.2.3.6 Process Instantiation

The rule for process instantiation can be succinctly stated.

$$\mathcal{B}''[\![\,P\,]\!]_{(d)} \triangleq \bigsqcup_j \mathcal{F}_B^j(\bot) \quad \text{where}$$

$(P := B) \in d$ and
$$\mathcal{F}_B^j(\bot) \triangleq \mathcal{F}_B(\mathcal{F}_B(\dots \mathcal{F}_B(\bot)\dots))$$
with j repetitions of $\mathcal{F}_B$ on the right-hand side.

However, this belies a good deal of theoretical complexity, which is required in order to support this statement. This complexity is focused on the derivation of a suitable fixed point theory to handle recursive process definitions. As was the case for the other denotational semantics we have considered, the trace semantics of Chapter 3 and the (untimed) bundle event structure semantics of Chapter 4, it is beyond the scope of this book to present the necessary fixed point theory in full detail. However, the required semantic constructions are very closely related to those presented in [107], have similarities to those given in [32] and are presented in detail in [46]. To give an informal perspective on this theory, the mathematical constructions in [46] ensure that the above definition characterises the (unique) least timed bundle event structure, according to a complete partial order, denoted $\preceq$, that satisfies $\Psi = \mathcal{F}_B(\Psi)$.

$\mathcal{B}''[\![P]\!]_{(d)}$ for $P := B$ is defined using standard fixed point theory. A complete partial order $\preceq$ is defined (see [46]) on timed bundle event structures with the empty event structure (i.e. $\mathcal{B}''[\![stop]\!]_{(d)}$) as the least element, denoted $\bot$. Then, for each definition $P := B$, a function $\mathcal{F}_B$ is defined that substitutes a timed bundle event structure for each occurrence of P in B, interpreting all operators in B as operators on timed bundle event structures. (Due to the compositionality of our semantics this approach is feasible.)

$\mathcal{F}_B$ is shown to be continuous with respect to $\preceq$, which means that $\mathcal{B}''[\![P]\!]_{(d)}$ can be defined as the least upper bound of the chain (under $\preceq$) $\bot, \mathcal{F}_B(\bot), \mathcal{F}_B(\mathcal{F}_B(\bot)), \dots \dots$ Such a chain reflects the unfolding of a recursive process definition, with the nth unfolding of the process definition being larger, in the sense of $\preceq$, than the $n-1$ previous unfoldings. Furthermore, [46] gives a definition of $\bigsqcup$, such that $\bigsqcup_i \Psi_i$ is the least upper bound of such a chain; i.e. it is the smallest TBES that is larger according to $\preceq$ than all TBESs in the chain.

We illustrate this mathematical construction with a simple example of a recursive process:

$$Q := x\,[2,4]\,;\,(\,hide\;x\;in\;(\,z\,[3,6]\,;\,stop\;|||\;Q\,)\,)$$

Our semantics would yield the series of timed bundle event structure approximations to $\mathcal{B}''[\![Q]\!]_{(d)}$ shown in Figure 10.13.

As a further example, consider the channel from the multimedia stream specification of Section 9.3.2:

$$Channel := sourceOut\,;\,(\,(\,i\,[80,90]\,;\,sinkIn\,[0]\,;\,stop$$
$$[]\;i\,[0,90]\,;\,stop\,)$$
$$|||\;Channel\,)$$

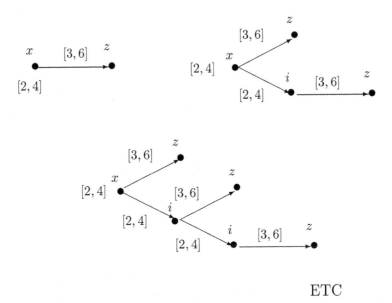

ETC

Fig. 10.13. Example Fixed Point Approximations

Figure 10.14 presents the true concurrency model resulting from this behaviour. The triangle informally denotes further recursive unfolding of the
event structure. We have not included the interleaved interpretation, because
the parallel interleaving of time and action transitions makes it too complicated to draw. In fact, even without showing time transitions, the labelled
transition system is highly complex. This example illustrates one of the major
benefits of the true concurrency approach: avoidance of state-space explosion.

10.2.4 Anomalous Behaviour

As noted in [47], some situations of degenerate behaviour that arise when
tLOTOS is given an operational semantics (see Section 9.4) do not arise in
the true concurrency setting. In particular, the direct link between unguarded
recursion and timelocks is lost when event structure semantics are considered.
In addition, zeno processes can be given a natural interpretation in a rather
straightforward way. We discuss these issues in this section.

Consider, for example the unguarded recursion introduced in Section 9.4.

$$unguarded := (\, x\,[2,6]\,;\, stop\,)\ |||\ unguarded$$

The interleaving semantics of tLOTOS generates a timelock for this behaviour.
In contrast, the timed bundle event structure semantics for an instantiation
of *unguarded*,

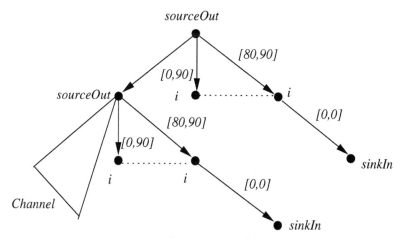

Fig. 10.14. True Concurrency Model of Multimedia Stream Channel

$$
\begin{array}{cccc}
x & x & x & x \\
\bullet & \bullet & \bullet & \bullet \quad \cdots\cdots \\
[2,6] & [2,6] & [2,6] & [2,6]
\end{array}
$$

does not timelock. This event structure allows (amongst others) a trace of
infinite length consisting of events all labelled with x that occur in the interval
$[2,6]$. For *unguarded* $||| \, (i\,(t)\,;\, success\,;\, stop)$ and arbitrary t $(t \neq \infty)$, the
occurrence of *success* is not prevented: an event labelled i followed by an
event labelled *success* can happen after any finite sequence of xs.

Notice the difference with the process,

$$unguarded' := hide \; x \; in \; unguarded$$

which leads to the timed bundle event structure,

$$
\begin{array}{cccc}
i & i & i & i \\
\bullet & \bullet & \bullet & \bullet \quad \cdots\cdots \\
[2,6] & [2,6] & [2,6] & [2,6]
\end{array}
$$

Now, *unguarded'* $||| \, (i\,(t)\,;\, success\,;\, stop)$ only permits *success* to happen if
$t \leq 6$. For $t > 6$ there exist an infinite number of urgent events that should
occur before the right-hand side i.

Unguarded recursion is the only one of the anomalous behaviours considered in Section 9.4 that behave fundamentally differently in the true concurrency setting. However, timed bundle event structures yield compact representations for instant recursion and zeno behaviour. For example, an instant
recursion, such as

$$R := x\,(0)\,;\, R$$

which we discussed in Section 9.4, will give rise to the timed bundle event
structure:

$$\underset{x}{\overset{[0,0]}{\bullet}}\xrightarrow{[0,0]}\overset{x}{\bullet}\xrightarrow{[0,0]}\overset{x}{\bullet}\xrightarrow{[0,0]}\overset{x}{\bullet}\longrightarrow \dots\dots\dots$$

This structure can perform infinitely many events labelled x without passing time, however, again, nothing forces the nontime-passing run, thus, this is not a timelock.

A zeno process, such as

$$zeno := zzeno(1)$$
$$zzeno(k : nat) := x \,;\, wait\ [2^{-k}]\ zzeno(k{+}1)$$

which was introduced in Section 9.4, yields the timed noninterleaving semantics,

$$\underset{x}{\bullet}\xrightarrow{2^{-1}}\overset{x}{\bullet}\xrightarrow{2^{-2}}\overset{x}{\bullet}\xrightarrow{2^{-3}}\overset{x}{\bullet}\longrightarrow \dots\dots\dots$$
$$\quad e_1 \qquad\qquad e_2 \qquad\qquad e_3 \qquad\qquad e_4$$

The infinite sequence $(e_1, t_1)(e_2, t_2)\dots$ is a timed proving sequence of this timed bundle event structure if $t_{j+1} \geq t_j + 2^{-j}$ for all $j \geq 1$. In particular, for $t_1 = 0$ and $t_{j+1} = t_j + 2^{-j}$ we obtain a proving sequence in which infinitely many events happen before time 1. However, $zeno$ does not stop time.

10.2.5 Discussion

One of the current limitations of the field of timed extensions of event structures is that development relations have not, to date, been explored. However, it is likely that relations of the style of those considered in Section 4.6 could be applied in this context. This then remains a topic awaiting further research.

In fact, within the format of this book, we have only been able to explore a subset of the full timed bundle event structure theory. In a somewhat broader context than that considered here, in [107], Katoen gives a comprehensive account of the TBES theory. In addition, within the context of tLOTOS-like calculi, [47] and [46] go beyond the theory presented here by also giving (event-based) operational semantics for a tLOTOS-like calculus and showing that these semantics characterise the same set of timed proving sequences (called timed event traces in that work) as the timed bundle event structure semantics.

11

Timed Communicating Automata

11.1 Introduction

Timed automata are one of the most successful techniques for modelling and verifying real-time systems. This is particularly evident from the success of region graph-based model-checking techniques, implemented in tools such as Uppaal [16][1], Kronos [66] and HyTech [92]. Different timed automata models and extensions are described in the literature and adopted by tools. For example, Uppaal's model supports shared variables (where types include bounded integers and arrays of clocks and integers) and different forms of synchronisation, including binary and (nonblocking) broadcast synchronisation (through broadcast channels.[2]) In addition, clocks in Uppaal's timed automata can be reset to any positive integer value. Urgent behaviour can be expressed through invariants, urgent channels (resulting in urgent binary synchronisation), and urgent and committed locations. Kronos, on the other hand, does not have such a rich automata language, but supports multiway synchronisation. Yet, other timed automata models represent progress conditions with deadlines or urgency types [30, 35].

Here we describe a simple model that nevertheless suffices to explain the concepts underlying timed automata frameworks. This model basically corresponds to that of *Safety Timed Automata* [91], but communication between automata follows a CCS-style [148] binary synchronisation. In this sense, the model can be seen as a timed extension of finite state communicating automata (Chapter 8). Furthermore, the reader will find that many results and discussions offered in this chapter particularly apply to Uppaal, and in many cases are also based on Uppaal developments in recent years.

A timed automaton is a finite automaton (i.e. a set of locations and transitions) extended with *clocks*, which allows for the representation of quantitative timed behaviour. For example, timed automata can describe that a

---

[1] http://www.uppaal.com.

[2] Uppaal's *channels* play a similar role to half actions in process calculi.

system cannot remain for more than five time units in a given state, or that two actions cannot be executed more than three time units apart. Clocks are variables in $\mathbb{R}^{+0}$ which increment synchronously, thus representing the passage of time. Time can only pass in locations; transitions are considered instantaneous. Transitions are annotated with *guards*, these are clock constraints which determine when the transition is enabled. Transitions may also include a *reset set*, which corresponds to a set of clocks whose values are set to zero when the transition is performed.

Timed automata are a natural extension of communicating automata (chapter 8) to model real-time systems. Complex systems can be represented as a network of timed automata executing in parallel. Concurrency is modelled by interleaving, and communication is synchronous, where synchronisation between components is modelled through half actions. The semantics of the network correspond to those of the product automaton (which results from parallel composition). At any given time, either (a) a completed action is performed, in some component automaton; or (b) two synchronising half actions are performed simultaneously, yielding a completed action; or (c) some time passes without any transition being performed.

Notice that, unlike in (untimed) communicating automata, it is not guaranteed that enabled transitions in timed automata are eventually executed. In many applications, though, it is necessary to model actions that must be executed in some time interval (provided they are enabled). In order to express this kind of situation, locations in a timed automaton can be annotated with clock constraints called *invariants*, with the following (informal) semantics: at any location, time progress is allowed only as long as the resulting clock valuations satisfy the corresponding invariant. In a network, time progress must satisfy the invariant of the current location in every component (i.e. the conjunction of all current invariants). Thus, when time cannot pass any longer in a given location (invariants usually express upper bounds), enabled transitions will be considered *urgent* and performed (if possible) without delay. This modelling of urgency gives rise to the occurrence of *timelocks* in timed automata specifications. For example, if some invariant prevents time from passing any further, and no transition is enabled at that point (possibly by a mismatched synchronisation), control will remain in that location indefinitely, and (semantically) time stops. Worryingly, a timelock originating in one component will propagate globally, bringing any possible execution to a halt. This issue is discussed in detail later, in Chapter 12.

This chapter is organised as follows. The timed automata model is formally defined in Section 11.2. This includes syntax, semantics and some explanatory examples. Then, Section 11.3 elaborates on automatic verification of timed automata (real-time model-checking); symbolic states, forward reachability, and techniques adopted by Uppaal and Kronos are discussed. Throughout the chapter, the multimedia stream protocol (Section 9.3.2) is used as a running example.

11.2 Timed Automata – Formal Definitions

This section formally defines the syntax and semantics of timed automata. The model presented here has some differences with others frequently found in the literature. For example, the CCS-like synchronisation adopted in our model closely resembles that of Uppaal, but is different from the multiway synchronisation adopted by Kronos. Nevertheless, the reader will find that our timed automata model represents all the main elements of the theory, and that other models can be easily studied by taking this as a starting point.

Before we concern ourselves with formal definitions, let us first present an introductory example. Figure 11.1 shows a network composed of two timed automata, and its corresponding product automaton. Initial locations are distinguished with a double circle; the initial value for clocks is assumed to be 0. Transition $a!$[3] has a guard $3 < x \leq 5$, meaning that it is enabled in the time interval $(3, 5]$. As we have discussed in the timed process calculus setting, this does not imply that $a!$ must be performed at some point in that interval; in fact, an execution where the automaton remains permanently in location 1 is possible. Synchronisation between $a!$ and $a?$ results in transition a in the product automaton, with guards conjoined. Location 2 is assigned the invariant $x \leq 6$, meaning that time is allowed to pass in that location only as long as the value of x is less than 6. If the value of x reaches 6 while in location 2, transition b becomes urgent and must be performed without delay. Notice that (immediate) interleaving with other actions is still possible: for example, even if b is urgent, transition c can be performed before b, although time would not be able to pass until b is performed. This can be seen in the product automaton, if the lowest branch $\langle 2, 5 \rangle$ c $\langle 2, 6 \rangle$ b $\langle 3, 6 \rangle$ is executed when the value of x reaches 6 in $\langle 2, 5 \rangle$ (at any location vector, the invariant results from conjoining the invariants of the component locations). Finally, note that x is reset in b, and so its value is zero when location 3 is entered.

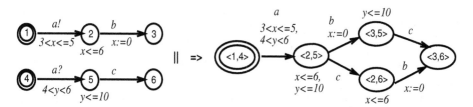

Fig. 11.1. A Simple Network of Timed Automata, and Its Product Automaton

---

[3]In this, and following chapters, we depart from our process calculus notation and use a, b, etc. to denote action labels (either for completed actions or half actions), and x, y, etc. to denote clocks.

11.2.1 Syntax

Basic Sets and Notation. *TA* denotes the set of all timed automata. The sets *CAct* (completed actions), *HAct* (half actions), and *Act* (all actions) are defined as for communicating automata (Section 8.2.2.2). $\mathbb{C}$ is the set of clocks, all of which take values in $\mathbb{R}^{+0}$. *CC* is a set of clock constraints, whose syntax is given by

$$\phi ::= \textit{false} \mid \textit{true} \mid x \sim c \mid x - y \sim c \mid \phi \wedge \phi$$

where $c \in \mathbb{N}$, $x, y \in \mathbb{C}$, $\phi \in CC$ and $\sim \in \{<, >, =, \leq, \geq\}$. *Clocks*$(\phi)$ is the set of clocks occurring in $\phi \in CC$. Let $C \subseteq \mathbb{C}$ denote the set of clocks of a given timed automaton. CC_C is the set of constraints over clocks in C. Similarly, $\mathbb{V} : \mathbb{C} \to \mathbb{R}^{+0}$ is the space of possible clock valuations, and $\mathbb{V}_C : C \to \mathbb{R}^{+0}$ the space of valuations restricted to clocks in C.

Given ϕ a clock constraint and v a valuation, we use $v \models \phi$ to denote that v satisfies ϕ (or, equivalently, that v is in the solution set of ϕ). If r is a reset set, and $d \in \mathbb{R}^{+0}$ a delay, we define $v + d$ to be the valuation such that $(v + d)(c) = v(c) + d$, for all $c \in C$. Also, we use $r(v)$ to denote the valuation that results from v by resetting to zero all clocks in r, i.e. $r(v) = v'$, where $v'(c) = 0$ whenever $c \in r$ and $v'(c) = v(c)$ otherwise.

Timed Automata. A timed automaton $A \in TA$ is a tuple (L, TL, T, l_0, C, I), where

- L is a finite set of locations;
- $C \subseteq \mathbb{C}$ is a finite set of clocks;
- $TL \subseteq Act$ is a finite set of transition labels;
- $T \subseteq L \times TL \times CC_C \times \mathcal{P}(C) \times L$ is a transition relation, where transitions $(l, a, g, r, l') \in T$ are usually denoted,

  $l \xrightarrow{a,g,r} l'$

  where $a \in TL$ is the *action*, $g \in CC_C$ is the *guard* and $r \in \mathcal{P}(C)$ is the *reset set*;
- $l_0 \in L$ is the initial location; and
- $I : L \to CC_C$ is a mapping which associates invariants with locations.

11.2.1.1 Example: A TA Specification for the Multimedia Stream

Let us revisit the example of the multimedia stream, introduced in Section 9.3.2 (see Figure 9.1). The *Source* process generates a continuous sequence of packets which are relayed by the *Channel* to a *Sink* process which displays the packets. Three basic interprocess communication actions support the flow of data (see Figure 9.3.2 again), *sourceOut*, *sinkIn* and *play*, which respectively transfer packets from the *Source* to the *Channel*, from the *Channel* to the *Sink* and display them at the *Sink*. Here we assume that the *Channel* is reliable;

the *Source* transmits a packet every 50 ms; packets arrive at the *Sink* between 80 ms and 90 ms after their transmission (the latency of the *Channel*) and that whenever the *Sink* receives a packet, it needs 5 ms to process it, after which it is ready to receive the next packet.

Figure 11.2[4] shows a possible timed automata specification, where the *Channel* is represented by two one-place buffers, *Place1* and *Place2*. Notice, in contrast to the tLOTOS specification in Section 9.3.2, that in timed automata we cannot (directly) specify a channel with an unbounded number of places. Nevertheless, it can be shown[5] that two one-place buffers represent a safe implementation of an infinite-capacity channel, in the sense that synchronisation between *Source* and either *Place1* or *Place2* is always possible (in other words, a packet can always be put into the *Channel*).

Every component in the network includes a local clock: $t1$, $t2$, $t3$ and $t4$. The initial location in the *Source*, *State0*, is annotated with the invariant $t1 = 0$ to ensure that the first packet (*sourceOut!*) is sent immediately. The guard $t1 = 50$ and reset $t1 := 0$ enable *sourceOut!* in location *State1*, once every 50 ms. The invariant at *State1*, $t1 \leq 50$, makes the *sourceOut!* urgent as soon as it is enabled. Notice that, because *sourceOut!* is a half action, it will only be performed if *sourceOut?* is enabled in either *Place1* or *Place2* (otherwise a timelock would occur). Now consider the model for a buffer, say *Place1*. At location *State1*, transition *sourceOut?* is offered to synchronise with a *sourceOut!* from the *Source*. Should this happen (notice that the *Source* may nondeterministically synchronise with *Place2* instead), the clock $t4$ is reset and the automaton moves to location *State2*. The value of $t4$ represents the time elapsed since the last packet was transmitted. The invariant $t4 \leq 90$, together with the guard $t4 \geq 80$ enabling transition *sinkIn!*, effectively represent the *Channel*'s latency: packets arrive at the *Sink* between 80 and 90 ms after they have been sent. The *Sink* synchronises with the *Channel* (i.e. with *Place1/Place2*) by offering a *sinkIn?* action. The action *play* is performed 5 ms after a packet has arrived, representing the speed at which the *Sink* can process and play packets.

11.2.2 Semantics

The semantics of a timed automaton, say $A = (L, TL, T, l_0, C, I)$, can be interpreted in terms of a timed transition system (S, Lab, T_S, s_0), which describes all possible executions of A. S denotes a set of states[6] of the form $s = [l, v]$, where l is a location in A and v a possible valuation for its clocks. $s_0 = [l_0, v_0]$ is the starting state, where l_0 is the initial location in A, and v_0 is the initial valuation, which sets all clocks to 0. $Lab = TL \cup \mathbb{R}^+$ is a set of transition

---

[4]This is based on a model presented in [43].

[5]A report on the verification of this and other correctness properties using Uppaal can be found in [43].

[6]Also referred to as *concrete* states.

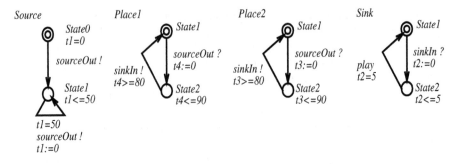

Fig. 11.2. Timed Automata Specification of the Multimedia Stream

labels. The transition relation $T_S \subseteq S \times Lab \times S$ represents the set of all possible executions of A (also called *runs*). For any (reachable) state, a transition denotes one possible step the current execution can take. Thus, transitions can be of one of two types: *action transitions*, e.g. (s, a, s'), where $a \in Act$, or *time transitions*, e.g. (s, d, s'), where $d \in \mathbb{R}^+$ and the passage of d time units is denoted. Transitions are denoted[7]

$$s \xrightarrow{\gamma} s'$$

where $\gamma \in Lab$. We use $s \xrightarrow{\gamma}$ to denote $\exists\ s'.\ s \xrightarrow{\gamma} s'$. Usually, we refer to action transitions simply as *actions*.

Semantic transitions (time and action transitions, e.g. $s \xrightarrow{a} s'$) are not to be confused with the *syntactic* transitions (or edges, e.g. $l \xrightarrow{a,g,r} l'$) in a timed automaton graph. Indeed, transitions and locations in a timed automaton are finite. On the other hand, the TTS describing the semantics of the automaton will be, in most cases, infinite. This is due to clocks taking valuations in a dense space, $\mathbb{R}^+$ (a similar point was made in Section 10.1.1). In general, whenever the automaton is allowed to remain in a given location l for $d \in \mathbb{R}^+$ time units, the TTS contains infinitely many time transitions

$$[l, v] \xrightarrow{d'} [l, v + d'],$$

$d' \in \mathbb{R}^+$, $0 \leq d' \leq d$. Figure 11.3 below illustrates these concepts.

The timed automaton depicted in Figure 11.3(i) can remain in location 1 for 5 time units. Transition a can be performed at any time in $[2, 5]$, and is urgent when $v(x) = 5$. Once in location 2, any amount of time can pass before transition b is executed. Moreover, and unlike in untimed communicating

---

[7]In the presentation of TTS in Section 10.1.1 we have used $\rightarrow$ and $\rightsquigarrow$ to denote, respectively, action and time transitions. Also, Section 10.1.3 introduced $\longrightarrow\!\!\!\!\twoheadrightarrow$ to denote the union of these two types of transitions. Here we use $\longrightarrow\!\!\!\!\twoheadrightarrow$ for the same purpose, but we do not use $\rightarrow$ and $\rightsquigarrow$ separately, to avoid confusion with syntactic transitions (edges) in timed automata (denoted $\rightarrow$).

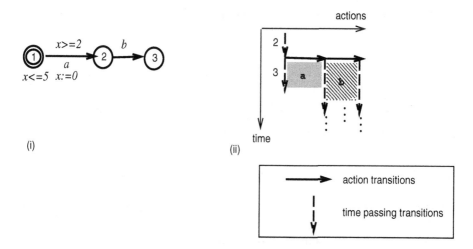

Fig. 11.3. A Timed Automata (i) and (Part of) Its TTS (ii)

automata (chapter 8) here there is no guarantee that b is ever executed: the timed automaton may remain in location 2 permanently. This results in an infinite TTS, part of which is sketched in Figure 11.3(ii). For example, the following runs are two particular instances of the timed automaton's execution.

$$\rho_1 = [1,0] \xrightarrow{2} [1,2] \xrightarrow{a} [2,0] \xrightarrow{3.3} [2,3.3] \xrightarrow{b} [3,3.3] \cdots$$

$$\rho_2 = [1,0] \xrightarrow{3.5} [1,3.5] \xrightarrow{a} [2,0] \xrightarrow{7} [2,7] \cdots$$

where, for every state $[l,v]$, l denotes a location in the automaton and v the current value of x in that state. The first run, ρ_1, denotes a partial execution where the automaton remains in location 1 for 2 time units, takes transition a, then remains for 3.3 time units in location 2 and takes transition b. Another possible partial execution is represented by ρ_2: the automaton takes a when $v(x) = 3.5$ and then remains in location 2 for 7 time units without performing any action.

Some other aspects of timed automata semantics are worth observing. For example, the action transition $[2,3.3] \xrightarrow{b} [3,3.3]$ in ρ_1 confirms the instantaneous nature of transitions in a timed automaton: notice that x is not incremented (which is consistent with all the models considered in this book). Similarly, $[1,2] \xrightarrow{a} [2,0]$ illustrates the reset of x in transition a. The time transition $[1,0] \xrightarrow{2} [1,2]$ in the same run shows that time only elapses in locations. And, as we have mentioned before, time is allowed to progress only as long as it does not invalidate the current invariant. For example, a run like ρ_3 below is not possible because the invariant $x \leq 5$ in location 1 would be invalidated by time-progress (equivalently, a must be performed before more than 5 time units have elapsed in location 1):

$$\rho_3 = [1, 0] \xrightarrow{\;6\;}\!\!\!\twoheadrightarrow [1, 6] \xrightarrow{\;a\;}\!\!\!\twoheadrightarrow [2, 6]$$

11.2.2.1 Runs

A *run* starting from state $s \in S$, is a finite or infinite sequence ρ defined as follows,

$$\rho \triangleq s_1 \xrightarrow{\gamma_1}\!\!\!\twoheadrightarrow s_2 \xrightarrow{\gamma_2}\!\!\!\twoheadrightarrow s_3 \xrightarrow{\gamma_3}\!\!\!\twoheadrightarrow \ldots$$

where $s_1 = s$, $s_i \in S$, and $\gamma_i \in Act \cup \mathbb{R}^+$, for all $i \geq 1$. We use $s \xrightarrow{\gamma}\!\!\!\twoheadrightarrow s' \in \rho$ to denote that $s \xrightarrow{\gamma}\!\!\!\twoheadrightarrow s'$ is a (action or time) transition in the sequence ρ. We define $delay(\rho)$ as the sum of all delays in the run ρ:

$$delay(\rho) \triangleq \Sigma \{\gamma \mid \gamma \in \mathbb{R}^+ \wedge s \xrightarrow{\gamma}\!\!\!\twoheadrightarrow s' \in \rho\}$$

We define $Runs(A)$ to be the set of all runs of a timed automaton A. A *divergent run* is a run ρ s.t. $delay(\rho) = \infty$, i.e. an infinite run where time diverges. Nondivergent runs are called *convergent runs*. A *zeno run* is a convergent, infinite run with infinitely many actions. $ZRuns(A) \subseteq Runs(A)$ is the set of all zeno runs of A.

As we have mentioned, runs represent possible system executions. However, finite runs are considered valid executions only if they end in a state where no transition (either action or time passing) is enabled. Notice that here we drop the liveness hypothesis of finite state communicating automata (see our discussion in Section 8.2.4), where action transitions, if enabled, will eventually be performed. Timed automata, on the contrary, can remain at any location for as long as the invariant in that location allows. In this model, the intended (urgent) execution of actions must be indicated explicitly through invariants. Moreover, one must be precise in quantifying the intended execution time (through guards and invariants): there is no way to enforce the execution of actions at some (unspecified) point in the future.

11.2.2.2 Parallel Composition

The behaviour of a network can be defined in terms of the parallel composition of the component automata. Composition results in a single automaton, called the *product automaton*, whose semantics correspond to that of the network. The parallel composition of timed automata is just an extension of the same operation defined for (untimed) communicating automata (Section 8.2.2.2). In addition, here we note that component guards and reset sets are conjoined as a result of synchronisation, and that component invariants are conjoined in location vectors. Formally, the product automaton can be defined as follows. Let $|A = |\langle A_1, \dots, A_n \rangle$ be a network of TAs, where

$$A_i = (L_i, TL_i, T_i, l_{i,0}, C_i, I_i)$$

for $1 \leq i \leq n$. Let u, u' be location vectors. The product automaton, which represents the behaviour of the network $|A$, is defined as

$$\Pi = (L, TL, T, l_0, C, I)$$

where

- $L = \{ l_0 \} \cup \{ u' \mid \exists u \in L, a, g, r \cdot u \xrightarrow{a,g,r} u' \}$;

- $TL = \bigcup_{i=1}^{n} TL_i$;

- T is as defined by the following rules $(1 \leq i \neq j \leq n)$[8],

$$(P1) \ \frac{u_i \xrightarrow{a?,g_i,r_i}_i l \quad u_j \xrightarrow{a!,g_j,r_j}_j l'}{u \xrightarrow{a,g_i \wedge g_j, r_i \cup r_j} u[l \to i, l' \to j]} \qquad (P2) \ \frac{u_i \xrightarrow{a,g,r}_i l \quad a \in CAct}{u \xrightarrow{a,g,r} u[l \to i]}$$

- $l_0 = \langle l_{1,0}, \dots, l_{n,0} \rangle$;

- $C = \bigcup_{i=1}^{n} C_i$; and

- $I(\langle u_1, \dots, u_n \rangle) = \bigwedge_{i=1}^{n} I_i(u_i)$.

Example: Product Automaton for the Multimedia Stream. Figure 11.4 shows part of the product automaton which corresponds to the multimedia stream specification (Figure 11.2). We have omitted unreachable locations; these result from transitions that will never be enabled.[9] For example, location $\langle 0, 1, 1, 1 \rangle$ corresponds to *Source.State0, Place1.State1, Place2.State1* and *Sink.State1*. Transition *sourceOut*, from $\langle 0, 1, 1, 1 \rangle$ to $\langle 1, 2, 1, 1 \rangle$, results from synchronisation between *sourceOut!* in *Source.State0* and *sourceOut?* in *Place1.State1* (a similar transition exists from $\langle 0, 1, 1, 1 \rangle$ to $\langle 1, 1, 2, 1 \rangle$, which corresponds to initial synchronisation between *Source* and *Place2*). The invariant $t1 \leq 50 \wedge t4 \leq 90$ in location $\langle 1, 2, 1, 1 \rangle$ corresponds to the conjunction of invariants in *Source.State1, Place1.State2, Place2.State1* and *Sink.State1*.

---

[8] As for communicating automata in Chapter 8, we use $a?$, $a! \in HAct$ to denote half actions.

[9] Notice that these locations and transitions are still part of the product automaton. Reachability can only be determined by semantic analysis.

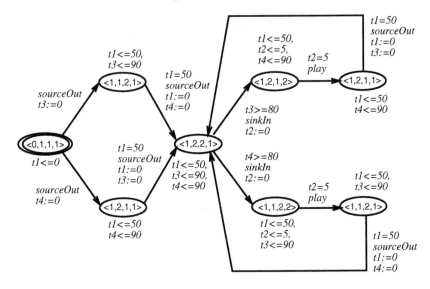

Fig. 11.4. Product Automaton (TA) For The Multimedia Stream

11.2.2.3 A TTS Semantics for Timed Automata

Here we present a formalisation of semantics in terms of TTSs. We assume that an automaton with half actions cannot be executed in isolation (this corresponds, for example, to the semantics of Uppaal models), and as such it does not have a semantics related to it. Therefore, the semantics offered in this section correspond to automata where all actions are completed. Note (as for communicating automata in Chapter 8) that this does not prevent us from offering a semantics for a network of TAs: the behaviour of a network corresponds to the TTS semantics for its product automaton (Section 11.2.2.2).

Let $A = (L, TL, T, l_0, C, I) \in TA$ be a timed automaton where all actions are completed (i.e. $TL \subseteq CAct$). The semantics of A is given by the TTS (S, Lab, T_S, s_0), where

- $S \subseteq L \times \mathbb{V}_C$ is the set of reachable states; i.e.

$$S = \{ s_0 \} \cup \{ s' \mid \exists s \in S, \gamma \in Lab \,.\, s \xrightarrow{\gamma} s' \}$$

- $s_0 = [l_0, v_0]$ is the starting state, where v_0 (the initial clock valuation) is s.t. $\forall c \in C$, $v_0(c) = 0$;

- $Lab = TL \cup \mathbb{R}^+$ is the set of transition labels;

- $T_S \subseteq S \times Lab \times S$ is the transition relation, defined by the following inference rules,

$$\text{(R1)} \; \frac{l \xrightarrow{a,g,r} l' \quad v \models g \quad r(v) \models I(l')}{[l,v] \xrightarrow{a} [l',r(v)]} \qquad \text{(R2)} \; \frac{\forall d' \leq d, \, (v + d') \models I(l)}{[l,v] \xrightarrow{d} [l,v+d]}$$

The first transition rule, (R1), gives an interpretation to invariants in which locations cannot be entered if the invariant is false. This *strong-invariant* interpretation is the most commonly adopted both in the literature and tools (e.g. Uppaal). In contrast, a *weak-invariant* interpretation, in which the invariant in the target location is not required to hold for a transition to be performed, is given by the following rules,

$$\text{(W1)} \; \frac{l \xrightarrow{a,g,r} l' \quad v \models g}{[l,v] \xrightarrow{a} [l',r(v)]} \qquad \text{(W2)} \; \frac{\forall d' \leq d, \, (v + d') \models I(l)}{[l,v] \xrightarrow{d} [l,v+d]}$$

The difference between these two interpretations can be observed in rules (R1) and (W1), which govern when a transition can be performed; rules (R2) and (W2), which determine when time is allowed to elapse, are the same in both interpretations. For example, if the semantics of the automaton shown in Figure 11.5 is considered with respect to the strong-invariant interpretation, then a would only be performed in the interval $[0,5]$. After that, the invariant in location 2 is not valid and so that location cannot be entered. On the other hand, with a weak-invariant interpretation, a can be performed at any time. If a is performed after 5 time units have passed, then b must be performed immediately afterwards. Consider, for example, the following run.

$$\rho = [1,0] \xrightarrow{6} [1,6] \xrightarrow{a} [2,6] \xrightarrow{b} [3,6] \cdots$$

Fig. 11.5. Strong and Weak Invariants

Such a run waits for 6 time units in location 1 and then performs a. This is not possible with a strong-invariant interpretation, because performing a when $v(x) = 6$ would invalidate the invariant in the target location ($x \leq 5$ in location 2). On the other hand this run is possible with weak invariants, and b is performed urgently after a.

11.2.2.4 Discussion: Urgency in Timed Automata and tLOTOS

The form of urgency expressed by invariants can be compared to that obtained through explicit urgency operators in process calculi, discussed in Section 9.2.2. With invariants, urgency can be enforced on both completed and half actions (which corresponds to urgency in internal and observable actions in process calculi). Consequently, this form of urgency is stronger than the one adopted by tLOTOS, which is enforced only on internal actions. Therefore, the use of invariants in timed automata may cause timelocks due to synchronisation mismatches, whereas this cannot occur in tLOTOS, as observable actions are never urgent.

11.3 Real-time Model-checking

In general, *real-time model-checking* refers to a collection of formal automatic verification methods in which a system, modelled as a network of timed automata, is checked against a property expressed in some temporal logic. Predominantly, properties will be expressed in some subset of TCTL (Timed Computation Tree Logic) [6], a real-time extension of CTL [57] (Section 8.2.5.1). Because the state space of a network is infinite, these methods rely on the computation of abstractions, which map an infinite number of states in the network's TTS (which we call *concrete* states) to a finite number of *symbolic* states. In general, a symbolic state consists of a location vector and a number of clock constraints, which represent a space of clock valuations: every single valuation in this set, together with the location vector, define one reachable concrete state.

Indeed, we can say that progress in the area of automatic verification of timed systems, and in particular of timed automata, has a milestone in the seminal work of Alur and Dill [7]: a *region graph* partitions the infinite state-space into a finite number of equivalence classes: for any guard g, all valuations in a region satisfy g, or none does. The fundamental drawback of the region graph is its size: the number of regions grows exponentially with the number of clocks and the maximum constants (per clock) used in clock constraints. In practice, real-time model-checkers use a coarser abstraction, the *forward reachability graph*, which can be much smaller (in number of symbolic states) than the corresponding region graph.

The key observation here is that, in order to determine whether a certain state is reachable, the fine discrimination of valuations introduced by regions is not necessary. Instead, the forward reachability graph divides the infinite state-space into *zones*. Like regions, zones are conjunctions of clock constraints and can be seen as symbolic states in the execution of a timed automaton. Zones characterise all valuations that are reachable on a given automaton's location, from the time that location is entered and as long as the location's invariant allows. However, unlike regions, it is not required that all valuations in a zone satisfy the same guards. Therefore, more valuations can be considered part of the same zone, and so the (infinite) state-space is divided into a smaller number of symbolic states.

Also, model-checkers cope with complex systems thanks to *on-the-fly* verification: properties can be checked while the reachability graph is being generated. Therefore, and depending on the property at hand, it may not be necessary to construct the whole graph to determine whether the system satisfies a property. Moreover, and because the verification algorithms work over the reachability graph, the construction of the product automaton is not necessary to model-check a network of TAs.

11.3.1 Forward Reachability

Model-checkers can verify a number of different TCTL formulae, including reachability, safety and liveness properties (including bounded-response[10]). In general, TCTL extends CTL by allowing the specification of time intervals. For example, a TCTL formula $EF_{\leq n}\phi$ is satisfiable in given state s, if there exists a run ρ (i.e. a path in the computation tree) starting from s where a state s' is reachable, such that ϕ is satisfiable in s' and the accumulated delay in ρ, up to s', is in the interval $[0, n]$, $n \in \mathbb{R}^{+0}$. Although some model-checkers (notably, Kronos) are able to deal with general TCTL formulae, this section is concerned just with reachability formulae of the form $EF\phi$, where ϕ is given in the BNF,

$$\phi ::= g \mid l \mid \phi \wedge \phi \mid \neg \phi$$

where g is a clock constraint in CC and l is a location in a given timed automaton. Notice that, even when delays are not explicitly specified in the TCTL formula, they can be naturally modelled as part of the clock constraint g. In practice, TCTL formulae without explicit delays have proved to be expressive enough for real-time verification. For example, Uppaal verifies a subset of TCTL without explicit delays, and where modalities cannot be nested: formulae include $EF\phi$, $AG\phi$, $EG\phi$ and $AF\phi$; but ϕ cannot contain path (A/E) or temporal (F/G) operators.

Furthermore, reachability analysis remains the core of the verification engine, in all real-time model-checkers. One reason for this is that reachability analysis is versatile. For example, we have seen already that safety properties can be expressed in terms of reachability properties: $AG\phi$ is satisfiable if $EF\neg\phi$ is not. Also, a number of methods are known that augment the timed automata specification (e.g. with test automata [4], or extra clocks and Boolean variables) and allow the verification of bounded-response properties to be expressed in terms of basic safety properties [16]. The other reason why reachability analysis is crucial to model-checking is that the verification of more complex formulae, such as general liveness properties (e.g. $AGEF\phi$), can be realised by nested reachability checks (see, e.g. [189]). Mostly, then, development in both model-checking theory and tools has focused on efficient reachability algorithms (and on the data structures used by these algorithms).

---

[10]In TCTL, bounded-response properties usually take the form $AG(\phi \Rightarrow AF_{\leq n}\psi)$, for some $n \in \mathbb{N}$ denoting the maximum delay between a ϕ-state and a ψ-state.

We now describe forward reachability in detail. Our discussions are based on a single timed automaton, but definitions readily accommodate networks of automata (if we apply these definitions to the product automaton). Given a timed automaton A and a state formula ϕ (a formula given in the BNF mentioned above), an algorithm will determine whether there exists a symbolic state in the forward reachability graph for A, which satisfies ϕ. In what follows, we assume $A = (L, TL, T, l_0, C, I)$.

11.3.1.1 Symbolic States and Operations on Zones

This section presents the main theoretical elements underlying symbolic model-checking of timed automata. Because this area is still under active research, we decided to keep our discussions at a conceptual level, without delving too deep into current implementations (such as Uppaal or Kronos). These and other issues are further discussed in Section 11.3.3, where pointers to relevant literature are also offered.

Symbolic States. A symbolic state is a pair (l, Z), where $l \in L$ is a location in A and $Z \in CC_C$ (called a *zone*) is a clock constraint. Symbolic states are finite abstractions of infinite sets of (concrete) states. In this sense, a symbolic state (l, Z) encodes the set $\{ [l, v] \mid v \models Z \}$; that is, the set of all concrete states with location l and valuation v satisfying the constraints in Z. We use $s \in (l, Z)$ to denote $s = [l, v]$, and $v \models Z$.

Symbolic states constitute the nodes of the reachability graph. We show that, given a symbolic state in the reachability graph, the derivation of its direct successors is a crucial operation in the reachability algorithm. This, in turn, consists of a number of operations on zones. Figure 11.6 below illustrates some of these basic operations, where zones (over $\{x, y\}$) are represented through their solution sets.

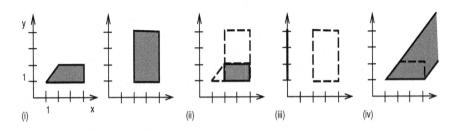

Fig. 11.6. (i) Z and Z', (ii) $Z \wedge Z'$, (iii) $r(Z')$, $r = \{x\}$, (iv) $Z^\uparrow$

Conjunction. Let Z and Z' be two zones; conjunction is defined in the usual way and corresponds to the set of valuations satisfying both Z and Z'.

$$Z \wedge Z' \triangleq Z \cap Z'$$

Figure 11.6(i) shows the zones,

$$Z = x \geq 1 \wedge x \leq 4 \wedge y \geq 1 \wedge y \leq 2 \wedge x - y \geq 0$$

$$Z' = x \geq 2 \wedge x \leq 4 \wedge y \geq 1 \wedge y \leq 4$$

Conjunction (Figure 11.6(ii)) gives the expected,

$$Z \wedge Z' = x \geq 2 \wedge x \leq 4 \wedge y \geq 1 \wedge y \leq 2$$

Reset. Let Z be a zone and r a reset set. The reset of Z with respect to r, denoted $r(Z)$, corresponds to the set of valuations in Z where the value of every clock in r is set to zero.

$$r(Z) \triangleq \{ r(v) \mid v \models Z \}$$

For example, the reset of Z' with respect to $r = \{x\}$ (Figure 11.6(iii)) yields,

$$r(Z') = x = 0 \wedge y \geq 1 \wedge y \leq 4$$

Forward projection. Given a zone Z, its forward projection, $Z^\uparrow$, is defined as follows,

$$Z^\uparrow \triangleq \{ v + d \mid v \models Z \wedge d \in \mathbb{R}^{+0} \}$$

The forward projection of Z is the set of valuations that can be reached from any valuation in Z by letting some time pass. This operation preserves the lower bounds imposed by Z, but allows time to diverge, maintaining the uniform clock speed.[11] Figure 11.6(iv) depicts the forward projection of Z, which yields

$$Z^\uparrow = y \geq 1 \wedge x - y \geq 0 \wedge x - y \leq 3$$

Normalisation. Let $c_{\max} \in \mathbb{N}$ be the greatest constant occurring in any guard or invariant in A. Let Z be a zone, and $m \in \mathbb{N}$, $m > c_{\max}$. We define $norm(Z)$ as the zone which can be obtained from Z by removing all constraints $x \sim m$, $x - y \sim m$ ($\sim \in \{<, \leq\}$), and replacing all constraints $x \sim m, x - y \sim m$ ($\sim \in \{>, =\}$) with $x > c_{\max}$ and $x - y > c_{max}$, respectively.

Normalisation (not shown in Figure 11.6) guarantees a finite number of zones in the forward reachability graph, and therefore is necessary to ensure that the

---

[11] As we have mentioned before, timed automata synchronise on the passage of time, and thus, clocks advance at the same speed. Effectively, the time model of TA assumes an implicit global clock.

reachability algorithm terminates. We now explain the necessity for normalisation through a small example.[12] Consider the timed automaton depicted by Figure 11.7,

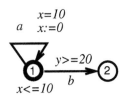

Fig. 11.7. Clock Drift

The clock y is allowed to "drift" unbounded in location 1, generating an infinite number of symbolic states $(1, Z_i)$, where

$$Z_0 = x \leq 10 \wedge x = y$$
$$Z_1 = x \leq 10 \wedge y \leq 20 \wedge y - x = 10$$
$$Z_2 = x \leq 10 \wedge y \leq 30 \wedge y - x = 20$$
$$Z_3 = x \leq 10 \wedge y \leq 40 \wedge y - x = 30$$
$$Z_4 = x \leq 10 \wedge y \leq 50 \wedge y - x = 40$$
$$\vdots$$

The state $(1, Z_0)$ denotes that, initially, the automaton can remain in location 1 for 10 time units. State $(1, Z_1)$ is reachable from $(1, Z_0)$: Z_1 represents the set of valuations that can be reached in location 1 after transition a is performed (and letting time pass as much as the invariant allows). The clock x is constrained to $x \leq 10$ by the invariant in location 1; however, after a is performed, the value of y and the difference between y and x increase: this is so because a resets x and y is not constrained by the invariant. Consequently, an infinite number of zones $Z_0, Z_1, \ldots$ are reachable, and so the reachability algorithm may not terminate (this would be the case, for example, when the property to check cannot be verified until the whole of the state-space has been explored).

Notice that $v_2(y) \in [20, 30]$, $v_3(y) \in [30, 40]$ and $v_4(y) \in [40, 50]$, where $v_2 \models Z_2$, $v_3 \models Z_3$ and $v_4 \models Z_4$. Transition b, therefore, does not distinguish among these different valuations: all that matters is that b is enabled because $v(y) \geq 20$. Therefore, removing the constraint $y \leq 30$ from Z_2 produces a "normalised" zone, $norm(Z_2)$, which is, in the sense just mentioned, equivalent to Z_2. Similarly, removing $y \leq 40$ and replacing $y - x = 30$ with $y - x > 20$ in Z_3 results in the equivalent zone $norm(Z_3)$ (which is also equivalent to $Z_4, Z_5, \ldots$). We have, then:

---

[12]This is inspired by an example in [13].

$$norm(Z_2) = x \le 10 \wedge y - x = 20$$
$$norm(Z_3) = x \le 10 \wedge y > 20 \wedge y - x > 20$$

Normalisation, then, is an operation on zones that produces an equivalent zone with respect to timed automata tests (i.e. guards and invariants). For explanatory purposes, our definition of normalisation is just a simplified description of the procedures currently implemented in Uppaal or Kronos. Section 11.3.3 offers some pointers to some literature on this topic.

11.3.1.2 The Forward Reachability Graph

Consider, once again, the timed automaton shown in Figure 11.7. The corresponding TTS contains, for example, a time transition

$$[1, x = y = 0] \xrightarrow{10} [1, x = y = 10]$$

that will trigger the immediate execution of action a. In general, the TTS contains infinitely many time transitions of the form:

$$[1, x = y = 0] \xrightarrow{d} [1, x = y = d]$$

where $d \le 10$, $d \in \mathbb{R}^+$, which denote that time can initially elapse by 10 time units in location 1. Similarly, there exist infinitely many action transitions of the form:

$$[1, x = 0 + d \wedge y = 20 + d] \xrightarrow{b} [2, x = 0 + d \wedge y = 20 + d]$$

for any $d \le 10$, $d \in \mathbb{R}^{+0}$. These action transitions denote that b can be performed at any time during the interval [20,30].

We could argue that the distinction between these infinitely many transitions (that is, the different ways in which time can pass up to a certain point) is not relevant to the execution of the timed automaton. What is important, though, is whether time has elapsed by a certain relevant quantity: this is determined by guards, invariants and resets in the automaton.

The forward reachability graph, then, provides an abstraction for the elapsing of time in the form of clock constraints (zones). Every node in the graph is represented by a symbolic state (l, Z), where l is a location in the automaton A and Z is a zone. The starting node is (l_0, Z_0), where l_0 is the initial location of A and Z_0 is the zone describing the maximum time-progress allowed in l_0 (notice that this depends on the invariant in l_0). Given a node (l, Z), the forward reachability graph contains a direct successor (l', Z') for every transition $t = l \xrightarrow{a,g,r} l'$ in A. The zone Z' represents the maximum time-progress allowed in the target location l', after t has been performed. Z' is calculated from the current zone Z, the transition's guard g and reset set r, and the target location's invariant $I(l')$. In what follows, we give formal definitions for symbolic successors and the forward reachability graph, and illustrate these concepts with a small example.

Symbolic Successors. Let $t = l \xrightarrow{a,g,r} l'$ be a transition in A and (l, Z) be a symbolic state, where $l \in L$ is a location in A and $Z \in CC_C$ is a zone. Let Z_t be a zone defined as follows,

$$Z_t \triangleq r(Z \wedge g) \wedge I(l')$$

The symbolic state (l', Z_t) represents the set of all concrete states that can be reached from any concrete state in (l, Z), by performing transition t. Hence, the following holds,

$$\forall s' \in (l', Z_t), \exists s \in (l, Z) . s \xrightarrow{a} s'$$

It is not difficult to see that, if a concrete state $s' = [l', v'] \in (l', Z_t)$ is reachable from some state $s \in (l, Z)$, by taking transition t, then so is any state $s'' = [l', v' + d]$, $d \in \mathbb{R}^{+0}$, $v' + d \models I(l')$ (just by allowing time to elapse in the target location l'). Then, the set of immediate successors of any node (l, Z) is given by,

$$Successors(l, Z) = \{ (l', norm(Z_t^{\uparrow} \wedge I(l'))) \mid t = l \xrightarrow{a,g,r} l' \}$$

Forward Reachability Graph. Let

$$Z_0 \triangleq I(l_0) \wedge \bigwedge_{x,y \in C} x = y$$

be the initial zone. The forward reachability graph, $G = (N, E)$, where N is a finite set of nodes and E is a finite set of edges, can be defined inductively as follows,

$$N = \{ (l_0, Z_0) \} \cup \bigcup_{(l,Z) \in N} Successors(l, Z)$$

$$E = \{ (l, Z) \rightarrow (l', Z') \mid (l, Z) \in N \wedge (l', Z') \in Successors(l, Z) \}$$

Notice that normalisation guarantees finiteness of N. The graph can be interpreted as a finite abstraction of the concrete, operational (TTS) semantics given in Section 11.2.2. Effectively, a node $(l, Z) \in N$ represents the set of time transitions,

$$\{ [l, v] \xrightarrow{d} [l, v + d] \mid d \in \mathbb{R}^+ \wedge v \models Z \wedge v + d \models Z \}$$

and an edge $(l, Z) \rightarrow (l', Z') \in E$ represents the set of action transitions,

$$\{ [l, v] \xrightarrow{a} [l', v'] \mid a \in Act \wedge v \models Z \wedge v' \models Z' \}$$

An Example. Consider the automaton of Figure 11.7. The starting node in the reachability graph is the symbolic state $(1, Z_0)$, where

$$Z_0 = x \le 10 \wedge x = y$$

This state denotes that initially (location 1) time can pass up to 10 time units and that clocks x and y have the same value. One of the direct successors of the starting node is given by $(1, Z_1)$, where

$$Z_1 = x \le 10 \wedge y \le 20 \wedge y - x = 10$$

This new symbolic state represents all the concrete states that are reachable from (l, Z_0) by performing transition a, and then letting some time pass in the target location.

11.3.1.3 A Forward Reachability Algorithm

The reachability algorithm is shown in Figure 11.8. This is sketched as a Boolean function *reachable*(A, ϕ) (where $A \in TA$ and ϕ is a state formula) which can be thought of as exploring the forward reachability graph, generating its nodes on demand. The algorithm starts with the starting node of the graph, and then generates, at every step, the set of successors for the node under consideration. This is repeated until a node is found which satisfies the reachability formula (line 7), or until the whole graph has been explored and no node has been found to satisfy ϕ (line 19).

Termination is guaranteed by the normalisation of zones performed during the generation of successors, and by keeping a set *Visited* of visited nodes. The set *Waiting* contains the nodes to be explored. Notice (line 10) that successors are generated only for unvisited nodes. Indeed, given two symbolic states (l, Z) and (l, Z_v) s.t. $Z \subseteq Z_v$, all states which are reachable from (l, Z) are also reachable from (l, Z_v). Thus, there is no need to explore (l, Z) if (l, Z_v) has been visited already.

We note that this algorithm just sketches those currently implemented in tools such as Uppaal and Kronos, where many optimisations have been realised both in terms of data structures and the algorithm itself (see Section 11.3.3). To conclude this section, then, let us briefly comment on some ways to improve the algorithm of Figure 11.8.

- The algorithm could be modified to avoid keeping visited states in the *Waiting* list. Notice that successors are generated and stored in *Waiting* regardless of whether they have been previously visited (line 14), thus potentially wasting memory (until they are eventually checked in line 5).[13]

---

[13]Indeed, Uppaal implements a unified *Waiting-Visited* list, minimising the storage of symbolic states during exploration (see, e.g. [62]).

Function $reachable(A, \phi)$
1 **begin**
2         $Visited \leftarrow \emptyset$;
3         $Waiting \leftarrow \{(l_0, Z_0)\}$;
4   **while** $Waiting \neq \emptyset$ **do**
5   Choose $(l, Z) \in Waiting$;
6            $Waiting \leftarrow Waiting \setminus \{(l, Z)\}$;
7   **if** $(l, Z) \models \phi$ **then return TRUE**;
8   **end if**
9   **if** $\nexists (l, Z_v) \in Visited. \ Z \subseteq Z_v$ **then**
10                $Waiting \leftarrow Waiting \cup Successors(l, Z)$;
11                $Visited \leftarrow Visited \cup \{(l, Z)\}$;
12   **end if**
13   **end while**
14   **return FALSE**;
15 **end.**

Fig. 11.8. A Simple Forward Reachability Algorithm

- One can observe that the construction of the product automaton is not necessary for the reachability analysis of a network. Every location in a symbolic state would correspond to a location vector in the product, and synchronisation will be solved on demand when successor states are generated.
- It is not difficult to modify this algorithm so as to generate the set of traces that witness the satisfiability of ϕ. These traces correspond to paths in the reachability graph, from the initial symbolic state to the state which was found to satisfy ϕ (for example, a simple implementation would consider storing the current path in a stack for later retrieval). Indeed, trace generation is a standard and necessary feature of model-checkers, as usually this is the main source for debugging. This is particularly important in the verification of safety properties: if a safety property is not satisfied, then "observing" the system execution which leads to the error state is much more useful than just knowing that such an error state is reachable. Uppaal, for example, provides the means to generate and visualise both the shortest trace (in terms of number of symbolic states) and the fastest trace (in terms of accumulated delay).

11.3.1.4 Difference Bound Matrices (DBMs): A Data Structure to Represent Zones

Difference Bound Matrices (DBMs) [71] are efficient data structures to represent conjunctions of clock constraints (and hence, zones). Consequently, symbolic operations such as forward projection, conjunction, reset and normalisation will have their counterparts implemented over DBMs [13,189]. Here we give just a brief introduction to the representation of zones using DBMs.

Let Z be a zone over the set of clocks $C_Z = \{x_1, x_2, \ldots, x_n\}$. Let x_0 be a special clock denoting the constant 0; i.e. $v(x_0) = 0$ for any valuation v. Then, Z can be rewritten using just clock-difference constraints of the form $x_i - x_j \sim k$, where $x_i, x_j \in C_Z \cup \{x_0\}$, $\sim \in \{<, \leq\}$ and $k \in \mathbb{Z}$.

Given, then, a zone Z written as a conjunction of clock-difference constraints over $C_Z \cup \{x_0\}$, a DBM representing Z will be a matrix M of dimension $(n+1) \times (n+1)$, where the M_{ij} element of the matrix stores the bound for the difference $x_i - x_j$ in Z. Formally,

1. M_{ij} is set to $(k, \sim)$, for every constraint $x_i - x_j \sim k$ occurring in Z;
2. M_{ij} is set to ∞, for every clock difference $x_i - x_j$, $i \neq 0$, $i \neq j$, which is not constrained in Z;
3. M_{ii} is set to $(0, \leq)$, denoting that the difference between a clock and itself is zero; and
4. M_{0i} is set to $(0, \leq)$, for every clock difference $x_0 - x_i$ which is not constrained in Z. This denotes that every clock is positive.

For example, the zone

$$Z \text{ defined as } x_1 \geq 5 \wedge x_1 \leq 10 \wedge x_3 > 20 \wedge x_1 - x_2 = 3$$

can be rewritten as

$$
\begin{aligned}
Z' = \; & x_0 - x_1 \leq -5 \; \wedge \\
& x_1 - x_0 \leq 10 \; \wedge \\
& x_0 - x_3 < -20 \wedge \\
& x_1 - x_2 \leq 3 \; \wedge \\
& x_2 - x_1 \leq -3
\end{aligned}
$$

and its corresponding DBM is

$$
\begin{pmatrix}
(0, \leq) & (-5, \leq) & (0, \leq) & (-20, <) \\
(10, \leq) & (0, \leq) & (3, \leq) & \infty \\
\infty & (-3, \leq) & (0, \leq) & \infty \\
\infty & \infty & \infty & (0, \leq)
\end{pmatrix}
$$

11.3.2 Example: Reachability Analysis on the Multimedia Stream

Section 11.2.1.1 described a timed automata specification (Figure 11.2) for the multimedia stream, where the *Channel* was modelled as a pair of automata *Place1* and *Place2*, each one representing an independent one-place buffer synchronising with the *Source* (which puts packets in the buffer via a *sourceOut!* action) and the *Sink* (which receives packets via a *sinkIn?* action).

One important correctness requirement for this specification is that at least one buffer must be empty every time a packet is to be sent, or, equivalently, that there does not exist a reachable state in which the *Source* is attempting to send a packet and both *Place1* and *Place2* are currently transmitting a packet. Notice in Figure 11.2 that this set of reachable states is characterised by both *Place1* and *Place2* being in *State2*, and by $v(t1) = 0$ or $v(t1) = 50$ (i.e. those times at which *sourceOut!* is enabled). Therefore, we can verify the correctness requirement by testing that $reachable(\Pi, \phi)$ does not hold, where Π denotes the product automaton corresponding to the network $|A = |\langle Source, Place1, Place2, Sink\rangle$, and ϕ stands for the following state formula (where $A.l$ denotes that l is a location of A),

$$\phi = ((Source.State0 \wedge t1 = 0) \vee t1 = 50) \wedge Place1.State2 \wedge Place2.State2$$

Figure 11.9 shows a fragment of the forward reachability graph, where we have annotated the edges with the components involved in their generation. The Figure depicts a 5-state path in the graph; every symbolic state being composed of a vector location and a zone. For example, $S0$ corresponds to the initial symbolic state, in which the location vector $\langle 0, 1, 1, 1\rangle$ corresponds to *Source.State0, Place1.State1, Place2.State1* and *Sink.State1*; and the initial zone represents that all clocks are initially set to zero. Moreover, because of the constraint $t1 \leq 0$, time is not allowed to pass. The outgoing edge corresponds to the initial, urgent *sourceOut* between the *Source* and *Place1*, and connects $S0$ with one of its successors, $S1$. Notice that, although it is not shown in the Figure, a similar edge does exist which corresponds to a *sourceOut* between *Source* and *Place2*, because at this point the *Source* may synchronise with either buffer. The zone in $S1$ confirms the intuition that, after performing the first *sourceOut* action, control can remain in *Source.State1* and *Place1.State2* as long as $v(t1) \leq 50$ and $v(t4) \leq 90$. Following a similar reasoning, $S4$ represents all those states which can be reached after the first packet has been played and before the second packet arrives at the *Sink*, provided the first packet was initially put in *Place1*.

11.3.3 Issues in Real-time Model-checking

Canonical zones. In general, a given set of valuations can be described by an infinite number of zones. However, every zone can be converted to a *closed* form (also called a *canonical* form) such that no constraint can be strengthened without reducing the solution set. Working with zones in closed form has the advantage of fast inclusion checking (which, as we have seen, occurs at every step of the reachability algorithm), and thus, operations on zones are implemented on DBMs in such a way that they yield closed zones, or resulting zones are "closed" as a final step [13].

Unfortunately, the algorithm used to obtain zones in closed form usually produces zones with redundant constraints. The work of Larsen et al. [116,117]

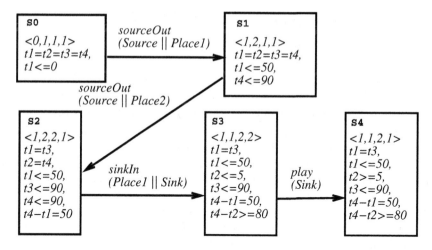

Fig. 11.9. Reachability Graph (Fragment) for the Multimedia Stream

provides a step further towards minimal representation of zones. The authors describe a minimisation algorithm for DBMs, which reduces the space requirements for zones, obtaining a closed representation that is minimal in the number of constraints. This also results in faster zone-related operations, e.g. checking for zone-inclusion, and thus might improve the time requirements of reachability analysis in general. The authors present, as well, a technique which proposes to store, as visited, just a particular subset of all symbolic states generated by the reachability algorithm. It is shown that this particular subset is sufficient to guarantee termination of reachability checking, while reducing the space requirements as fewer states need to be kept as visited. These states are identified based on static information: certain key locations are detected that are entry points for loops in the timed automaton graph. Bengtsson [12] and David et al. [63] describe techniques for efficient storage of symbolic states in Uppaal.

Normalisation. Normalisation can be efficiently implemented if zone constraints are reduced with respect to individual upper bounds (i.e. the greatest upper bound per clock), instead of one single upper bound for all clocks. This is currently done in Uppaal and Kronos (see [13] for a description of the technique). More efficient abstractions have been recently found [11], which take into account both upper and lower bounds for clocks.

Over- and under-approximation. These two abstractions are used to reduce the state-space during verification, at the expense of potentially inconclusive answers. With over-approximation [9, 67], the union of zones, which could be related to the same location is replaced by its convex hull. Because the set of clock valuations satisfying a convex hull can be a proper superset of those satisfying the corresponding union of zones, it cannot be concluded that a given state is reachable. This abstraction can, though, guarantee that a given state is unreachable. Over-approximation has been implemented both in Kronos and Uppaal.

With under-approximation [12, 98, 186, 200], a hash signature is computed for every symbolic state, and only this signature is kept as a record of visited states. With a small probability, a number of symbolic states might have the same hash signature, and so a new symbolic state found during reachability will be assumed to be visited if some other state with the same signature has already been visited. This may yield situations in which some parts of the state-space remain unexplored when the reachability analysis is finished (i.e. those symbolic states which could only be reachable from a state that was wrongly assumed to be visited). Consequently, the results of under-approximation are inconclusive if a state is "found" to be unreachable. Under-approximation is available in Uppaal.

Clock reduction. Daws and Yovine [68] describe a static algorithm which identifies those clocks which are irrelevant during reachability analysis. Informally, a clock is said to be *active* from the point where it is reset up to the point where it is tested (i.e. in a guard or invariant), without being reset on the way. For every location in the timed automaton, then, a set of active clocks can be computed (the technique is compositional, and thus generalises to location vectors for networks of automata). Later, during reachability analysis, zones are generated so as to include just those constraints which refer exclusively to the active clocks related to the corresponding location. This may result, not only in smaller zones, but also in fewer symbolic states (e.g. different symbolic states related through the same location might become indistinguishable when inactive clock constraints are removed from the corresponding zones). Clock reduction has been implemented both in Kronos and Uppaal.

Symmetry reduction. Hendricks et al. [88] describe an extension to Uppaal with symmetry reduction, aiming to limit the state-explosion problem. The user is expected to provide a number of *scalarsets* [100] representing the (full) symmetries of the system. This (and other static information) is used to derive an abstraction that partitions the set of symbolic states (as generated by the forward reachability graph) into a number of equivalence classes: all states in a class are regarded as symmetric upon a notion of state swap. Moreover, the authors show how, for any given symbolic state, a unique representative of the state's equivalence class can be efficiently computed. In this way, the forward reachability graph can be generated just among representative states. Experiments described in [88] confirm that, for systems which present a high degree of symmetry, the gain in space-performance can even approach a factorial magnitude. Symmetry reduction is expected to be a standard feature of forthcoming Uppaal releases.

Beyond reachability checking. Aceto et al. [3] present a temporal logic $L_{\forall S}$ which characterises the set of properties whose verification can be reduced to reachability checking. Given a property in $L_{\forall S}$, a *test automaton* can be derived which contains a distinguished "rejecting" state. The property is considered satisfied if this reject state is not reachable when the system is composed with the test automaton. In this way, for example, some properties can be verified in Uppaal even when they cannot be directly expressed in its specification language (which is a subset of TCTL).

In contrast with the branching-time properties (TCTL) usually considered, Tripakis [189] presents algorithms to model-check linear-time properties, expressed as Timed Büchi Automata (TBA), and ETCTL$_\exists^*$ properties, a logic which is strictly more expressive than both TCTL and TBA. Also, Tripakis shows how existing untimed model-checking techniques and tools (e.g. the CADP toolset [81]) could also be used to verify timed systems. This involves the generation of a *quotient graph*, an untimed automaton, which is (time-abstracting) bisimilar to the original system. This reduction from a timed to an untimed system can also be used to check whether two timed automata are behaviourally equivalent, by checking that their quotients are bisimilar with respect to an untimed bisimulation. Most of these techniques have been included in Kronos.

12

Timelocks in Timed Automata

12.1 Introduction

Informally speaking, a system can "timelock" if a state can be reached where time cannot diverge in any possible run.[1] Timelocks can arise for a number of reasons, and different classes of timelock need to be handled in different ways. In particular, we can distinguish between *time-actionlocks*, which are states where neither time nor action transitions can be performed, and *zeno-timelocks*: states where time is unable to pass beyond a certain point, but actions continue to be performed. In other words, a zeno-timelock can be seen as a situation where an infinite number of actions are performed in a finite period of time.

It is important to realise that timelocks are quite different from action-locks, which are the analogue of deadlocks in untimed specifications. Critically, actionlocks allow time to pass; even when the automaton is unable to perform any further "useful" computation, it does not prevent other component automata from passing time. Timelocks, on the other hand, propagate to the rest of the network; this is a consequence of timed automata implicitly synchronising on the passage of time.[2]

In most cases (if not all), real-time model-checking is meaningful only for specifications that are free from timelocks. For example, consider the network shown in Figure 12.1. Notice that the automaton $A1$ contains a timelock when $v(x) = 1$ (this could have been a consequence, for example, of the designer forgetting to reset x in transition a). Consider the verification of the (TCTL) safety property $AG \neg A2.E$, which expresses the unreachability of a certain error-state in the network (represented by location E in $A2$). Now, this error-state can only be reached after 2 time units have passed; i.e. after transition

---

[1]Notice that this is consistent with the intuition of timelocks in timed process calculi (Section 9.2.2).

[2]The same applies to tLOTOS, because parallel processes synchronise on the passage of time (Section 10.1.2).

b is performed. However, this will never happen, because the timelock in A_1 does not allow time to progress beyond 1 time unit. Then, the safety property will be found satisfiable (because no error-state can ever be reached), giving false confidence in the model's correctness (and so we are left with validation problems). Undetected, this error-state might still be present at some later implementation stage; after all, a system that "stops time" is not physically realisable.

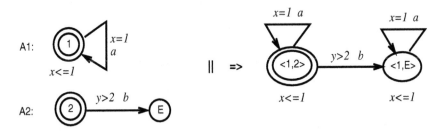

Fig. 12.1. Timelocks and Safety Properties

In this chapter we present a classification of deadlocks in timed automata, and discuss solutions for every class. In particular, we describe timed automata with deadlines [29] which are, by construction, free from time-actionlocks (also known as time reactiveness). In addition, the chapter includes an analytical method to ensure absence of zeno-timelocks (also called nonzenoness), which builds upon the notion of *strong nonzenoness* [190]. This method extends earlier results and broadens the class of timed automata specifications that can be guaranteed to be nonzeno. Also, the more general concept of *inherently safe* automata is introduced. This embodies a number of properties that can be checked at the level of the automaton's syntax (in particular, loops) and guarantee that a zeno-timelock does not occur.

Detecting zeno-timelocks at a syntactic level is usually efficient, and in many cases compositional (i.e. depending on the check, nonzeno components guarantee that the network itself is also nonzeno). Also, syntactic properties are usually general enough to analyse most specifications, as zeno-timelocks seldom occur. However, these properties are sufficient-only, in the sense that they can only guarantee nonzenoness: if the properties are not fulfilled, then a zeno-timelock *may or may not* occur, but neither case can be proved.

For some systems, where a complete confidence in the nonzenoness status must be established, sufficient-only methods are not enough. This motivates a discussion of sufficient-and-necessary conditions for nonzenoness. In particular, a condition is presented that can be reduced to simple reachability analysis. The method works at the level of the product automaton, using first sufficient-only conditions to identify those loops that do not produce zeno-timelocks. A certain kind of reachability formula will then be derived, syntactically, from the remaining loops. The satisfiability of these formulae is both sufficient and necessary to decide whether a zeno-timelock occurs in the automaton.

This chapter is organised as follows. Section 12.2 presents a classification of the different kinds of deadlocks that may occur in timed automata. Later, Section 12.3 elaborates on time-actionlocks, and discusses a solution based on timed automata with deadlines (Section 12.3.1). Section 12.4 describes zeno-timelocks in detail, and presents both sufficient-only and sufficient-and-necessary conditions for nonzenoness. Finally, Section 12.5 gives an overview on the detection of timelocks in Uppaal and Kronos. Let us note that, whenever not defined otherwise, this chapter follows the timed automata notation and definitions given in Chapter 11.

12.2 A Classification of Deadlocks in Timed Automata

In a broad sense, deadlocks are states where the system is unable to progress further. In untimed systems, deadlocks are states where the system is unable to perform any action. However, in timed automata, transitions correspond either to time-progress or the execution of actions. Consequently, in this setting, the ways of violating the requirements of progress can vary.

Generally speaking, an *actionlock* is a state where, for however long time is allowed to pass, no action transition can be performed. Formally, given $A = (L, TL, T, l_0, C, I) \in TA$ with TTS (S, Lab, T_S, s_0), a state $s \in S$ is an actionlock if

$$\forall d \in \mathbb{R}^{+0}, \ s + d \in S \ \Rightarrow \ \nexists a \in Act . s + d \xrightarrow{a}$$

where, if $s = [l, v]$, then $s + d = [l, v + d]$. On the other hand, a *timelock* is a state $s \in S$ where time is not able to progress beyond a certain limit. Equivalently, s is a timelock if every run starting from s, $\rho(s)$, converges:

$$\forall \rho(s) \in Runs(A), \ delay(\rho) \neq \infty$$

A timed automaton A is actionlock-free (timelock-free) if none of its reachable states is an actionlock (timelock). Actionlocks and timelocks can be further classified as *pure-actionlocks*, *time-actionlocks* or *zeno-timelocks* (also called pure timelocks), which are explained next.

Pure-actionlock. A pure-actionlock is a state where the system cannot perform any action transitions, but time is allowed to progress. Figure 12.2(i)[3] shows an example of a timed automaton with a pure actionlock: no action is enabled once the automaton reaches location 2, however, time is not prevented from passing. Formally, a state s is a pure-actionlock if

---

[3]Omitted guards and invariants are assumed to be *true*.

$$\forall d \in \mathbb{R}^{+0}, s + d \in S \wedge \nexists a \in Act . s + d \xrightarrow{a} \!\!\!\!\!\!\not\rightarrow$$

Time-actionlock. Time-actionlocks are states where neither action nor time transitions can be performed. For example, Figure 12.2(ii) shows a time-actionlock produced by a mismatched synchronisation between two automata. Transition $a!$ in the upper automaton is urgent when $v(x) = 5$, but it cannot synchronise with $a?$ in the lower automaton, because this transition is not enabled at that time. Consequently, the system enters a time-actionlock state at $v(x) = 5$. Formally, $s \in S$ is a time-actionlock if,

$$\nexists a \in Act, d \in \mathbb{R}^+ . s \xrightarrow{a} \!\!\!\!\!\!\not\rightarrow \vee s \xrightarrow{d} \!\!\!\!\!\!\not\rightarrow$$

Zeno-timelock. In such a state, systems can still perform transitions (which can be either action or time transitions), but time cannot pass beyond a certain point. This represents a situation where the system performs an infinite number of actions in a finite period of time. For example, any reachable state in the automaton shown in Figure 12.2(iii) is a zeno-timelock, because time can only pass up to 5 time units and transition a is always enabled. Hence, a becomes urgent at $v(x) = 5$ and will be performed infinitely often, without time-passing at all. Formally, $s \in S$ is a zeno-timelock if there exists at least one infinite run starting from s, and all such runs are zeno; i.e.

$$\exists \rho(s) \in ZRuns(A) \wedge \forall \rho(s) \in Runs(A), \rho(s) \in ZRuns(A)$$

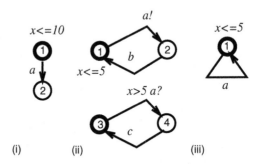

Fig. 12.2. (i) Pure-actionlock (ii) Time-actionlock (iii) Zeno-timelock

12.2.1 Discussion: Justifying the Classification of Deadlocks

One reason for presenting this classification is that we believe that different types of deadlocks bring different types of problems and, hence, should be treated differently. Firstly, although pure actionlocks may be undesirable within the context of a particular specification, they are not of themselves counterintuitive situations. It is wholly reasonable that a component or a system might reach a state from which it cannot perform any actions, as long as such an actionlock does not stop time. Thus, although analytical tools that detect pure-actionlocks certainly have value, we do not believe there is any fundamental reason why actionlocks should be prevented (by construction) at the level of the specification notation.

In contrast, we are strongly of the opinion that time-actionlocks are counterintuitive. In particular, and as previously discussed, a local "error" in one component has a global effect on the entire system, even if other components have no actions in common with the timelocked component. Because of these particularly counterintuitive aspects, we believe that time-actionlocks should be prevented *by construction*; i.e. the timed automata model should be reinterpreted in such a way that time-actionlocks just cannot arise.

Finally, to come to zeno-timelocks: our position here is that analytical methods should be provided to check on a specification-by-specification basis whether zeno-timelocks occur. Our reasons for advocating this approach are largely pragmatic, because it is not clear how the timed automata model could be changed in order to constructively prevent such situations. In particular, any mechanism that ensured at the level of the semantics that a minimum time (say ϵ) was passed on every cycle, would impose rigid constraints on the specifier's ability to describe systems abstractly. Sections 12.4.2 and 12.4.3 consider just such an analytical method for detecting zeno-timelocks.

12.2.2 Discussion: Timelocks in Process Calculi

It is interesting to mention that in the early work on timed concurrency theory, which largely focused on timed process calculi (see Chapter 9), the problem of timelocks was noted and partially resolved. As a result most timed process calculi only allow urgency to be applied to internal actions, and so timelocks due to synchronisation mismatches cannot happen. Indeed, they often enforce the so-called *as soon as possible* (asap) principle [168] that we have mentioned in Section 9.2.2; in such an interpretation, internal actions are considered implicitly urgent and will be performed as soon as they are enabled.

In timed process calculi with asap, a hiding operator can be used to make synchronisation urgent without causing a time-actionlock (see Sections 9.2.10 and 9.4). The hiding operator turns observable into internal actions, which are, as we just mentioned, urgent as soon as they are enabled. Because observable actions correspond to *successful* synchronisation between half actions, synchronisation is only made urgent if it is possible. This rules out most time-actionlocks in timed process calculi with asap (as we have discussed in Section 9.4, unguarded recursion can though also generate time-actionlocks).

Unlike timed process calculi, timed automata do not incorporate a hiding operator, and so it is not possible to selectively take an observable action that results from synchronising half actions and turn it into an (urgent) completed action. Instead, urgency can only be specified individually for half actions, regardless of whether synchronisation is possible.

12.3 Time-actionlocks

As previously discussed, perhaps the most counterintuitive aspect of the time-lock story is the manner in which timelocks can arise from mismatched synchronisations (e.g. Figure 12.2(ii)). If we consider how this problem arises, we can see that it is caused by the particular interpretation of urgent interaction employed in timed automata.

It is undoubtedly true that facilities to express urgency are required; otherwise certain important forms of timing behaviour could not be expressed (e.g. timeouts; see Section 9.2.2). However, it is our perspective that although urgency is needed, currently it is given an excessively strong formulation. We illustrate this issue with a modified specification for the multimedia stream example.

Consider the model shown in Figure 12.3, where now packets can be sent to the *Sink* by two different sources, *Source1* and *Source2*. The behaviour of the new added *Source2* is similar to that of *Source1*, although (a) it can send the first packet at any time (notice that there is no invariant attached to *Source2.State0*) and (b) following packets are sent faster than in *Source1* (1 packet every 25 ms). This, however, will produce a time-actionlock in the network.

Consider the following scenario. *Source1* sends its first packet to *Place1*, at time $t = 0$. Later, say at $t = 10$, *Source2* sends its first packet to *Place2*. By the time that *Source2* attempts to send the second packet ($t = 35$), neither *Place1* nor *Place2* can offer a matching *sourceOut?*, as the transmission of the previous packets is not yet finished (the transmission delay is at least 80 ms). At this point, a time-actionlock occurs: because *sourceOut!* in *Source2* is urgent at $t = 35$, time is prevented from passing and no action is enabled.

The time-actionlock occurs because *Source2* makes the *sourceOut!* action urgent *even when it is not enabled*, as both *Place1* and *Place2* are currently transmitting packets and synchronisation cannot be achieved. Moreover, the time-actionlock propagates to all other components because time is prevented from passing. We would argue, then, that it should only be possible to make an action urgent if it is enabled, i.e.

> *must requires may or, in other terms, you can only force what is possible.*

Such an interpretation of urgency arises in *Timed Automata with Deadlines* (TADs) [29, 30], which are discussed in the next section. In particular, certain time constraints (so-called deadlines) are attached to actions denoting those time intervals where the action is considered urgent. Because every deadline implies the action's guard, only enabled actions can be urgently performed,

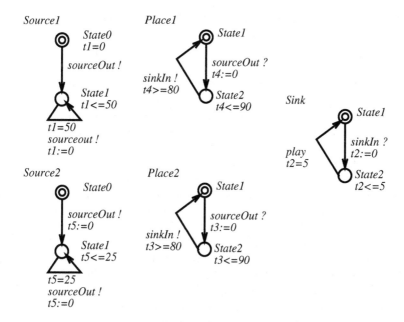

Fig. 12.3. A Multimedia Stream with Two Sources and a Time-actionlock

and therefore time-actionlocks are ruled out by construction (although zeno-timelocks, on the other hand, can still occur). Timed automata with deadlines, then, guarantee time reactiveness (i.e. the absence of time-actionlocks) by construction.

12.3.1 Timed Automata with Deadlines

Informally speaking, timed automata with deadlines [29, 30, 34, 35] can be described as timed automata where the time progress condition is expressed by *deadlines*, instead of invariants. Importantly, TADs are time reactive; i.e. time-actionlocks cannot occur. Different variants of TADs have been proposed, which differ in the treatment of parallel composition (although all of them preserve time reactiveness), e.g. standard TADs, sparse TADs and TADs with minimal priority escape transitions [34]. Our presentation of TADs in this section follows the model of *Sparse-TADs*, developed by Bowman in [34, 35].

Deadlines are clock constraints attached to transitions (in contrast with invariants, which are attached to locations), which determine when the transition is considered urgent. However, in TADs, time cannot be prevented from passing by an "urgent" transition not being enabled. This is an important difference between invariants and deadlines: unlike in TAs, urgency in TADs does not cause time-actionlocks. Let us illustrate this issue with the following example.

Figure 12.4(i) shows a network of two TADs[4], and the corresponding product automaton to the right. Assuming all clocks are initially set to zero, transition $b!$ is enabled in the time interval $[1, \infty)$, and is urgent in $[2, \infty)$: the deadline $(x \geq 2)$ expresses that, during $[2, \infty)$, synchronisation must happen *as soon as possible*. In the second automaton, $b?$ is enabled during $[3, \infty)$, and is urgent in $[4, \infty)$. But then, what happens when $v(x) = v(y) = 2$? Clearly, at this point in execution, transition $b!$ is enabled and enters its urgency period, but $b?$ is not yet enabled, and so synchronisation cannot occur! Deadlines on half actions enforce urgency only if synchronisation can be achieved. Equivalently, synchronisation is urgent as soon as: (a) one of the parties is urgent, and (b) both parties can synchronise (i.e. when both half actions are enabled).[5] As a result, $b!$ "waits" for $b?$ to become enabled, and so synchronisation is immediately performed when $v(x) = v(y) = 3$. It is important to note that time passes until synchronisation is possible, and so synchronisation mismatches cannot cause time-actionlocks. This behaviour is evident from the structure of the product automaton: the guard on b results from conjoining the component guards, and the deadline assigned to b is defined as the disjunction of the component deadlines, conjoined with the component guards. In this way, the deadline on b implies its guard. Furthermore, by construction, *every* deadline in a TAD specification implies the corresponding guard: this is true for half actions, completed actions in components and completed actions which result from synchronisation. It is not difficult to see, then, that time-actionlocks cannot occur in TAD specifications.

The TA specification in (ii), on the other hand, shows that invariants enforce a stronger form of urgency than deadlines. Notice that the network of TAs shown in (ii) "intends" to mimic the network of TADs in (i); for example, the invariant $x \leq 2$ (in location 1), makes $b!$ urgent at $v(x) = v(y) = 2$. However, unlike the network of TADs, the network of TAs enters a time-actionlock at $v(x) = v(y) = 2$: synchronisation cannot yet occur, but the invariant in location 1, $x \leq 2$, prevents time from passing any further. Even though, in this example, half actions are not urgent until they are enabled (e.g. $b!$ becomes enabled at $v(x) = 1$, and is not urgent until $v(x) = 2$), invariants will enforce this "local" urgency regardless of whether synchronisation is possible. This can be seen in the product automaton: the invariant in $\langle 1, 3 \rangle$ prevents time from passing beyond $v(x) = v(y) = 2$, even though b is not yet enabled.

12.3.1.1 Formal Definitions: Timed Automata with Deadlines

Here we just highlight the basic elements of the theory, and refer the reader to [29, 30, 34, 35] for a more comprehensive presentation. Unless stated oth-

---

[4]In our TAD figures, deadlines are shown in brackets; "," denotes conjunction; and "|" denotes disjunction.

[5]Notice that tLOTOS adopts a similar approach: internal actions (in particular, those which result from synchronisation) are urgent on their upper bounds (Section 9.2.10).

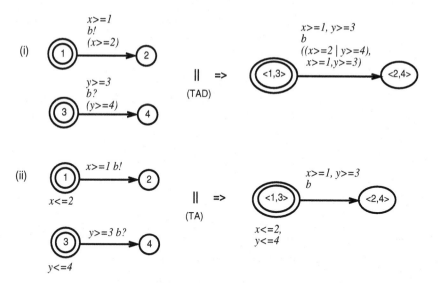

Fig. 12.4. Parallel Composition in TADs and TAs

erwise, the notation used here respects the sets and conventions defined for timed automata in Section 11.2.

Syntax. A timed automaton with deadlines (or simply, TAD) is a tuple of the form $A = (L, TL, T, l_0, C)$, where L is a finite set of locations ($l_0 \in L$ is the initial location); $TL \in Act$ is a set of labels; T is a transition relation and C is a set of clocks. Transitions in T are denoted $l \xrightarrow{a,g,d,r} l'$, where $l, l' \in L$ are automata locations; $a \in TL$ is the action labelling the transition; $g \in CC_C$ is a guard; $d \in CC_C$ is a deadline; and $r \in \mathcal{P}(C)$ is a reset set. In addition, deadlines and guards satisfy the following conditions.

1. Deadlines imply guards,

$$(C1) \quad l \xrightarrow{a,g,d,r} l' \implies (d \Rightarrow g)$$

2. If both a deadline and its corresponding guard denote the same solution set, then this set must denote a left-closed time interval,

$$(C2) \quad l \xrightarrow{a,g,d,r} l' \implies ((d = g) \Rightarrow \exists v . (v \models g) \wedge \forall v' , (v' \models g) \Rightarrow v' \geq v)$$

Let us illustrate the necessity for condition (C2) with the following example. Assume a transition with guard $g = x > 1$ and deadline $d = x > 1$, where $x \in C$. Notice that both g and d denote the same solution set, which corresponds to the left-open interval $v(x) \in (1, \infty)$. This transition will be urgent as soon as it is enabled, but the constraint imposed by the d does not allow time to progress beyond $v(x) = 1$ (to see why, check the semantic rule S2 below). It should not be difficult to see, then, that TADs that do not fulfill (C2) are not guaranteed to be time reactive, even if deadlines imply guards (C1).

Semantics. Let $A = (L, TL, T, l_0, C, I)$ be a TAD where all actions are completed (i.e. $TL \subseteq CAct$). The semantics of A are given by the TTS (S, Lab, T_S, s_0), where

- $S \subseteq L \times \mathbb{V}_C$ is the set of reachable states; i.e.

$$S = \{ s_0 \} \cup \{ s' \mid \exists s \in S, \gamma \in Lab \,.\, s \xrightarrow{\gamma} s' \}$$

- $s_0 = [l_0, v_0]$ is the starting state;
- $Lab = TL \cup \mathbb{R}^+$ is the set of transition labels;
- $T_S \subseteq S \times Lab \times S$ is the transition relation, defined by the following inference rules,

$$\text{(S1)} \quad \frac{l \xrightarrow{a,g,d,r} l' \quad v \models g}{[l, v] \xrightarrow{a} [l', r(v)]}$$

$$\text{(S2)} \quad \frac{\forall l', l \xrightarrow{a,g,d,r} l' \;\Rightarrow\; \forall t' < t \in \mathbb{R}^+, v + t' \not\models d}{[l, v] \xrightarrow{t} [l, v + t]}$$

At the beginning of this section, we elaborated on the relation between deadlines and invariants; let us carry on with this comparison a bit further. Urgency, as expressed by deadlines in TADs, has more in common with a weak interpretation of invariants in TAs (Section 11.2.2), than it does with the strong interpretation. For example, the TAD shown in Figure 12.5(i) can perform transition a at any time (*false*-deadlines model non urgent actions), but it will take b immediately after that. This behaviour corresponds to the timed automaton with weak invariants in (ii). Notice that, if the same automaton would be given a strong invariant interpretation, no transition (not even a) can ever be performed, as locations with *false*-invariants cannot be entered. On the other hand, the timed automaton with strong invariants shown in (iii) achieves the same behaviour as the TAD in (i), at the expense of adding a clock x, which is reset in a, and attaching the invariant $x = 0$ to location 2. In any case, as we have discussed before (and illustrated by Figure 12.4), the semantics of networks of TADs cannot always be expressed by networks of TAs.

Parallel Composition (Sparse TADs). Let $|A = \langle A_1, ..., A_n \rangle$ be a network of TADs, where

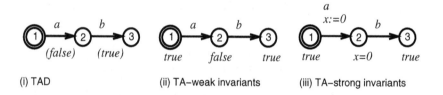

(i) TAD   (ii) TA–weak invariants   (iii) TA–strong invariants

Fig. 12.5. Deadlines, Weak Invariants and Strong Invariants

$$A_i = (L_i,\, TL_i, T_i, l_{i,0}, C_i)$$

for $1 \le i \le n$. Let u, u', etc. denote location vectors. Once again, here we follow the substitution notation introduced in Section 8.2.2.2. The product automaton is defined as

$$\Pi = (L,\, TL, T, l_0, C)$$

where

- $L = \{\, l_0 \,\} \,\cup\, \{\, u' \mid \exists u \in L, a, g, d, r \,.\, u \xrightarrow{a,g,d,r} u' \,\}$;

- $TL = \bigcup_{i=1}^{n} TL_i$;

- T is as defined by the following rules $(1 \le i \ne j \le n)$,

$$(\text{TAD1}) \quad \frac{u_i \xrightarrow{a?,g_i,d_i,r_i}_i l \quad u_j \xrightarrow{a!,g_j,d_j,r_j}_j l'}{u \xrightarrow{a,g',d',r_i \cup r_j} u[l \to i, l' \to j]}$$

$$(\text{TAD2}) \quad \frac{u_i \xrightarrow{a,g,d,r}_i l \quad a \in CAct}{u \xrightarrow{a,g,d,r} u[l \to i]}$$

  where $g' \triangleq g_i \wedge g_j$ and $d' \triangleq g_i \wedge g_j \wedge (d_i \vee d_j)$;

- $l_0 = \langle l_{1,0}, \dots, l_{n,0} \rangle$; and

- $C = \bigcup_{i=1}^{n} C_i$

Rule (TAD1) defines synchronisation in TADs. As in TAs, guards and reset sets of component transitions (matching half actions) are combined in the resulting transition in the product automaton (completed action). Two things must be noticed in the definition of the resulting deadline. First, the disjunction of component deadlines ensures that synchronisation is made urgent if at least one of the involved half actions is urgent. Second, and as it is necessary to ensure time-reactiveness, conjoining the component guards ensures that deadlines in the product automaton's transitions imply their guards. In other words, synchronisation is urgent only if it can be performed. Finally, rule (TAD2) gives the standard interpretation for completed actions in component TADs.

12.3.2 Example: A TAD Specification for the Multimedia Stream

Figure 12.6 shows a TAD specification for the multimedia stream, corresponding to the example discussed in Section 12.3. Transitions have been annotated
with the necessary deadlines (shown in brackets): for example, *sourceOut?*
in *Source1.State1* is made urgent as soon as it is enabled (with a deadline
$t1 = 50$). Let us revisit the scenario which caused a time-actionlock in the TA
specification (see again Figure 12.3). *Source1* sends at $t = 0$; *Source2* sends
at $t = 10$ and attempts to send the second packet at $t = 35$. At this point,
Source2 blocks because synchronisation with *sourceOut?* in either *Place1* or
Place2 is not possible. However, unlike in the TA specification, time is not
prevented from passing and all the other components can evolve normally.
This is so because deadlines attached to half actions are only enforced if synchronisation can be achieved (rule TAD1).

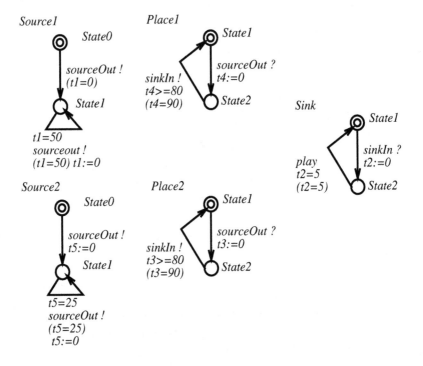

Fig. 12.6. A TAD Specification for the Multimedia Stream (with Two Sources)

12.4 Zeno-timelocks

This section elaborates on a number of methods to detect nonzenoness [44, 190]. Before discussing these approaches in detail, let us introduce some basic concepts and notation which appear throughout the section.

Preliminaries. Let $A \in TA$. A simple loop is a cycle in the timed automaton graph; i.e. a sequence of locations and transitions of the form,

$$l_0 \xrightarrow{a_1, g_1, r_1} l_1 \xrightarrow{a_2, g_2, r_2} \ldots \xrightarrow{a_n, g_n, r_n} l_n$$

where $l_0 = l_n$ such that $l_i \neq l_j$ for all $0 \leq i \neq j < n$. A nonsimple loop is, correspondingly, a sequence of locations and transitions that starts and ends in the same location, and also contains other repeating locations.

Unless otherwise stated, when we talk about loops we are referring to simple loops. Usually, we refer to loops (both simple and nonsimple) through their component transitions. For example, Figure 12.7 shows two simple loops, $\langle ab \rangle^6$ and $\langle cd \rangle$, and one nonsimple loop, $\langle acdb \rangle$. The entry point (a location through which the loop is reachable) in these loops is location 1, where x is previously set to 0.

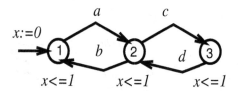

Fig. 12.7. Simple and Non Simple Loops

Let $Loops(A)$ be the set of all loops in A, and lp a given loop in A. $Loc(lp)$ is the set of all locations of lp; $Clocks(lp)$ is the set of all clocks occurring in any invariant of lp; $Trans(lp)$, $Guards(lp)$ and $Resets(lp)$ are, respectively, the sets of all transitions of lp, all guards of lp, and all clocks that are reset in lp; and $Act(lp)$ is the set of all actions labelling transitions in lp. A *half loop* is a loop that contains at least one transition labelled with a half action. A *completed loop* is a loop which is not a half loop, i.e. a loop where all transitions are labelled with completed actions.

12.4.1 Example: Zeno-timelocks in the Multimedia Stream

Figure 12.8 shows a multimedia stream similar to the one described in Section 12.3 (Figure 12.3), but where a new component *Source3* has been added.

---

[6] The notation for loops must not be confused with that we have used for location vectors, e.g. $\langle 1, 3 \rangle$.

This automaton models an unreliable source, which will attempt to send packets at a speed of 1 packet per 100 ms but, occasionally, a *failure* may occur, which forces the source to enter an *Offline* state. *Source3* will remain in *Offline* for an unspecified period of time, and then it will restart the sequence again.

Consider, once more, the scenario which in Figure 12.3 caused a time-actionlock: *Source1* sends at $t = 0$ to *Place1*; *Source2* sends at $t = 10$ to *Place2* and attempts to send again at $t = 35$, but is blocked because synchronisation with *sourceOut?* in either *Place1* or *Place2* is not possible. At this point, $v(t5) = 25$, and so the invariant $t5 \leq 25$ in *Source2.State1* prevents time from passing any further. However, and unlike in the specification of Figure 12.3, a time-actionlock does not occur because transition *failure* at *Source3.State0* is enabled. Moreover, notice that all infinite runs starting at *Source3.State0* converge, because the loop ⟨*failure, reset*⟩ can be visited infinitely often while time is blocked by *Source2*. A zeno-timelock occurs, then, at a state $s = [l, v]$ where l is a location vector denoting *Source1.State1, Source2.State1, Source3.State0, Place1.State2, Place2.State2* and *Sink.State1*, and v is s.t. $v(t) = 25$ for $t \in \{t3, t5\}$ and $v(t) = 35$ for $t \in \{t1, t2, t4, t6\}$.

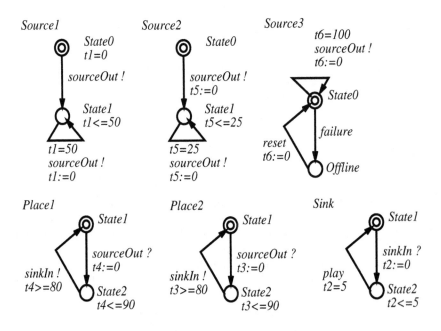

Fig. 12.8. A Multimedia Stream with Three Sources and a Zeno-timelock

12.4.2 Nonzenoness: Syntactic Conditions

Tripakis [190] showed that the absence of zeno-timelocks (nonzenoness) in a timed automaton can be determined from the syntactic structure of its loops. By definition, a zeno-timelock occurs when some state can be reached in the automaton where actions are performed infinitely often, in a finite period of time. Now, actions can only be performed infinitely often if they are part of some loop. Thus, in order to ensure that no zeno-timelock can ever occur, it is sufficient to check that any loop allows time to diverge, if visited infinitely often.

Following this argument, the *Strong NonZenoness* (SNZ) property is a condition on the guards and resets of a loop, which, if satisfied, guarantees that in every iteration of the loop time passes at least by d time units ($d \in \mathbb{N}$, $d > 0$). Hence, every run that visits a SNZ-loop infinitely often is guaranteed to be divergent (notice that, by definition, such an infinite run contains infinitely many actions). Clearly, if all loops in a given automaton are SNZ, then all infinite runs with infinitely many actions are divergent, and so no zeno-timelock can occur in the automaton. Moreover, strong nonzenoness is a compositional property: if every automaton in a network is SNZ (i.e. all its loops are SNZ), then so is the network itself (and it is thus free from zeno-timelocks). Some necessary definitions, and the strong nonzenoness property itself, are presented below.

Bounded from Below. Given a clock constraint $\phi \in CC_C$, a clock $x \in C$ is said to be *bounded from below* in ϕ, if ϕ contains a term $x \sim c$, or a term $x - y \sim c$, where $y \in C$, $c \in \mathbb{N}$, $c > 0$ and $\sim \in \{=, >, \geq\}$.

Bounded from Above. Given a clock constraint $\phi \in CC_C$, a clock $x \in C$ is said to be *bounded from above* in ϕ, if either:

1. ϕ contains a term $x \sim c$, where $c \in \mathbb{N}$, $c > 0$ and $\sim \in \{=, <, \leq\}$;
2. ϕ contains a term $x - y \sim c$, where $y \in C$, $c \in \mathbb{N}$, $c > 0$, $\sim \in \{=, <, \leq\}$ and y is bounded from above in ϕ; or
3. ϕ contains a term $y - x \sim c$, where $y \in C$, $c \in \mathbb{N}$, $c > 0$, $\sim \in \{=, >, \geq\}$ and y is bounded from above in ϕ.

Strong Nonzenoness (SNZ). A loop lp in $A \in TA$ is called *Strongly NonZeno* (or an SNZ-loop) if there exists a clock which is both reset in the loop, and bounded from below in some guard in the loop. If every loop in A is SNZ, then A is said to be SNZ.

Figure 12.9 shows an example of a strongly nonzeno loop: the clock x is bounded from below in a (with guard: $x > 1$), and is reset in b. It is not difficult to see that at least 1 time unit must pass between any two consecutive iterations of the loop. This means that runs which visit the loop infinitely often accumulate at least a 1 time unit delay in every iteration, and so they diverge.

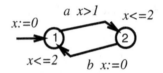

Fig. 12.9. A Strongly Nonzeno Loop

Lemma 12.1 (which was proved in [190]) formalises the relationship between SNZ-loops and nonzenoness, and the compositionality of SNZ. This lemma suggests a static verification method in which a network can be guaranteed to be nonzeno if every loop is found to be SNZ.

Lemma 12.1. *If $A \in TA$ is strongly nonzeno then A does not contain zeno-timelocks. Moreover, if $A_1, \ldots, A_n \in TA$ are strongly nonzeno then $|A = |\langle A_1, \ldots, A_n \rangle$ is also strongly nonzeno.*

It so happens that Lemma 12.1 can be weakened, in the sense that not every loop in a network must necessarily be SNZ to guarantee that the network itself is nonzeno. Indeed, every loop in the product automaton results either from a completed loop in the component automata, or from the synchronisation of two matching half loops. If every completed loop in the network is SNZ, then every loop in the product resulting from these is also SNZ: by construction, guards and resets in completed loops are preserved in the product (see Section 11.2.2). Similarly, if at least one of two matching half loops in the network is SNZ, then every loop in the product resulting from these is also SNZ. Once again, by construction, if a clock x is bounded from below and reset in a half loop, then x will also be bounded from below and reset in every loop in the product that is derived from this half loop. For example, Figure 12.10 shows the composition between a SNZ loop and a non-SNZ loop, which results in two SNZ loops in the product automaton. Both loops, $\langle abc \rangle$ and $\langle acb \rangle$ are SNZ because x is bounded from below in a and reset in b.

We conclude that synchronisation between a SNZ loop and any other loop (even a non-SNZ loop) must be considered safe. This is in contrast with Lemma 12.1; in particular, the conditions imposed by this lemma cannot guarantee that the network of Figure 12.10 is nonzeno. The following method (and the corresponding Lemma 12.2 below, which is proved in [44]) refines the compositional results of Lemma 12.1, so a more comprehensive class of nonzeno systems can be analysed positively. Nonzenoness can be verified, then, as follows.

1. Pair all complementary half loops in the network, i.e. those loops which may synchronise on some transition;

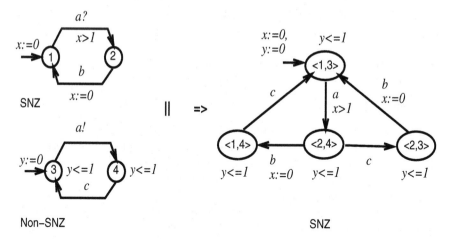

Fig. 12.10. Composition Preserves Strong Nonzenoness

2. If at least one loop in every resulting pair is SNZ, and every completed loop in the network is SNZ[7], then the network itself is nonzeno.

Lemma 12.2. *Let* $|A = |\langle A_1, \ldots, A_n \rangle$ *be a network of TAs. Let* $HL(|A)$ *be the set of matching half loops, and* $CL(|A)$ *the set of completed loops in the network, where*

$$HL(|A) = \{ (lp, lp') \mid \exists i, j \, (1 \le i \ne j \le n) . lp \in Loops(A_i) \wedge lp' \in Loops(A_j)$$
$$\wedge \exists a? \in Act(lp). a! \in Act(lp') \}$$

$$CL(|A) = \{ lp \mid \exists i \, (1 \le i \le n) . lp \in Loops(A_i) \wedge \forall a \in Act(lp), a \in CAct \}$$

If at least one loop in every pair in $HL(|A)$ *is strongly nonzeno and every loop in* $CL(|A)$ *is strongly nonzeno, then the product automaton obtained from* $|A$ *is strongly nonzeno. Equivalently,* $|A$ *is nonzeno.*

In general, there exist a number of ways in which a loop can be syntactically guaranteed not to produce a zeno-timelock. We discuss, in what follows, a number of nonzenoness conditions that work very much in the same way as strong nonzenoness: if fulfilled, they guarantee that in every iteration of the loop time passes at least by d time units ($d \in \mathbb{N}$, $d > 0$) and so, time will necessarily diverge if the loop is visited infinitely often.

Because these conditions are defined in terms of invariants and not transitions, they characterise some kinds of safe loops that are not SNZ, and thus they can be used to complement the analysis of a broader class of TA specifications. Before presenting these syntactic conditions, let us define the

---

[7]Non-SNZ completed loops in components are inherited by the product. Therefore, if this is the case, the network cannot be considered nonzeno.

general concept of *inherently safe* loops, and the related (and straightforward) Lemma 12.3.

Inherently Safe Loops. We say that a loop is *inherently safe* if it can be guaranteed, by syntactic means, not to contain a zeno-timelock.

Lemma 12.3. *If every loop in $A \in TA$ is inherently safe, then A is nonzeno.*

A number of nonzenoness conditions (including strong nonzenoness) are presented below in Lemma 12.4 (proofs can be found in [44]) to characterise loops that are inherently safe (the definition of *smallest upper bound*, which comes before, is necessary to formulate one of the syntactic conditions enumerated in the lemma). It is important to realise that this list of syntactic conditions is, by no means, comprehensive: other interactions between guards, resets and invariants can possibly be found to guarantee nonzenoness.

Smallest Upper Bound. Let lp be a loop in $A \in TA$, and $x \in Clocks(lp)$ where at least one invariant in the loop contains a term of the form $x \sim c$, where $c \in \mathbb{N}$, $c > 0$ and $\sim \in \{=, <, \leq\}$. We define $c_{\min}(x, lp) \in \mathbb{N}$ to be the smallest upper bound for x occurring in any invariant in lp, i.e. $c_{\min}(x, lp) \leq c'$, for any term $x \sim c'$ occurring in any invariant of the loop ($c \in \mathbb{N}$, $c > 0$ and $\sim \in \{=, <, \leq\}$).

Lemma 12.4. *Let lp be a loop in $A \in TA$, where lp satisfies at least one of the following conditions.*

1. *lp is strongly nonzeno.*
2. *There exists at least one invariant in lp where no clock is bounded from above.*
3. *There exists a clock $x \in Resets(lp)$ s.t. x is bounded from below in some invariant in lp.*
4. *There exists at least one invariant in lp of the form*

$$\bigwedge_{i=1}^{n} x_i \leq c_i,$$

   where, for all $1 \leq i \leq n$, either (a) $c_i > c_{\min}(x_i, lp)$, or (b) $x_i \in Resets(lp)$ and $c_i > 0$.

Then, lp is inherently safe.

Figure 12.11 helps to understand the last three conditions enumerated in Lemma 12.4. Figure 12.11(i) shows a loop which satisfies condition (2): notice that location 2 has a *true*-invariant, and so it does not impose upper bounds on any clock occurring in the loop. This guarantees the existence of divergent runs in the loop (which just idle in location 2).

   The loop shown in (ii) satisfies condition (3): x is reset in transition b and bounded from below in location 2 ($1 < x \leq 2$). Then, a delay of at least 1 time unit is guaranteed between consecutive iterations of the loop.

Figures 12.11(iii) to (vi) illustrate condition (4), which involves the smallest upper bound of the loop. Notice in (iii), that location 1 always allows time to pass by 1 time unit, because x is reset in b and it is the only clock occurring in that location. Correspondingly, the loop satisfies condition (4) in the lemma. On the other hand, we cannot guarantee that the loop shown in (iv) allows time to pass in every iteration: the clock y is not reset in the loop, it occurs in every invariant and all invariants impose the same smallest upper bound on y ($c_{\min}(y, lp) = 1$) (thus, condition (4) is not satisfied). In particular, notice that the state $s = [1, v]$ is a zeno-timelock, where $v(y) = 1$ and $v(x) = v(z) = 0$.

The loop in Figure 12.11(v) is also guaranteed to be inherently safe: all conjuncts in the invariant of location 2 refer to constants that are greater than the smallest upper bound for every clock. Notice that the difference between the upper bounds in locations 1 and 2 confirms that time is allowed to pass by at least 1 time unit in location 2 (if so, we will end up with a time-actionlock, but no zeno-timelock can be contained in this loop). Finally, the loop in (vi) shows a slightly different arrangement of upper bounds, but cannot be guaranteed to be inherently safe. Notice that there does not exist an invariant where every clock is either greater than its smallest upper bound, or reset in the loop. In fact, the loop contains a zeno-timelock $s = [1, v]$, $v(x) = v(y) = 1$.

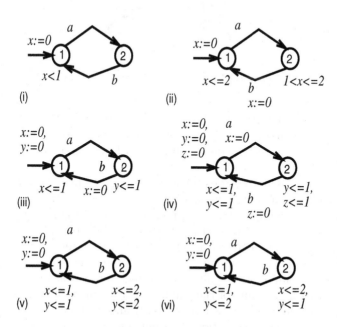

Fig. 12.11. Syntactic Conditions

Syntactic Conditions Are Sufficient-only. The syntactic conditions enumerated in Lemma 12.4 are sufficient-only in the following sense: if they are satisfied by every loop in a given $A \in TA$, then every such loop is inherently safe and so Lemma 12.3 guarantees that A is nonzeno. However, nothing about A can be said if some of its loops are not inherently safe. This is to say, some nonzeno automata do exist where some (or all) of its loops do not satisfy any of the conditions enumerated in Lemma 12.4.

For example, the loop $\langle a \rangle$ in Figure 12.12 does not satisfy any of the four conditions stated in Lemma 12.4, and therefore it cannot be considered inherently safe. Nonetheless, the automaton is nonzeno! The key point here is that, even when zeno runs do exist in the automaton (e.g. the run starting in location 1, which remains there, performing an infinite number of a-transitions in 1 time unit), there is no state in the system that prevents the existence of divergent runs. Notice that b is always enabled in location 1, and time is always allowed to diverge in location 2. This is strongly related to the notion of *escape transitions*, which is exploited in Section 12.4.3 to define a sufficient-and-necessary condition for nonzenoness.

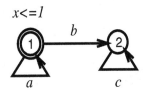

Fig. 12.12. Lemma 12.4 Is Sufficient-only

On the Compositionality of Syntactic Conditions. It is interesting to consider some results regarding the compositionality of the conditions stated by Lemma 12.4. As we have discussed previously, strong nonzenoness is compositional.

Condition (2) is not compositional because new upper bounds can occur as the result of conjoining invariants during the construction of the product automaton. For example, both component loops in Figure 12.13(i) satisfy condition (2), because there exists at least one location in every loop with a *true*-invariant (i.e. there exists at least one invariant where no clock is bounded from above). Consequently, both component loops are inherently safe. However, composition results in a product automaton with a single loop, which does not satisfy any of the conditions in Lemma 12.4. In fact, a zeno-timelock occurs at $s = [l, v]$, where $l = \langle 1, 3 \rangle$ and $v(x) = v(y) = 1$.

For the same reason, condition (4) is not compositional either. Once again, the component loops in Figure 12.13(ii) can be considered inherently safe, as they satisfy condition (4) in Lemma 12.4. Notice that, in every component loop, there exists at least one invariant where all the clocks are bounded from above by a constant bigger than the corresponding smallest upper bound. However, composition yields a loop which contains the zeno-timelock $s = [l, v]$, where $l = \langle 1, 3 \rangle$ and $v(x) = v(y) = 1$.

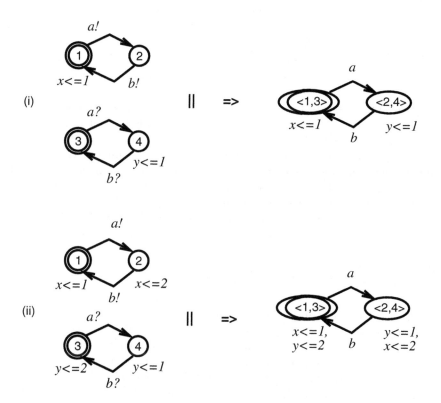

Fig. 12.13. Noncompositional Syntactic Conditions

On the other hand, condition (3) is compositional, although it is not commonly found in practice.[8] Nevertheless, it remains an interesting alternative given the fact that, at least in principle, invariants with lower bounds might occur when modelling real-time constraints (e.g. $1 < x \leq 2$).

To conclude, we can say that, in general, checking that all components in a network are inherently safe does not guarantee that the product automaton is nonzeno. Nevertheless, Lemmas 12.4 and 12.3 are important as they can be applied to the product automaton itself: if every loop in the product is inherently safe according to Lemma 12.4, then by Lemma 12.3 the product is nonzeno.

---

[8]For instance, Uppaal does not allow lower bounds in invariant expressions.

12.4.3 Nonzenoness: A Sufficient-and-Necessary Condition

The syntactic conditions presented in the previous section provide sufficient-only conditions for nonzenoness. One may argue that in most systems the presence of zeno-timelocks during modelling stages is rare, and for that reason, a sufficient-only check is generally enough to ensure that a system is nonzeno. However, there is always the possibility of systems that fail to satisfy the static properties, in which case, nonzenoness cannot be formally proved (or disproved). Here we show that reachability analysis, based on syntactic information obtained from a timed automaton's structure, can be used to provide a sufficient-and-necessary condition to guarantee nonzenoness.

This sufficient-and-necessary condition, however, does not come for free. Among some other minor syntactic restrictions, this nonzenoness condition can only be obtained from a single timed automaton where all actions are completed. This means that we do not have a compositional method to guarantee nonzenoness for an arbitrary network of automata: the analysis has to be performed on the product automaton. Depending on the model at hand, the resulting product automaton might be too big, even though many location vectors are actually unreachable. Notice that reachability will be governed by clock valuations in possible executions, i.e. "semantic" information that is not available when the product is built. Nevertheless, the construction of the product automaton is a purely syntactic operation, and so we could expect the method to scale up reasonably well.

Loops and Local Zeno-timelocks. Intuition suggests that a zeno-timelock can only occur if a loop is visited infinitely often, and time is not allowed to pass in any iteration. Although not trivial to prove, this observation can be strengthened: a zeno-timelock occurs *if and only if* execution reaches a state in a loop lp (i.e. a state $s = [l, v]$, $l \in Loc(lp)$) where all subsequent infinite runs are convergent and visit *just* transitions in lp. We say that this state is a zeno-timelock *local* to lp, and the nonzenoness condition we elaborate on in this section is concerned only with the detection of local zeno-timelocks.

For example, consider the loop $\langle cd \rangle$ in Figure 12.14. This loop can be reached either through transitions a or b. The reader will notice that this loop is not inherently safe according to Lemma 12.4: nonzenoness cannot be determined by any of the proposed syntactic conditions. However, reachability analysis can help to determine whether a zeno-timelock is produced by this loop.

For a zeno-timelock to occur in $\langle cd \rangle$, a state $s = [l, v]$ must be reached where $l \in \{1, 2\}$ and v is a valuation (which we call *maximal*) which

1. Enables all invariants in the loop,
2. Enables all transitions in the loop,
3. Assigns 0 to all clocks that are reset in the loop, and
4. Satisfies at least one upper bound occurring in every invariant in the loop.

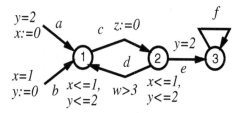

Fig. 12.14. Zeno-timelocks: Loops, Maximal Valuations and Escape Transitions

Clearly, if conditions (1) to (3) are fulfilled, then there exists at least one infinite run starting from s, which visits the loop infinitely often. Condition (4) guarantees that v makes all transitions in the loop urgent, and, therefore, no further execution will change the value of any clock. Consequently, all infinite runs that visit just transitions in the loop are guaranteed to be convergent.[9]

If we observe Figure 12.14 again, it is not difficult to convince ourselves that a state $s = [1, v]$ could be reached in $\langle cd \rangle$ through a, where v is s.t. $v(x) = v(z) = 0$, $v(y) = 2$ and $v(w) > 3$ (we can assume the values of z and w are such that this valuation is possible). This valuation satisfies all conditions (1) to (4). However, notice that in this case, v also enables an infinite run starting from s that visits a location outside the loop, and diverges: this run starts at s, takes c, then e and visits the loop $\langle f \rangle$ infinitely often (passing, say, 1 time unit between consecutive f-steps). Thus, s is not a zeno-timelock, because not every infinite run starting from s converges. This proves that conditions (1) to (4) are necessary for a zeno-timelock to occur, but not sufficient. We also need to ensure that the maximal valuation does not enable any transition leading to a location outside the loop (which we call an *escape* transition).

Escape transitions witness the existence of runs that visit some transition outside the loop, providing a counterexample for the occurrence of a zeno-timelock, which is *local* to that loop. See Figure 12.14 again. A zeno-timelock $s' = [1, v']$ may occur in $\langle cd \rangle$, where $v'(y) = v'(z) = 0$, $v'(x) = 1$ and $v'(w) > 3$. With this valuation (which can be reached through transition b), transition e is not enabled and therefore all infinite runs starting from s' visit just transitions in the loop, and are convergent.

Using Reachability to Guarantee Nonzenoness. It turns out, then, that a sufficient-and-necessary condition for the occurrence of zeno-timelocks in a given loop can be expressed as a reachability problem. A loop lp contains a zeno-timelock *if and only if* a state in lp can be reached where the valuation is maximal, and it does not enable any transition leading to a location outside lp. Moreover, we show that such a state can be characterised by a formula con-

---

[9]Moreover, because clocks cannot change their values, such a run is unique.

structed out of information derived from the syntactic structure of the loop, provided this structure respects certain restrictions. Now, let us be formal.

Let $A \in TA$ be a timed automaton where all actions are completed, and all invariants respect the following syntax (I is an invariant, x is a clock and $c \in \mathbb{N}$),

$$I ::= true \mid x \leq c \mid I \wedge I$$

Let lp be a loop in A which is not inherently safe.[10] We define a state formula $\phi \triangleq A.l \wedge \alpha(lp) \wedge \beta(lp)$, where $l \in Loc(lp)$, s.t.

> *A state s satisfying ϕ is reachable in A, if and only if A contains a zeno-timelock, which is local to lp.*

The formula $\alpha(lp)$ characterises the set of maximal valuations of lp, and $\beta(lp)$ represents the set of all valuations that simultaneously disable all escape transitions from lp. Next, we show that these formulae can be defined in terms of the syntactic structure (guards, invariants and resets) of lp.

$$\alpha(lp) \triangleq \bigwedge_{l \in Loc(lp)} I(l)$$
$$\wedge \bigwedge_{g \in Guards(lp)} g$$
$$\wedge \bigwedge_{y \in Resets(lp)} y = 0$$
$$\wedge \bigvee_{conj \in SUBs(lp)} conj$$

where (for $Loc(lp) = \{\, l_1, \ldots, l_n \,\}$)

$$SUBs(lp) \triangleq \{\, x_1 = c_1 \wedge \ldots \wedge x_n = c_n \mid x_i \leq c_i \in LocSUBs(l_i, lp), 1 \leq i \leq n \,\}$$

$$LocSUBs(l, lp) \triangleq \{\, x \leq c \mid x \leq c \text{ occurs in } I(l) \text{ and } c = c_{\min}(x, lp) \,\}$$

Here, every element of $SUBs(lp)$ is a conjunct representing that at least one clock in every invariant has reached its smallest upper bound (every element of $LocSUBs(l, lp)$ is a term of $I(l)$ that refers to a smallest upper bound). Note, because lp is assumed not to be inherently safe, every invariant in the loop contains at least one term of the form $x \leq c_{\min}(x, lp)$ (otherwise, condition 4 in Lemma 12.4 would be satisfied, and so lp would be inherently safe). Therefore, the set $LocSUBs(l, lp)$ cannot be empty, and so the conjuncts in $SUBs(lp)$ are always well-formed.

As we mentioned before, $\alpha(lp)$ denotes the set of all maximal valuations of a given loop lp. A maximal valuation v of lp must satisfy all invariants and

---

[10]We can check this by applying, for example, Lemma 12.4. We know that inherently safe loops do not produce zeno-timelocks.

guards in lp, and assign 0 to all clocks that are reset in lp. This ensures that, if a state $s = [l, v]$, $l \in Loc(lp)$ is reached, then there exists a run ρ starting from s, which visits lp infinitely often, without changing its clock valuation (i.e. v). These conditions are expressed in $\alpha(lp)$ by

$$\bigwedge_{l \in Loc(lp)} I(l),$$

$$\bigwedge_{g \in Guards(lp)} g, \quad \text{and}$$

$$\bigwedge_{y \in Resets(lp)} y = 0$$

A maximal valuation must also satisfy at least one smallest upper bound in every invariant of lp^{11}, which ensures that v not only enables every transition in lp, but also makes them urgent (when v is reached, every invariant in the loop has reached an upper bound). This is characterised by

$$\bigvee_{conj \in SUBs(lp)} conj$$

Thus, ρ represents an infinite run starting from s, which visits lp infinitely often (and visits just locations in lp) and does not allow time to progress beyond v (i.e. it is a zeno run). An intricate example is shown in Figure 12.15, which results in the following expression,

$$\begin{aligned}
\alpha(lp) = \quad & (x \leq 1 \wedge y \leq 2) \wedge (z \leq 2 \wedge y \leq 3) \wedge \\
& (y \leq 2 \wedge w \leq 1) \wedge (t \leq 0) \\
\wedge \ & (z > 1 \wedge y = 2) \\
\wedge \ & (t = 0 \wedge w = 0) \\
\wedge \ & (\ (x = 1 \wedge z = 2 \wedge y = 2 \wedge t = 0) \ \vee \\
& (x = 1 \wedge z = 2 \wedge w = 1 \wedge t = 0) \ \vee \\
& (y = 2 \wedge z = 2 \wedge y = 2 \wedge t = 0) \ \vee \\
& (y = 2 \wedge z = 2 \wedge w = 1 \wedge t = 0) \ )
\end{aligned}$$

Now, for a state $s = [l, v]$ to be a zeno-timelock *local* to lp, we need to ensure, in addition to the conditions expressed by $\alpha(lp)$, that v does not enable any escape transition from lp. This would guarantee that the run ρ, described above, is the only infinite run starting from s which visits lp infinitely often (and, as we saw, convergence of ρ is guaranteed by $\alpha(lp)$). With this in mind, we define a function $\beta(lp)$ that characterises the set of all valuations that simultaneously disable all escape transitions from lp. Let us first define an

---

[11] Note, if v is a maximal valuation of lp, and x is a clock occurring in any invariant in lp, then $v(x) \leq c_{\min}(x, lp)$. Otherwise, v would invalidate all invariants in lp that contain the term $x \leq c_{\min}(x, lp)$ (we know that, because lp is not inherently safe, there must exist at least one such invariant), which contradicts its maximality.

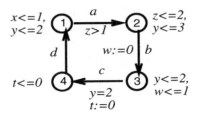

Fig. 12.15. A Complex Loop: Calculating $\alpha(lp)$

auxiliary function, $IsEnabled(g, r, l')$ (where x is a clock, g is a guard, r is a reset set and l' is a location):

$$IsEnabled(g, r, l') \triangleq g \wedge \bigwedge_{conj \in Target(l', r)} conj$$

$$Target(l', r) \triangleq \{ x \le c \mid x \le c \text{ occurs in } I(l') \text{ and } x \notin r \}$$

The function $IsEnabled(g, r, l')$ checks whether a given outgoing transition t, with guard g, reset set r and target location l', is enabled by the current valuation. It is not difficult to realise that t (the escape transition) is enabled by the current valuation, v say, if v satisfies (a) the transition's guard g, (b) the invariant in the source location and (c) the invariant in the target location, after the reset (i.e. $r(v)$ must satisfy $I(l')$). However, notice the following.

1. The invariant of the source location is not considered in $IsEnabled(g, r, l')$. Note that $\beta(lp)$, and therefore, $IsEnabled(g, r, l')$, is meant to be checked in conjunction with $\alpha(lp)$, which represents the maximal valuations in the loop. Then, by definition of maximal valuation, the invariant in the source location (which is a location in the loop) is satisfied whenever $\alpha(lp)$ is.
2. Conjuncts in the invariant of the target location, which refer to clocks that are reset in t, are not considered in $IsEnabled(g, r, l')$ (note the definition of $Target(l', r)$). Let us show you why this is the case. Suppose that $x \le c$ is one of such conjuncts in the target invariant[12], i.e. x is reset in t ($x \in r$). When t is performed, the value of x is set to zero, and so $x \le c$ is trivially satisfied. Therefore, for any v that holds before t is performed, $r(v)$ satisfies the target invariant ($I(l')$) if and only if v satisfies all conjuncts in $I(l')$ that do not refer to clocks in r (i.e. all conjuncts in $Target(l', r)$).

Let $Esc(lp) = \{ l_1 \xrightarrow{a_1, g_1, r_1} l'_1, \dots, l_n \xrightarrow{a_n, g_n, r_n} l'_n \}$ be the set of escape transitions of lp, i.e. transitions where $l_i \in Loc(lp)$ and $l'_i \notin Loc(lp)$, for all $1 \le i \le n$. We can now define $\beta(lp)$:

$$\beta(lp) \triangleq \bigwedge_{i=1}^{n} \neg IsEnabled(g_i, r_i, l'_i)$$

---

[12]Remember, as in Uppaal, that we disallow invariants with lower bounds.

For example, $Esc(lp)$, $\alpha(lp)$ and $\beta(lp)$, are calculated below for the loop $\langle cd \rangle$ in Figure 12.14 (redundant terms have been removed):

$$Esc(\langle cd \rangle) = \{2 \xrightarrow{e,\ y=2,\ \{\}} 3\}$$

$$\alpha(\langle cd \rangle) = (x \leq 1 \wedge y \leq 2) \wedge$$
$$(w > 3) \wedge$$
$$(z = 0) \wedge$$
$$(x = 1 \vee y = 2)$$

$$\beta(\langle cd \rangle) = \neg\ (y = 2)$$

Taking $\phi = A.1 \wedge \alpha(\langle cd \rangle) \wedge \beta(\langle cd \rangle)$, the reachability algorithm $reachable(A, \phi)$ (Figure 11.8) would confirm that there exists a state that satisfies ϕ, and therefore that the loop $\langle cd \rangle$ contains a local zeno-timelock.

The following theorem (proved in [44]) formalises a sufficient-and-necessary condition for nonzenoness in a timed automaton.

Theorem 12.5. *Let $A \in TA$. A contains a zeno-timelock if and only if there exists a loop in A, lp, such that $reachable(A, \phi)$ holds, where ϕ is defined as follows, $\phi \triangleq A.l \wedge \alpha(lp) \wedge \beta(lp)$, $l \in Loc(lp)$.*

Zeno-timelocks and Nonsimple Loops. Clearly, the application of Theorem 12.5 requires the detection of all loops in the automaton in question (most likely, this will be the product automaton for a given network). One would expect that simple loops are enough to accomplish the task. Unfortunately, some zeno-timelocks can only be considered local to nonsimple loops. Consider again Figure 12.7: the state $s = [1, v]$, $v(x) = 1$, is a zeno-timelock local to the nonsimple loop $\langle acdb \rangle$. However, s is neither local to the simple loop $\langle ab \rangle$ (v enables the escape transition c) nor is it local to $\langle cd \rangle$ (v enables the escape transition b).

In practice, however, detection of all nonsimple loops in the automaton may not be required. Nonzenoness detection might proceed in a number of steps, where each step ideally reduces the number of possible loops worth considering. Arguably, this avoids the detection of nonsimple loops as much as possible, making the overall process much more practical.[13] We conclude this section, then, with a method to analyse nonzenoness in a given network (a more detailed algorithm is offered in [44]),

1. Initially, sufficient-only conditions can be applied to the components of the network, possibly identifying a small number of unsafe loops (completed loops, or pairs of half loops, as discussed in Section 12.4.2). Let L_0 be that set of unsafe loops.

---

[13]We note that this method is presented here only for the sake of completeness; better strategies can be found and are definitely worth exploring.

2. Then, when the product automaton (Π) is constructed, the completed loops that result just from loops in L_0 can be identified. Let L_1 be this new set of loops in the product, all of which are not inherently safe. Notice that, so far, we are just dealing with simple loops.
3. Now, we could reduce L_1 by removing those loops that do not reach maximal valuations (this, as we have seen, is a necessary condition for the occurrence of zeno-timelocks). These loops $lp \in L_1$ are such that $reachable(\Pi, \phi_\alpha)$ does not hold, where ϕ_α is defined by the following relationship $\phi_\alpha \triangleq A.l \wedge \alpha(lp)$, $l \in Loc(lp)$.[14] Then, let $L_2 \subseteq L_1$ be the set of simple loops that do reach maximal valuations.
4. We can remove, from L_2, those loops that can be guaranteed to contain a local zeno-timelock, i.e. those loops $lp \in L_2$ for which $reachable(\Pi, \phi)$ holds, where ϕ is defined as $\phi \triangleq A.l \wedge \alpha(lp) \wedge \beta(lp)$, $l \in Loc(lp)$. It is important to mention that, most likely, the analysis will be concluded here: once a zeno-timelock is found, the model will be corrected before nonzenoness is checked again. In the worst case, though, let us assume that we want to continue the analysis with the rest of the loops, say $L_3 \subseteq L_2$.
5. L_3 is such that every loop is a simple loop that reaches maximal valuations, and every such maximal valuation enables one or more escape transitions. As a final step, then, we consider from Π only those nonsimple loops that could be obtained by combining (where possible) simple loops in L_3. For every such nonsimple loop, the sufficient-and-necessary condition ($\phi \triangleq A.l \wedge \alpha(lp) \wedge \beta(lp)$) is tested again.

12.5 Timelock Detection in Real-time Model-checkers

12.5.1 Uppaal

Currently, Uppaal only supports a limited form of timelock detection. The formula `A[]not deadlock`[15] can be verified, which guarantees absence of actionlocks. This clearly implies time reactiveness. However, if the specification does not verify `A[]not deadlock`, no facilities are available to detect whether the cause is just a pure actionlock, or a time-actionlock.

Nonzenoness can be detected in Uppaal by adding a new component to the network, usually referred to as a *test automaton*. This automaton looks like the one shown in Figure 12.16(i), where t is a local clock and a is a completed action. In networks augmented with such a test automaton, nonzenoness can

---

[14]Notice that we do not need to check, at this stage, for escape transitions. Thus, formula $\beta(lp)$ is not included in this check.

[15]This corresponds to a TCTL formula `AG`$\neg$(*Deadlock*), where *Deadlock* is a state formula that holds whenever no action transition is enabled in the current state.

be guaranteed if the Uppaal formula (t==0)-->(t==1)[16] is satisfiable. This corresponds to the TCTL formula $AG((t = 0) \Rightarrow AF(t = 1))$, which is satisfiable only if for every state $s = [l, v]$ in which $v(t) = 0$, a state $s = [l', v']$ in which $v(t) = 1$ is reachable in *every* possible run starting from s (l and l' denote arbitrary location vectors). In other words, this guarantees that the network is always able to elapse 1 time unit.

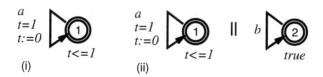

Fig. 12.16. Test Automaton (i) and a Nonzeno System (ii)

The combined use of a test automaton and a leads-to formula provides an ingenious solution to guarantee nonzenoness, and is good evidence of the versatility of Uppaal in respect of verification of nontrivial properties. However, this approach has a few drawbacks. One problem is that verification of a leads-to formula is computationally demanding; algorithms would typically include some sort of nested reachability verification. The other problem is that the approach is sufficient-only: there exist some networks that do not satisfy (t==0)-->(t==1), yet they are nonzeno. The system shown in Figure 12.16(ii) illustrates such a case. Notice that the system does not contain zeno-timelocks, although it contains zeno runs. For example, transition b can be performed infinitely at $v(t) = 0$, generating a zeno run that is a counterexample to (t==0)-->(t==1). To convince ourselves that this is so, we only need to observe that this zeno run is a run starting from a $(t = 0)$-state in which no $(t = 1)$-state is reachable.

It turns out that, considering again a network augmented with a test automaton such as the one shown in Figure 12.16, a sufficient-and-necessary condition for nonzenoness is given by the TCTL formula $AG((t = 0) \Rightarrow EF(t = 1))$. Indeed, a system is timelock-free if there exists *at least* one run starting at every $(t = 0)$-state, where a $(t = 1)$-state is reachable. Notice that this formula provides a "weaker" condition than the Uppaal leads-to formula (t==0)-->(t==1), in the sense that just one divergent run is enough to prove nonzenoness. Unfortunately, such a formula cannot be written in Uppaal.

Despite these drawbacks, Uppaal remains probably the most usable and efficient real-time model-checker available. This has motivated recent research, which aims to complement the timelock-detection facilities in Uppaal [44, 45]. In particular, this research is concerned with the integration of the syntactic and sufficient-and-necessary nonzenoness conditions presented in Sections 12.4.2 and 12.4.3.

---

[16] A *leads-to* formula [16].

12.5.2 Kronos

Kronos handles an expressive TCTL subset, which allows for the verification of the TCTL formula $\texttt{AGEF}_{=1}\,true$. This formula characterises models where, from every reachable state, at least 1 time unit is always allowed to pass. Unlike Uppaal's leads-to formula, this one represents itself as a sufficient-and-necessary nonzenoness condition [49]. However, this formula is also difficult to verify, and Kronos' engine is not as efficient as Uppaal's. This means that for some specifications, checking nonzenoness in Kronos would be the most expensive requirement to check and the need to check it could prevent a complete verification.

13

Discrete Timed Automata

13.1 Infinite vs. Finite States

The attractiveness of timed automata as a formal method is the possibility it raises of efficient and automatic verification (real-time model-checking). However, automatic verification comes at a price: systems must exhibit a behaviour where "discrete changes" are finite, e.g. systems that can be modelled using finitely many automata locations and variables in finite domains (e.g. Uppaal [16]).

Unfortunately, many interesting systems that present infinite behaviour cannot be represented using timed automata. For example, reasoning about this sort of behaviour comes about naturally when dealing with parameterised communication protocols. Formal notations for timed infinite-state systems (see, e.g. [1,113,134,135,142,178]) have been developed for a number of years to respond to this issue, providing specification and verification solutions in those domains where automatic techniques, such as model-checking, cannot be applied. The evolution in formal frameworks for timed, infinite state systems is witnessed by several pieces of work, e.g. [82,84,85,110]. The main disadvantage of infinite-state frameworks is the lack of fully automatic verification support. Typically, properties will have to be verified deductively, where proofs are developed by hand or aided by theorem provers. Therefore, a considerable degree of user interaction and expertise is usually needed. But on the other hand, deductive proofs strongly encourage a deep understanding of how the system works.

Here we discuss *Discrete Timed Automata* (DTAs) [84, 85] as a representative notation for infinite-state, real-time systems. This notation is a natural timed extension of infinite state communicating automata, presented in Section 8.3, and it embodies many of the principles that are present in other formalisms, e.g. *timed I/O automata with urgency* [82]. The main elements of this theory are enumerated below, and formally introduced in Section 13.3.

1. A DTA is composed of a set of variables and a number of actions.

2. Variables define the state-space of an automaton (every state corresponding to one possible valuation) and can be local to an automaton, or declared externally and shared with other components in a network of DTAs. DTAs have been developed so MONA [111], a satisfiability checker for the *Weak Monadic Second-order Theory of 1 Successor* (WS1S), can be used to support the deductive verification of safety properties. One consequence of this is that variables in DTAs are typed, and types must be supported by MONA, which offers natural numbers, Boolean values, enumerations and finite sets of natural numbers. Other relatively complex data types, such as finite arrays on finite domains, can also be derived from the basic types [181].

3. Actions are defined in terms of a label, a precondition, a deadline and an effect. Preconditions, deadlines and effects are defined as MONA (WS1S) formulae over the automaton's variables. A precondition defines the set of states where the action is enabled; correspondingly, the effect defines the states reachable when the action is performed. As in timed automata with deadlines (Section 12.3.1), a deadline defines the states where the action *must* be performed. Equivalently, time is not allowed to progress in any state where some action's deadline holds. Also, deadlines are required to imply preconditions, hence DTAs are time reactive by construction (i.e. time-actionlocks cannot occur).

4. Time is discrete, represented by a designated shared variable $T \in \mathbb{N}$ (called the *time variable*), and a special action, *tick*, that increments the value of T (by 1 time unit). T can be read by any action, but updated only by the *tick* action. Time constraints (occurring in preconditions and deadlines) will refer to T, and be expressible in WS1S. This, and the fact that T represents a natural number, allows DTA specifications to be expressed in MONA.

5. Systems are modelled as networks of synchronising DTAs. A set of shared variables, which includes the time variable T, is related to the network. Among other well-formedness conditions, one automaton in the network (and just one) is required to include the *tick* action. In general, shared variables can be read and updated by any component, with the following exceptions: (a) T is only updated by one component (the one that includes the *tick* action) and (b) shared variables cannot be simultaneously updated by two synchronising half actions.

6. Concurrency is modelled by interleaving; at any point in execution a given action is nondeterministically chosen from the set of actions enabled at that point. Communication is achieved through binary CCS-like synchronisation; actions are classified as completed, input or output actions, and communication takes place when two matching actions (input/output actions with the same label in two different components in a network) are executed at the same time. There is no value-passing in communication, but this can be achieved with shared variables with one restriction: either

the input or output matching action can modify a shared variable, but not both (to prevent simultaneous, inconsistent updates).

As in timed automata with deadlines, parallel composition preserves time reactiveness: synchronisation will only be considered urgent if both matching actions are enabled (i.e. if synchronisation is possible).

7. Verification of properties in DTAs is deductive: proofs can be developed by hand or supported by theorem provers. Here we focus, in particular, on the verification of safety properties (i.e. those stating that error-states are never reachable) by the well-known method of invariance proofs [137]. We show that crucial to these proofs is the satisfiability checking of certain MONA formulae, which characterise the successful execution of DTA actions.

Example: A DTA Specification of an Alarm Clock. Figure 13.1 shows a DTA specification of a simple alarm clock. V_L denotes the automaton's local variables, Θ_L denotes the initialisation formula for variables in V_L, TL is a set of action labels, and $\mathcal{A}$ the automaton's actions; *true*-preconditions, *false*-deadlines and effects which do not change the current valuation are omitted. The network of DTAs is composed of two automata, *Clock* and *Alarm*. V_S denotes the set of shared variables related to the network (note, in this example only T is shared) and Θ_S denotes the initialisation formula (which sets T initially to zero).

The *Clock* component models a 24-hour clock, where the alarm is set to 5:30. Local variables s, m and h denote, respectively, the seconds, minutes and hours elapsed so far (assuming the granularity of *tick* is to the second). Actions *minute* and *hour* calculate the current minute and hour; *hour* and *reset* keep the values of m and h between 0 and 60, and 0 and 24, respectively. To keep the specification simple, s is allowed to drift unbounded. All these actions are internal to the automaton; on the other hand *sound_alarm!* is an output action, which synchronises with the input action *sound_alarm?* in *Alarm*. Once synchronisation happens, the alarm will ring for 15 seconds and *stop*. The following general points are worth observing,

- All actions, save for *tick* and *sound_alarm?*, are made urgent as soon as they are enabled: the set of states denoted by deadlines and preconditions are the same.
- Local variables such as s and d, which are referred to as *time capture variables*, are kept implicitly synchronised with the global time, by resetting them to the current value of T.
- The value of a variable, say v, after an action has been performed, is denoted by its primed version, v'.

Network: $|\langle Clock,\ Alarm \rangle$
$V_S :\ \{T \in \mathbb{N}\}$
$\Theta_S :\ T = 0$

DTA: *Clock*
$V_L :\ s, m, h \in \mathbb{N}$
$\Theta_L :\ s = 0\ \wedge\ m = 0\ \wedge\ h = 0$
$TL :\ \{tick,\ minute,\ reset,\ hour,\ sound\_alarm!\}$
$\mathcal{A} :\ tick$

       eff: $T' = T + 1$

    minute

       prec: $T = s + 60\ \wedge\ m < 60$

       deadline: $T = s + 60\ \wedge\ m < 60$

       eff: $m' = m + 1\ \wedge\ s' = T$

    hour

       prec: $m = 60\ \wedge\ h < 24$

       deadline: $m = 60\ \wedge\ h < 24$

       eff: $h' = h + 1\ \wedge\ m' = 0$

    reset

       prec: $h = 24$

       deadline: $h = 24$

       eff: $h' = 0$

    sound_alarm!

       prec: $h = 5\ \wedge\ m = 30$

       deadline: $h = 5\ \wedge\ m = 30$

DTA: *Alarm*
$V_L :\ d \in \mathbb{N},\ on \in \mathbb{B}$
$\Theta_L :\ d = 0\ \wedge\ on = false$
$TL :\ \{sound\_alarm?,\ stop\}$
$\mathcal{A} :\ sound\_alarm?$

       eff: $on' = true\ \wedge\ d' = T$

    stop

       prec: $on\ \wedge\ T = d + 15$

       deadline: $on\ \wedge\ T = d + 15$

       eff: $on' = false\ \wedge\ d' = 0$

Fig. 13.1. A Simple Alarm Clock

13.2 Preliminaries

This section gives the necessary information on fair transition systems, invariance proofs, the logic WS1S and MONA.

13.2.1 Fair Transition Systems and Invariance Proofs

Fair Transition Systems (FTSs) are a well-known computational model for (untimed) infinite-state systems [136]. Here we include a brief description of FTS, as this model can elegantly express the semantics of DTAs[1].

An FTS, $F = (V, \Theta, \mathcal{T})$, includes a finite set of typed variables V (types are not part of the theory, but assumed, instead, to be application-dependent), an initial condition Θ and a finite set of transitions $\mathcal{T}$. V determines the state-space of the system, each state corresponding to a possible valuation. Θ and transitions in $\mathcal{T}$ are expressed as assertions in a first-order language (predicate logic). Θ is an assertion, which defines a set of possible starting states (i.e. initial valuations for V).

A transition $\tau \in \mathcal{T}$ is represented by an assertion ρ_τ on variables in V and their primed versions, where V' denotes the set of primed variables with respect to V. If $V'(\tau)$ denotes the set of variables in V that are modified by τ, then ρ_τ (here referred to as a *transition formula*) is usually written as

$$\rho_\tau \triangleq p_V \wedge \bigwedge_{v \in V'(\tau)} v' = E_V$$

where p_V is an assertion which imposes a certain valuation for some variables in V, representing the set of states where τ is enabled; and

$$\bigwedge_{v \in V'(\tau)} v' = E_V$$

where E_V is an expression on V, indicates a new valuation for some variables in V after τ has been performed (i.e. it defines the next state). Notice that terms of the form $v' = E_V$ determine a unique next state. For example, the assertion $\rho_\tau : x > 0 \wedge x' = x + 1$, characterises a transition τ, which can only be performed in those states where $x > 0$, and whose effect is to increment the value of x by 1. $\mathcal{T}$ is also assumed to include the *idling transition*,

$$\rho_{idle} \triangleq \bigwedge_{v \in V} v' = v$$

which does not change the current state. All other transitions in $\mathcal{T}$ are referred to as *nonidle*.

A *computation* is an infinite sequence of states $s_0, s_1, s_2, \ldots$ such that (a) s_0 satisfies Θ, (b) for each $i \geq 0$ there is some enabled transition $\tau \in \mathcal{T}$ that is performed at s_i and results in s_{i+1}, and (c) the sequence contains either infinitely many nonidle steps (i.e. the result of performing a nonidle transition) or a terminal state (i.e. a state where the only enabled transition is the idling transition). Every state in a computation is referred to as a *reachable state*.

Concurrency is modelled by interleaving: at any given point in a computation, a transition is executed, being nondeterministically chosen from the set of

---

[1]Although, in this work, we are not concerned with fairness in DTAs.

enabled transitions at that point. *Fairness conditions* are enforced to prevent computations that do not correspond to executions of real-life systems. This is achieved by marking transitions in an FTS as *just* or *compassionate*. A just transition cannot be continuously enabled (i.e. enabled in every state of some computation's suffix), but performed only finitely many times. A compassionate transition cannot be enabled infinitely often, but performed only finitely many times. Compassionate transitions respond to stronger fairness conditions than just transitions. Notice that a transition can be enabled infinitely often without being continuously enabled; hence, marking this transition as "just" will not guarantee its eventual execution.

A *safety property* is an assertion about the system that holds in all reachable states (see Section 8.2.5.1). Formally, a safety property can be specified as an LTL (Linear Temporal Logic) [137] formula $\Box\phi$, where ϕ is, in general, an LTL past formula. If $\Box\phi$ holds then ϕ holds in every reachable state. In this chapter, ϕ just refers to a state assertion (i.e. a formula without LTL temporal operators), which is usually called an *invariant*[2]. Invariants can be formally verified over FTS using the rule presented below.

$$
\begin{array}{ll}
\text{P1} & \varphi \rightarrow \phi \\
\text{P2} & \Theta \rightarrow \varphi \\
\text{P3} & \forall\, \tau \in \mathcal{T},\ \rho_\tau \wedge \varphi \rightarrow \varphi'
\end{array}
$$
$$\overline{\qquad\qquad\qquad \Box\phi \qquad\qquad\qquad}$$

This deductive rule guarantees the invariance of ϕ, provided the existence of a (usually stronger) invariant φ such that (P1) φ implies ϕ, (P2) φ holds in every starting state and (P3) φ is "preserved" by all transitions in $\mathcal{T}$ (i.e. if φ holds whenever τ is enabled, then it also holds after τ is performed). The formula φ' can be obtained by replacing, in φ, all variables v by their primed version v', where v' occurs in ρ_τ.

It is not difficult to see that, if all premises hold, then ϕ is satisfiable in every reachable state. Manna et al. [137] also proved that, if $\Box\phi$ is valid, then an assertion φ exists which satisfies the rule premises. Unfortunately, methods to obtain such an assertion φ (called an *inductive* invariant) are not complete. It turns out that, for any assertion φ, premises may be found to be unsatisfiable for some valuations, even in those cases when φ is, indeed, an invariant. The following discussion explains this issue in more detail.

Without loss of generality, let us assume that $\varphi = \phi$ is a good guess to start our deductive proof. Suppose that a valuation is found that invalidates either premise P2 or P3, and which, therefore, does not allow us to conclude the validity of $\Box\phi$. Now, if this valuation denotes a reachable state, then ϕ is guaranteed not to be an invariant, as there exists a reachable state in which it does not hold. On the other hand, if the valuation in question denotes an unreachable state, then ϕ may or may not be an invariant, but neither case can be confirmed yet. In addition, the problem becomes more difficult to tackle as

---

[2]Not to be confused with invariants in timed automata.

to determine whether a valuation denotes a reachable or unreachable state is, in general, far from straightforward. Notice, as well, that this issue is inherent to the nature of transition formulae: they represent a set of states where the transition is enabled, but not every state in this set is necessarily reachable.

One way to approach this problem is to assume $\varphi = \phi$ initially, and then to strengthen it (on demand) with auxiliary invariants, which rule out unreachable states. It is hoped that this process results in a formula φ for which the deductive rule provides a definite answer; φ will typically have the form:

$$\varphi \triangleq \phi \wedge \bigwedge_{i=1}^{n} \alpha_i$$

where α_i, for all $1 \leq i \leq n$, is an auxiliary invariant describing some known relationship between the system variables. Note that ingenuity is needed here to propose convenient auxiliary invariants, and to prove that these assertions are, themselves, invariants. In consequence, it is often the case that the verification of a safety property requires several applications of the deductive rule.

Nevertheless, the case is far from hopeless, as many heuristics have been proposed in the literature to guide the invariant strengthening process (see, e.g. [19, 20]). It is also worth mentioning that other deductive rules have been devised to prove the invariance of more general LTL past formulae [137], which can also be applied to verify more complex safety properties in DTA specifications.

13.2.2 The Weak Monadic Second-order Theory of 1 Successor (WS1S) and MONA

This section gives the necessary background on WS1S and MONA (further details can be investigated in [111]). WS1S [55, 72, 188] is a decidable logic interpreted over finite sets of natural numbers, with the following (minimal) syntax:

$$\phi ::= p = q + 1 \mid p \in X \mid \neg \phi \mid \phi \vee \phi \mid \exists\, p.\phi \mid \exists\, X.\phi$$

where ϕ denote a WS1S formula, p, q two first-order variables and X a second-order variable. WS1S is interpreted over $\mathbb{N}$; first-order variables range over natural numbers, second-order variables range over finite sets of natural numbers and operators $=, +, \in, \neg, \vee$ and $\exists$ have the classic interpretation. Other operators can be derived from these, e.g. $\Rightarrow$, $\leq$, and $\subseteq$, in the usual way.

MONA [111] implements a decision procedure for WS1S based on a translation from WS1S formulae to DFA (Deterministic Finite Automata) [55, 72]. The syntax of MONA is that of WS1S augmented with syntactic sugar, that is, no expressive power is added. A MONA specification consists of a declaration section and a formula section.

Boolean, first-order and second-order variables can be declared (these are declared by `var0`, `var1` and `var2`, respectively). Other relatively complex data types, such as finite arrays on finite domains, can also be represented in MONA [181]. Predicates can also be declared, which instantiate a given formula with actual parameters.

Formulae are built using the usual logic connectives, such as ~ (negation), & (conjunction), | (disjunction) and => (implication). Expressions on first-order variables include relational operators (e.g. `t1>=t2`), addition of constant values (`t+n`) and quantification (`ex1 t:`φ, `all1 t:`φ). Expressions on second-order variables include `min T`, `max T` (minimum and maximum element in a set), `t in T` (membership), `T1 sub T2` (set inclusion), quantification (`ex2 T:`φ, `all2 T:`φ) and other typical set operations such as intersection, difference and union.

MONA translates a WS1S formula to a minimum DFA that represents the set of satisfying interpretations. Models of the formula are then expressed by paths from the starting state to an accepting state (MONA returns only the shortest model). Similarly, counterexamples are represented by paths leading to rejecting states. For example, MONA returns `X={0,1,2}` and `Y={1,2,3}` as a model for the following formula (`X={}` and `Y={}` are respectively returned as a counterexample),

```
var2 X,Y;
X={0,1,2} & all1 k:k in X => k+1 in Y;
```

Despite the nonelementary complexity of the decision problem, MONA has been applied in many nontrivial problems, such as controller synthesis [174], protocol verification [181] and theorem proving [158], [10] (more applications can be found in [111]). MONA's successful applications can be explained by optimisations performed during the translation process as well as by the fact that the decision procedure is nonelementary in the worst case, which may not arise so frequently in practice.

13.3 Discrete Timed Automata – Formal definitions

13.3.1 Syntax

Discrete Timed Automata. DTAs always stand as components of a given network. A single DTA can be defined as a tuple,

$$A = (V_L, \Theta_L, TL, \mathcal{A}, V_S, \Theta_S)$$

where

- V_L is a finite set of local, MONA-typed variables (these include Boolean values, natural numbers and finite sets of natural numbers);

- Θ_L is a MONA formula representing the initial valuation for variables in V_L;

- $TL \subseteq Act$ is a finite set of action labels;

- $\mathcal{A}$ is a finite set of actions; and

- V_S, which includes the time variable T, is a set of shared variables with initial valuations given by Θ_S. Both V_S and Θ_S are declared (globally) in the network where A sits. In what follows, we use $V = V_L \cup V_S$ to denote the set of variables accessible by the automaton.

Actions in $\mathcal{A}$ are tuples (a, p, d, e), where $a \in TL$ is the action's label, p, d are MONA formulae on V, respectively denoting the action's precondition and deadline; and e is a MONA formula on variables in V and their primed versions, which denotes the action's effect. As in infinite state communicating automata (Section 8.3.1.1), effect formulae are of the form

$$e \triangleq \bigwedge_{v \in V'(e)} v' = E_V$$

where $V'(e) \subseteq V$ is the set of variables modified by e, and E_V is a MONA expression on V. As in timed automata with deadlines (Section 12.3.1), time reactiveness in DTAs is guaranteed by restricting deadlines to imply preconditions[3],

$$\forall (a, p, d, e) \in \mathcal{A}, \, d \Rightarrow p$$

The set of actions $\mathcal{A}$ is further partitioned into sets of completed, input and output actions; that is,

$$\mathcal{A} = COMP(\mathcal{A}) \cup IN(\mathcal{A}) \cup OUT(\mathcal{A})$$

Internal, input and output actions are labelled with $a \in CAct$, $x? \in HAct$ and $x! \in HAct$, respectively. Note that many actions in the same partition (completed, input or output) may share the same label; in this way we naturally model actions that have different effects depending on the state. The time action is a completed action,

$$(tick, true, false, T' = T + 1) \in COMP(\mathcal{A})$$

Notice that the time action is always enabled (the precondition is *true*), and never urgent (the deadline is *false*).

Network of DTAs. A network of DTAs, $|A = (|\langle A_1, \ldots, A_n \rangle, V_S, \Theta_S)$, is a tuple, where $A_i = (V_L^i, \Theta_L^i, TL_i, \mathcal{A}_i, V_S, \Theta_S)$, for $1 \le i \le n$, and the following well-formedness conditions[4] apply.

---

[3]Left-closed intervals are naturally obtained in DTAs due to discrete time.

[4]Notice that the first two conditions are inherited from those imposed on networks of ISCAs (see Section 8.3.1).

1. The time variable, $T \in \mathbb{N}$, is included in V_S, and initialised $(T = 0)$ by Θ_S.

2. Local variables are disjoint among the components,

$$\forall i, j \, (1 \leq i \neq j \leq n), \, V_L^i \cap V_L^j = \emptyset$$

3. The set of completed actions in any component is disjoint from the set of actions (completed, output and input actions) in any other component in the network,

$$\forall i, j \, (1 \leq i \neq j \leq n), \, COMP(\mathcal{A}_i) \cap \mathcal{A}_j = \emptyset$$

4. One (and only one) automaton in the network must include the time action *tick*, and T can only be updated by *tick*. Formally,

$$\exists i \, (1 \leq i \leq n) \, . \, tick \in TL_i \wedge \forall j \, (1 \leq i \neq j \leq n), \, tick \notin TL_j$$

$$\forall i \, (1 \leq i \leq n), \, (\, (a, p, d, e) \in \mathcal{A}_i \implies (T \in V'(e) \iff a = tick) \,)$$

5. The set of shared variables modified by input actions is disjoint from the set of shared variables modified by matching output actions. Let $V_S'(e) = V_S \cap V'(e)$ be the set of shared variables modified by a given effect formula e. Then,

$$\forall \, i, j \, (1 \leq i \neq j \leq n),$$
$$\forall \, (x?, p_i, d_i, e_i) \in IN(A_i), \, (x!, p_j, d_j, e_j) \in OUT(A_j),$$
$$V_S'(e_i) \cap V_S'(e_j) = \emptyset$$

13.3.2 Example: A DTA Specification for the Multimedia Stream

Figure 13.2 shows a DTA specification for the multimedia stream example of Section 11.2.1.1, and is worth comparing with the TA specification given in Figure 11.2. The network of DTAs is composed of the following automata: *Source*, *Place1*, *Place2* and *Sink*, representing the components of the stream, and *Clock*, representing the passage of time (it declares both the time variable T and the time action *tick*).

The *Source* declares a variable *SourceState* $\in \{0, 1\}$ to represent the current control state of the automaton, and a time capture variable $t1$ to keep track of the time elapsed between two consecutive transmissions. Control states will denote that the automaton is ready to transmit the first packet (when *SourceState* $= 0$), or that it is ready to transmit the next packet in the sequence (when *SourceState* $= 1$). Transmissions are represented by two *sourceOut!*s: one for the first packet, and the other one for any subsequent packet. Deadlines ensure that the first packet is transmitted urgently when

$T = 0$, and that every subsequent packet is transmitted 50 ms after the previous one. This is achieved by setting the value of $t1$ to the current time immediately after a packet is sent ($t1' = T$), and sending the next packet only when the difference between $t1$ and the current time is 50 ms (as expressed by the deadline $T = t1 + 50$).

Similarly, it is not difficult to analyse the behaviour of the other components in the network. For example, the action *sinkIn!* in *Place1* is enabled as soon as at least 80 ms have passed since a packet was received (i.e. since *sourceOut?* was performed), and must be performed before 90 ms have passed since then (notice that the deadline in *sinkIn!* does not allow time to pass beyond $T = t4 + 90$).

13.3.3 Semantics

Let $A = (V_L, \Theta_L, TL, \mathcal{A}, V_S, \Theta_S)$ be a DTA where all actions are completed (i.e. $\mathcal{A} = COMP(\mathcal{A})$). Notation is as defined for infinite state communicating automata (Section 8.3); the main difference being that $\models$ here denotes satisfiability with respect to WS1S semantics. The semantics of A are given by an LTS (S, TL, T_S, s_0), where

- S denotes the set of all type-consistent valuations for variables in $V_L \cup V_S$;
- $s_0 \in S$ is the starting state, which satisfies $s_0 \models \Theta_L \wedge \Theta_S$;
- $T_S \subseteq S \times TL \times S$ is the transition relation, where transitions $(s_1, a, s_2) \in T_S$ are denoted, as usual, $s_1 \xrightarrow{a} s_2$. T_S is defined by the following inference rules,

$$(D1) \quad \frac{a \neq tick \quad s_1 \models p \quad (s_1, s_2) \models e}{s_1 \xrightarrow{a} s_2}$$

$$(D2) \quad \frac{a = tick \quad s_1 \models p \quad (s_1, s_2) \models e \quad \nexists (a_1, p_1, d_1, e_1) \in \mathcal{A}. \, s_1 \models d_1}{s_1 \xrightarrow{tick} s_2}$$

where $(a, p, d, e) \in \mathcal{A}$. Notice that rule (D2) only allows time to pass in states where no deadline is enabled (i.e. where no action is urgent). Time-actionlocks cannot occur because deadlines imply preconditions, and so, only enabled actions can be considered urgent (hence, $s_1 \models d_1 \Rightarrow s_1 \models p_1$ is implicit in the rule's premises). The set of reachable states is, then,

$$S_{reach} = \{s_0\} \cup \{s_2 \mid \exists \, a \in TL, \, s_1 \in S_{reach}. \, s_1 \xrightarrow{a} s_2\}$$

Parallel Composition. Parallel composition for DTAs is inspired by sparse TADs (Section 12.3.1), and also preserves time reactiveness (i.e. timelocks cannot occur in DTA specifications). For any given network DTAs, the resulting product automaton is a single DTA whose semantics (according to the LTS defined in the previous section) correspond to that of the network. By

Network: $|\langle Clock, Source, Place1, Place2, Sink\rangle$
$V_S : \{T \in \mathbb{N}\}$
$\Theta_S : T = 0$

DTA: *Clock*
$V_L : \emptyset$
$\Theta_L : true$
$TL : \{tick\}$
$\mathcal{A} : tick$

  eff: $T' = T + 1$

DTA: *Source*
$V_L : SourceState \in \{0, 1\}, \ t1 \in \mathbb{N}$
$\Theta_L : SourceState = 0 \ \wedge \ t1 = 0$
$TL : \{sourceOut!\}$
$\mathcal{A} : sourceOut!$

  prec: $SourceState = 0 \ \wedge \ T = 0$
  deadline: $SourceState = 0 \ \wedge \ T = 0$
  eff: $SourceState' = 1$

 sourceOut!

  prec: $SourceState = 1 \ \wedge \ T = t1 + 50$
  deadline: $SourceState = 1 \ \wedge \ T = t1 + 50$
  eff: $t1' = T$

DTA: *Place1*
$V_L : Place1State \in \{1, 2\}, \ t4 \in \mathbb{N}$
$\Theta_L : Place1State = 1 \ \wedge \ t4 = 0$
$TL : \{sourceOut?, \ sinkIn!\}$
$\mathcal{A} : sourceOut?$

  prec: $Place1State = 1$
  eff: $Place1State' = 2 \ \wedge \ t4' = T$

 sinkIn!

  prec: $Place1State = 2 \ \wedge \ T > t4 + 80$
  deadline: $Place1State = 2 \ \wedge \ T \geq t4 + 90$
  eff: $Place1State' = 1$

DTA: *Sink*
$V_L : SinkState \in \{1, 2\}, \ t2 \in \mathbb{N}$
$\Theta_L : SinkState = 1 \ \wedge \ t2 = 0$
$TL : \{sinkIn?, \ play\}$
$\mathcal{A} : sinkIn?$

  prec: $SinkState = 1$
  eff: $SinkState' = 2 \ \wedge \ t2' = T$

 play

  prec: $SinkState = 2 \ \wedge \ T = t2 + 5$
  deadline: $SinkState = 2 \ \wedge \ T = t2 + 5$
  eff: $SinkState' = 1$

Fig. 13.2. Multimedia Stream as a Network of DTAs. Only one place is shown; the other is similar.

construction (and well-formedness of the network), this product automaton contains just completed actions, and declares both the time variable and the time action.

Let $|A = (||\langle A_1, \ldots, A_n \rangle, V_S, \Theta_S)$ be a network of DTAs, where

$$A_i \triangleq (V_L^i, \Theta_L^i, TL_i, \mathcal{A}_i, V_S, \Theta_S)$$

for $1 \leq i \leq n$. The resulting product automaton is a DTA,

$$\Pi \triangleq (V_L, \Theta_L, TL, \mathcal{A}, V_S, \Theta_S)$$

where

- $V_L \triangleq \bigcup\limits_{i=1}^{n} V_L^i$

- $\Theta_L \triangleq \bigwedge\limits_{i=1}^{n} \Theta_L^i$

- $TL \triangleq \bigcup\limits_{i=1}^{n} TL_i$

- $COMP(\mathcal{A}) \triangleq \bigcup\limits_{i=1}^{n} COMP(\mathcal{A}_i) \cup$
  $$\{(x, p, d, e) \mid \exists i, j \, (1 \leq i \neq j \leq n).$$
  $$(x?, p_i, d_i, e_i) \in IN(\mathcal{A}_i) \wedge$$
  $$(x!, p_j, d_j, e_j) \in OUT(\mathcal{A}_j) \wedge$$
  $$(p = p_i \wedge p_j) \wedge$$
  $$(d = p_i \wedge p_j \wedge (d_i \vee d_j)) \wedge$$
  $$(e = e_i \wedge e_j)\}$$

- $IN(\mathcal{A}) \triangleq OUT(\mathcal{A}) \triangleq \emptyset$

Notice that all actions in the product automaton are completed, where synchronisation has been resolved by producing one completed action from every two matching input/output actions in the components. By way of example, Figure 13.3 below shows the product automaton corresponding to the network of DTAs of Figure 13.2. In particular, observe that the product includes four completed actions *sourceOut*, each one representing a possible synchronisation between a *sourceOut!* in *Source* and a *sourceOut?* in either *Place1* or *Place2* (see Figure 13.2 again).

13.4 Verifying Safety Properties over DTAs

Invariance proofs can be applied on networks of DTAs to verify safety properties, by mapping[5] the network's product automaton to an equivalent FTS

---

[5]The soundness of this mapping is proved in [85].

Network: $|\langle \Pi \rangle$
$V_S : \{T \in \mathbb{N}\}$
$\Theta_S : T = 0$

DTA: Π
$V_L : t1,\ t2,\ t3,\ t4 \in \mathbb{N}$
   $SourceState \in \{0, 1\},$
   $Place1State,\ Place2State,\ SinkState \in \{1, 2\}$
$\Theta_L : t1 = 0 \ \wedge\ t2 = 0 \ \wedge\ t3 = 0 \ \wedge\ t4 = 0 \ \wedge$
   $SourceState = 0 \ \wedge$
   $Place1State = 1 \ \wedge\ Place2State = 1 \ \wedge\ SinkState = 1$
$TL = \{sourceOut,\ sinkIn,\ play\}$
$\mathcal{A} : tick$

   eff: $T' = T + 1$
   sourceOut
      prec: $SourceState = 0 \ \wedge\ T = 0 \ \wedge\ Place1State = 1$
      deadline: $SourceState = 0 \ \wedge\ T = 0 \ \wedge\ Place1State = 1$
      eff: $SourceState' = 1 \ \wedge\ t4' = T \ \wedge\ Place1State' = 2$
   sourceOut
      prec: $SourceState = 0 \ \wedge\ T = 0 \ \wedge\ Place2State = 1$
      deadline: $SourceState = 0 \ \wedge\ T = 0 \ \wedge\ Place2State = 1$
      eff: $SourceState' = 1 \ \wedge\ t3' = T \ \wedge\ Place2State' = 2$
   sourceOut
      prec: $SourceState = 1 \ \wedge\ T = t1 + 50 \ \wedge\ Place1State = 1$
      deadline: $SourceState = 1 \ \wedge\ T = t1 + 50 \ \wedge\ Place1State = 1$
      eff: $t1' = T \ \wedge\ t4' = T \ \wedge\ Place1State' = 2$
   sourceOut
      prec: $SourceState = 1 \ \wedge\ T = t1 + 50 \ \wedge\ Place2State = 1$
      deadline: $SourceState = 1 \ \wedge\ T = t1 + 50 \ \wedge\ Place2State = 1$
      eff: $t1' = T \ \wedge\ t3' = T \ \wedge\ Place2State' = 2$
   sinkIn
      prec: $Place1State = 2 \ \wedge\ T > t4 + 80 \ \wedge\ SinkState = 1$
      deadline: $Place1State = 2 \ \wedge\ T \geq t4 + 90 \ \wedge\ SinkState = 1$
      eff: $Place1State' = 1 \ \wedge\ t2' = T \ \wedge\ SinkState' = 2$
   sinkIn
      prec: $Place2State = 2 \ \wedge\ T > t3 + 80 \ \wedge\ SinkState = 1$
      deadline: $Place2State = 2 \ \wedge\ T \geq t3 + 90 \ \wedge\ SinkState = 1$
      eff: $Place2State' = 1 \ \wedge\ t2' = T \ \wedge\ SinkState' = 2$
   play
      prec: $SinkState = 2 \ \wedge\ T = t2 + 5$
      deadline: $SinkState = 2 \ \wedge\ T = t2 + 5$
      eff: $SinkState' = 1$

Fig. 13.3. DTA Product Automaton for the Multimedia Stream

(Section 13.2.1). In particular, deadlines in the product automaton can be expressed as (semantically equivalent) preconditions for the *tick* action; because the product automaton does not contain half actions, time progress conditions can be independently obtained from every deadline.

Let $|A = (|\langle A_1, \ldots, A_n \rangle, V_S, \Theta_S)$ be a network of DTAs, and

$$\Pi \triangleq (V_L, \Theta_L, TL, \mathcal{A}, V_S, \Theta_S)$$

the corresponding product automaton. Let ρ_{tick} be defined as follows,

$$\rho_{tick} \triangleq (T' = T + 1) \wedge \bigwedge_{(a,p,d,e) \in \mathcal{A}} \neg d$$

Then, Π is semantically equivalent to the FTS $F_\Pi = (V, \Theta, \mathcal{T})$, where

$$V \triangleq V_L \cup V_S$$

$$\Theta \triangleq \Theta_L \wedge \Theta_S$$

$$\mathcal{T} \triangleq \{\rho_{tick}\} \cup \{\rho_\tau \triangleq p \wedge e \mid \tau = (a, p, d, e) \in \mathcal{A}, \ a \neq tick\}$$

Consider again the multimedia stream example, and the product automaton Π depicted by Figure 13.3. Figure 13.4 shows the equivalent FTS F_Π (superscripts have been used to distinguish the transition formulae that correspond to actions with the same label).

Given F_Π, then, invariance proofs can be used to confirm that synchronisation between *Source* and either *Place1* or *Place2* is always possible, i.e. that packets can be put in the *Channel* whenever the *Source* is ready to send them. This safety property[6] can be expressed by the LTL formula $\Box \phi$, where

$$\phi \triangleq \neg((T = 0 \vee T = t1 + 50) \wedge Place1State = 2 \wedge Place2State = 2)$$

As discussed in Section 13.2.1, the verification of $\Box \phi$ is achieved by applying the deductive rule,

$$\begin{array}{ll} \text{P1} & \varphi \rightarrow \phi \\ \text{P2} & \Theta \rightarrow \varphi \\ \text{P3} & \forall \tau \in \mathcal{T}, \ \rho_\tau \wedge \varphi \rightarrow \varphi' \\ \hline & \Box \phi \end{array}$$

In particular, Figure 13.5 offers a list of assertions, which can be used as auxiliary invariants in the verification of $\Box \phi$. The predicate $mult50(n)$ can be expressed in WS1S and holds whenever n is a multiple of 50.

---

[6]Section 11.3.2 discusses the verification of an equivalent (branching-time) reachability property, for a TA specification of the multimedia stream.

$V : \{T,\ t1,\ t2,\ t3,\ t4 \in \mathbb{N}$
$\quad SourceState \in \{0,1\},\ Place1State,\ Place2State,\ SinkState \in \{1,2\}$
$\quad \}$
$\Theta : T = 0\ \wedge\ t1 = 0\ \wedge\ t2 = 0\ \wedge\ t3 = 0\ \wedge\ t4 = 0\ \wedge$
$\quad SourceState = 0\ \wedge\ Place1State = 1\ \wedge\ Place2State = 1\ \wedge\ SinkState = 1$
$\mathcal{T} : \{\ \rho_{tick} : \quad \neg(SourceState = 0\ \wedge\ T = 0\ \wedge\ Place1State = 1)\ \wedge$
$\qquad\qquad\qquad \neg(SourceState = 0\ \wedge\ T = 0\ \wedge\ Place2State = 1)\ \wedge$
$\qquad\qquad\qquad \neg(SourceState = 1\ \wedge\ T = t1 + 50\ \wedge\ Place1State = 1)\ \wedge$
$\qquad\qquad\qquad \neg(SourceState = 1\ \wedge\ T = t1 + 50\ \wedge\ Place2State = 1)\ \wedge$
$\qquad\qquad\qquad \neg(Place1State = 2\ \wedge\ T \geq t4 + 90\ \wedge\ SinkState = 1)\ \wedge$
$\qquad\qquad\qquad \neg(Place2State = 2\ \wedge\ T \geq t3 + 90\ \wedge\ SinkState = 1)\ \wedge$
$\qquad\qquad\qquad \neg(SinkState = 2\ \wedge\ T = t2 + 5)\ \wedge$
$\qquad\qquad\qquad T' = T + 1$

$\rho^1_{sourceOut} : SourceState = 0\ \wedge\ T = 0\ \wedge\ Place1State = 1\ \wedge$
$\qquad\qquad\quad\ SourceState' = 1\ \wedge\ t4' = T\ \wedge\ Place1State' = 2$

$\rho^2_{sourceOut} : SourceState = 0\ \wedge\ T = 0\ \wedge\ Place2State = 1\ \wedge$
$\qquad\qquad\quad\ SourceState' = 1\ \wedge\ t3' = T\ \wedge\ Place2State' = 2$

$\rho^3_{sourceOut} : SourceState = 1\ \wedge\ T = t1 + 50\ \wedge\ Place1State = 1\ \wedge$
$\qquad\qquad\quad\ t1' = T\ \wedge\ t4' = T\ \wedge\ Place1State' = 2$

$\rho^4_{sourceOut} : SourceState = 1\ \wedge\ T = t1 + 50\ \wedge\ Place2State = 1\ \wedge$
$\qquad\qquad\quad\ t1' = T\ \wedge\ t3' = T\ \wedge\ Place2State' = 2$

$\rho^1_{sinkIn} : \quad Place1State = 2\ \wedge\ T > t4 + 80\ \wedge\ SinkState = 1\ \wedge$
$\qquad\qquad\ Place1State' = 1\ \wedge\ t2' = T\ \wedge\ SinkState' = 2$

$\rho^2_{sinkIn} : \quad Place2State = 2\ \wedge\ T > t3 + 80\ \wedge\ SinkState = 1\ \wedge$
$\qquad\qquad\ Place2State' = 1\ \wedge\ t2' = T\ \wedge\ SinkState' = 2$

$\rho_{play} : \quad SinkState = 2\ \wedge\ T = t2 + 5\ \wedge$
$\qquad\qquad\ SinkState' = 1\ \}$

Fig. 13.4. FTS F_Π for the Multimedia Stream

Notice that all formulae occurring in the deductive rule, that is $\varphi,\ \varphi',\ \phi,\ \Theta,$
the transition formulae ρ_τ, and the premises themselves would be instantiated
with WS1S formulae and, as such, they are expressible in MONA. Therefore,
MONA can be used to check whether a particular premise is valid. In the
case where the premise is not valid, MONA will return a given valuation (i.e.
a state) as a counterexample, and user interaction will be needed to assess
whether such a valuation is reachable in the system. As we have mentioned in
Section 13.2.1, if we are in the presence of a *reachable* state then $\Box\phi$ can be
immediately guaranteed *not* to hold. If, on the other hand, the MONA coun-

(1) $Place1State = 2 \;\wedge\; Place2State = 2 \Rightarrow (t3 \geq t4 + 50 \vee t4 \geq t3 + 50)$
(2) $t1 \geq t3 \;\wedge\; t1 \geq t4$
(3) $SourceState = 0 \Rightarrow T = 0 \;\wedge\; Place1State = 1 \;\wedge\; Place2State = 1$
(4) $(T > t4 + 90 \Rightarrow Place1State = 1) \;\wedge\; (T > t3 + 90 \Rightarrow Place2State = 1)$
(5) $T \geq t1 \;\wedge\; T \geq t2 \;\wedge\; T \geq t3 \;\wedge\; T \geq t4$
(6) $mult50(t1) \;\wedge\; mult50(t3) \;\wedge\; mult50(t4)$
(7) $t2 = T \;\wedge\; T > 0 \Rightarrow ((Place1State = 1 \;\wedge\; T \leq t4 + 90 \;\wedge\; T > t4 + 80)\vee$
$\qquad\qquad\qquad\qquad (Place2State = 1 \;\wedge\; T \leq t3 + 90 \;\wedge\; T > t3 + 80))$
(8) $SinkState = 2 \Rightarrow T \leq t2 + 5$
(9) $T \leq t1 + 50$

Fig. 13.5. Example Auxiliary Invariants

terexample denotes an *unreachable* state, then verification might proceed by strengthening φ with other auxiliary invariants, and checking all rule premises again. Figure 13.6 shows, as an example, the MONA specification that checks whether the invariant ϕ is preserved by the time action, i.e. to check the validity of the WS1S formula (part of rule premise $P3$),

$$\rho_{tick} \wedge \phi \Rightarrow \phi'$$

```
% Variables

var1 T,T',t1,t3,t4,t2,
     SourceState where SourceState in {0,1},
     Place1State where Place1State in {1,2},
     Place2State where Place2State in {1,2},
     SinkState where SinkState in {1,2};

% ρtick  ∧  φ ⇒ φ' as a MONA formula
% for  φ ≜ ¬((T = 0 ∨ T = t1 + 50) ∧ Place1State = 2 ∧ Place1State = 2)

~(SourceState=0 & T=0 & Place1State=1) &
~(SourceState=0 & T=0 & Place2State=1) &
~(SourceState=1 & T=t1+50 & Place1State=2) &
~(SourceState=1 & T=t1+50 & Place1State=1) &
~(Place1State=2 & T>=t4+90 & SinkState=1) &
~(Place2State=2 & T>=t3+90 & SinkState=1) &
~(SinkState=2 & T=t2+5) &
T' = T+1 &
(~((T=0 | T=t1+50) & Place1State=2 & Place2State=2))
=>
(~((T'=0 | T'=t1+50) & Place1State=2 & Place2State=2));
```

Fig. 13.6. MONA Specification to Verify $\rho_{tick} \wedge \phi \Rightarrow \phi'$

Other quality of service properties can also be verified for the multimedia stream, such as throughput (i.e. the number of packets delivered to the *Sink* in a given period of time), and latency (i.e. the end-to-end delay between the time a packet is sent by the *Source*, and the time it is played by the *Sink*). As shown in [85], a few modifications to the original DTA specification allow these properties to be expressed as invariants, and be verified by MONA.

13.5 Discussion: Comparing DTAs and TIOAs with Urgency

A detailed comparison between DTAs and other similar notations (e.g. clock transition systems [135]) escapes the format of this book (the reader is referred, instead, to [85]). Nevertheless, this section highlights some differences and common points between DTAs and timed I/O automata with urgency (TIOAUs, for short) [82].

Both notations, DTAs and TIOAUs, are influenced (among other frameworks) by timed I/O automata [110] and TAD (Section 12.3.1). As a result of this, a number of similarities can be observed. In both notations, DTA and TIOAU, automata are composed of variables, which define the state-space, and actions, which model instantaneous state changes (i.e. discrete events). Actions are characterised by a label, a precondition, an effect and a deadline. The set of actions is partitioned into internal (or completed) and external (input or output) actions. Automata can be composed to describe complex systems, and interaction among components is realised via message passing (matching external actions). Also, DTA and TIOAU specifications are time-reactive (although, zeno-timelocks can occur in both models). But here the similarities end, and the models differ in a number of ways.

Synchronisation and Parallel Composition. DTAs adopt CCS-like binary synchronisation, and only allows one level of parallel components. Effectively, a network of DTAs results in a product automaton where synchronisation is resolved, and all actions are completed. Thus, the product automaton cannot participate in further synchronisations, and so parallel composition cannot be applied incrementally. Notice that this is consistent with the communicating automata models described in this book: finite- and infinite-state communicating automata (chapter 8), and timed automata (chapter 11).

On the other hand, TIOAUs are closer to process calculi such as CSP or LOTOS. TIOAUs adopt multiway synchronisation, and parallel composition can be incrementally applied to build larger systems (as discussed in Section 2.3.6.4, this suits a constraint-oriented style of specification). In TIOAU, parallel composition can be thought of as yielding a new automaton, where synchronisation between matching output and input actions results in a new output action (and not a completed action, as in DTAs). Also, and unlike DTAs, TIOAUs are *input enabled*; i.e. input actions are enabled in any state.

This is consistent with the intention of TIOAUs to model open systems, in which input actions are assumed to be under the control of the environment (hence, it can be argued that input actions should not be constrained by the system). These different approaches to specification have been discussed in Section 8.2.6.2, in the context of communicating automata and process calculi. In general, the same conclusions apply here, and thus we can argue that the expressiveness of TIOAUs facilitates the specification of complex systems, whereas the verification of DTA specifications is easier to automatise.

Time. Discrete time in DTAs is represented by a time-passage action, whereas in TIOAUs continuous time is represented by trajectories (which describes how variables, i.e. the state, change over time). It is argued [110], that trajectories are more convenient than time-passage actions, as they lead to simpler mathematical proofs. On the other hand, a time-passage action, such as the *tick* action in DTAs, seems to be a more natural choice if invariance proofs are to be applied (because both discrete events and the passage of time are represented by the same kind of actions, mapping DTAs to FTSs is straightforward).

Expressiveness of the Specification Language. Representing complex specifications with TIOAUs can be considerably easier than doing so with DTAs. For example, TIOAUs support continuous time domains, parameterised actions, more general data types and a powerful assertion language (for writing preconditions and effects). On the other hand, the expressiveness of DTAs is limited to allow MONA to be used as a verification tool, whereas proofs for TIOAUs specifications are usually developed by hand.

References

1. M. Abadi and L. Lamport. An old-fashioned recipe for real time. *ACM Transactions on Programming Languages and Systems*, 16(5):1543–1571, September 1994.
2. S. Abramsky. Observation equivalence as a testing equivalence. *Theoretical Computer Science*, 53:225–241, 1987.
3. L. Aceto, P. Bouyer, A. Burgueño, and K. Larsen. The power of reachability testing for timed automata. *Theoretical Computer Science*, 1-3(300):411–475, 2003.
4. L. Aceto and D. Murphy. On the ill-timed but well-caused. In *CONCUR'93: Concurrency Theory*, Lecture Notes in Computer Science, N0. 715. Springer-Verlag, 1993.
5. A. Aho and J. Ullman. *Foundations of Computer Science*. Computer Science Press, 1992.
6. R. Alur, C. Courcoubetis, and D. Dill. Model-checking in dense real-time. *Information and Computation*, 104(1):2–34, May 1993.
7. R. Alur and D. Dill. A theory of timed automata. *Theoretical Computer Science*, 126:183–235, 1994.
8. J.C.M. Baeten, J.A. Bergstra, and J.W. Klop. On the consistency of Koomen's fair abstraction rule. *Theoretical Computer Science*, 51:129–176, 1987.
9. F. Balarin. Approximate reachability analysis of timed automata. In *IEEE Real-Time Systems Symposium*, pages 52–61, 1996.
10. D. Basin and S. Friedrich. Combining WS1S and HOL. In D.M. Gabbay and M. de Rijke, editors, *Frontiers of Combining Systems 2*, volume 7 of *Studies in Logic and Computation*, pages 39–56. Research Studies Press/Wiley, Baldock, Herts, UK, February 2000.
11. G. Behrmann, P. Bouyer, K.G. Larsen, and R. Pelanek. Lower and upper bounds in zone based abstractions of timed automata. In *Proceedings of TACAS'04*, LNCS 2988, pages 312–326. Springer, 2004.
12. J. Bengtsson. Efficient symbolic state exploration of timed systems: Theory and implementation. Technical Report 2001-009, Department of Information Technology, Uppsala University, 2001.
13. J. Bengtsson and W. Yi. Timed automata: Semantics, algorithms and tools. In W. Reisig and G. Rozenberg, editors, *Lecture Notes on Concurrency and Petri Nets*, LNCS 3098. Springer, 2004.

14. B. Berard, M. Bidoit, A. Finkel, F. Laroussinie, A. Petit, L. Petrucci, and P. Schnoebelen. *Systems and Software Verification.* Springer, 2001.

15. J.A. Bergstra and J.W. Klop. Algebra for communicating processes with abstraction. *Journal of Theoretical Computer Science,* 37:77–121, 1985.

16. G. Berhmann, A. David, and K. Larsen. A tutorial on UPPAAL. In M. Bernardo and F. Corradini, editors, *Formal Methods for the Design of Real-Time Systems. International School on Formal Methods for the design of Computer, Communication and Software Systems, SFM-RT 2004. Revised Lectures,* LNCS 3185, pages 200–236. Springer, 2004.

17. C. Bernardeschi, J. Dustzadeh, A. Fantechi, E. Najm, A. Nimour, and F. Olsen. Transformations and consistent semantics for ODP viewpoints. In H. Bowman and J. Derrick, editors, *FMOODS'97, 2nd IFIP Conference on Formal Methods for Open Object Based Distributed Systems.* Chapman & Hall, July 1997.

18. M. Bernardo and R. Gorrieri. A tutorial on empa: A theory of concurrent processes with nondeterminism, priorities, probabilities and time. *Theoretical Computer Science,* 202:1–54, 1998.

19. N.S. Bjørner. *Integrating Decision Procedures for Temporal Verification.* PhD thesis, Computer Science Department, Stanford University, November 1998.

20. N.S. Bjørner, A. Browne, and Z. Manna. Automatic generation of invariants and intermediate assertions. *Theoretical Computer Science,* 173(1):49–87, February 1997.

21. G. S. Blair, L. Blair, H. Bowman, and A. Chetwynd. *Formal Specification of Distributed Multimedia Systems.* UCL Press, 1998.

22. E. Boiten, H. Bowman, J. Derrick, and M. Steen. Viewpoint consistency in Z and LOTOS: A case study. In J. Fitzgerald, C.B. Jones, and P. Lucas, editors, *FME'97: Industrial Applications and Strengthened Foundations of Formal Methods,* LNCS 1313, pages 644–664. Springer-Verlag, September 1997.

23. E. Boiten, J. Derrick, H. Bowman, and M. Steen. Consistency and refinement for partial specification in Z. In M.-C. Gaudel and J. Woodcock, editors, *FME'96: Industrial Benefit of Formal Methods, Third International Symposium of Formal Methods Europe,* LNCS 1051, pages 287–306. Springer-Verlag, March 1996.

24. T. Bolognesi and E. Brinksma. Introduction to the ISO specification language LOTOS. *Computer Networks and ISDN Systems,* 14(1):25–29, 1988.

25. T. Bolognesi and F. Lucidi. LOTOS-like process algebras with urgent or timed interactions. In *FORTE'91.* North-Holland, 1991.

26. T. Bolognesi, F. Lucidi, and S. Trigila. Converging towards a timed LOTOS standard. *Computer Standards & Interfaces,* 16:87–118, 1994.

27. G. Booch. *Object-oriented Analysis and Design.* Benjamin/Cummings, 1994.

28. M. Boreale, P. Inverardi, and M. Nesi. Complete sets of axioms for finite basic LOTOS behavioural equivalences. *Information Processing Letters,* 43:155–160, 1992.

29. S. Bornot and J. Sifakis. On the composition of hybrid systems. In *Hybrid Systems: Computation and Control,* LNCS 1386, pages 49–63. Springer, 1998.

30. S. Bornot, J. Sifakis, and S. Tripakis. Modeling urgency in timed systems. In *Compositionality: The Significant Difference, International Symposium, COMPOS'97, Bad Malente, Germany, September 8-12, 1997. Revised Lectures,* LNCS 1536, pages 103–129. Springer, 1998.

31. G. Boudol and I. Castellani. Flow models of distributed computations: Three equivalent semantics for CCS. *Information and Computation*, 114:247–314, 1994.

32. H. Bowman. A true concurrency approach to time extended LOTOS (revised version). Technical Report 17-96, Computing Laboratory, University of Kent at Canterbury, 1996.

33. H. Bowman. A LOTOS based tutorial on formal methods for object-oriented distributed systems. *New Generation Computing*, 16:343–372, 1998.

34. H. Bowman. Modelling timeouts without timelocks. In *ARTS'99, Formal Methods for Real-Time and Probabilistic Systems, 5th International AMAST Workshop*, LNCS 1601, pages 335–353. Springer-Verlag, 1999.

35. H. Bowman. Time and action lock freedom properties for timed automata. In M. Kim, B. Chin, S. Kang, and D. Lee, editors, *FORTE 2001, Formal Techniques for Networked and Distributed Systems*, pages 119–134, Cheju Island, Korea, 2001. Kluwer Academic.

36. H. Bowman, L. Blair, G.S. Blair, and A. Chetwynd. Time versus abstraction in formal description. In R.L. Tenney, P.D. Amer, and M.U. Uyar, editors, *Formal Description Techniques VI, FORTE'93*, pages 467–482, Boston, October 1993. North-Holland.

37. H. Bowman, E.A. Boiten, J. Derrick, and M. Steen. Viewpoint consistency in ODP, a general interpretation. In E. Najm and J. Stefani, editors, *First IFIP International Workshop on Formal Methods for Open Object-based Distributed Systems*, pages 189–204, Paris, March 1996. Chapman & Hall.

38. H. Bowman, C. Briscoe-Smith, J. Derrick, and B. Strulo. On behavioural subtyping in LOTOS. In H. Bowman and J. Derrick, editors, *FMOODS'97, Second IFIP International Conference on Formal Methods for Open Object-based Distributed Systems*. Chapman & Hall, 1997.

39. H. Bowman and J. Derrick. Extending LOTOS with time; a true concurrency perspective. In M. Bertran and T. Rus, editors, *Proceedings 4th Amast Workshop on Real-Time Systems, Concurrent and Distributed Software*, LNCS 1231. Springer-Verlag, 1997.

40. H. Bowman and J. Derrick. A junction between state based and behavioural specification. In *Formal Methods for Open Object-based Distributed Systems*, pages 213–239. Kluwer, February 1999.

41. H. Bowman and J. Derrick, editors. *Formal Methods for Distributed Processing, A Survey of Object-Oriented Techniques*. Cambridge University Press, 2001.

42. H. Bowman, J. Derrick, P. Linington, and M. Steen. Cross viewpoint consistency in open distributed processing. *IEE Software Engineering Journal*, 11(1):44–57, January 1996.

43. H. Bowman, G. Faconti, and M. Massink. Specification and verification of media constraints using UPPAAL. In *5th Eurographics Workshop on the Design, Specification and Verification of Interactive Systems, DSV-IS 98*, Eurographics Series. Springer-Verlag, August 1998.

44. H. Bowman and R. Gomez. How to stop time stopping. Submitted for publication, 2005.

45. H. Bowman, R. Gomez, and L. Su. A tool for the syntactic detection of zeno-timelocks in timed automata. In *Proceedings of the 6th AMAST Workshop on Real-Time Systems*, Stirling, July 2004.

46. H. Bowman and J. Katoen. A true concurrency semantics for ET-LOTOS. Technical Report 12/97, Univeristy of Erlangen, 1997.

47. H. Bowman and J. Katoen. A true concurrency semantics for ET-LOTOS. In *CSD'98 International Conference on Application of Concurrency to System Design*. IEEE Computer Society, 1998.

48. H. Bowman, M.W.A. Steen, E.A. Boiten, and J. Derrick. A formal framework for viewpoint consistency. *Formal Methods in System Design*, 21:111–166, 2002.

49. M. Bozga, C. Daws, O. Maler, A. Olivero, S. Tripakis, and S. Yovine. Kronos: A model-checking tool for real-time systems. In *Proceedings of the 10th International Conference on Computer Aided Verification*, pages 546–550. Springer-Verlag, 1998.

50. E. Brinksma. A theory for the derivation of tests. In S. Aggarwal and K. Sabnani, editors, *Protocol Specification, Testing and Verification, VIII*, pages 63–74, Atlantic City, USA, June 1988. North-Holland.

51. E. Brinksma, J. Katoen, R. Langerak, and D. Latella. Performance analysis and true concurrency semantics. In *Theories and Experiences for Real-time System Development (ARTS'93)*, pages 309–337. World Scientific, 1994.

52. E. Brinksma and G. Scollo. Formal notions of implementation and conformance in LOTOS. Technical Report INF-86-13, Dept of Informatics, Twente University of Technology, 1986.

53. E. Brinksma, G. Scollo, and C. Steenbergen. Process specification, their implementation and their tests. In B. Sarikaya and G. V. Bochmann, editors, *Protocol Specification, Testing and Verification, VI*, pages 349–360, Montreal, Canada, June 1986. North-Holland.

54. R.E. Bryant. Graph-based algorithms for Boolean function manipulation. *IEEE Transactions on Computers*, C-35(8), 1986.

55. J.R. Büchi. On a decision method in restricted second-order arithmetic. *Zeitschrift für Mathemathische Logik and Grundlagen der Mathematik*, 6:66–92, 1960.

56. CCITT Z.100. *Specification and Description Language SDL*, 1988.

57. E. Clarke and E. Emerson. Design and synthesis of synchronization skeletons using branching-time temporal logic. In D. Kozen, editor, *Logic of Programs, Workshop, Yorktown Heights, New York, May 1981*, LNCS 131, pages 52–71. Springer-Verlag, 1982.

58. E.M. Clarke, O. Grumberg, and D.A. Peleg. *Model Checking*. The MIT Press, 1999.

59. J. Courtiat and R.C. de Oliveria. RT-LOTOS and its application to multimedia protocol specification and validation. In *International Conference on Multimedia Networking*, pages 30–47. IEEE Computing Press, 1995.

60. E. Cusack and G. H. B. Rafsanjani. ZEST. In S. Stepney, R. Barden, and D. Cooper, editors, *Object Orientation in Z*, Workshops in Computing, pages 113–126. Springer-Verlag, 1992.

61. E. Cusack, S. Rudkin, and C. Smith. An object oriented interpretation of LOTOS. In *Proceedings 2nd International Conference on Formal Description Techniques (FORTE'89)*. North-Holland, December 1989.

62. A. David, G. Behrmann, K. Larsen, and W. Yi. A tool architecture for the next generation of UPPAAL. In *UNU/IIST 10th Anniversary Colloquium. Formal Methods at the Cross Roads: From Panacea to Foundational Support*, LNCS 2757. Springer, 2003.

63. A. David, G. Behrmann, K. Larsen, and W. Yi. Unification & sharing in timed automata verification. In *SPIN Workshop 03*, volume 2648 of *LNCS*, pages 225–229, 2003.

64. J. Davies. *Specification and Proof in Real-time CSP*. Cambridge University Press, 1993. Distinguished Dissertations in Computer Science.

65. J. Davies, J.W. Bryans, and S.A. Schneider. Real-time LOTOS and timed observations. In D. Hogrefe and S. Leue, editors, *Formal Description Techniques VIII*. Chapman & Hall, 1995.

66. C. Daws, A. Olivero, S. Tripakis, and S. Yovine. The tool KRONOS. In *Hybrid Systems III, Verification and Control*, LNCS 1066. Springer-Verlag, 1996.

67. C. Daws and S. Tripakis. Model checking of real-time reachability properties using abstractions. In *TACAS*, pages 313–329, 1998.

68. C. Daws and S. Yovine. Reducing the number of clock variables of timed automata. In *RTSS '96: Proceedings of the 17th IEEE Real-Time Systems Symposium (RTSS '96)*, page 73. IEEE Computer Society, 1996.

69. J. Derrick and E. Boiten. *Refinement in Z and Object-Z: Foundations and Advanced Applications*. Springer, FACIT Series, 2001.

70. J. Derrick, E.A. Boiten, H. Bowman, and M. Steen. Supporting ODP - translating LOTOS to Z. In *First IFIP International workshop on Formal Methods for Open Object-based Distributed Systems*, Paris, March 1996. Chapman & Hall.

71. D. Dill. Timing assumptions and verification of finite-state concurrent systems. In *Proceedings of the International Workshop on Automatic Verification Methods for Finite State Systems*, pages 197–212. Springer-Verlag, 1990.

72. C.C. Elgot. Decision problems of finite automata design and related arithmetics. *Trans. Amer. Math. Soc.*, 98:21–51, 1961.

73. A. Fantechi, S. Gnesi, and G. Ristori. Compositional logic semantics and LOTOS. In L. Logrippo, R. L. Probert, and H. Ural, editors, *Protocol Specification, Testing and Verification, X*, Ottawa, Canada, June 1990. North-Holland.

74. K. Farooqui and L. Logrippo. Viewpoint transformations. In J. de Meer, B. Mahr, and O. Spaniol, editors, *2nd International IFIP TC6 Conference on Open Distributed Processing*, pages 352–362, Berlin, Germany, September 1993.

75. J. Fernandez. An implementation of an efficient algorithm for bisimulation equivalence. *Science of Computer Programming*, 13(2–3):219–236, 1990.

76. J. Fernandez and L. Mournier. On-the-fly verification of behavioural rquivalences and preorder. In *3rd Workshop on Computer-Aided Verification*, 1991.

77. C.J. Fidge. A comparative introduction to CSP, CCS and LOTOS. In *FORTE 92 Tutorial*, Lannion, France, 1992.

78. C.J. Fidge. A constraint-oriented real-time process calculus. In M. Diaz and R. Groz, editors, *FORTE 92, Formal Description Techniques V*, Lannion, France, 1993. North-Holland.

79. A.C.W. Finkelstein, D. Gabbay, A. Hunter, J. Kramer, and B. Nuseibeh. Inconsistency handling in multiperspective specifications. *IEEE Transactions on Software Engineering*, 20(8):569–578, August 1994.

80. K. Fisher and J.C. Mitchell. Notes on typed object-oriented programming. In *Proceedings of Theoretical Aspects of Computer Software (TACS '94)*, Sendai, Japan, LNCS 789, pages 844–886. Springer, 1994.

81. H. Garavel, F. Lang, and R. Mateescu. An overview of CADP 2001. Technical Report RT-254, INRIA, France, December 2001. Also see http://www.inrialpes.fr/vasy/cadp/.

82. B. Gebremichael and F. Vaandrager. Specifying Urgency in Timed I/O Automata. Technical Report NIII-R0459, Radboud University Nijmegen, Netherlands, December 2004.

83. A. Goldberg and D. Robson. *Smalltalk-80: The Language and its Implementation.* Addison-Wesley, 1983.

84. R. Gomez and H. Bowman. Discrete timed automata and MONA: Description, specification and verification of a multimedia stream. In H. Konig, M. Heiner, and A. Wolisz, editors, *Formal Techniques for Networked and Distributed Systems - FORTE 2003. Proceedings of the 23rd IFIP WG 6.1 International Conference, Berlin, Germany, September/October 2003*, LNCS 2767, pages 177–192. Springer, 2003.

85. R. Gomez and H. Bowman. Discrete timed automata, invariance proofs and mona: An alternative approach to the specification and verification of real-time systems. Submitted for publication, 2004.

86. D. Gries and F.B. Schneider. *A Logical Approach to Discrete Math.* Springer-Verlag, 1993.

87. D. Harel. Statecharts: A visual formalism for complex systems. *Science of Computer Programming*, 8:231–274, 1987.

88. M. Hendriks, G. Behrmann, K. Larsen, P. Niebert, and F. Vaandrager. Adding symmetry reduction to UPPAAL. In K. Larsen and P. Niebert, editors, *Proceedings of FORMATS 2003*, LNCS 2791, pages 46–59. Springer-Verlag, 2004.

89. M. Hennessy. *Algebraic Theory of Processes.* MIT Press, 1988.

90. M. Hennessy and R. Milner. Algebraic laws for non-determinism and concurrency. *Journal of the ACM*, 32(1):137–161, 1985.

91. T. Henzinger, X. Nicollin, J. Sifakis, and S. Yovine. Symbolic model checking for real-time systems. *Information and Computation*, 111(2):193–244, 1994.

92. T.A. Henzinger and Pei-Hsin. HyTech: The Cornell HYbrid TECHnology tool. In *Proceedings of TACAS, Workshop on Tools and Algorithms for the Construction and Analysis of Systems*, 1995.

93. H. Hermanns. *Interactive Markov Chains.* PhD thesis, University of Erlangen, 1998.

94. J. Hillston. *A Compositional Approach to Performance Modelling.* Cambridge University Press, 1996. Distinguished Dissertations in Computer Science.

95. C.A.R. Hoare. Communicating sequential processes. *Communications of the ACM*, 21(8):666–677, 1978.

96. C.A.R. Hoare. *Communicating Sequential Processes.* Prentice-Hall, 1985.

97. G. Holzmann. *The SPIN MODEL CHECKER: Primer and Reference Manual.* Addison-Wesley, 2003.

98. G.J. Holzmann. *Design and Validation of Computer Protocols.* Prentice-Hall, 1991.

99. International Standards Organization. *Belgium-Spanish Proposal for a Time Extended LOTOS*, December 1994.

100. C. Ip and D. Dill. Better verification through symmetry. *Formal Methods in System Design*, 9(1-2):41–75, 1996.

101. ISO. Information processing systems – Open Systems Interconnection – LOTOS – A formal description technique based on the temporal ordering of observational behaviour, 1989. IS 8807.

102. ISO. *Time Extended LOTOS.* International Standards Organization, 1997. Available at ftp://ftp.dit.upm.es/pub/lotos/elotos/.

103. ISO. *Information Technology - E-LOTOS, ISO/IEC 15437:2001, International Standard.* ISO, 2001.

104. ISO 8807. *LOTOS: A Formal Description Technique based on the Temporal Ordering of Observational Behaviour*, July 1987.

105. ISO 9074. *Estelle, a Formal Description Technique based on an extended state transition model*, June 1987.

106. ITU Recommendation X.901-904 — ISO/IEC 10746 1-4. *Open Distributed Processing - Reference Model - Parts 1-4*, July 1995.

107. J. Katoen. *Quantitative and Qualititative Extensions of Event Structures*. PhD thesis, University of Twente, The Netherlands, 1996.

108. J. Katoen, D.Latella, R. Langerak, E. Brinksma, and T. Bolognesi. A consistent causality-based view on a timed process algebra including urgent interactions. *Journal of Formal Methods in System Design*, 12(2):189–216, 1998.

109. J. Katoen, D. Latella, R. Langerak, and E. Brinksma. On specifying real-time systems in a causality-based setting. In B. Jonsson and J. Parrow, editors, *Formal Techniques in Real-Time and Fault-Tolerant Systems*, LNCS 1135, pages 385–405. Springer-Verlag, 1996.

110. D. Kaynar, N. Lynch, R. Segala, and F. Vaandrager. Timed I/O automata: a mathematical framework for modelling and analyzing real-time systems. In *Proceedings 24th IEEE International Real-Time Systems Symposium (RTSS03)*, pages 166–177. IEEE Computer Society, 2003.

111. N. Klarlund and A. Möller. *MONA Version 1.4 User Manual*. BRICS, University of Aarhus, Denmark, January 2001.

112. D. Kozen. Results on the propositional mu-calculus. *Theoretical Computer Science*, 27:333–354, 1983.

113. L. Lamport. Hybrid systems in TLA+. In *Hybrid Systems*, LNCS 736, pages 77–102. Springer-Verlag, 1993.

114. R. Langerak. *Transformations and Semantics for LOTOS*. PhD thesis, University of Twente, The Netherlands, 1992.

115. K. Lano. Specification of distributed systems in VDM++. In *FORTE'95*. Chapman & Hall, 1995.

116. K. Larsen, F. Larsson, P. Pettersson, and W. Yi. Efficient verification of real-time systems: Compact data structures and state-space reduction. In *Proceedings of the 18th IEEE Real-Time Systems Symposium*, pages 14–24. IEEE Computer Society Press, December 1997.

117. K. Larsen, F. Larsson, P. Pettersson, and W. Yi. Compact data structure and state-space reduction for model checking real time systems. *Real-Time Systems*, 25(2):255–275, September 2003.

118. K. Larsen and A. Skou. Bisimulation through probabilistic testing. In *6th ACM Symposium on Principles of Programming Languages*, 1989.

119. K.G. Larsen, B. Steffen, and C. Weise. A constraint oriented proof methodology based on modal transition systems. Technical Report RS-94-47, University of Aarhus, 1994.

120. G. Leduc. *On the Role of Implementation Relations in the Design of Distributed Systems using LOTOS*. PhD thesis, University of Liège, Liège, Belgium, June 1991.

121. G. Leduc. An upward compatible timed extension to LOTOS. In *FORTE'91*. North-Holland, 1991.

122. G. Leduc. A framework based on implementation relations for implementing LOTOS specifications. *Computer Networks and ISDN Systems*, 25:23–41, 1992.

123. G. Leduc and L. Leonard. A timed LOTOS supporting a dense time domain and including new timed operators. In *FORTE'92*, Lannion, France, October 1992. North-Holland.

124. L. Leonard. *An Extended LOTOS for the Design of Time-Sensitive Systems.* PhD thesis, University of Liege, Belgium, 1997.

125. L. Leonard and G. Leduc. An enhanced version of timed LOTOS and its application to a case study. In P. Amir R. Tenney and U. Uyar, editors, *FORTE'93*, pages 483–498, Boston, October 1993. North-Holland.

126. L. Leonard and G. Leduc. An introduction to ET-LOTOS for the description of time-sensitive systems. *Computer Networks and ISDN Systems*, 29:271–292, 1996.

127. L. Leonard, G. Leduc, and A. Danthine. The tick-tock case study for the assessment of timed fdts. In *The OSI95 Transport Service with Multimedia Support*, pages 338–352. Springer-Verlag, 1994.

128. O. Lichtenstein and A. Pnueli. Propositional temporal logics: Decidability and completeness. *Logic Journal of the IGPL*, 8(1), 2000.

129. P. F. Linington. RM-ODP: The architecture. In K. Raymond and L. Armstrong, editors, *IFIP TC6 International Conference on Open Distributed Processing*, pages 15–33, Brisbane, Australia, February 1995. Chapman and Hall.

130. B. Liskov and J. M. Wing. A new definition of the subtype relation. In O. M. Nierstrasz, editor, *ECOOP '93 - Object-Oriented Programming*, LNCS 707, pages 118–141. Springer-Verlag, 1993.

131. R. Loogen and U. Goltz. Modelling nondeterministic concurrent processes with event structures. *Fundamenta Informaticae XIV*, pages 39–74, 1991.

132. N. Lynch and M. Tuttle. An introduction to input/output automata. *CWI Quarterly*, 2(3):219–246, September 1989.

133. N. Lynch and F. Vaandrager. Forward and backward simulations: I. untimed systems. *Information and Computation*, 121(2):214–233, 1995.

134. N. Lynch and F. Vaandrager. Forward and backward simulations—Part ii: Timing-based systems. *Information and Computation*, 128(1):1–25, July 1996.

135. Z. Manna, Y. Kesten, and A. Pnueli. Verifying clocked transition systems. In *Hybrid Systems III*, LNCS 1066, pages 13–40. Springer-Verlag, 1996.

136. Z. Manna and A. Pnueli. *The Temporal Logic of Reactive and Concurrent Systems: Specification.* Springer-Verlag, 1992.

137. Z. Manna and A. Pnueli. *Temporal Verification of Reactive Systems: Safety.* Springer-Verlag, 1995.

138. R. Mateescu and M. Sighireanu. Efficient on-the-fly model-checking for regular alternation-free mu-calculus. In I. Schieferdecker S. Gnesi and A. Rennoch, editors, *FMICS'2000, 5th International Workshop on Formal Methods for Industrial Critical Systems, GMD Report 91*, pages 65–89, 2000.

139. A. Mazurkiewicz. Basic notions of trace theory. In *Linear Time, Branching Time and Partial Order in Logics and Models of Concurrency*, LNCS 354. Springer-Verlag, 1988.

140. K. McMillan. *Symbolic model checking: an approach to the state explosion problem.* PhD thesis, Carnegie Mellon University, Pittsburgh, PA, 1992.

141. P. Merlin and D.J. Farber. Recoverability of communication protocols - Implications of a theoretical study. *IEEE Transactions on Communications*, COM-24:1036–1043, September 1976.

142. M. Merritt, F. Modugno, and M. Tuttle. Time-constrained automata. In *CONCUR: 2nd International Conference on Concurrency Theory*. LNCS, Springer-Verlag, 1991.

143. C. Miguel, A. Fernandez, and L. Vidaller. Extending LOTOS towards performance evaluation. In M. Diaz and R. Groz, editors, *Formal Description Techniques, V*, Lannion, France, October 1992. North-Holland.

144. G.J. Milne. CIRCAL and the representation of communication concurrency and time. *ACM Transactions on Programming Languages and Systems*, 7(2):270–298, 1985.

145. R. Milner. *A Calculus of Communicating Systems*. LNCS 92. Springer-Verlag, 1980.

146. R. Milner. Calculi for synchrony and asynchrony. *Journal of Theoretical Computer Science*, 25:267–310, 1985.

147. R. Milner. Process constructors and interpretations. In *Information Processing 86*. Elsevier Publishers, 1986.

148. R. Milner. *Communication and Concurrency*. Prentice-Hall, 1989.

149. R. Milner, J. Parrow, and D. Walker. A calculus of mobile processes. *Information and Computation*, 100:1–77, 1992.

150. H.B. Munster. Comments on the LOTOS standard. Technical Report DITC 52/91, National Physical Laboratory, Teddington, Middlesex, UK, September 1991.

151. E. Najm, J. Stefani, and A. Fevrier. *Introducing Mobility in LOTOS*. ISO/IEC JTC1/SC21/WG1 approved AFNOR contribution, July 1994.

152. A. Nakata, T. Higashino, and K. Taniguchi. Lotos enhancement to specify time constraint among non-adjacentactions using 1st-order logic. In *FORTE'93*. North-Holland, 1993.

153. R. De Nicola and M. Hennessy. Testing equivalences for processes. *Journal of Theoretical Computer Science*, 34:83–133, 1984.

154. X. Nicollin and J. Sifakis. An overview and synthesis on timed process algebra. In *Real-time Theory in Practice*, LNCS 600, pages 549–572. Springer-Verlag, June 1991.

155. M. Nielsen, G. Plotkin, and G. Winskel. Petri nets, event structures and domains, part 1. *Theoretical Computer Science*, 13, 1981.

156. O. Nierstrasz. Regular types for active objects. In *Object-oriented Software Composition*, pages 99–120. Prentice-Hall, 1995.

157. J.S. Ostroff. *Temporal Logic for Real-Time Systems*. Research Studies Press, 1989.

158. S. Owre and H. Rueß. Integrating WS1S with PVS. In E.A. Emerson and A.P. Sistla, editors, *Computer-Aided Verification, CAV '2000*, LNCS 1855, pages 548–551. Springer-Verlag, 2000.

159. R. Paige and R. Tarjan. Three partition refinement algorithms. *SIAM Journal of Computing*, 16(6), 1987.

160. D. Park. Concurrency and automata on infinite sequences. In *Proceedings of 5th GI Conference*, LNCS 104, pages 167–183. Springer-Verlag, 1981.

161. C.A. Petri. Fundamentals of a theory of asynchronous information flow. In *Information Processing 1962, Proceedings of the IFIP Congress 62*, pages 386–390, Munich, Germany, 1962. North Holland Publishing Company.

162. A. Pnueli. The temporal logic of programs. In *Proceedings of the 18th IEEE Symposium Foundations of Computer Science (FOCS 1977)*, pages 46–57, 1977.

163. F. Puntigam. Types for active objects based on trace semantics. In *First IFIP Workshop on Formal Methods for Open Object-Based Distributed Systems*, Paris, March 1996. Chapman & Hall.

164. J. Quemada and A. Fernandez. Introduction of quantitative relative time into lotos. In *Protocol Specification, Testing and Verification, VII*, pages 105–121. North-Holland, 1987.

165. J. Quemada, D. Frutos, and A. Azcorra. Tic: A timed calculus. Technical Report 28040, University of Madrid, Madrid, Spain, July 1991.

166. J. Quemada, C. Miguel, D. de Frutos, and L. Llana. *Proposal for Timed LOTOS.* ISO/IEC JTC1/SC21/WG1, 1994.

167. T. Regan. *Process Algebra for Timed Systems.* PhD thesis, University of Sussex, Sussex, UK, 1991.

168. T. Regan. Multimedia in temporal LOTOS: A lip synchronisation algorithm. In *PSTV XIII, 13th Protocol Spec., Testing & Verification.* North-Holland, 1993.

169. W. Reisig. *Petri Nets, An Introduction.* Springer-Verlag, 1982.

170. A. Rensink. Posets for configurations! In *CONCUR'92*, LNCS 30. Springer-Verlag, 1992.

171. A.W. Roscoe. *The Theory and Practice of Concurrency.* Prentice-Hall, 1997.

172. G.A. Rose. Object-Z. In S. Stepney, R. Barden, and D. Cooper, editors, *Object Orientation in Z*, Workshops in Computing, pages 59–78. Springer-Verlag, 1992.

173. S. Rudkin. Inheritance in LOTOS. In K.R. Parker and G.A. Rose, editors, *Formal Description Techniques, IV*, Sydney, Australia, November 1991. North-Holland.

174. A. Sandholm and M.I. Schwartzbach. Distributed safety controllers for web services. In E. Astesiano, editor, *Fundamental Approaches to Software Engineering (FASE'98)*, LNCS 1382, pages 270–284. Springer-Verlag, 1998.

175. S. Schneider. Timewise refinement for communicating processes. *Science of Computer Programming*, 28:43–90, 1997.

176. S. Schneider. *Concurrent and Real-time Systems, the CSP Approach.* Wiley, 2000.

177. S. Schneider, J. Davies, D.M. Jackson, G.M. Reed, J.N. Reed, and A.W. Roscoe. Timed CSP: Theory and practice. In *Real-Time: Theory in Practice*, LNCS 600, pages 640–675. Springer-Verlag, 1991.

178. R. Segala, R. Gawlick, J. Sogaard-Andersen, and N. Lynch. Liveness in timed and untimed systems. *Information and Computation*, 141(2):119–171, 1998.

179. S. Singh. *Fermat's Last Theorem.* Walker, 1997.

180. G. Smith. Extending $\mathcal{W}$ for Object-Z. In J. Bowen and M. Hinchey, editors, *9th International Conference of Z Users*, LNCS 967, pages 276–295. Springer-Verlag, 1995.

181. M.A. Smith and N. Klarlund. Verification of a sliding window protocol using IOA and MONA. In T. Bolognesi and D. Latella, editors, *Formal Methods for Distributed System Development*, pages 19–34. Kluwer Academic, 2000.

182. I. Sommerville. *Software Engineering.* Addison-Wesley, 1989.

183. J.A. Stankovic and K. Ramamiritham. *Tutorial - Hard Real-time Systems.* IEEE Computer Society Press, 1988.

184. M. Steen, H. Bowman, and J. Derrick. Composition of LOTOS specifications. In P. Dembinski and M. Sredniawa, editors, *Protocol Specification, Testing and Verification*, Warsaw, Poland, 1995. Chapman & Hall.

185. M. Steen, H. Bowman, J. Derrick, and E.A. Boiten. Disjunction of LOTOS specifications. In *Formal Description Techniques and Protocol Specification, Testing and Verification, 1997*, pages 177–192. Kluwer, 1997.

186. U. Stern and D.L. Dill. Improved probabilistic verification by hash compaction. In *Proceedings of the Advanced Research Working Conference on Correct Hardware Design and Verification Methods*, pages 206–24, 1995.

187. A. Tanenbaum. *Computer Networks*. Prentice-Hall, 1989.

188. W. Thomas. Automata on infinite objects. In *Handbook of Theoretical Computer Science*, volume B, pages 133–191. MIT Press, Elsevier, 1990.

189. S. Tripakis. *The analysis of timed systems in practice*. PhD thesis, Universite Joseph Fourier, Grenoble, France, December 1998.

190. S. Tripakis. Verifying progress in timed systems. In *ARTS'99, Formal Methods for Real-Time and Probabilistic Systems, 5th International AMAST Workshop*, LNCS 1601. Springer-Verlag, 1999.

191. R.J. van Glabbeek. The refinement theorem for ST-bisimulation semantics. In *Programming Concepts and Methods*. Elsevier Science Publishers, 1990.

192. R.J. van Glabbeek. The linear time - branching time spectrum (I and II). In *Concur'90 and Concur'93, LNCS 458 and LNCS 715*. Springer-Verlag, 1990 and 1993.

193. R.J. van Glabbeek and G.D. Plotkin. Configuration structures. In *10th Annual Symposium on Logic in Computer Science*. IEEE Computer Society Press, 1995.

194. M.Y. Vardi. Branching vs linear time: Final showdown. In T. Margaria and W. Yi, editors, *TACAS'2001, Tools and Algorithms for the Construction and Analysis of Systems, held as part of ETAPS'01*, LNCS 2031. Springer-Verlag, 2001. invited talk.

195. C. A. Vissers, G. Scollo, M. van Sinderen, and E. Brinksma. On the use of specification styles in the design of distributed systems. *Theoretical Computer Science*, 89(1):179–206, October 1991.

196. C.A. Vissers, G. Scollo, and M. van Sinderen. Architecture and specification styles in formal descriptions of distributed systems. In *Protocol Specification, Testing and Verification, VIII*, pages 189–204. North-Holland, 1988.

197. P. Wegner. Why interaction is more powerful than algorithms. *Communications of the ACM*, 40(5):80–91, 1997.

198. G. Winskel. An introduction to event structures. In *Linear Time, Branching Time and Partial Order in Logics and Models of Concurrency*, LNCS 354, pages 364–397. Springer-Verlag, 1988.

199. G. Winskel. *The Formal Semantics of Programming Languages, an Introduction*. MIT Press, 1993.

200. P. Wolper and D. Leroy. Reliable hashing without collision detection. In *CAV'93*, pages 59–70, 1993.

201. Wang Yi. Ccs + time = an interleaving model for real-time systems. In *Automata, Languages and Programming 18*, LNCS 510, pages 217–228. Springer-Verlag, 1991.

202. S. Yovine. Kronos: A verification tool for real-time systems. *Springer International Journal of Software Tools for Technology Transfer*, 1997.

203. P. Zave and M. Jackson. Conjunction as composition. *ACM Transactions on Software Engineering and Methodology*, 2(4):379–411, October 1993.

14

Appendix

14.1 Enabling as a Derived Operator

The following sections (14.2 and 14.3) present congruence proofs for bisimulation equivalences over the pbLOTOS operators. To avoid one case in each of these proofs, we use the fact that enabling can be encoded using hiding and parallel composition.[1]

The mapping works as follows. Take d as a distinguished action and then assume a mapping, denoted $tr^{>>}$, which takes a behaviour, and rewrites all occurrences of *exit* with d; *stop* and ensures that all parallel threads synchronise on d. Then it should be straightforward to see that

$$B_1 >> B_2 \sim hide \ \mathsf{d} \ in \ (tr^{>>}(B_1) \ |[\mathsf{d}]| \ \mathsf{d}; B_2)$$

14.2 Strong Bisimulation Is a Congruence

This section includes a proof of the fact that strong bisimulation equivalence (see Definition 5 in Section 3.3.3.1) is a congruence over the pbLOTOS operators.

Theorem 14.1.
If we assume that $B_1 \sim B_2$, then $C[B_1] \sim C[B_2]$, if $C[.]$ is any allowable pbLOTOS context, i.e. could be generated from any of the operators of the calculus.

Proof
Assume $B_1 \sim B_2$ and that R is a corresponding strong bisimulation containing (B_1, B_2). We step through the pbLOTOS operators, showing that substitution into the corresponding context preserves $\sim$.

---

[1]In fact, a similar observation was made by Milner, see Section 8.2 of [148].

Action Prefix

Let $P_1 := a\,;\, B_1$ and $P_2 := a\,;\, B_2$ (where $a \in Act \cup \{i\}$). Further assume that $S = \{(P_1, P_2)\} \cup R$. We claim that S is a strong bisimulation relation. To show this, take $(Q_1, Q_2) \in S$ and assume that $Q_1 \xrightarrow{b} Q_1'$. We have two cases to consider.

Case 1 ($Q_1 = P_1$ and $Q_2 = P_2$).
But, then, $Q_1' = B_1$, $a = b$ and $Q_2 \xrightarrow{a} B_2$. The result follows because $(B_1, B_2) \in R \subseteq S$.

Case 2 ($Q_1 \neq P_1$ or $Q_2 \neq P_2$).
But, then, $(Q_1, Q_2) \in R$ and the result follows.

Symmetric arguments can be given from Q_2 to Q_1.

Choice

This case is simpler than that for parallel composition and is omitted.

Parallel Composition

Let $P_1 := B \,||[G]||\, B_1$ and $P_2 := B \,||[G]||\, B_2$ (where $G \subseteq Act$). Further assume that $S = \{(D \,||[G]||\, D_1, D \,||[G]||\, D_2) \mid D, D_1, D_2 \in Beh \,\wedge\, (D_1, D_2) \in R\}$. We claim that S is a strong bisimulation relation. To show this, take $(Q_1, Q_2) \in S$, assume that $Q_1 \xrightarrow{a} Q_1'$, $Q_1 = D \,||[G]||\, D_1$ and $Q_2 = D \,||[G]||\, D_2$. We have two cases to consider.

Case 1 ($a \notin G \cup \{\delta\}$).
This yields two subcases.

Case 1.a ($D \xrightarrow{a} D'$).
But then, $Q_1' = D' \,||[G]||\, D_1$, $Q_2 \xrightarrow{a} Q_2'$ and $Q_2' = D' \,||[G]||\, D_2$. The result follows because $(D' \,||[G]||\, D_1, D' \,||[G]||\, D_2) \in S$.

Case 1.b ($D_1 \xrightarrow{a} D_1'$).
But then, $Q_1' = D \,||[G]||\, D_1'$ and (because $(D_1, D_2) \in R$), $D_2 \xrightarrow{a} D_2'$ and $(D_1', D_2') \in R$. It follows then that $Q_2 \xrightarrow{a} Q_2'$ and $Q_2' = D \,||[G]||\, D_2'$. The result follows because $(D \,||[G]||\, D_1', D \,||[G]||\, D_2') \in S$.

Case 2 ($a \in G \cup \{\delta\}$).
But then, $D \xrightarrow{a} D'$ and $D_1 \xrightarrow{a} D_1'$ and $Q_1' = D' \,||[G]||\, D_1'$. However, because $(D_1, D_2) \in R$, $D_2 \xrightarrow{a} D_2'$ and $(D_1', D_2') \in R$. It follows then that $Q_2 \xrightarrow{a} Q_2'$ and $Q_2' = D' \,||[G]||\, D_2'$. The result follows because, $(D' \,||[G]||\, D_1', D' \,||[G]||\, D_2') \in S$.

Symmetric arguments can be given from Q_2 to Q_1.

Enabling

The encoding, presented in Section 14.1, of $>>$ using hiding and parallel composition means that this case does not have to be separately considered.

Hiding

Let $P_1 := hide\ G\ in\ B_1$ and $P_2 := hide\ G\ in\ B_2$ (where $G \subseteq Act$). Further assume that $S = \{(hide\ G\ in\ D_1, hide\ G\ in\ D_2) \mid D_1, D_2 \in Beh \land (D_1, D_2) \in R\}$. We claim that S is a strong bisimulation relation. To show this, take $(Q_1, Q_2) \in S$, assume that $Q_1 \xrightarrow{a} Q_1'$, $Q_1 = hide\ G\ in\ D_1$ and $Q_2 = hide\ G\ in\ D_2$. We have two cases to consider.

Case 1 ($a \neq i$).
But then, $a \notin G$ and $D_1 \xrightarrow{a} D_1'$. However, because $(D_1, D_2) \in R$ we know that $D_2 \xrightarrow{a} D_2'$ and $(D_1', D_2') \in R$. Hence, $Q_2 = hide\ G\ in\ D_2 \xrightarrow{a} Q_2' = hide\ G\ in\ D_2'$ and because $(Q_1', Q_2') = (hide\ G\ in\ D_1', hide\ G\ in\ D_2') \in S$, the result follows.

Case 2 ($a = i$).
This yields two subcases.

Case 2.a ($D_1 \xrightarrow{i} D_1'$).
This case proceeds as per Case 1 above and is omitted.

Case 2.a ($D_1 \xrightarrow{x} D_1' \land x \in G$).
But then because $(D_1, D_2) \in R$ we know that $D_2 \xrightarrow{x} D_2'$ and $(D_1', D_2') \in R$. Hence, $Q_2 = hide\ G\ in\ D_2 \xrightarrow{i} Q_2' = hide\ G\ in\ D_2'$ and because $(Q_1', Q_2') = (hide\ G\ in\ D_1', hide\ G\ in\ D_2') \in S$, the result follows.

Symmetric arguments can be given from Q_2 to Q_1.

Relabelling

Follows similar lines to hiding and is omitted.

Process Instantiation

The proof here is somewhat more involved, because we need to handle recursive definitions. We closely follow Milner's proof for CCS [148].

Assume definitions of the form $P := E$, where E only references the process variable X. We only deal with the case of single recursion. However, the argument can easily be generalised to multiple recursive equations.

We write recursive equations as $P := E[P/X]$.[2] Expressions of the form $E[B/X]$ can be defined by induction on the structure of E in the obvious way.

---

[2] The overloading of the $[c/d]$ notation, which is already used for action relabelling, will not cause any confusion.

In addition, we actually work with a generalisation of strong bisimulation to behaviour expressions containing references to process variables. Again, only dealing with the single recursion case, assuming that E and F only reference the process variable X, we define

$$E \sim^* F \text{ iff } \forall B \in Beh , \; E[B/X] \sim F[B/X]$$

Now, the result we require is that, assuming that E and F only reference the process variable X,

$$(E \sim^* F \; \wedge \; P := E[P/X] \; \wedge \; Q := F[Q/X]) \implies P \sim^* Q$$

Now, on the assumption that E and F only reference the process variable X, and $E \sim^* F \; \wedge \; P := E[P/X] \; \wedge \; Q := F[Q/X]$, we show that,

$$S = \{ (C[P/X], C[Q/X]) \,|\, C \text{ only references } X \}$$

is a strong bisimulation, which is as required because the case $C = X$ gives us that $P \sim^* Q$.

In fact, we show that

$$C[P/X] \xrightarrow{a} B' \implies \exists D', D'' \cdot C[Q/X] \xrightarrow{a} D'' \sim^* D' \wedge (B', D') \in S.$$

In all cases, there will exist symmetric arguments to justify the corresponding result from $C[Q/X]$ back to $C[P/X]$. We prove this result by transition induction (see Section 2.10 of [148]) on the depth of the inference by which the transition $C[P/X] \xrightarrow{a} B'$ is generated. So, assume that $C[P/X] \xrightarrow{a} B'$; we have the following cases.

Case 1 ($C = X$).
But then, $C[P/X] = P$ and thus, $P \xrightarrow{a} B'$. It follows then that $E[P/X] \xrightarrow{a} B'$ by a shorter inference, and thus, $E[Q/X] \xrightarrow{a} D'' \sim^* D' \; \wedge \; (B', D') \in S$. However, because $E \sim^* F$, we know that $F[Q/X] \xrightarrow{a} D''' \sim^* D'$ and, because $Q := F[Q/X]$, we have $C[Q/X] = Q \xrightarrow{a} D''' \sim^* D'$ and $(B', D') \in S$, as required.

Case 2 ($C = a ; C'$).
But then, $C[P/X] = a ; C'[P/X]$ and $B' = C'[P/X]$. Also, we know that $C[Q/X] = a ; C'[Q/X] \xrightarrow{a} C'[Q/X]$ and clearly $(C'[P/X], C'[Q/X]) \in S$, as required.

Case 3 ($C = C_1 \,[]\, C_2$).
Proceeds by a similar, but simpler, line of argument to the parallel composition case and is, thus, omitted.

Case 4 ($C = C_1 \,|[G]|\, C_2$).
But then, $C[P/X] = (C_1 \,|[G]|\, C_2)[P/X] = C_1[P/X] \,|[G]|\, C_2[P/X]$. We have two subcases.

Case 4.a ($a \notin G \cup \{\delta\}$).
Without loss of generality, assume $C_1[P/X] \xrightarrow{a} B_1'$ and $B' = B_1' \,||G||\, C_2[P/X]$, which is by a shorter inference, thus, $C_1[Q/X] \xrightarrow{a} D_1'' \sim^* D_1' \wedge (B_1', D_1') \in S$. But, then we know that, $C[Q/X] = C_1[Q/X] \,||G||\, C_2[Q/X] \xrightarrow{a} D'' \sim^* D'$, where $D'' = (D_1'' \,||G||\, C_2[Q/X])$ and $D' = (D_1' \,||G||\, C_2[Q/X])$. But, we also know that $(B_1', D_1') \in S$, therefore, $\exists H \,.\, B_1' = H[P/X] \wedge D_1' = H[Q/X]$. It follows then that

$$(B', D') = (\, B_1' \,||G||\, C_2[P/X],\, D_1' \,||G||\, C_2[Q/X]\,)$$

$$= (\, H[P/X] \,||G||\, C_2[P/X],\, H[Q/X] \,||G||\, C_2[Q/X]\,)$$

$$= (\,(H \,||G||\, C_2)[P/X],\, (H \,||G||\, C_2)[Q/X]\,) \in S$$

which is as required.

Case 4.b ($a \in G \cup \{\delta\}$).
Follows similar lines to Case 4.a and omitted.

Case 5 ($C = C_1 \gg C_2$).
This does not have to be separately dealt with, because of the encoding of enabling into hiding and parallel composition discussed in Section 14.1.

Case 6 ($C = hide\ G\ in\ C'$).
But then, $C[P/X] = (hide\ G\ in\ C')[P/X] = hide\ G\ in\ C'[P/X]$. We have two subcases.

Case 6.a ($a \neq i$).
But then, $C'[P/X] \xrightarrow{a} D_1$ (where $B' = hide\ G\ in\ D_1$), which is by a shorter inference, therefore, $C'[Q/X] \xrightarrow{a} D_2 \sim^* D_3 \wedge (D_1, D_3) \in S$. Thus, $C[Q/X] = (hide\ G\ in\ C')[Q/X] = hide\ G\ in\ C'[Q/X] \xrightarrow{a} D'' \sim^* D'$, where $D'' = hide\ G\ in\ D_2$ and $D' = hide\ G\ in\ D_3$. But, we also know that $(D_1, D_3) \in S$, therefore, $\exists H \,.\, D_1 = H[P/X] \wedge D_3 = H[Q/X]$. It follows then that

$$(B', D') = (\,(hide\ G\ in\ D_1),\, (hide\ G\ in\ D_3)\,)$$

$$= (\,(hide\ G\ in\ H[P/X]),\, (hide\ G\ in\ H[Q/X])\,)$$

$$= (\,(hide\ G\ in\ H)[P/X],\, (hide\ G\ in\ H)[Q/X]\,) \in S$$

which is as required.

Case 6.b ($a = i$).
This case is similar to Case 6.a, and is omitted.

Case 7 ($C = C'[H]$).
Similar to Case 6, and omitted.

Case 8 ($C = R$, where X does not occur).
Holds automatically, because $C[P/X] = C[Q/X]$.
○

14.3 Weak Bisimulation Congruence

This section includes a proof that justifies our use of the term weak bisimulation congruence; see Definition 8 in Section 3.3.3.1.

Theorem 14.2.
If we assume that $B_1 \approx_c B_2$, then $C[B_1] \approx_c C[B_2]$, if $C[.]$ is any allowable pbLOTOS context, i.e. could be generated from any of the operators of the calculus.

Proof
Assume $B_1 \approx_c B_2$ and that R is a corresponding weak bisimulation congruence containing (B_1, B_2). We step through the pbLOTOS operators, showing that substitution into the corresponding context preserves $\approx_c$.

Action Prefix

Let $P_1 := a; B_1$ and $P_2 := a; B_2$ (where $a \in Act \cup \{i\}$). Further assume that $S = \{(P_1, P_2)\}$. We claim that S is a weak bisimulation congruence. To show this, take $(Q_1, Q_2) \in S$ and assume that $Q_1 \xrightarrow{b} Q'_1$. Now, we know that $Q_1 = P_1$ and $Q_2 = P_2$. But, then, $Q'_1 = B_1$, $a = b$ and $Q_2 \xrightarrow{a} Q'_2 = B_2$ (note, whether $a = b = i$, or not, $\xRightarrow{a}$ will have the same effect). The result follows because, as $\approx_c \subset \approx$, we now that $B_1 \approx B_2$.

Symmetric arguments can be given from Q_2 to Q_1.

Choice

Let $P_1 := B [] B_1$ and $P_2 := B [] B_2$. Further assume that $S = \{(P_1, P_2)\}$. We claim that S is a weak bisimulation congruence. To show that this is the case, take $(P_1, P_2) \in S$ and assume that $P_1 \xrightarrow{b} P'_1$. We have two cases to consider.

Case 1 ($B \xrightarrow{b} B'$).
But then, $P'_1 = B'$ and $P_2 \xrightarrow{b} B'$ and $P_2 \xRightarrow{b} B'$. The result follows because $(B', B') \in Id \subset \approx$.

Case 2 ($B_1 \xrightarrow{b} B'_1$).
But then, $P'_1 = B'_1$ and, because $B_1 \approx_c B_2$, we know that $B_2 \xRightarrow{b} B'_2$ and $(B'_1, B'_2) \in \approx$. Therefore, we know that $P_2 \xRightarrow{b} B'_2$.[3] The result follows because $(B'_1, B'_2) \in \approx$.

Symmetric arguments can be given from P_2 to P_1.

---

[3]It is this deduction, from $B_2 \xRightarrow{b} B'_2$ to $P_2 \xRightarrow{b} B'_2$, that is dependent upon the use of $\xRightarrow{}$, because, with this relation, we know that choice is resolved when B_2 performs b. If we had used $\xRightarrow{}$ with $b = i$, this would not have been certain.

Parallel Composition

Let $P_1 := B \,||[G]||\, B_1$ and $P_2 := B \,||[G]||\, B_2$ (where $G \subseteq Act$). Further assume $S = \{(P_1, P_2)\}$ and $R = \{(D \,||[G]||\, D_1, D \,||[G]||\, D_2) \,|\, D, D_1, D_2 \in Beh \,\wedge\, (D_1, D_2) \in \approx\}$. We claim that S is a weak bisimulation congruence, with R the associated weak bisimulation. We verify these two statements in turn.

Case 1 (to show that S is a weak bisimulation congruence).
Take $(P_1, P_2) \in S$ and assume that $P_1 \xrightarrow{a} P_1'$. We have two cases to consider.

Case 1.a $(a \notin G \cup \{\delta\})$.
This yields two subcases.

Case 1.a.i $(B \xrightarrow{a} B')$.
But then, $P_1' = B' \,||[G]||\, B_1$, $P_2 \xrightarrow{a} P_2'$ and $P_2' = B' \,||[G]||\, B_2$. Therefore, $P_2 \stackrel{a}{\Longrightarrow} P_2'$ and because $\approx_c \subseteq \approx$ and $B_1 \approx_c B_2$, we have that $(P_1', P_2') = (B' \,||[G]||\, B_1, B' \,||[G]||\, B_2) \in R$, as required.

Case 1.a.ii $(B_1 \xrightarrow{a} B_1')$.
But then, $P_1' = B \,||[G]||\, B_1'$ and (because $B_1 \approx_c B_2$), $B_2 \stackrel{a}{\Longrightarrow} B_2'$ and $(B_1', B_2') \in \approx$. It follows then that $P_2 \stackrel{a}{\Longrightarrow} P_2'$ and $P_2' = B \,||[G]||\, B_2'$. The result follows because $(B \,||[G]||\, B_1', B \,||[G]||\, B_2') \in R$.

Case 1.b $(a \in G \cup \{\delta\})$.
But then, $B \xrightarrow{a} B'$, $B_1 \xrightarrow{a} B_1'$ and $P_1' = B' \,||[G]||\, B_1'$. However, because $(B_1, B_2) \in \approx_c$, $B_2 \stackrel{a}{\Longrightarrow} B_2'$ and $(B_1', B_2') \in \approx$. It follows then that $P_2 \stackrel{a}{\Longrightarrow} P_2'$ and $P_2' = B' \,||[G]||\, B_2'$ and because $(P_1', P_2') = (B' \,||[G]||\, B_1', B' \,||[G]||\, B_2') \in R$, the result follows.

Symmetric arguments can be given from P_2 to P_1.

Case 2 (to show that R is a weak bisimulation equivalence).
To show this, take $(Q_1, Q_2) \in R$ and assume that $Q_1 \xrightarrow{a} Q_1'$. Let $Q_1 = D \,||[G]||\, D_1$ and $Q_2 = D \,||[G]||\, D_2$. We have two cases to consider.

Case 2.a $(a \in G \cup \{\delta\})$.
But then, $D \xrightarrow{a} D'$ and $D_1 \xrightarrow{a} D_1'$ and $Q_1' = D' \,||[G]||\, D_1'$. However, because $(D_1, D_2) \in \approx$, $D_2 \stackrel{a}{\Longrightarrow} D_2'$ and $(D_1', D_2') \in \approx$. It follows then that $Q_2 \stackrel{a}{\Longrightarrow} Q_2'$ [4] and $Q_2' = D' \,||[G]||\, D_2'$. The result follows because $D_1' \approx D_2'$ and, thus, $(Q_1', Q_2') = (D' \,||[G]||\, D_1', D' \,||[G]||\, D_2') \in R$.

Case 2.b $(a \notin G \cup \{\delta\})$.
The two subcases here are both easier than Case 2.a above; both follow the Case 2.a strategy and are both omitted.

Symmetric arguments can be given from Q_2 to Q_1.

---

[4]Note, any i actions that D_2 performs before or after the a in $\stackrel{a}{\Longrightarrow}$ would be inherited as (nonsynchronising) internal actions of $D \,||[G]||\, D_2$, allowing $\stackrel{a}{\Longrightarrow}$ also at this level.

Enabling

The encoding, presented in Section 14.1, of $>>$ using hiding and parallel composition means that this case does not have to be separately considered.

Hiding

Let $P_1 := hide\ G\ in\ B_1$ and $P_2 := hide\ G\ in\ B_2$ (where $G \subseteq Act$). Further assume $S = \{(hide\ G\ in\ D_1, hide\ G\ in\ D_2) \mid D_1, D_2 \in Beh\ \wedge\ (D_1, D_2) \in \approx_c\}$ and $R = \{(hide\ G\ in\ C_1, hide\ G\ in\ C_2) \mid C_1, C_2 \in Beh\ \wedge\ (C_1, C_2) \in \approx\}$. We claim that S is a weak bisimulation congruence and R is a weak bisimulation equivalence. We show these two results in turn.

Case 1 (to show that S is a weak bisimulation congruence).
Take $(Q_1, Q_2) \in S$; assume that $Q_1 \xrightarrow{a} Q_1'$, $Q_1 = hide\ G\ in\ D_1$, $Q_2 = hide\ G\ in\ D_2$ and $D_1 \approx_c D_2$. We have two cases to consider.

Case 1.a $(a \neq i)$.
But then, $a \notin G$ and $D_1 \xrightarrow{a} D_1'$. However, because $(D_1, D_2) \in \approx_c$ we know that $D_2 \stackrel{a}{\Longrightarrow} D_2'$ and $(D_1', D_2') \in \approx$. Hence, $Q_2 = hide\ G\ in\ D_2 \stackrel{a}{\Longrightarrow} Q_2'$ [5], $Q_2' = hide\ G\ in\ D_2'$ and because $(Q_1', Q_2') = (hide\ G\ in\ D_1', hide\ G\ in\ D_2') \in R$, the result follows.

Case 1.b $(a = i)$.
This yields two subcases.

Case 1.b.i $(D_1 \xrightarrow{i} D_1')$.
Follows Case 1.a, and thus, omitted.

Case 1.b.ii $(D_1 \xrightarrow{x} D_1' \ \wedge\ x \in G)$.
But then because $(D_1, D_2) \in \approx_c$ we know that $D_2 \stackrel{x}{\Longrightarrow} D_2'$ and $(D_1', D_2') \in \approx$. Hence, $Q_2 = hide\ G\ in\ D_2 \stackrel{i}{\Longrightarrow} Q_2' = hide\ G\ in\ D_2'$ [6] and because $(Q_1', Q_2') = (hide\ G\ in\ D_1', hide\ G\ in\ D_2') \in R$, the result follows.

Symmetric arguments can be given from Q_2 to Q_1.

Case 2 (to show that R is a weak bisimulation equivalence).
Take $(Q_1, Q_2) \in R$, assume that $Q_1 \xrightarrow{a} Q_1'$, $Q_1 = hide\ G\ in\ D_1$ and $Q_2 = hide\ G\ in\ D_2$ and $D_1 \approx D_2$. We have two cases to consider.

Case 2.a $(a \neq i)$.
But then, $a \notin G$ and $D_1 \xrightarrow{a} D_1'$. However, because $(D_1, D_2) \in \approx$ we know

---

[5] Note, any i actions that D_2 performs before or after the a in $\stackrel{a}{\Longrightarrow}$ would be inherited by $hide\ G\ in\ D_2$, allowing $\stackrel{a}{\Longrightarrow}$ also at this level.

[6] Note, $D_2 \stackrel{x}{\Longrightarrow} D_2'$ ensures that $\exists D, D'$ (possibly equal to D_2, D_2', respectively) such that D is reachable from D_2 by $\stackrel{\epsilon}{\Longrightarrow}$ and $D \xrightarrow{x} D'$ and $D' \stackrel{\epsilon}{\Longrightarrow} D_2'$. Now, applications of (HD.ii) ensure that $hide\ G\ in\ D_2 \stackrel{\epsilon}{\Longrightarrow} hide\ G\ in\ D$ and $hide\ G\ in\ D' \stackrel{\epsilon}{\Longrightarrow} hide\ G\ in\ D_2'$ and (HD.i) ensures that $hide\ G\ in\ D \xrightarrow{i} hide\ G\ in\ D'$.

that $D_2 \overset{a}{\Longrightarrow} D_2'$ and $(D_1', D_2') \in \approx$. Hence, $Q_2 = hide\ G\ in\ D_2 \overset{a}{\Longrightarrow} Q_2' = hide\ G\ in\ D_2'$ and because $(Q_1', Q_2') = (hide\ G\ in\ D_1',\ hide\ G\ in\ D_2') \in R$, the result follows.

Case 2.b ($a = i$).
This yields two subcases.

Case 2.b.i ($D_1 \overset{i}{\rightarrow} D_1'$).
But then, $D_2 \overset{i}{\Longrightarrow} D_2'$ and $(D_1', D_2') \in \approx$. Hence, $Q_2 = hide\ G\ in\ D_2 \overset{i}{\Longrightarrow} Q_2'$ [7], $Q_2' = hide\ G\ in\ D_2'$ and because $(Q_1', Q_2') = (hide\ G\ in\ D_1',\ hide\ G\ in\ D_2') \in R$, the result follows.

Case 2.b.ii ($D_1 \overset{x}{\rightarrow} D_1' \wedge x \in G$).
But then because $(D_1, D_2) \in \approx$ we know that $D_2 \overset{x}{\Longrightarrow} D_2'$ and $(D_1', D_2') \in \approx$. Hence, $Q_2 = hide\ G\ in\ D_2 \overset{x}{\Longrightarrow} Q_2' = hide\ G\ in\ D_2'$ and moreover because $(Q_1', Q_2') = (hide\ G\ in\ D_1',\ hide\ G\ in\ D_2') \in R$, the result follows.

Symmetric arguments can be given from Q_2 to Q_1.

Relabelling

Follows similar lines to hiding and is omitted.

Process Instantiation

Again, we closely follow Milner's proof for CCS [148]. We generalise weak bisimulation congruence to behaviour expressions containing references to process variables. Again, only dealing with the single recursion case, assuming that E and F only reference the process variable X, we define

$$E \approx_c^* F \text{ iff } \forall B \in Beh\ ,\ E[B/X] \approx_c F[B/X]$$

Now, the result we require is that, assuming that E and F only reference the process variable X,

$$(E \approx_c^* F \wedge P := E[P/X] \wedge Q := F[Q/X]) \implies P \approx_c^* Q$$

Now, on the assumption that E and F only reference the process variable X, and $E \approx_c^* F \wedge P := E[P/X] \wedge Q := F[Q/X]$, we show that

$$S = \{\,(C[P/X], C[Q/X]) \,|\, C \text{ only references } X\,\}$$

is a weak bisimulation congruence. This is as required because the case $C = X$ gives us that $P \approx_c^* Q$.

---

[7]The only slight difference between the argument here and the argument with $\overset{i}{\Longrightarrow}$ in the corresponding case, (1.b.i), is that $Q_2 = Q_2'$ and $D_2 = D_2'$ are possible here, but this does not cause any problems for the reasoning.

In fact, we show that

$$C[P/X] \xrightarrow{a} B' \implies \exists D', D'' . C[Q/X] \xRightarrow{a} D'' \approx_c^* D' \wedge (B', D') \in S.$$

In all cases, there will exist symmetric arguments to justify the corresponding result from $C[Q/X]$ back to $C[P/X]$. We prove this theorem by transition induction (see Section 2.10 of [148]) on the depth of the inference by which the transition $C[P/X] \xrightarrow{a} B'$ is generated. So, assume that, $C[P/X] \xrightarrow{a} B'$; we have the following cases.

Case 1 (C = X).
But then, $C[P/X] = P$ and thus, $P \xrightarrow{a} B'$. It follows then that $E[P/X] \xrightarrow{a} B'$ by a shorter inference, and thus, $E[Q/X] \xRightarrow{a} D'' \approx_c^* D' \wedge (B', D') \in S$. However, because $E \approx_c^* F$, we know that $F[Q/X] \xRightarrow{a} D''' \approx_c^* D'$ [8] and, because $Q := F[Q/X]$, we have $C[Q/X] = Q \xRightarrow{a} D''' \approx_c^* D'$ and further $(B', D') \in S$, as required.

Case 2 (C = a ; C').
But then, $C[P/X] = a ; C'[P/X]$ and $B' = C'[P/X]$. Also, we know that $C[Q/X] = a ; C'[Q/X] \xrightarrow{a} C'[Q/X]$. Therefore, $C[Q/X] \xRightarrow{a} C'[Q/X]$ Furthermore, it is clear that $(C'[P/X], C'[Q/X]) \in S$, as required.

Case 3 (C = C_1 [] C_2).
But then, $C[P/X] = (C_1 [] C_2)[P/X] = C_1[P/X] [] C_2[P/X]$. Without loss of generality, assume $C_1[P/X] \xrightarrow{a} B'$, which is by a shorter inference, thus, $C_1[Q/X] \xRightarrow{a} D'' \approx_c^* D' \wedge (B', D') \in S$. However, then we know that $C[Q/X] = (C_1 [] C_2)[Q/X] \xRightarrow{a} D'' \approx_c^* D'$, where $(B', D') \in S$ and the result follows.

Case 4 (C = C_1 |[G]| C_2).
But then, $C[P/X] = (C_1 |[G]| C_2)[P/X] = C_1[P/X] |[G]| C_2[P/X]$. We have two cases to consider.

Case 4.a (a $\notin G \cup \{\delta\}$).
Without loss of generality, assume $C_1[P/X] \xrightarrow{a} B_1'$ and $B' = B_1' |[G]| C_2[P/X]$, which is by a shorter inference, thus, $C_1[Q/X] \xRightarrow{a} D_1'' \approx_c^* D_1' \wedge (B_1', D_1') \in S$. However, then we know that $C[Q/X] = C_1[Q/X] |[G]| C_2[Q/X] \xRightarrow{a} D'' \approx_c^*$ D', where $D'' = (D_1'' |[G]| C_2[Q/X])$ and $D' = (D_1' |[G]| C_2[Q/X])$. But, we also know that, $(B_1', D_1') \in S$, therefore, $\exists H . B_1' = H[P/X] \wedge D_1' = H[Q/X]$. It follows then that

---

[8]Notice, the deduction here is more complex than the corresponding deduction for strong bisimulation. Specifically, there must be a derivation that witnesses $E[Q/X] \xRightarrow{a}$, possibly involving i transitions. Now, because $E \approx_c^* F$, we can walk along this path turning it into a (possibly longer, i.e. containing more i transitions) path to witness $F[Q/X] \xRightarrow{a}$.

$$(B', D') = (B'_1 \|[G]\| C_2[P/X], D'_1 \|[G]\| C_2[Q/X])$$

$$= (H[P/X] \|[G]\| C_2[P/X], H[Q/X] \|[G]\| C_2[Q/X])$$

$$= ((H \|[G]\| C_2)[P/X], (H \|[G]\| C_2)[Q/X]) \in S$$

which is as required.

Case 4.b $(a \in G \cup \{\delta\})$.
Follows similar lines to Case 4.a and omitted.

Case 5 $(C = C_1 \gg C_2)$.
This does not have to be separately dealt with, because of the encoding of enabling into hiding and parallel composition discussed in Section 14.1.

Case 6 $(C = hide\ G\ in\ C')$.
But then, $C[P/X] = (hide\ G\ in\ C')[P/X] = hide\ G\ in\ C'[P/X]$. We have two subcases.

Case 6.a $(a \neq i)$.
But then, $C'[P/X] \xrightarrow{a} D_1$ (where $B' = hide\ G\ in\ D_1$), which is by a shorter inference, therefore, $C'[Q/X] \overset{a}{\Longrightarrow} D_2 \approx_c^* D_3 \wedge (D_1, D_3) \in S$. Thus, $C[Q/X] = (hide\ G\ in\ C')[Q/X] = hide\ G\ in\ C'[Q/X] \overset{a}{\Longrightarrow} D'' \approx_c^* D'$, where $D'' = hide\ G\ in\ D_2$ and $D' = hide\ G\ in\ D_3$. But, we also know that $(D_1, D_3) \in S$, therefore, $\exists H\ .\ D_1 = H[P/X] \wedge D_3 = H[Q/X]$. It follows then that

$$(B', D') = (hide\ G\ in\ D_1, hide\ G\ in\ D_3)$$

$$= (hide\ G\ in\ H[P/X], hide\ G\ in\ H[Q/X])$$

$$= ((hide\ G\ in\ H)[P/X], (hide\ G\ in\ H)[Q/X]) \in S$$

which is as required.

Case 6.b $(a = i)$.
This case is similar to Case 6.a, and is omitted.

Case 7 $(C = C'[H])$.
Similar to Case 6, and omitted.

Case 8 $(C = R, where\ X\ does\ not\ occur)$.
Holds automatically, because $C[P/X] = C[Q/X]$.
○

14.4 Timed Enabling as a Derived Operator

The following sections (14.5, 14.6 and 14.7) investigate substitutivity of tLO-TOS operators with respect to timed bisimulation equivalences. As was the case in the untimed setting (see Section 14.1), to show that enabling does not fundamentally complicate the question of substitutivity, we show that, in the tLOTOS context, enabling can be encoded using hiding and parallel composition.

The mapping works as follows. Take d as a distinguished action and then assume a mapping, denoted $tr_t^{>>}$, which takes a behaviour, and rewrites all occurrences of $exit\,I$ with $d\,I\,;\ stop$ and ensures that all parallel threads synchronise on d. Then the following holds.

$$B_1 >> B_2 \ \sim_t \ hide \ \text{d} \ in \ (\,tr_t^{>>}(B_1) \ |[\text{d}]| \ \text{d} \,;\ B_2\,)$$

14.5 Hiding is Not Substitutive for Timed Bisimulations

In fact, because of our handling of urgency of internal actions, hiding fails to be substitutive for all the timed bisimulation equivalences that we consider. The following serves as a counter-example for all these equivalences. So, for an arbitrary t in $\mathbb{R}^{+0}$ assume the following definitions.

$$observable_1 := (\,x\,[0,t]\,;\ stop \ [] \ x\,;\ stop\,)$$
$$observable_2 := x\,;\ stop$$
$$hidden_1 := hide\ x\ in\ observable_1$$
$$hidden_2 := hide\ x\ in\ observable_2$$

Now, $observable_1$ and $observable_2$ are equivalent by any of our timed bisimulation relations: they both allow time to pass arbitrarily and immediately, or after any such time passing transition, both can perform an x and evolve to deadlock. However, $hidden_1$ and $hidden_2$ are behaviourally very different and fail to be equivalent according to any one of our timed bisimulation equivalences. In fact, $hidden_1$ is equivalent to $i\,[0,t]\,;\ stop$, because i becomes urgent at time t and, thus, $hidden_1$ cannot pass time beyond t time units. However, $hidden_2$ can pass time arbitrarily.

14.6 Substitutivity of Timed Strong Bisimulation

Leonard [124] provides a timed strong bisimulation congruence for a calculus (ET-LOTOS) that has similarities to tLOTOS. In order to reuse some of these results, we provide the following mapping from tLOTOS to Leonard's ET-LOTOS, which is typed as

$$toETLOT : tLOTOS \longrightarrow ET\text{-}LOTOS$$

and is defined as follows.

$$toETLOT(B) \triangleq B \quad, \text{ if } B \in \{ \, stop, \, B_1 \, [] \, B_2, \, B_1 \, |[G]| \, B_2$$
$$B_1 \gg B_2, \, hide \, G \, in \, B', \, P \, \}$$

$$toETLOT(exit \, I) \triangleq \Delta^{\downarrow I} \, exit \, [\uparrow I - \downarrow I]$$

$$toETLOT(x \, I; \, B) \triangleq x@t \, [t \in I] \, ; \, toETLOT(B)$$
$$\text{for } t \text{ a fresh time variable}$$

$$toETLOT(i \, I; \, B) \triangleq \Delta^{\downarrow I} \, i \, [\uparrow I - \downarrow I] \, ; \, toETLOT(B)$$

$$toETLOT(wait \, [t] \, B) \triangleq \Delta^t \, toETLOT(B)$$

The requirement that t be a fresh variable in the third clause of this definition is needed to ensure that t does not appear in $toETLOT(B)$. Relabelling would be translated via ET-LOTOS process definition and instantiation in the obvious way and tLOTOS process definition can also be translated in the obvious way.

From a consideration of the ET-LOTOS semantics (Section 3.4 of [124]) it is not hard to see that the meaning of the following tLOTOS operators is preserved by this mapping: stop, exit, (internal and external) action prefix, delay, choice, parallel composition, relabelling and process instantiation. However, because tLOTOS and ET-LOTOS (which enforces maximal progress when an observable or successful termination action is hidden) handle hiding and enabling differently, we cannot reuse Leonard's proof in these two cases. As a result, we have the following theorem.

Theorem 14.3.
For $B_1, B_2 \in tBeh$, if we assume that $B_1 \sim_t B_2$, then $C[B_1] \sim_t C[B_2]$, where $C[.]$ is a tLOTOS context using any operator apart from hiding and enabling.

Proof
This result follows from Leonard's congruence proofs in Section 3.6.2 of [124] using the $toETLOT$ mapping.
○

However, the tLOTOS hiding and enabling operators are not substitutive.

Hiding. The example in Section 14.5 demonstrates hiding's lack of substitutivity. In particular, $observable_1 \sim_t observable_2$, which can be justified as follows. First, if we let,

$$R_d := (\, x \, [0, t - d]; \, stop \,) \, [] \, (\, x; \, stop \,) \quad \text{and}$$

$$T \triangleq \{ \, (R_d, observable_2) \, | \, d \in \mathbb{R}^{+0} \, \} \cup \{ \, (stop, stop) \, \}$$

noting that

$$(observable_1, observable_2) = (R_0, observable_2) \in T$$

we can show that T is a timed strong bisimulation. We argue as follows.

take $d \in \mathbb{R}^{+0}$ and for $v \in \{x\} \cup \mathbb{R}^{+}$ let $R_d \overset{v}{\longrightarrow\!\!\!\!\rightarrow} R$

There are two cases to consider depending upon the type of v.

Case 1 $(v = d' \in \mathbb{R}^{+})$
Now, because

$$observable_2 = x[0, \infty) \,;\, stop = x([0, \infty) \ominus d') \,;\, stop$$

and thus,

$$observable_2 \overset{d'}{\rightsquigarrow} x([0, \infty) \ominus d') \,;\, stop = observable_2$$

we know that $R = R_{(d-d')}$ and therefore $(R, observable_2) \in T$, as required.

Case 2 $(v = x$ and $R = stop)$
But then, $observable_2 \overset{x}{\longrightarrow\!\!\!\!\rightarrow} stop$ and $(stop, stop) \in T$, as required.

The other direction of the definition of $\sim_t$ follows similarly.

This confirms that $observable_1$ and $observable_2$ are timed strong bisimilar. However, $hidden_1 \not\sim_t hidden_2$, because

$$hidden_2 \overset{t+k}{\longrightarrow\!\!\!\!\rightarrow} \text{ for } k \in \mathbb{R}^{+}, \text{ but } hidden_1 \overset{t+k}{\longrightarrow\!\!\!\!\not\rightarrow}.$$

Enabling. In addition, enabling is not substitutive with respect to timed strong bisimulation. In fact, due to the encoding of enabling using hiding and parallel composition given in Section 14.4, this lack of substitutivity can be tracked back to the previously discussed problem with hiding. However, for completeness, we offer a counter-example expressed directly using enabling. Thus, take $t \in \mathbb{R}^{+0}$ and assume the following definitions.

$$Exit_1 := exit\,[0, t]\ [\,]\ exit$$
$$Exit_2 := exit$$
$$Enab_1 := Exit_1 \gg stop$$
$$Enab_2 := Exit_2 \gg stop$$

But then it is straightforward to show that $Exit_1 \sim_t Exit_2$. However, $Enab_1 \not\sim_t Enab_2$, because, $\forall d \in \mathbb{R}^{+}$, $Enab_2 \overset{t+d}{\longrightarrow\!\!\!\!\rightarrow}$, but $Enab_1 \overset{t+d}{\longrightarrow\!\!\!\!\not\rightarrow}$.

14.7 Substitutivity of Timed Rooted Weak Bisimulation

This section includes a proof that justifies that, apart from hiding and enabling, all tLOTOS operators are substitutive with respect to timed rooted weak bisimulation, as introduced in Definition 44 of Section 10.1.3. First though, we justify that hiding and enabling are not substitutive in this context. In fact, we can reuse the examples used for timed strong bisimulation.

That is, with respect to hiding, considering the definitions first highlighted in Section 14.5, it is not hard to see that $observable_1 \approx_r^t observable_2$, but $hidden_1 \not\approx_r^t hidden_2$. In addition, with respect to enabling, consider the definitions highlighted in the discussion of enabling in Section 14.6. The following relations obtain, $Exit_1 \approx_r^t Exit_2$ and $Enab_1 \not\approx_r^t Enab_2$.

Now we move to our main result.

Theorem 14.4.
If we assume that $B_1 \approx_r^t B_2$, then $C[B_1] \approx_r^t C[B_2]$, where $C[.]$ is any tLOTOS context that does not contain hiding or enabling.

Proof
Assume $B_1 \approx_r^t B_2$. We step through the tLOTOS operators, showing that substitution into the corresponding context preserves $\approx_r^t$.

Observable Action Prefix

Assume that $S = \{ (x\,I\,;\,D_1\,,\,x\,I\,;\,D_2) \mid D_1 \approx_t D_2 \wedge x \in Act \}$, noting that $(x\,I\,;\,B_1, x\,I\,;\,B_2) \in S$, because $\approx_r^t \subset \approx_t$. We will show that S is a timed rooted weak bisimulation.

First, let $P_1 := x\,I\,;\,D_1$ and $P_2 := x\,I\,;\,D_2$ and $D_1 \approx_t D_2$. Second, let $P_1 \xrightarrow{v} P_1'$. There are two cases to consider.

Case 1 ($v = d \in \mathbb{R}^+$).

But then, $P_1' = x\,(I \ominus d)\,;\,D_1$ and $P_2 \xrightarrow{d} x\,(I \ominus d)\,;\,D_2 = P_2'$. In addition, $(P_1', P_2') \in S$, as required.

Case 2 ($v = x$).

But then, $P_1' = D_1$ and $0 \in I$. From which it is clear that $P_2 \xrightarrow{x} D_2$, which implies that $P_2 \xRightarrow{x} D_2$ and because $D_1 \approx_t D_2$, the result follows.

Symmetric arguments can be given from P_2 to P_1.

Internal Action Prefix

Assume $S = \{ (i\,I\,;\,D_1, i\,I\,;\,D_2) \mid D_1 \approx_t D_2 \}$, noting that, because $\approx_r^t \subset \approx_t$, it is also the case that $(i\,I\,;\,B_1, i\,I\,;\,B_2) \in S$. We will show that S is a timed rooted weak bisimulation.

Firs, let $P_1 := i\,I\,;\,D_1$ and $P_2 := i\,I\,;\,D_2$ and $D_1 \approx_t D_2$. Second, let $P_1 \xrightarrow{v} P_1'$. There are two cases to consider.

Case 1 ($v = d \in \mathbb{R}^+$).
But then, $P_1' = i\,(I \ominus d)\,;\,D_1$ and $d \leq\uparrow I$. From which it is straightforward to see that $P_2 \xrightarrow{d} i\,(I \ominus d)\,;\,D_2 = P_2'$. In addition, $(P_1', P_2') \in S$, as required.

Case 2 ($v = i$).
But then, $P_1' = D_1$ and $0 \in I$. From which it is clear that $P_2 \xrightarrow{i} D_2$, which implies that $P_2 \xRightarrow{i} D_2$, and, because $D_1 \approx_t D_2$, the result follows.

Symmetric arguments can be given from P_2 to P_1.

Wait

Assume that $S = \{(wait\,[t]\,D_1,\,wait\,[t]\,D_2)\,|\,D_1 \approx_r^t D_2\} \cup \approx_r^t$, noting that $(wait\,[t]\,B_1, wait\,[t]\,B_2) \in S$. We will show that S is a timed rooted weak bisimulation.

First, let $P_1 := wait\,[t]\,D_1$ and $P_2 := wait\,[t]\,D_2$ and $D_1 \approx_r^t D_2$. Second, let $P_1 \stackrel{v}{\twoheadrightarrow} P_1'$. There are three cases to consider.

Case 1 ($v = a \in Act \cup \{i, \delta\}$).
But then, $D_1 \stackrel{a}{\longrightarrow} D_1'$ and $t = 0$. From which it is clear that $P_1' = D_1'$, $D_2 \stackrel{a}{\Longrightarrow} D_2'$ and $D_1' \approx_t D_2'$. But then, $P_2 = wait\,[0]\,D_2 \stackrel{a}{\Longrightarrow} D_2'$ (note, any i transitions that enables $D_2 \stackrel{a}{\Longrightarrow}$ will be inherited by $P_2 \stackrel{a}{\Longrightarrow}$). The result follows because $D_1' \approx_t D_2'$.

Case 2 ($v = d \in \mathbb{R}^+ \wedge d \leq t$).
But then, $P_2 \stackrel{d}{\leadsto} wait\,[t-d]$; $D_2 = P_2'$, $P_1' = wait\,[t-d]$; D_1 and $(P_1', P_2') \in S$, as required.

Case 3 ($v = (d+t) \in \mathbb{R}^+$).
But then, $D_1 \stackrel{d}{\leadsto} D_1'$ and $P_1' = D_1'$. Furthermore, because $D_1 \approx_r^t D_2$, we know that $D_2 \stackrel{d}{\leadsto} D_2'$ and $D_1' \approx_r^t D_2'$. But then, $P_2 \stackrel{d+t}{\leadsto} P_2'$ and $P_2' = D_2'$. The result follows, because $(P_1', P_2') \in S$.

Symmetric arguments can be given from P_2 to P_1.

Choice

Assume that $S = \{(D\,[]\,D_1, D\,[]\,D_2)\,|\,D_1 \approx_r^t D_2\}$, noting that, by definition, $\forall B, (B\,[]\,B_1, B\,[]\,B_2) \in S$. We will show that S is a timed rooted weak bisimulation.

First, let $P_1 := D\,[]\,D_1$ and $P_2 := D\,[]\,D_2$ and $D_1 \approx_r^t D_2$ (symmetric arguments can be given if it is the first argument that varies). Second, let $P_1 \stackrel{v}{\twoheadrightarrow} P_1'$. There are two cases to consider.

Case 1 ($v = a \in Act \cup \{i, \delta\}$).
Proceeds as per the untimed case (Theorem 14.2).

Case 2 ($v = d \in \mathbb{R}^+$).
But then, $D \stackrel{d}{\leadsto} D'$, $D_1 \stackrel{d}{\leadsto} D_1'$ and $P_1' = D'\,[]\,D_1'$. In addition, because $D_1 \approx_r^t D_2$, we know that $D_2 \stackrel{d}{\leadsto} D_2'$ and $D_1' \approx_r^t D_2'$. It follows then that $P_2 \stackrel{d}{\leadsto} P_2'$ and $P_2' = D'\,[]\,D_2'$. The result follows because $(P_1', P_2') \in S$.

Symmetric arguments can be given from P_2 to P_1.

Parallel Composition

Assume that $S = \{(D \;||[G]||\; D_1, D \;||[G]||\; D_2) \,|\, D_1 \approx_r^t D_2\}$, noting that, by definition, $\forall B, (B \;||[G]||\; B_1, B \;||[G]||\; B_2) \in S$. We will show that S is a timed rooted weak bisimulation.

First, let $P_1 := D \;||[G]||\; D_1$ and $P_2 := D \;||[G]||\; D_2$ and $D_1 \approx_r^t D_2$ (symmetric arguments can be given if it is the first parameter that varies). Second, let $P_1 \overset{v}{\longrightarrow\!\!\!\rightarrow} P_1'$. There are two cases to consider.

Case 1 ($v = a \in Act \cup \{i, \delta\}$).
Proceeds as per the untimed case (Theorem 14.2).

Case 2 ($v = d \in \mathbb{R}^+$).
But then, $D \overset{d}{\rightsquigarrow} D'$, $D_1 \overset{d}{\rightsquigarrow} D_1'$ and $P_1' = D' \;||[G]||\; D_1'$. In addition, as $D_1 \approx_r^t D_2$ we know that $D_2 \overset{d}{\rightsquigarrow} D_2'$ and $D_1' \approx_r^t D_2'$. It follows then that $P_2 \overset{d}{\rightsquigarrow} P_2'$ and $P_2' = D' \;||[G]||\; D_2'$. The result follows because $(P_1', P_2') \in S$.

Symmetric arguments can be given from P_2 to P_1.

Relabelling

Straightforward.

Process Instantiation

Again, we closely follow Milner's proof for CCS [148]. We generalise timed rooted weak bisimulation to behaviour expressions containing references to process variables. Again, we only deal with the single recursion case. Assuming that E and F only reference the process variable X, we define,

$$E \approx_r^{t*} F \;\; \text{iff} \;\; \forall B \in tBeh, \; E[B/X] \approx_r^t F[B/X]$$

Now, the result we require is that, assuming that E and F only reference the process variable X and do not contain hiding or enabling,

$$(E \approx_r^{t*} F \,\wedge\, P := E[P/X] \,\wedge\, Q := F[Q/X]) \implies P \approx_r^{t*} Q$$

Now, on the assumption that E and F only reference the process variable X, do not contain hiding or enabling, and $E \approx_r^{t*} F$, $P := E[P/X]$ and $Q := F[Q/X]$, we will show that

$$S = \{(C[P/X], C[Q/X]) \,|\, C \text{ only references } X$$
$$\text{and does not use hiding or enabling}\}$$

is a timed rooted weak bisimulation. This is as required because the case $C = X$ gives us that $P \approx_r^{t*} Q$.

In fact, we will show that

$$C[P/X] \xrightarrow{d} B' \implies \exists D', D'' \, . \, C[Q/X] \xrightarrow{d} D'' \approx_r^{t*} D' \wedge (B', D') \in S$$

and

$$C[P/X] \xrightarrow{a} B' \implies \exists D', D'' \, . \, C[Q/X] \xRightarrow{a} D'' \approx_t D' \wedge (B', D') \in S.$$

In all cases there will exist symmetric arguments to justify the corresponding result from $C[Q/X]$ back to $C[P/X]$. We prove this theorem by transition induction (see Section 2.10 of [148]) on the depth of the inference by which the transition $C[P/X] \xrightarrow{v} B'$ ($v \in \mathbb{R}^+ \cup Act \cup \{\delta, i\}$) is generated. So, assume that $C[P/X] \xrightarrow{v} B'$, we have the following cases.

Case 1 ($C = X$).
But then, $C[P/X] = P$ and thus, $P \xrightarrow{v} B'$. It follows then that $E[P/X] \xrightarrow{v} B'$ by a shorter inference, from which we have two cases.

Case 1a ($v = d \in \mathbb{R}^+$).
$\exists D', D'' \, . \, E[Q/X] \xrightarrow{d} D'' \approx_r^{t*} D' \wedge (B', D') \in S$. However, because $E \approx_r^{t*} F$, we know that $F[Q/X] \xrightarrow{d} D''' \approx_r^{t*} D'$. Therefore, because $Q := F[Q/X]$, we have $C[Q/X] = Q \xrightarrow{d} D''' \approx_r^{t*} D'$ and $(B', D') \in S$, as required.

Case 1b ($v = a \in Act \cup \{\delta, i\}$).
$\exists D', D'' \, . \, E[Q/X] \xRightarrow{a} D'' \approx_t D' \wedge (B', D') \in S$. However, because $E \approx_r^{t*} F$, we know that $F[Q/X] \xRightarrow{a} D''' \approx_t D'$ (this step follows as per the untimed case (Theorem 14.2)). Therefore, because $Q := F[Q/X]$, we have $C[Q/X] = Q \xRightarrow{a} D''' \approx_t D'$ and $(B', D') \in S$, as required.

Case 2 ($C = a\,I \, ; \, C'$).
But then, $C[P/X] = a\,I \, ; \, C'[P/X]$. From which there are four cases to consider.

Case 2a ($a = x \in Act \wedge v = d \in \mathbb{R}^+$).
But then, $B' = x\,(I \ominus d) \, ; \, C'[P/X]$. Also, $C[Q/X] = x\,I \, ; \, C'[Q/X] \xrightarrow{d} D' = x\,(I \ominus d) \, ; \, C'[Q/X]$. Furthermore, it is clear that

$$(B', D') = (\, x\,(I \ominus d) \, ; \, C'[P/X] \, , \, x\,(I \ominus d) \, ; \, C'[Q/X] \,)$$

$$= (\, (x\,(I \ominus d) \, ; \, C')[P/X] \, , \, (x\,(I \ominus d) \, ; \, C')[Q/X] \,) \in S$$

as required.

Case 2b ($a = v = x \in Act$).
But then, $B' = C'[P/X]$ and $0 \in I$. Also,

$$C[Q/X] = x\,I \, ; \, C'[Q/X] \xrightarrow{x} D' = C'[Q/X].$$

Furthermore, it is clear that $C[Q/X] \xRightarrow{x} D' = C'[Q/X]$ and the result follows because $(B', D') = (C'[P/X], C'[Q/X]) \in S$.

Case 2c ($a = i \land v = d \in \mathbb{R}^+$).
But then, $B' = i\,(I \ominus d)\,;\, C'[P/X]$ and $d \leq\uparrow I$. From which we know that
$C[Q/X] = i\,I\,;\, C'[Q/X] \overset{d}{\rightsquigarrow} D' = i\,(I \ominus d)\,;\, C'[Q/X]$. Furthermore, it is clear
that

$$(B', D') = (\,i\,(I \ominus d)\,;\, C'[P/X]\,,\, i\,(I \ominus d)\,;\, C'[Q/X]\,)$$
$$= (\,(i\,(I \ominus d)\,;\, C')[P/X]\,,\, (i\,(I \ominus d)\,;\, C')[Q/X]\,) \in S,$$

as required.

Case 2d ($a = v = i$).
Proceeds as per Case 2b.

Case 3 ($C = wait\,[t]\,C'$).
But then, $C[P/X] = wait\,[t]\,C'[P/X]$, from which there are three cases to
consider.

Case 3a ($v = d \in \mathbb{R}^+ \land d \leq t$).
But then, $B' = wait\,[t - d]\,C'[P/X]$. In addition, it follows immediately that
$C[Q/X] = wait\,[t]\,C'[Q/X] \overset{d}{\rightsquigarrow} D' = wait\,[t - d]\,C'[Q/X]$. Furthermore, it is
clear that

$$(B', D') = (\,wait\,[t - d]\,C'[P/X]\,,\, wait\,[t - d]\,C'[Q/X]\,)$$
$$= (\,(wait\,[t - d]\,C')[P/X]\,,\, (wait\,[t - d]\,C')[Q/X]\,) \in S,$$

as required.

Case 3b ($v = (t + d) \in \mathbb{R}^+$).
But then, $C'[P/X] \overset{d}{\rightsquigarrow} B''$ and $B' = B''$, which is by a shorter inference.
Therefore, we know that $\exists D', D''\,.\, C'[Q/X] \overset{d}{\rightsquigarrow} D'' \approx^{t*}_r D' \land B'SD'$. But
then, $(wait\,[t]\,C')[Q/X] = wait\,[t]\,C'[Q/X] \overset{t+d}{\rightsquigarrow} D'' \approx^{t*}_r D' \land B'SD'$, as
required.

Case 3c ($v = a \in Act \cup \{\delta, i\}$).
But then, $t = 0$ and $C'[P/X] \overset{a}{\longrightarrow} B''$ and $B' = B''$, which is by a shorter inference. Therefore, we know that $\exists D', D''\,.\, C'[Q/X] \overset{a}{\Longrightarrow} D'' \approx_t D' \land B'SD'$.
But then, $(wait\,[0]\,C')[Q/X] = wait\,[0]\,C'[Q/X] \overset{a}{\Longrightarrow} D'' \approx_t D' \land B'SD'$, as
required.

Case 4 ($C = C_1 \,[\!]\, C_2$).
But then, $C[P/X] = (C_1 \,[\!]\, C_2)[P/X] = C_1[P/X] \,[\!]\, C_2[P/X]$. We have two
cases to consider.

Case 4.a ($v = d \in \mathbb{R}^+$).
Thus, $C_1[P/X] \overset{d}{\rightsquigarrow} C_1'$, $C_2[P/X] \overset{d}{\rightsquigarrow} C_2'$ and $B' = C_1' \,[\!]\, C_2'$. However, these two
time transitions are by a shorter inference, thus, we know that

$$\exists D_1', D_1'', D_2', D_2''. \; C_1[Q/X] \stackrel{d}{\rightsquigarrow} D_1'' \approx_r^{t*} D_1' \;\wedge\; (C_1', D_1') \in S \;\wedge$$

$$C_2[Q/X] \stackrel{d}{\rightsquigarrow} D_2'' \approx_r^{t*} D_2' \;\wedge\; (C_2', D_2') \in S.$$

But then,

$$C[Q/X] = C_1[Q/X] \;[]\; C_2[Q/X] \stackrel{d}{\rightsquigarrow} D'' \approx_r^{t*} D'.$$

where $D'' = (D_1'' \;[]\; D_2'')$ and $D' = (D_1' \;[]\; D_2')$. But, we also know that, for $j \in \{1,2\}$, $(C_j', D_j') \in S$, therefore, $\exists H_j . \; C_j' = H_j[P/X] \;\wedge\; D_j' = H_j[Q/X]$. It follows then that

$$(B', D') = (C_1' \;[]\; C_2', D_1' \;[]\; D_2')$$
$$= (H_1[P/X] \;[]\; H_2[P/X], H_1[Q/X] \;[]\; H_2[Q/X])$$
$$= ((H_1 \;[]\; H_2)[P/X], (H_1 \;[]\; H_2)[Q/X]) \in S$$

which is as required.

Case 4.b $(v = a \in Act \cup \{\delta, i\})$.
Without loss of generality, assume $C_1[P/X] \stackrel{a}{\longrightarrow} C_1'$ and $B' = C_1'$, which is by a shorter inference, thus, $\exists D', D''. C_1[Q/X] \stackrel{a}{\Longrightarrow} D'' \approx_r^{t*} D' \;\wedge\; (B', D') = (C_1', D') \in S$. However, then we know that

$$C[Q/X] = (C_1 \;[]\; C_2)[Q/X] = C_1[Q/X] \;[]\; C_2[Q/X] \stackrel{a}{\Longrightarrow} D'' \approx_r^{t*} D'$$

where $(B', D') \in S$ and the result follows.

Case 5 $(C = C_1 \;||[G]||\; C_2)$.
Arguments used for timed transitions are similar to those given in Case 4a and for discrete / action transitions are as per the untimed case (Theorem 14.2).

Case 6 $(C = C'[H])$.
Straightforward.

○

Index